# Key Issues in
# Hunter-Gatherer Research

# Explorations in Anthropology

*A University College London Series*

Series Editors: Barbara Bender, John Gledhill and Bruce Kapferer

---

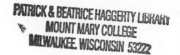
# Key Issues in Hunter-Gatherer Research

*Edited by*
**Ernest S. Burch, Jr.,** *and* **Linda J. Ellanna**

# BERG
*Oxford / Providence*

Published in 1994 by
Berg Publishers, Inc.
Editorial offices:
221 Waterman Street, Providence, RI 02906, U.S.A.
150 Cowley Road, Oxford OX4 1JJ, UK

**A CIP catalogue record for this book is available from the British
Library.**

**Library of Congress Cataloging-in-Publication Data**
Burch, Ernest S. and Ellanna, Linda J.
    Key issues in Hunter-Gatherer research / edited by
Ernest S. Burch, Jr., and Linda J. Ellanna.
        p.    cm.
    Includes bibliographical references and index.
    ISBN 0–85496–375–8.—ISBN 0–85496–376–6 (pbk.)
    1. Hunting and gathering societies.    I. Burch, Ernest S., Jr., 1938-
II. Ellanna, Linda J., 1940-
GN388.K49    1993
306.3—dc20

Front cover photograph: Lawrence *Ilugtun* Sage with part of an
evening's harvest of ringed seals, Kivalina, Alaska, June 26, 1964.
Photo by E. S. Burch, Jr.

Back cover photograph: Biaka Pygmy women and child at a stream
near Djoko, Central African Republic.
Photo by Marion McCreedy, 1989.

Printed in the United Kingdom by Short Run Press, Exeter.

# Contents

To

*Alfred Reginald Radcliffe-Brown*
*(1881-1955),*

*and*

*Julian Haynes Steward*
*(1902-1972),*

*who initiated the scientific study*
*of hunter-gatherer societies*

# List of Figures

## List of Tables

# 1

# Introduction

*Ernest S. Burch, Jr., and Linda J. Ellanna*

Societies with economies based entirely on hunting and gathering have existed ever since the evolution of the first humans.[1] However, it was only in the mid-twentieth century, when the last of such societies were about to disappear, that they began to attract widespread scholarly attention. It is true that hunter-gatherers have fascinated Westerners for a long time. It is even true, as Bettinger (1991: 1) has claimed, that, "hunter-gatherer research has traditionally been undertaken within explicit theoretical frameworks and all but the most recent and doctrinaire interpretations of hunter-gatherers . . . are constructed out of arguments and assumptions that are hundreds, sometimes thousands, of years old." But the theoretical frameworks of which he writes belonged to political philosophy, not science, and the arguments and assumptions were based more on fantasy than fact. Typically they were framed in terms of such stereotypes as "the noble savage" or people living lives that were "solitary, poor, nasty, brutish, and short." It rarely, if ever, occurred to their proponents to view such notions as hypotheses to be tested against empirical evidence. Field studies of hunting and gathering peoples were carried out, of course, but most of them were purely descriptive and they were read by relatively few people.

Theoretical interest in hunter-gatherer societies was stimulated in North America primarily by the pioneering work of Julian Steward (1936, 1938, 1955). Steward's contributions lay in his discussion of bands as the foundation of foraging societies and in his efforts to reinstate social evolution as a legitimate subject of academic inquiry. In other parts of the world interest in an empirical-

1. We thank Lois M. Myers for the extraordinary attention, care, and effort she put into helping us make this book a reality. We also thank Pam Odum, Cheryl Worthen and Deb Varner for their help, and the Department of Anthropology at the University of Alaska Fairbanks for its support. Finally, we thank our colleague-contributors to this volume for their cooperation and patience.

1

ly grounded theory of hunter-gatherer societies was stimulated
primarily by A. R. Radcliffe-Brown's (1930, 1931) models of Australian Aborigine societies. V. Gordon Childe's (1925, 1951: 22)
evolutionary distinction between "food gatherers" (i.e., hunter-
gatherers) and "food producers" (i.e., societies with agriculture
and/or husbandry) also created some interest, as did the early
field studies of nonhuman primates (e.g., DeVore, ed. 1965) and
the search by prehistorians for ethnographic models to help interpret archaeological assemblages (e.g., Kleindienst and Watson
1956). In the late 1950s and early 1960s these trends led to an
unprecedented surge of theoretically oriented field research on
hunter-gatherer societies.

The combination of serious theoretical concerns and the acquisition of large quantities of new field data led to a series of conferences. The first was the Conference on Band Organization in
1965 (Damas, ed. 1969a). The other two, held in 1966, were the
Conference on Cultural Ecology, in which foraging societies held
center stage (Damas, ed. 1969b), and the Man the Hunter Conference (Lee and DeVore, eds. 1968), in which such societies constituted the sole topic of discussion. Together, the three conferences
and their published proceedings had the effect of moving hunter-
gatherer research from the backwaters of anthropology into the
mainstream.

In the quarter century since the proceedings of the three
"founding" conferences appeared, hunter-gatherer research has
expanded enormously, so much so that it is difficult to keep track
of developments in the field. Thus, it is useful from time to time
to pause and take stock, which is the purpose of this book.

The nineteen papers that comprise the core of this volume are
grouped into several sections according to the general issue they
address. The themes are gender, territories and territoriality,
hunter affluence, social stratification, culture contact, government
intervention, native perspectives, and the future of the field.[2]
Each is comprised of an editorial introduction followed by one or
more chapters, each of which deals with a specific problem within the general category. Since most of our own points are made in
the editorials, the balance of this general introduction is devoted
to putting the volume as a whole into context.

2. A number of the more philosophical issues affecting hunter-gatherer studies
were recently discussed in a paper by Richard Lee (1992).

## Conceptual Distinctions

There has been much greater variation among hunter-gatherer societies than is realized by many, or admitted by most, hunter-gatherer specialists. At one extreme within the historical/ethnographic record are the Calusa of southern Florida, who had substantial material wealth and a fully developed class system. At the other extreme are peoples such as the Basarwa of Botswana,[3] the Hadza of Tanzania, and various African Pygmy groups, all of whom had almost nothing in the way of material possessions and minimal social stratification.

Most specialists on hunter-gatherer societies have dealt with this variation by ignoring it. A few have attempted to deal with it by dividing the general class of hunter-gatherers into subcategories according to various criteria. Since these distinctions are referred to in some of the chapters and in most of the editorials, it is appropriate to introduce them here.

### Hunter-Gatherer Versus Gatherer-Hunter

Historically, "hunter" took precedence over "gatherer" in referring to this class of societies, because it was assumed that hunting was more important to people's livelihood than gathering. As is made clear in the section on gender, recent evidence demonstrates otherwise. In fact, in many societies, gathering has contributed more to the food supply than hunting. On the basis of this finding, it has been suggested that the components of the label be reversed, so that the class would be referred to as gather-

3. The people referred to here and in the several editorials as Basarwa were labelled Bushmen in the earlier anthropological literature, and as San or Khoisan in more recent writings. All of these terms are unsatisfactory for one or a combination of the following reasons: (a) they are considered insulting by the people to whom they are applied; (b) the boundaries of the group being referred to are vague; (c) it is not clear whether biological, linguistic, or other criteria are used to delimit the population(s) concerned. Efforts to replace those terms with alternatives have not been satisfactory, either because they are beset by the same problems, or because they involve native designations that are so specific that they have no meaning to people who are not specialists in the area. Our choice of Basarwa is based on the fact that it is the term used officially by the government of Botswana to designate the several relevant groups. For discussions of this issue, see Lee (1979: 29 ff.), Silberbauer (1981: 3 ff., 1991), and Wilmsen (1989a: 27). We thank George Silberbauer for clarifying the relevant issues for us in a personal communication.

er-hunter; or, that the class be divided into two subclasses depending on whether hunting or gathering are more important: hunter-gatherer and gatherer-hunter. Both types are represented in this volume.

To some authors this is important; to us it is not an issue. Whenever the reference is to the class as a whole, we think the two labels should be considered complete equivalents; when applied to specific cases, we think that an author should be free to follow his or her own inclinations (or the evidence) regarding which label to use. As it happens, all of the contributors to the present volume chose to use the phrase hunter-gatherer, but there was no requirement or suggestion that they do so.

A supposedly neutral alternative is the term "forager," which is said to refer without prejudice to either gatherers or hunters, or to both. But even this term is not altogether free of sentiment, since it often has been used to refer to the raping and pillage that medieval (and many other) armies inflicted on local populaces as they traversed the countryside.

Again, we do not consider this to be a problem. For the purposes of this volume, the designations hunter-gatherer, gatherer-hunter, and forager are absolute equivalents. In addition, because the peoples among whom the two of us have done most of our research do a great deal of fishing, we wish to emphasize that all three labels encompass that activity as well.

A more fundamental question is whether the hunter-gatherer class of societies, regardless of the label by which it is known, is fruitfully differentiated from all other types of society. This *is* an issue, one that is addressed in the final section of this book.


*Immediate-Return Versus Delayed-Return Societies*

The distinction between immediate- and delayed-return societies was developed in somewhat different ways by James Woodburn (1980, 1982) and Alain Testart (1982).[4] As summarized by Barnard

---

4. Testart's scheme focuses on the specific issue of food storage. The presence or absence of storage affects whether or not a return is immediate or delayed. Although narrower in scope than the immediate/delayed-return distinction, it is also more complex in Testart's formulation. For a discussion of the differences between the two schemes, see Barnard (1983: 204-208). See also Marciniak, Watanabe, and Testart (1988).

and Woodburn (1988: 11), immediate-return societies are those "with economies in which people usually obtain an immediate yield for their labor, use this yield with minimal delay and place minimal emphasis on property rights." (Examples of immediate return societies discussed in the present volume are the !Kung and the Hadza, particularly as portrayed in the paper by Blurton Jones, Hawkes, and Draper.) Delayed return societies are all others, hence most of the societies known to science. This distinction has not been widely used except by its original proponents, although it has come more into vogue in recent years.

We find the distinction between immediate-return and delayed-return societies useful for differentiating the least complex hunter-gatherer societies (immediate-return) – who have dominated the recent literature on foragers – from the rest. Furthermore, both Woodburn and Testart have explored the implications of this essentially economic distinction for a wide array of other aspects of social life. Few immediate-return societies have been described by anthropologists, but their theoretical significance is considerable because they represent the simplest economic systems ever studied.

*Simple Versus Complex Hunter-Gatherers*

Complexity in this case connotes the degree of internal differentiation and specialization of the components of a system. The more differentiation and specialization, the more complex the system; the less the differentiation and specialization, the simpler or less complex the system (see Price and Brown 1985:7). There are three important features of the concept thus defined. First, the simple-complex dimension is a continuum, not a dichotomy. Second, complexity is a characteristic of a system, not a component (although a component may itself be a system, depending on the level of analysis). Third, there are no moral or other evaluative connotations to the terms "simple" and "complex" when used in this context. To say that a given society is simpler than another does not imply that it is somehow inferior, nor does it imply that its members are less intelligent than those living in the more complex system.

As far as we know, no one has developed an absolute scale of social complexity, according to which one society could be said to be at level X, while another would be at level Y.[5] Thus, we are forced to use relative measures, according to which a given society is said to be more or less complex than another. As a practical matter, however, students of gatherer-hunter societies tend to speak of them in dichotomous terms, as being either simple or complex; the middle gets left out of the discussion. This is disturbing, partly on general grounds and partly because the societies with which we are both most familiar, in northern and western Alaska, fall into the middle range of forager complexity.

The matter of societal complexity is a subject that crosscuts the others addressed in this volume, although it is not mentioned in most of the chapters. We make an issue of it in some of the editorials, partly to place the chapters into context and partly because we wish to stress the fact that foraging societies exhibit a wide range of variation with regard to complexity. This variation is ignored too often in general works on hunter-gatherer societies.

## Omissions

Two themes that hold a prominent place in current hunter-gatherer literature are not given special attention in this volume. It is appropriate to conclude this general introduction by briefly summarizing them, and by stating why they are not included. The two are "revisionism" and optimal foraging theory.

### *"Revisionism"*

The repeated challenging and testing of hypotheses are essential parts of the scientific enterprise. Indeed, they are the primary sources of the objectivity that science strives to achieve. Thus, it should be accepted as a matter of course that major research findings in anthropology are subject to critical scrutiny, tested and retested by other investigators. When a scientific field is as poorly developed as anthropology, it also should come as no surprise to find the results of earlier studies being disproved by later ones more often than not.

---

5. In principle it should be possible to do this, although measurement obviously would be difficult in the case of very complex systems.

In view of the above considerations, a natural scientist skimming over recent literature on gatherer-hunter societies likely would be surprised by the prominence of the epithet "revisionism"; revisions should be expected in such a young field. Older anthropologists who have not kept up to date with the literature on foragers might be forgiven for thinking that "revisionism" referred to the attacks by Berndt (1959), Elkin (1950, 1953), Hiatt (1962, 1965, 1966), Hiatt, ed. (1984), Meggitt (1962: 70), and others on the generalizations of Radcliffe-Brown (1918, 1930, 1931) about the structure of Australian Aborigine societies.[6] In fact, "revisionism," as the term is presently used, refers exclusively to attacks, particularly by Schrire (1980, 1984: 10) and Wilmsen (1983, 1989a, 1989b; Wilmsen and Denbow 1990) on the work of George Silberbauer (1981), Jiro Tanaka (1980), and especially Richard Lee (1979) and his colleagues (e.g., Lee and Devore, eds., 1976) on the Basarwa of Botswana.

The "revisionist" critique and the "traditionalist" defense deal with a variety of issues, the most important of which, in our view, is the extent to which historic foragers can be considered representative of prehistoric ones. The reason we do not include a section on the debate in this book is that numerous papers on the subject have appeared very recently,[7] and more will appear in the near future. However, the subject is addressed briefly in the final chapter by Burch.

## Optimal Foraging Theory

Optimal foraging theory is "an attempt to explain hunter-gatherer subsistence activities as part of general strategies for optimal resource procurement" (Durham 1981: 219). Drawing on the work of evolutionary ecologists and economists, it "assumes that hunter-gatherer survival and reproduction are maximized when the techniques of resource harvest optimize the returns per unit of time and/or energy expended" (Durham 1981: 219; see also

6. See also the exchange between Elkin (1953) and Radcliffe- Brown (1954, 1956), the paper by Birdsell (1970), and the discussion in Lee and Devore, eds. (1968: 146-149).

7. Other relevant works include Barnard (1992), Kent (1992), Lee (1992), Lee and Guenther (1991), Silberbauer (1991), Solway and Lee (1990), Stiles (1992), and Yellen (1990).

Smith 1991b: 41). Its practitioners make extensive use of formal models in developing hypotheses, which they test against evidence concerning how gatherer-hunters operate in the real world. We do not include a section on optimal foraging theory in this book for the same reasons we do not have one on revisionism. The approach has a number of enthusiastic proponents and critics who are actively publishing, and little would be gained by having a special section devoted to it here.[8]

8. Proponents include Belovsky (1988); many of the contributors to the volume by Cashdan, ed. (1990); Hawkes, Hill, and O'Connell (1982); Smith (1987b, 1991b); Smith and Winterhalder (1985); Winterhalder (1986); Winterhalder, et al. (1988); and Winterhalder and Smith, eds. (1981). Critics include Jochim (1988), Keene (1983), and Martin (1983).

# Part 1

## Gender

# Editorial

The word "man" in the *Man the Hunter* volume (Lee and DeVore, eds., 1968) probably was understood by many when it first appeared to refer to humans in general, not just male humans. Despite this possibility, it does not take a very careful reading of the book to reveal that, of the twenty-nine contributors, only two were females, and that males or male activities were the primary focus of attention in almost every chapter where gender was a relevant consideration.

The reaction was not long in coming. Only three years after *Man the Hunter* appeared, Sally Linton (1971) challenged the notion – especially as developed by Washburn and Lancaster (1968) in that book – that hunting and maleness were the only factors, or, indeed, even particularly important factors, in explaining human evolution. Subsequently, Tanner (1981) and Zihlman (1981) turned the original argument on its head by maintaining, with considerable success, that females were more important than males as determining factors in human evolution.

Other critics pointed out that, even though it may be true that men did most of the hunting in many hunter-gatherer societies, the gathering that was undertaken by women in those societies often made an enormous contribution to the food supply. Hunn (1981), for example, showed that, on the Columbia-Fraser Plateau of northwestern North America, three-quarters of people's food energy needs were acquired from plant foods harvested by women!

Out of such studies, the view emerged that men hunted and women gathered, a notion encouraged by the title of the book *Woman the Gatherer* (Dahlberg, ed. 1981).[1] At the very least, it had to be acknowledged that gathering was or is a much more important enterprise than most anthropologists had realized previously. In some cases, indeed, such as among the Agta (Estioko-Grif-

1. See also Tanner's (1983) review of this book.

11

fin and Griffin 1981) of northeastern Luzon (Philippines), and among the Biaka pygmies described here by McCreedy, women do much of the hunting. Where fishing (Burch 1975: 88) or shell-fishing (Meehan 1982) are important, women often play a major role, even if they do not do much hunting in the usual sense of the term. Finally, in many if not most foraging societies, women perform the crucial functions of processing and distributing food and food products (Hawkes and O'Connell 1981).

We now recognize that there has been considerable variation in the extent and nature of the involvement of females in the food quest in hunting-gathering societies. In virtually every case they have filled a major role in gathering, and the foods they have gathered often have been of enormous importance. (In many cases males also have been involved in gathering activities.) In some instances, such as the Chipewyan described here in Sharp's paper, females do indeed gather but do not hunt. In a few societies, females have hunted big game, in others they have cooperated with males in the pursuit of big game, and in quite a few they have hunted small game and have fished, with or without male assistance. Even where they have not actively participated in hunting, females often have played a major part in the rituals that have helped to ensure hunting success. In short, the general importance of females in food production in hunter-gatherer societies has been established beyond any reasonable doubt.

Once the economic aspect of female roles in hunter-gatherer societies was well documented, primary attention shifted to political issues, particularly to the allocation of power along gender lines. In this area, once again, evidence frequently has challenged theory. Useful studies include Leacock's (1978) survey of women's status in egalitarian societies, Lee's (1981b, 1982) summary of the situation among the !Kung, and several works (Brock, ed. 1989; Gale, ed. 1978; Mearns, this volume; Merlan 1988) on the Australian Aborigines. More generally, Begler (1978) determined, on the basis of a literature review, that the conventional view of universal male dominance in hunter-gatherer societies was not always borne out, even by the evidence that already was available. Instead, the literature showed that there was a range of variation extending from virtual equality between males and females, at one extreme, to clear-cut male dominance at the other; to our knowledge, female dominance over males never has been demonstrated on a society-wide basis.

Both extremes are represented in the following chapters. Marion McCreedy's paper deals with the Biaka pygmies, where females seem to have every bit as much power as males. Henry S. Sharp's paper concerns the Chipewyan, among whom male domination is thought by most observers to be overwhelming. Neither author dwells on these basic points, however, for each is interested primarily in more subtle issues relating to how the social system actually works.

The questions that interest McCreedy and Sharp concern how power was wielded, particularly by females, in certain contexts. Thus, McCreedy explores the interaction between women, who were the only ones who could perform a certain crucial ritual, and men, who had to persuade them that the conditions requiring its performance existed. Sharp, on the other hand, shows how a Chipewyan woman used her alleged weakness to exercise control over her husband in a potentially volatile situation. His account supports the more general thesis that even where male dominance is institutionalized, it is often more ideological or symbolic than substantive; women use a variety of means to achieve their goals.

Perhaps the most fundamental point made by these authors is that gender issues are only analytically distinct from many other issues. One cannot really make sense of the division of labor along gender lines in a given society without reference to the allocation of power and responsibility, ritual, symbolism, communication, and emotional expression. The straightforward focus of many early gender studies on the amount of time males and females spent in different activities is no longer sufficient.

# 2

# The Arms of the *Dibouka*
*Marion McCreedy*

In the *bobanda* ritual, Biaka women are legitimate actors in economic and ritual domains, having control over their own particular forms of power. Prolonged hunting failure creates a state of
crisis in a Biaka community. Failure on the hunt is a technical crisis that implies a crisis in social relations. Through the medium of
oratory, individuals (primarily men) convince everyone of the
state of crisis, calling for the most drastic measure to be taken: a
*bobanda* ritual. As the women are reluctant to perform this ritual,
it is up to the community to convince them of the seriousness of
the situation and the need for their economic and ritual labor.
This paper is an examination of the *bobanda* net-hunting ritual of
the Biaka pygmies and its implications.[1]

> The women are the arms of the dibouka.[2]
> If they refused to participate in the bobanda,
> it could not take place,
> because it is the women who
> are responsible for the spirit of the bobanda. (Makanda)

In the anthropological analysis of male-female relations, Marilyn
Strathern (1981:167) draws a distinction between, on the one
hand, "gender stereotypes, the symbolic representation of the

1. Earlier versions of this paper were presented at the Sixth International Conference on Hunting and Gathering Societies in Fairbanks, Alaska (May, 1990) and
at the University of Chicago (April, 1990). Thanks go to Laura Bohannan, Sylvia
Vatuk, Misty Bastian, Robert Moise, Michelle Kisliuk, Ernest S. Burch, Jr., Paul
Hockings, Jim Metcalf, and Jerry Kopecky for helpful comments and suggestions
on revisions. Most important, I acknowledge and thank all my friends at Djoko
(especially Epolo, Maya, Mandjobe, Makanda, Mossongo, and Lembe) and the
government of the Central African Republic, all of whom have shown me kind-
ness, generosity, patience and cooperation. To Justin Mongosso: I have nothing
but respect and gratitude for all the years of guidance and patience you have
shown me. And to Jerry and Lydia, it is for you that I do this.
2. A *dibouka* is a "throw of the nets." During the *dibouka* the nets are set up, animals are driven by beaters to guardians waiting at the nets, and the nets are taken
down. This process is repeated from four to six times during a day of net hunting.

sexes, and the way these often underpin formal relations of authority or power," and, on the other hand, "how women adapt to their position, the maneuvers and stratagems to which they resort, their informal power and interpersonal influence." Close attention to women's strategies and motives indicates that even in situations of overt sex role asymmetry, women have a good deal more power than conventional theorists have assumed (Rosaldo and Lamphere 1974: 9). Peggy R. Sanday (1974: 192) acknowledges the importance of the degree to which women have "defacto or recognized decision-making powers that affect activities at the economic and/or political levels."

## Biaka Pygmies[3]

The Biaka pygmies[4] inhabit the tropical rain forest of the Central African Republic on the southwestern border with the Popular Republic of the Congo. They generally hunt and live deep in the dense Congo Brazza forest between the Sangha and Oubangui rivers. They are mobile hunter-gatherers whose subsistence strategy incorporates a trade relationship of wild game, forest products, and labor for agricultural and Western products from sedentary village agriculturalist neighbors. Most Biaka are also beginning marginal forest farming.

Barry Hewlett (1988: 265) states that the Biaka are primarily patrilineal and usually patrilocal. Primarily and usually are the key words in this case. Most residential communities are made up of a kin group connected through common descent from male ancestors, but this affinity with "their male ancestors" only goes back a generation or two – the Biaka do not think in terms of lineages and rarely can remember details from long ago. They con-

3. My fieldwork was carried out among the Biaka Pygmies of the Lobaye region in the Central African Republic (including nine months of residence with one community) from April 1984 through May 1985. My primary study group was a band of 108 people associated with the village of Lombo in the rural community of Bagandou. Their camp is known as Djoko. My initial research was designed and executed with a friend and colleague, Robert Moise. Although the project began as a joint venture, we have since chosen to write separately and on different subjects. I made a second field trip, alone, to the same region and worked with my primary study group again in July and August 1989.

4. These people are referred to as Biaka or Bayaka, depending on regional variation and accent (Michelle Kisliuk 1991), plural, or Moaka, singular, which is how the Pygmies call themselves. They are more commonly referred to as Aka, the root word, in scientific literature. Their language is Diaka, which is classified as a Bantu language.

ceive of residential communities first by familiarity and by the people with whom they grew up, and the majority of the time this connection is through their male ancestors. Each residential group is usually composed of two to four subgroups (termed "sub- bands" by Ichikawa [1978: 151] and "segments" by Dodd [1984: 6]), based on affective ties and associations. While the residential community is usually based on relationships with the father, the smaller subgroups can be based on several things: relationships with the mother or father, or affective ties. Unless there are serious problems between subgroups, residential units tend to remain relatively stable over time. A man often lives in the camp of his father except for the first few years of marriage, when he fulfills his "marriage service" in the camp of his wife's family.[5] The newly married couple often stays in the wife's camp until the birth of their first child, but, it is not uncommon for the couple to remain in the wife's camp instead of returning to her husband's natal camp. As with most other aspects of Pygmy life, marriage and kinship rules are flexible and are adapted to situational constraints.

Pygmy social organization and political life are characterized as distinctly "egalitarian."[6] Godelier (1977) characterizes Mbuti political rules and practice as lacking of any significant inequality in political status or authority between individuals, men, and women, or between generations, the old, the adult, and the young.[7] Lamphere (1974: 100) proposes that societies where domestic and political spheres are integrated are those in which domestic authority is shared by both men and women. There are no persons of ultimate authority in a Biaka home or community, and there are very few Biaka status roles, which results in the maintenance of egalitarian balance within the society.

5. The amount of time required for a man to fulfill his marriage service is flexible. Marriage involves long term obligations to affines, and it is not unusual for a man to give labor and goods to them throughout the course of his marriage. This, of course, depends upon many things, including how many children his wife has borne, how well he completed his original marriage service, and his relationship with his wife's family, etc.

6. See Bahuchet (1985, 1988), Dodd (1984), Godelier (1977), Hewlett (1987, 1988), Ichikawa (1978), Kisliuk (1991), McCreedy (1987), Meillassoux (1973), Moise (1992), Pedersen and Wæhle (1986), Putnam (1948), Tanno (1976), Turnbull (1965a, 1965b, 1981), and Woodburn (1982).

7. The inequality that does exists favors adult men in relation to women, old men in relation to others, and men over women in young generations. (Godelier 1977: 56)

Even though there is no person commanding ultimate authority in a Pygmy camp and there is no male head of household who
controls the nest, there are positions of respect, knowledge, and
experience. A *kombeti* is an older and respected adult male who
exerts his opinions and influence in subsistence, camp movement, and intercamp relationship decisions in unassertive and
indirect ways. The wife of the *kombeti* also commands great
respect and often is sought out for advice and influence in matters that concern the women. Even if he or she offers a suggestion
in solving a problem at hand, there is no guarantee that it will be
acted upon, and there is no system in place to enforce it. The
*nganga* is a specialist in traditional medicines and healing who
leads divination hunt rituals, and who is trained in healing cases
of natural illnesses and sorcery. The *ntuma* is an elephant hunting
leader and ritual specialist.[8] In the time of the great elephant and
big game hunts, or in regions where elephant hunting still exists,
he leads important seasonal and hunting rituals. The *ntuma* and
the *kombeti* are very often the same person, and in all cases they
are men. Michelle Kisliuk (1991: 262) offers a fourth specialized
status role, the *ginda*, a title the Biaka accord to the master of an
*eboka* (dance) style. Unlike the other three roles, usually filled by a
man, a *ginda* can be a man or woman, depending on the particular
dance form.

In the roles of *kombeti*, *ntuma*, *nganga*, and *ginda*, status is
afforded as long as the activity is relevant to their area of specialization. It does not carry over into other areas or activities. Leadership is minimal and no attempts are made to control or dominate either the human (social) or geographical environments. For
the Baka in Southern Cameroun, Dodd (1984: 2–3) states that
"this very same kind of authority is present in a hunting and
gathering society which, like the Hadza, has no leaders, no officers and no power groups; but where consensus depends upon a
daily recognition of how things ought to be, brought about
through co-operation not only in food production activities, but
also through a view of the world (the forest) and the position of
the Baka within it."

8. Most *ntumas* in the Lobaye region are very old. Since it is now rare to see an
elephant in the Lobaye (although there is still an abundance of elephants in the
Haute Sangha, the forest region to the west of the Lobaye), young adults are not
being trained as *ntumas*.

Louise Lamphere (1974: 109) has shown that in societies where authority is egalitarian, women's and men's interests coincide; women have autonomy or a great deal of influence in many domestic decisions; and their strategies for cooperation are similar to those of men. These elements characterize African Pygmy groups.

With the Biaka, the avoidance of differentiation between the sexes is consistent with the principle of egalitarianism that dominates their life. Although Turnbull (1981: 219) states that sexual differentiation is a major principle of social organization and is used with age as a structural means of dividing the labor and authority, sexual differentiation exists among the Biaka without any sense of superordination or subordination. A woman is in no way the social inferior of a man, and there is little absolute division of labor along sex lines. Turnbull, however, feels that the quality of interdependence and a balance of intradependence between the sexes dominates.

Moreover, as Meillassoux (1973: 195) observes, "the weak development of any division of labor and the participation of women in most of the men's activities, in particular net-hunting parties, helps to keep the sexes on an almost equal social footing." There is also general agreement that in their relations with each other, Pygmy individuals exhibit a high degree of autonomy in most aspects of their lives (Dodd 1984; Turnbull 1965b; Bahuchet 1985; Hewlett 1987, 1988; McCreedy 1987). Individual autonomy is valued above all else; thus the order and organization that the Biaka achieve must be produced without resorting to hierarchy, coercion, or force. No one has the right or means to direct, order, or coerce another individual to do anything against his or her wishes. It is a quality that dominates their mode of production, music and dance, social relations, parenting, and political life. These aspects of Biaka life are characterized by cooperation between the sexes. Biaka women have a great deal of autonomy and influence, and the strict division of labor along gender lines is not a significant organizational principle for them. Decisions are made by common consent. Men and women have equal say, as hunting and gathering are equally important to the economy.

Marilyn Strathern (1981: 186) points out that "at the same time, insofar as an extremely high cultural value is put upon autonomy, people are not, as it were, only social creatures. . . . Whereas prestige must rest upon the opinions of others, self-interest has its own ends, and the exercise of autonomy, whatever others may think, is a payoff in itself." Self-interest can be equal to community interest, which is often the situation with the Biaka. Social rewards for self-interest often coincide with the public good, which can be seen by looking at the motives and methods used by the actors in any ritual, economic, or domestic situation.

### Activities of Females and Males in Economic, Ritual, and Domestic Fields

Godelier (1977: 51) states that Mbuti women's contribution of mollusks, mushrooms, tubers, and other wild plants accounts for half of their food resources. On average, the Biaka spend about 56 percent of their subsistence time hunting, 27 percent of their time gathering, and 17 percent of their time working in the village[9] (Bahuchet 1988: 131). Women are seen as the source of food, as all food that is either hunted or collected must be (and is) cooked by them. Men control the distribution of meat, and women, as principal gatherers and sole food preparers, are the primary food providers.[10]

The loose division of labor practiced by the Biaka divides the daily chores into the responsibility of the women or the men, and again, into the young, the adults, and both (see Table 2.1).

This division of labor is not adhered to strictly, as often the majority of the tasks are practiced by the opposite sex and different age groups. Work is something men and women do for each other; there exists an acknowledged sense of interdependence necessary for survival. Survival and an individual's level of expertise were given as the most frequent responses as to why Biaka do the things they do. It is not unusual to see a man perform a task that is technically his wife's responsibility or vice versa. With the exception of building a hut, I have seen or heard of a member of the opposite sex performing, without reservation, the other's task. Both Turnbull and Bahuchet have noted this flexibility: "Activities will create a difference and distance between male and female but there is no accompanying sense of superiority

9. But values fluctuate between 26 percent and 90 percent for hunting, 8 percent and 56 percent for gathering, and between 0 percent and 34 percent for village work.

10. The women complain a lot, and have great influence over the final result, if they do not agree with their husbands' distribution of the meat.

**Table 2.1:** Biaka Division of Labor[a]

| Male | Female | No Distinctions in Gender or Age |
|---|---|---|
| Felling dead trees for family firewood (usually done on a family or romantic outing); Felling large trees to make forest camp | Hut building (including collection and transportation of materials for construction) | Participation on net hunt[b] |
| | Meal preparation | Singing |
| Big game hunting (elephant, gorilla, forest pig, etc.) | Cleaning areas in and around dwelling | Dancing |
| | | Collecting caterpillars |
| Trap hunting and crossbow hunting | Collecting and transporting firewood | Garden/farm chores |
| Making hunting nets (including collection and transportation of materials for construction) | Collecting and transporting water | Washing clothes (if appropriate) |
| | Caring for infants | Collect and transport vine from which hunting nets are made |
| Collecting honey | If practiced, making mud walls for permanent dwellings | Most ritual activities and performances |
| Constructing smoking racks | Gathering forest products (wild yams, fruits, mushrooms, nuts, vegetables) | |
| If practiced, construction of permanent dwellings (including collection and transportation of materials for construction) | Making baskets | |
| | Making skirts | |
| Making bark clothes (out of practice) | Making mats | |
| | Making digging sticks | |
| Making honey baskets | Butchering and transporting animals | |
| Making spear, ax, and knife handles | Fishing | |
| Making dance costumes | | |
| Making drums | | |
| Drumming | | |
| Tapping palm wine | | |
| Most ritual leadership | | |

[a] This breakdown of activities is loosely adhered to as the majority of tasks are often practiced by the opposite sex and different age groups.

[b] Net hunting is defined to include the attracting and killing of animals, and following the proper behavior and rituals needed to maintain successful and amiable social relations.

or exclusive authority" (Turnbull 1981: 207). "What especially characterizes food-getting strategies is the mental versatility of the Aka, that is, the shrewdness of perception that allows them to take advantage immediately of any opportunity they encounter" (Bahuchet 1988: 133).

Loosely, the following are areas of female activity: building huts, which includes collecting the construction materials; preparing meals for the family; cleaning the area in and around the house; collecting and transporting firewood, although the men help to fell the dead trees; collecting and transporting water; caring for the infants; making the mud walls for the more permanent structures; gathering forest products, such as wild yams, fruit, mushrooms, nuts, vegetables, etc.; making baskets, skirts, mats, and digging sticks; fishing (by creating dams); butchering and transporting animals; and collecting and transporting the vine from which the hunting nets are made. Activities usually considered male are: hunting big game, such as elephant, gorilla, forest pig, etc.; trap hunting; bow hunting; making hunting nets, which includes collecting all net materials; collecting honey; constructing smoking racks; constructing permanent houses (where practiced), which includes collecting and transporting the construction materials; making dance costumes and drums, which includes collecting the materials; making bark cloth clothes (now no longer done); making honey baskets; making spears, axes, and knife handles; and tapping palm wine. All other activities, such as singing, dancing, collecting caterpillars, working on their farms, participating on the net hunt, washing, etc., are free from any gender distinctions and are practiced equally by both sexes and among all ages.

Men are basically responsible for most ritual leadership and some performance, while women are active participants and often specific specialists. At times they have also been the channel through which ritual knowledge is revealed. The *nganga* (and *kombeti*) of my primary study camp received his magical knowledge through the dreams of Lembe, his wife. Maya (the *nganga*) was staying by Lembe's side during a long and nearly fatal fever, at which time she saw and heard many powerful and strange things in her repeated dreams. As she explained to me, in one of her later dreams, "the spirits urged me to take the power to be a healer" and insisted upon putting her to some tests. "It was very powerful, too powerful for me and it scared me. The grand spirits came and said they wanted to give me the power but after several tests they remarked that I could never support it. They decided to grant my wish to transmit this power to Maya because he is very courageous. Since that day, it is Maya who has had the power" (McCreedy 1989). Today, Maya is one of the most respected *ngangas* in the region and he never fails to mention that this came about as a result of Lembe's vision.

Laughter, jokes, and imitation are vital elements in Biaka conflict solving. Women have great power through mimicry and imitation. They act out events relating to and explaining the current situation or conflict, or one in the recent past. It is not at all uncommon to see a woman or group of women suddenly burst into a reenactment of an event, at center stage for all to see, bringing on crowds howling with laughter. They are excellent actors and as a result exert influence and power through their dramas of reenactment. Men often state that they wish to avoid being made fun of by the women because it can be embarrassing. If a man has problems with a woman (typical complaints were not making love frequently enough with one's wife, and not bringing in a lot of animals), the woman will tell all the other women, and the ridicule that follows is very hard for the man to bear.

In discussing Mbuti ridicule, Turnbull (1981: 211) states that "ridicule is an important element in all conflict resolution; only the old women come out in the open, in the middle of the camp, and make explicit criticisms. Many men use the same central position, which commands attention, but only to grumble or complain and perhaps make minor and rather petty criticisms that are most likely to be ignored."

In regard to Biaka net-hunting and sharing practices, the hunt involves cooperation and reciprocity between members of the group, irrespective of sex or age. Both sexes and all ages work equally hard. Each household in a Biaka community owns a hunting net, which belongs to the adult male member of the household. During a net hunt, these nets are placed end to end to form a semicircle, into which game is driven by beaters to the waiting "guardians." This process of putting up the nets, chasing game into it, and then taking the nets down (a *dibouka*) usually takes less than an hour and is repeated between four and six times a day, changing the location and the type of hunt each time. Animals killed on the hunt belong to the household owning the net in which they were captured. Based on a principle of general reciprocity, the animals are butchered and the owners of the meat distribute portions of it to those individuals within the camp whose nets did not catch anything and/or to individuals who aided in the capture of the game.[11]

Net hunting has a number of unique characteristics that distinguish it from other forms of hunting. In most hunting and gathering societies, hunting is a male activity. For the Biaka, hunting is essentially the men's responsibility, but it is everyone's concern. The execution of the net hunt is a large scale, cooperative effort involving a significant number of people. It is not an individual affair, but involves the camp as a whole. No one segment of the community is large enough to accomplish it. The net hunt is therefore an effort of the entire community: men, women, the young and the old participate. Only the very young or infirm are excluded.

While the women participate technically in the net hunt, their primary interest is in gathering. Whenever they have the chance, they search for wild foods (nuts, fruits, and vegetables). While gathering is mostly a female activity, it may be and often is done by men when necessary. During the hunt the women most often fulfill the role of guardian of the net, standing ready to capture the game as their husbands or brothers drive (beat) the game toward them. While waiting, they explore the immediate area for food to collect or for future gathering.

The Biaka have five types of net hunts in their repertoire of hunting techniques. In four of them the men act as beaters, driving the animals a short distance toward the women, who are waiting as guardians.[12] The men also perform all associated ritual activity in these hunts. In the fifth type, the *mbembo* hunt, women act as the beaters while the men wait near the nets. As the women approach the men, the latter take over as beaters and the women become guardians.

The *mbembo* hunt is the only type of hunt associated with the *bobanda* ritual. In contrast to the other four, all of which employ a strategy of making minimal noise until the moment of attack, the *mbembo* requires an enormous amount of noise from the outset. It

11. There is a very precise and established system of dissection and distribution of the game captured in Biaka net hunting, which is detailed in the work of Bahuchet (1985).

12. It is interesting to note that among the Mbuti, net hunters of the Ituri forest, the women normally perform the role of beaters and, on the average, their participation in the hunt was greater than that of the men (Harako 1976: 53).

also requires the beaters to travel farther out before beginning to drive the game. Also in contrast to the other four, women involved in the *mbembo* hunt participate equally with men as ritual actors in the exhausting, daylong hunt.

## Hunting Failure

Hunting provides the basis of Pygmy economic systems, and as a result it is clear that hunting (as opposed to gathering) success is more important for Pygmy groups than it is for many other hunting-gathering groups.[13] While a few days with no luck on the hunt is the norm and can be tolerated, prolonged hunting failure for a Pygmy community quickly can become a crisis. There is a level of fluctuation that is considered "natural" in hunting success. Consistent failure is not "natural." After numerous days of hunting with continual failure to capture sufficient game, the Biaka view the failure as an indication of the influence of some outside agent.

The flow of animal resources received in exchange for the investment of labor is considered vulnerable to the influence of the actions of all the members within, and occasionally outside, the community. A wide range of behaviors is thought to be capable of interrupting it: eating taboo foods and breaking taboo rules, such as the participation of menstruating women and/or their husbands on the hunt, or the consumption of meat by menstruating women and/or their husbands, the existence of negative feelings between individuals (especially jealousy), contagious bad luck, or the harboring or expression of negative thoughts through sorcery.

To solve a crisis in social relations associated with a case of hunting failure, the Biaka apply the same resolution technique they use when faced with other problems: a verbal discussion I call the "parole."[14] (Dodd [1984: 12] calls this technique "kalo" for the Baka, and Pedersen and Wæhle [1986: 84] call it "nightly speeches" for the Bamgombi [Baka].) The "parole" functions as

13. The only notable exception is the BaGyeli of Southwestern Cameroun, for whom fishing and agriculture play major economic roles (Joiris 1986).

14. "Parole" is the French word for a speech. This is how Justin Mongosso, my research assistant, and I referred to these discussions while in the field. As the Biaka have no word for these discussions, I chose to call them as I referred to them while at Djoko.

the primary method a community uses to make its plans, solve problems, and resolve disputes involving any matter of community concern. Since most personal matters have the potential to become community matters, almost everything and anything can be discussed during the "parole."

The "parole" occurs in camp when the majority of the community is present. It is held either in the morning before people have left for the hunt or to perform other activities in the forest, or during the evening when everyone has returned to the camp and people are relaxing or cooking around their huts. I have even heard of a "parole" taking place during the middle of the night while most people are trying to sleep. A "parole" is begun by an individual simply raising his or her voice and talking until all other conversations cease and the group's attention is focused on the speaker. After an introduction, summarizing the situation and its potential causes, the individual presents his or her idea on the causes of the failure. Once this has been done, the remainder of the discourse is an act of persuasion: trying to convince others in the community to agree with a particular recommendation enough to invest their energies in the ritual and hunting activity being suggested. Inspiration is the vehicle by which individuals are convinced of the need to invest their energies in the collective. As they cannot be coerced or forced to do so, they must be persuaded. All these acts of persuasion are directed towards the same goal: creating within the individual an awareness of the needs of the whole community, and inspiring each individual to mobilize his/her energies for participation in a collective action to restore order.

Once the Biaka determine the causes of failure, they seek a solution in the realm of ritual. In the case of prolonged hunting failure, four major rituals are employed and used in a developmental "sequence of intensification," corresponding with increasing amounts of dramatic and symbolic action. As hunting success falters and meat shortages commence, the ritual activity of camp increases. Three of these four rituals are beyond the scope of this paper; the fourth and most dramatic of the rituals, the *bobanda*, is what concerns us here.[15]

15. For a more detailed description of Biaka ritual activity see Moise (1992) and Bahuchet (1985).

*Bobanda Ritual and Hunt*

Unlike the minor net hunt rituals, the *bobanda* ritual and hunt is drastic and spectacular.[16] In the minor ones, men handle the ritual and technical action of the hunt, but when the crisis is severe enough, as with the *bobanda*, women are drawn into the normally male domain of ritual and the driving or beating of game. The *bobanda* is performed over the course of a hunting day and the preceding evening. Full and complete *bobandas* are not always performed (the evening activities are often neglected), but what will be described here is a full performance.

During a "parole" discussion, if a *bobanda* ritual hunt has been decided upon and the women have agreed to participate, very often a ritual leader, a *bobanda nganga*, will be picked to direct the ritual and hunting activity. This position is held only for the day and any adult male is eligible for it. The leader picks a male assistant and a female *bobanda nganga* to help him. The choice of the assistant appears to be arbitrary, but the female *bobanda nganga* is often the leader's wife, sister, or an "aunt" of the camp. The leader is responsible for the necessary ritual, including the preparation of both magical substances and ritual sites, the *mabangbe*. All adult male hunters possess the relevant knowledge to be a leader.

The night before the *bobanda* hunt a dance is performed. Below are edited excerpts from my field notebook describing this event:

Makanda, the *kombeti's* wife, began by addressing the group, saying that they had to do something to increase their luck tomorrow and get rid of the *ekila* (bad spirits) that might be causing the bad luck. She then started singing in the middle of the camp. Then the *bokala* (bachelors, eight years and older) started playing the drums. They played the drums on and off for twenty minutes. But once the drummers got

16. For the archers of the Ituri, Turnbull (1965b: 162), Schebesta (in Turnbull 1965a: 172–3), Harako (1976: 54), and Terashima (1983: 79) describe the annual *begbe* hunt as having qualities similar to the *bobanda* in that it involves a corresponding hunting technique and festive atmosphere. As the women never participate on the hunt, the *begbe* is remarkably like the net hunt of their Mbuti neighbors in technique and social function. The major difference is the lack of nets. Terashima (1983: 76–8) also describes the *musilo* hunt, which involves the symbolic participation of a few women. While these hunts are more symbolic than practical (they are not done in times of hunting failure and crisis), they are done as a demonstration of cooperation and the collective, and in this way they are similar to the *bobanda* of the Biaka.

going, everyone assembled. All the women had *ebobos* (batons made from wrapped bunches of leaves, like what they use when beating on the hunt), which they beat against the ground in time with the music. They were singing one song over and over.

Soon the *kombeti* went into the center of the circle of singers and began dancing. Once he started dancing, the men joined in with the beating of the leaves. Maya (the *kombeti*) did the same dance over and over. He was imitating an animal and danced in a crouched position. He would start out on a stroll, just cruising around, minding his own business, enjoying himself. Then he would perk his head up like an animal as if he knew something was going on, but he still paraded around, with a watchful eye.

Then he would become frantic, and start running here and there, trembling and shaking. This motion would mount to a frenzy. He then noticed something through the frenzy and danced toward the singers. He danced up to the circle, and, in a frenzy, fell into it.

The singers would always start out with the normal song, but as time progressed, they would start yelling, shaking the leaves and the tension would mount (like it does when they see an animal on the hunt) until it was at a feverish pitch. Then the *kombeti* would fall into the circle. Once the *kombeti* fell, they would yell in unison "ohhhh" and then they would start cracking up with more than just laughter.

They kept doing this over and over with Maya (the *kombeti*) as the only dancer. At one point, between songs, Maya delivered a soliloquy about how they would have to be fast in chasing the animals. They would have to run fast and be quick with their spears. He acted this out in the dance. The dance is called the *bobanda* dance.

After the dance, while preparing for bed, the *kombeti* warns the hunters to leave the women alone tonight, and for the women to keep their legs together because no sex is allowed before a *bobanda* hunt. (The hunters now say that they do not abide by this rule much.) The following morning the appointed male *bobanda nganga* begins alone, at daybreak, without eating breakfast (he must have an empty stomach), by preparing several ritual sites. He prepares a number of small sites along the path leading from the camp to the hunting area, where each individual is obliged to perform a collective ritual action. These sites are small structures built from thick red vines, or else carvings and drawings on small trees. He also prepares a more elaborate site, the *mabangbe*, where he sits and waits for the arrival of the hunters, who are followed by the dancing and singing women. Usually, all participants are required to gather some nearby leaves, spit on them, and deposit them on a designated pile.

Throughout the period of my field study, the variation in site elaboration was great, depending upon product availability in each area of the forest. A consistent feature of the *mabangbe* was a gateway, through which or under which everyone passed, made from the same thick red vine used for the sites along the path, from which various leaves are cut and hung. The small trees surrounding the area are also carved and drawn in geometric patterns and designs. The male *bobanda nganga* usually builds a separate area for himself which often has a small bench. He sits with his back to the group and to the fire, where he burns leaves that will aid in the capture of game.[17]

It is at the *mabangbe* where the male assistant joins the *bobanda nganga* and takes up a pair of percussion sticks[18] made on the spot, which he beats continually in a rhythmic pattern. The *bobanda nganga* also makes a sharp noise by cupping a leaf in his hands and clapping so as to make a loud pop. The rest of the group waits at the *mikando*, where the nets have been left and protected overnight in the forest, and where everyone gathers the following morning. The percussive sounds and the leaf popping lead the camp members to the *mabangbe*. The males from the camp arrive first, followed by the women, who arrive in single file. As the women arrive, they sing and dance with great vitality around the leader, "beating" him lightly with branches.[19] He sits in total silence throughout these activities. Once all the women have bestowed their blessings upon the male *bobanda nganga*, he solemnly gets up and departs, without uttering a word, leading the rest to where the first *dibouka* will occur. The following edited observations from my field notes provide a vivid description of the *mabangbe*:

17. Turnbull writes of a similar ritual of fire and smoke in connection with the hunt, particularly the *begbe* hunt of the Mbuti archers. "The archers also may light a special fire and cover it with leaves so that a thick smoke rises. The God of the Undergrowth sees the smoke, smells its fragrance, and hears the *segbe* pipes. [See my notes 20 and 21.] His attention is thus drawn to the plight of his 'children'" (Turnbull 1965a: 190).

18. Bahuchet (1985: 452) identifies these sticks as *mbanda*, which he believes is the origin for the name of the ritual.

19. The beating of branches is used in other rituals as a means of transferring negative and positive forces (Bahuchet 1985: 438–40).

The action of the ritual seems to rest with the leader, his male assistant (on the sticks), and the women. The leader has a very solemn, silent attitude. He does not talk to anyone. At the *mbenguis* (rest and discussion locations) he always stays away from the group, out of sight. When the group is ready to depart, he appears and leads the procession.

The women contribute to the ritual as well, but in a different way. Their attitude is not solemn. Instead they are very lively. They are like the batteries that charge the event. They keep yelling "Oka," "Oka" (Let's go), singing loudly and yelling, laughing and dancing around. Their purpose seems to be to stir things up. During the *dibouka*, the women participate in the beating and it is very loud and lively.

The male *bobanda nganga* leaves behind, at the *mabangbe*, mixtures of magical red and black powders, which the women use to paint their foreheads, faces, and hair. He also paints himself with these powders, which are used to revitalize one's productive self (Bahuchet 1985: 452). The female *bobanda nganga* puts a magical cord around her ankle, which the male *bobanda nganga* has made for her. He also wears a magical cord on his ankle. The cords are used to make the drive more effective by producing an abundance of animals within the semicircle of nets. He leaves a paste, which he paints around his eyes, for the female *bobanda nganga* and other women so that they can do the same. This paste enables them to see the animals better.[20] In general, all the ritual decorations at the *mabangbe* are also for personal use. The cut leaves and red vines are taken down, and hats, headbands, and sashes are fashioned from them for both male and female hunters, to increase their personal luck during the hunt. After they have applied the various magical substances to their bodies and decorated themselves, they join the others in setting up the nets.

The male *bobanda nganga* and his male assistant sit at the center point of the nets, the *dikai*, producing percussion and wind sounds in an attempt to attract game. The *bobanda nganga* creates sounds on a flute-like instrument made from a duiker hoof, similar to the *segbe* pipes used by the Efe and the Mbuti.[21] The male

20. Turnbull (1965a: 225) mentions a paste, called *anjo*, which the Efe "sometimes smeared on the face to heighten the senses of smell, sound and sight." Tanno (1976: 109) writes of the Mbuti that in their methods of net hunting "they burn snapped twigs with green leaves, the charcoal of which they smear around their eyes, on their foreheads and noses as they like. They maintain that this ritual aids in procuring a large catch."

21. Both Schebesta and Putnam refer to pipes and whistles used by both the Efe archers and the Mbuti net hunters to "call" game (cited in Turnbull 1965a: 173,

assistant plays the rhythm sticks mentioned earlier. After the nets are prepared, a signal is given and the male *bobanda nganga* hooks the two nets at the *dikai*, places the rhythm sticks at the base of the nets, and then hangs the flute from the top of the net. There they rest until the nets are taken down. They then join the female *bobanda nganga* and the other women who are waiting for them at the head of the nets (*mossoko*). Together, they go a great distance away from the nets and lead the driving of game toward the nets in an *mbembo* hunt. The women drive the game by hitting the ground with batons made from tightly rolledup branches, making sharp explosive sounds that send the animals running toward the men waiting at the nets. Throughout the day it is the women who hold the responsibility of executing the exhausting *mbembo*. Excluding the performances at the initial ritual site, the technical and ritual actions of the *ngangas*, the assistant, and the women are repeated each time the nets are set up and the game is driven for the remainder of the day.

The powerful ritual aspects of the *bobanda* are what make it so clearly the best weapon in the Biakas' arsenal of remedies. Two forms of power attempt to fix the state of crisis: the individual male power of the *bobanda nganga*, focused on the knowledge of magical materials; and the collective power and energy of the females displayed in their vitality as a group. The women show their vitality symbolically as a group through their singing and dancing, transferring this power and energy to the male leader by "beating" him with leaves. He sits receiving this power silently. In most other net hunting rituals, the men beat the nets to bring success, but in the *bobanda* ritual, the women beat the *bobanda nganga*, transmitting to him their power and energy. This energy is maintained and reinforced throughout the day as the women physically display it in their coleadership and efforts during the numerous *mbembos*, an expression of dual gender participation in rituals.

Technically, a *bobanda* hunt day is filled with five or six *mbembos*, but has no ritual action. On the average, three or four *mbembos* are performed each week. When one is performed, it is done only once that day. Even though it is a highly effective and pro-

---

190, 192, 240). There were incorporated in the hunting net for the hunter to blow to attract the antelope. The *segbe* pipes are able to deflect storms, attract game, or defeat the enemy.

ductive type of hunt and guarantees results, the vast amount of the forest that is covered in driving the game toward the nets makes it is physically exhausting. It requires the women to perform extra labor, and although four or five times a week is tolerable, four or five times a day requires some persuasion.

The "parole" is the medium through which the men try to persuade and convince the women to perform the *bobanda*. Emphasizing their ideology of unity and community and stressing the whole over the individual, the men convince the women of the need of a *bobanda*. The women's enthusiasm is necessary for it to be successful, indicating the power of women's actions and their effect on hunting success. Women have the potential and the power to greatly affect the net hunt. They are rarely convinced in one discussion that the situation requires the amount of energy being asked of them. It takes many discussions with the men as a group, first directing the address toward the full community and then toward the women to generate the necessary enthusiasm. The men (and the entire community) are at the mercy of the women and must convince them to perform. The women cannot be coerced. They must be motivated from within to identify their interests with those of the community.

Collective action must be based on a perceived mutuality of interest and it is up to the men to convince the women that the situation requires their cooperation. When one is hungry enough it does not take much convincing. But when the nets of only a few households are empty and there is not yet a serious shortage of meat, it requires a considerable amount of persuasion to convince the women that the men's problems are also theirs. Even if the women do not need any convincing, they hold back. As Lembe once explained to me, sometimes it is better to make the men a little nervous before agreeing to perform – "otherwise, they might take advantage of us and make us do it too often." Since a crisis of the hunt is everyone's crisis, once the women agree it is a crisis, they never refuse to perform the *bobanda*.[22]

As the *bobanda* ritual is asked for and performed in a time of crisis, it indicates that women are a source of power to be summoned to effect the success of the hunt. They are called upon and formally recognized by the men as the most powerful remedy to

22. The women refuse to participate if they do not believe that the shortage is a crisis that necessitates a *bobanda* hunt and ritual.

solve the most serious problem. When the individual magical knowledge of the men in camp breaks down and fails to remedy the hunting failure, the collective energy and power of the women are needed. Through their displays of vitality in singing and dancing, the transference of power to the *bobanda nganga*, coleadership of the beating of the game, the wearing of magical cords, the smearing of magical powders and pastes, and the wearing of magical leaves and cords, the women indeed must be viewed as an important source of power. Also, through the role they play in preparation for this ritual and its execution, women are seen as political actors who employ strategies to achieve particular communal and personal ends.

### Emic Perspective of Bobanda Ritual (Female)

On several occasions Mossongo, Makanda, Lembe and I would have conversations concerning the *bobanda* ritual. As the three of them were wives of respected hunters and active participants in the unit, their comments were both insightful and helpful. The following are excerpts from those conversations (McCreedy 1989).

> "The *bobanda* has not changed since our youth. The structure and the formulas have remained. The ritual *bobanda* requires the necessary cooperation of the women and the men. " (Mossongo)

> "The only difference since our youth, is that in the past the women put on a outfit (uniform) of skirts well put together with leaves." (Lembe)

> At one point I asked if the women could lead the *bobanda* ritual in the same way as the men. Mossongo replied, "No. The biggest power of the fetishes, the cords, the leaves, the roots, and the vegetable powder is only led by the men. The woman can not go in the early morning, but she waits for the other hunters and she only begins to assist the *nganga* during the *dibouka*. She receives from the *nganga* a cord she wears on her ankle with the power to attract animals toward the hunters. She leads the other arm of the *dibouka*."

> "The *bobanda* is a ritual that is realized by male and female hunters. After many repeated defeats and shortages of meat, the decision [to perform a *bobanda*] is made in the evening. In that which concerns the fetishes, it's the male *nganga* that possesses the secret. During the performance, the wife of the *nganga* or one of the sisters or aunts of the camp receive the fetishes from him (the *bobanda nganga*). She leads the

other side of the *dibouka*. The women are the arms of the *dibouka*. If
they refused to participate in the *bobanda*, it could not take place,
because it is the women who are responsible for the spirit of the *bobanda*." (Makanda)

## Conclusion

In recent years, more research has focused on women's roles and
influences on hunting and its ritual practices. For example, in *I
Am Not the Great Hunter, My Wife Is*, Barbara Bodenhorn (1990: 1)
states that women are considered pivotal to successful hunting
because they ritually attract the animals, and are thus categorized
as hunters by Iñupiaq men. While among the Iñupiat, hunting is
considered "hard work" and women frequently speak of their
husband's labors with respect and appreciation, the husbands
openly recognize their wives' contributions as well: "Animals
give themselves up to men whose wives are generous and skillful; it is also the man's responsibility to treat the animal properly,
but it is the woman to whom the animal comes" (Bodenhorn
1990: 5). In her work with the Baka Pygmies of Southeastern
Cameroun, Veronique Joiris has found that even though the
women are excluded from the technical process in the *grand chas-
se á l'elephant*, they contribute nonetheless. They are essential in
the ritual processes surrounding the hunt, and without their
intervention the hunters could never enter the forest world and
succeed. In these rituals the women perform divination, acting as
mediators between the human world and the forest world to
locate and call the animals, in the hope of aiding the cynegetic
activities of the men. It is the women who can restore an individual's "luck" and thus ensure successful hunting (Boursier, cited
in Joiris 1990: 20).

As with the Iñupiat and the Baka, Biaka women have great
influence and are considered vital to successful hunting. In conclusion, the implications presented in this examination of the
*bobanda* ritual are: women are seen as important economic and ritual actors, who have control over their own particular forms of
power; and women are seen as the ultimate solution to economic
and social problems. Once the community is in a state of economic and social crisis, it is the women and only the women who can
provide a solution and restore the community to a state of economic and social viability.

# 3

# The Power of Weakness

*Henry S. Sharp*

This paper examines a mechanism through which individuals categorized as inferior are able to exercise control and power over individuals categorized as superior in power or knowledge. This mechanism is broadly based in Chipewyan culture, independent of gender relations, but particular attention is paid here to a situation of apparent male domination.[1]

The Chipewyan are not well known outside of Canada and little known even within their own country. What is known about the Chipewyan both in Canadian popular culture and in the academic literature is controlled by images of primitiveness, harshness, and male domination (Sharp in press [b]). These images held by Canada's English-speaking public are part of its cultural legacy; a folk understanding of the time when the lives of white Canadians were economically, socially, and politically dominated by the presence of Canada's native peoples. The images of the past are constantly reformed and reinforced by the confusion and misunderstanding of white administrators, tourists, seasonal workers, and others who experience the Chipewyan as the cultural "other"; by experiences and interpretations formed in circumstances that often are alien as well as physically and emotionally stressful, which then are carried by word of mouth into the larger cultural domain.

The Chipewyan themselves (Irimoto 1981; Jarvenpa 1976, 1980, 1982; Sharp 1988a; D. M. Smith 1973, 1982, 1990a; J. G. E. Smith 1970, 1978; VanStone 1965) are Athapaskan speakers now living

1. I wish to thank Edie Turner and Richard Slobodin for their keen insights and helpful comments on earlier drafts of this paper. A previous version of this paper was summarized at the Sixth International Conference on Hunting and Gathering Societies (CHAGS-6) in Fairbanks, Alaska, in May 1991, where it generated some smoke and a number of useful insights, for which I am grateful. I am appreciative of these insights, but responsibility for the arguments made here rests with me, as does responsibility for any errors.

in the Prairie Provinces and the Northwest Territories. Aboriginally, they were a small scale hunting society existing at population densities rarely exceeding one person per hundred square miles. Traditional Chipewyan diet consisted almost entirely of animal tissue; the use of plants for food was minimal. Their dependence upon animal tissue was so great that they form an extreme case within the general class of hunter-gatherers, so much so that academic discussions of hunter-gatherers often ignore them and other northern hunters altogether (e.g. Stiles 1992). Neither the land, the climate, nor the ecology of the Chipewyan has struck a positive chord in Canadian popular culture (or in academic culture, for that matter), and Canadian public opinion about Chipewyan lands has tended to be more favorable than Canadian public opinion about the Chipewyan people. This pattern of thought has existed in popular writing at least since the original publication of Samuel Hearne's widely known and highly influential *Journal* (1971 [1795]).

Hearne spent several years living among the Chipewyan, primarily among travelling parties organized for trade and raiding, in the course of his multiyear search for fabulous copper deposits in the then unknown lands of the present-day Northwest Territories. He was little impressed by the life of the ordinary Chipewyan who were not greatly involved in the fur trade. Their lives were based upon a seasonal round of subsistence activities that even Hearne felt obliged to acknowledge was more secure than the life of the Chipewyan traders drawn into commerce with the Hudson's Bay Company (Hearne 1971 [1795]: 82–83).

The overriding environmental image Hearne presented was of deprivation – of food, shelter, comfort, and security. This image of bare survival, of life hanging in only the most tenuous balance in a land of starvation, continues to this day in spite of anthropological rejection of the view (Sharp in press [b]; Farb in Wilson 1992: 17). As both cause and effect, this negative image of the Chipewyan blends well with Canadians' more general perception of their environment and the native peoples (Atwood 1972).

No culture – including the contemporary ones of European derivation – has ever been able to support itself through agriculture within the range of the Chipewyan. The success of the Chipewyan as hunters has been contingent upon their ability to make large seasonal kills of game and has been aided by their knowledge of preservation techniques for long-term meat storage. The extremely cold and dry climate, large numbers of astonishingly mobile (Burch 1972) – but often highly concentrated – prey animals, fish, and birds, and the limited needs of a small population all contributed to the success and maintenance of the Chipewyan hunting culture. The Chipewyan carefully constructed alliances of kinship and affinity that facilitated food distribution (Sharp 1977). These alliances, in combination with a body of empirical knowledge about the process of obtaining subsistence that was carefully attuned to the effects of both short-term and long-term variations in geographic, climactic, and seasonal variables upon the indigenous prey species, enabled the Chipewyan to construct for themselves a relatively secure existence in the absence of epidemic disease.

Congruent with the image that Hearne presented of the harshness of the Chipewyan homeland was the image he presented of the harsh life endured by all Chipewyan, especially the lives of the elderly and the women. His *Journal* presents a spectacular vision of male dominance (primarily by males in the middle period of their lives), in which the elderly were routinely abandoned to starve and women were forced to exist in a state of extreme deprivation and degradation. Women not only were allocated as chattel in marriage, but they could be purchased, and were unconsulted prizes in contests even after they were married (Slobodin 1975). Their lives included rape, beatings, hunger, abandonment, and hard work.

The contemporary reality of Chipewyan life simply is not compatible with the Canadian historical folk image of deprivation and male domination. Neither can historical accounts of Chipewyan life sustain that image in the light of contemporary ethnographic interpretation. However, understanding the Chipewyan construction of gender is complicated by the pervasive negative symbolic and linguistic categorization of the category "female" in Chipewyan culture. "Female" is a symbolic classification that is extensively developed through canid metaphors (Sharp 1976, 1986, 1988a, 1988b) and it is deeply embedded in the Chipewyan language through the contrasting values placed upon hunting and scavenging (Carter 1974). It is because of the persistence of Western civilization's negative image of the Chipewyan (in spite of the readily observable fact that the daily reality of

Chipewyan social life does not conform to that image) and because of the heavy asymmetry between the categories of "Male" and "Female" internal to Chipewyan culture that their mode of constructing gender is of particular interest.

If, to borrow a metaphor from Roy Wagner (1981), the meaning of events is sometimes negotiated in the shadow space cast by symbols, so power and control may exist in the shadows cast by dominant symbolic forms. This chapter examines one general mechanism in Chipewyan culture through which members of social categories (including gender categories) that are defined as inferior or weaker are able to exercise power over members of social categories (including gender categories) that are defined as superior or stronger. Chipewyan classification schemes make far greater use of polythetic (nonbinary) categories (Needham 1972, 1975) than do English language classification schemes, often giving a relativistic aspect to categorizations that may confound a binary analysis. The general examination of this mechanism will focus upon situations that seem to be clear-cut examples of dominance or hegemony in order to minimize this problem, and in order to isolate the dynamics of the interactions. The detailed analysis of a specific case will show how the very assertion of negative valuation can draw upon other cultural beliefs to place control of a given situation in the hands of the apparently weaker, or dominated actor.

## Complementarity and Dominance

This analysis is predicated upon the importance of gender complementarity in human cultures, a position in marked contrast to the contemporary focus upon dominance and hegemony in the analysis of gender relations. The emphasis upon complementarity demands some specification of the reasons for my unease with the concept of dominance (Sharp 1981: 221–22; 1982: 425–27; in press [b]). I assume that complementarity in gender relationships is a direct product of the reciprocity fundamental to human social organization (Durkheim 1964, 1965; Huntington 1973; Mauss 1967), and that that reciprocity has been based on the evolutionary biology of the species since the introduction of food-sharing. Of more immediate relevance, I presume that a model of gender complementarity provides a more dynamic model of society than does a dominance model. The implications of the complementarity model lead research conducted under that model toward a more comprehensive examination of interpersonal relationships in human society than does research conducted under a dominance model.

A dominance model, whether expressed in terms of domination, hegemony, or oppression, is reductionist. The logic of the model focuses research attention upon attempts to isolate relations of presumed coercion, relations that are essentially binary and of the logical order of $A > B$. When a dominance model is used without explicit reference to some broader model of society, its focus upon dichotomous power relations creates by default a linear model (Coveney and Highfield 1990: 158–169) of society, in which society is presumed to be the summation of those isolated relationships. As a minimalist model of society, the power of the dominance approach lies precisely in its demand for the isolation of power relations from their context, but that power is achieved at the cost of the context within which those relations exist.

In contrast to a dominance model, the implicit theoretical view of society embedded in a complementarity model is on the logical order of $A + B = 1$. Two immediate differences are apparent. The logic of a complementarity model readily allows for the consideration of multiple variables, $A + B + \ldots N = 1$, within the same set of dynamics. This factor becomes increasingly relevant as the nonbinary nature of gender becomes increasingly conspicuous ethnographically. The second difference is the complementarity model's demand for the inclusion of power relationships within their broader social context. Where the logic of a dominance approach calls for the discovery and explication of the mechanisms of dominance, the complementarity model demands that those relations be considered along with the countervailing mechanisms and values controlling human interaction. As a practical issue, a complementarity model makes a different assessment of the nature of human gender relations than that made by the more restricted assumptions of a dominance model. The complementarity model leads the investigator into a broader search for the mechanisms of power in human relationships. If the driving force in a dominance model is the search for the locus and nature of the domination, the main issue in a complementarity model is, What holds them together?

**The Power of Weakness: I**

Culture is obligatory (Durkheim 1964, 1965). It is more typical for social anthropology to speak of society than of culture and to emphasize that society exists through shared values, but the obligatory nature of the sharing of values is not diminished through this focus. Sharing is coercive interaction. Whether the sharing is of objects (Mauss 1967) or of values, it is always a total social phenomenon. It is the coerciveness of the sharing of values within a cultural context that provides a key to understanding the way Chipewyan women exercise power in the situations examined here.

Several decades ago, in the course of some brief but subtle ethnographic examinations of the Kutchin (hereafter called Gwich'in), Richard Slobodin (1962, 1969) touched upon their ideas about the danger of incompetent or ignorant individuals bringing harm to themselves or others, and the necessity of preventing such behavior. The consequences of the harm that can result from an individual's incompetence or ignorance do not stop with the immediate victims. Among the Gwich'in, responsibility for those consequences is felt by others who, having superior competence or knowledge, failed to prevent that harm from occurring.

In a culture that is egalitarian to the degree that any attempt to direct the thoughts, decisions, or actions of another person is offensive (MacNeish 1956; Ridington 1990), attempting to change the behavior of an adult (which is necessary to prevent harm from occurring) on the presumption that one person possesses knowledge or competence that is superior to that of another presents a difficult situation for the Gwich'in. Yet, as noted most clearly by Slobodin (1962) in his analysis of leadership in a trapping party, individual Gwich'in would go far out of their way, even if it required substantial camouflage, to prevent others from undertaking activities that might bring them to harm. These actions would be undertaken precisely because the momentarily "superior" Gwich'in would be concerned that other Gwich'in in the wider social domain would hold them responsible for any harm that resulted from the former's inaction.

I am not aware that Slobodin's insight into the Gwich'in has been pursued further either in Gwich'in ethnography or in the ethnography of any other Northern Athapaskan culture. This omission may exist because the behavior pattern discussed in the preceding paragraphs appears to be an expression of guilt, which is already a much examined component of the "Northern Atha-paskan personality." Guilt may well be the means by which this mechanism operates in the individual and, for a psychological mechanism, that may be sufficient explanation. As a social mechanism, this pattern of assuming responsibility for preventing the actual or potential harm that might be a consequence of the action (or inaction) of others, is considerably more complex. If society is marked by shared values, it is also marked by the processes of that sharing. Since one does not assume responsibility for the consequences of the actions that unknown others (whether strangers, "bushmen," or animate beings of unknown categorization) bring upon themselves, the response pattern Slobodin identified among the Gwich'in is a defining marker of the social field within which the Gwich'in share their values.

For the Chipewyan as with the Gwich'in, this behavior pattern is an indicator that the actors are internal to the social field of the Chipewyan that is defined by them through the sharing of cultural values.[2]

Assuming the responsibility for preventing the harmful consequences that the actions of others within the social field might bring upon themselves or others is subject to cultural definitions and conventions of patterning beyond those involved in defining the social field. These conventions are little talked about among the Chipewyan and are not systematically formulated. They are part of implicit cultural knowledge that is acquired largely through stories and by observing social life. It is knowledge that manifests itself only when individual Chipewyan find themselves in similar situations. This is an area of culture where the similarity in response between individuals comes not from the explicit verbal mechanisms of the culture but from the creation of similar cultural beings who tend to respond in similar ways in similar circumstances.

What makes the behavior observed by Slobodin into a power dynamic is that the assumption of responsibility is only half of

2. The idea of social field, as I am using it here, is not precisely bounded and does not correspond closely to the customary idea of culture as a clearly bounded entity. The Chipewyan include aspects of the resident white population, particularly those aspects relating to their public roles within their social field, although the whites clearly belong to another culture. This situation is analogous to the discussion of "part-worlds" in the section "Gender And Power," and will be a topic of future work.

the process. Responsibility can also be projected. This projection is a process that can be conscious, rational, and knowing; unconscious and nonrational; or even be unknowing and unintentional. It is a general cultural dynamic in interactions between a number of categories of unequals (such as adult-child), of which gender inequality is but a specific case.

## Exploring the Dynamic

Perhaps the best initial demonstration of the projection of responsibility onto an individual categorized as "superior" as a means of exercising power over that "superior" individual is found in one of the techniques some Mission Chipewyan (Sharp 1979, 1988a) used to separate some of Mission's resident white teachers from small quantities of their goods. The economic and political relations the Mission Chipewyan had with the outside world were substantially controlled by white Canadian administrators, educators, and missionaries, even the most impoverished of whom individually controlled capital resources far in excess of the wealthiest of the Chipewyan. Separating whites from some of those resources had a long and honorable tradition among the Mission Chipewyan.

One particular form of Chipewyan exploitation of the teachers occurred frequently enough to become a performance, the script of which was as well known to the resident whites as it was to the Chipewyan. Recounting these performances was a favorite pastime of both Chipewyan and the whites, although for different reasons. These stories circulated widely enough within Mission – although more among whites than among Indians – that they served, through the limitations of the context in which they were told and through restrictions determining the audience to whom they were told, as boundary markers between the two populations. They also served as a means for the one population to define the nature of the other.

The performance involved an Indian (either male or female) who would appear at the rear door of a teacher's townhouse after the store was closed, usually on a Saturday night or a Sunday. The Chipewyan would relate a story of deprivation and poverty at the center of which was grave and immediate peril to a nursing Chipewyan infant. There were inevitably three parts to the story: there was no condensed milk at home for the infant, there was no place open where milk could be purchased for it, and there was no money with which to pay for the milk if any place had been open. The history of past performances and the context of mutual familiarity (if not understanding) that existed between the resident whites and the Chipewyan had honed the script to precision. The ensuing performance almost always came off smoothly, with successful results for the Chipewyan.

The Chipewyan would humbly relate the tale of abject misery and powerlessness, emphasizing how poverty now endangered the nursing child. The white teacher would question the Chipewyan performer closely in order to determine if the deprivation was "real" or a scam. The teachers and the Chipewyan knew each other as members of contraposed ethnic groups. Sometimes they knew each other slightly as individuals on the basis of their interactions involving the school and its pupils, but there were always gaps in mutual knowledge created by the cultural context of colonialism and ethnicity. The teachers were a tiny minority in a sea of natives that created its family structure and social life according to principles alien and unknown to the teachers. They rarely knew the limits of any Chipewyan individual's domestic life, family boundaries, or social responsibilities. The presence or absence of a dependent infant was always something of a mystery to them. Conversely, the Chipewyan knew the teachers as public figures. Their knowledge of the teachers' domestic life as manifested in the residential situation of Mission was much greater than the teachers' knowledge of them. However limited and imperfect the knowledge may have been that each had about the other, the advantage in knowledge of the other almost always rested with the Chipewyan.

The teacher's opening response to the story related by the Chipewyan visitor would be typically Western, an attempt to determine the "facts" of the situation through a determined and hostile questioning of the visitor. In the teacher's ideological framework, the gift of a can of milk could be justified only if the teacher became convinced that there was a genuine need for the milk. The questioning, independent of the conclusions drawn from it, provided the teacher with a platform for the assertion of a superior moral and economic station. In fact, the teacher's performance asserted precisely those Western economic and rational values, the inculcation of which in the Chipewyan was perceived by the teachers as the primary reason for their presence at Mis-

sion. Once superiority had been asserted through this performance, the teacher would close the drama by delivering a moral
pronouncement about forethought and planning – along with a
can of milk.

Few humans, especially in circumstances as relatively affluent
as those at Mission, would gamble the well-being of a child upon
the chance charity of something so trivial as a can of condensed
milk. Seeking the can of milk was a scam. The teachers knew that
a can of condensed milk had a token value of one dollar in the
local card games and that it was interchangeable with a dollar bill
or a pack of cigarettes. The teachers also knew that trade in a card
game was the milk's intended use. The Chipewyan, in turn, knew
that the teachers understood that the milk was for use in the card
games. Everyone knew the performance was a scam, but it virtually always worked. Intercultural exploitation in a colonial situation is always complex and the one at Mission is worthy of analysis in its own right (Sharp 1991), but the salient factor here is the
Chipewyan ability to project responsibility for the fate of the
probably nonexistent child onto the white teachers. The actions of
the Chipewyan were invasive, an intrusion upon the teachers'
very different sense of privacy, leading to a forceful assertion of
the very incompetence and lack of planning that the teachers presumed it their task to remove from Chipewyan culture.

The intrusion into the private space and private time of the
teachers was an aggression upon Western values not shared by
the Chipewyan. They projected their own incompetence by playing off of the teachers' own values, values (again) not shared by
the Chipewyan (who hardly regard themselves as incompetent).
Yet, in a situation bearing the classic hallmarks of political and
economic "domination", the success of the Chipewyan in obtaining the can of milk was contingent upon their ability to force the
whites to acknowledge their own inclusion within the
Chipewyan social field; an inclusion that was possible only
through the recognition of their mutual participation as Indian
(inferior) and white (superior) in the process of acculturating the
Indian.

The dynamic, if not its projection, should possess a certain
familiarity. It is not unknown to Western philosophy and similar
dynamics are widely and explicitly recognized in our own culture, in the various ideologies of military rank ("rank hath its
privileges," but also "rank hath its responsibilities"), obligation,

dependency, and hierarchy. It is but one example of a theoretical proposition basic to anthropology since Sir Henry Maine (1972) published *Ancient Law* in 1861: rights and obligations come together.

What is less apparent is how the obligatory mutuality can give to the inferior the ability to bind and control the superior; power by even the most traditional definition. A strong analog to the operation of this Chipewyan cultural dynamic is that of gift exchange in Mauss's (1967) classic formulation. To refuse a gift is to refuse to enter into the social domain of the giver; to presume superiority without recognizing responsibility for the inferior is to deny participation in the same social domain. Where we, as outsiders, tend to see only oppression and dominance in the assertion of superiority, the Chipewyan create mutuality of interaction as part of the total social phenomenon inherent in that assertion.

Part of the logic of what may seem paradoxical lies in the strongly egalitarian nature of Chipewyan culture. Denying the right of others to direct the behavior of the individual is widespread in Native American cultures (e.g. Weltfish 1965: 6–9) and is certainly characteristic of Northern Athapaskan cultures (MacNeish 1956; Ridington 1988, 1990). In the Chipewyan, egalitarianism operates primarily through denying others the right of control over one's behavior (Sharp 1988a). Under the conventions of Chipewyan culture, a face to face assertion of the categorical[3] inferiority or incompetence of any individual is a powerful statement. It binds those who assert superiority as fully as it binds those who accept categorization as the inferior. To assert superiority and deny the obligation to protect the "inferior" from the consequences of their inferiority is to push the inferior beyond the social field and to deny all relationship with them.

## Gender and Power

This dynamic is most conspicuous to the outside observer when the Chipewyan engage in the performance of the routine physical tasks related to subsistence and domestic life in the course of their travels in the bush. The elderly people who cannot put up their own tents have this task done for them without their having to

3. It is important to note the emphasis upon categorical definition. To assert superiority (e.g., "I am stronger") between those defined as categorical equals (e.g. adult male to adult male) is a very different kind of statement and leads to very different results!

ask; food is shared with those unable to hunt or fish; those who are younger and stronger help those who are older or weaker to carry their goods over a portage. Those categorized as (or who assume themselves to be) more capable assume responsibility for those who are categorized as less capable or incapable.[4]

This power dynamic is particularly evident in situations in which the projection of weakness is a function of the symbolic values of Chipewyan gender categories. For example, a woman, who happens to observe several spruce grouse sitting in a tree near the camp, may walk into the camp and tell the men about them. She is perfectly capable of picking up a rifle and shooting them herself and has a greater probability of success since she has the advantage of knowing their exact location. However, the provision of food through the use of a weapon is something the Chipewyan presume to be an aspect of maleness and a task at which males are superior to women (Sharp 1976); indeed, hunting is arguably the most fundamental aspect of maleness in Chipewyan ideas of gender (Sharp 1988a, 1988b; in press [a], in press [b]). Refusing to perform tasks of which they are capable is more than a simple reinforcement of ideas of gender, it is also a fundamental way in which women bind men into their roles and emphasize their obligations toward women.

One of the more conspicuous uses of this dynamic as a form of manipulation and control was displayed by young women in the early stages of their marriages. The 1970s, when most of my fieldwork at Mission was conducted, were a period of transition between the earlier conventions of arranged marriage and emerging conventions of self-selected marriage based upon mutual attraction and consent. Most of these more modern marriages involved women in their late teens married to husbands who were only slightly older. Practically the sole economic experience of these women was being dependent children in a household where their parents exercised the basic authority and decision making. These women had had no opportunity to establish separate economic identities in either the traditional economy or in the emerging wage labor/welfare economy, and their husbands were only marginally less dependent.

4. The slipperiness of the wording here reflects the polythetic nature of Chipewyan classification. The issue of relative competence or superiority, particularly between males, segues into issues of *inkoze* and the definition of maleness that are not relevant here (Sharp 1988a).

These marriages rarely initiated new village households.[5] The couples generally contributed to the subsistence of the larger domestic groupings to which they belonged, but remained dependent upon those groupings for their food and shelter. The transition from dependent child to wife meant primarily the transfer of the responsibility for providing luxury goods from the parents to the husband. This transfer was often accomplished without either spouse having any real understanding of the need to budget resources or of the requirements of an independent household. The pressure of the economic demands was aggravated by the emerging paradigm of romantic love in the simultaneously emerging consumer society in which the young women of Mission were coming to view a husband's gifts to his wife as a measure of her status and of the value of their marriage. In the context of the times, these young wives had rapidly rising expectations and little realistic understanding of their husbands' ability to meet them. The substitution of husband for parents as provider was solidly within the role expectations of a husband, but the demands often were much greater than even the most successful young men could meet.

When husbands were unable (or unwilling) to meet their wives' demands for particular items, the women often resorted to a form of nagging to obtain satisfaction, a manipulation technique that was a variation of a form of childhood begging. Once the demand was made, and refused, the wife would repeat the demand and follow it with the phrase "hina'h." This phrase, for which I can provide no effective translation, was repeated every few seconds. The repetition could continue for days at a time throughout all the waking moments the couple were together and was subject to considerable elaboration and variation in length, tone,[6] pronunciation, and phraseology. There was no discussion of the demand or of its practicality, there was simply the sustained repetition of the almost phatic substitute for the demand. The surface effect, when used by either children or these young wives, was the assertion of the inferiority of the speaker. The practical import of the practice was the declaration of the legitimacy of the demand, and the implied obligation of the more

5. New families that participated in bush activities generally established their first separate household in the bush. The establishment of a separate household in the village often followed only years later.

6. The Chipewyan language has two tones.

powerful actor to meet it. The longer the performance continued – and I have seen them last for days, the wife following her husband about the household area for more than an hour at a time – the greater the dichotomy between the two was emphasized.[7]

Begging is degrading.[8] The longer the "hina'h" routine continues, the more the dependency of the speaker is emphasized. As the degree of the speaker's dependency increases, the greater becomes the expectation that the person being solicited should meet the demand. And as the expectation that the solicited person should meet the demand increases, his failure to meet it becomes more and more problematic until the weight of the unmet demand threatens to destroy his status as superior actor. This is a difficult situation for a young husband who is not able to obtain the goods his wife desires. The "hina'h" performance is difficult for him to stop without capitulation, a loss of status, or a recourse to violence – all three of which, if the marriage relationship is thought of as a struggle for power between husband and wife, yield a form victory for the wife.[9]

So far, this examination has been restricted to ethnographic situations that are not overly complex. What has been accomplished is exposure to several difficult points: Chipewyan self-perception provides a set of conventions under which individuals will take action to prevent other individuals from engaging in activities that might have harmful consequences; the assumption of "responsibility" for the consequences of the actions or inaction of others is part of a broader set of Chipewyan conventions about capability and competence; it is possible to activate this sense of responsibility in others, projecting it onto them; and the projection of this sense of responsibility is a potential mechanism for the control of those who assume that responsibility.

7. I do not have any evidence of the practice being carried on outside of the household. Within the household it may be carried on in the presence of strangers, and will be carried on in the presence of even the most remote of kin. There is probably a set of conventions restricting the practice in "public" areas outside the household, but I have only the negative evidence of not having observed it there.

8. What the Chipewyan do to obtain goods from whites, as with the milk example cited above, is seen more as a skill or form of trickery akin to those practiced in gambling, rather than as begging.

9. Marital violence is too complex an issue to take on in this paper but sometimes, in a culture that emphasizes individual self-control, reducing someone of supposed superior status to the point of violence represents a significant victory, especially if the violence is directed toward the "inferior" person (Sharp 1975, 1979).

The dynamic of power has been treated thus far as a simple mechanical model applicable to relationships subsumed under a binary distinction between capable and incapable. As applied to gender categories, several observations merit elaboration. First, the greater the implication that contrasting gender categories represent differences in capability, the greater the obligation becomes for the gender category categorized as more capable to assume responsibility for, and to meet the needs of, the gender category categorized as less capable. Second, the lack of capability can be asserted, projected upon the more capable person as a form of obligatory responsibility. The concept of "responsibility" should be understood here to extend to and encompass the full range of the behaviors related to a gender role. What is projected upon the other person is not just the obligation to protect or take care of the "inferior" person according to the "superior" person's actual capabilities, but rather the full range of stereotypic behaviors and characteristics associated with the gender status or role. Third, this dynamic works at both the level of individuals in idiosyncratic situations and the level of groups and categories. Fourth, any lack of capability can be either actual or categorical, just as any capability can be either actual or categorical.

In the broadest sense, the issue is the symbolic attribution of competence and ability, and relates to a now substantial set of writings on Chipewyan gender and causality published over the last twenty years. If the Chipewyan had a uniform system of binary categorization in which it could be presumed that both male and female understood the same verbal categories to have the same meaning, explication of the operation of this dynamic of power would be relatively simple. Unfortunately, this is not characteristic of the Chipewyan. The Chipewyan, in addition to making extensive use of polythetic classification, do not emphasize either the clarification or the precise definition of the categories themselves or seek such clarification in the process of explanation. This has long been recognized in various ways (e.g. Scollon and Scollon 1989: 1009, quoting Fang Kuei Li) but only recently has become a topic of examination. This built-in imprecision makes the perception and interpretation of "reality," causality, and meaning heavily contingent upon the gender of the interpreter. From an observer's perspective, Chipewyan men and women may live in the same physical and social universe, but from inside, their different part-worlds of meaning and causality are often dramatically different and the Chipewyan themselves are frequently unaware of (or indifferent to) the role and function of gender in their constructions of reality (Sharp 1986, 1987, 1988a, 1991; D. M. Smith 1973, 1982, 1985, 1990a, 1990b; Slobodin 1970, 1975).

## The Power of Weakness: II

To explicate more fully the exercise of power by women in situations of apparent male domination, it is necessary to consider a more complex ethnographic situation. The following case revolves around the threat of violence between husband and wife in a domestic conflict where alcohol is the precipitating agent, a combination of factors among the most salient to the current North American debate on gender relations.

The Chipewyan response to alcohol, as is the case in any culture, is at least as much cultural as it is physical. Whatever chemical effects the drug has upon human physiology, an individual's translation of those effects into behavior, and the interpretation of that behavior by others is heavily conditioned by culture. In the summer of 1970, whiskey was difficult to obtain at Mission and it was very expensive. Most of the population there consumed alcohol infrequently or not at all. What little alcohol could be obtained was consumed under highly regulated, almost ritualized circumstances. Heavy or frequent consumption of the drug was restricted to a small number of addicts or individuals temporarily responding to circumstances of stress or transition. The "normal" use of alcohol (i.e., by nonaddicts) was in a celebration of solidarity between kin and close friends of the same gender. The intent of these celebrations was to reach a state of "feeling good" while still retaining control over one's awareness and actions (Sharp 1975). The overlay of social factors upon the physical effects of the drug was conspicuous in the behavior of the Chipewyan both during and after consumption. I have seen an adult male Chipewyan, weighing more than one hundred eighty pounds, consume but a fraction cf an ounce of rye whiskey and continue talking quietly with his companions for nearly an hour before quietly walking the several hundred yards through the village to his home, where, in that protected social environment, he then became roaring drunk and remained in that state for several hours. The physical effect of the alcohol was far less significant than the fact of its consumption and the display of that consumption among persons willing to tolerate and protect the man making it.

A couple, in their early fifties at the time and with whom I worked closely throughout the 1970s, had a history of domestic conflict during the early years of their marriage. One component of that conflict had involved the husband's drinking. The husband was normally a very controlled and affable man, but when he drank alcohol he became abusive. Alcohol was not the root cause of their problems. Rather than causing the loss of control that our culture attributes to drunkenness, his use of alcohol followed a widespread Chipewyan practice: using the consumption of alcohol as a charter for the expression of hostilities and fears that otherwise are beyond public expression (VanStone 1965). There was, as far as I can determine, little relationship between the amount he drank and his physical expression of hostility. The loss of control that we attribute to the influence of alcohol is a real phenomenon, but the expression of that phenomenon is so heavily conditioned by culture that the actual physical effects of the drug are difficult to determine. By the time of my fieldwork, he had for years partaken of alcohol in only the most minimal way. His wife and all of their children, who ranged from their mid-thirties to their early teens, remembered or had been told of the changes that occurred in their father's personality and behavior when he drank. These memories centered on the aggressiveness that he had sometimes displayed toward their mother during or after drinking. By now, any drinking on his part was referred to as "being drunk" by his family regardless of the amount of alcohol he actually had consumed. Any conjunction between him and alcohol served as an acute family symbol for the history of domestic turmoil and for the unpleasant memories that were held by the wife and the children. His wife was now adamantly opposed to the possession or consumption of any alcoholic beverage by any member of her family, most particularly in the case of her husband.

One of the presumptions regarding gender in Chipewyan culture is that men are stronger than women. This carries the expectation that women are not able to defeat men in a fight.[10] This assumption is promulgated by both men and women, and, as is

10. Native statements of this order are not commonly heard. Reviewing my field experience, I realized that I actually have heard statements like this made by

the case for the analogous set of assumptions in our own culture, it is not a valid statement regarding the differences between men and women regarding physical strength, temperament, fighting skill, aggressiveness, physical condition, health, or stage in the life cycle.[11] In Mission, this convention was maintained in spite of everyday evidence that it was not an accurate reflection of the circumstances of life there, which included a widely known (and enjoyed) body of gossip about numerous marriages in which the wife routinely defeated the husband in domestic fights.

In the summer of 1970, the husband was given a long-promised bottle of whiskey by a friend who had just returned from Uranium City, where he had paid a visit to the provincial liquor store. In spite of the vociferous objections of his wife – which she had begun to make known several days before, while the friend was still planning his trip – the bottle was accepted. Later that afternoon the husband took out the bottle and seated himself at the table in their cabin. He had not invited any friends over to share a drink with him, the invitation of which normally would have been a sign that he had not planned to consume the alcohol in its entirety. He carefully poured himself a drink into the enameled tin cup that was a favored Chipewyan drinking container.

As soon as he poured himself the drink his wife began to scream and ran out of their house. She ran into the adjacent home of her eldest still married son. Within a few moments of arriving there she was in an apparently hysterical state of semiconsciousness, moaning incoherently. She was immediately attended to by several of her daughters who had gathered at their brother's

---

women much more frequently than I have heard them made by men, and that almost all of these statements were made in reference to the nature and abilities of children rather than those of adults.

11. In American and Canadian culture the statement that males are stronger than females is contingent upon cultural conventions regarding the "fair fight" between opponents matched in age, physical condition, and social status (Dyck 1980). Similar ideas hold for the Chipewyan, although the specifics of what constitutes both a fight and a fair fight differ from our own. The observable social reality of violence is that gender categories crosscut categories of age, physical condition, marital and social status, willingness and/or ability to use weapons, and willingness to attack when the opponent is vulnerable (e.g., sleeping) that are left out of the cultural equation. Males and females are much more evenly matched in terms of their quickness, strength, endurance, capability for violence, and willingness to use violence than either culture recognizes in its construction of the attributes and characteristics of the gender categories Male and Female.

house because of the impending crisis between their parents. All of her other children present in the village were quickly contacted, and they soon came to her side. The eldest of the daughters present began spoon-feeding her a weak sugar-water solution and mopping her brow with a damp cloth, while the other children vituperated their father for his drunkenness and his brutality toward their mother. Their expressions of animosity toward their father were passionate, strong, and loud.

The woman remained in this state for several hours. I found her physical condition so alarming that I feared she had had a heart attack. I went to the school and used their shortwave radio to contact the public health nurse in the neighboring town to come examine her. The nurse did not have a radio so she had to be summoned to talk with me. All of this communication had to be conducted over a public communication link, open to anyone within hearing distance of a receiver. News of the situation quickly became public knowledge, and her situation provided ample opportunity for commentary from many people of both cultures. When the nurse got to a radio link and heard of the circumstances, there was no land vehicle readily available, so she chartered a floatplane to make the sixteen-mile trip to Mission. Once the nurse had arrived at Mission, she was quickly able to determine that there had been no heart attack and that the wife's condition did not represent a medical emergency. The nurse declared that the woman was "just hysterical" and advised me that, while the condition could appear to be very serious, there was no physical danger. I was a bit nonplussed but the nurse said that the condition was common among the women of Mission. She said that she "saw it all the time," particularly in cases of conflict between spouses.

While the woman was semiconscious and under the care of her children, her eldest son (a widower, not the son in whose house their mother was sequestered) went next door to his parent's home to check on his father's condition. His father was sitting quietly at the table in the empty dwelling with the largely unconsumed bottle of whiskey on the table before him. His demeanor was calm and he was quite sober. He was irritated by his wife's behavior, by the presumption that he was going to lose control of himself, by the assumption that he would become drunk and abusive, and by the attention directed toward him. He was acutely aware of the emptiness of his house and of the concentration of his children in his son's house next door. I presume that he had been able to hear at least some of the louder comments that his children had made about him and the whiskey. In any case, he was certainly aware of the dynamics of the situation, of his position as a focus of public attention, and of his physical, moral, and social isolation.

After the eldest son made several trips back and forth between the two dwellings, and after some discussion and negotiation with his siblings, the eldest son obtained his father's assent to remove the troublesome bottle and took it into his possession. The wife remained in her quietly hysterical state, showing no awareness of the discussions and negotiations that were being conducted between her children and their father. When the whiskey bottle was surrendered by her husband, she quickly recovered consciousness, and, within the hour, returned home, and the normal pace of domestic life quietly resumed. Considering the dynamic of power, this situation has some parallels to the cases in Slobodin's work among the Gwich'in focusing on the issue of guilt. The psychological dynamics of the wife's response are not relevant here. It does not matter whether her actions were true "hysteria", whether they were consciously induced or faked, whether they were a rational performance or a conditioned cultural response that should not be categorized by the label "hysteria." The issue is the way in which her response to the situation drew upon the cultural categorization of the relative strength and aggressiveness of males and females, allowing her to emphasize the attributes of her classification as female to effect an acceptable outcome of the situation.

This domestic confrontation was conditioned by cultural values that presume males to be stronger and more aggressive than females, and that charter alcohol consumption as an occasion for the release of the social and psychological controls preventing the expression of aggression. Chipewyan gender categories obviated the possibility of the wife standing up to the husband in a physical confrontation, even if he had been incontinently drunk. The Western "reflex" interpretation is one of male domination, in which the wife is seen as a victim driven by fear into a state of hysterical passivity. Thinking of this situation in terms of male dominance and the male potential for violence creates a false understanding of the situation. Through her actions, the wife was not only capable of exercising power, but in fact defined the nature of the situation and exercised control over it. A "male-dominance" perspective on these events reduces the wife to the status of an object by categorizing her only as a potential victim of abuse who was incapable of interacting equally with her husband, let alone having the power to control the situation. My argument, constructed in terms of a gender complementarity model, is more compatible with the actual outcome of the situation, which was clearly in the favor of the wife.

To begin with, there was little indication that the husband's receiving the gift of the liquor would lead to a physical confrontation even if he were to become drunk. Even if a physical confrontation were perceived as a probable outcome of his possession of the liquor, there were a number of simple and effective courses of action available to the wife that would have quietly defused the situation and avoided any potential for confrontation between them. One option would have been for her to visit with her children until the possibility of a confrontation had passed. Another option would have been for her to encourage her adult sons to share the bottle with their father; their joint presence and consumption of the liquor would have converted its consumption into a ritual of solidarity that would have regulated the situation and prevented the possibility of violence. That the situation became a confrontation over values was as much her choice as it was his.

The behavior of the wife indicated that, either consciously or unconsciously, she had chosen to play an active role in gaining and exercising control over the situation. It might fly in the face of Western values to see a state of hysterical unconsciousness as a viable exercise of power in political relations – for the audience for this drama was far wider than the domestic unit of the couple, so their actions were imbued with a political significance in this small-scale society (Sharp 1988a: xv) – but her performance was an effective tool for the exercise of power. The success of her performance was contingent precisely upon her ability to project upon her husband the disparity between the perceived potentials for strength and inclination for violence that are attributes of the Chipewyan gender categories male and female. This projection involved not only her children, but the wider social body of Mission that tuned into the events through the system of gossip – the primary source of social sanctions in Chipewyan culture (Sharp 1975, 1986, 1987, 1988a). Her actions, her apparent fear and hysteria, defined the situation in such a way that she was perceived as being incapable of protecting herself from an aggressive and potentially violent male. Her successful projection of this image forced others (directly, through the agency of their children, and indirectly, through the coercive power of gossip in the wider social body at Mission) who were categorically defined as more powerful than her to assume the responsibility for her protection. The apparent outcome she desired, protection from her husband, was achieved by obtaining a more basic outcome, the reassertion of her husband's obligations, as male and as husband, toward her through his abandonment of the alcohol and through the reinforcement of the understanding that he should not drink.

The response of this family to the sudden availability of liquor is related to their specific family history. Any situation is tied to the history of the personal relationships involved, and I do not mean to imply that the responses of this family were typical for all of the Mission Chipewyan. However, the pattern of their responses played upon a widely reported feature of Northern Athapaskan kinship: the sentiment attached to the status of mother offsets the more formal structural attachment to the status of father (see Sharp 1988a: 136–40). In situations of stress, the nature of the attachment to the two parents is different and, in cases where conflict produces real polarization, the pull the two parents are able to exert upon their offspring is very different in nature; the weaker and more vulnerable the wife is seen to be, the greater is her ability to coerce others into actions that conform to her goals, and the greater is her control over the situation.

Power through the operation of categorically determined vulnerability can operate at a collective level as well as at an individual level. I have presented an example of this process in some detail in a recent account (Sharp 1988a: 96–120) of the bushman figure among the Mission Chipewyan. I shall not repeat that analysis here, but I wish to emphasize one of its salient points. The attention paid by the women of that group to the newly discovered bushman figure stressed the weakness and vulnerability inherent in their gender role while simultaneously emphasizing the protective aspects embodied in the male gender role. In that group, trying to resolve the stresses of incipient fission, the women's collective assertion of their vulnerability to the bushman was also a coercive assertion that the collective obligations the men owed the women overrode even the rivalries that had developed between the men.

## Discussion: Complementarity and Dominance

Any theoretical model risks becoming a search for the justification of its initial propositions – and the validity of the cultural
context within which the theory exists – rather than a search for
an explanation of the ethnographic situation. Dominance and
complementarity approaches are implicit theoretical models of
society, each of which directs attention to particular kinds of
questions about society and the role of gender within it. They are
analytical tools for the conduct of research, not moral philoso-
phies. To assert that one approach offers a broader and more
comprehensive framework of analysis than the other is not to
denigrate the significance or relevance of the other.

Gender is a uniquely politicized topic in North American culture and anthropology is not immune to such politicization of the
topic. In a more general theoretical context, gender dominance is
a condition that needs to be demonstrated – rather than assumed
– in each ethnographic context. The assumption of gender dominance expresses the contemporary social and intellectual currents
of our cultural context and, as such, acts as a guide to the social
context of anthropology rather than as an indicator of the needs
of ethnographic analysis. Without a contrasting search for the
operation of gender complementarity, the search for hegemony
can hinder our recognition of how power is exercised by those we
presume to be oppressed. My use of a complementarity model
here ultimately reflects my discomfort with the traditional ethnographic and historical record of the Chipewyan as constructed
under a dominance model. The dynamics examined in this paper
are invisible from a dominance perspective, hidden by the lack of
a need to look for them.

The issue of male dominance in the analysis of culture is a
topic far broader than can be satisfactorily addressed in this
paper, but I do wish to comment on one more aspect of this complex issue. The conceptualization of gender relations in terms of
dominance (and at this level of abstraction I regard the concepts
of dominance, oppression, and hegemony as no more than variants of the same conceptual issue) risks becoming no more than a
symbolic and emotional inversion of the quasibiological arguments of Konrad Lorenz, Robert Ardrey's popularization of the
ideas of Sir Arthur Keith, and numerous other writers who were
popular several decades ago. Those works were tremendously

influential in forming the intellectual context in which the interests of the current generation of anthropologists developed. These arguments differed enormously in their specifics, but all of them excluded females from active consideration in their theory building. Creating analytic frameworks in which females appear primarily as wronged victims of male domination (almost as belated compensation for the excesses of those models) are as false as those early models of male dominance.

Females, just as much as males, are active creators of and contributors to the cultures in which they live. The presumption of male dominance in Chipewyan history and ethnology effectively prevents determination of the range of mechanisms through which the Chipewyan negotiate gender relations. My point is not to prove the superiority of one perspective or set of assumptions over another, but to emphasize the need for comparison in the process of ethnographic analysis. The two sets of theoretical assumptions about the nature of human culture need to be positioned against each other in the interpretation of the ethnography of the Chipewyan just as they need to be positioned against each other in the ethnography of any other human society.

# Part 2

Territories and Territoriality

# Editorial

The subject matter commonly subsumed under the headings of territories and territoriality relates to the distribution of people: how many and which people are located where, and when and why they are there. Answers to the first set of questions require map and census data; answers to the second require data on the seasonal round (annual cycle), genealogical and social networks (and their boundaries), land use, land disputes, and a number of environmental variables. Research in all of these areas is relatively straightforward in principle, but usually difficult and time-consuming in practice. The practical problems are exacerbated by the fact that many hunter-gatherers live in small, widely dispersed, mobile groups, whose memberships undergo frequent changes in both size and composition.

The general impression conveyed by the literature (e.g., Lee and DeVore 1968: 7 ff.) is that both social and spatial boundaries among hunter-gatherers are extremely flexible with regard to membership and geographic extent, respectively. As Smith (1988: 244) put it, the conventional view is that foragers live on land that "is one vast commons." However, this view is based almost exclusively on data from the Basarwa of the Kalahari Desert (Cashdan 1984; Lee 1972b: 177–178; 1976: 77–79; 1979: 334 ff.; Lee and DeVore, eds. 1968; Silberbauer 1981: 141, 189 ff.), the Hadza of Tanzania, (Woodburn 1968a, 1972, 1979) and the Australian Aborigines (Maddock 1982: 42 ff.; Myers 1982: 184–86; 1986: 127 ff.; Sharp 1958; Stanner 1965). All of these peoples were at or near the minimum extreme of the known ethnographic range of variation in these respects. Hunter-gatherer societies that were somewhat more complex, such as the Alaskan Eskimos (Burch 1980, 1981; Fienup-Riordan 1984; Shinkwin and Pete 1984), have been ignored by writers attempting to generalize about forager territoriality. Among the Alaskan Eskimos, both social and spatial boundaries were clearly defined, and territories were defended by force if necessary (Burch 1974, 1988c; Fienup-Riordan 1989). Still more complex hunter-gatherer societies, such as those of the Northwest Coast Indians of North America, have been treated by most writers on hunter-gatherer territoriality either as though they do not exist, or as though they represent an entirely different order of phenomena. All of these groups are represented in the papers presented here.

An enormous amount of the hunter-gatherer literature has been devoted, either explicitly or (mostly) implicitly, to territorial questions. The matter of who lives where is a basic ethnographic issue, one that must be dealt with before practically any kind of systematic fieldwork can proceed. Consequently, at least some data on this and related subjects have been collected by virtually every serious field investigator. Land-related issues were particularly important during the 1960s and 1970s because of native land claims, especially in Australia (e.g., Berndt, ed. 1982; Hiatt, 1989; Hiatt ed. 1984; Peterson and Langton, eds. 1983; Williams 1986) and northern Canada (e.g., Brice-Bennett, ed. 1977; Dyck 1983; Feit 1976, 1983, 1989; Freeman 1976), and a huge volume of new information was acquired. However, most of both the older ethnographic work and the newer land-claims research were primarily descriptive. Territoriality, as a scientific problem, remained largely an "unexamined concept" (Myers 1986: 127).

Conceptual and theoretical issues have been addressed in a few recent studies (e.g., Cashdan 1983; Dyson-Hudson and Smith 1978; Hill, King, and Cashdan, 1983; Ingold 1980: 152 ff.; 1987: 130 ff.; Peterson, ed., 1976; Peterson and Long 1986; Smith 1988: 244 ff.), but many problems remain to be resolved. Unfortunately, an exhaustive treatment of these problems would require a volume in itself. Here we deal with just three: the environmental basis of territoriality, the environmental basis of territory size, and land as a factor in personal and group identity.

The environmental basis of territoriality is examined in the paper by Elizabeth Andrews. She assesses data on the Akulmiut, an Eskimo society in southwestern Alaska, using the model propounded by Dyson-Hudson and Smith (1978). In her example, the members of a bounded social unit have exclusive use of the resources of a bounded geographic territory, and she wants to know why. In her attempt to answer that question, Andrews describes the sociocultural features that have helped the Akulmiut maintain exclusive use of their territory over a long period of time. She finds that, by focusing on the distribution and abundance of critical resources, as suggested by the model, she can explain Akulmiut territoriality. She also shows that the appropriate analytical unit for examining territoriality among Alaskan Eskimos is the regional group, or society, not a single village or band.

The environmental basis of territory size is discussed in the paper by Leland Donald and Donald Mitchell in the light of data on the Wakashan-speaking peoples of the Northwest Coast. The investigation of this general issue was actually initiated as long ago as 1953, when Joseph Birdsell, in a classic study, examined the relationship between regional variations in the amount of rainfall, on the one hand, and human population size and distribution, on the other, in the Australian desert. In more complex settings, however, the size of the resource base is usually much more difficult to measure, and such concepts as the "carrying capacity" of a given environment have proven devilishly difficult to measure. In the Wakashan language area the sizes of the territory and population of the seventy-nine local groups on which there are data vary considerably. Donald and Mitchell want to know why they vary the way they do. In their attempt to answer this question, they focus their attention on a single resource, salmon, to see if data on the size and stability of the salmon run will account for the relevant phenomena. They find that knowledge of the salmon run does, indeed, help predict the size of the human population of a given territory. However, they also discover that territories are more than just social spaces, the extent of which is determined solely by environmental factors. They are also the outcome of intentional human behavior designed to improve the resource base of the people involved.

The papers by Andrews and Donald and Mitchell both represent the materialist approach to the study of territoriality, although the latter go beyond materialist explanations in their conclusions. That is, they attempt to explain the relevant phenomena exclusively or primarily by reference to the physical conditions within which the given systems operate. The final paper, by George Silberbauer, takes the very different "mentalist" approach. His interest is in land as a factor in individual and group identity, which he investigates by contrasting the Pitjantjatjara, of Australia, with the G/wi, of Botswana. He is interested in what used to be known as "world view" – the basic perception that people have of the world and their place in it. This phenomenon is difficult, if not impossible, to explain in materialist terms – the terms in which territoriality is almost always discussed.

To our knowledge, no one has ever explained in empirical terms why a given people view the world as they do. It is even conceivable that chance or historical accident may play a part in the matter. However, regardless of how people's perceptions of the world originate, these perceptions have enormous implications for how people act. In the present instance, for example, Silberbauer finds that, for whatever reason, there are important differences between the Pitjantjatjara and the G/wi regarding how they perceive their places in the landscape. Despite the fact that they both live in desert environments, their contrasting views of the world result in different interpersonal relations, different ecological relations, and differing responses to pressures placed by outsiders on their use of land. The basic point here is that while material conditions always must be part of an explanation of how and why the members of a given hunter- gatherer society distribute themselves the way they do, material conditions are probably never the only ones that need to be considered.

# 4

# Territoriality and Land Use Among the *Akulmiut* of Western Alaska

*Elizabeth F. Andrews*

This essay tests an ecological model (Dyson-Hudson and Smith 1978) that helps explain the nature of socioterritorial organization among Alaskan Eskimos as demonstrated by its application to the *Akulmiut*,[1] a Yup'ik Eskimo society. *Akulmiut* territorial dimensions were analyzed in terms of critical food resources, spatial organization, and mechanisms used for maintaining exclusive use. It is shown, consistent with the theory, that between regional groups or societies, the *Akulmiut* exhibited a territorial system of land use and occupancy when critical resources were predictable in time and location, and were abundant or dense. Spatial organization and sociocultural features were important in maintaining exclusive use.[2]

## Introduction

Territory is defined as an area occupied exclusively by one group by repulsing other groups through overt defense or through some means of communication (Dyson-Hudson and Smith 1978; Wilson 1975). It has been recognized universally in the literature that most hunting-gathering groups had geographic use areas, but the extent to which these areas were exclusively occupied or defended against intrusion by outsiders has not been clearly

1. Words set in italics are Yup'ik Eskimo written in the phonemic system described in Jacobson (1984), except where scientific names for fish and wildlife species used for subsistence foods are provided.

2. I appreciate the financial and logistical support of the Alaska Department of Fish and Game for the study upon which this paper is based. I thank the people of Nunapitchuk for their cooperation and interest in the study. Key participants in the research on territorial aspects of land and resource use were the late Andrew Tsikoyak and Nastasia Keene of Nunapitchuk, the late John and Martha Parka of Napakiak, and Anna Alexie, also of Napakiak. Their contributions are gratefully acknowledged.

defined. The question of territoriality among hunting-gathering societies has revolved around two principal theoretical generalizations. One holds that the territorial band was the characteristic form of hunter-gatherer social organization (Service 1962), while the other states that groups were flexible and fluid, their form varying according to ecological factors (Lee and DeVore, eds. 1968). Some researchers (Lee, Pilling, and Hiatt 1968) have questioned whether there were boundaries at all among hunting and gathering societies. These earlier discussions were hampered by the lack of a clear definition of territoriality and were complicated by the variation evident from the ethnographic descriptions of socioterritorial organization (Damas 1968).

In a more general view, "territory" has been used to refer to a more or less delimited area, within which a population carries on resource harvesting activities over the course of a year in a customary pattern. The extent to which areas and resources were exclusive has not been examined systematically for Alaskan Eskimo groups. Accounting for the variability in socioterritorial organization between Eskimo regional groups or tribes remains an important issue.

## Research Problem

In anthropological studies of Alaskan Eskimos, territoriality has not been systematically addressed in terms of defining how exclusive use of an area is maintained, nor has the interrelationship of territorial space and associated resources been defined. Some researchers (Burch 1980, 1981; Ray 1967) argue that Alaskan Eskimos were clearly territorial, but did not pursue the nature of this behavior. Their work has focused on Eskimo societies in northwest Alaska. Occurrences of overt defense among the Point Hope Inupiat of the Arctic coast region and use of a well-defined area allude to territoriality (Burch 1980, 1981). More specifically, Burch (1980: 274) emphasized that "the structured relations that operated within societies contrasted with those that operated between them," demonstrating the "social distinctiveness" of socioterritorial groups in northwest Alaska. However, at particular times of the year, certain neighboring groups harvested resources within the otherwise delimited area:

> The summer movements of the members of different societies into and out of one another's territories were so precisely articulated that

almost no conflict resulted from them. The members of one society entered another territory either after it had been vacated by its owners, or else under the long-established truce conditions which existed at certain times of the year. Comparable movements at other times of year would have resulted in considerable bloodshed. (Burch 1980: 276)

Among Alaskan Eskimos of the Bering Strait region, ethnographic data indicate maintenance of an area for exclusive use, if not by overt defense, by some symbolic means or sociopolitical institutions (Ray 1967). For example, members of groups were informed of areas where they could go with safety. Again, under certain conditions, members of several groups could harvest resources in the same areas. After receiving permission from the chief to use foreign territory to obtain wild foods, individuals had to be sponsored by a relative, and use of areas was reciprocal (Ray 1967: 385):

> When islanders used the mainland it was understood that they were to give products more or less unobtainable in their borrowed territory in return. Such products as walrus hides or seal oil were often traded at that time . . . Mainland families were permitted to live on the islands with relatives for a winter or longer, the visiting families returning home in spring after the ice had broken up. They were sometimes accompanied by island relatives who would then reside in mainland villages of their alliance. (Ray 1967: 386)

Among Bering Strait Eskimos, warfare resulted primarily from trespass or invasions and took place near territorial boundaries (Ray 1967: 388).

Other researchers (Lantis 1946; Oswalt 1967) maintain that exclusive and defended territories among Alaskan Eskimos were less defined. Oswalt (1963: 154, 155) reported that Yup'ik Eskimos at the lower Kuskokwim River community of Napaskiak were characterized by a "restricted territoriality" with "sometimes vague territorial limits." The eastern and western limits of areas exploited for subsistence harvests were delineated, but the northern and southern limits were not mentioned (Oswalt 1963: 82). Perhaps for this reason he classified this community as "central-based wandering" (Beardsley, et al. 1956: 138), a community which has a central base from which it ranges seasonally and to which it may or may not return in subsequent years. However, Beardsley also notes that "community rights of prior or exclusive access to certain food resources" were considered a feature of the central-based wandering community pattern (Beardsley, et al. 1956: 138). It is noteworthy that Oswalt's findings apply to a single community and not the larger regional group, the *Kusquqvagmiut*, which was probably the socioterritorial unit.

It is believed that the Yup'ik society (*Nunivaarmiut*) of Nunivak Island had no tribal or political organization (Lantis 1946: 249, 256). Whether or not the *Nunivaarmiut* maintained an area exclusively is not known. Community or extended family groups among the *Nunivaarmiut* did not maintain geographic areas for exclusive use. However, warfare did occur between the *Nunivaarmiut* and other Yup'ik regional groups, though not often, reportedly to avenge the killing of a relative. Among other Yup'ik societies, war was waged to retaliate for a specific violent act or aggression by another group (Fienup-Riordan 1989), not precluding retaliation for trespass. Overt defense was rare.

What contributes to territorial behavior has not been clear in these studies. Instead, in this area of inquiry, typologies derived from ethnographic description are more developed in the anthropological literature than are general theoretical principles to explain the variation observed in socioterritorial organization. These typologies of northern hunting-gathering systems (Chang 1962; Damas 1969; Graburn and Strong 1973) were developed for classifying observed variability in resource utilization and settlement patterns rather than to explain the nature of socioterritorial organization. Settlement pattern, subsistence economy, or social organization was classified (Chang 1962; Damas 1969; Graburn and Strong 1973; Helm 1975). One typology (Chang 1962) simply classifies circumpolar societies based on their settlement patterns – those with a year-round settlement or those with a "complex" of seasonal settlements. Subtypes are identified within each class. Another typology of northern Athapaskan Indian societies bases the classification on the subsistence economy. The three types, "inland riverine, inland hunting-snaring, intensive riverine/maritime," subsumed most ethnographic examples, although not all could be classified into one of these categories (Graburn and Strong 1973).

An analysis of Arctic drainage Indians identified tribal organization among northern hunting and gathering societies and noted the relationship of wild food resources and tribal territories (Helm 1975). The "linked-family" band was distinguished from, but a part of, the larger "regional" band. Along a continuum, the subsistence "task group" was the smallest level of organization and the enduring "tribe" was the most encompassing. The tribe was characterized by a "shared orientation . . . to an extensive exploitative zone or territory – its biotal resources, their sites, and the routes of access . . . to those sites . . . " (Helm 1975: 376).

While ethnographic studies of northern societies reported close relationships between resources, their utilization, and group organization (Damas 1968; Helm 1975; Rogers 1969), the extent to which groups had either social or geographic boundaries and maintained them was not systematically examined. As a result, the issues of how to account for variation in socioterritorial organization and how to explain the relationship between spatial organization, resources, and resource utilization were not addressed.

Nevertheless, these and other studies contributed to a broad theoretical framework that linked subsistence patterns with patterns of resource distribution and abundance in the natural environment. Customary law recognized distinct geographic areas associated with particular human societies (Ellanna, Sherrod, and Langdon 1985: 56–58). Other studies began to explore the existence and maintenance of boundaries, both social and geographic, among hunting and gathering societies (Burch 1974, 1980, 1981; Burch and Correll 1972; Fienup-Riordan 1984; Ray 1967, 1975; Shinkwin and Pete 1984). However, the conditions that gave rise to territorial behavior remained undefined.

More recently, a model was developed that uses ecological variables for explaining the presence or absence of exclusive, defended areas. This theory holds that diversity in human spatial organization can be accounted for by examining the distribution of critical resources in terms of their density and predictability (Dyson-Hudson and Smith 1978). The model predicts that the occurrence of a territorial system is associated with critical food resources that are predictable in time and location and are dense or abundant, because the benefits of increased availability of certain resources exceed the costs of defending use of those resources. In contrast, territoriality will not evolve where food resources are sparse or very mobile because the cost of defense would exceed the benefits gained. This theoretical proposition is worth examining among Alaskan Eskimos because, although resources are characteristically dispersed or mobile, their occurrence is fairly predictable and in large enough quantities for these seminomadic people to make a good living.

This essay uses the results of an ethnohistoric and ethnographic study of nineteenth and twentieth century land and resource use of a Yup'ik-speaking Eskimo society, the *Akulmiut* (Andrews 1989) to test this theory. The study addressed the question of whether the society was territorial. The variables examined in the analysis were wild resource utilization, the distribution of critical food resources in terms of density and predictability, spatial organization, and mechanisms used for maintaining exclusive use.

## Research Setting

The subsistence economy and geographic location of the *Akulmiut* were unique among Alaskan Eskimos. The name *Akulmiut* means "inhabitants of the settlements of the area in between," where the area "in between" refers to the area between the Yukon and Kuskokwim Rivers. The secondary meaning of *Akulmiut* is "the people of the tundra." The *Akulmiut* were a hunting, fishing, trapping, and gathering society distinct from other Yup'ik regional groups or tribes (see Figure 4.1) (Andrews 1989; Shinkwin and Pete 1984; Fienup-Riordan 1984; Pratt 1984; Ray 1975). About one thousand *Akulmiut* resided in three year-round villages in 1983: Atmautluak, Kasigluk, and Nunapitchuk. These villages were located about five hundred air miles west of Anchorage and twenty-six air miles northwest of the regional service center of Bethel. None of these communities was linked by road.

The *Akulmiut* subsisted on the fish and wildlife resources characteristic of low, marshy areas of moist and wet tundra ecosystems. They harvested northern pike (*Esox lucius*), several species of whitefish (*Coregonus sp.*), Alaska blackfish (*Dallia pectoralis*), mink (*Mustela vison*), muskrat (*Ondatra zibethicus*), and numerous waterfowl species. Ethnographic literature on Alaskan Eskimos describes human adaptations centered around the harvest of marine mammals (Burch 1980, 1981; Ellanna 1983; Lantis 1946; Rainey 1947), large game (Gubser 1965; Spencer 1959), or major fish runs, such as Pacific salmon (*Oncorhynchus* sp.) (Oswalt 1963). Within western Alaska, *Akulmiut* resource use was distinct from that of other Yup'ik societies, such as the *Naparyaarmiut*, whose harvest focused on marine mammals (Stickney 1984); the *Qaluyaarmiut*, who harvested Pacific herring (*Clupea harangus pallasi*) (Pete, Albrecht, and Kreher 1987); and the *Kusquqvagmiut* and *Kuigpagmiut*, who harvested Pacific salmon (Oswalt 1963; Wolfe

**Figure 4.1:** General locations of the *Akulmiut* among Yup'ik societies of western Alaska, c. 1900-present (adapted from Shinkwin and Pete [1984])

1979). The inland tundra adaptation, such as that of the *Akulmiut*, has been documented only recently (Andrews 1989). These data were derived from fieldwork, primarily in the *Akulmiut* community of Nunapitchuk, and historical sources.

The time period examined was from roughly 1820, the outset of Russian commercial presence in the region (Andrews 1989:

117), to 1983. Throughout this period, *Akulmiut* were distributed primarily in the large lakes region of the Johnson River drainage, where the largest and most permanent settlements have been situated. Several villages were identified that were occupied "at the time of wars" or intersocietal warfare (prior to 1820) (Andrews 1989: 292); three of these were occupied through the mid-twentieth century. In spite of their permanence and proximity to the Kuskokwim River, the first record of any *Akulmiut* village by name came from Edward Nelson's (1882: 669, map) 1878-1879 winter journey between the mouths of the Yukon and Kuskokwim rivers, when six villages in the large lakes district were noted. Village population ranged from thirty to one hundred people according to the 1880 census (Petroff 1884: 100), forty years after the 1838 smallpox epidemic, which reduced the regional population considerably (Michael, ed. 1967: 200).

Just prior to 1900, four villages were occupied along with four satellite communities or hamlets associated with them (Andrews 1989: 290-94). Two villages were reportedly so large they had two *qasgit* (pl.; men's residential and community/ceremonial houses) apiece (Andrews 1989: 292). In 1900, *Akulmiut* population was decimated again, by an influenza and measles epidemic (Wolfe 1982: 108) which resulted in the abandonment, consolidation, and relocation of some villages between 1900 and 1915 (Andrews 1989: 294-96). By 1940, the census reported about 360 *Akulmiut*, similar to the population reported in the 1880 census prior to the 1900 epidemic. This population more than doubled by 1983 when *Akulmiut* were situated in three year-round villages in the large lakes district referred to in historic sources.

## Research Findings

### Wild Resource Utilization and Distribution

*Akulmiut* wild resource utilization was characterized by aggregation during part of the year and dispersal at other times. Aboriginally, and in the earlier part of the twentieth century, subsistence activities were conducted from permanent winter villages, seasonal settlements, such as spring hunting and fishing camps and summer fish camps, and from temporary settlements and campsites. The shift to permanent, year-round settlements occurred about the middle of the twentieth century. In the 1980s, the har-

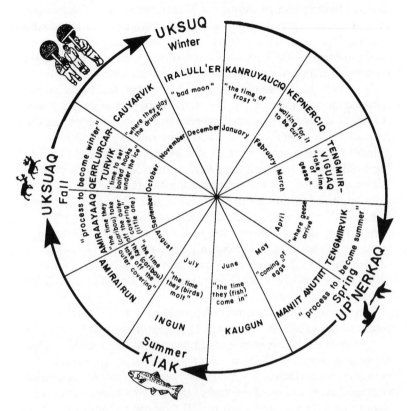

**Figure 4.2:** An *Akulmiut* calendar showing Yup'ik names for seasons and months, c. 1900-1983

vest of fish and wildlife for subsistence use continued to require the use of seasonal settlements and temporary camps.

Historic monthly subsistence activities are reflected in the *Akulmiut* calendar (see Figure 4.2). In spring (*Up'nerkaq*; March through May), families were dispersed, fishing for blackfish, hunting muskrat, mink, land otter (*Lutra canadensis*), and birds, such as ptarmigan (*Lagopus lagopus*) and various duck species. After breakup, gill nets were set for taking whitefish and northern pike. These species concentrate during their return to summer feeding areas among the large lakes of the Johnson River drainage. With the onset of summer (*Kiak*; June through August), some families moved from their spring camps to the seasonal salmon fishing camps along the Kuskokwim River. However, other families stayed in the Johnson River area and harvested whitefish and pike. Collecting berries, especially cloudberries (*Rubus chamaemorus*), and taking molting waterfowl in drives were other major summer subsistence activities for all.

In fall (*Uksuaq*; September through November) fishing for whitefish was the major activity, although northern pike were also taken. Again, as in spring, whitefish were concentrated as they left the Johnson River drainage in late September and October. Permanent villages were situated near these sites. Whitefish, preserved by drying and freezing, was a primary food source for use throughout the winter. Processed fish were stored at the village sites.

In late fall, families returned to the same camps they had used in spring. Wicker traps made of split spruce wood and willow or spruce root lashing were set under the ice to harvest blackfish, a species that can survive in oxygen-depleted waters. The carcasses of furbearers such as beaver (*Castor canadensis*), mink, and land otter, as well as blackfish, were sources of food during fall for humans and dogs.

Winter (*Uksuq*; December through February) marked the return of dispersed family groups to winter villages or permanent settlements. Blackfish were caught in traps at key locations relatively near winter settlements. Snares were set for ptarmigan and hare (*Lepus americanus, L. othus*), but previously stored foods also provided sustenance. At the end of the winter season, many families returned to camps used in fall and spring, again hunting mink, land otter, and beaver, and fishing for blackfish.

In the early 1980s, this annual round of subsistence activities remained essentially the same for *Akulmiut* communities (Andrews 1989; see Figure 4.3). Northern pike and whitefish were taken in fall using large dip nets at fish fences constructed across the Johnson River and tributaries adjacent to the communities. They were also taken with set gill nets in late spring, as the fish ascended the Johnson River, and in summer, at sites throughout the drainage where the fish dispersed. Blackfish were also taken, using small cylindrical traps set beneath the ice – the same way as they were taken in the past. The seasonal round in 1983 was different than it had been in the past in that, beyond the area customarily used by the *Akulmiut*, seal (*Phoca hispida, P. largha*, and *Erignatus barbatus*) were taken along the Bering Sea coast and northern pike were taken in the deeper waters of the Kuskokwim

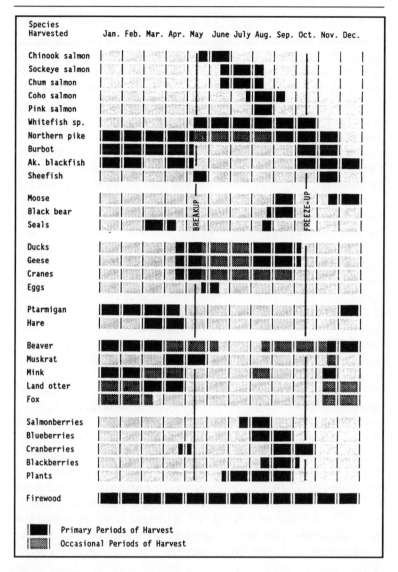

**Figure 4.3:** Seasonal round of subsistence activities at Nunapitchuk, 1983

River. Salmon, which do not occur in the Johnson River drainage, were harvested in the Kuskokwim River by some families throughout the summer.

The prevalence of whitefish species, northern pike, and Alaska blackfish in the *Akulmiut* diet, and the characterization of those species as "critical foods" is documented in a report of the results of a wild food harvest study conducted in 1983 (Andrews 1989) and in historical references. By species, northern pike, whitefish, and blackfish accounted for seventy-one percent of the total pounds of edible weight of all wild foods harvested per capita within the area of the *Akulmiut* (see Table 4.1). Even when considering the harvest of nonlocal species, such as seal and salmon, the per capita harvest of freshwater fish species is considerable and accounts for forty-four percent of the harvest. Other species that were harvested historically in larger quantities than in 1983 were mink, muskrat, and waterfowl. Even so, greater harvest levels in the past (Burns 1964; Klein 1966) indicate that these resources still would not have constituted as large a proportion of the total harvest (in edible pounds per capita) as would northern pike, whitefish, and blackfish combined. When the naturalist Edward Nelson (1882) described his travels through the *Akulmiut* area in the winter of 1878–1879, he noted the Johnson River drainage's unique abundance of whitefish and blackfish based on the dominance of these foods at the *Akulmiut* villages. The predominance of these species also was noted in missionary accounts (Kilbuck ca. 1890–1910) and in an educational survey (Anderson and Eels 1935).

The seasonal round of subsistence activities showed that whitefish and pike were taken when concentrated, as they left the large lakes of the Johnson River drainage in late September and October, when the water bodies became shallow and oxygen-depleted as they began to freeze. They were harvested again in late spring and early summer (May and June) as they moved into the drainage. These occurrences were predictable in both time and location. Large fish fences were constructed for intercepting whitefish and pike as they moved out of the large lakes into the narrow streams of the area descending to the deeper waters of the Kuskokwim River. The fences were located in the area where the stream bottlenecked, constricting the flow of water and fish. There is a narrow window of time in the fall during October when the fish migrate from the drainage into the deeper waters where they overwinter, and conversely, when they move back into the drainage after the numerous lakes and streams have thawed.

In contrast, blackfish was taken during winter months and was a critical food resource in winter (November through March).

**Table 4.1:** Household and per capita harvests of fish, game, and plant resources within *Akulmiut* territory for sampled Nunapitchuk households, 1983

| Fish or Wildlife Resource | Percentage of Sampled Households Harvesting (N=17) | Mean Harvesting Household Harvest (pounds) | Mean Household Harvest (pounds) (n=17) | Per Capita Harvest (pounds) (n=111) | Total Pounds Edible Weight | Percentage of Total Pounds Harvested | Total Harvest Numbers |
|---|---|---|---|---|---|---|---|
| Pike | 100.0 | 1,153.94 | 1,153.94 | 176.73 | 19,617.0 | 22.04 | 6,539 |
| Salmon, chinook | 64.7 | 1,411.36 | 913.24 | 139.86 | 15,525.0 | 17.44 | 1,035 |
| Salmon, chum | 64.7 | 1,021.82 | 661.18 | 101.26 | 11,240.0 | 12.63 | 2,248 |
| Blackfish (gal.) | 52.9 | 1,185.47 | 627.60 | 96.12 | 10,669.3 | 11.99 | 1,146 |
| Whitefish sp. | 94.1 | 548.81 | 516.53 | 79.11 | 8,781.0 | 9.86 | 2,927 |
| Salmonberries (gal.) | 100.0 | 208.76 | 208.76 | 31.97 | 3,549.0 | 3.99 | 507 |
| Salmon, sockeye | 58.8 | 305.00 | 179.41 | 27.48 | 3,050.0 | 3.43 | 610 |
| Beaver | 52.9 | 255.11 | 135.06 | 20.68 | 2,296.0 | 2.58 | 82 |
| Seal sp. | 29.4 | 437.00 | 128.53 | 19.68 | 2,185.0 | 2.45 | 19[a] |
| Salmon, coho | 41.2 | 307.71 | 126.71 | 19.41 | 2,154.0 | 2.42 | 359 |
| Moose | 23.5 | 525.00 | 123.53 | 18.92 | 2,100.0 | 2.36 | 3 |
| Duck sp. | 88.2 | 103.20 | 91.06 | 13.95 | 1,548.0 | 1.74 | 1,032 |
| Burbot (loche) | 76.5 | 112.85 | 86.29 | 13.22 | 1,467.0 | 1.65 | 326 |
| Goose sp. | 82.4 | 78.11 | 64.32 | 9.85 | 1,093.5 | 1.23 | 243 |
| Blackberries (gal.) | 100.0 | 51.29 | 51.29 | 7.86 | 872.0 | 0.98 | 218 |
| Mink | 47.1 | 82.81 | 38.97 | 5.97 | 662.5 | 0.74 | 265 |
| Ptarmigan | 88.2 | 38.50 | 33.97 | 5.20 | 577.5 | 0.65 | 770 |
| Cranberries (gal.) | 76.5 | 37.23 | 28.47 | 4.36 | 484.0 | 0.54 | 121 |
| Hare | 58.8 | 30.66 | 18.04 | 2.76 | 306.6 | 0.34 | 73 |
| Crane | 58.8 | 27.90 | 16.41 | 2.51 | 279.0 | 0.31 | 31 |
| Black bear | 11.8 | 125.00 | 14.71 | 2.25 | 250.0 | 0.28 | 2 |
| Swan | 41.2 | 28.77 | 11.85 | 1.81 | 201.4 | 0.23 | 19 |
| Eggs (gal.) | 35.3 | 5.83 | 2.06 | 0.32 | 35.0 | 0.04 | 25 |
| Sheefish | 11.8 | 11.25 | 1.32 | 0.20 | 22.5 | 0.03 | 3 |
| Land otter | 11.8 | 15.75 | 1.85 | 0.28 | 31.5 | 0.03 | 3 |
| Muskrat | 17.6 | 5.13 | 0.91 | 0.14 | 15.4 | 0.02 | 22 |
| Fox[b] | 23.5 | - | - | - | - | - | 8 |
| Totals | | 8,114.26 | 5,236.01 | 801.90 | 89,012.2 | 100.00 | |
| Totals less salmon and seal[c] | | 3,482.89 | 2,009.07 | 494.21 | 54,858.2 | | |

[a] An additional 8 seals and 70 gallons of seal oil were purchased.
[b] Fox are not eaten and therefore pounds edible weight was not calculated.
[c] Salmon and seal species do not occur within *Akulmiut* territory

Unlike other fish species, blackfish do not leave the large drainage lakes in winter. Even though the shallow lakes freeze to a considerable depth and the remaining water becomes oxygen-depleted, the unique biology of blackfish enables them to survive. Blackfish then concentrate in open water areas amidst ice and obtain atmospheric oxygen. Such areas are dispersed and fluctuate from year to year. Because blackfish was the only major winter food resource in the area, extended family groups dispersed throughout much of the delimited area to harvest them as well as furbearers, especially mink. Compared to whitefish and pike, blackfish are a less dense and less predictable key resource.

### Spatial Organization

There have been three or four primary *Akulmiut* villages, both in historic and contemporary times, all of which have been located within twelve miles of each other along the large lakes and associated tributaries of the Johnson River drainage (see Figure 4.4). In contrast, seasonal settlements were dispersed and situated

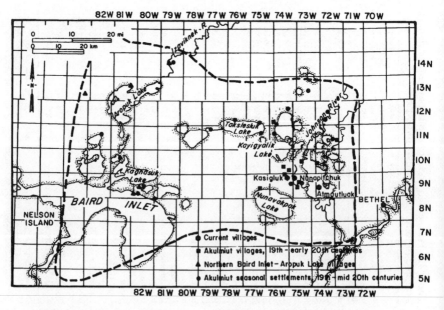

**Figure 4.4:** *Akulmiut* villages noted in historic and modern records, 1882-1950

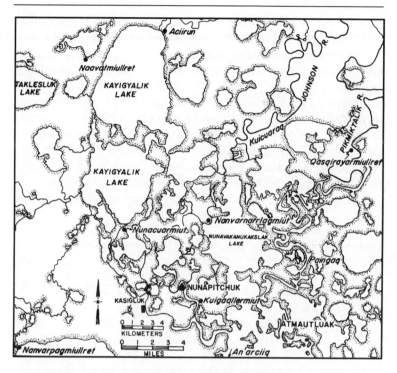

**Figure 4.5:** *Akulmiut* villages and seasonal settlements

along lakes and tributaries throughout the Johnson River drainage area (see Figure 4.5).

*Akulmiut* villages were characterized primarily by the presence of a *qasgiq* (sing.; "kasgi," "kashim," "men's house"). However, the *qasgiq* at some of these villages (specifically, a hamlet or *nunacuaq*, literally "little village") was used solely as a residence/bathhouse/workshop for men – not for ceremonies. Members of those villages went to other villages to participate in intravillage and interregional ceremonies held in a *qasgiq*, as was customary. Furthermore, each late nineteenth and twentieth century *Akulmiut* village was characterized by its location at a place suitable for constructing a fence used to intercept large quantities of whitefish during their annual migration. All of these places were located along the relatively narrow streams below the large lakes of the lower Johnson River drainage (again see Figure 4.4). The funneling aspect of the geography was important for intercepting not only whitefish, but also pike, during their annual migrations into and out of the complex of lakes and sloughs.

The population of *Akulmiut* primary villages historically has been at least thirty to fifty, with communities relocating when there were fewer individuals. Declining population was not the sole factor in relocation; famine, depletion of fish resources, and increased population of villages (upwards of about one hundred to one hundred twenty) also were cited. The social composition of villages based on genealogical reconstructions for 1920 shows that the larger communities consisted of five to seven extended family groups, which included sets of siblings, their parents, spouses, and children, and also cross-cousins, spouses, and chil-

**Table 4.2:** Core family composition of three *Akulmiut* villages, c. 1920

| VILLAGE | | NUMBER AND PERCENTAGE OF VILLAGE POPULATION |
|---|---|---|
| **NANVARNARRLAK** | | |
| *Family 1:* | 1 brother, 2 sisters | |
| adjunct: | 1 daughter-in-law and her sibling | 38 (46%) |
| *Family 2:* | 2 brothers, 3 sisters | 18 (22%) |
| *Families 3, 4, 5:* | husband and wife (from another village) | 4 (5%) |
| | | 5 (6%) |
| | | 5 (6%) |
| *Family 6:* | wife and husband (from another village) | 3 (4%) |
| *Family 7:* | husband and wife (both from village) | 9 (11%) |
| | | 82 (100%) |
| **PAINGAQ** | | |
| *Family 1:* | 1 brother, 2 sisters | 9 (19%) |
| *Family 2:* | 3 brothers, 2 sisters | 16 (33%) |
| *Family 3:* | 2 brothers, 1 male cross cousin | 15 (31%) |
| *Family 4:* | 1 brother, 2 sisters | 5 (11%) |
| *Family 5:* | husband and wife (both from village) | 3 (6%) |
| | | 48 (100%) |
| **NUNAPICUAQ** | | |
| *Family 1:* | 2 brothers, 1 sister, 2 male cross cousins | |
| adjunct: | 1 sister-in-law | 27 (64%) |
| *Family 2:* | 2 sisters and their husbands all from another village | 10 (24%) |
| *Family 3:* | husband and wife | 5 (12%) |
| | | 42 (100%) |

dren (see Table 4.2). The core of these families generally consisted of a set of siblings in both fledgling communities, such as *Nunapicuaq*, and long-established ones, such as *Nanvarnarrlak* and *Paingaq*.

Seasonal settlements, on the other hand, were used by one or several extended family groups in early winter and spring and were not reported in any historic or modern references until recently (Andrews 1989: 299–303). These sites were readily identified as seasonal camps in that there was no *qasqiq* ("kasgi" or "kashim") associated with them. These were places where families seasonally relocated for several months to harvest multiple species, such as blackfish, mink, land otter, beaver, ptarmigan, and hare. In addition, there were places where temporary camps were set up for specific hunting, fishing, and trapping activities of short duration (overnight to several weeks).

Other means for identifying the distribution of the *Akulmiut* population are found in historic sources and Yup'ik place-names. The earliest historic reference to the *Akulmiut* is found in the Lieutenant Zagoskin's (Michael, ed. 1967) accounts of his travels and explorations in the 1840s for the Russian-American Company. Based on encounters with *Akulmiut* trading at the Russian post along the lower Yukon River, "Ikogmiut" (*Iqugmiut*) near Russian Mission, it was understood that they resided between the mouth of the Kuskokwim River and the Kashunuk River, which was generally correct, although their distribution was not as far west (again see Figure 4.1). Other historic sources (Holmberg 1985; Kilbuck *ca.* 1890–1910; Nelson 1882, 1899) also mention the *Akulmiut* and note that they occupied the area of large lakes of the Johnson River drainage and were distinct from the "Kashunamiut" or *Qissunarmiut*, who occupied the Kashunuk River, and the "Tshananayamiut" or *Caninermiut*, of the coastal and inland areas west of the lower Kuskokwim River (again see Figure 4.1) (Kilbuck *ca.* 1890–1910; Waskey 1950). These sources clearly identify the "big lakes" of the Johnson River drainage as the loci of *Akulmiut* villages (again see Figures. 4.4 and 4.5).

The boundaries of the *Akulmiut* also were indicated by place names. Place names tend to end at boundaries. The area used and occupied by the *Akulmiut* was delineated by Yup'ik place-names (Andrews 1989), the distribution of which corroborated historic accounts that associated the area between the Yukon and Kuskokwim Rivers with the *Akulmiut*. Former settlements, noted

above, were identified with Yup'ik place-names, and their locations were recorded on U.S. Geological Survey maps (1:63,360
scale) along with all other named places considered to be within
the area of the *Akulmiut* (Andrews 1989: 500–547). The place-name
data more specifically indicated the area used and occupied by the
*Akulmiut* as extending from the middle and lower Johnson River
drainage west to Baird Inlet, including the large lakes or "big lakes
country" noted in the historic literature (again see Figure 4.5).

Finally, the distribution of land parcels applied for by *Akulmiut* as native allotments indicated the geographic extent of places
occupied, some as early as the beginning of the twentieth century
(Andrews 1989: 305–309). This distribution corresponds closely
with the locations of previously occupied villages and seasonal
settlements, Yup'ik place-names, and historic accounts. It covers
approximately three thousand square miles extending from the
Johnson River drainage west to Baird Inlet and Aropuk Lake. The
majority of place names (60 percent) was located in the immediate vicinity of the large lakes area of the Johnson River drainage
where, as noted earlier, villages were located during the nineteenth and twentieth centuries.

## Territoriality Among the Akulmiut

Territoriality refers to the exclusive use of resources or occupation of an area by means of overt defense or some form of communication or advertisement (Dyson-Hudson and Smith 1978: 22;
Wilson 1975: 256). Defense can be overt, along a boundary, or be
by patterned, mutual avoidance which acknowledges "keep-out
signals" (Davies and Houston 1984: 149, 189). In terms of the
model proposed by Dyson-Hudson and Smith (1978) described
earlier, exclusively maintained areas are expected to occur where
critical food resources are dense and predictable in time and location. The *Akulmiut* employed several ways of maintaining exclusive use, both by overt defense and symbolic means. They maintained territory through warfare and fighting, which was occasional; symbolic ceremonies that delineated areas of exclusive use
and that intimidated neighbors; naming conventions, including
place names and personal names; and kinship and marriage patterns.

Examples of overt defense, although few, were evident in war
stories and certain place names that referred to encounters with

the enemy, specific non-*Akulmiut* groups. Although information on offense and defense was not elicited, it is reasonable to assume that techniques used by other Yup'ik societies in the region were applied (see Fienup-Riordan 1989). Defensive techniques included the construction of secret tunnels connecting houses and the *qasgiq*, secret hideaways for children, skylight coverings made of slats to prevent the penetration of arrows, and shields made of wooden slats (Lantis 1946: 168). *Akulmiut* tales of war noted the use of long, interconnected, ingenious entryways. Offensive techniques also included wearing specially tailored unconstrictive clothing that promoted freer action, also described by Fienup-Riordan (1989) for other western Alaska Yup'ik societies. One account depicted a technique used by a legendary *Akulmiut* man when he was approached by the enemy. The man repeatedly changed into different clothing to give the appearance of more people at the site than were actually there.

*Akulmiut* place-names were found that refer to places where enemy intrusions into *Akulmiut* territory occurred, with one exception downstream from and relatively near *Akulmiut* villages, just within the southern extent of *Akulmiut* territory. A devastating raid was made on only one of the *Akulmiut* primary villages, and it was the most remote village. Still, warfare occurred near territorial boundaries, as noted among Bering Strait Eskimo (Ray 1967: 388).

*Akulmiut* and non-*Akulmiut* people also could be readily identified by certain forms of communication, namely clothing design and the style of the kayak bow. *Akulmiut* men were identified by the pattern of their parka, which had no hood; a general style of boot; and a labret in the lower lip (Nelson 1899: 32, 37–38, 41, 46). Differences in parka design and decorative details of the bodice and bust of the *Akulmiut* women's parka distinguished them from those of the coastal communities and lower Kuskokwim and lower Yukon rivers (see also Fienup-Riordan 1989). The type of fur used in making clothing also distinguished different Yup'ik groups (VanStone, ed., 1973: 52–53, 60).

It has been noted by *Akulmiut* respondents and in other accounts (Nelson 1899: 265, 327; Fienup-Riordan 1989) that intertribal warfare ceased in western Alaska after the established presence of Russian traders in the region. Even after the end of intersocietal warfare around 1820, interregional travel was still undertaken cautiously. Tribal boundaries were duly noted and respected.

Explorers' accounts for the 1800s characteristically note locations where native guides refused to embark further with nonnative expeditions (Jacobsen 1977; Michael, ed. 1967; Oswalt 1980; Wrangell 1980). By the 1840s the Russian-American Company had instituted a system by which "trading chiefs" were appointed to facilitate Russian trading activities, creating a mechanism whereby designated Eskimo and Indian natives could travel fearlessly into other tribal areas for the purpose of trade with the Russians (Oswalt 1980; Michael, ed. 1967). Even near the end of the Russian period in the 1860s in Alaska, Russian-American Company traders themselves had not succeeded in venturing into all native-occupied areas to trade, including the area of the *Akulmiut*.

Interregional ceremonies were symbolic means for communicating to others the composition of the *Akulmiut* in terms of its people, but also in terms of the land and resources they used. Ceremonies were conducted during late fall and winter (late October to March). Only one of these ceremonies, *Kevgiq* (the Messenger Feast), took place between *Akulmiut* and members of neighboring regional groups or societies (Andrews 1989: 257, 274–80). In fact, one elderly *Akulmiut* man remarked that he had heard that *Kevgiq* replaced warfare, prior the to Euroamerican presence in the area (*c.* 1820), and that it reflected "a new foreign policy," that is, an intersocietal policy, whereby the Yup'ik competed through dance and gift giving. This phenomenon also developed among other Yup'ik societies in the region (Morrow 1984; Shinkwin and Pete 1984; Fienup-Riordan 1989).

One major function of *Kevgiq* was that it informed each regional group of their respective people, places, and subsistence products. The following recollection of *Kevgiq* was provided by an elderly *Akulmiut* man (Tsikoyak 1987a):

> [After their arrival] the guests would sing a song about the things that were requested by the hosts. At the same time, they would slowly bring in [to the *qasgiq*] the gifts. The next morning, the hosts would make available to their guests all the things they would need during their stay. This is the second day [*kalukaq* – eating food part of the ceremony]. [On] the third day, hosts and their guests changed places. The guests would do the receiving and the hosts the giving. This is called *mumigulluuteng* [exchanging places or positions].

The three-day ceremony required contributions from both the hosts and the guests, and required large stores of food to be served and distributed to participants:

*Kevgiq* didn't happen all the time. You would take what you had even though the host, as a joke, could ask for something special of his cross cousin or joking partner. You were supposed to share what you had. That's what people did at the ceremony. You took what you could, what you had, from your area (Tsikoyak 1987a).

From the analytical perspective of territoriality or maintenance of exclusive use, this important ceremony, the only interregional or intersocietal one, is viewed as a mechanism for communicating the composition of the social group or tribe and delineating the areas or the territory they used and occupied. The type of exchange that characterized *Kevgiq* informed each group of the associated people, places, and products. Travel to and from the host village required knowledge of major travel routes and place names that guided access into foreign tribal areas. Communication between guests and hosts required knowledge of personal names and kinship. Through communication, guests and hosts learned how to identify groups of people and their relationships simply by having knowledge of personal names which tended to be group-specific (Beaver 1982; Shinkwin and Pete 1984).

Ceremonies also required vast stores of food to be provided by the host community. Aside from sustenance, this was a lavish and somewhat intimidating display of the regional group's local subsistence products, including the primary ones, such as whitefish, pike, and blackfish among the *Akulmiut*. Supplemental products, such as waterfowl and cloudberries, also were displayed. Items not indigenous to the area that had to be obtained through trade, such as sea mammal skins and oil, were evident, and these advertised the extent of *Akulmiut* resource use. By having a large group of people from different societies come together at a single place for several days, the activities of each were monitored through direct communication. In this fashion a relatively large area was maintained exclusively without the high costs of time and energy associated with actual defense of a perimeter.

Kinship also served to reinforce territorial boundaries. Boundaries were defined by a marriage universe. As the literature states frequently, Eskimos did not trust people who were not relatives. There was an aversion toward strangers. An elderly *Akulmiut* man commented, "You wouldn't travel so far that you wouldn't have some kinship." Genealogical reconstructions showed that the *Akulmiut* were primarily endogamous in the 1920s (see Table 4.3). At that time, nearly two-thirds of one *Akulmiut* village was

**Table 4.3:** Source of spouse for couples of three *Akulmiut* villages, c. 1920

| VILLAGE | TOTAL MARRIED COUPLES | BOTH SPOUSES FROM VILLAGE | WOMAN FROM VILLAGE AKULMIUT, MAN | MAN FROM VILLAGE, AKULMIUT WOMAN | WOMAN FROM VILLAGE NON-AKULMIUT MAN | MAN FROM VILLAGE, NON-AKULMIUT WOMAN | ONE SPOUSE FROM VILLAGE; OTHER UNKNOWN | OTHER |
|---|---|---|---|---|---|---|---|---|
| NANVARNARRLAK | 25 | 13 (52%) | 2 (8%) *(Nunacuaq)* | 1 (4%) *(Paingaq)* | 5 (20%) *(Cuukvagtuliq; Kwethluk; Napaskiak; Tuntutuliak)* | 2 (8%) (Bethel; Kuskokwim R.) | 1 (4%) | 1 (4%) *(Nunacuaq woman and Cuukvagtuliq man)* |
| PAINGAQ | 13 | 5 (38%) | 1 (8%) *(Kuigaallermiut)* | 1 (8%) *(Nunacuaq)* | 3 (23%) (Akiak, Napaskiak) | 2 (15%) (Eek, Napaskiak) | 1 (7%) | 1 (7%) (Napaskiak woman and Bethel or Russian Mission man) |
| NUNAPICUAQ | 9 | 0 | 0 | 5 (55%) *(Nanvarnarrlak; Paingaq; Akulmiut)* | 1 (11%) (Eek) | 0 | 1 (11%) | 3 (33%) *(Paingaq woman and Napaskiak man; Nunacuaq woman and Paingaq man; Nunacuaq woman and man)* |

endogamous as were over one-half of two others. The exceptions were some spouses from lower Kuskokwim River villages (*Kusquqvagmiut*). In 1983, endogamy also prevailed in at least one of the contemporary communities where more than 60 percent of married couples included spouses who were both *Akulmiut*.

Families and groups of related families were associated with the use of some areas during some or many years. The expansive resource base of winter could be defended with little energy when families were distributed throughout the area. This dispersal signaled their use of the area, but also monitored it for signs of intrusion. Mobility was not so great that families moved frequently; they remained at fall and spring camping sites which were identified easily through common knowledge of place names. In this fashion, spring and fall camps were essentially outposts that served to protect the relatively broad winter resource base. They also encompassed the area important for harvesting the major winter food resource, blackfish.

Withholding geographic knowledge of an area from others was another means by which exclusive use to an area and its resources could be maintained. In the absence of maps, *Akulmiut* place-names facilitated travel and resource use among the group. The uninformed were disadvantaged. Within the area of the *Akulmiut*, the immense complex of lakes, sloughs, and other waterways was a challenge for the uninitiated traveler. Without signs or experience, it was difficult to locate many travel routes and resource areas. Knowledge of place names greatly aided travel and access.

That the *Akulmiut* area was not open to access by neighboring Yup'ik societies is evident in the existence of designated travel routes that could be used only by some regional groups and communities at certain times of the year. During open water, the lower Johnson River was the primary means of entry into the tundra region from the south. This route provided access to the *Akulmiut* villages along the Johnson River and the large lakes draining into it, and the Pikmiktalik River. The Pikmiktalik River was used by the *Akulmiut* and the *Akiacuarmiut*. The *Akiacuarmiut* ascended it and the upper Johnson River (*Kuicaraq*) in fall as they went to camps for hunting mink. In spring, the area was used by *Akulmiut, Akiacuarmiut,* and occasionally by others for hunting muskrats. Its use was explained in the following way:

Nobody asked, but you know they used it. Not [generally] Napakiak [along the lower Kuskokwim River], but some may have used it . . . like in spring if people heard about the abundance of muskrats, you'd expect to see people from other places such as Napakiak or Ohagmiut [along the lower Yukon River]. They would go if they knew also, convening on the area without asking. [Also], about this time of year [October] if [fish] were plentiful then, like Napakiak, people would come. You tell your relatives (Tsikoyak 1987b).

The upper Johnson River (*Kuicaraq,* "the way to go to the river") was a route used both in open water and when frozen to reach the lower Yukon River near Russian Mission. Baird Inlet to the west, and beyond to the Bering Sea coast, were accessed by means of portages and water routes along an east-west route, which was still used in the 1980s during open water (see Figure 4.6). The route extended from the large lake, Nunavakanukakslak Lake (*Nanvarnarrlak),* through *Pulayarrat* to *Arviyaraq* ("the way to go across") to upper and lower Kayigyalik Lake (*Qayigyalek).* From two points, portages and streams provided access into Taksleslak Lake (*Taklirrlak),* which provided access to the west. This was accomplished by means of streams and lakes, such as Puk Palik Lake (*Paq'pal'aaq),* which then flowed southwest to Baird

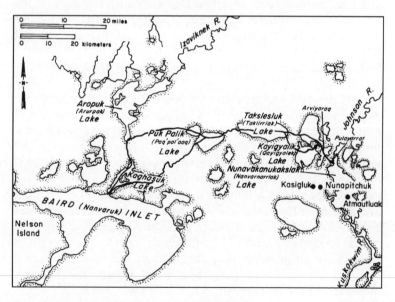

**Figure 4.6**: East-west travel routes in the *Akulmiut* area

Inlet (*Nanvaruk*) or northwest into Aropuk Lake (*Arurpak*). The elderly respondent (born 1901) noted:

> [In the early 1900s] people used this trail to bring things to trade [to and from the coast]. It was used by *Akulmiut* or *Cenarmiut* and whoever needs to when traveling this way or through here [*Qaluyaarmiut* and *Kusquqvagmiut* were mentioned also]. All these trails were open to anybody. Nobody gets a second look when you use a travel route (Tsikoyak 1987b).

Travel routes were open to members of some other groups, at certain times of the year, for specific purposes.

## Discussion

Whether defense is overt or by some form of communication, in both cases, time and energy are expended to maintain a territory. It makes little difference whether territories are maintained by physical combat or by occupation – "through individuals avoiding each other by the use of simple movement rules" (Davies and Houston 1984: 149). *Akulmiut* boundaries did not include the Kuskokwim or Yukon Rivers, or the Bering Sea coast. With no direct access to salmon or marine mammals, why were their boundaries as delineated? The answer is found in their utilization of critical fish resources. It is argued here that the nature of Alaskan Eskimo socioterritorial organization can be explained by an ecological analysis of critical resource distribution and abundance.

Both whitefish and northern pike are dense and predictable resources in a strategically located catchment area that defined the core area of the *Akulmiut*. Villages were situated to support the harvest of whitefish primarily, and the harvest of pike at certain times of the year when abundant and concentrated at a few strategic stream locations. These sites were characterized by storage and processing facilities such as caches and storage pits. Furthermore, each had at least one *qasgiq*, a multipurpose structure that functioned as a residence for men and male youth, men's workshop, community hall, and ceremonial and spiritual center. The village *qasgiq* was also where foods were redistributed during intravillage, intervillage, and interregional ceremonies. The *Akulmiut* village was the economic, social, and political center of *Akulmiut* life and was occupied by most families as much as eight months of the year. The site of the *Akulmiut* village carried with it a guaranteed food supply. On the other hand, the distribution of blackfish defined the peripheral boundaries of the *Akulmiut* area. Seasonal settlements occupied by one or several families were dispersed – found where blackfish and furbearers could be harvested readily – throughout the area to its boundaries.

Studies of north Alaskan Eskimo indicated that some societies such as the Point Hope Eskimo (*Tikirarmiut*[3]) had definable and defended territories (Burch and Correll 1972; Burch 1974, 1981). Warfare was endemic among north Alaskan Eskimo groups until nonnative contact and trade essentially terminated native warfare (Burch 1974: 1,2; 1988c: 238). Although no attempt was made to discuss or explain the nature of Eskimo territoriality, mechanisms for defending and advertising an area of exclusive use have been described. Knowledge of place names, dispersion to fringe or "less productive" areas at certain times, and restricted travel routes open for members of some regional groups for traveling across tribal "boundaries" to participate in intersocietal trade events helped maintain a territorial system (Burch and Correll 1972: 25). Particular conventions were followed when leaving the borders of the group's territory and for traveling through intervening territories (Burch 1974: 5–6). However, what accounted for the existence of a territorial system in the first place has not been examined.

An explanation for, or the predictability of, territoriality among the *Tikirarmiut* could emerge from a systematic analysis using the Dyson-Hudson and Smith (1978) ecological model. However, several questions must be answered first. Which marine mammal species utilized were key resources or "critical foods" for the *Tikirarmiut*? Were these predictable in time and location and dense in abundance? Was the primary settlement of the *Tikirarmiut* at Point Hope situated to maintain exclusive use of critical resources with little time and energy expended in defending them?

The data for the *Tikirarmiut* (Burch 1981) showed that, as with the *Akulmiut*, the primary settlement was the site for a guaranteed food supply (several marine mammal species), but also where food was stored. Predictable and dense resources and stored food supplies likely generated the *Tikirarmiut* territorial system. Although the *Tikirarmiut* were settled much of the year at a large

3. This is an Iñupiaq Eskimo word written in the phonemic system used by Burch (1981).

village site, families dispersed in summer to different areas used for fishing, netting belukha whale, or hunting caribou. Determining whether these or other species constituted a critical resource for the *Tikirarmiut* would help to explain the maintenance of the exclusively used area described by Burch (1981) as being well beyond the village, as found for the *Akulmiut*. Furthermore, the seeming puzzle noted by Burch (1981) for *Tikirarmiut* defense of areas of "low productivity" appears to be accounted for by the model. As among the *Akulmiut*, one of the critical resources was probably dispersed, and the costs of defense over a large area may have been reduced by dispersing small family groups throughout the area.

The socioterritorial organization of the Bering Strait Eskimo (Ray 1967, 1975) is another example to which this type of analysis can be applied to enhance our understanding of the relationship between resource distribution and utilization and the nature of Eskimo territoriality. Among the Kauwerak,[4] an Iñupiaq society, Ray (1967) alluded to caribou and fish (species not identified) as being critical resources of the Kauwerak. Research findings suggested that areas were defended, although analysis did not use resource distribution and utilization variables to conclude that the Kauwerak were territorial. Again, as among the north Alaskan Eskimo, overt defense was rare. There was no defense of a perimeter, nor were there village fortifications. Rather, several mechanisms helped monitor incursions into their territory to protect Kauwerak from offending neighboring groups. As with the *Akulmiut*, the *qasgiq* organization was central for putting these mechanisms into operation. The sociopolitical aspects of *qasgiq* life aided monitoring land and resource use by Kauwerak and their neighbors, and enforced appropriate conduct in land and resource use, such as requesting permission for hunting or fishing in the area of an allied society or tribe. Place names, knowledge of names of older persons in the society, and unique boat styles all contributed to distinguishing the Kauwerak from their neighbors, as among the *Akulmiut*.

Ray (1967: 386) also described "alliance sanctuaries," areas that were used in common for harvesting seals and fish. The occur-

---

4. This is an earlier spelling used by Ray (1967) of an Iñupiaq Eskimo word, *Qawiaraq* (see Woodbury [1984: 56] for an explanation of the phonemic system used in more recent orthography).

rence of these sanctuaries may be explained readily by the ecological model, by determining whether the resources harvested were critical resources, the distribution of which was dense and predictable. If they were not, this would explain their use by multiple groups. Certainly our present limited understanding of the nature of Alaskan Eskimo socioterritorial organization can only be enhanced by an ecological analysis of resource distribution and abundance and spatial organization as suggested here. In turn, these analyses could lead to broad generalizations of territorial behavior among Eskimo societies.

## Conclusion

In conclusion, the theory that territoriality will occur where critical food resources are dense and predictable (Dyson-Hudson and Smith 1978) gives an explanation of why there is a separate Eskimo society where the *Akulmiut* are today because of the distribution and abundance of their critical food resources: whitefish, pike, and blackfish. The *Akulmiut* harvested these key food resources that were dense, predictable, and abundant. They had a territorial system of land use and occupancy as predicted by the model.

The population was compressed at times and dispersed at others. The territory had a core area of intensive usage with an outer cortex used and occupied less frequently. Their spatial organization showed that all primary villages and storage and processing facilities were situated at a few strategic river bottlenecks, where whitefish and northern pike could be intercepted easily twice a year during their annual migrations. The sites were centers for *Akulmiut* social, political, and ceremonial life.

The Alaska blackfish, another critical resource, was dispersed and relatively ubiquitous. Family groups moved seasonally to more remote areas to harvest them. The family-group distribution throughout the area signaled the use of land and resources by the *Akulmiut*, but also served to monitor the area for signs of intrusion. This dispersion marked the farthest edge of the *Akulmiut* area. The *Akulmiut* distinguished themselves by several means. They did not need to resort to overt defense or actual defense of a perimeter. Instead, they used other mechanisms, such as ceremonies, naming conventions, kinship, and place names to communicate and delineate a unique area and its resources. Data for the *Akulmiut* show, as analyses of other Alaskan Eskimo groups may also show, that even with dispersed or mobile resources, predictability and abundance of critical food resources secure these hunting-gathering people with a nearly guaranteed food supply, contributing to a territorial system of land and resource use.

The theoretical model used to guide this analysis has considerable value for addressing the relationship among resource distribution and spatial organization and resource use among Alaskan Eskimos. It provides a means to analyze systematically territorial dimensions of these societies in a comparative context, and provides an understanding of the nature of Eskimo socioterritorial organization. That is, according to this ecological model, each Eskimo society that, like the *Akulmiut*, has a defended territory, will be located where a critical food resource is dense and predictable, and can be harvested efficiently. The promise this type of analysis holds for explaining Alaskan Eskimo territorial behavior points to the contribution that data on Alaskan native societies can make to the general theory of human territoriality.

# 5

# Nature and Culture on the Northwest Coast of North America: The Case of Wakashan Salmon Resources

*Leland Donald and Donald H. Mitchell*

This article reconstructs the territories controlled by seventy-nine Wakashan-speaking local groups. Using escapement data, relative salmon resources of each stream and territory are estimated. Salmon resources of territories are not only larger but more predictable than those of streams: the construction of territories that control more than one stream stabilizes the resource base. There is also much variation between territories in both size of resource base and resource variability. Territories were created as a base for group activities and some local groups controlled territories with larger and, equally important, more stable salmon resources. Salmon resources were found to be moderately good predictors of population and of some other cultural features of Wakashan groups. [1]

Of the many anthropologists who have worked on the Northwest Coast, Franz Boas remains the most important and dominant figure in Northwest Coast ethnography. Even though he was trained in physical geography, his earliest ethnographic work, *The Central Eskimo* (Boas 1888) was "the only one in which the geographic setting is given other than perfunctory or minimal consideration" (Kroeber 1935: 543). In thousands of pages of Northwest Coast ethnography, he and his followers pay almost no attention to the natural environment. Such lack of interest in the environment contributed to a model in which the resource base was viewed as so rich that it offered no constraints on Northwest Coast culture. This model was not seriously challenged until the work of Wayne Suttles in the 1960s. Although Suttles's papers

1. We gratefully acknowledge the support of the University of Victoria's Committee on Faculty Research and Travel.

(1960, 1962, 1968) have been well received and frequently cited, they represent suggestive rather than systematic treatment of the resource base and its relation to society and culture: model building without benefit of empirical verification. As such, they left the way clear for equally unsupported counterclaims of environmental irrelevance (see, e.g., Drucker and Heizer 1967: 139). Since the 1960s there have been few published studies that consider the relationships between the resource base and other aspects of culture in a systematic or empirical manner.[2]

In this paper we describe one major Northwest Coast resource, salmon, in some detail for one set of Northwest Coast cultures, the Wakashan speakers. We are specifically interested in the variation of salmon from territory to territory and in possible relationships between the resource base and other aspects of society and culture. Salmon are chosen both because we have access to good data about the resource and because they play such a large role in all aspects of Northwest Coast culture – especially as an important source of food.

The Wakashan-speaking peoples of the Northwest Coast culture area include those commonly referred to in the ethnographic literature as the Makah and Nootka (by their own preference, the latter will be referred to hereafter as the Nuuchahnulth) and the Kwakiutl – including Southern Kwakiutl (who now wish to be identified as Kwakwaka'wakw), Owikeno, Heiltsuk (or Bella Bella), Xaixais, and Haisla. Their territories range from Cape Flattery in the state of Washington to Douglas Channel on the northern coast of British Columbia. This study includes all Wakashan but the Makah.

## Data Used in This Study

Our basic approach has been to compile estimates of the salmon resources available to Wakashan local groups. We have done this by reconstructing the territories of seventy-nine groups and by assuming that, in the absence of information to the contrary, each local group made exclusive use of salmon spawning in the streams of its territory. The local group, our fundamental unit of analysis, is a set of people who share a common winter village

2. For some exceptions, see Donald and Mitchell 1975; Langdon 1979; Mitchell and Donald 1988; and Schalk 1977, 1981.

and who act as an independent social unit. Traditionally, each was essentially politically autonomous. Our identification of groups and reconstruction of their holdings pertain to the early nineteenth century.

## Identification of Territories

Many ethnographic and historic sources provided data on the seventy-nine local group territories, although precise boundary information was rarely available. Knowledge of a local group's seasonal settlement locations and the identification of streams or beaches it exploited helped determine the area used by each group, and then boundaries were drawn separating such territories along watershed divisions, through remote headlands or beaches, and across major bodies of water. Once drawn, all streams falling within such boundaries then were assigned to the local group, even if a specific reference to the use of a stream could not be found.

## Estimates of Local Group Salmon Resources

Because a major goal is to compare the resources of local groups, useful and reliable information is needed about the salmon available aboriginally in each definable territory. Since salmon populations are known to vary cyclically, we also wish to investigate variations over time within and between territories.

Pacific salmon are anadromous (i.e., they ascend rivers from the sea to spawn) and most aboriginal capture took place at the mouths of rivers or after the fish had entered streams to spawn. This means that the information on salmon we seek is how many fish on average entered a territory's salmon streams and how much variation there might be around this average over the years. We require such information not merely for a few streams or territories, but for every stream in every reconstructible territory. Such a demand for completeness cannot be met by relying on the early historical observations available for a few streams. We must turn to relatively recent attempts at systematic and comprehensive record keeping. There are two twentieth century sources of salmon run information: escapement estimates compiled each year by the Canadian Department of Fisheries and Oceans; and statistics relating to the annual commercial, sport, and native subsistence catches of salmon in British Columbia waters. Together these sources should account for nearly all the mature salmon in British Columbia waters in a given year (missing will be those fish taken by other predators, such as seals, sea lions, and killer whales).

The Canadian Department of Fisheries and Oceans has estimated escapements according to species and on a stream by stream basis since 1934. Since about 1950, these estimates have included virtually all coastal streams with a salmon run of any consequence. Escapement estimates, however, have a major missing piece: those fish caught before they reach their natal stream. Unfortunately, catch cannot be added to escapement, because for most species in most areas catches cannot be attributed to particular streams and, hence, particular territories. In the long run, the effect of catch on different streams should even out so that all are affected equally, but these missing fish mean that escapement estimates cannot be used to reconstruct the absolute amount of salmon available in a territory – only the relative amount. Escapement data allow us to compare territories with respect to their relative quantities of salmon, but we cannot use these estimates to speak of total pounds of fish, kilograms of protein, calories, etc., that were available from salmon to the aboriginal population of a given territory.

There is an additional obstacle to estimating total salmon available in a given territory. In the early 1950s, chum salmon runs abruptly declined to about one-half the levels for the earlier part of this century and have never recovered (Aro and Shepard 1967: 254). Other species also have declined significantly since the 1820s and 1830s. Thus, any reconstruction of absolute salmon available in a given stream or territory aboriginally would not only have to combine escapement and catch statistics in some way, but would have to deal with historical declines as well.

Escapement estimates are compiled from the reports of fisheries protection officers who visit and make visual evaluations of the number of fish ascending the river to spawn. Since these reports are based on sight counts only, there is the possibility of considerable measurement error (Aro and Shepard 1967: 227; Brett 1952: 454). The few studies undertaken to determine the accuracy of the counting methods suggest that there is probably relatively little difference between observers (Hunter 1959: 839); that for moderate runs, the counting error is in the neighborhood of 2.5 to 5 percent (Wood 1970); and that errors are greatest when the actual escapement is in excess of 100,000 fish, at which level the runs may be underestimated by over 50 percent (Brett 1952: 454).

In deciding to use escapement, we have assumed that certain kinds of errors will tend to cancel out when long runs of observations are pooled to make territorial resource estimates, an assumption also made by Neave (1953) in justifying the use of these data. The underestimation of large runs, in particular, is not a serious problem for our study area, as there are few streams in the region with single species escapements of more than 100,000 fish.

For this study, the estimates used span the period from 1950 to 1967. After 1967 the decline in small stream populations in particular is too marked to allow us to assume that the salmon populations reported relate in any useful way to pre-contact conditions. Although counts are available for some streams on the coast back to the 1930s, we were able to obtain comparable stream data for all local group territories only after 1950. Thus, for most streams usable data were available for an eighteen year period.

Escapement data we have used are for five species of Pacific salmon: pinks (*Oncorhynchus gorbuscha*), chum (*O. keta*), coho (*O. kisutch*), sockeye (*O. nerka*), and chinook (*O. tshawytscha*). These salmon spend the first part of their lives in freshwater lakes and streams, the majority of their time in open ocean feeding grounds and their final months returning to reproduce at or near their freshwater birthplace. All die after spawning.

Variation among the species affected their availability and importance to the Wakashan groups. The following discussion relies primarily on Hart (1973). Average weights relate to the commercial catch from 1951 to 1963 in British Columbia and are calculated from data in Aro and Shepard (1967).

Pinks (or humpbacks) are widespread, but their numbers are concentrated in a few large rivers, most of which lie beyond the Wakashan territories. They are all but absent from the southern part of Vancouver Island. Pinks are on a two year cycle, and some areas have very different numbers returning to spawn in alternate years. There are also differences in the sizes of individuals belonging to these two populations, odd-year pinks averaging almost 50 percent larger than even-year ones. The overall average size is 4.84 pounds. They spawn between late August and late October.

Chum (or dog salmon) enter a great many streams in the Wakashan territories and are, in some localities, late spawners, appearing generally from September to November but sometimes well into winter. Their return cycle is anywhere from two to seven years (usually three to five), with the sizes of maturing salmon varying considerably from year to year. The average size of the chum salmon is 11.72 pounds. Hart (1973: 114) notes that they were favored by the native population because they smoked well, which may be a result of their comparatively low fat content.

Coho (or silver salmon) spawn in a great many streams, both large and small, along the whole coast. They usually run in October or November at the end of a two to four year cycle. Their average size is 7.09 pounds.

Sockeye (or red or blueback) are more restricted in their distribution than the preceding species. They usually reproduce in river systems that drain accessible lakes. Most sockeye return to spawn in their fourth year, but the recorded range is from three to eight years (Foerster 1968: 356). They average 6.16 pounds in weight and spawn in the late summer or fall.

Chinook (or spring, tyee, or king) average 12.80 pounds, but, as the largest Pacific salmon, may weigh more than 100 pounds. Most return in their fourth or fifth years, with some arriving in their second year and others arriving as late as their sixth. Comparatively few streams are used by spawners. Although maturing fish may return at almost any time of year, peak runs commonly fall within the late summer and early fall months (from August to October).

The data for each stream were coded by year for each of the five Pacific salmon species. The species vary considerably in size, as noted, so we standardized by dividing the average size of individuals of that species by the average size of the smallest species, pinks. Thus all fish numbers are reported in units of "standard fish" (s.f.).

Two measures were selected to assess different aspects of salmon escapement into a stream. The median escapement for the eighteen year period was chosen as a measure of central tendency. For many streams the number of fish fluctuates considerably from year to year, so the mean often would be very unstable and thus unsuitable, especially given that only eighteen years are used in the calculations. The most familiar measure of variation is the standard deviation. It, however, is based on the mean as a measure of central tendency, a measure we have just rejected. The measure of variation adopted here is the average deviation around the median. This is calculated by summing the absolute values of the deviations from the median and dividing by the number of cases. However, since the size of stream medians ranges so widely, absolute values are difficult to compare. Instead, we use the coefficient of relative variation around the median ($CRV_{md}$), obtained by dividing the average deviation from the median by the median. This expresses the average deviation as a proportion of the median – making comparison of variation meaningful, even where absolute sizes of the medians are very different. A $CRV_{md}$ of zero means that there is no variation around the median and all values are equal, while a $CRV_{md}$ of fifty means that, on average, yearly values are 50 percent larger or 50 percent smaller than the median. Thus, a $CRV_{md}$ of near zero reflects salmon escapements that are relatively stable, whereas one much larger than zero reflects salmon escapements that fluctuate considerably from year to year.

## The Salmon Resources of Wakashan Territories

Of the seventy-nine territories included in this study, two had no streams with recorded salmon escapements. Both (the Yalakai-idox and Yutlinuk) occupied small clusters of islands exposed to the open sea. Given the emphasis on salmon as a food source in the Northwest Coast culture area, it is perhaps surprising that any territories without salmon streams existed. Such streamless territories serve as a reminder that salmon, though important, perhaps was not essential to a local group's existence. However, when the precipitous population decline of the first half of the nineteenth century occurred and many formerly autonomous groups began to amalgamate, these salmonless populations seem to have been among the first to disappear as independent political and territorial entities.

### Number of Streams

Wakashan territories contained from zero to twenty-five salmon streams. The median number per territory is 3.9 and the mean, 5.1. Seventy-seven percent of group territories controlled six or fewer streams, while only one had more than seventeen streams. Streams per territory are not normally distributed. And data transformation by taking the logarithm of the number of streams does little to normalize this distribution (goodness-of-fit test for normality, where $p < .01$).[3]

The interquartile range of streams is from two to six. Territories falling within this range may be thought of as ordinary with respect to number of streams controlled. The most unusual territories outside the range have already been mentioned: those with no streams. The Koskimo territory, with twenty-five streams, is an extreme outlier at the other end of this distribution. It is comprised of many small water courses, producing a total median escapement of 32,000 s.f. One of its neighbors on the northwest coast of Vancouver Island, the Koprino, has thirteen streams and about the same median escapement (32,800 s.f.), while its two other nearest neighbors, the Klaskino and Quatsino, have six and four streams respectively, but only 13,600 and 8,100 s.f.

Ten local groups had access to one or more streams shared with at least one other local group. By and large, this was not a case of a stream being divided between up-river and down-river groups, but of one (or several) groups having rights to fishing stations on streams well inside another's territory. Four of these groups with shared access were on the west coast of Vancouver Island: Opetchisat and Seshart; Nitinat and Carmanah. The other six form a cluster in the core of the Queen Charlotte Sound region: Awaitlala, Fort Rupert, Nenelkenox, Nimpkish, Mamalillikulla, and Tlawitsis.

## Overall Escapements

The seventy-nine reconstructed Wakashan territories have a wide range of median escapements. In addition to the two territories with no salmon streams, one other has such a low escapement that we treat it as a virtual zero. This is the Tatchuath territory, which, although it has two streams, has runs too small and sporadic to achieve a minimum median of even 100 standard fish. At the other extreme is the Tlawitsis territory with a median escapement of 426,800 standard fish. The median of territory escapements is 48,580 s.f. (See Table 5.1 for this and other descriptive statistics of territory characteristics.) The distribution of median

3. In this instance, a goodness-of-fit test determines the likelihood that the distribution of the logarithms of the numbers of streams per territory comes from a normal distribution. The test results suggest that there is less than one chance in one hundred that the distribution is normal.

**Table 5.1:** Salmon Resources of Wakashan Territories

| STATISTIC | MEDIAN | $CRV_{md}$ |
|---|---|---|
| Range | 0-426,800 s.f. | 12.1-283.1 % |
| Mean | 812,400 | 72.9 |
| Median | 485,500 | 56.8 |
| 1st quartile | 174,000 | 45.2 |
| 3rd quartile | 1,003,000 | 93.3 |
| Territories with runs <100 | 3.8 % | |
| Territories with runs >1,000 | 93.7 | |
| Territories with runs >10,000 | 81.0 | |
| Territories with runs >100,000 | 26.6 | |

**Notes:**
1. N=79.
2. Territories with salmon escapement <100 excluded from calculation of $CRV_{md}$.

escapements has a marked skew toward the lower values, and a long upper tail. Most territories (79.7 percent) have median escapements of more than 10,000 s.f.

The distribution of territory medians is not normal (goodness-of-fit test for normality, where $p < .01$). The interquartile range is from 17,400 to 100,300 s.f., and the 50 percent of territories that fall within or near these limits can be taken as typical territories. At the lower end of the scale, the most unusual cases are the three territories with little or no fish. The very large territories are Awaitlala (208,200 s.f.), Owikeno (249,700 s.f.), Kitlope (260,500 s.f.), Kynoch (271,300 s.f.), Nenelkenox (366,200 s.f.), Nimpkish (393,100 s.f.), Fort Rupert (395,500 s.f.), and Tlawitsis (426,800 s.f.).

The largest territory has an escapement that is 1,067 times the size of the smallest median escapement recorded (400 s.f. for Tlaaluis)! This is an enormous difference in relative resource potential – one that outstrips any possibility of actual utilization, as it is very doubtful that the largest local group exceeded the smallest in population by a ratio of more than 200 to 1, and even this assumes a largest local group of the unlikely size of 5,000 persons. Obviously, in the most richly endowed territories, the resource base was not fully exploited. One consequence is that differences in median escapement between territories on the lower end of the scale are more significant than differences of the same size between territories at the upper end of the scale. The addition of 10,000 s.f. to the escapement of a territory such as that of the Hesquiat (9,400 s.f.) would have a much greater impact on the local group than would the same 10,000 added to the Awaitlala or Owikeno, with their 208,200 s.f. and 249,700 s.f., respectively.

The decreasing importance of additional fish as escapement size increases provides a strong rationale for transforming escapement data. The result of log transformation is not a normal distribution of the log values (goodness-of-fit test for normality, where $p < .01$) and the skew toward the lower values has been turned into one toward the higher values, but the spread in log units is only 5.6 (Tlaaluis to Tlawitsis). A log transformation of these data also focuses attention on a different set of "extreme" cases for territory medians. Under the log transformations (median, 4.69; interquartile range, 4.24 to 5.00) even the four largest cases fall relatively near to the main body of territories, while the divergent character of the smaller cases is emphasized. Now the unusual cases are the territories of the Clo-oose (3,200 s.f.), Uwigalixdox (600 s.f.), Tlaaluis (400 s.f.), and the three salmonless territories. These smallest territories would need to add several thousand standard fish to make even modest progress toward the main body of escapements in the log distribution (i.e., an increase of at least 1.0 log units), while the largest territories could gain as many as 500,000 more standard fish and not move a significant distance away from the main body of the log distribution.

As the preceding discussion shows, there are two foci on the edges of the distribution of territory escapements: the small territories and the large territories. Untransformed data draw attention to territories with large escapements; log-transformed data focus on territories with small escapements. In terms of environmental constraints, the territories at the smaller end of the scale faced the greatest problems.

## Species Escapements

In fifty-nine of the territories, a single species contributes over half of the median escapement. This relatively high dependence on a single species is especially marked on the west coast of Vancouver Island. Although some territories have very large single species escapements, few depend on but a single species – only five, in fact. And many contain runs of at least four of the five species (54.7

percent). The five one-species territories are all in the Rivers Inlet area, where groups apparently depended on sockeye alone.

Chum is the most important species of Pacific salmon in the Wakashan area. It not only has the largest median territorial escapement of any of the five species (19,400 s.f.; the next largest species median is coho, 3,200 s.f.), but it is the major contributor to individual territorial escapements much more often than any other species. The most striking patterns are the relative dominance of chum on the west coast of Vancouver Island and the northernmost part of the Wakashan-speaking area, while species dominance is much more mixed in Queen Charlotte Sound.

Despite the importance of chum, the largest single species escapements into any territory are sockeye runs, a few of which are very large indeed. The most important sockeye streams in the area are the Nimpkish River and the complex of streams emptying into Rivers Inlet. Because of streams in these two small regions, five local groups have access to sockeye escapements in excess of 100,000 s.f. each: Tlawitsis, Nimpkish, Fort Rupert, Nenelkenox, and Owikeno. Three local groups have access to median chum escapements of over 100,000 s.f.: Kynoch, Uwitlidox, and Tlawitsis, although four other local groups come close, having access to chum escapements in excess of 90,000 s.f. The largest pink and coho median territorial escapements are somewhat smaller (77,300 s.f. and 57,200 s.f., respectively) and the largest spring median is much smaller (23,700 s.f.).

*Annual Variation*

Salmon streams exhibit marked annual variation in the number of fish available in a typical year, and, as would be expected, there is also considerable variation in territorial escapement from year to year. The coefficient of relative variation around the median for territories ranges from 12.2 to 283.1 percent. The median $CRV_{md}$ is 56.89 percent and the interquartile range is from 45.2 to 93.3 percent. The distribution of territory coefficients is not normal but has a marked skew toward the lower values. One territory is an extreme outlier in this distribution, for although Asxwilan territory has a $CRV_{md}$ of 283.1, the next largest $CRV_{md}$ is 159.6 (Nohuntsitk territory). These are neighboring groups at Rivers Inlet, and both depend on single streams and a single species (sockeye).

If the territory coefficients are log transformed, the distribution has a more symmetrical shape, although it is still not a normal distribution. The high annual variation of the Asxwilam territory keeps it an extreme case even under log transformation, but attention is now also called to the unusually low annual variation of Clo-oose territory (12.1 percent).

*Relations Among Territory Characteristics*

It would seem that the logical way for a Wakashan group to improve its resource base would be to add salmon streams to its territory. And indeed, although we did not discuss the number of streams in territories, our previously published work on Southern Kwakiutl salmon resources (Donald and Mitchell 1975) is sometimes interpreted as showing that there is a relationship between the number of streams a group controls and the resources available to it. In fact, the relationship between number of streams in a territory and median escapement of a territory is quite modest; Pearson's r = .23 (i.e., 5.3 percent variation explained).[4] But we have already shown that log transformations are appropriate for both of these variables, and the relationship between the log of number of streams and log of territory medians is considerably higher than that for the raw data, Pearson's r = .53 (i.e., 25 percent of variation explained). The 95 percent confidence interval for this r is from .34 to .67. Thus, although there is some tendency for median escapement to increase as the number of streams increases, the number of streams will not account for a very large proportion of variation in territory escapement. Even allowing for considerable sampling error, number of streams is very unlikely to account for even as much as 50 percent of the variation in territory escapement. The relationship between median escapement and $CRV_{md}$ is also modest; r = -.35. Log transformation of the two variables lowers the strength of the relationship to -.28 (or only 7.8 percent of the variation). Although an r of this magnitude is statistically significant ($p \leq .008$), the 95 percent confidence interval (-.04 to -.51) suggests that, even allowing for considerable sampling error, neither of these variables can account for much of the variation in the other. Number

---

4. Pearson's r is the correlation coefficient, which measures the strength of the relationship between two numerical variables.

of streams is not related at all to annual variation. Pearson's r for untransformed data is -.10, and for the log data, Pearson's r is -.06.

That most territories do not depend on a single species for their escapement is emphasized by the fact that individual species escapement is only moderately related to overall escapement (correlations range from .43 for sockeye to .56 for chum). Thus, although number of streams and median escapements are modestly related, in general, territory characteristics are not highly predictive of each other.

*Regional Comparison*

The Wakashan area is large enough to have considerable environmental diversity. In this section we divide the area into three regions and investigate differences and similarities within and among the regions.

Two of these regions, although differing from one another, each have a certain overall internal environmental unity, for the west coast of Vancouver Island has much open shoreline and a relatively small amount of protected water. The Queen Charlotte Strait area is almost entirely sheltered water. The third region, in the northernmost part of the Wakashan area, includes a mix of sheltered channels and inlets and open coast. The west coast of Vancouver Island region contains thirty-two territories, the Queen Charlotte Strait region twenty-three territories, and the northern region twenty-four territories.

As was shown in the preceding section, there is a modest relationship between the log of the median escapement of a territory and the log of the number of streams in that territory (r = .53). This relationship holds by region as well, although in Queen Charlotte Strait only 14 percent of the variance is accounted for. The overall relationship between the log of median escapements and the log of $CRV_{md}$ is only -.28. This overall relationship is largely the product of the relationship between median escapement and annual variation in one of the regions, Queen Charlotte Strait, where 59 percent of the variance is explained (r = -.77). In the other two regions there is essentially no relationship between these two variables (for the west coast of Vancouver Island, r = .09; for the northern region, r = -.11). The Queen Charlotte Strait correlation is significantly different from the correlations in either of the other two regions ($p < .003$ for the west coast of Vancouver

Island/Queen Charlotte Strait difference, for example). Thus, in Queen Charlotte Strait, unlike in the other two regions, there is a fairly good relationship between typical territory escapements and annual variation: the higher the escapement the lower the annual variation. Overall, we found no relationship between number of streams and annual variation, which is true for individual regions as well.

There are important differences in median overall escapements by region. At 31,050 s.f., the west coast of Vancouver Island has a much lower median than the other two regions with 65,600 s.f. (Queen Charlotte Strait) and 51,600 s.f. (north). These differences are statistically significant at conventional levels (Kruskal-Wallis one way analysis of variance for ranks, $p < .05$).[5] The regional differences between median $CRV_{md}$ or median number of streams per territory are neither large nor statistically significant.

The difference in typical territory medians reflects another regional difference. If territories are classified by region and by the "quality" of a territory's salmon resource base, using a four step assessment (poor: <1,000 s.f.; mediocre: 1,000 to 9,999 s.f.; good: 10,000 to 99,999 s.f.; and excellent: >100,000 s.f.), the quality of territories is not distributed at random over the regions ($Chi^2 = 12.72$, $p < .05$). The major deviation from the expected distribution, if region made no difference to territory quality, is that the west coast of Vancouver Island area is under-represented in the "excellent" category.

The species component of territories also varies from region to region. When we test for whether at least one of the regions differs from the others, we find that pink, coho, and spring escapements all surpass conventional significance levels, but that sockeye and chum do not. This is not surprising for chum, since it is the mainstay species for most territories in all regions. Sockeye is distributed too sporadically for a regional difference to appear, especially since each area contains at least one sockeye "hot spot."

5. Because of the small sample size and the skewed nature of escapement distributions, a distribution-free test was used in the regional analysis. The Kruskal-Wallis test is a test of significance. It estimates the probability that one's results are an artifact of sampling error rather than a reflection of the true characteristics of the population one is studying. In this instance, the chances are less than five out of one hundred that differences between the territories of the three regions are the result of sampling error rather than real differences between regions. Other significance tests used later in this chapter include the Median Test, the Mann-Whitney Test and the Chi-square test.

Overall, the major regional differences involve the west coast of Vancouver Island, where territories tend to have markedly fewer pinks and lower overall escapement, and where there are fewer territories with escapement of over 100,000 s.f. The north region tends to have fewer coho and spring, while the Queen Charlotte Strait region stands out as the only one with a moderately strong relationship between typical escapement and annual variation.

### Ethnolinguistic Group Patterns

Wakashan speakers form two major linguistic divisions – Northern and Southern – which are typically separated into four main language groups of Northern Wakashan speakers (Haisla, Heiltsuk, Oowekyala, and Kwakwala) and three main language groups of Southern Wakashan speakers (Nootkan, Nitinat, and Makah). The language groups form contiguous blocks and only one (Kwakwala) falls into more than one region. The conventional ethnic or "tribal" divisions conform fairly closely to linguistic divisions, although in most discussions of Nuuchahnulth, Nitinat speakers are rarely distinguished from Nootkan speakers. In addition, Boas's work on the "Southern Kwakiutl" focused on the Fort Rupert groups and the other Kwakwala speakers who regularly potlatched with them, so that we have less information about the groups at some distance from Fort Rupert (such as Klaskino, Goasila, or the Lekwiltok groups: Wiwiakay, Tlaaluis, Kweeha, and Wiwiakum), and they tend to be overlooked in discussions of the "Kwakiutl."

Comparison of ethnolinguistic groups with respect to salmon resources is made difficult by the fact that only two of the usual comparison units contain even modest numbers of local groups – Kwakwaka'wakw with twenty-seven and Nuuchahnulth with twenty-eight; the next largest is Heiltsuk with ten. Comparison of ethnolinguistic groupings also may not be very meaningful from a cultural point of view since none had any overall political or other organizational unity. Local groups intermarried and had ceremonial relations with other local groups both within and without so-called ethnic or tribal boundaries. They also went to war and raided for slaves both inside and outside such groupings. The hypothesis that local groups probably had more positive relations within the larger ethnic groupings and more negative relations outside these groupings might be supported by the facts, although, to our knowledge, no one has attempted such an analysis on a systematic basis. Were this analysis attempted, we suspect it might be very difficult to show that ethnic similarity is a more powerful predictor of the quality of relations between local groups than is simple geographic propinquity.

In spite of the preceding remarks, since discussion of the ethnic cluster of local groups is the conventional way to proceed in the Northwest Coast literature, we briefly consider the characteristics of ethnic group salmon territories. The first point to recognize has already been made: ethnic groupings tend to fall within regional groupings. This means that when we compare ethnic groupings we may be covertly comparing regional groupings once again. For the two largest ethnic groupings, we perform only a slightly modified regional comparison: the difference in Kwak-waka'wakw and Nuuchahnulth medians is largely accounted for by the difference in the medians for the west coast of Vancouver Island and Queen Charlotte Strait. All of the ethnic/regional discrepancy is accounted for by a shift of four territories on the northern end of the west coast of Vancouver Island region into the Kwakwaka'wakw ethnic grouping, which otherwise occupies the entire Queen Charlotte Strait region.

### Streams and Territories Compared

Wakashan local group territories are cultural and social phenomena. They are not simply random collections of neighboring streams whose salmon characteristics reproduce those of individual streams. As this section will show, territories are the product of cultural action on the possibilities offered by the natural environment.

Since most territories (78.2 percent) involve access to more than one spawning stream, and the 377 streams are held or shared by only seventy-nine groups, the typical territorial escapement will be larger than the typical stream escapement. The difference is very large indeed: the stream median escapement is 2,400 s.f., while the median for territories is 48,580 s.f. It is interesting and unexpected that when territories are constructed out of the raw material of stream characteristics, not only do they have larger medians, but the shape of the distribution of these medians is quite different. When both stream and territory median escapements are log transformed, we get two asymmetrical frequency distributions. The "bulge" in the stream distribution is to the lower end of the log scale, while the bulge in the territory distribution is to the higher end of the scale. If we use the same class interval scale having fifteen equal width divisions to divide up both the stream and territory median escapements, and then take the modal class interval of stream medians as a cutting point, 81.8 percent of streams fall at or below this point while only 21.7 percent of territory medians fall at or below this point.

There are differences in annual variation as well. The median territory $CRV_{md}$ is 56.8 percent compared to 100.6 percent for streams, and the territory interquartile range is 45.2 to 93.3 percent compared with 74.8 to 131.2 percent for streams. If we log-transform both distributions, a change in distribution shape also occurs with respect to annual variation. As with median escapements, neither distribution is normal or log-normal, but this time the shape of the distribution shifts toward the lower values when we move from streams to territories. When both sets of values are log transformed, and the same fifteen equal width class intervals are used for each distribution, and we take the modal class interval of territory coefficients of relative variation around the median as a cutting point, 51.9 percent of territories fall at or below this point while the corresponding figure for the streams is only 10.5 percent.

The effects of the Wakashan territory building process are clear: median escapements grow larger and variation is decreased. Equally important, as one moves from streams to territories, the shape of the distributions undergoes considerable change. For both median escapements and relative variation, territories are more alike than are streams. Territory building cancels out much of the variation present in nature.[6]

*The Relationship between Local Group Resources and Population*

Given that salmon was the most important food resource for many Wakashan groups, one might expect that group size and size of salmon resource would be related – an association we had earlier found to hold true for a set of Kwakwa'wakw local groups

---

6. These differences are not merely effects of the fact that territories frequently contain more than one stream. In a series of simulations too complex to report in detail here, we found that "territories" randomly constructed out of sets of contiguous streams had characteristics much more like those of streams than like these of actual Wakashan territories.

(Donald and Mitchell 1975). To investigate this, we obtained estimates of Wakashan local groups for two times: the 1830s and
1840s (drawn from Hudson's Bay Company estimates) and the
1880s (relying on Department of Indian Affairs censuses). Earlier
estimates are too spotty to be of any use and even the numbers
we have used must be considered with caution because, especially for the earlier period, these are estimates rather than census figures. Missing data are a serious problem. Figures were available
for fifty-two groups in the 1830s and 1840s and forty-three in the
1880s. Because we have greater confidence that those providing
the estimates knew the relative size of the various groups than the
exact numbers, we have chosen to rank them and then have
sought relationships between population rank and rank on several of our salmon resource characteristics.

Overall there is a modest relationship between the population
of the 1830s and 1840s and median salmon escapement (Spear-
man's *rho* = .42, *p* < .01).[7] The only other characteristics that have
a statistically significant relationship with population in either
time period are rank of number of streams in a territory with
1830s/1840s population rank (*rho* = .30, *p* = .03) and the rank of
median salmon with rank on 1880s population (*rho* = .30, *p* < .05).

The results are not much better if we break the Wakashan
down into ethnolinguistic units. Given missing data, only two are
large enough to warrant analysis: Kwakwaka'wakw and
Nuuchahnulth. For twenty-five Kwakwaka'wakw groups, rank
on median salmon is significantly related to rank on population
in both time periods (for the 1830s, *rho* = .47, *p* < .01; for the 1880s,
the coefficient is slightly smaller). For the Nuuchahnulth there are
no significant relationships with territorial salmon characteristics,
although the largest correlation is between rank on median
salmon and rank on 1840s population (*rho* = .38, *p* = .10, *n* = 19).

These results suggest that for the two periods considered,
either salmon resources are only one of many factors contributing
to local group size, or available estimates of population are too
crude to pick up the full extent of the relationship. Some results
reported below suggest that population and salmon resources
come together more meaningfully in more specific cultural and
political contexts.

7. Spearson's *rho* is the rank correlation coefficient, which measures the strength
of the relationship between two ranked variables.

## Local Group Salmon Resources and Other Variables

*Kwakwaka'wakw Local Group Rank*

Throughout the nineteenth century, many Kwakwaka'wakw local groups were organized into a feasting hierarchy that involved a relatively fixed order of precedence. At least sixteen local groups were integrated into this hierarchy. We have two rankings with which to work: one of eleven groups collected by Boas in the nineteenth century, and one containing an additional five groups collected in this century by Ford. As we have shown previously (Donald and Mitchell 1975), both rank on population and rank on salmon resources strongly correlate with local group rank in the prestige hierarchy. The relationship between median salmon and population in the 1830s is much stronger within the feasting circle than it is among the Kwakwaka'wakw overall (*rho* = .85 for the eleven-group set, .74 for the sixteen-group set, and .47 for all the Kwakwaka'wakw). The relationship between rank on median salmon and place in the prestige hierarchy is *rho* = .73 for the eleven-group set and .86 for the sixteen-group set. Obviously, salmon resources, population, and place in the prestige hierarchy are interrelated.

*Kwakwaka'wakw Expansion*

Details of changes in the territories controlled by the various Wakashan groups at different periods have yet to be worked out satisfactorily. To the extent that this can be done, an important problem to pursue will be determining the relationship between territorial change and change (especially improvements) in the resource base. Some preliminary work suggests that this will be a fruitful approach. For example, the possible original (before 500 B.C.) territory of the Southern Kwakiutl of Boas was the northern end of Vancouver Island, from Brooks Peninsula to the mouth of the Nawitti River. The median salmon escapement into this region was 125,000 s.f. If we can assume approximately the same number of group territories in this area as in the 1830s, the average local group had access to median escapements of about 18,000 s.f. By the 1830s Wakashan territory had expanded considerably, and in just the southern part of their new lands alone (from Smith Inlet to Havannah Channel) had added about 1.5 million s.f. to their median salmon escapement, and the average resident local group had access to median salmon escapements of almost 100,000 s.f.

The protohistoric or historic move of the Koskimo from the north end of Vancouver Island to Quatsino Sound (Dawson 1887: 70) represented a marked gain in salmon resources. From what can have been no more than 3,000 s.f., they moved up to 32,000. The contemporaneous Quatsino expansion southward to replace the Koprino at the entrance to Quatsino Sound (Dawson 1887: 68) saw the invading group's salmon base increase from 8,100 s.f. to 41,000 s.f.

## Nuuchahnulth Federations

Nuuchahnulth local groups were the basic sociopolitical unit on the west coast of Vancouver Island, but some local groups joined together to form federations that resided together in summer villages. We are able to reconstruct the territories controlled by twenty independent Nuuchahnulth polities: fourteen independent local groups and six federations. In addition, we can reconstruct the territories of eleven of the local groups that joined one of the federations. One might expect federations to control richer territories than independent local groups, and the difference between the federation median of 93,000 s.f. and the unattached local groups median of 50,800 s.f. seems to support this. But the Median Test shows that this difference is not significant at conventional levels ($p = .25$).

There is, however, a significant difference between the salmon resources of attached and unattached local groups. The median escapement for the eleven attached groups is 23,500 s.f., which is much smaller than the median for unattached groups (50,800 s.f.) (Mann-Whitney U test, $p < .01$). This suggests that one of the reasons local groups joined federations is that they could indirectly improve their resource picture with respect to salmon. Except where drift whales were concerned, federated groups do not seem to have pooled resources or to have shared access to resources, but they did form feasting hierarchies, and one of the outcomes of joint feasting is the distribution (redistribution) of food within the feasting unit. There is not, however, a difference between the two types of local groups with respect to variability. The median $CRV_{md}$ is 64 percent for attached local groups and 52 percent for unattached local groups, but the difference is not statistically significant ($p = .19$).[8]

## Discussion and Conclusions

This study of Wakashan salmon resources has established the following points:

First, it cannot be argued, as Drucker and Heizer (1967) have done, that Suttles's model relating resources to society is not applicable outside of the Salish area because the important resources are not significantly variable. There may be other reasons why it cannot be applied, but, as we have shown, one of those is not an absence of salmon variability. Different local groups controlled territories with different – sometimes vastly different – salmon resources, in the average amount of fish available and in the annual variation in numbers of fish. There were enormous differences in the salmon resources available in the richest and poorest territories (the richest territorial escapement is more than 1,000 times that of the poorest). The richest groups almost certainly had more salmon than they could exploit, but the poor groups were not so fortunate and must have been at a considerable disadvantage.

Second, we also have shown that there was a cultural response to this variation. Territories grouped streams together in a way that not only reduced the variation in resources available from territory to territory as compared to streams, but also reduced the relative annual variation within territories. Culture, in the form of territories, is more regular than nature.

Third, we found a modest relationship between a local group's median salmon resources and its population (rank on salmon "explains" roughly 17.5 percent of the variance in rank on population). Our estimates of population date from the 1830s and 1840s, several generations after European contact and its impact on aboriginal populations. Contact led to overall population declines as a result of new diseases (such as smallpox, measles), although these were not uniform for all groups. In addition, trade opportunities were not the same for all local groups, and these opportunities both directly and indirectly affected group size, as they created new opportunities for ambitious leaders to acquire

8. For further discussion of Nuuchahnulth political processes, see Morgan 1981.

additional followers by fueling the competitive side of the prestige system through trade, including the slave trade, and warfare.[9] In addition, other resources also made important contributions to most groups' food supply. Given the large number of variables that could affect group population, even 17.5 percent variance explained remains a considerable contribution by one resource.

Fourth, connections between variation in the resource base and other aspects of culture are clearest among those Kwakwaka'wakw groups who formed a feasting hierarchy. Among the groups in this hierarchy, both a group's rank in the prestige system and its population are strongly associated with its salmon resources.

For those Kwakwaka'wakw local groups that belonged to the nineteenth century feasting circle, median salmon escapement accounts for about 65 percent of the variance in local group population. Among all of the Kwakwaka'wakw local groups, median salmon escapement accounts for only 22 percent of the variance in population (twenty-five local groups). Poor data quality could be invoked to explain this difference. We think it more likely that systems display the characteristics of systems – that is, the nineteenth century Kwakwa'wakw feasting circle ordered and organized the interactions of a number of winter village populations, and the most obvious manifestation of this order was the local group prestige hierarchy itself. A community's position in this feasting circle was heavily dependent on its population (rank on population accounts for perhaps 80 percent of rank in the prestige hierarchy), which, in turn, was strongly associated with size of salmon resource base. The leaders of high ranking groups probably found it easier to attract and keep followers than did the leaders of low ranking communities. This would reinforce the association between population and hierarchy and place stronger (larger) communities in a better position to keep or add to their salmon resources.

Fifth, ownership of salmon streams also probably played an important role in political behavior. This can be seen in the tendency of Nuuchahnulth local groups who did join federations to rank lower in salmon than those who did not. Joining a federation

9. Examples of the interaction of leadership, trade, and warfare in the nineteenth century are provided in Mitchell 1984, Donald 1987, and references cited therein.

at least indirectly strengthened a group's salmon resource base. And, as indicated above, an improvement in salmon resources certainly accompanied the territorial expansions we examined.

Sixth, we know from Swadesh's (1948) work that Nuuchah-nulth territories changed as a result of warfare, and that the motivation behind some Nuuchahnulth fighting was territorial gain to improve the resource base. Kwakwa'wakw expansion at the expense of the Salish or other Kwakwa'wakw was almost certainly the result of similar motivations. The fit among the Kwakwa'wakw feasting hierarchy of group salmon resources, population, and group rank also suggests adjustment of or addition to the resource base. Unfortunately, we lack clear accounts of this process or of the conscious motivations of the actors involved.

Our overall results support the idea that territories not only had an impact through the reflection of differential resources, but also were conscious cultural products designed, at least in part, to improve the resource base available to particular local groups.

# 6

# A Sense of Place

*George B. Silberbauer*

Social anthropology aims to explain human social and cultural behavior. Reality is refracted through a people's world view and how they make sense of it, and their responses are made sensible by their vernacular logic. Unless a people's construction of reality is integrated in an explanation of its behavior, the explanation is incomplete or invalid. The human-land concepts of G/wi are characterized as "humans-in-society on the land"; while Pitjant-jatjara see themselves as a more intimate component of the orderly existence and functioning of the land. This article discusses the implications for internal and external relations of these peoples.

The Zimbabwean anthropologist, Angela Cheater (1989), once told me that she did not think that anthropology was worth doing unless it could be applied. By this she did not mean that only applied anthropology was worthy, but that one's research eventually should have some application. What she rejected was the kind of anthropology that is merely a word game, played solely for the delectation of the players. I think that she and I agreed that the business of anthropology is the explanation of human social and cultural behavior, and therefore I am not misrepresenting her position by saying that what one does in the discipline should be of eventual application to that task. Our conversation took place in the late 1980s, when enthusiastic Marxist anthropologists were becoming rare; what made the experience unique for me was that she was a joyful Marxist and I found myself in warm sympathy with her vision of anthropology. Until then I had found Marxist anthropologists to be a dismal breed whose vision was quite alien to my own (I remain unconverted, or, as the case may be, unenlightened).

Epstein (1967) gave anthropology the epithet of craft, which is probably a reasonable view of its de facto state. However, the discipline is scientific in its orientation and intention. By that I mean that its data should be verifiable empirically, and should be interpreted by logical, valid argument to reach nontrivial conclusions that can be tested. (These conditions are necessary but not sufficient for that which is scientific. As far as I know, the full complement has yet to be listed, and science has yet to be defined adequately.)

Now that there remain so few people who live principally by hunting and gathering, there is correspondingly little opportunity for collecting fresh data about "live" hunter- gatherer societies. Instead, activity in the anthropology of foragers is confined virtually to two areas. The first of these areas is research among peoples who get their food from additional or other sources, but who still see themselves as directly connected with their hunting and gathering tradition, and for whom that tradition continues to furnish social and cultural meanings. The second field of activity is interpreting extant ethnography, and formulating generalized statements about hunter-gatherers.

Both types of inquiry are worth pursuing, and we need to explore them. Ethnography of recent ex-foragers is not just "rescue anthropology"; rather, it is the investigation of a somewhat neglected but very important phase of social change. The people concerned are real and they are crossing, or recently have crossed, what anthropology has viewed as a cultural and social Rubicon. Among many other aspects, their situation gives us the opportunity of establishing whether or not there was a river there and, if so, what its characteristics might be. I do not claim that the significance of this type of change is illusory; we have not investigated it fully in hunter-gatherer anthropology. We need to know more about it.

In both types of research activity – the active collection of fresh ethnographic data, and interpretation of ethnography – we need to give proper attention and emphasis to the ways in which the people concerned see themselves, their world, and themselves in their world. Be it cosmology, *Weltanschauung*, religion, science, or value system, a people's social construction of reality is a necessary element in understanding its social and cultural behavior. To leave out of account their way of construing their experience of reality is to present the people as bereft of rationality, or, for lack of anything better, to impose on them the anthropologist's own set of constructions. I am a determined relativist; I cannot see how it is possible to make sense of the behavior of others without including their assumptions, logical structures and perceptions in the explanation. If I were to insist on using my assumptions and perceptions to analyze the behavior of others, inevitably they would come out of it looking rather silly (as would I if their assumptions and perceptions were the basis of explaining my behavior in my own social and cultural setting). It is, for instance, often necessary to take economic, demographic, or ecological variables into account when attempting to understand people's behavior, but what directs them in their own process of accounting for and responding to these factors are the meanings that they accord to these factors. These meanings are derived from vernacular metaphysical concepts, and it is with these that the anthropologist respectfully must come to grips in formulating explanations of social and cultural behavior.

Social anthropology is a relativistic discipline – which does not mean, however, that we must forever have our heads stuck in the bucket of cultural minutiae. There is a hierarchy of levels of abstraction and generality: particular facts; these facts in their own frame of reference (the relative); and then the general, which comprehends, but transcends both the particular and the relative. When we can make statements of that level of generality, then we shall be able to extend our vision beyond the narrow confines of the bucket, correcting the distortion that neglecting the relative surely brings.

It is legitimate to consider a limited range of factors – such as economic, demographic, or ecological variables – without taking a relativist perspective, as long as this approach is recognized as a form of reductionism. Although reductionism was once highly regarded among philosophers and practitioners of science as an analytic and explanatory strategy, it has deservedly less prestige among the biological and social sciences, in which the eventual context of explanation is a complex whole of interdependent and interacting entities. Reductionism does, however, have one valuable characteristic: although its use narrows the scope of information yielded by the analysis or explanation, its reliability is likely to be higher. So, if the particular anthropological activity is one in which it is profitable to trade away breadth of explanation in return for reduced uncertainty, then a reductionist strategy is indicated.

To illustrate my point: The use of Newtonian mechanics to explain a traffic accident will yield a very reliable explanation of the collision and damage done to the vehicles. But it will explain nothing at all of the behavior of the drivers who were in control of the vehicles. For that information, one needs to widen the scope of inquiry to include such physiological and psychological factors as visual acuity, blood-alcohol levels, driving skill and experience, and the interaction of these factors. Road design and drivers' attitudes are also relevant. By the time one has accounted for all these factors, explanation has become far less certain, but is nevertheless more helpful than the bare Newtonian solution if one's goal is to understand the nature of the mishap.

In examining relationships between hunter-gatherers and their land, interpretations and generalizations that do not include the people's own construction of those relationships reduce the people to generalized human beings, whose behavior is governed mechanistically by cultural lowest common denominators. Such generalizations are all that is needed if the relevant aspect of the relationship is something like the rate of caloric extraction; that is, establishing that a particular population did, in fact, inhabit a given tract of land. At a higher level of complexity, reductionist analyses showed that the fission-fusion cycles of African Mbuti Pygmies, !Kung, and G/wi Basarwa did not synchronize, and that Australian Western Desert Aborigines appear not to have had any periodicity. Considering another pattern, G/wi ate their way outward from waterholes; it has been shown that others ate their way inward. These behavioral traits could be correlated logically with differences in the amount and timing of rainfall in the various habitats; or with small, ephemeral waterholes versus large, permanent, or semipermanent ones to give an explanation that we all accept as being reasonable. But these would be explanations of correlation; before arguing causation it would be prudent to consider the vernacular view. A good explanation not only tells why something is done; it also tells why something else is not done. My quibble with my own and others' use of reductionist explanation is that it leaves us blind to the possibility of alternative patterns and to additional relevant factors. By restricting the equation to lowest common denominators of culture, we confine inquiry to the restricted scope of information allowed by a reductionist frame of reference. We may come up with something very plausible, but we also risk finding ourselves in the predicament of eighteenth century chemists explaining combustion in terms of phlogiston –the hypothesis answers the questions we ask now, but inhibits the asking of other questions, and could turn out to be hopelessly wrong if those other questions are asked later.

If we can include the vernacular rationale of a behavioral pattern in our net of causation, then we can be more confident that the hypothesis will enable us to see further and to formulate questions that did not arise at the earlier stage of inquiry, and may alert us to new factors of which we were ignorant. These wider, deeper questions and the search for their answers only make sense if people's interaction with their land is explained in terms that include their cultural perceptions and constructions as guided by their logic based on their axioms. How do they perceive human beings? How do they perceive the nature of the land and its resources? As they see it, what happens when they interact with the land? Which actions are good, or bad, or insignificant in that relationship?

Consider the nature of attachment to locality in central Australian Pitjantjatjara society and how it differs from what previously obtained among the central Kalahari G/wi Basarwa.

## The Pitjantjatjara

By 1969 a long drought had brought into Ernabella, Fregon, and Amata in northern South Australia a number of bush people to join the more sedentary, older residents of these settlements. As the drought began to break, the move back into the bush gathered up some of the more sedentary people in its momentum; this was the beginning of the outstation movement in Central Australia, which eventually led to the establishment of self-constituted, nearly autonomous communities of Aborigines away from the formally organized, white-run settlements.

This development was much discussed during my stay in Central Australia and the appropriate location of any household or individual was a frequently raised topic. Not that access would be denied to anybody, but there did appear to be a ranking of places for each person. This was not a matter of prescription; rather, it was something to be weighed and pondered in the light of one's kinship position, marriage, ancestry, and circle of close acquaintances. As many kinship links were multiplex (i.e., two people could be related in more ways than one) there were several possible configurations of other than immediate kin. Consequently, there was seldom an unequivocal ranking of locations, and, although preferences could always be explained, they could not always be predicted. The structures of kinship and the other paradigms within which preference could be understood were not prescriptive in a deterministic sense, but rather provided a set of rules within which ranking could be negotiated.

This way of distributing the population in two-dimensional space is remote from a reductionist model of optimal density. The overall results were quite commonly consistent with the model, in that resulting density neither overloaded resources nor was so low as to indicate that too much time and energy had been spent in using resources. However, the model could not give any indication of who went where, and why. It models the mechanics of choosing locations and not the logic of placing people in them and, hence, the social dynamics of relationship and interaction. This is not simply to take a leaf from Levi-Strauss's book and say that spatial placement mirrors Pitjantjatjara social statuses; but it is to say that the two are connected.

The Pitjantjatjara view of the world and of the human role in it is similar to that of other Western Desert peoples. This uniformity is hardly surprising as they cooperated with and encountered one another in their journeyings and in the performance of large ceremonies. This view is formulated here and elsewhere in Australia within the concept of *Tjukurpa*, The Dreaming. It has been variously outlined and extensively discussed by such ethnographers as Myers (1986), Spencer and Gillen (1899), Stanner (1956, 1965, 1966), Strehlow (1947), and many eminent others. According to this view, people are not imposed upon and external to the environment; they are an integral part of it, as are streams and mountains, plants and animals. Humans (here, specifically Pitjantjatjara) have an essential and reciprocal role in the maintenance of the orderly operation of natural processes, and, through their proper conduct and performance of ceremonies, humans are necessary to the causal chain of these processes. Neglect of these functions will impair the natural order, such that the health and survival of flora and fauna will be endangered, as will be the general well-being of the people and their environment.

In Pitjantjatjara geomorphology, the genesis of many of the landforms and features of the countryside is found in the acts of mythical heroes. These Beings travelled across the land, raising mountain ranges or cleaving abysses. They carved valleys or froze other Beings into masses of rock, or they themselves became petrified. Each of these acts became an episode in the myth relevant to the particular hero. The route travelled by each is thus signposted and closely identified with the Being concerned. Land is not an anonymous, impersonal topography; it is differentially imbued with the personality of Beings – here powerfully charged by Malu (Red Kangaroo), elsewhere by Ili (Fig), Kuninka (Native Cat), or Milpali (Perentie lizard). The routes cross and stretch into neighboring countries of other Western Desert peoples, crossing language boundaries without changing identity, sometimes going beneath the surface to emerge further on, potentially covering the whole of Australia (and, at least in the case of Malu, actually extending from the southwest Indian Ocean coast to the northeast Pacific shore).

There is a special, totemic relationship between individuals and mythical heroes that is acquired by birth and descent, and, less intimately, by marriage. Because descent and marriage are socially structured, totemic relationships reflect that structure and constitute criteria for membership in certain social groups. A totemic group is not corporate in nature, but its members share particular rights and obligations to respect the land that is associated with the hero's route. Because these rights and obligations are shared, joint, or at least, coordinated, action is sometimes required of the members. Totemic relationships are complex and extensive, and they constitute an important aspect of individual and social identity. It is a relationship of interdependence, in which the individual both maintains and expresses identity by social interaction and by appropriate observances and participation in ceremonies that also serve to foster the well-being of the mythical heroes. The intimate link between hero and land, between hero and individual, and between individual and social group amounts to a similarly intimate connection between social group and land. Maintaining the health of the land, its resources, and the well-being of people is assisted by humans fulfilling their obligations toward their totemic identities.

Although each social group is responsible for its local area, this is not an ideology of exclusiveness. Rather, there is a ranking of competence and concomitant responsibility. Potentially, any group may be capable of the requisite action, but the one with the most immediate links to a locality has the greatest capability and is therefore preferred. In this social dimension of the man-land relationship, reciprocity also obtains, as one group may act for or support another. This can look deceptively like territoriality, which is certainly not absent from Pitjantjatjara land relations.

However, territoriality is exercised in the context of the control and use of resources. Territory is the space surrounding a group, not the fixed area of land for which some group has the closest bonds of responsibility. Locality is ephemeral; a person or group stays in a place for a shorter or longer period in association with others. The structure of this association reflects, but is not determined by, mythical geography. In another place, the group will be composed differently and structured differently but will have control of local resources for the duration of its composition and stay. Primary competence in and responsibility for maintaining proper relations with a specific area rests with a number of persons who belong to an appropriate totemic category. To confuse the alien onlooker, the two sets of relations with land sometimes coincide but can be distinguished by their respective functions. Responsibility entails decision making and leadership in interacting with the environment. Participation in following leadership is not exclusive, but inclusive – the focus is on ways in which a group or individual can be integrated, rather than on seeking barriers that might be used to exclude them. Those who are thus included participate on a temporarily equal footing.

As I have indicated, kinship is an important organizing principle. The universalist character of Pitjantjatjara kinship, within which many are included as kin by reason of their kinship with other kin, lengthens and proliferates the vectors along which connections can be established. Even if one were so remote a stranger as to have no discoverable shared kin, invoking an additional system of fictive kinship can create an attachment. Thus it was that a Thursday Islander could be incorporated into Ernabella kin groups, and so could my family and I. Fictive kinship illustrates the way in which the structures provide the framework and rules for negotiating order – in this case, relationships. When the fictive status is accorded to an individual she or he is thus provided with an opportunity to develop the relationship. Until it has been "grown" the status is somewhat tentative, impermanent. In due course, after the Thursday Islander had created a pattern of interaction in accordance with the expectations of conventional kinship, the Islander was regarded increasingly as an "ordinary" relative and eventually became eligible to choose, and be chosen by, a suitable wife. In the case of my family and me, fictive kinship guided our behavior in interacting with members of the community, opening some doors to us and closing others. It gave to the

Islander and to us meaningful relationships with land, so that we no longer blundered about in limbo. In this aspect the tentative nature of the fictive kinship status was easier to discern; there was not the complication of shyness and reserve that often must be overcome in relationships with people. Rather, it was a matter of getting to know the land, and learning proper attitudes, beliefs, and practices in an orderly sequence, learning each new step after comprehension of the previous ones had been demonstrated. I felt that I progressed as far as was necessary to allow for my comfortable inclusion in group discussions and activities, under the guidance and encouragement of one of my fictive elder brothers. To have gone further would have committed me, by implication, to a relationship with the land and to concomitant practices that I could not fulfill as a visitor, living there for only nine months. My relationships "grew", but only to stunted stature. Had I come back on a third visit, they would have grown further.

My status in Ernabella allowed me to progress across the chessboard of kinship to have links with people and land as far afield as Warburton Ranges and Docker Creek when I travelled beyond Pitjantjatjara country into that of the Pintupi. Clearly, the ideology was one of inclusiveness.

An individual's status is an important aspect of identity in this matrix. Myers (1986) has described and discussed this in the Pintupi context with lucid and convincing insight. I believe that the Pitjantjatjara concept is closely comparable. Self is defined, sensed, and expressed in the context of group membership and relationship to land. A discontinuity in either will disrupt the other, diminishing or negating Self. (Group membership and relationship to the land are as intimate and important as are learning and knowledge to one's Self; were these to be taken away, identity and Self would be diminished.) As Margaret Bain has argued (in press), to exist in an identity requires meaningful action which expresses that identity – in order to Be, one has to Do. This also entails reciprocal interaction with the land, one receives from and gives to the land, affirming the Being of both it and oneself.

In the late 1960s people at Ernabella bought nearly all their food from the store. From a purely economic perspective, they were low-income shoppers. From an empirical nutritional point of view, the additional and frequent forays that these people made into the bush simply served to add garnishes and delicacies to their store-bought diet. But in the eyes of the Ernabellans, hunting and gathering met their strong need to affirm their existence as social identities. The time and energy dedicated to hunting and gathering, rather than to wage-earning activities, would appear to be economically irrational if Pitjantjatjara reality were ignored. It is, however, completely rational to invest time and effort in maintaining oneself in a state of Being, without which nothing – not even wage earning – would be possible.

Bain and Sayers (1990) have pointed out the close link between Aborigine knowledge and concrete reality; that this link is not abstract, but exists in the process of its use ("knowledge is doing"). There is a comparable attitude in large-scale societies toward certain types of knowledge: for instance, one cannot validly claim to know a language unless one can speak and/or read and write it. In the Pitjantjatjara view, knowledge extends to its realization in action, and not beyond that. That is not to say that it is limited in its potential to its present state. One can imagine knowing more than one presently does, and can proceed to learn or discover more. But until one is able to do that which one imagines learning, it has not been learned and does not constitute part of one's knowledge. Furthermore, knowledge must be realized in its appropriate social context; that is, its realization in action must have social meaning. It cannot exist as a purely private thing to which only the knower is privy. Hypothetical or conditional knowledge is seen as a nonsensical notion, as is private knowledge. The concept is viewed as a contradiction in terms: "If I knew the declination of a heavenly body, and could measure its altitude at its meridian passage, I could calculate my latitude." (But I do not know its declination and am therefore just wasting words on the wind.) As knowledge and being require social action for their realization, knowledge is more than a personal attribute; it is an actual component of identity and Self. The requirement of social action imposes on knowledge an unusually heavy functional load: It must bear a burden greater than that of instrumental efficacy; it must also serve as currency of interaction. Because of its heavy load and expression in concrete action, knowledge tends to be conservative and pragmatic. That functional mass does not, however, preclude endogenous growth and change, and there is abundant historical evidence of these processes such as the progressive discoveries of the extent of Malu's travels across the continent. Nor does this concept of knowledge imply any diminution or impairment of intellectual capacity – this concept in no way reduces the need for or exercise of ingenuity and creativity in the application and development of knowledge. The concept serves to tie the people closely to their social matrix, which, in turn, entails continuing connection with the land in, and with which they have status.

## The G/wi

During my fieldwork among them in the fifties and sixties, the central Kalahari G/wi had a very different view of the nature of the universe, the world, and how human beings fit in. They saw themselves as having been created by N!adima as but one of the many forms of life. N!adima's purpose in creating life and the other components of the known world was, as are most things about him, inherently unknowable – a mystery. Order was believed to be an intrinsic aspect of creation, in which life forms had been given certain properties and characteristics. These were complementary to or matched those of other creatures. The outcome was a system of functional interdependence. N!adima was a deity of order, rather than one of morals, laws, and love. Having made an ordered, self-regulating and self-sustaining world, He was able to withdraw from it and leave it to exist and function without His constant intervention. He was not, however, absent in His withdrawal, but was omnipresent and omniscient, free, within the bounds of the order of His own creation, to intervene when He chooses. A set of built-in condign punishments for acts of disruption of mundane order served to discourage the unruly, greedy or over-adventurous.

Following creation, it was incumbent on each life form to devise its own way of living within the constraints and capabilities with which it and others had been created. Herbivores had to find grazing areas to sustain them, but also had to try to avoid becoming food for predators. Although it might cost a clump of grass dearly to be grazed, and an antelope even more to be killed and eaten, all creatures could legitimately exploit others – this was seen as an expression of the order of creation – but not beyond reasonable need. Any method of exploitation could be used provided it did not belittle the creature concerned – this would be an implied slight of N!adima. Inflicting unnecessary pain or indignity on the victim would be examples of such wrongful behavior.

Ethnographers of other Basarwa – for example, John Marshall in his film *The Hunters* – have often referred to killing rites that hunters performed to restore what has been disturbed by their killing. I did not see any G/wi do this and they stated that they had no such practice. There was, however, a keen sense of respect for prey animals. Even when a prey animal was seen as silly in its attempts to evade the hunters, its actions might be laughed at, but without scorn.

As creator, N!adima was seen to be the owner of the world, free to do with it what He chose. He could capriciously do away with a person or any other creature, and although this would cause the same distress as would death by any other means, it would not bring resentment against Him. For with the same unpredictability, He would favor an individual or group with unusual good fortune. No attempts were ever made to influence N!adima; there was no special means of communicating with Him and, as He was omniscient, none was needed.

Thus humans in nature were seen simply as creatures among many other creatures, without special favor or disadvantage. Mankind had been given a unique but not otherwise special set of abilities to meet a corresponding set of needs through respectful use of the resources that could be found in the habitat, using any methods that would not cause offense to N!adima.

Their account of the world and of their place in it held no certain promise for the G/wi of safety and security. If they survived it was by their own lonely efforts and ingenuity. Techniques of successful struggle had to be discovered and developed, as much by them as by other peoples and creatures. Knowledge and ability were essential, but not sufficient in themselves. The company and cooperation of one another were also necessary, and these were best gained by the establishment and maintenance of harmonious relationships. The G/wi repeatedly spoke of harmonious relationships as something toward which to strive, to be desired, and, when experienced, to be celebrated. Good fortune, pleasure, and contentment were referred to in terms of being shared. To experience them on one's own was a contradiction, an irony in which the greater the good fortune, the deeper was the frustration of being alone. Solitude was an everyday experience. Although both women and men preferred to gather and hunt with at least one companion, both would make shorter or longer forays alone. Loneliness, however, was a truly frightening prospect. It was the metaphor for fear beyond the physical and was the most extreme punishment that a human being could suffer. When there was company – which was most of the time – it was maximally appreciated. Interpersonal communication by touch, gesture, eye contact, and speech was almost constant. If it was possible to share an activity, one or two others would be drawn into it, even if only as commenting spectators. Except during times of stress caused by hunger, thirst, or inclement weather, much of the spare time was spent in activities like playing games, dancing, or making music. These activities varied the modes of interaction by bringing forth different facets of participants' skills, moods, and idioms of self-expression.

Identity was more group-referenced than individual. That is, a person would identify herself or himself with reference to kin or some other group. Considering the intense intimacy of band life, it is perhaps to be expected that both social identity and Self should have included this prominent element of the social matrix as means of definition and orientation. The language reflects the sharp awareness of the group; for instance, G/wi positional pronouns (such as "this," "that," and "yonder" in English) include mandatory reference to the person addressed: "this, nearer to me than to you," "this, nearer to you than to me," etc., through four different positions. Personal pronouns ("I," "you," etc.) require an indication of whether the person addressed or referred to is part of any plural identity conveyed by the pronoun: "she-and-her- household" vs. "she-alone." This is not to say that a G/wi band was like the proverbial flock of sheep. Each person was vivid as an individual, with charm, vanity, warts, and beauty. But if one were uncharitable about one wart then many vanities would be ruffled; if one praised another's beauty, many would return the compliment with charm. (This is not to say that jealousy and spite were absent – to remark on a blemish could bring unkind delight to some.) With no significant differences in wealth or status within G/wi society and with no external reference point or source of authority (such as communication with N!adima), the G/wi were dependent on their collective resources for the formulation, validation, and interpretation of their values and rationale for action.

In their search for knowledge and competence in devising their modus vivendi, the G/wi undoubtedly learned some things from others but they incorporated that knowledge into their own style (as if, for instance, my colleagues and I were to all learn Iñu-piaq and then develop a distinctive Monash dialect, complete with variant vocabulary and grammatical quirks). They also made their own discoveries and inventions, as is indicated by the substantial parts of their knowledge that were not shared with those with whom they had contact, and by the fact that they rejected their neighbors' knowledge as false or irrelevant (such as sorcery, of which they had a fair understanding, but no belief or practice). To the G/wi, knowledge was a plastic and pragmatic entity; they could lose some of it, or acquire more. Some of what had been lost was regretted (such as certain hunting techniques and medicinal practices) but it could be replaced, they hoped, by new discoveries and learning. Knowledge was neither sacred nor esoteric, but some might be harmful or erroneous. Little of what constituted good knowledge and legitimate belief could be vali-dated by any religious or supernatural source. G/wi theology enjoined the avoidance of offending N!adima, but was practically silent on positive virtues. These were overtly coined by the peo-ple themselves, as was much of their value system. Its only vali-dation came from consensus among and within the bands. G/wi were thus more dependent on intrinsic resources for assessing and maintaining their position in the world than are most peo-ples. Their view of themselves was not so much as "people in nature" but as "people-in-society" who had to make do with nature, and nature was the dynamic and constantly adjusting middle world of N!adima's creation. Interactions with the world clearly comprised the doings of individuals: picking fruit, or killing a tortoise or a springhare was the act of one woman or one man. The identity of that person, however, was not an isolate but extended to include her or his household, band, the G/wi people, and, in greater and greater dilution, her or his direct and indirect social contacts. These people would have benefited or been touched somehow by the proceeds of the picking or killing because of their social relationships; they were comparably involved in the act because those same relationships constituted part of the woman's or man's identity.

To see identity in terms of one's social setting is, of course, com-monplace. In G/wi society, however, identity was wholly con-nected to social setting and was not derived from location or pat-tern of activity in any significant extent. Location was used as a label – one was a -xade, Tsxobe, or Tshokudu person – but place was a metaphor for group. Territoriality was institutionalized in that a band exercised exclusive control over the right to use the resources of a defined area. The rules or etiquette of territoriality were strictly observed, and, to the extent of my knowledge, were never seriously breached. This was so, I think, largely because the fundamental rule was not that a law be observed but that relations among people be as harmonious as possible. Territorial boundaries were reached by agreement among neighboring bands with the intention of providing each band with convenient security in the use of its resources. If resources were utilized by a coherent group like a band, acting as a coordinated whole, then each member would know not only the present and foreseeable state of resources, but also would have a say in deciding their future state. This would be much more difficult if not impossible if resources were also subject to use and disturbance by others whose intentions were not known. When territory boundaries were crossed, it was important to know whether there had been a need to do so and whether that need had been greater than the need of the resident band. For instance, if neighbors in hot pursuit followed wounded prey into a part of the band's territory remote from the current camp, the neighbors' need would be plain, and the residents' disadvantage would be trifling, or none. However, it would be very bad form indeed to gather esculent plants in a neighbor's territory, thus diminishing resources which would probably be used in the near future. The basis of boundary maintenance was represented to me as a commonsense way of managing resources when close coordination (between neighbors) was too complicated. Again, the emphasis on the integrity of society and land was a necessary but incidental aspect of that aim.

Band membership, though fairly stable, could be changed easily. Such facility indicated that the group rather than the place was the critical factor in defining identity. People invoked descent and other kinship links and previous residence as grounds for gaining membership in a band. This did not constitute a claim with the force of law, it had only the force of logic: "I know those people and they know me (or us)" was the reason given for wishing to join the band, and for the band to accept the claimant. The band exercised its exclusive control over the right of resource use by agreement with neighboring bands, not as a power that it could take to itself. Through this device, popular opinion would immediately side with a band aggrieved by a neighbor's incursion, a prospect that served as adequate protection. In the same way, a household was protected from invasion of its range during the period of winter isolation because its area had been apportioned by the band's agreement. Band territories and winter ranges each contained and constituted a convenient nexus of resources. In the Central Kalahari, the resources needed for hunter-gatherer survival were not uniformly distributed. To make their use feasible, there needed to be a clumping of the necessary resources. The number of places where this occurred was limited and, as a consequence, restricted the number of areas that would have presented convenient territories. This situation could have been exploited in various ways, but the way the G/wi chose was to allocate one resource-rich territory to each band, and for the band to limit its size to match the resources. New bands were formed and occupied new territories when the parent band's size approached the upper limit set by its territorial resources. Overall population numbers were historically limited by periodical cataclysms of epidemic illnesses and drought-induced famine. One might speculate (with no evidence other than that of its patent feasibility in the light of the above behavioral patterns) that migration followed by assimilation to other Basarwa groups could have been a safety valve had natural disasters not cruelly culled the population.

I was able to observe the process of band formation at various stages from inception to initiation of the next cycle. There was no mark of final separation of identity from the old to the new. The fiat of geographical relocation entailed day-to-day operation of an autonomous social, economic, and hence political entity. This entity gradually would acquire a distinctive character and have fewer and fewer direct links with the old band. Conceptually, however, the bonds of kinship remained forever. There was no evidence of the band members' formal establishment of their relationship with the territory. This is consistent with the notion that the primary relationship is people-in-society.

Interband migration was similarly free of formal establishment of relationships with land, but involved the negotiation of acceptance into the social unit. There was a practice of ceremonially greeting babies and young children when they first came into the band or had been absent for some months; this, too, was unequivocally "incorporation" into the social group and had no explicit reference to land. In her menarcheal ceremony, a girl was introduced to the territory of her band: "This is the country [n!uma] of all of us, and of you. You will always find food here" ["You will always be at home here"]. I do not interpret this as linking the girl to a specific stretch of land, but rather to the world in which she must make her living; the other parts of the ceremony were directed wholly toward the social rather than the spatial incorporation of her identity.

There were many G/wi stories that accounted for topographical features. The fossil Okwa Valley, for instance, was formed by the agonizing passage of G//amama (after N!adima, the other supernatural Being – in some respects the equivalent of the Devil) after he had been bitten by a python at Gobabis (a long way to the west). In European science this valley was the course of an ancient river. Part of its course is distinguished by a series of right-angled bends, apparently reflecting geological faults beneath the sand mantle. In the G/wi account, each of these marks a change of G//amama's course as he was outwitted by various adversaries; the calcrete (caliche)-floored tributary at each of these bends is the spill of his vomit provoked by each encounter. Such tales make it clear that the world was formed at the time of N!adima's creation, and features like the Okwa and its tributaries were imposed subsequently in much the same way as the tracks made by the passage of my vehicles (although not with quite the same satanic connotations, I hope). Nor was there any idea that the Okwa was imbued with the essence of G//amama. Other features, such as the Tsao Hills, had no specific mythical origin but dated from the time of creation. A grave would be haunted by the postmortem spirit for some time after burial of the corpse, and its vicinity would be avoided because of the danger this presented to the living. But once enough time had passed to allow the spirit's dangerous power to dissipate, the place would have no special quality and eventually would return to the category of usefulness that it had had before becoming a burial site.

## Comparison

At first glance, the G/wi might appear likely to have close attachment to place because of their well-marked territoriality in residential and resource-utilization patterns. However, as a closer look has shown, territory was a social solution to the economic and ecological problems of subsistence and to the spatial disposition of the population that the G/wi had devised for themselves in the circumstances of their habitat. It was the customary solution and was practiced with little or no questioning. However, it was not the only solution. The (then) Bechuanaland Protectorate government drilled and equipped a borehole at G/oma//a, near -xade, in the early 1960s. It was a time of deepening drought, and when the water flowed, people from near and distant bands flocked into the -xade territory, creating a food shortage, social chaos, and misery. Late in the decade, when the drought persisted, the government again activated the borehole. This time, the people adapted their patterns of residence and land-resource allocation to accommodate the influx. (See the difference between Tanaka's [1980] observations of this period and mine of earlier years.) This was coherent change in that the people themselves devised the new formations by an ingenious variation of an existing pattern and contrived to keep intact their sets of social meanings of behavior. This is not to say that the G/wi could be shunted around the countryside at will; their relations with the land and their sense of place was a function of a properly operating, thoroughly understood, autonomous social order. But in maintaining that order, it is apparent that the G/wi were capable of working out new relationships and matching practices with the land and habitat resources.

Because of their great mobility and the apparent freedom with which they form and change residential groups, the Pitjantjatjara, by contrast, might be assumed to have a very easygoing attitude to changes in their relationships with land. It is true that the nature of their social organization and the wide range of ways in which it can be expressed in land relationships give them many different options, but these are not random. There are clear concepts of what is right and wrong among the theoretically possible configurations. These are not rigid structures, but rather judgments made of a finite stochastic process. The proper composition of a population for a particular place at a specified time depends on who is already there or who is nearby and therefore can be expected to join the group at that place. It is a species of Markov chain – a sequence of events or states, the probability of each of which depends only on the one immediately preceding it. Certain possibilities are excluded by the principles of group formation, but the probability of any particular choice of additional members depends on the existing composition of the group already in residence at the place at the time. What is common to all probabilities is that there must be present at least some members who stand in the correct totemic relationship to the place in question. As I have indicated above, this does not necessarily mean that they be of the local totemic group; they may stand in a relationship with members of that group, which enables them to function on the latter's behalf in interacting with the land. Another constant in the human:land equation is that no one should be a stranger to a place that she or he occupies for any length of time. If a social relationship does not already exist, the individual must find one with somebody who has a link with that place. By the doctrine of universalist kinship, that link can be extended to the incoming individual and place her or him in a relationship with the land, thus conferring fitting social meaning on that person's presence, behavior toward the land, and identity while at that place.

The constraints on movement and residence are exacting in both the G/wi and Pitjantjatjara instances. That these constraints appear never to have been so onerous as to close off survival options to either people is a reflection of the great number of permutations of place and group permitted by each system, each of which retains the principles of social order as perceived, understood, and practiced by these two peoples. These permutations, never written down, but retained only in people's memories, are a very impressive demonstration of the power of human intellect.

These examples do not provide a sufficient basis for generalizations; all one can do is to see the contrasts and commonalities. More examples of other comparable peoples are needed for any useful general statement about relations between place and people in hunter-gatherer societies.

At the time of which I write – the 1950s and 1960s – the G/wi were politically autonomous. The Bechuanaland Protectorate government turned Nelson's telescope on the Central Kalahari, so the G/wi, their neighbors, and their doings remained out of official sight. These ethnically diverse Basarwa, Kgalagari, and other Bantu-speaking peoples interacted sporadically in patterns evidently reached by mutual consent for one another's convenience. The G/wi participated in a network of exchanges that brought them metal, tobacco, and other commodities that were preferred substitutes for indigenous ones. These exchanges expressed and necessitated social links between themselves and others, but because they were not imposed on them by others, they did not significantly diminish the political, economic, or social autonomy of the G/wi. They retained their own constructions of reality, choosing which aspects of others' knowledge and beliefs they would accept or reject. They were in effective control of their own destiny in their own country, and were free to devise and practice their own responses to the shocks and strains that challenged their survival. To the extent that these shocks and strains were predictable, they were markedly cyclical: cold, dry winters followed hot summers with average rainfall variability of 60 percent (extremes were 50 percent and 500 percent) from the mean. Flora and fauna were characterized by physiological and/or behavioral adaptations to this regime. A result was an annual rise and fall in habitat biomass and a consequent fluctuation in the supply of food and water, amplified by drought and rare floods (which were even more damaging than the droughts) or narrowed by a season of good but not excessive rainfall. To these difficulties were added periodic epidemics of smallpox, poliomyelitis (to which Central Kalahari Basarwa appear to have succumbed at a rate higher than the normal 4 to 8 percent of infected persons [see Kocen 1984: 21, 60]), and measles, which directly and indirectly caused many deaths. The G/wi response to fluctuations in food supply and their own numbers was to change their residential groupings so as to match the density of the localized population with that of the resources on which they depended. (The whole band would move every two to four weeks to a new campsite in the plentiful season, from about November to about June, and then each household would disperse to an isolated winter range until November.) Because of the seasonality of fluctuations in the amount and variety of available food, there was a corresponding cyclical tendency in their residential patterns.

The broad principles on which their strategies of social organization were based allowed many permutations of form, size, and location of grouping, without the intolerable loss of social coherence or order. After disastrous epidemics or widespread drought, those bands that had lost too many members to continue to bear alone the burden of sadness and short-handed survival could coalesce without having to devise completely new social arrangements. Those whose territories had been blighted by local drought and ensuing famine could disperse or move en masse to others' territories for shorter or longer periods. Location was limited by the availability of necessary resources, but not by particular links between people and land. Comparable mobility was open to those who felt the psychological or social need to move their attachment from one band to another because of irreconcilable conflict, boredom, or the pull of a more attractive person or group.

Those who are new to the Central Kalahari might be tempted to hypothesize that it is so featureless that there is simply insufficient topographical contrast to provide the distinctive features characteristic of Aborigine mythology. This would be a confession of very ethnocentric blindness. It does look unrelievedly flat and monotonous at first. However, familiarity eventually reveals enough distinctiveness to enable accurate navigation by surface features, even by moonlight, of an aircraft flying at an altitude of 35,000 feet at 500 knots. G/wi passengers who had not flown previously were able to locate themselves precisely, and to recount afterward with complete accuracy tracks flown in daylight at 100 feet at 200 knots within and beyond their own band territories. As I have mentioned above, hunter-gatherers require a nexus of resources for their survival. Not only do they need to know where these are located, but they also must be able to find their way back to camp at the end of occasionally very long chases after wounded game. The G/wi navigational technique was to use known (usually named) markers combined with impressively accurate distance-and-bearing geometry; they gave enviably accurate estimates of arrival times. Visits to and beyond neighboring bands also required competent navigation. The destination was the currently occupied camp, which was located actuarially in the light of knowledge of the territory's resources and the effect on these of recent rainfall. If the first estimate turned out to be wrong, the next best estimate was sought, and so on, until tracks of the band's members were found and followed to their camp.

The Pitjantjatjara experience little periodicity in their supply of rain-dependent food resources. Central Australia averages roughly 250 to 350 millimeters of rain per year, with an annual variability of 1.5 to 2.0 (index = [90 percentile - 10 percentile] ÷ 50 percentile) of nearly uniform seasonal distribution with a slight summer peak.[1] Drought risk is 0.6 in the northern region, rising to

1. Variability of 1.5 to 2 means that it can be one and one-half to twice as much. Drought risk, like probability, is measured as between zero and one. Here it means that the risk of drought is six-tenths of certainty or nine-tenths of certainty.

0.9 in the Simpson Desert in the southeast. The actual recorded occurrence from 1965 to 1980 was, respectively, 20 percent and 40 percent (Reynolds, Watson, and Collins 1983). The flora is adapted to this regime, and, although there is species-specific seasonality, its variety and versatility always provide a dramatic increase in the supply of esculent plants after good rains in any season. Central Australia's geologically ancient hills and mountains provide vigorous drainage and numerous large pools, in which great amounts of water may collect and remain for several years.

The nearly random distribution in time and space of rainfall is reflected by an opportunistic pattern of varying the size and location of the residential groups. Plentiful food and water near a site that is mythologically and ritually important provide the opportunity to gather in large numbers for the ceremonies that are required for the establishment, statement, and maintenance of proper relationships among individuals, totemic and kin groups, and land. At the other end of the scale, a residential group may be as small as a single household that moves about the country, directed by the availability of food and water in those areas to which their totemic identity in its ramifications give them legitimate access, and by the location and movements of other groups like their own. Although this may seem like a de jure limitation, the rich permutational logic of kinship and totemic affiliation is invoked to give a very wide set of choices. It is not, however, an infinitely wide choice. Eventually one reaches the end of the country in which one is "at home" and the range of even a universalistic kinship system. In a strange land among strangers with whom not even fictive kinship can be established, a Pitjantjatjara woman or man would be lost. In that state, she or he would be diminished, much like any other person dislodged from the web of cultural meanings by which personal identities, prestige, and social statuses are understood, expressed, and reckoned. There is no matrix of meaning within which to perform or respond to accustomed roles. Instead there is an informational wilderness in which one is unable to decode and encode sequences of social action, and in which one is left powerless, anomic, and alienated.

In the incorporation (with different types and degrees of incompleteness) of G/wi and Pitjantjatjara into their respective nation-states, very different problems arose in the formulation of national policies pertaining to land relationships. In both countries, the law is intended to serve all subjects equally. To this end, it frequently errs by making the tacit or explicit assumption that all are similar. The difficulty here is in the implication that all people share a common set of perceptions and values, as well as similar rules for interpreting these. The outcome is that, although the laws relating to land differ in Australia and Botswana, both sets are unsuited to the legal regulation of Pitjantjatjara and G/wi relationships with land.

The status of a landholder in Australia who considers herself or himself to have ownership is essentially that of tenant in fee simple, not outright owner.[2] This derives from the principle that land is the property of the Crown, which consequently has the potential power to take any of the rights that constitute ownership or even enjoyment of land. Title to land (i.e., tenancy in fee simple) is both alienable and transferable, potentially by compulsion, as are the individual rights that constitute this species of tenancy. This defeasible tenancy is inimical to the tripartite Pitjantjatjara nexus. Not only may the state fractionate a person's rights to a piece of land and dispose of them to others, but even those rights that are not taken away may be diluted by extending interest in them to other persons. Thus, minerals under "my" land may be mined by others who will obtain a right of passage over whatever I may retain of "my" property. Despite the appearance to the contrary of the Australian Land Rights legislation, recent and current practice and debate over this matter indicate that there is no real security against the incursions of miners, State and Commonwealth government agencies (e.g., when building roads), and others.

Furthermore, with the negligible exception of consecrated ground, and then virtually *de speciali gratia*,[3] Australian law takes no cognizance of the sacredness of a locality. There is no effective protection against others' incursions and behavior that would constitute desecration and consequent damage to the health of the Pitjantjatjara group's relationship with the place. It is possible that

2. A tenant is one who holds lands, etc., of another and has the use and occupaments to hold to him, and his heirs, forever, without mentioning what heirs, but referring that to her or his own pleasure or to the disposition of the law. The underlying assumption here is that all lands and tenements in the hands of subjects are held mediately, or immediately by the Crown. A tenant in fee simple is a mediate holder, but the Crown remains the ultimate owner.

3. *De speciali gratia* would best translate as "by grace and favor," i.e., as distinct from by right.

such action could be construed as trespass and/or a tort, but to contrive this outcome in a court could only bring retrospective compensation, and do little if anything to effectively prevent repetition.

The law could move to recognize the nature of Pitjantjatjara and other Aborigine concepts of relationship with land. While in the field of commerce it has moved quite slowly to come to terms with the notion of intellectual property, it has nevertheless undergone radical change in the last decades. There appears to be no reason other than apathy why it should not be at least equally accommodating of a different concept of proprietorial interest in land.

I see the G/wi case as being somewhat less difficult. Botswana inherited Roman-Dutch law from the Colony of the Cape of Good Hope. This confers nearly absolute ownership, not only of the surface, but also of what is above and beneath it. Ownership has been reduced extensively by subsequent legislation in other countries in which Roman-Dutch law obtains, but the archaic principle is more intact in Botswana. However, legislation in the Protectorate era of Botswana's history prohibited the alienation of erstwhile "tribal" land, and vested ownership of the remainder in the Crown (now the State). This latter land can be alienated, potentially to the full extent of ownership. Difficulty arises in relation to the G/wi, as ownership must be vested in a legal person. Unless those comprising a band or any other group of G/wi were to incorporate themselves as such a person, they could not obtain ownership. Whether G/wi social organization could adapt to the fixed group membership that such incorporation would entail is doubtful.

A possible remedy might lie in the old Protectorate provision in the legislation relating to the judiciary. With the assistance of assessors expert in the relevant principles and practice, a judge or magistrate could hear cases argued in terms of vernacular usage, custom, or law, and come to a legal decision. This sort of ad hoc administration of the law would cause both practitioners and bureaucrats to go prematurely grey, but it worked well enough in my experience and practice of it, and my grey head and beard were sometimes mistaken as a sign of wisdom.

There is not simply a conflict of laws here, nor only a matter of frustration of the respective peoples' (i.e., the State and its representatives, and Pitjantjatjara citizens) sets of expectations of one another's behavior and the attendant confusion, conflict, and unhappiness. For the Pitjantjatjara, the Australian law's presently very limited ability to recognize and deal with the vernacular conceptualization of the person-society-locality nexus is, at best, to leave it unprotected and open to the hazards of others' incursion onto land. It is true that a permit from the relevant (Aboriginal) Lands Council is required before entering its area and that some conditions may be endorsed on the permit; compared with the many forms of protection the law affords my rather different interests in my land (as a white Australian) this is scant security. At worst, the law denies the nature of the link with the land, and thus denies the very identity of the person. Inadvertent as this may be, it is a savage alienation of Pitjantjatjara Self, for which neither the individual nor the group has any recognized remedy. Instances of this alienation and examples of the consequences are legion. It says much for the people's courage and ingenuity that they have managed to contrive at least palliative measures of an informal nature.

A comparable and even more distressing alienation of G/wi people has occurred where their social order has been dislocated to the extent that groups have been stripped of their capacity to regulate and conduct their own relationships with one another and the land they occupy.

This brief, superficial, and very incomplete excursion into the legal aspects of the contrast between the respective positions of Pitjantjatjara and G/wi is to illustrate the need for those who make and administer decisions of public policy to exercise caution in formulating or accepting generalizations about peoples who identify with a hunting-gathering tradition in their perception of their relationship with land. Comparable caution is necessary for anthropologists; although we have little capacity to decide matters of public policy, our utterances and writings do sometimes influence those who have that power. Less important, it is poor science to cantilever inference and conclusion beyond the limits of what their logical bases can support.

# Part 3

# Hunter Affluence?

# Editorial

Thirty years ago the general view among anthropologists was that hunter-gatherers had to toil from dawn to dusk in the quest for food in order to eke out a life that was nasty, brutish, and short. Then, at the Man the Hunter Conference in Chicago in 1966, it dawned on several people that the conventional view simply was not true. On the basis of fieldwork done by Lee (1968) among the !Kung Basarwa, and by McCarthy and McArthur (1960) on the Australian Aborigines, Marshall Sahlins (1968a) pointed out that people whose wants and needs were limited, like many hunter-gatherers, could achieve a comfortable life with little time and effort. Instead of working all day every day, these people spent much of their time simply lounging around.

Seizing on a phrase originally coined by the economist John Kenneth Galbraith (1958) in a famous book on highly modernized societies, Sahlins (1968a, 1972) characterized the class of foraging societies involving people whose wants were easily satisfied as "the original affluent society." Dismissing as aberrant such people as the Netsilik Eskimos (Balikci 1968), where the new model failed to meet the test of evidence, Sahlins (1968a: 85, n. 1; 1972: 32) and Lee (1968: 40–41) clearly implied that all hunter-gatherers lived in a state of affluence.

The affluence model was totally at variance with the earlier view of forager subsistence. Characterized by a catchy phrase, and based on enough evidence to make it plausible, the affluence model became the new stereotype. It was, however, subjected to some empirical testing. In a few cases, such as among the !Kung (Lee 1979: 72, 440; 1984: 50 ff.), it did account for the evidence. In many, however, it did not (e.g., Altman 1984; Hawkes and O'Connell 1981; Hawkes et al. 1985). Barnard and Woodburn (1988: 11) and Bird-David (1992) pointed out that much depends on whether or not a society is characterized by a delayed-return or an immediate-return system. According to their analyses, the affluence model is supported by the facts to a much greater extent in the latter type of economy than in the former. This, of course, is the irony that made the hypothesis so intriguing in the first place: the most "affluent" hunters in terms of leisure time are also the poorest in terms of material possessions.

The three papers presented here all question the notion of affluence in hunter-gatherer societies, but in very different ways. In the first, David Yesner does not explicitly address the Sahlins hypothesis, but looks instead for evidence of seasonal resource stress in two prehistoric populations of complex hunter-gatherers – and finds lots of it. The evidence shows that the individuals involved suffered such severe hunger that they completely stopped growing for a period of almost every year. Obviously, if people were regularly suffering from food shortages that were serious enough for evidence of the fact to appear in the archaeo-logical record hundreds of years later, their wants were not being met in a very satisfactory manner. Yesner finds such evidence in two study populations. This casts further doubt on the usefulness of the notion of affluence beyond the simplest immediate return economy (see Testart 1988a). He also summarizes old evidence and presents new evidence showing that resource diversity and seasonal variability are critical factors: the greater the diversity and the lower the seasonal variability, the less resource stress there is likely to be.

Yesner's conclusions are supported in the second paper, where Victor Shnirelman examines the original affluence model in the light of historical data on the Itel'men, relatively complex hunter-gatherers living in far eastern Eurasia. These people, like the Northwest Coast Indians discussed in the previous section by Donald and Mitchell, were primarily fishermen. The author describes at length the quantities of fish they caught and the means used to capture them. It is probably fair to say that he writes about quantities of food that !Kung and Australian Aborig-ines never would have imagined in their wildest dreams. In order to acquire it, the Itel'men sometimes had to work hard for days at a time – but for only a limited part of the year. Despite this appar-ent affluence, sometimes things went wrong; early rains, or bad fish runs spoiled everything. The result was an entire season of hunger, and often death from starvation. As in the cases described by Yesner, limited resource diversity and pronounced seasonal variability were the underlying factors in the Itel'man case. In light of this evidence, Shnirelman concludes that it is not useful to think of the traditional Itel'men as having lived in a state of affluence.

In the third and final paper, Nicholas Blurton Jones, Kristen Hawkes, and Patricia Draper take a novel approach to the question of affluence by examining the part played by children in the food quest among two African peoples, the Hadza and the !Kung. Both have immediate-return economies, and both provided part of the evidence that led to the development of the notion of "original affluence" in the first place. The point of departure for the paper is the fact that Hadza children are active and independent foragers from a very young age, whereas !Kung children are discouraged from independent foraging because adults are afraid to let them wander far from camp. The questions arise, are the !Kung therefore more affluent than the Hadza, and, if so, is this the best way to explain the differences in the children's behavior? The authors consider the evidence on these points and find that, while one could argue in their support, other explanations are much more fruitful.

These three studies, plus most of those cited earlier, establish pretty clearly that "affluence" in any useful sense of the term is not characteristic of many hunter-gatherer societies. It seems to occur only in societies at the simplest end of the complexity continuum. However, nowhere in the relevant literature is there any discussion of a possible range of variation with regard to affluence; the issue is always presented as a matter of all or nothing.[1] Whether elaboration of the affluence model in this direction proves more fruitful than the alternatives to it remains to be seen.

1. The possibility of a range of variation is present in models where risk, rather than affluence, is the focus of attention; see, for example, Gould (1982) and Smith (1988). However, these are invariably presented as complete alternatives to the affluence model.

# 7

# Seasonality and Resource "Stress" Among Hunter-Gatherers: Archaeological Signatures

*David R. Yesner*

Evidence for episodic seasonal population stress is widespread among hunter-gatherers in arctic, temperate, and arid regions where resource seasonality existed. These effects were not limited to "simple" hunter-gatherers with low population densities in resource-poor environments; they were also found among "complex" or "affluent" hunter-gatherers, in coastal regions, for example. Greater sedentism, larger populations, and the resulting greater intensification of local resource exploitation among such societies elevated seasonal resource imbalances to a different level; technological and settlement pattern solutions were sought, but their effect was limited.

A quarter of a century ago, when *Man the Hunter* appeared, our primary concerns involved challenging accepted nomothetic notions of hunter-gatherers as uniform societies in terms of subsistence, technology, demography, and sociopolitical organization, with the latter including the prevalent patrilocal band model.[1] As a part of this variability, it was acknowledged that

1. This paper was originally presented in the symposium on "Nutrition among Hunter-gathers Past and Present," organized by George Armelagos for the Sixth International Conference on Hunting and Gathering Societies. It benefited greatly from earlier work by Armelagos and Alan Goodman, as well as by specific comments made by Alan Goodman at the time of the conference. The "stress" models developed in this paper were conceived through undergraduate work with Brooke Thomas at Cornell University more than two decades ago, and have been influenced by work from Jane E. Buikstra, Richard A. Gould, Lewis R. Binford, and others. Research discussed here was supported by funding from the U.S. Department of the Interior (through the Maine Historic Preservation Commission), as well as by archaeology field schools at the University of Maine, Portland, and the University of Alaska Anchorage. Study of the human skeletal material from Moshier Island was made possible by kind permission of the landowner, Dr. Charles Harriman. Nathan D. Hamilton of the University of Southern Maine was

some hunter- gatherers had larger population densities and more complex sociopolitical organization; by the 1980s, these had become known as "complex hunter-gatherers." Nevertheless, it was suggested that hunter-gatherers in general – with the possible exception of high arctic and subarctic peoples – were "affluent," in the sense of being able to supply their basic needs with an average work level of a few hours per day. This supposedly led to a general lack of concern about what tomorrow might bring. However, at the Man the Hunter Conference and in a series of subsequent papers, Binford (1968, 1978, 1980) cogently argued that hunter-gatherers differ greatly in "logistical" strategies, largely as a function of latitudinal differences in the seasonality of resources. At higher latitudes, where the seasonality of resources increases and the diversity of resources declines, food storage developed, along with more complex settlement patterns involving base camps and more ephemeral task group sites. In Binford's (1968: 90) original view, such behaviors were developed in order to increase the "time utility" of resources, by maintaining subsistence input levels "in a steady state despite seasonal fluctuations in yield from the standing crop of available resources."

Latitudinal gradients, however, are by no means the only significant axes of seasonal variation in resource biomass and/or diversity for traditional hunter-gatherers. For example, coastal and interior regions within single latitudinal belts often have very different resource configurations, with resulting differences in population levels and settlement patterns (Yesner 1977, 1980). The full set of adaptations of groups to local resource configurations includes responses to the abundance, diversity, distribution, temporal variability, and sequential pattern of availability of those resources, both individually and collectively. The nutritional content of the resources may also be a factor (Keene 1985;

the field supervisor at Moshier Island and analyzed the artifactual data from the site. Access to human skeletal material from the Kachemak tradition was provided by William Workman of the University of Alaska Anchorage (for Kachemak Bay) and by Neal Crozier of the U.S. Bureau of Indian Affairs (for Kodiak Island). Figure 7.1 was provided by Nathan D. Hamilton (University of Southern Maine), and Figure 7.4 was provided by Ellen McKay (University of Alaska, Anchorage). The radiographs in Figure 7.2 were provided by Dr. Russell M. Briggs, Radiology Department, Maine Medical Center (Portland, ME), and were converted into prints by Ronald Dies, Radiology Department, Providence Hospital (Anchorage, AK). Revision of the manuscript was enhanced by review from Ernest S. Burch, Jr. I retain sole responsibility for the views voiced herein.

Yesner 1987). In this context, the development of food storage and other "logistical" strategies in the late Pleistocene era, along with shifts in subsistence toward increasing the use of maritime and other resources, and eventually the domestication of plants and animals, all may be viewed as attempts to even out such temporal and spatial discontinuities in energy flow.

In examining the nutritional "stress" levels affecting hunter-gatherers, therefore, we are actually measuring the ability of societies to track these resource variations with appropriate cultural responses. "Appropriate" responses are those that do not tax the individual or system more than the original stressor. A biological example would be the lack of genetically based skin temperature responses (or somatotype responses, for that matter) to night cold stress in the desert by either Australian Aborigines (Macpherson 1966: 439) or South African Basarwa (Wyndham 1966: 229). A cultural example might be the lack of storage behavior among hunter-gatherers, such as the !Kung, who inhabit temporally and spatially homogeneous low-latitude environments (Lee 1979; Yellen and Lee 1976), where large deviations in resource availability (either scarcity or abundance) are infrequent and unpredictable (Goland 1991).

"Stress," in either individuals or systems, results from a lag between the impact of stressors and the ability of the individual or system to respond. This may be the result of an impact that is so great that homeostatic mechanisms cannot respond effectively; or may occur through a failure in the response mechanisms, be they biological or cultural. Our ability to measure the "stress" levels in populations often depends upon the way in which such stresses are distributed within the population – whether the stresses are felt evenly by all (or most) members of the population, or whether they are unevenly (i.e., hierarchically) distributed. Our ability to measure stress levels also may be a function of the length of the time lag between impact and response; if it is too short, it cannot be viewed archaeologically (and, in any case, may be meaningful only as adaptive "noise"), while if it is too long, dysfunction leads to death of individuals and/or systems, which then pass more quickly out of the archaeological record. What remain in the archaeological record are numerous patterns of intermediate-level stress, reflecting the pervasive but limited impact of stressors.

**Archaeological Signatures of Episodic Stress**

Archaeological signatures of such intermediate-level stress episodes depend on whether the response is biological and/or cultural in nature. Among biological responses that affect bone are features of nonspecific etiologies ("indicators of episodic stress"), including radiologically opaque lines of growth arrest, enamel hypoplasias, and other dental microdefects. Cultural responses include changes in subsistence, including intensified use of marginal resources as reflected in animal bone assemblages inventories; and shifts in settlement patterns, allowing intensified use of marginal environments, or environments in which marginal (i.e., high cost) resources are more abundant. Ultimately, this may lead to total changes in diet or abandonment of habitats.

The participants in the original Man the Hunter Conference considered the nutritional status of hunter-gatherers on the basis of data available at that time. Dunn (1968: 223) concluded that:

> While hunter-gatherers are exposed to *relative* dietary deficiencies leading to malnutrition, they may, exceptionally, be faced with *gross* deficits. In tropical and temperate regions...starvation has undoubtedly been the exception, occurring only in individuals incapacitated for other reasons. In the arid tropics only an unusually prolonged drought may be expected to imperil the food supply . . . In the Arctic and Subarctic winter, on the other hand, starvation has probably always been a relatively important cause of death. (emphasis in original)

How has the research of the intervening twenty-five years affected our current understanding of the paleonutritional status of hunter-gatherers? The special characteristics of the arctic region were apparently confirmed in studies by Buikstra (1976) of Caribou Eskimo skeletal remains, of which a high proportion (roughly 50 percent) contained lines of growth arrest ("Harris lines"). The marked periodicity in these lines was attributed to a recurrent annual stress cycle, most probably late winter famine. Similarly, Lobdell (1984) found evidence for Harris lines in four out of five bodies recovered from Mound 44 at the Utqiagvik Village site near Barrow in northern Alaska; the even spacing of these lines again suggested regular, periodic nutritional deficiencies, probably in late winter or early spring.

Other studies, however, have shown that these features were also present among hunter-gatherers in arid regions, such as in the Central Desert of Australia (Gill 1968; Webb 1989). Harris lines also were found in prehistoric California populations, where they were more prevalent among interior desert than coastal populations (Dickel, Schulz and McHenry 1984). Among the coastal California groups, earlier populations showed greater numbers of Harris lines than did later populations (McHenry 1968), suggesting that "the apparent good health of the later populations reflects the diversification of their economy...which would provide a buffer against periodic deprivation" (Cohen 1981). In all of the above cases, signs of periodic subsistence stress were more frequent among populations dependant upon a lower diversity of resources, in that sense mimicking the situation for arctic peoples. In the above cases, the "richness" component of resource diversity (total number of different species in the diet) may be high, but the "homogeneity" component of resource diversity (the number of species found in abundance) may be relatively low, as may be the relative temporal variance in that abundance. The skeletal record, therefore, suggests that correlations between hunter-gatherer resources and seasonal stress depend less on latitude than on a combination of resource diversity (in the broadest sense) and temporal variability. Cook (1984), for example, has noted that, in comparison to both earlier hunter-gatherers and later intensive maize farmers, "transitional" early farmers in west-central Illinois not only experienced a mortality decline, but also showed fewer examples of episodic stress in the form of Harris lines. For these groups, the combination of food storage – providing a more reliable diet – and a more diverse diet than was achieved by later intensive farmers, allowed a reduction of such episodic stress.

Although much argument has ensued about the value of Harris lines as a measure of episodic stress, Goodman et al. (1984: 24) concluded that they are "potentially an excellent source of data obtainable in no other way." Alternative measures of resource stress, such as enamel hypoplasias, seem less related to acute episodic stress than to chronic deficiency conditions, which, in turn, are more likely to be related to the resource specialization, greater population densities, and differential access to resources seen among many farmers but among relatively few hunter-gatherers. Thus, McHenry and Schulz (1976, 1978) found inverse correlations between Harris lines and enamel hypoplasias among California hunter-gatherers, suggesting that they respond to different biological signals.

One real advantage to the study of Harris lines is the degree to which they can act as specific indicators of nutritional insults to subadult members of the population. They have provided evidence, for example, of the "weaning effect" in which the nutritional protection of human breastmilk is removed. Among prehistoric California populations of all time periods, McHenry and Schulz (1978) have found evidence for peaks in both Harris lines and enamel hypoplasias at the age of four.

Underscoring the acute nature of the episodic stress recorded by Harris lines is the fact that there are generally low correlations between these lines and other diseases expressed in bone (Goodman et al. 1984; Mensforth et al. 1981). This is important to consider in looking at the biological evidence for stress associated with more "complex" hunter-gatherers, including coastal groups. Meiklejohn et al. (1984), in a survey of Mesolithic societies, found little evidence for gross pathologies in bone, but apparently no attempt was made to look for evidence of growth arrest lines. On the British Columbia coast, Cybulski (1977) found evidence of nutritional disorders in gross skeletal pathologies limited to cribra orbitalia (reflecting iron deficiency anemias), but again, no apparent attempt was made to look for episodic stress markers. Is there, in fact, evidence for such stress markers among other "complex" hunter-gatherer populations?

The following discussion focuses on the evidence for periodic seasonal stress among "complex" hunter-gatherers in coastal regions of North America. Examples are drawn from two recent areas in which I have worked: the southern coast of Maine (in the northeastern United States), and the coast of southcentral Alaska.

### Coastal Algonkians (northeastern United States)

Although there is some debate concerning the prehistoric ancestry of Coastal Algonkians of the northeastern United States, archaeologists appear agreed that Woodland (Ceramic) period populations of the last three thousand years represent direct antecedents of historically known groups in the region. To the south of Massachusetts, such groups had adopted horticulture by Late Woodland times, but in the Maine-Maritimes region of the extreme northeastern United States and adjacent Canada, groups remained hunter-gatherers until the time of European contact

(Sanger 1975; Yesner 1984). Although these groups may have desired to obtain storable vegetable foods to even out the highly seasonal energy flow characteristic of the region (ethnographic accounts suggest that aboriginal trade in such foodstuffs may have extended northward as far as Nova Scotia), the lack of 100-day frost-free seasons limited their capability to integrate maize farming into their subsistence pattern effectively (Yesner 1988). As among other North American hunter-gatherers, late winter/early spring appears to have been the time of greatest food stress. At that time of year, populations in many areas evidently shifted from the interior to the coast to make use of low-calorie but reliable shellfish resources (Yesner 1980). Food resources, however, appear to have been sufficiently abundant to have supported dense regional populations. In fact, there is considerable evidence that Late Woodland groups on the southern Maine coast were expanding into wider areas, occupying more marginal ecological niches (particularly for shellfish exploitation) that had been ignored by earlier populations (Yesner 1984). While Late Woodland populations may not have been quite as complex as the earlier "Maritime Archaic" tradition peoples of the Late Archaic period (around 5,500 to 4,500 years ago; see Bourque, Cox and Spiess 1983), during this period there appears to have been a resurgence of widespread ceremonialism, trade in exotic items, and personal ornamentation suggesting the evolution of some status differentiation.

While poor preservation conditions have generally limited the availability of skeletal data from the northeastern United States, an opportunity to examine the lifestyles of Late Woodland Coastal Algonkians in more detail was provided through the excavation of the Moshier Island burial site in Casco Bay on the coast of southern Maine during 1978-1987 (Yesner 1989; see Figure 7.1). There, fourteen individuals were recovered from a point of land extending northeastward into the bay. The context of the burials suggested a single episode of internment, and possibly represented a single extended family group (only three individuals were fully adult; the balance were juveniles and infants; see Table 7.1). The burials of all individuals were oriented toward the east. Grave goods and items found in the adjacent, contemporaneous midden – including shark's teeth, shell beads, and exotic copper beads – suggest that this was a locus of ceremonial behavior (Hamilton 1988).

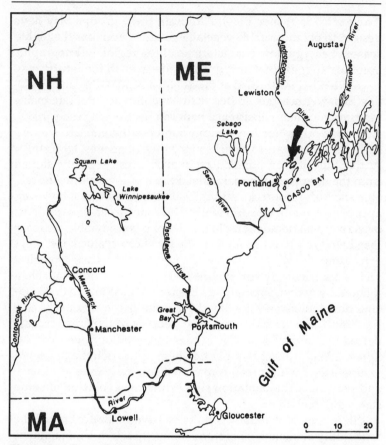

**Figure 7.1:** Casco Bay, Maine, showing the location of Moshier Island. Reproduced by permission of the Archaeological Association, Department of Archaeology, University of Calgary.

As a part of a general examination for paleopathological indicators, the radius, ulna, tibia, and fibula, as well as distal humerus and femur, were examined radiologically for growth arrest lines (Yesner 1989). Of the ten individuals recovered from the site over the age of two years, eight showed multiple lines of growth arrest (see Figure 7.2); the two exceptions were juvenile males. Most burials displayed from two to six lines per skeletal element, although one burial (Burial D, an adult male) had as many as fourteen lines in the proximal tibia and fifteen in the distal fibula (see Table 7.2). That individual apparently also was suffering from chronic osteomyelitis (Yesner 1989).

The growth arrest lines displayed in these individuals were extremely regular in their spacing. In particular, the distal fibulae from Burial D, which had some of the most distinct lines found on any of the burials (fifteen lines on the right distal fibula and six on the left distal fibula), showed highly regular spacing (see Figure 7.3). For the right distal fibula, these lines varied from 0.16 to 0.37 mm. in interlineal distance, with a mean interlineal distance of 0.23 mm. and a standard deviation of only 0.06 mm.; for the left distal fibula, these lines varied only from 0.34 to 0.39 mm. in interlineal distance, with a mean interlineal distance of 0.36 mm. and a standard deviation of only 0.02 mm. Burial E (a juvenile, between six and seven years old) also showed a highly regular series of lines on the right and left distal radii (see Table 7.1), varying in one case from 0.11 to 0.14 mm. in interlineal distance (with a standard deviation of only 0.01 mm.), and in the other case from 0.10 to 0.25 mm. (with a standard deviation of 0.05 mm.). The regularity of these lines is best interpreted as the result of acute seasonal metabolic stress related to nutritional deprivation and restoration.

**Table 7.1:** Summary of Demographic Features, Moshier Island Burials, Casco Bay, Maine

| Burial | Sex | Age |
|---|---|---|
| A | F | 30-40 |
| B | M | 20-25 |
| C | ? | Fetal |
| D | M | 35-50 |
| E | ? | 6-7 |
| F | ? | 7-8 |
| G | ? | <1 |
| H | ? | <1 |
| J | ? | <1 |
| K | M | 25-30 |
| L (fragmentary) | ? | Juvenile |
| M | ? | <1 |
| N | ? | <1 |
| 14.9#1 | M | 25-35 |
| 14.9#2a | ? | 2 |
| 14.9#2b | ? | <1 |

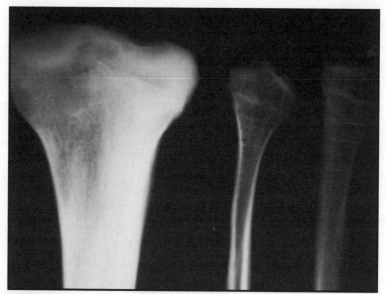

2a

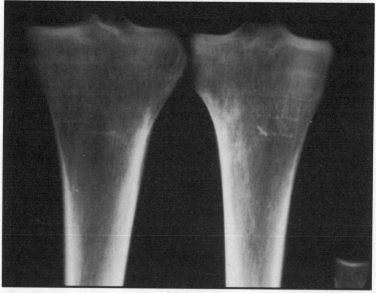

2b

**Figure 7.2:** Radiographs showing Harris lines in distal fibulae and proximal tibiae, Burial D, Moshier Island. 2a: fibulae; 2b: tibiae.

**Table 7.2:** Statistical analysis of Harris Line Interlineal Distances, Burial D, Moshier Island

| Statistic | Tibia 1 | Tibia 2 | Fibula 1 | Fibula 2 |
|---|---|---|---|---|
| No. of cases | 14 | 6 | 15 | 6 |
| Minimum distance (mm) | 0.150 | 0.200 | 0.160 | 0.340 |
| Maximum distance (mm) | 1.500 | 1.160 | 0.370 | 0.390 |
| Range (mm) | 1.350 | 0.960 | 0.210 | 0.050 |
| Mean distance (mm) | 0.401 | 0.407 | 0.229 | 0.357 |
| Variance | 0.129 | 0.142 | 0.004 | 0.000 |
| Standard Deviation | 0.359 | 0.376 | 0.061 | 0.021 |
| Standard Error | 0.096 | 0.154 | 0.016 | 0.008 |
| Skewness | 2.225 | 1.645 | 1.391 | 0.635 |
| Kurtosis | 4.400 | 0.925 | 1.020 | -1.025 |

Analysis of age patterns from the Moshier Island burials (see Yesner 1989), utilizing the methods developed by Allison, Mendoza, and Pezzia (1978) for the tibia, demonstrates that most Harris lines were developed before the age of eight, with a great likelihood that one line was developed during the "hard" season (late winter/early spring). There is, however, also evidence here for the "weaning effect." Not a single growth arrest line was found in the skeletons of any of the seven individuals from the site under the age of two years. As indicated above, this is an indication that the protective nutritional effects of lactation quickly disappeared after weaning.

## Kachemak Eskimo (Southcentral Alaska)

Eskimo peoples of the Kachemak tradition, who occupied lower Cook Inlet and Kodiak Island in Southcentral Alaska from around three thousand to one thousand years ago, have been described by Jordan (1987) and others as complex hunter-gatherers. Their diverse subsistence base, including sea mammals, anadromous fish, deep-sea fish, shorebirds, and shellfish, supported a large, stable population for two thousand years. Although the population density in lower Cook Inlet may have been somewhat smaller and more easily disrupted (see Work-

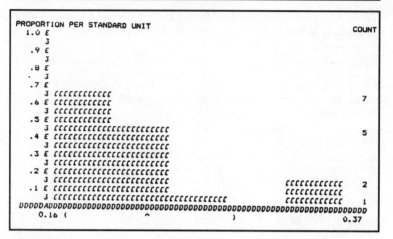

**Figure 7.3:** Harris line interlineal distances for right distal fibula, burial D, Moshier Island. Reproduced by permission of the Archaeological Association, Department of Archaeology, University of Calgary.

man, Lobdell and Workman 1980), there is abundant evidence for permanent log house structures, ornamentation, ceremonialism, and chronic warfare, including dismemberment and reinternment of human remains (Yesner 1990), all of which suggest linkage with the complex Pacific Eskimo cultures known historically from the region.

The largest series of Kachemak tradition skeletons for which Harris lines have been studied derive from the Cottonwood Creek site on lower Cook Inlet in Southcentral Alaska (see Figure 7.4). Of the seven well-preserved skeletal remains from the site, six demonstrated evidence for Harris lines in distal femora (Lobdell 1980: 81-82). The remaining individual, however, along with two of the burials that displayed Harris lines, showed evidence of enamel hypoplasias. (In one individual, enamel hypoplasias was found on both upper medial incisors; in a second, it was found on the lower left canine and right first premolar; and in the third, it occurred on all upper incisors and canines, both lower lateral incisors, and the right first premolar, right canine, and left second premolar.) Again, regular spacing of Harris lines was present, indicative of patterns of regular seasonal stress.

### Interpreting the Evidence

In reviewing the evidence for nutritional deficiency conditions among prehistoric California hunter-gatherers, Cohen (1981) sug-

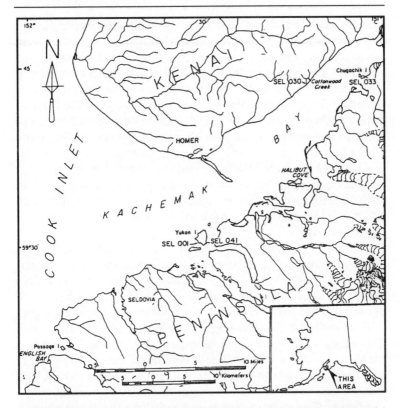

**Figure 7.4:** Kachemak Bay, southcentral Alaska, showing the location of Cottonwood Creek and Chugachik Island. Source: Workman,Lobdell and Workman. (1980). Reproduced by permission of the Arctic Institute of North America.

gested that these derived essentially from the growth of these "affluent" human populations. As population density increased, physical mobility became limited; "populations which were once able to move away from the failure of specific resources...now found adjoining territory occupied and emergency resources already exploited" (Cohen 1981: 287). In addition, the resource specialization that may have triggered the growth of regional populations among such "affluent" hunter-gatherers required such sedentism and territorial exclusion. Paradoxically, the result may have been a greater risk of famine, or at least the depletion of higher ranked food resources. When faced with such conditions, hunter-gatherers appear to have intensified their resource base through increased utilization of higher ranked food resources, and through broadening the subsistence base to include larger numbers of lower ranked resources that had lower yields, were more costly to obtain, or both. Archaeological signatures of such activities are found in both the subsistence inventory and in settlement pattern changes. The former, for example, would provide evidence in the archaeofaunal record for the increased use of lower ranked, often "emergency" food resources such as shellfish; for the greater utilization of specific species that are more costly to obtain because they require higher search times and do not aggregate; and for the increased use of smaller (lower yield) or older (less fatty) individuals within species. The latter would include settlement pattern evidence for more intensive utilization of "marginal" habitat zones where such resources are available (Yesner 1984).

Abundant evidence is available to corroborate this linkage between biological and archaeological signatures of seasonal stress in both the Maine and Alaskan coastal groups. In Maine, there is evidence from Moshier Island itself for intensification of the subsistence base, with increased utilization of shellfish in general, as well as the decreasing size of individuals (Yesner 1984). Simultaneously, groups were expanding outward to utilize smaller islands (with less diverse resources), coves with smaller shellfish beds, islands more distant from seal rookeries, and islands more distant from the mainland (thus increasing transportation costs to base camps and reducing the availability of deer and anadromous fish populations). There is good reason to believe that this settlement pattern change involved the fragmentation of a small number of larger base camps into a larger number of smaller nuclear family exploitation units, the kind of pattern that may have been present at the time of European contact (Yesner 1983). At the end of the prehistoric period there is evidence for the final filling up of the local habitat, and the development of trade in horticultural foodstuffs to supplement the hunter-gatherer economy.

A similar situation may have prevailed among the Kachemak Eskimo in lower Cook Inlet, except that the filling up of the habitat and subsistence intensification took place at an earlier point in time. Lobdell (1980) suggests that, at Cottonwood Creek and on Chugachik Island in Kachemak Bay (Figure 7.4), increased utilization of shellfish took place toward the end of the Kachemak tradition, associated with some changes in shellfish types. At the same time, there is evidence for intensification of seal exploitation, which Lobdell (1980) suggests may have been a factor in the ultimate demise of the Kachemak tradition. Workman (1980; Workman, Lobdell, and Workman 1980; Workman and Workman 1988) also suggests that increased utilization of more marginal habitats was taking place during late Kachemak times, with greater population fragmentation (similar to the Casco Bay case) perhaps producing greater risk of population decimation. Why the intensification solution ultimately did not work in this area is explored below.

**Discussion**

Hayden (1981) has suggested that resource intensification could be accomplished through technological "research and development" among hunter-gatherers. Technological intensification, however, has its limits. Cohen (1981), and more recently Hayden (1990b) himself, have suggested that removal of mobility as a solution to restoring population and resource imbalances among "affluent" hunter-gatherers necessitated the development of "new homeostatic mechanisms of a political nature," including storage systems, the "banking" of subsistence surplus by conversion to durable goods, interregional trade, and ceremonial systems. The latter help to insure the flow of goods and the continued viability of trade channels during hard times through the addition of prestige factors and luxury items into the economy, the function of which is to create elastic, open-ended demand even in the face of increasing inequality in both prestige and possessions. Theoretically, this helps to insure the long-term survival of the population. Under these conditions, I would argue, further relaxation of population growth controls is likely to take place, since additional family members become a source not only of greater labor (thus potentially providing more resources within increasingly fixed territories), but also of greater access to prestige and luxury items, both by "banking" resources in trade relations and by conducting ceremonial activities. Even greater increases in corporate labor, and concomitant increases in storable goods, prestige, and long-term survival (beyond that which can be provided by natural human reproduction) then can be achieved only through the slavery that is associated with the warfare system of the most "complex" coastal hunter-gatherers. This helps to generate even greater demand (or justification) for political centralization. The upper limit for labor intensification, of course, is set by both region-wide resource availability and the ultimate costs of chronic warfare.

How successful were these mechanisms in ultimately achieving the goal of restoring population/resource imbalances? In the case of the two "complex" hunter-gatherer populations discussed here – the Northeast Coastal Algonkians and the Kachemak Eskimo – the answer is "not very." Although there may be relatively few signs of gross skeletal pathologies, the retention of Harris lines in both populations suggests that for both groups, neither technological or settlement pattern changes, nor sociopolitical changes, had much final impact in promoting increased resistance to seasonal resource fluctuations. Sociopolitical factors, however, may help us to understand the demise of the Kachemak tradition population in lower Cook Inlet. The lower Cook Inlet (Kachemak Bay) area was probably not large enough to maintain the population in the face of resource reduction or overexploitation, and limited local anadromous fish populations probably did not allow the degree of open-ended resource intensification that occurred in some other areas. Unlike the Northeast Coastal Algonkians, furthermore, the lower Cook Inlet Eskimos were isolated from potential trading partners among relatives on Kodiak Island to the southwest. Any significant change in resource availability or resource overexploitation (see Yesner 1992) probably could not be compensated for quickly through reciprocal trade relations. On Kodiak Island itself, however, a larger population base and the greater availability of anadromous fish resources probably allowed for continued subsistence intensification and the eventual emergence of the historic Koniag Eskimo configuration.

## Conclusion

Evidence for episodic seasonal population stress appears to be widespread among hunter-gatherers in arctic, temperate, and arid regions where any degree of resource seasonality existed. These effects were not limited to "simple" hunter-gatherers with low population densities in resource-poor environments; they were also found among so-called "complex" or "affluent" hunter-gatherers in coastal regions. Greater sedentism, larger populations, and the resulting greater intensification of local resource exploitation among such societies simply elevated seasonal resource imbalances to a higher level. Technological and settlement pattern solutions were sought to restore population and resource imbalances among these groups, but their response was limited, and they often created higher levels of population growth. Eventually, sociopolitical solutions developed to address these problems, but their primary success was in insuring long-term population survival rather than doing away with all seasonal resource fluctuations. Their most important consequence, of course, was the development of economic inequalities and differential access to resources.

Eventually, where possible, some hunter-gatherer groups developed the ultimate solution to seasonal resource imbalances: domestication. Although arctic and arid environments did not allow this to take place, evidence of environmental manipulation, resource management, and even quasi-domestication is found among Australian Aborigines, native Californians, and Northwest Coast peoples (see Hayden 1990b), all telling evidence of the importance of reducing resource seasonality. In spite of this, as far as we can tell, nearly all hunter-gatherers living in seasonal environments continued to be affected by that seasonality with some degree of episodic stress. However, the relative degree of severity of those episodes among "simple" and "affluent" hunter-gatherers is difficult to judge from the record of Harris lines, since no procedures have been developed yet for interpreting the degree of thickness or continuity of such lines in any consistent way. It may be, as Cohen and Armelagos (1984: 590) have concluded, that "minor, regular hunger periods among hunter- gatherers have been traded for more irregular and more severe stresses of farming life." Further economic inequalities and differential access to resources have occurred in the process.

# 8

## *Cherchez le Chien:* Perspectives on the Economy of the Traditional Fishing-Oriented People of Kamchatka

*Victor A. Shnirelman*

This paper examines the hypothesis of "original affluence" in the light of data on the Itel'men, complex hunter-gatherers who lived on the Kamchatka Peninsula. The evidence reveals a pattern of prosperity alternating with hardship during precontact and early contact times. Thus, even complex hunter-gatherers did not always have a stable resource base. Therefore the hypothesis of "original affluence" needs to be modified or discarded.

### Introduction

One of the main reasons for *perestroika* in the former U.S.S.R. was the negative trend in Soviet economic development over the past several decades.[1] This trend was expressed not only in the main industrial regions, but also in the outlying areas of the country. Included among the latter were several areas that were inhabited by traditional hunter-gatherers until well into the twentieth century. Indigenous peoples in these areas were almost completely deprived of ways to maintain their traditional way of life due to forced changes in their economies, technology, social organization, educational patterns, and decision-making procedures. Moreover, their natural environments were largely destroyed in many areas. Therefore, one of the most crucial problems for the indigenous populations today is how to effect economic and cul-

1. I gratefully ackknowledge the help of my colleagues, Igor I. Krupnik, Olga A. Murashko, and Anna V. Smoliak, with whom I have discussed the ideas propounded in this paper, and whose friendly remarks were valuable to me inproducing this final version. I also thank Linda Ellanna, Ernest S. Burch, Jr., Igor Krupnik, and Lois Myers for their help in preparing the manuscript for publication.

tural development. This is an especially important consideration given the transition to a market economy in Russia.

One of the solutions that has been recommended by some scholars is that indigenous peoples should return to their traditional ways of life. Even the creation of a kind of special reservation for native peoples has been suggested. This view is not new in the former U.S.S.R., since it was defended by some well-known Soviet anthropologists in the 1920s (Gurvich, ed. 1987: 15). It is based on a romantic notion of the condition of traditional hunter-gathering economies, which are assumed to have operated without crises. The idea is apparently similar to that of the "original affluent society" (Sahlins 1972). In my view, first one should carefully analyze the real potential of traditional economies before arriving at such conclusions.

While putting forward the idea of "original affluence" among hunters and gatherers, Sahlins (1972) quite consciously stressed the situation observed among nomadic hunters and gatherers. However, at the same time he wondered if "marginal hunters such as the Basarwa of the Kalahari [were] any more representative of the paleolithic condition than the Indians of California or the Northwest Coast" (Sahlins 1972: 38).

Disregarding Paleolithic economies, one may now reasonably argue that sedentary and semisedentary complex hunters were found in many parts of the world, at least during the Holocene period (Shnirelman 1986: 126–27; 1989: 401). These peoples, which include fishermen, deserve more attention than they have received until recently.

Studies of complex hunter-gatherers will demonstrate the natural and economic conditions under which a sedentary way of life emerged, the size and density of populations increased, and social organization became more complex. What were the relationships among these variables? What kind of prosperity was required for the development of a complex social structure? Were sedentary or semisedentary hunter-gatherers, in fact, "the original affluent societies"?

An enormous volume of data concerning the economic characteristics of hunter-gatherer societies and their evolutionary trends during the past two hundred to three hundred years is now in the hands of Russian scholars. Specifically, these include economic and demographic statistics, which have been collected regularly in Russia since the late nineteenth century. These data may serve as the foundation for a more accurate reconstruction of the traditional way of life of hunters and gatherers than do the circumstantial and fragmentary ones used by Sahlins (1972). Recently, the great scientific importance of these data was demonstrated by Krupnik (1989) in his construction of ecological models for evolutionary trends among some Arctic populations.

The aims of the present paper are to test and supplement Krupnik's (1989) conclusions. At the same time, I hope to provide new insight into the problems presented by the Sahlins model.

## Historical Background

Here I analyze the main features of the economies of the traditional fishermen of the Kamchatka Peninsula. The original inhabitants of Kamchatka were the Itel'men, whose livelihood depended primarily on riverine fishing. Several mixed Itel'men-Russian populations emerged during the last two hundred and fifty years, after Russian colonization, which commenced at the beginning of the eighteenth century. However, although the local culture was transformed to some extent under Russian influence, the earlier way of life not only survived but was borrowed in part by Russian "old-settlers"; they also became intensive fishermen. The majority of Itel'men local groups, in turn, developed a type of horticulture and kept livestock as a result of Russian colonization. However, these occupations were of little importance compared to fishing, which preserved its significant role even into the late nineteenth century (Murashko 1985). Therefore, the nonfishing aspects of the economy will be ignored in the present paper.

In the late nineteenth century, the same settlement pattern characterized both groups of riverine fishermen, Itel'men and Itel'men-Russians, as was the case in late precontact and early contact times. The great majority of permanent villages were situated on river banks several miles from the sea. The traditional winter village contained one or more multifamily semisubterranean dwellings and several smaller houses elevated on piles, the latter functioning as storehouses in winter and as nuclear family dwellings in summer. The former were replaced by Russian-style log houses occupied by individual households, composed of about six to eight persons, during the nineteenth century. The latter preserved their earlier function until very recent times.

In some areas there were also separate temporary fishing

camps near the river mouths in summer, which were occupied by several able-bodied men and women for brief periods. Old people, small children and cripples lived in winter settlements year round (Antropova 1949a; Krasheninnikov 1949: 374–77; Starkova 1976: 41; Steller 1927: 24–27). Most of the winter settlements were known by names dating from at least the early eighteenth century, indicating that they had remained stable in location through time. This provides evidence of the substantial longevity of fishermen's settlements (see Figure 8.1).

People usually fished from March or April until October. But the most important fishery occurred in summer, during the time of the main salmon migration. The king salmon run occurred in May and early June. However, this species was relatively rare in Kamchatka, and provided poor yields. Kings were followed by red salmon, from May until August. Chum salmon were available from late June until the end of August, pink salmon from late June until September, and silver salmon in August and September. The precise time and the scale of the runs varied from year to year and from place to place. The intensity of the salmon migration was of much importance for the local inhabitants, since their ability to lay up a sufficient supply of food for the winter depended on it. However, the most intensive runs were strictly limited in time. The silver and pink runs lasted from two to four weeks, but that of the reds lasted for only three to eight days (Geineman 1912: 6–7; Krasheninnikov 1949: 302–305; Slunin 1895: 71–73; 1900: I, 543–45; Unterberger 1912: 30–31).

The prosperity of the local community in winter depended on the success of fishing activities during a few weeks in summer. Therefore, all able-bodied people were engaged in fishing during this crucial period. Men did the majority of the fishing, while women processed the catch and old people and children helped hang the fish up to dry (Prozorov 1902: 153; Steller 1927: 37). This was a collective task for the working group, which ranged from a few households to a majority of the local community. The yield was divided among the participating households, each of which stored its share separately (Geineman 1912: 8; Krasheninnikov 1949: 705; Krynin 1913: 187; Slunin 1900: I, 549–50; Tjushov 1906: 65).

Kamchatkan fishermen used weirs and nets (Geineman 1912: 7; Krasheninnikov 1949: 300–305; Lesseps 1801: 109; Prozorov 1902: 239–40; Slunin 1900: I, 546–47; Starkova 1978; Steller 1927: 37). There were several types of weirs made from rows of poles

**Figure 8.1:** The villages of the Kamchatka fishers mentioned in the text

stretched across the river with holes between them, which led to funnel-shaped basket traps. There were also several types of nets, originally made of nettle fiber – large ones for kings, and small ones for other species.

The activity of storing food was of vital importance during the summer, since it was the main means of supplying people with food during severe winter months. Originally, two types of fish preservation were practiced: *yukola*, or dried fish, and fermented fish seasoned in special pits dug into the ground. *Yukola* was made primarily from chums, while fermented fish was made mostly from pinks. Fish were cut into three pieces to make *yukola*: two pieces of edible flesh were prepared for people, while the third, including the head and spine, was stored as "dog *yukola*," or "bone." Whole fish were thrown into pits for fermentation. People ate *yukola* as an ordinary food, while fermented fish was saved for guests during special occasions. Dogs were fed with "bone" while traveling, and with a soup of fermented fish on days when they were not working.

The sedentary or semisedentary fishermen of Kamchatka and those of other far eastern areas of what is now Russia should be distinguished from other groups of settled fishermen and hunters of sea mammals in that they kept dogs for transport since prehistoric times. It is worth noting that elements of dog sledges (also known as sleds) were excavated by Soviet archaeologists in several regions of the Russian Far East. They dated from the tenth to thirteenth centuries, and possibly even from the first to fifth centuries A.D. (Orekhov 1987; Vasil'evskii 1977). Itel'men, however, acquired dog sledges comparatively recently, possibly just prior to Russian colonization (Ponomarenko 1985: 188).

Originally Itel'men did not travel far from home (Steller 1927: 47, 72). A light sledge, pulled by four or five dogs, was usually used in precontact and early contact times for personal trips and for transporting light loads, such as water, fuel, and *yukola* from summer camps to winter villages (Krasheninnikov 1949: 384, 395–400; Lesseps 1801: 111; Steller 1927: 74). However, heavy sledges became widespread with the development of the fur trade, and transport in Kamchatka during the contact period required the use of dog teams of about nine to eleven animals (Antropova 1949b; Starkova 1976: 74–81).

## Analysis

As we have seen, seasonal fishing for anadromous species of fish in Kamchatka formed the economic basis for the majority of the indigenous people until just a few decades ago. What was the efficiency of traditional fishing methods? Information on single or one-day harvests, although scarce and fragmentary, is sufficient to suggest some tentative conclusions. A single weir produced about 500 fish per day during the average salmon run in a stream in the Avacha area, and about 1,000 fish per day in the Tigil' River (Slunin 1895: 68; 1900: I, 550). Krynin (1913: 186) noted that each fish trap, which could hold between 150 and 200 fish, was filled in just a few minutes at the time of the main run. There were several such traps in a weir, and a village owned one or two weirs. It took from half an hour up to an hour to clean the fish from each trap (Slunin 1900: I, 549).

Other traditional fishing methods were no less successful. One person could take more than 700 fish per day with a dip net during the main salmon run (Krynin 1913: 186). Additionally, one could harvest between fifty and eighty fish every one to two hours with the help of a hook attached to a pole (Pravdin 1928: 223) during peak periods. Eight fishermen were able to catch up to 4,000 salmon per day with a seine (Slunin 1895: 69). The yield was certainly much greater than even these data indicate over the whole fishing season. For instance, seven men caught about 32,000 chum salmon with a net during the summer of 1921 in the Gizhiga region (Arsen'yev 1925: 28), a year that was considered by the indigenous people to be an unfavorable one for fishing.

Yields were much smaller at the end of the fishing season. For example, during three October days in 1894, six fishermen caught about 3,600 brook char and 360 silver salmon with the help of a small net in a western Kamchatka stream, this yield being referred to as "good" for this time of the year (Tjushov 1906: 65).

What do these data mean? Let's take one of the largest villages of the late nineteenth century – Vorovskoye – as an example. The population of the community was about 120 persons in the 1890s, when residents obtained the largest yields in Kamchatka – up to about 100,000 salmon per summer (see Table 8.1). Thus, the people of Vorovskoye had to have caught between 3,000 and 4,000 salmon per day in only one month, or between 1,500 and 2,000 salmon per day over two months, to achieve this yield. Conceivably it would not have been a difficult task for villagers, since there were no less than twenty-five adult males in the population. In fact, it is documented that intensive fishing continued for less than a month. However, even if it continued for only two weeks, it was quite possible to have enormous yields under these conditions.

**Table 8.1:** The main characteristics of yields and communities' size among the Kamchatka fishermen in 1891–1896*

| Name of Village | Size of Community | No. of Dogs | Mean Yields (fish) | $CRV_{md}$ | Mean No. of Fish for Yukola | Mean Stores of Fish for Yukola and Fermentation |
|---|---|---|---|---|---|---|
| Khajrjuzovo | 247 | 335 | 72,740 | 35.0 | 13,143 | 55,743 |
| Apachi | 122 | 208 | 59,073 | 40.2 | 17,217 | 40,557 |
| Vorovskoye | 120 | 250 | 77,031 | 25.1 | 11,537 | 70,053 |
| Oblukovino | 116 | 195 | 36,241 | 21.5 | 8,513 | 31,980 |
| Moroshechnoye | 112 | 138 | 21,195 | 33.7 | 5,404 | 17,732 |
| Kolpakovo | 104 | 180 | 32,914 | 36.6 | 9,371 | 31,638 |
| Kavran | 100 | 128 | 50,173 | 53.2 | 12,057 | 39,624 |
| Sedanka | 99 | 120 | 11,859 | 56.9 | 6,017 | 10,901 |
| Mashura | 97 | 175 | 23,443 | 23.2 | 5,617 | 15,967 |
| Malka | 93 | 159 | 41,657 | 44.1 | 10,769 | 35,360 |
| Ganaly | 93 | 158 | 53,882 | 32.8 | 11,986 | 47,536 |
| Sopochnoye | 90 | 84 | 27,236 | 27.1 | 7,379 | 26,449 |
| Utkholok | 80 | 102 | 38,344 | 42.6 | 14,544 | 30,259 |
| Amanino | 79 | 83 | 13,893 | 69.4 | 3,371 | 9,614 |
| Krutogorovo | 78 | 157 | 48,531 | 16.6 | 8,396 | 47,729 |
| Tolbachik | 77 | 162 | 41,634 | 31.3 | 11,360 | 35,102 |
| Icha | 76 | 100 | 34,619 | 31.1 | 10,875 | 30,708 |
| Kresty | 75 | 116 | 26,545 | 47.0 | 8,292 | 19,058 |
| Kamaki | 75 | 120 | 22,943 | 5.3 | 13,800 | 13,800 |

**Table 8.1:** *Continued*

| NAME OF VILLAGE | SIZE OF COMMUNITY | NO. OF DOGS | MEAN YIELDS (FISH) | $CRV_{md}$ | MEAN NO. OF FISH FOR YUKOLA | MEAN STORES OF FISH FOR YUKOLA AND FERMENTATION |
|---|---|---|---|---|---|---|
| Verkhne-Kamchatsk | 72 | 167 | 31,061 | 22.7 | 11,654 | 21,729 |
| Kolovskoye | 67 | 144 | 48,013 | 24.1 | 10,267 | 43,100 |
| Kikhchiki | 67 | 166 | 45,754 | 36.9 | 11,071 | 39,488 |
| Kozyrevskoye | 61 | 117 | 18,079 | 24.2 | 4,938 | 10,421 |
| Napana | 60 | 79 | 25,249 | 61.6 | 7,771 | 19,875 |
| Kirganik | 55 | 116 | 21,230 | 16.7 | 7,825 | 17,555 |
| Sheromy | 54 | 121 | 26,934 | 29.1 | 7,975 | 20,608 |
| Kharchino | 53 | 71 | 13,964 | 7.5 | 7,533 | 10,478 |
| Shchapino | 51 | 83 | 23,966 | 12.8 | 7,875 | 18,883 |
| Yelovka | 51 | 73 | 20,533 | 46.8 | 6,020 | 14,317 |
| Utka | 50 | 93 | 56,948 | 53.8 | 11,514 | 48,648 |
| Golygino | 47 | 62 | 32,715 | 33.2 | 9,623 | 26,832 |
| Ushki | 46 | 101 | 14,887 | 49.5 | 3,877 | 8,533 |
| Belogolovoye | 45 | 58 | 15,548 | 43.3 | 4,181 | 11,067 |
| Yavino | 43 | 101 | 45,327 | 32.9 | 16,654 | 39,838 |
| Nachiki | 43 | 86 | 56,868 | 39.5 | 16,183 | 51,550 |
| Pushchino | 26 | 47 | 17,853 | 20.9 | 5,258 | 15,308 |

*After Slunin 1900:II, with the author's calculations

Even groups of about forty to fifty persons could have comparable yields. For instance, summer yields sometimes were as great as 90,000 to 100,000 fish (see Table 8.1) in Nachiki village (forty-three persons). In this case, the task was accomplished by only twelve to thirteen adult males. Thus, the size of the yield did not necessarily correspond to the number of productive members of the community. This conclusion may be confirmed by data on other Kamchatka villages.

It is likely that the data on fish yields gathered in the late nineteenth century were not very accurate, since it was not possible to count the exact harvest of fish. For example, some fish were consumed by people and dogs almost immediately, and fish for fermentation were thrown into storage pits very quickly. This may explain the discrepancies in the accounts of different scholars (Krynin 1913: 191; Prozorov 1902: 242; Slunin 1900: I, 574). However, the actual number of fish harvested was apparently underestimated rather than overestimated in the harvest figures. The effectiveness of traditional Kamchatka fishermen was fairly high due to intensive work, which could last more than twelve hours a day if necessary, and due to the efficiency of fishing devices, the number and capacity of which were subject to manipulation.

Kamchatka fishermen harvested fewer fish in practice than the theoretical potential, however. In this sense, Sahlins's (1972: 52 ff.) opinion about the underproduction and underuse of labor resources in hunter-gatherer societies is as valid for Kamchatka fishermen as it is for many other populations. As Slunin (1900: I, 549) pointed out, the fish traps were emptied once a day (or, more rarely, two or three times a day), and sixty people could be at leisure almost all day if there were only twenty to thirty fish traps in a weir. Indeed, twenty to thirty traps could produce 3,000 to 4,000 salmon, even if they were emptied only once a day. Therefore 30,000 to 45,000 fish could be harvested in only ten days, quite enough for an average-sized community.

What were the limitations on an increase of productivity of the traditional subsistence economy? The main goal of intensive summer fishing was the preparation of foodstuffs for winter, principally the storage of *yukola*. Therefore, it was not enough to obtain a good yield; fish had to be processed as quickly as possible, since they would otherwise rot in the hot summer sun (Smoliak 1989). Women's work was of crucial importance, for it was they who made the *yukola*. According to some experts (Arsen'yev

1925: 19; Krjukov 1894: 85–86), a woman was able to process one chum every 2.5 minutes during twelve hours of continuous labor. However, the accounts in question may have overestimated the real number of fish.

It is known that residents processed from 10,000 to 20,000 fish for *yukola* in Vorovskoye village in 1891–1896 with the labor of no less than twenty to twenty-five mature women. Thus, it is easy to calculate that it must have taken less than two weeks to accomplish this task. Additionally, women may have been engaged in only part-time production, since their work was not very intensive even during this short period of time.

On the other hand, just the two or sometimes three weeks of intensive fishing were critical periods that affected the stability of the traditional ways of life and culture throughout the year. The *yukola* should have been prepared and put into storehouses before mid-July – that is, before the season of wet mists and heavy rains, since the moisture could undo the results of an entire season's work (Komarov 1912: 114). As was already mentioned, the main chum run usually began in mid-June and sometimes even later. Pink runs sometimes coincided with the chum run, but more often followed it. That is why Kamchatka inhabitants preferred to make *yukola* from chums and even reds rather than from pinks, since it was much easier to obtain a satisfactory amount of the former than of the latter before the rainy period. And it was not accidental that, according to Krasheninnikov (1949: 305), pinks were a primary source of dog food.

In what measure could summer fishing adequately supply local populations with food during winter months? To answer this question one must make some theoretical calculations and then compare the results with the empirical data. Since winter in Kamchatka lasted for about six months or 183 days, one can calculate the quantity of fish individual households and village communities consumed if they ate only fish. A Kamchatka fishing household averaged seven to eight persons (ranging from six to nine). Most local communities were of moderate size (from fifty to one hundred persons), and only a few were smaller or larger. How many fish did a household have to preserve for winter to meet the normal requirement of 2,500 kilogram calories (kcal) per person per day in high latitudes (Krupnik 1989: 53) if the main part of the catchment consisted of chums and pinks?

The average weight of a Kamchatka chum is about 3 kilograms, and that of a pink about 1.4 kilograms (Berg 1948: 175, 184). The edible part of the former is about 1.8 kilograms, and that of the latter is about 0.8 kilogram. A kilogram of edible chum flesh may supply 1,260 kcal of energy, and a kilogram of pink flesh, 1,350 kcal (Budagjan, ed. 1961). Thus, about 1,450 to 1,650 chums, or 2,900 to 3,300 *yukolas*, had to be preserved to feed a household of seven to eight persons with *yukola* only. To put it another way, no less than 8,200 to 10,250 fish (16,400 to 20,500 *yukolas*) were required for a small community; 10,250 to 20,500 fish (20,500 to 41,000 *yukolas*) for a middle-sized one; and more than 20,500 fish (41,000 *yukolas*) for a large one.

The reliability of these calculations may be tested against Krejnovich's data (1973: 465) on a Nivkh household of nine persons, who preserved 7,680 *yukolas* from 3,840 fish (2,880 pink, each weighing about 1.4 kilograms; 720 summer chums, each weighing about 1.7 kilograms; and 240 fall chum, each weighing about 4.5 kilograms) for winter. This supply guaranteed 2,957 kcal to each person – that is, it was more than adequate. The anomalous status of this household in our calculation may be the result of its large size. Second, it also may be the result of an unusually large volume of stores in comparison to other Nivkhan households. Finally, it may be the consequence of the much smaller size of pink and summer chums, the primary source of Nivkhan stores, in comparison to Kamchatka fish that were twice as large.

Even so, only a few Kamchatka communities really managed to prepare such large *yukola* stores as was calculated above, and even they did so very infrequently. In fact, their stores were much more limited in size: about 4,000 to 16,500 fish in small villages; about 5,000 to 14,500 fish in medium-sized ones; and about 9,000 to 17,000 fish in large ones (see Table 8.1).

However, Kamchatka fishermen's stores contained not only *yukola* but fermented fish as well. Thus, a household of seven to eight persons would preserve about 1,900 to 2,200 fish for a winter if chums and pinks were caught in equal proportion. It meant that about 11,000 to 13,800 fish per small village were required; 13,800 to 27,600 fish were required for a medium-sized one; and 27,600 to 33,120 fish were required for a large one. In fact, the stores ranged from 8,000 to 51,500 (median 25,500) in small villages; from 10,500 to 48,000 (median 24,700) in medium-sized ones; and from 18,000 to 70,000 (median 41,000) in large ones (see Table 8.1).

Now it is useful to compare these findings with data obtained by other scholars. According to Slunin (1900: I, 575), a household of five to eight persons required from 1,800 to 2,200 fish to feed themselves and their dogs in winter. Gurvich (1963: 32) mentioned that Kamchadals preserved about 2,000 fish per household during the 1930s and 1940s. These accounts correspond closely to our theoretical calculations. But these authors did not define the species of fish being preserved.

Geineman (1912: 9) cited much larger quantities – 2,000 to 6,000 *yukolas* and 3,000 to 10,000 fermented fish per household (including dogs) per winter. Alternatively, they used from 4,000 to 10,000 fish or more to make their winter stores. In general, these data correspond to the volume of actual winter stores made by Kamchatka fishermen in the period from 1891 to 1896, according to the figures provided by Slunin (1900: II). If one ignores the smallest numbers, which were observed very infrequently, it may be apparent that the average size of the winter supply was usually much larger than was required under normal conditions. Why store so many fish?

It was already mentioned that Kamchatka fishermen kept large dog teams in the nineteenth century. In fact, there were about 1.8 dogs per person (or 12.3 dogs per household) in the period from 1896 to 1897 among Kamchatka River inhabitants; about 1.9 dogs per person (15.8 dogs per household) among southwestern Kamchatka inhabitants; and about 1.2 dogs per person (13.1 dogs per household) among west-central Kamchatka inhabitants. Unfortunately, the information provided by different scholars (Antropova 1971: 43; Arsen'yev 1925: 20–21; Sergeev 1936: 619–20; Slunin 1900: I, 576) on the winter food requirements of dogs is inconsistent. However, it is known that dogs were fed with "dog *yukola*" or "bones," and also with boiled fermented fish (Krasheninnikov 1949: 254; Lesseps 1801: i, 110; Slunin 1900: I, 572, 630–31). When calculating the norms of winter feeding, many scholars erroneously segregated fish prepared for dogs from those prepared for human beings. In fact, it was one and the same fish: its flesh was stored for people, and its "bones" were kept for dogs.

Regrettably, there is no direct information on the requirements for dog food in winter. Therefore, I shall use other data for the calculations in this paper. The evidence regarding food stores in the summer of 1892 is of special importance, since there was high dog mortality due to hunger during the winter of 1892–1893. According to my calculations, the volume of stores in general varied between different groups of Kamchatka fishermen (see Table 8.1). If a person's diet consisted only of fish, then a dog's diet should be much poorer in the Kamchatka River valley and west-central Kamchatka than it was in southwestern Kamchatka. This can be explained by the fact that the role of horticulture and cattle keeping was somewhat higher in the Kamchatka River valley (Murashko 1985), whereas the role of sea mammal hunting was of some importance in west-central Kamchatka, in contrast to southwestern Kamchatka. I do not include these occupations in my calculations, but one should not entirely ignore them. The southwestern Kamchatka data seem to be the most reliable. A high level of dog mortality due to starvation was revealed there when the volume of their winter food stores was one-third that of people in 1892. Moreover, there were about 1.2 dogs per person in this critical year.

If one knows that dogs were fed with one "bone" per animal per day, or with boiled fermented fish, then the large-scale fish preservation mentioned above is well understood. However, the winter diet was not limited to preserved food. Kamchatka fishermen also caught fish in unfrozen streams and lakes, which are not uncommon in Kamchatka (Krynin 1913: 193). Therefore, the accounts of winter food referred to above should not be treated as absolute. Moreover, one should consider that Kamchatka fishermen hunted sea and land mammals, if only to a limited extent, storing their fat and meat (Krasheninnikov 1949: 247 ff., 271 ff.; Slunin 1900: I, 571); and they preserved silver salmon fat as well. These stores were of secondary importance, but they should not be ignored.

Thus, one may conclude that sedentary Kamchatka fishermen had a fairly satisfactory diet, and even a surplus of food at times. Nevertheless, that is not proof of the existence of an "affluent society." In fact, starvation was not an infrequent phenomenon in this region because of inadequate yields or of unsuccessful storage. *Yukola* decayed if one was not able to prepare it before the rainy season began. People were doomed to hunger in winter when this happened, as it did in Tigil' village in 1897 (Slunin 1900: I, 563).

Rain was not the only enemy of *yukola*, since flies laid their eggs on fish hung for drying. If one failed to prevent this from happening, the larvae ate the entire *yukola* except the skin (Komarov 1912: 114; Krjukov 1894: 86; Krynin 1913: 185).

Low harvests were the most significant reason for starvation, which occurred once every several years due to regular fluctuations in the size of salmon runs. These cyclical fluctuations in the volume of salmon runs are well documented in the scientific literature (Berg 1948:180, 187–88; Kaganovskij 1949; Krogius and Krokhin 1956). The fluctuations in question could happen every two, four, six, or more years, depending on the species and on ecological factors. Tables 8.2 and 8.3 demonstrate a cycle on the order of approximately five to seven years, with a decrease of yields in Kamchatka in general in 1892 and 1897. A similar phenomenon can be observed in the Lower Amur region in 1907 and 1908. Moreover, a very low yield occurred in Kamchatka in 1890, when many dogs died of starvation (Slunin 1900: I, 630).

Unfortunately, there is no similar information previous to the late nineteenth century. However, there are accurate data on the occurrence of famines in Kamchatka and in neighboring regions

**Table 8.2:** Fish yields, population size of river fishermen and dog numbers in Kamchatka, 1891-1897

|                 | 1891      | 1892      | 1893      | 1894      | 1895      | 1896      | 1897      |
|-----------------|-----------|-----------|-----------|-----------|-----------|-----------|-----------|
| Yields (fish)   | 2,025,930 | 1,441,830 | 1,933,724 | 1,927,874 | 2,393,411 | 2,733,638 | ?         |
| *Yields (fish)  | ?         | ?         | ?         | 2,114,694 | 2,980,844 | 2,596,095 | 1,327,591 |
| Population size | 2,695     | 2,703     | 2,792     | 2,873     | 2,874     | 2,964     | ?         |
| Dog number      | 3,655     | 4,583     | 3,961     | 4,652     | 5,281     | 6,037     | ?         |

* Data derived from Prozorov (1902). All other data from Slunin (1900:II).

**Table 8.3:** Fish yields, population size, and dog numbers in eight Penzhina region villages, 1890-1896*

|                 | 1890    | 1891    | 1892    | 1893    | 1894    | 1895    | 1896    |
|-----------------|---------|---------|---------|---------|---------|---------|---------|
| Yields (fish)   | 129,010 | 230,406 | 334,237 | 258,181 | 318,024 | 538,777 | 592,670 |
| Population size | 785     | 803     | 797     | 825     | 857     | 853     | 894     |
| Dog number      | 708     | 718     | 977     | 877     | 1,035   | 1,285   | 1,687   |

*1890 data derived from Starkova (1976); 1891-1896 data derived from Slunin (1900:II)

during the eighteenth and especially the nineteenth centuries. The most severe hardship was known in Kamchatka during 1769, 1770, 1788, 1816, 1818–1820, 1837, and 1883–1886; in the adjacent Gizhiga region in 1815–19, 1883, 1886 and 1897; and in the Okhotsk region to the south in 1815–1819, 1824, 1826–1827, 1832, 1837, 1842, and 1843 (Slunin 1900: I, 577). However, the data are incomplete. For instance, Slunin (1900: I, 579) mentioned the famine of 1879 as well, when about three hundred persons died from starvation. These data, together with the above mentioned evidence of the fluctuation of yields, may serve to show that unfavorable ecological conditions for sedentary fishermen occurred quite regularly once every five to ten years. This corresponds fairly well to Krupnik's (1989: 119–45) idea of the biological "pendulum" that works persistently in northern regions and affects all living organisms.

What was the influence of such a biological "pendulum" on human population dynamics? The natural increase in population in the Kamchatka region was about 18.8 per 1,000 in 1872 and 20.4 per 1,000 in 1873, which were relatively favorable years (Slunin 1900: I, 415–16). If one regards the extended period of time from 1880 to 1896, the natural increase of population averaged 14.2 per 1,000 among the Kamchatka River valley inhabitants; 7.9 per 1,000 in southwestern Kamchatka; and 23.6 per 1,000 in westcentral Kamchatka. This occurred despite the hardships of 1883–1886 and 1889, which had to be an important limiting factor.

If one takes an even more extended period, the indices would be more modest. For instance, the population increase was on the order of six per one thousand per year in five Penzhina region villages during the period 1853–1897 (Starkova 1976: 39) – that is, four times slower than during 1880–1896. Apparently, it was the result of high mortality during a time of famine, which, as mentioned, killed about three hundred persons throughout Kamchatka in 1879 (Slunin 1900:I, 579). However, the Russian administration increased its help to local inhabitants after the 1880s, and this led to a decrease of mortality from starvation (Slunin 1900: I, 579).

Starvation affected primarily dogs in the latter period, since their diet was inadequate at the time of the famine. In some cases they were intentionally killed (Arsen'yev 1925: 20). This may be seen in Table 8.2, where a decrease in dog numbers is demonstrated after the famine of 1892–1893. A more significant decrease in the number of dogs occurred during the period 1890–1891, when the dog population declined by half (Slunin 1900: I, 630).

## Discussion

By no means should one maintain that the way of life of sedentary fishermen developed under especially favorable ecological conditions, as is continuously argued by some scholars (e.g., Kabo 1986; Sahlins 1968a; Service 1962). While opposing the idea of absolute prosperity associated with traditional ways of life in the Northwest Coast of North America, Donald and Mitchell (1975: 331–33) reasonably pointed out that the local environment was far from paradise for the indigenous people, since it was subjected to severe fluctuations in the size of its resource base. This may be demonstrated by the variation in the number of salmon available at any given time. According to Donald and Mitchell's (1975) calculations, a coefficient of relative variation around the median (CRV $_{md}$) salmon escapement ranged from 35.6 to 211.6 (CRV $_{md}$ was 59.4) in various rivers in the area occupied by the southern Kwakiutl. To put it another way, the yields fluctuated significantly from year to year. This variability was much greater for some groups than for others.

I have made similar calculations for yields in Kamchatka during the 1890s (Table 8.1). It appears that the coefficient of relative variation was much smaller among Kamchatka fishermen than it was among the southern Kwakiutl. The former ranged from 5.3 to 49.5 (CRV $^{md}$ was 27.6) in the Kamchatka River valley; from 16.6 to 53.8 (CRV $^{md}$ was 32.8) in southwestern Kamchatka; and from 27.1 to 69.4 (CRV $^{md}$ was 45.3) in west- central Kamchatka. In other words, the situation was much more stable and reliable in Kamchatka than in the region occupied by the southern Kwakiutl.

However, subsistence efficiency was apparently very different between the Kamchatka fishermen and the southern Kwakiutl. This is demonstrated in Table 8.4, which contains demographic data on precontact and early contact situations for both groups (see also Figure 8.2). The figures suggest that efficiency was much greater among the Kwakiutl than in Kamchatka. Possibly this is one of the reasons why scholars so far have failed to find anything similar to potlatch-like relations,

**Table 8.4:** Some demographic variables among different groups of Itel'men in the late seventeenth century* and of southern Kwakiutl in the 1830s**

| Ethnic Group | Population Density (pers/km2) | Settlement Density (km2 settl) | Mean Settlement Size (pers) |
|---|---|---|---|
| Kamchadal | 0.16 | 863 | 138 |
| Avacha Itel'men | 0.19 | 79 | 68 |
| Bol'shaja River Itel'men | 0.11 | 970 | 107 |
| Western Itel'men | 0.14 | 1,586 | 222 |
| Khajrjuzovo Itel'men | 0.18 | 870 | 134 |
| Southern Kwakiutl | 0.69 | 728 | 420 |

*After Dolgikh (1960) and Ogryzko (1961), with author's calculations
**After Schalk (1981)

which were well known among the Kwakiutl, among traditional Kamchatka fishermen. The other explanation may be related to Russian colonial politics, which destroyed the traditional system of power immediately after Kamchatka was occupied by the Russians.

However, was it a result of colonization that Kamchatka fishermen became subject to regular hardships as may be discerned from Sahlins's (1972: 1–39) arguments? It is useful to test this idea against the available evidence. If Itel'men local groups ranged from 100 to 200 persons in the precontact period (see Table 8.4), then according to our calculations, each of them would have stored about 30,000 to 60,000 fish for the winter. This figure is not excessive, since much smaller groups succeeded in achieving this harvest using traditional fishing methods in the late nineteenth century. If there were about 13,000 Itel'men in Kamchatka at the very end of the seventeenth century, as was calculated by Dolgikh (1960: 571), then they would have stored about 3.5 million fish (considering 276 fish as the consumptive norm per person per winter in Kamchatka). In fact, about 3,000 Kamchatka fishermen caught between 900,000 and 1.5 million fish per year in the 1890s, preserving from 800,000 to 1.3 million for *yukola* and fermented fish. If the proportions held constant, 13,000 Itel'men would have been able to catch from 3.9 million to 6.5 million fish per year, with roughly 3.5 to 5.6 million of these being preserved

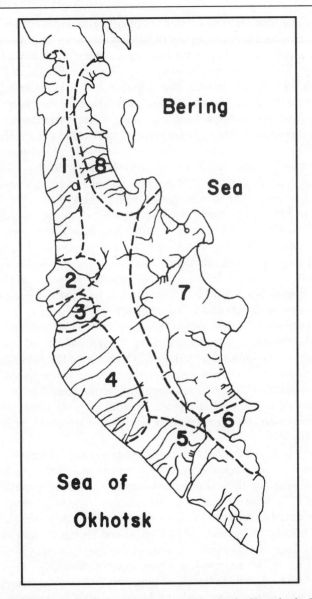

**Figure 8.2:** Itel'men and Koriak subgroup areas on the Kamchatka Peninsula in the late seventeenth century: (1) Palana Koriak; (2) Tigil' Koriak; (3) Khajrjuzovo Itel'men; (4) Western Itel'men; (5) Bol'shaja River Itel'men; (6) Avacha Itel'men; (7) Kamchadals; (8) Karaga Koriak (after Dolgikh 1960 and Ogryzko 1961)

for *yukola* and fermented fish. People could satisfy their food requirements even during unfavorable years with such stores.

However, not only people, but dogs, depended on winter food stores. Dog feeding required no less than one-half of all stored fish in the 1890s, when the dog population was between 1.5 and 2.0 times as large as the human population. Since there were about four to five dogs in the usual dog team in precontact time, there were two to three times fewer dogs in that period than in the 1890s. Thus, canine requirements were more modest then. Additional calculations reveal the actual quantity of food required for dogs. If an Itel'men household averaged seven to eight persons in the seventeenth century, then there were about 1,600 to 1,800 households during that time. If, as I have calculated, the requirements of dogs were no less than thirty percent of the number of fish required for people, the number of people and dogs being equal, then this number should be decreased to fifteen to twenty percent if the number of dogs was half that of people. Now, if each household had four dogs at its disposal, then there were between 6,500 and 7,000 dogs among Itel'men at the very end of the seventeenth century. Thus, they required about 500,000 to 700,000 fish in winter, omitting "dog's *yukola*" or "bone." Therefore, the general volume of fish stores in the seventeenth century had to have been no less than four million fish. These data suggest that the Itel'men were doomed to hardship and starvation during unfavorable years, even in the precontact period, as is suggested by some ethnohistorical sources (such as Steller 1927: 46–47).

There is no doubt that the Itel'men were quite "original" in the precontact period. However, they were apparently by no means as "affluent" as they should have been according to Sahlins's model. The idea of the "original affluent society" should be reconsidered and revised in the light of accurate data from a variety of traditional systems of ecological and economic adaptation. The traditional economic system of the Itel'men was far from ideal and could not protect them against hardship. This fact should be kept in mind by those people who have recommended a return to the economic system of former times.

# 9

# Differences Between Hadza and !Kung Children's Work: Original Affluence or Practical Reason?

*Nicholas Blurton Jones, Kristen Hawkes, and Patricia Draper*

Hadza children between the ages of five and fifteen forage successfully. !Kung children seldom forage. The behavior of !Kung children has been attributed to the low dependent to producer ratio by Lee (1979: 7), and could reflect the "original affluence" of the !Kung. We report interviews with !Kung adults to explore hypotheses about "practical reasons" for the difference.

!Kung children appear at considerable risk of getting lost if they wander into the bush. Furthermore, data to be presented elsewhere show that because of the way food is distributed in the environment, !Kung children cannot acquire much food without travelling far from dry season camps that are near permanent water. Hadza children have many landmarks by which to navigate, and acquire much food close to camp.

We compare evolutionary ecology arguments with arguments from the producer: dependent ratio, and "original affluence." We conclude that the former account for more data more parsimoniously.[1]

## Introduction

Hadza children forage frequently and successfully (Blurton Jones, Hawkes, and O'Connell 1989). !Kung children forage very little (Draper 1976; Draper and Cashdan 1988; Lee 1979 [Table

1. We are grateful to the Office of the President, Republic of Botswana for permission to do research in Botswana; to the National Science Foundation for support; to /"Ashe Kumsa, /Oma Bau, /=Oma Kxau, and N/=isa Kxau for assistance in our quadrat survey; to Timon Mbatara for interpreting and other assistance in the field. Kristen Hawkes and Nicholas Blurton Jones would like to thank Patricia Draper and Henry Harpending for their hospitality and advice in the field. Harpending and Draper were supported by a grant from the National Institute of Aging.

9.3]). Is this best explained by the concept of original affluence, or
are there practical reasons that explain the difference? The question is important not only as a test of theory but also because we
propose that the difference in children's foraging is a key factor
underlying other differences in demography and social behavior
between these two populations. In this paper we consider some
practical explanations for the difference in children's behavior
and report some of the data collected to evaluate them. We compare the ability of the competing explanations to account for
other differences between the !Kung and the Hadza.

Sahlins characterized foragers as the original affluent societies,
in which people's wants were easily satisfied, because they
desired little. This continues to be an influential counter to economic and ecological explanations of forager life. Sahlins's concept rested on two observations, best documented in Lee's (1968,
1972b, 1979) pathbreaking quantitative studies. Working hours
were short, and some categories of people (including children)
did no work at all. The work hour issue has been critically examined by Hawkes and O'Connell (1982), Hawkes et al. (1985), E. A.
Smith (1987a), and Winterhalder (1983). Here we offer some data
and analysis concerning children, a class of people among the
!Kung who do no work at all.

Blurton Jones, Hawkes, and O'Connell (1989) proposed that
the acquisition of food by Hadza children should have important
ecological, demographic, and behavioral consequences. It would
lower the cost of raising children, which would lead to higher fertility in Hadza women (as is indeed reported by Dyson 1977 and
Blurton Jones et al. 1992), and to differences in child rearing practices between the two populations (Blurton Jones 1993). Further,
there may be implications for the reproductive strategies of men,
and ultimately for the greater "separation" between men and
women among the Hadza than among the !Kung, which are
reflected in the writings of Lee (1979: 454) and Woodburn (1968a,
1968b). These arguments rest on the assumption that since the
reproductive advantages to the Hadza mother from her child's
foraging are so striking, there must be some good practical reason
why !Kung mothers do not persuade their children to forage.

Lee (1979: 71), offers another explanation for !Kung children
not working, which also could explain some of the differences
between Hadza and !Kung. He reverses part of our "chain of consequences": whether children forage is influenced by the ratio of

dependents to producers. Only where there are many children and few adults do adults fail to provide all the food that children need, and in these circumstances !Kung children can be seen to forage. Thus, one could argue that while Hadza children must forage because their mothers are so fertile, the !Kung children's leisure is leisure of choice: they could forage if they wanted, but why bother if mother brings in all they need? But could !Kung children forage if they wanted to? Would it be worthwhile for mothers to allow or encourage them to forage? What would children get if they foraged? What costs would they incur and what risks might they take? In fieldwork on the !Kung in July and August 1988 (in the middle of the dry season) we tried to assess the potential costs and benefits of !Kung children foraging.

Recently Wilmsen (1989) forcefully criticized all previous approaches to the study of the !Kung for their neglect of history and the processes by which neighboring and remoter societies may have restricted, or even removed, economic opportunities for the !Kung, and the effects of the need to interact with these neighbors upon !Kung society. Similar arguments could be applied, perhaps more easily, to the Hadza, even those studied by Hawkes et al. (1989), O'Connell, Hawkes, and Blurton Jones (1988a, 1988b, 1990), and Blurton Jones, Hawkes, and O'Connell (1989), who, for substantial stretches of time, obtain less than 5 percent of their food from agricultural sources. But in both cases, since farming and herding are not readily available options, the daily demand for food must set in motion some interaction between people and the ecology and economics of foraging. Our research concerns aspects of this ecology, particularly for the period of the lives of the people studied by Lee (1968, 1979) and by Howell (1979).

### Introductions to the Hadza and the !Kung

The approximately 750 eastern Hadza occupy an area of 2500 square kilometers in the eastern rift valley southeast of Lake Eyasi in northern Tanzania. They are best known to English speaking anthropologists from the work of James Woodburn (1968a, 1968b), and from a series of physical anthropology studies directed by Nigel Barnicot (Barnicot et al. 1972; Bennett et al. 1970, 1975; Hiernaux and Hartono 1980). Earlier investigators wrote in German, notably Kohl-Larsen (1958) and Obst (1912).

The region has a warm, dry climate, with a marked six- to seven- month rainy season (mean annual rainfall is 300–600 mm [Schultz 1971]); medium and large animals are locally abundant. When first described, the Hadza appear to have been the main occupants of the area, and to have lived entirely by hunting and gathering. Incursions by non-Hadza pastoral and agricultural groups were reported by Obst and his informants. Archaeological evidence indicates the periodic presence of farmers and pastoralists over several centuries (Mehlman 1988). Non-Hadza settlement has increased in recent years, being heaviest at Mangola in the Balai delta, the location of a major onion growing industry.

During the past fifty years, various segments of the Hadza population have been subjected to a series of government- and mission-sponsored settlement schemes designed to encourage them to abandon foraging in favor of full-time farming (McDowell 1981; Ndagala 1988). None of these schemes has been successful; and in every case, most of the Hadza involved have returned to the bush, usually within a few months. In each instance some Hadza have managed to avoid settlement altogether, and have continued to live as full-time hunters and gatherers. One settlement scheme, at Yaeda, was more substantial than most. Scores of Hadza were moved there in 1964, and many children attended the local school. The settlement faded away in the mid-1970s. Throughout this period and before, Hadza families also farmed at the village of Munguli to the south (Woodburn 1964; Cooper 1947). A school and clinic were built there by missionaries, who have since left. The village remained a thriving Hadza community until 1990.

The research referred to in this paper was conducted in an area the Hadza denote as Tli'ika, the southern part of the hills that separate Lake Eyasi from the Yaeda valley. Camp sizes and compositions and other features of Hadza social life seem to resemble closely the accounts given by Woodburn on the basis of his fieldwork between 1959 and 1962. During the years of our fieldwork these people obtained less than 5 percent of their food from agricultural sources. The plant foods obtained by women and by children include several species of roots and tubers, baobab fruit, and berries of several species. Much the same species are used in other Hadza localities. In the Mangola and Siponga regions, some Hadza work for farmers some of the time and are paid in maize or sweet potatoes, but continue to forage extensively.

The !Kung live in northwestern Botswana and northeastern Namibia. A substantial literature describing this population has accumulated (Howell 1979; Lee 1979; Lee and DeVore 1976; Marshall 1976; Yellen 1977). These sources deal primarily with !Kung social organization, economy, demography, and archaeology. Most authors writing on the !Kung describes them as hunter-gatherers, yet in recent decades many !Kung show increasing contact with non-!Kung peoples, and substantial changes in their economy and demography. In the past, !Kung lived by a variety of economic strategies. Some !Kung lived in nomadic bands part of the time, and subsisted primarily by hunting and gathering. Other groups of !Kung, for varying periods of time, lived as servants to Bantu- speaking pastoralists. Today, all of the !Kung of western Botswana have become permanently settled around year-round water sources and they live by a combination of gardening, stock raising, hunting and gathering, and government distribution of famine relief foods. They live in small villages ranging in size from about ten to thirty or more people related to each other by kinship and marriage. Except for irregular food relief from the government, the !Kung subsist on foods they provide for themselves. Because of the remoteness of the area and lack of economic development, there are virtually no wage-paying jobs to be had in the region.

## The Evidence That !Kung Children Do Not Forage and That Hadza Do

Before we describe our efforts to find out what would happen if !Kung parents persuaded children to forage, we should review the evidence that they seldom forage, and that Hadza children often do.

### !Kung Children

Draper (1976) and Draper and Cashdan (1988) present quantitative data that shows that !Kung children aged 4 to 14 years who were living in the bush did virtually no foraging, ran few errands, and did extremely little of anything else that could be called work. Draper was careful to test for the effects of her own activity (as did Blurton Jones, Hawkes, and O'Connell 1989). She examined the frequency with which a child next on the list for observation could not be found (a mere 3.4 percent of observations of girls; 2.5 percent for boys). Even if all the missing children were foraging, this still represents a very small amount of time spent foraging. Her category of "work" was met by girls only 6 percent of the observation time, and for boys only 2 percent of the time. She states "the children of foraging camps are seldom called upon to work, either as babysitters or as assistants to adults." Work, as defined by Draper and Cashdan (1988), includes processing food. Though Draper's subjects at /Du/da obtain few mongongo nuts, Lee comments (presumably based on his time in the Dobe and /Xai/xai areas) that "children over 8 do most of their own cracking" of the mongongos that they eat (Lee 1979: 277).

Draper's (1976) "spot observations" on girls show that they were foraging on only eight out of seventy-six observations, and seven of these were observations of children less than three years old carried by their mother. Spot observations of boys showed them to be out gathering on seven out of ninety-three occasions, and all of these were children less than three years old out with their mothers. Draper's systematic, quantitative observations are supported by Lee's quantitative data on !Kung work in July and August 1964, and in numerous comments in his book based on less rigorously scheduled observation. Lee's (1979: 260) Table 9.3 shows children gathering on four person-days out of 304 child-days of observation. Some ethnographies (and our interviews) suggest that !Kung children forage from time to time in the wet season, such as when the family is camped in a nut grove. But note that Draper's observations covered both wet and dry seasons.

*Hadza Children's Foraging*

Blurton Jones, Hawkes, and O'Connell (1989) report the returns from foraging by Hadza children in Tli'ika, a region in which about one third of the eastern Hadza live. Not only were their returns quite high (high enough to provide half of the child's caloric requirements in two hours of work), but children clearly were spending roughly two hours each day collecting and processing food. Some was done while accompanying women, but more was done during independent excursions from camp by small groups of children unattended by adults. Observations in subsequent years and various seasons support these findings and supplement them with data on a wider range of foods, including berries and nestling birds. On some of the berry trips children accompanied women quite far from camp.

These findings are foreshadowed in the literature. Woodburn comments that boys successfully hunt birds and small game. Jelliffe et al. (1962: 908) claim "it is not uncommon for a boy of 10 to be able to shoot enough birds and small game to feed himself and for such a child to leave his parents and join another band". Many authors mention foraging by children accompanying women to gather berries, roots or baobab (Bleek 1931; McDowell 1981; Obst 1912; Tomita 1966; Vincent 1985; Woodburn 1968 and Woodburn and Hudson 1966). Bleek (1931: 279) comments that the "appellation workers for the big girls and boys is deserved; it is their duty to fetch water and wood; when game has been shot the lads must carry it to the huts." Among these authors, Cooper and Obst are the only ones to have worked primarily in Tliika, like us. While Cooper (1949) comments on the great numbers of children, he discusses only the archery of small boys. Obst (1912) describes women and children going to the bush at seven each morning, and returning with roots, berries, and baobab. He does not specify whether they go together or separately. We conclude from these reports that foraging by Hadza children is nothing new.

It seems clear that there was a substantial difference in the amount of foraging done by Hadza children and by !Kung children. Despite this striking difference in "work," there is little difference in play. In both cultures, one can observe much social play: rough and tumble, dramatic play, and some formal games with rules. Children in both cultures sing and dance. Hadza children in particular hold long, noisy song and dance sessions in the evenings, especially if there are some young teenage girls in camp. The reader must not suppose that Hadza children's foraging is accompanied by a lack of play or by any particular solemnity even while foraging. Children's foraging is conducted with more enthusiasm, pride, and humor than adult foraging.

### The Environments

Two features of these environments seemed significant to us even before we conducted the fieldwork reported here. It is relatively easy to navigate in Hadza country and very difficult in !Kung country. Distribution of water is very different during the dry season. For the !Kung, there are a few well known and substantial water holes where the calcrete (caliche) is penetrated on major "underground water courses"; for the Hadza, there are many small water holes dotted all over the hills, some in "stream beds" and dry rivers, hand dug anew each camp move, some at the foot of a slope or rock, some in baobab trees.

Like others before us, we accept that the different water distribution shapes the annual schedule. !Kung are tied to the few major water sources for their lengthy dry season, moving away into the bush when rain leaves pools of water in the bush. Hadza are able to move camp more easily, at any time of year, and are reported by Woodburn to move very frequently.

The 9000 sq. km. Dobe area (Yellen and Lee 1976) shows a "parallel structure" of soil types, dunes, and valleys. Lines of sand dunes (bearing the mongongo nut groves) run approximately west-southwest and east-southeast, parallel with low lying "molapos" that contain water in the wet season, but not quite parallel to two main valleys. These two valleys, the !Kangwa valley and the /Xai/xai valley, contain significant amounts of underground water capped with calcrete, partly covered with hardpan soil. Seven of the nine permanent, dry season water holes in the Dobe area lie in these two valleys. The water holes occur where the calcrete is penetrated by natural or man made apertures. We refer to the !Kangwa valley and the /Xai/xai valley collectively as "underground water courses."

Dry season camps are located along these "underground water courses" within a mile of accessible permanent water. !Kung forage out from camp over great distances, collecting roots and berries en route as well as the highly localized staple, mongongo nuts. Lee (1979: 92–96) defines four habitat types or "associations" of plants, soil, and altitude. Highest are dunes on which mongongo nut trees grow, with loose reddish soil. Intermediate are "flats" with loose reddish and white soil, where productive berry bushes grow. Two kinds of "lowland" habitat are molapos, hollows between dunes with gray harder soil, and hardpan, in the calcrete capped major underground water courses.

The country is very flat. Views of the distant Aha hills, which "rise only 100 metres above the surrounding plain" (Lee 1979: 87), are rare. The flatness, and the thickness of the bush (even the small berry bushes severely limit visibility), mean that the traveller walks along in a small circle of visibility, with the bush always close at hand. !Kung camps of the 1960s, when Draper made her observations of children, were small, relatively insubstantial places, often with the bush growing up against the backs of the huts, except in dry season (probably the most important season for our argument), when people burned off vegetation outside the village to avoid having wild bushfires burn their camp. Even in the dry season, when people approach a known camp placed in a burned out area, they do not actually see the huts until they come close. The Kalahari terrain is flat or gradually undulating on a scale of five to ten kilometers, but on a scale of one-half to one kilometer, it incorporates swales and hummocks. This factor, together with the flatness and thickness of the bush, makes it oddly featureless. On foot the lay of the land is not at all obvious. Everyday examples of how the !Kung themselves recognize the featurelessness of their environment are easy to cite. Favorite playthings for !Kung children were termite hills, usually not more than eight to ten feet high. Children climbed to the top and exclaimed about how far they could see, apparently meaning that for the first time in days they could get a glimpse of the horizon. When women gather nuts in the mongongo groves, they separate into several parties of two or three collectors. Once divided up and out of each other's sight, the women of the different parties sing a characteristic song, which they say is for the purpose of keeping oriented to the other foragers.

In contrast, expansive vistas are common where Blurton Jones, Hawkes, and O'Connell (1989) worked with the Hadza, in a ridge of hills rising to 1551 meters between the flat and open Yaida valley and the Lake Eyasi basin (at about 1020 meters). Hadza often camp near the western edge of these hills and have views of Lake Eyasi, the rift valley escarpment (35 kilometers to the northwest and rising to 1900 meters), and of Oldeani mountain (70 kilometers to the north; at 3214 meters, this mountain rises some 2200 meters above the lake). The hills are dissected by many small streambeds and pocked with small rocky outcrops. The open woodland is in most places well forested with giant Baobab trees (up to thirty-two baobab trees per square kilometer). There are many small dry season water sources dotted over the hills. The choice of available dry season camp sites is immense. Women and children forage very near camp (women average twenty-five minutes walking to a gathering site; the range is four to sixty minutes), and they decide beforehand whether to pursue roots, berries, or baobab; thus they have particular locations in mind when they set off. The study area covers approximately 300 sq. km. of the total Hadza country area of 2500 sq. km. Although a camp can be invisible literally until a visitor has arrived, the pedestrian has an endless sequence of slopes, kopjies, stream beds, and baobab trees during the journey by which to chart a course.

Although Hadza country is much more heavily wooded than the better known rift valley localities, the walker nearly always can see something big, standing out as a beacon in one or another direction. One can look back and see where one has been, and forward and see where one is going. In the Kalahari, however, navigation by these means is not possible. With each step the bush closes behind one, and the vegetation and the unfolding vistas are less varied.

Two other differences between the environments could be important. There is much more shade available in Hadza country, so much digging is conducted in thick bush in dense shade and an observer has only the problem of selecting the best shade and the best view. In !Kung country, the observer of foraging women and children quickly gives up the quest for shade. Small children, for example, literally crouch in the shade cast by their own mother's bodies while the mothers dig. Plant foods may be distributed more patchily in Hadza country, or may contain a greater supply of resources in each patch. Hadza women and children often set off with a definite target location in mind, and once they settle down to dig, they do not travel much more. !Kung women change gathering locations more or less constantly while they forage. Even in the mongongo groves, they stop only briefly at each tree. These descriptions suggest that if !Kung children were trying to forage, they would have to go further and move from patch to patch more often than Hadza children. Both conditions would increase the risks apparent from these descriptions and hypothesized below.

### Hypotheses

In planning the fieldwork, we set out the following propositions:
1. The differences in the landscape suggest that it may be easier for children to get lost in the Dobe area.
2. Since !Kung adults are reported to travel increasingly far to

gather food, when anchored to dry season water (Lee 1979: 175, 191–92), significant returns for foraging only may be found far from camp. To match Hadza children's returns in the dry season, !Kung adults or children might have to travel very far from camp.

3. Assuming that predators stay clear of human habitation, the risks from predators might be greater when children have to travel far to forage productively.

4. Risks from exhaustion and heat stress might be greater on long journeys with little shade than on short journeys.

## Procedures

Several procedures were employed to pursue the first three hypotheses:

1. Interviews of older !Kung about children: these provided evidence about the costs of foraging, and actual accounts of children getting lost.

2. Experimental in-patch foraging to examine potential benefits from foraging in different locations: we took adults, teens, and children by truck into the bush to forage, and then we measured the amounts of food acquired by each person.

3. Quadrats surveying plant foods, and tracks of domestic livestock, people, predators, and game animals: these allowed us to examine such factors as the availability of food and the distribution of predators.

Here we report the findings from the interviews, which give us a good indication of the potential costs of !Kung children's foraging. The results of the other procedures will be reported elsewhere.

## Interviews: Evidence About Potential Costs of Children's Foraging

We wanted to see what the !Kung had to say about children foraging in "the old days" (and about other issues regarding location of food and the work levels of older women). Seven interviews were conducted by Draper (numbered consecutively 1 through 7), with nine people (four women, one man, and two couples) aged 40 to 80 years, with one or both coauthors in attendance. The interviews gave such a consistent pattern that it seemed unnecessary to keep Draper from her primary tasks to interview more people.

In each interview we began by asking whether in the old days children had collected food. We followed the informants' flow of conversation, but took care to insert questions to cover the following issues: Did children go into the bush to forage? Did they go without adults? Why not? When informants stated that adults told children to stay in camp and warned them of dangers in the bush, we asked whether these dangers were real, or whether they were something to tell children to make them obey. Next, we asked whether the informant knew any cases of children getting lost, and asked for the details-which were given at length without further prompting.

Since it is difficult to score interview data objectively, and easy to read into it what one hopes or expects to find, we quote our interviews at length under the headings of our question topics. The comments of these informants shed some light on related topics of !Kung life – particularly women's lives, making a little more plausible the suggestions of Blurton Jones and Sibly (1978) about the physical exertion and stress involved in foraging.

## Results

### Did Children Forage?

The interviews indicate that children stayed in camp in the dry season, but if food was close, such as in the rainy season, children did some gathering with adults and teenagers.

Interview 1. "If mother is gathering someplace close she takes them."
Interview 2. "It is so far they get tired. The walking is too far for them, and makes them tired. It's the distance that keeps children at home." Did children ever go? "No, they stay and play at the village." In the wet season? "In the rainy season food is close. Two kinds of food are close. Then children do go and get it." Don't elders call them back? "No because they can still see them. If they see one going too far, they call that one back and say `no, you have to stay close.' Some other day all [mothers and children] go off together." "Mothers are the ones who go far."
Interview 4. If they get hungry . . . ? "Older children [indicating a girl of twelve to fourteen years] would go. But here, where we are living now, there is no food close. It is far and so they give up, they can't get it when it is far." Before, would they go? "Children this age are fearful. They don't go by themselves."

## Foraging With Children is Inefficient

The problems associated with taking a child to the bush were spontaneously mentioned by several informants.
Interview 1. "The trouble is they cry and say `let's go back.' So you see this and don't let them come." "Thirst makes them cry." "The sun is hot."
Interview 7. "Thirst. Adults cause them to fear thirst and so children stay." About taking children to bush – wasn't that hard? "It was heavy but that's the way I've done it. One on my side, one on my shoulder, and the food behind. But what is really nice is when you feel the weight of food only. That's light."

## Why Did Children Stay in Camp? Why Didn't They Go on Their Own?

Informants volunteered that children feared getting lost and that adults indoctrinated them with this fear.
Interview 1. "Children fear they will get lost. If there is food in camp you leave it for them." "Adults tell them not to go into bush because they will get lost and thirsty."
Interview 5. "Older people and big children keep watch on them. Older children keep them close in the village, tell them if you go out you get lost."
Interview 7. What if little children go alone? "Little children don't. They will get lost. They still can't differentiate things – their eyes don't see well yet. There are big trees and lots of leaves. Too much vegetation. Even older children can get lost."

## What Do They Fear and is it a Realistic Fear?

Adults themselves fear that children would get lost if they left camp, and regard getting lost as very dangerous to children.
Interview 4. Is it true that it is dangerous out in the bush? "The adults are telling a true thing, because even if children don't see these things (leopards and lions) they will get lost."
Interview 5. "Its a true thing. Elders feel responsible and tell them."
Interview 6. What is it that the elders fear? "Getting lost. They think that if the children are alone together they will get lost. Once the child is lost he dies." What is it that kills the child? "Hunger, thirst and cold."

*Cases of Lost Children*

After the above issues had been discussed we asked whether the informants knew of any child who had gotten lost. Eight cases were reported. With one exception, it was easy to tell which cases were repeated reports of previous cases given to us by other informants. In nearly every case a search party was organized. Some children were not found until they had slept 1 – 2 nights in the bush. Two died. (These cases were examined and resolved by the local judicial authorities when they occurred.) One woman described her own experience:

Interview 6.(a) "Once when I was a big child I got lost. I remember following back on my own footprints. I cried and was afraid that I was lost. But I found my own footprints. I cried and cried and would stop and listen, walk and cry and stop and listen, and start all over. I was not little, by then I was a big child [she uses a term that means prepubertal]. No one was looking for me that time. But as I came close to the village I heard people calling me from the village. They were starting to search for me but I came in on my own. I remember running and crying that day and thinking to myself, `I've got to find my own footprints.'" (case 7)

She then reported another case:

Interview 6.(b) "Long ago some children at N//au's village were lost. they were /Gau, Kumsa, and /Oma. They slept one night in the bush and people followed them and found them at !Ubi." Who followed them? "Men. One was my younger brother, /I!ay, and one was Bo Haboutwe. They followed the boys' footsteps to !Ubi and brought them back to their village." How old were these boys then? "Some were like kxau [5 to 6 years old]. The other two were about 10 years old." What were they doing when they got lost? "They were running around playing and eating tree resin and they got lost." (case 8)

Most seemed to think predators were not much of a threat to children, though they expected children to be frightened by them, and everyone had heard of adults being killed or seriously injured. One case was reported in which a child was killed by a leopard at a water hole.

*Conclusions From the Interviews*

Two things stand out from these interviews: the fear of children getting lost, and the distance to food. The interviews seem to confirm that in the dry season, food was far away and children under fourteen did not forage, though they sometimes did in the wet season and whenever food was nearby; and that children who accompanied their mothers were handicaps to foraging. The risks to children who do get lost are extremely high (two deaths out of eight cases), and thus worth the adults' efforts to ensure that the children do not get lost.

The interviews were extraordinarily consistent, despite that they were conducted in several different villages, and with men and women. Other investigators have found the !Kung to be objective and reliable informants on factual data (Howell 1979; Draper [repeat reproductive histories taken from the same informants]; Blurton Jones and Konner 1976), but it is easy for the researcher to find what is desired or expected in this kind of material. However, no informant or bystander made any remarks to the effect that children had no need to forage because adults easily could provide all they need. And no one suggested that children could forage, easily or safely or that they often could forage near camp.

We regard the cases of lost children as accounts of real events. Not only were several of them independently confirmed by informants in different villages, but the case of a Herero child who died in Namibia was told in identical form to Konner and Blurton Jones in 1970. Konner and Blurton Jones also witnessed a panic-stricken instant mobilization of the camp at Dobe in 1970, when a mother realized that she did not know the location of her daughter (aged about five). People shouted for the child, a tracking party set out instantly, donkeys were saddled up. The child was found quickly with older children, about 20 meters beyond the edge of camp. Draper (1976: 207) describes a similar incident in 1969:

> One afternoon at #To//gana I was sitting with five women and a few infants. We were all huddled in the shade thrown by a single hut. It was almost too hot to talk; we all sat listlessly, waiting for the sudden lifting of the heat which came everyday at about 5:30 pm. Suddenly one woman jerked herself to a sitting position, neck arched, eyes darting to all directions. "Listen . . . listen!" she whispered. "Where are the children?" All the women leapt to their feet, looking about and calling to other people sitting farther off in the village. About that time we heard a child's voice calling in the distance and looking in that direction we saw the missing children [aged five, four, and nine] . . . who were walking through the bush toward the camp. The wave of alarm which had

galvanized the women, raised them from torpor, and scattered them twelve or more metres in a few seconds, subsided immediately.

It is impossible to overstate the degree of panic expressed by !Kung on these occasions.

We regard the interviews as highly suggestive evidence about the ecological issues. We conclude that these interviews support the observations of Draper and give us good reason to think that the distance from camp to food (particularly in the dry season) and the risks of getting lost were real contributors to the behavior of !Kung parents and children.

## Potential Benefits From Foraging: Comparison of !Kung and Hadza Children's Returns

Blurton Jones, Hawkes, and O'Connell (1989) found that Hadza children aged 5 to 10 years obtained 629 kilogram calories (kcal) per hour from collecting and processing baobab, and 163 kcal per hour digging roots; children aged 10 to 15 years get 1014 kcal per hour from baobab, 559 kcal per hour from roots, and 339 kcal per hour from honey. These measures, collected from spontaneous pursuits of only one resource at a time, include travel time and processing time.

Hadza children mostly forage within a quarter mile of camp and usually much closer, within sight, or at least within earshot. (We should interview Hadza, of course, about risks to children, although they show no concern when small children are out of camp, out of sight, or at an unknown location; foraging within sight or sound of camp seems to pose little risk of getting lost.)

Previous efforts to quantify !Kung foraging returns match those that we will be reporting. Hawkes and O'Connell calculate returns for a six hour mongongo nut trip (using figures from Lee 1968 and Lee 1979) at 670 kcals per hour. Sih and Milton (1982) show how this can reach 1302 kcals hour in the rainy season when the presence of water allows people to camp in the nut groves. It is important to remember that our data collection was conducted in the dry season, the season that we expect to be the most crucial for feeding children. O'Connell and Hawkes's 670 calories per hour is a little lower than the 725 that we calculate for hypothetical trips to Dobe nut grove, based on returns from foraging in more productive nut groves. This close agreement suggests that returns for mongongo nuts have not decreased significantly over the intervening years.

The data show rather firmly that Hadza children routinely get higher returns than !Kung adults, without having to travel far from camp. To match Hadza children's foraging returns, !Kung have to go at least as far as Dobe nut grove. Thus, !Kung children that attempted to get reasonable returns would risk getting lost.

### An Exception That Proves the Rule: The Boys of Bate

Lee (1979) supports a different view of !Kung children's foraging (elaborated in his dependent:producer ratio argument), as follows:

> Let us look more closely at LG 14/73. Here 13 adults lived with 16 children, but 5 of those children were strong lads aged 10 to 14, who made a real contribution to the food quest. Plate 3.3 shows the boys after a day's gathering in July 1973 bringing a load of marula nuts into camp. I suspect that had these boys been in a more typical living group, they would not have been working to provide food at such an early age. But the fact that they WERE working pinpoints the existence in the majority of !Kung camps of an unutilized reserve of labor power. (Lee 1979: 71; emphasis his)

We did not have Lee's book in the field, so we were unsure where Lee's observation took place. Our observations on this matter had, for us, a tantalizing air of blind prediction about them.

Within sight of the !Kung camps and water hole at Bate there are several marula trees and some baobabs. From the camp where Draper was interviewing an old lady we could see one baobab and two large marula trees. For the Hadza, this place would be a little sparse on baobabs, but it would be the sort of setting in which Hadza children routinely forage. If distance to food was the powerful factor that we believed it might be, then this would have been the place where !Kung children would forage.

It was. The boys in Lee's photograph (Plate 3.3) were from camp LG 14/73. Table 3.17 shows that camp LG 14/73 was at Bate. We think the boys of Bate were the exception that proved our rule as well as Lee's: !Kung children didn't forage because food was usually too far away. These boys did forage, because their food was near at hand. Obviously, our interpretation differs from Lee's; we doubt that these boys would be foraging if the nut trees were not so near at hand. Their parents might be working harder, or the children might be fewer, or less well nourished.

## Discussion

*Conclusions*

What would happen if !Kung children were to try to forage from dry season camps in a habitat like that surrounding the !Kangwa water course? The data from our foraging experiments suggest that they would get very little food, and the data reported here suggest they would run serious risks of getting lost.

Do the likely costs and benefits from children's foraging differ between the !Kung and the Hadza? Much greater returns are obtained by Hadza children, foraging right on their doorstep. For even adult !Kung to achieve similar return rates to Hadza children aged 5 to 10 years collecting baobab (or Hadza children of 10 to 15 years digging roots), adult !Kung must travel as far as Dobe nutgrove, 5.5 to 6 kilometers each way. Hadza children get higher foraging returns and appear to run much lower risks.

The interviews show a striking concern by adult !Kung about children getting lost, even when they do not try to go far. The risks to lost children evidently are high. The cost of avoiding these risks, sacrificing the very small contribution that a child could make to its food intake, do not seem very high. The small gain in food from encouraging children to forage seems unlikely to outweigh the great risks this entails. Although we have not interviewed Hadza on this topic, they display no concern about children getting lost. We described above our observations of the panic that sweeps a !Kung camp when a mother realizes she does not know where her child has gone. We have never seen such an episode in a Hadza camp. Hypothesized costs, including risks of getting lost or getting exhausted by the heat, must increase as the distance walked from camp grows greater (although the likelihood of encountering predator tracks was the same at any distance). Even if costs were generally the same in the Dobe area as they are in Hadza country, to attain returns comparable to those of the Hadza child, the !Kung child, by having to go further, would have to incur higher costs than the Hadza child.

Most of the counterarguments we can anticipate concern our foraging data and thus will be discussed in detail elsewhere. These arguments concern the extent to which our data represent typical or "presettlement" conditions. We acknowledge the difficulties of reconstructing the !Kung dry season environment of the

1950s and 1960s from data collected during two months of the 1988 dry season. Nonetheless, the data show extreme differences between the circumstances in which Hadza children forage and the circumstances in which !Kung children would forage if they did. The payoff for foraging by Hadza children must have been many times the potential payoff for !Kung children at most of the Dobe area dry season camps. This is still far from showing that !Kung parents who persuade their children of 4 to 14 years to stay in camp leave more descendents than those who take the risk of losing their children. But it does show that in exchange for this risk, the risk-taking parents would gain only a very small contribution to the food needed to raise their children.

We think the main reason for this difference is the simple matter of distribution of water holes. In the Dobe area, the richest food sources tend to be far from dry season water (as described by our !Kung informants, and evidenced by our data, and implied by Lee 1979: 175, 191–92, 203). The Dobe area has only nine permanent water holes. We have not counted the water holes in Hadza country, but doubt that we ever could obtain a complete count. We already know many that we and our Hadza hosts use routinely. Most are far too small to support livestock, or a large complex of camps, but there are dozens, close together, all over Tli'ika. If Hadza children were to deplete their resources near camp, it would be easy to move to another water hole.

### The Use of the Concept of Original Affluence

In criticizing "original affluence," we do not intend to turn the clock back to the perception of hunter-gatherer life as "nasty, brutish, and short," which may have excused well-meaning but ultimately brutal attempts to make foragers settle. The Hadza, for example, live as long as the !Kung, and show the same ideals of sharing and equality. And although some younger Hadza men are attracted to the political thrust toward the modern world, the clear majority of Hadza take great pride in their way of life. Nor do we dispute the observation that !Kung spend relatively little time out of camp looking for food.

We claim that the option of foraging is scarcely available to !Kung children in the dry season, that the leisure of !Kung children is forced upon them, and that they are deprived of the Hadza children's opportunity of controlling their own food intake. One still may wish to call this affluence, but it does not seem to make sense to argue that it resulted from a choice of limited wants, since the foraging option seems so unattractive for the !Kung.

However, we can make some use of the "original affluence" concept by thinking about other possible measures of "affluence" besides leisure. Does the Hadza child's control of its food intake enable it to grow fatter, or does the work involved cancel this out, or is the extra energy immediately expended in more energetic play (of which there is plenty), or do the opportunities for parental exploitation result in the Hadza child growing thinner than the !Kung child?

A rigorous test for differences in growth requires access to original data on !Kung children. However, the figures in Howell (1979) for girls, and in Truswell and Hansen (1976), allow some approximate comparisons of heights and weights. It appears that !Kung children are heavier and have a greater weight:height ratio early in life, especially just at that age (two to four years old) when !Kung children are still carried and occasionally suckled, and when Hadza children are being left home and weaned. However, from the age of about ten years, Hadza girls begin to race ahead. These little mothers, substantial providers for their tiny siblings, nephews, and nieces (and similar relatives of their friends), grow rapidly toward the adult difference between !Kung and Hadza. Adult heights are similar, but Hadza women are roughly 8 kilograms heavier than !Kung women (Hiernaux and Hartono 1980). Thus, neither population can be said to choose fatness consistently during development, nor to gain it from their greater leisure or from their greater control of their food intake. This in turn makes us wonder how the culture (or the theory) "decides" which measure of "affluence" to value.

Are there other outcomes of these differences in "affluence" that also may attract the label? By accepting the burden of partly feeding themselves, Hadza children gain the chance of acquiring more siblings, especially as they further assist their mother by helping to provide for their siblings. We were impressed with the core of adult siblings that sometimes formed the basis of a camp, and wondered whether there were advantages to having more siblings. Our 1985 census data show that women with more siblings have more live children ($r = 0.42$, $n = 35$, $p < .05$). (This effect does not seem to be the result of one's age but it could arise from regional differences in fertility.) But perhaps finally Hadza children get something for all that work!

The idea of "affluence" sent us in two interesting directions that other arguments had not suggested. But these explorations show us that the concept of affluence cannot be applied consistently across the board. If there is a "cultural" choice of limited wants, there is also a cultural choice by the !Kung of fatter children, and thinner teenagers and adults, and less chance of large numbers of helpful siblings. Which outcome would we predict that a culture would choose first? How could the concept of "original affluence" help us make this prediction? Perhaps every culture has its own idiosyncratic choice of a mixture of outcomes. Given this possibility, the explanatory value and even the summarizing value of the concept of "original affluence" is shrinking very fast!

The same might be true for other "idealist" explanations of the differences between Hadza and !Kung. For example, in conversation with fellow anthropologists, we have heard the argument that !Kung have few children and long interbirth intervals because !Kung society does not value children. Such an argument is used frequently in discussions of fertility differences and transitions. The logic used in this argument is not immediately clear, but let us suppose that an everyday usage of "valuing children" is intended, based on a personal and culture-bound intuition. We quickly get into trouble: if !Kung don't value children, why do they treat them so well and protect them so carefully, and why do they say that God is stingy with children – allowing one to have too few (Howell 1976: 147) and taking back too many? The list of differences that we attempt to account for in the next section aggravates the problem for "original affluence" and for "valuing children." In a society that values leisure or does not value children, would we expect men to have more or less effect on the survival of children, and to share more or less interests with women? Let us turn to what we think are more rigorous and productive arguments.

*Predicting and Explaining Differences Between the Hadza and the !Kung: Consequences of the Difference in Children's Foraging Opportunities*

A central aim of anthropology is to explain differences between human populations. Explanations that refer to extrinsic factors, like the environment, can avoid circular argument, appeals to random processes, and explanations that beg the question, disguising the fact that they require still further explanation. For example, if the explanation for low fertility in a certain population is said to be that the society does not value children, an additional explanation is necessary as to why that society does not value children. Or, if the higher work rate of Hadza women is explained on the grounds that they lack the values of "original affluence," then one must explain why they lack those values. It is also good to pursue one paradigm at a time, and to refrain from using a variety of explanatory principles. These invite post hoc shifts from one principle to another (the aspect of eclecticism that so dismays Harris).

In this study we claim to have anchored the difference in children's foraging to some simple environmental factors that distribute food far from water in the !Kung case, and intermingle food and water in the Hadza case; and that make it difficult for !Kung children to find their way, and easy for Hadza children to find their way. We thus claim that the option of foraging is costly and unrewarding for !Kung children in the dry season, and that they are deprived of the Hadza children's opportunity to control their own food intake. If !Kung parents wanted their children to forage, there would be little advantage and much risk.

We believe that we can derive a series of predictable and testable consequences of the difference in children's foraging opportunities when we assume that individuals tend to behave in ways that maximize their fitness or reproductive success (referred to below as the "reproductive strategy," or the "maximization" argument). But Lee's emphasis on the dependent:producer ratio (sometimes linked to "original affluence") can also be developed to provide alternative interpretations of several differences between the Hadza and the !Kung, though, unlike maximization, it cannot explain variation in the dependent:producer ratio itself. Here we wish to compare the application of these alternative principles to differences between the Hadza and the !Kung. The comparison should be examined at two levels. At the level of data it enables us to derive contrasting predictions about how Hadza might differ from !Kung. At the level of methodology, the two starting assumptions perform differently: the dependent:producer argument seems to need more additional principles and extrinsic factors to make it yield predictions.

*The Reproductive Strategy Argument*

Hadza children's ability to acquire food for themselves buffers them from the effects of the withdrawal or reduction of parental support. This buffer enables mothers to divert resources to the production of other children, with less risk to the survival of existing children than would be incurred by a !Kung mother. Thus, the effects of a decreasing interbirth interval upon mortality should be much less than shown for the !Kung by Blurton Jones (1986). The Hadza woman threatens her child less by inattentive child care, responding less to the child's survival needs and tending more to enlist its labor in caring for younger siblings and running errands for mother. Thus we expected shorter interbirth intervals and higher fertility among the Hadza than among the !Kung, less indulgent child care, and more enlistment of children in errands. Blurton Jones et al. (1992), like Dyson 1977, indicate that fertility is indeed higher than among the !Kung, while mortality remains similar. Our impressions during fieldwork were that Hadza women are much harsher and less indulgent mothers than the !Kung described by Draper and by Konner, and that Hadza children run more errands than do !Kung children.

If one potential component of a man's strategy is to give food to his own children, fathers also may be influenced by children's foraging opportunities. The advantage to the father's reproductive success that accrues from providing for his children might be less if his children have more alternative sources of food. Thus the costs of desertion or of distributing provisions elsewhere in a "show-off" strategy (Hawkes 1990, 1991) may be lower for Hadza fathers than for !Kung fathers. We might expect Hadza men (other things being equal – and they may well not be) to have less effect on their own children's survival than !Kung men might have on the survival of !Kung children. Some relevant data are available.

Although the evidence is indirect, and although there is no proof that the effect is due to food provided by the father, Pennington and Harpending (1988) claim that !Kung fathers have a significant effect on their children's survival. Recently, long after these predictions were committed to paper, we examined how many Hadza children who were under five years old in our 1985 census had survived through 1991. Although death of the mother was associated with a high rate of death of the children, death or departure of the father had no discernible effect (six children died out of the thirty-six who were less than five years old and whose fathers died or left, contrasted with thirteen who died out of fifty-one whose fathers survived and stayed with their mother). Thus this prediction is confirmed. We must note however, that Hadza children and their mothers receive much meat from men other than their fathers or stepfather (as in many hunter-gatherer societies, where meat is shared widely). Our observation is thus much less surprising than that of Pennington and Harpending. (We should also note that these authors found that a mother's "departure," ascertained by whether a man had more than one marriage, showed no effect upon child survival. If we subscribe to their method, then this result is contrary to what we would have expected).

Since Hadza fathers apparently have no effect on the survival of their small children, we might expect them to desert more readily, have shorter marriages, and move on sooner to younger and more fertile new wives, or develop additional liasons more than !Kung men do. Woodburn (1968b) emphasizes the ease with which Hadza marriages end. Much more work is needed to decide the logical expectations about marriage duration and who leaves first, and then to extract the relevant data.

Greater differences between the reproductive strategies of Hadza men and women could lie behind the separateness of the sexes described by Woodburn and the occasional indications of opposition and sexism (such as "the men's place," and the men's sacred eating ceremony that women are not allowed to see) – characteristics that are not reported among the !Kung. The difference in men's strategies related to costs of "desertion" may account for an apparent difference in hunting. Hadza men seem to hunt large game almost exclusively; small prey are ignored or eaten in the field and traps are not used. Although this behavior could be explained by the simple diet breadth model (which would not predict differences in proportion of small game eaten in the bush and not brought home), we might think of it as "prestige" or showing off (Hawkes 1990, 1991; Hawkes, O'Connell, Blurton Jones 1991), and contrast it with a stronger tendency in !Kung men to bring home small prey that will make a useful contribution to their household if not to the entire camp. The !Kung elaboration of traps and specialized devices for capturing animals as small as the spring hare might be related to this difference. We have not observed Hadza spontaneously use traps, and according to Obst (1912), the Hadza consider traps to be "unmanly."

While our impressions concur with Woodburn's account of the sexes as being very separated in Hadza society, we have yet to test for differences in duration of marriages, or for any measures of the separation of the sexes other than the greater spatial separation reported by O'Connell et al. (1991). Our data do not match the impression that the diets of men and women are distinct, which the reader could gain from Woodburn (1968a), or Woodburn and Hudson (1966). Furthermore, Woodburn (personal communication) pointed out that our data on Hadza children's foraging comes from only one region of Hadza country, and we are at risk of explaining the "sexism" that is rather general to Hadza society by a very local phenomenon.

Indeed our own impression, stimulated by suggestions from a Hadza informant, was that baobab (the most productive resource for children) were less available in other parts of Hadza country. If this were a real difference, there would be interesting predictions to test about the costs of children. However, we could not explain Hadza "sexism" by reference to our existing data (though even without baobab, Hadza children still might be cheaper to raise than !Kung children).

However, our data came from a region that contained one third of the population of eastern Hadza. In addition, recent results of an aerial survey show that baobab trees are more widely spread than we had realized, and thus may have been available to most Hadza children.

### The Dependent: Producer Argument

The explanations and expectations given by the dependent:producer argument could begin thus: since Hadza are more fertile than !Kung and have about the same mortality as !Kung, they have more dependents per producer. Thus Hadza women must work longer hours (they do spend longer hours in the bush foraging, according to Hawkes, O'Connell, and Blurton Jones [1989]), and may be too busy to be as indulgent and responsive to their children as !Kung parents. Children must work to help feed the greater number of dependents, and run errands because mother is short of time.

This leads to two predictions. If the dependent:producer ratio determines that Hadza children must forage to help their overworked mothers, then children in small or widely spaced Hadza families should work less; and short interbirth intervals should aggravate the problem still further, posing a greater threat to the survival of the Hadza child than to the !Kung child whose mother is said to be able to expand her work hours and enlist help ("spare productive capacity") from her children. We thus derive almost the opposite prediction about the effect of interbirth intervals upon mortality in the two populations. However, unlike the reproductive strategy argument, the dependent:producer ratio does not predict how the length of the interbirth interval might be adjusted in response to an increase in mortality.

Lee's discussion of the dependent:producer ratio leaves us needing an explanation for variation in fertility. Elsewhere, Lee (1972a, 1979) has accounted for long !Kung interbirth intervals and low fertility by a model of the work entailed in carrying children while foraging, visiting, and moving camp. The foraging journeys entail a feedback between number of children and work (upon which Blurton Jones and Sibly [1978] based their extension of Lee's [1972a] model) which would make the use of the dependent:producer argument to explain fertility part of a circular argument. If work is used to explain fertility, then fertility cannot be used to explain work. However, we could call on a new "extrinsic factor," based on Harpending's suggestions about diseases of the reproductive tract (venereal disease), and propose that Hadza fertility is less impaired by venereal disease than is !Kung fertility.

We can apply the dependent:producer ratio argument to fathers. High Hadza fertility leads to overworked mothers and children. Then the effect on a child's survival from a father who feeds it should be greater among the Hadza than among the !Kung, the reverse of our prediction from reproductive strategy arguments, and the reverse of what apparently is observed. But the dependent:producer argument gives us no reason to expect men to be interested in their children's survival or to be influenced by the effort needed by women and children to feed themselves. If we borrow this assumption from the strategy argument, or call upon "common sense" (another new unexplained principle, inevitably culture-bound), we would have to predict that Hadza men do more to enhance their children's survival, perhaps by having longer and more monogamous marriages and by directing more of the food that they obtain to their wife and children. (Neither the predictions nor the findings may be so clear: Hadza men bring in more meat than !Kung men, which we might decide fits with dependent:producer expectations, but little of the meat in children's diets may be due to living with their fathers, as opposed to being in a camp with good hunters, according to Hawkes, O'Connell, and Blurton Jones [1991].)

While the dependent:producer argument contains no explicit implications about how we expect men to respond to the effect of their provisioning upon child survival, we can draw in another interesting factor to account for the proposed differences between Hadza and !Kung men. Hypergamy (the tendency of women to marry richer neighbors, which Bailey [1988] suggests is a challenge confronting all contemporary hunter-gatherer men) appears to be a greater threat to !Kung men than to Hadza men. We might suggest that one way !Kung men can attract and keep wives in competition with the much richer Bantu men is to emphasize provisioning and domesticity. This directs us to a new puzzle: why would !Kung women so readily give up their famous leisure to marry Bantu? Why would Hadza women so seldom flee, and so often return to, their long work hours and sexist society?

The dependent:producer argument and the reproductive strategy argument thus give some contrasting predictions that are testable. The dependent:producer argument requires more explanations (about fertility, hypergamy, how men would be expected to react to busy wives and hungrier children) to be added to the argument to account for all the differences. It is also not clear that the dependent:producer argument could have been used a priori to generate hypotheses, in the absence of the challenge provided by the reproductive strategy argument. We also should not lose sight of the evidence presented in this paper that !Kung children seldom represented "spare productive capacity." The observation upon which the dependent:producer argument was founded seems to be explained easily by the foraging opportunities available. In contrast, the models and concepts of evolutionary ecology guide research toward a series of differences, which can be accounted for by a very small number of processes. Posthoc arguments using concepts such as "original affluence," when compared to arguments based on evolutionary ecology or to cultural ecology's dependent:producer argument, seem ill suited to explaining the differences between Hadza and !Kung behavior.

# Part 4

## Social Stratification

# Editorial

Social stratification may be defined as the particular type of role differentiation that distinguishes between higher and lower standing according to one or more criteria (Levy 1966: 149–50).[1] In most of the literature on hunter-gatherers, the subject is conspicuous by its absence. The reason for this absence was implied recently by Richard Lee (1992: 31), who wrote that "politically, gatherer-hunters are usually labeled as 'band' or 'egalitarian' societies in which social groups are small, mobile, and unstratified, and in which differences of wealth and power are minimally developed." In other words, there is no need to discuss stratification since there is so little of it. Like Elman Service (1979: 3) before him, Lee then briefly notes that there are some significant exceptions to this generalization, and proceeds to ignore them (see also Lee 1990: 231, 239). A more informative, although otherwise similar, characterization was presented by Barnard and Woodburn (1988: 7), who wrote that "social differentiation by age, and differentiation by sex, are frequently the only dimensions in which dominance is evident in hunting and gathering societies."

There is no question that some hunter-gatherer societies were characterized by very little, if any, stratification. Examples include several groups of pygmies (Turnbull 1978, 1981), the !Kung (Lee 1979: 244–48; 1981a), the G/wi (Silberbauer 1982), and the Hadza (Woodburn 1979, 1982) in Africa, and the western Shoshone (Thomas 1981) in North America. The situation is somewhat more complicated among Eskimos of the eastern and central Canadian Arctic (Briggs 1982; Damas 1963: 46 ff.; Rouland 1979), Australian Aborigines (Bern 1979; Edwards 1987; Hiatt

1. Flanagan (1989) recently published an excellent summary of issues relating to stratification in hunter-gatherer societies. His review had a different purpose than the present one, but we consider his views congenial to those expressed here. Another relevant survey was conducted by Paynter (1989).

1965; Keen 1989; Kolig 1989; Meggitt 1966; Sharp 1958; Tonkinson 1988), and even some Basarwa groups (Cashdan 1980). However, these peoples hardly cover the entire range of hunter-gatherer variation.

Among the northwest Alaskan Eskimos, for example, there is evidence of incipient ranking (Burch 1975: 205 ff.; 1980: 264 ff.; Sheehan 1985), and ranking was quite pronounced among hunter-gatherers around much of the North Pacific rim (Arnold 1992; Koyama and Thomas, eds. 1981; Townsend 1980; 1985). It is important to note that these so-called "exceptions" to the hunter-gatherer pattern of stratification not only lived exclusively by hunting, fishing, and gathering, but that many were not even in indirect contact with agrarian peoples until they first encountered Europeans. Finally, we must note the Calusa, a society in southern Florida characterized by both a foraging economy and a fully developed class system (Marquardt 1988; Widmer 1988).

Any comprehensive model of stratification among foragers must deal with the entire range of variation within the class, not with just part of it. Such a model has yet to be devised. At an intermediate level, however, there has been some stimulating work on how simple hunter-gatherers evolve into complex hunter-gatherers, a transformation in which increasing stratification plays a crucial part.[2] This type of work is exemplified by the entire set of papers in the volume edited by Price and Brown (1985), as well as by the paper by Hayden presented in this volume.

Virtually every author who has addressed the subject agrees that the transformation from simple to relatively complex hunter-gatherer societies depends on the presence of a suitably large local resource base of native plants and animals, and on the ability to exploit it effectively. Beyond that, attention focuses variously on population pressure (Cohen 1981, 1985; Keeley 1988), ability to store foods ("delayed-return") (Barnard and Woodburn 1988; Testart 1982; Woodburn 1982), patterned resource clumping (Schalk 1981), sedentism (Ames 1991; Brown 1985; Kelly 1991; Renouf 1991), and intensification (Ames 1985; Basgall 1987; Bender 1981; Bouey 1987; Lourandos 1985, 1988). We suspect that the feedback loops among these variables are so tight that they will

---

2. This focus is in contrast to the usual interest, which is the transformation of foraging societies into agrarian systems. See Bender (1990) for a useful discussion of stratification on both sides of the hunter/farmer boundary.

all have to be taken into account in any defensible theory of how and why foraging societies increase in complexity. It is interesting, however, that none of these theories takes into account the possible motivations of real people. That deficiency is remedied here in Hayden's paper.

The focus in Hayden's paper is competition – among individuals and families, for goods, and for control over other people's labor. This is in direct opposition to the view generally expressed on this subject. To most authors "egalitarian patterns of sharing; strong anti-authoritarianism; [and] an emphasis on the importance of cooperation in conjunction with great respect for individuality" are part of the essence of the forager way of life (Leacock and Lee 1982: 7–8; see also Ingold 1980: 144–62; Kaplan and Hill 1985). Winterhalder (1986) and Bettinger (1991: 124) have even demonstrated mathematically why this must be so. However, Burch (1988a) and Gould (1982), among others, have pointed out that the empirical situation does not always confirm that model even among relatively simple foragers. Barnard and Woodburn (1988: 27) have cautioned further that ubiquitous sharing is more characteristic of immediate-return systems than it is of delayed-return systems. Among the relatively complex hunter-gatherers studied by Hayden, competition was at least as much a fact of life as sharing.

Hayden begins with an insight first expressed by Cowgill (1975) to the effect that, in a rich enough environment, the prospect of gain through competition may occur even among foragers. In other words, where there is a real possibility of acquiring more wealth or more power than one's fellows, at least some people are likely to compete with others in order to get it. After just a few people have competed with even modest success, some sort of stratified system comes into existence. Hayden shows us how this process worked in the interior of British Columbia.

# 10

# Competition, Labor, and Complex Hunter-Gatherers

*Brian Hayden*

The main argument of this paper is that socioeconomic competition occurs only where adequate basic subsistence is guaranteed for all. The competitive feast is proposed as the primary mechanism for converting surpluses into storable wealth and for creating socioeconomic inequalities and competition. Where labor is an additional constraint on wealth-related resource acquisition, attempts can be anticipated to expand production by increasing the size of the production group. In these communities, economic competition and attempts to maximize control over key resources generally lead to the disenfranchisement of weaker members of the community, resulting in a "poor" segment of society denigrated by more powerful members.

Cultural ecology has tended to adopt the same perspectives that have rendered population and evolutionary ecology powerful paradigms in the natural sciences. The models used in cultural ecology, such as genetic self-interest, optimal foraging strategies, ecological systems, and territoriality, and even the basic units of measurement and conceptualizations of resources are derived from natural ecological studies. While borrowing models from natural ecology studies has generated very important insights, it sometimes has created conceptual blinders that have deterred anthropological researchers from developing their own cultural ecological theories, particularly in areas of human behavior that lack direct analogs in nonhuman species. Such is the case in approaches to competition, particularly among hunter- gatherers. This paper is an ecological exploration of competition (and complexity) among hunter-gatherers.

There are many kinds of competition in human societies: competition for mates, for social recognition, affection, ritual leadership, knowledge, territory, and for virtually every esteemed or

223

necessary role, resource, and service. Perhaps because of the many disparate contexts and goals of competition, relatively little insightful or nomothetic modeling of this aspect of human behavior has been attempted (some notable exceptions include Dyson-Hudson and Smith 1978; Vayda 1974, 1976; and others). Perhaps because of the inherent complexity in ethnographic accounts of competition and because of the paucity of modeling of competition, many ethnologists have adopted ecological models of competition from the natural sciences. In these models, competition occurs largely as a result of scarcity. Examples of such models for cultural groups come readily to mind – Turnbull's (1972) documentation of the Ik, tribal confrontations and displacements in the Australian Western Desert during severe droughts recorded by Strehlow (1965), and the numerous cases cited by Dirks (1980) in his famine studies. It is important to note that none of these cases of competition involved stabilized man-land relationships. All of them involved the dramatic deterioration of resources far below what might be considered expectable.

However, as early as 1975, Cowgill (1975) suggested that a much different scenario actually might account for the vast majority of human competitive behavior. Specifically, he suggested that the prospect of gain under prosperous conditions was the primary driving force behind most human competition. Thus, the most intense competition in contemporary societies has occurred not between the poorest nations, but between the richest. Cowgill's suggestion has been provocative in the context of my own research on complex hunter-gatherers in the interior of British Columbia, but his suggested relationships find no counterparts in the ecology of the natural sciences. In fact, such suggestions make little sense to most ecologists. I would like to develop Cowgill's suggested model further and show how it can be used to understand some important developments among complex hunter-gatherers.

## The Prosperity Model of Competition

In order to eliminate much of the confusion inherent in the subject, I will deal only with one type of competition: economically based competition, or competition in which economic resources are used either as ends in themselves or as means to gain desired status, power, or control over goods and services. I will not deal with purely ritual competition, competition for mates, artistic competition, or other noneconomically based forms of competition.

In order to make ecological sense of Cowgill's insight, it is necessary to explain why his scenario should operate among human societies but not among societies or species in the rest of the animal kingdom. I suggest that there is, in fact, a critical difference between animal behavior and human behavior. Among animals, resources can be used only for direct metabolic consumption, primarily by the individual that collects them. This places an absolute and relatively low limit on the amount of resources that an individual can use – that is, the amount that an individual can eat. It simply makes no sense to gather or control far more resources than can be consumed under conditions of abundance, because nothing can be done with the excess. Therefore, competition does not develop in animal populations under conditions of resource abundance, only under conditions of scarcity.

In dramatic contrast to this natural scenario, the combination of technology, culture, and social relations among human populations enables people to transform excess resources into other highly desired, scarcer goods and services. I argue that it is this potential that galvanizes entire communities into explosive competitive bouts under the appropriate conditions. This change in the "use potential" of excess resources means fundamentally that a human individual's appetite for resource consumption can be virtually limitless – provided that a means can be devised to transform excess resources into other scarce and desirable commodities. It is this change in the fundamental relationship between individuals and resources that accounts for the type of competition that Cowgill envisions under conditions of prosperity.

## Conditions Promoting Competition

From ecological and cultural studies, there can be no doubt that resource based competition does occur under conditions of rapidly contracting resources, as illustrated in the case of the Ik (Turnbull 1972), and in similar situations noted by Dirks (1980). However, the possibility is now being raised that conditions of abundance can also precipitate intense competition. If both abundance and extreme resource deterioration promote competition, are there any conditions under which economically based competition is maladaptive?

On the basis of the excellent cultural ecological analyses that have been conducted among hunter-gatherers over the past few decades, the answer is clearly affirmative. Where resources are relatively stable but are limited, predictably fluctuating, and vulnerable to over exploitation, economically based competition destroys resources and is self-defeating, if not self-destructive, for communities. In such communities, ownership over critical resources, hierarchical control by some community households over others, and competitive individualistic ethics are rarely tolerated. In contrast, the sharing of access to resources as well as the sharing of procured food in camps and most other possessions is generally mandatory. Among many groups, hunters are even forbidden to take directly any of the game animals that they have killed, or are given the last choice of meat portions in order to curtail any self-aggrandizing behavior that might result from their successful role in the community. Cashdan (1980), Ford (1972, 1977), Gould (1982), Harris (1971), Hayden (1981, 1982), Hennigh (1983), Minc (1986), Spielman (1986), Strehlow (1965), Wiessner (1977), Winterhalder (1986), and Yengoyan (1976), have documented this behavioral complex, and it is now one of the most robust ecological integrative models in the discipline. I refer to communities with these resource and adaptive characteristics as "simple hunter-gatherers" (Hayden 1981).

The proposition that requires more critical examination, since it is not expected by ecologists or functionalists, is the one that states that competition arises under conditions of abundance. There are three aspects of this proposition that I will address. The first deals with theoretical reasons why abundance should lead to competition. The second deals with mechanisms by which abundant resources can be converted to other desirable goods or services. The third aspect involves ethnographic and archaeological examples of abundance leading to competition.

## Theoretical Considerations

The core of my argument is that under conditions of resource abundance, competition will occur if there exists a way to transform abundant resources into highly desired, scarcer goods or services. This concept may be presented as a self-evident axiom.

This is probably the strongest of the theoretical arguments in the prosperity model of competition. However, there are other ecologically based arguments that also might be entertained in its support. Notably, it can be argued that whenever a new resource field or a new resource niche is opened up, it is advantageous for potential competitors to "scramble" to try to monopolize the new resources for themselves and their offspring. If they can exclude others from using the new resources, they will possess selective genetic advantages. These consequences have been well recognized by ecologists as "founder" effects, i.e., the first individuals successful in exploiting new habitats produce all subsequent generations. Thus, under conditions of expanding resources, competition theoretically can be viewed as adaptive, even in these "natural" situations. However, in practical terms, the difference between what a natural organism can control by means of exclusive access and what it can eat may not be very great, which appears to limit the development or expression of competition in such situations.

On the other hand, the cultural ability to produce and utilize excess resources on a regular basis might be viewed as a new resource niche that was hitherto unexploited. As such, some degree of competition over the control and utilization of this new resource niche could be expected for reasons of genetic fitness, just as "founder-effects" competition might be expected to occur between organisms attempting to exploit a new source of energy.

The ability to produce and use excess resources could confer important advantages to individuals and groups exploiting this new niche. Notably, control over extra resources could provide individuals with a larger and more secure support group and with greater reserve resources in times of stress. As the following section will show, individuals could benefit from increased wealth, power, defensive potential, and a greater number of offspring. Where conflict between communities occurred, the use and transformation of excess resources not only allowed communities to control greater absolute amounts of resources, but also structured the flow of energy in a more complex, hierarchical fashion, integrating and coordinating defense and offense. Because of these very real consequences for survival and differential genetic and cultural success, competition over abundant resources could be expected on theoretical grounds.

**Transformation Mechanisms**

The number of pathways that might be used to convert abundant resources into coveted goods and services is potentially unlimited. Practically, however, the number of effective mechanisms appears to be very limited, at least when beginning from a pristine simple hunter-gatherer base. Among simple hunter- gatherers, the major impediment to the transformation of excess resources into scarce goods involves the preexisting egalitarian sharing ethic as well as strong pressures from the majority of the community to preserve access to essential resources, especially during critical periods of shortages. "Functionalist" suggestions as to what mechanisms would be effective in transforming resources often center on trade, irrigation, religious control, ideological control, and military force. In order to evaluate the "functionalist" explanations in contrast to the "exploitative" models proposed by Gilman (1981) and others, I initiated an ethnoarchaeological project in Mesoamerica (Hayden and Gargett 1990). The results clearly indicated that early socio-economic inequality was not based on the functionalist needs of communities. Given the unwillingness of most people in communities to recognize any individual claims of superiority or differential control, functionalist suggestions appear inadequate to account for the abandonment of sharing behavior.

A further problem is how to motivate individuals to produce more than they need and surrender this surplus to someone else under conditions in which everyone's essential needs are met.

These considerations and my work with the Interior Plateau groups of British Columbia have led me to consider two factors to be most important for the transformation of excess resources into desirable goods and services.

*Restriction of Resource Access*

The first is the restriction of access by individuals or subgroups within communities to resources potentially useful in transformations. This may range from the exclusive use or ownership of wild resources procured by an individual, to the exclusive use of specific garden plots and produce on the part of an individual family, to the "ownership" of specific resource locations such as fishing stations by individuals, families, or corporate groups within communities.

If exclusive limited access to resources was anathema to surviving conditions of limited, fluctuating, and vulnerable resource conditions, then forms of resource ownership might be expected to occur only under conditions of more abundance, less fluctuation, and less vulnerability to the excessive exploitation of resources. This has an appealing economic and emic rationale. If I am unwilling to let other individuals exert exclusive access to resources within the community's range or even to let individuals have exclusive access to resources they have harvested or hunted because I fear that such exclusive access may jeopardize my future survival, then it stands to reason that the only conditions under which I will be willing to recognize exclusive use or access to resources will be when I believe that I will have access to enough resources to ensure my future survival. Alternatively, I may allow such selective access and use only if I feel that this use will not have an adverse impact on my own ability to procure resources in the future. These conditions can be met only when resources are abundant and when competition over resources will not lead to significant declines in resource stocks. Matson (1985: 246) similarly has suggested that abundant and reliable but geographically restricted resources are necessary for the development of complex societies with resource ownership or control. I have argued that the effective exploitation of *r*-selected types of resources[1] such as grass seeds and fish can provide a highly abundant resource base that is invulnerable to excessive exploitation where these resources are abundant and where adequate technology exists for effective exploitation and storage (Hayden 1981). Other types of resources such as large numbers of migrating herd animals also may satisfy these conditions.

The Interior Plateau groups situated around the most productive fisheries of the Fraser River provide an example of the exclusive access to and use of important resources within communities. There are two classes of fishing locations. The largest and most productive fisheries, such as the Six Mile fishery near Lillooet, are part of the public domain. No exclusive access is permitted at these sites, presumably because such limited access would deprive large segments of the community of necessary

---

1. The term "*r*-selected" refers to reproduction strategies involving numerous offspring with short maturation times so that populations are resilient to catastrophic environmental effects and high rates of harvesting.

resources. Smaller yet highly productive fishing sites, however, are privately or corporately owned (Romanoff 1985). Exclusive access to such sites does not jeopardize the survival chances of others in the community, for they have adequate access to resources of their own. Moreover, at many of the privately owned fishing places, labor intensive improvements such as platforms have been made by individuals. These improvements generally increase the productivity of the site and in some cases are necessary for any production. Individuals making such improvements logically have a claim on the use of resources procured at the site due to the unusual labor invested in the improvements. However, it is the sheer abundance of resources and lack of adverse impacts on resources that render community members favorably disposed to acknowledge these claims. Moreover, the fact that *r*-selected resources (salmon laying an average of 4,000 eggs per female) were involved that could not be excessively exploited by private ownership or by competition based on their exploitation meant that private ownership of fishing sites would not affect resource abundance in the Lillooet area.

Thus, abundance and invulnerability to excessive exploitation constitute the conditions under which exclusive use and access to resources can be expected to emerge. However, this is a necessary condition only for the emergence of a complex society and competition over resources.

## Competitive Feasts

A second factor also must be present in order to effect the transformation of abundant resources into desired goods and services. The major question is: What mechanisms work and which are most effective? In other words, what motivates people to participate in such resource production and transformation systems? I argue that there must be practical benefits, and that in egalitarian systems, the carrot is far more effective than the stick. Previous suggestions as to the nature of those benefits include trade (Rathje 1972), irrigation (Wittfogel 1957), and defense (Carneiro 1970). Objections have been raised to these and other factors that have been proposed as monocausal factors responsible for socioeconomic inequality. I suggest that there is another more widespread mechanism that has been largely overlooked, which provides the link between excess resources and their transformation into scarcer commodities and services. This mechanism is the competitive feast; it is the carrot that lured communities into complexity.

While feasts probably occur among all hunter-gatherers, they are generally celebratory or exclusively religious in content. The competitive feast differs in that economic resources are explicitly used as a major tool of status competition, and, more important, as a tool for creating debts and thereby exerting hierarchical control over the behavior of other community members. The essential features of the competitive feast, as it is represented in the *moka*, the potlatch, the Mesoamerican cargo system, and other variants, is that individuals are enticed into producing or surrendering a surplus by promises that the original surplus plus some payment for the use of the surplus (or some other compensatory benefits) will be returned at a future date to the supplier. Promised interest payments are frequently on the order of 50 percent to 100 percent, so that there is considerable inducement to loan surplus, and to produce surplus. The producer of surplus, in essence, is making an investment of his produce and he hopes to earn interest off of his loan. Without a mechanism to invest surplus production so that it is stored (in the form of loans or wealth objects) and can increase in value over time, there is no incentive to produce or surrender surpluses in egalitarian communities. At the lowest level, this provides tangible motivation and material benefits for individuals to participate in the competitive feasting system.

At the highest level, where organizers are concerned, individuals combine and orchestrate large volumes of loans and repayments, and play off major accumulations against rivals in other communities. There are several important benefits for the major players in these affairs. First, by the careful balancing of rates of interest for loans and borrowings, skillful individuals can manage to keep a certain percentage of all transactions for themselves, just as contemporary bankers do. Bad loans must be minimized if supporters are to be satisfied with the repayments on their loans – an essential element in keeping the system working. Second, and most important, those who orchestrate the most transactions can and do use their administrative position to increase their personal power and influence. Essentially, they use loans as means of establishing debt relationships that have a quasilegal basis for claims on goods and services.

The establishment of debts and hierarchical relationships constitutes the revolutionary character of the competitive feast. Big Men, or "accumulators," are the major power brokers. They try to give away as much as possible not only because that is the way to increase wealth (by investing surplus and earning interest), but also because it creates debts and increases individual personal influence and power. In sum, the key to success of accumulators is establishing control over labor. They do this through competitive feasts that promise profits on the one hand, and on the other hand establish control over the labor of others through debts (cf. Gosden 1989: 359). Accumulators use every means at their disposal to engage families in the competitive feasting complex. Those who refuse to participate are disparaged as "poor" and are often targets for disenfranchisement as community resources are increasingly appropriated by the more powerful members of the community and their supporters.

An additional characteristic, and perhaps the most important one, of competitive feasting systems is that they establish a means for organizers and supporters to convert abundant resources into desired scarcer goods and services. In order to entice individuals to participate in the system of loans, it is essential to provide those individuals with desirable items or services as part of the profit on loans or in exchange for loans. This constitutes the motivational energy that drives the system and maintains it. The most coveted things include rare kinds of plant foods and labor-intensive delicacies, specially fattened animals, exotic decorations, and material or social support for undertakings such as marriages or training for specialized roles like shamans. Organizers compete with each other to obtain all of these for themselves and, to the extent necessary, for their supporters.

The result of competitive feasts and the transformation of subsistence surpluses into more costly types of labor production is the development of regional exchange networks in exotic items including shells, beads, feathers, carvings, ivory, jade, obsidian, native copper, ochers, and similar materials. Interestingly, although surplus staples are the ultimate basis for exchange, the most important items from the organizers' viewpoints are the labor intensive and exotic items that embody the transformed value of surplus resources. Thus, subsistence fish species do not figure prominently in the crest and totem ideology that permeate Northwest Coast art. Nor are fish the most important class of items "given" at competitive feasts from the point of view of the participants. The most important potlatch exchanges involve items representing subsistence labor that has been transformed via loans and exchange into more costly types of labor, such as fine masks, rare beads, and textiles. Similarly, in rich European Upper Paleolithic sites, there is little relationship between the animals most important to subsistence and the animals most important ideologically, as represented in the cave art (Butzer 1986: 212).

Without items of transformed value, the system cannot function. Because of the high value these items come to acquire, they also are used as a medium for facilitating major social transactions, such as marriages or alliances between groups, or as blood money in repaying injuries. As socioeconomic inequality increases or becomes entrenched, these "primitive valuables" often become necessary for engaging in any major social transactions. It is the possibility of acquiring wealth and power that makes control of feasting systems competitive in nature. Internal battles of wealth as well as battles between communities using wealth and arms characterize these systems. It is only the relatively abundant and invulnerable resources that make this adaptive in any individual or group sense. The inflationary nature of this system ultimately must place great pressure on economic resources; and for this reason, too, such systems should emerge only under conditions of relative resource abundance and invulnerability to excessive exploitation. These essential aspects of the economically based competitive feast, then, give rise to socioeconomic inequality and all the related characteristics that ethnographers and prehistorians currently view as typifying "complex" hunter-gatherers. Such a scenario clearly is more consistent with the exploitative view of elites than with the functionalist view, although at this early stage of development, all participants appear convinced that they stand to gain by investing in competitive feasts. Although loans and exchanges certainly could be (and were) negotiated by individuals, the competitive feast consistently emerged because it provided a greater incentive for participation and production, and, most important, because ambitious individuals realized that competitive feasts provided much more expanded opportunities to concentrate control and wealth in their own hands. Accumulators succeeded in attracting and satisfying supporters to the extent that surpluses could be produced and to the extent that accumulators were socially and economically astute.

## An Ethnographic Example and the Importance of Labor

Complex hunter-gatherers differ from simple hunter-gatherers primarily in that the former have much denser populations (more than .4 persons per square kilometer), which indicates more abundant and more reliable resources; are semisedentary; focus large parts of their productive economy on one or a few staples; exhibit pronounced wealth and status differences within the community; in many cases support part-time specialists and slaves; and, most important for the present discussion, in that they participate in the pronounced development of competitive self-aggrandizing behavior ultimately based on the competitive use of resources that can be transformed into scarce commodities and services. Typically, the major staples of complex hunter-gatherers are abundant and invulnerable to excessive exploitation. Not enough information is currently available to determine whether resource fluctuations are less frequent or of less amplitude among complex hunter-gatherers than among simple hunter-gatherers.

The interior plateau around the town of Lillooet in British Columbia provides an excellent example of competitive complex hunter-gatherers. The dry Interior of this area also presents a simplified resource system that is comparatively easier to model than the economies of complex hunter-gatherers elsewhere. By all accounts, the fisheries in this area were among the best anywhere along the Fraser River. Moreover, the climate was ideal for drying salmon and the fat content of salmon at this stage in their spawning migrations was considered prime. Salmon combined the attributes of seasonally migrating species moving through a constricted area and the high reproductive rates of $r$-selected species that made it virtually impossible to overuse the salmon resources, no matter to what extent they were exploited in aboriginal competition. It comes as little surprise, then, that 70 percent of the protein consumed by individuals in this area was derived from salmon (Lovell et al. 1986).

It was above all the abundant salmon resource that was used to underwrite the competitive feasting and trading system described by Romanoff (1985, 1990) and Teit (1906). Excess salmon were converted into scarcer, highly desired goods and services. The limiting factor was not the salmon, but the labor required to procure and above all process, dry, and store the salmon. Under these conditions, labor was the key to wealth. Price (1984) has pointed out some of the important implications that labor, rather than resource constraints, have for social organization – including competition, feasting, and power decentralization. On the Northwest Coast, chiefs explicitly tried to attract labor (Ferguson 1984: 289). I suggest that, where labor rather than resource availability is the major limiting factor on wealth accumulation among complex hunter-gatherers, a variety of means will be used to impress, attract, and bind people to an accumulator's band of supporters or to a corporate group. These means can include any or all of the following: lavish rituals meant to impress; transcendent ecstatic initiations meant to emotionally bond members to a group (see Hayden 1987); sumptuous displays of wealth and economic power involving boastful consumption; the creation of labor intensive art and jewelry; construction of impressive buildings or commemorative monuments; and conspicuous use of food and costly materials in important marriages, alliances, burials, and assumptions of office. Such demonstrations and expenditures were required to attract and maintain the loyalty of laborers because the self-interest of good workers dictated that they would seek to join groups providing the maximum benefits (see Burch 1975: 227–28). No one would want to join a poor group that could not display wealth and that might not even be able to repay debts. Public displays and disbursements of surplus were empirical demonstrations of the economic power of specific corporate groups or "big man" support groups.

Examples of these types of societies include the Lillooet and many other northwest interior groups, as well as the Northwest Coast Indians, who also had high labor needs in the construction of boats and drying facilities, the filleting and drying of fish, and the capture of fish. I suspect that Upper Paleolithic communities along important animal migration routes had similar labor constraints in butchering, filleting, drying, smoking, and storing meat from large ungulates, as well as processing hides into fine, garment quality leather (Hayden 1990a).

Around Lillooet, we can conjecture that in order to attract and control as much labor as possible for exploiting the abundant salmon resources of the Fraser River, enterprising individuals used the competitive feasting system to distribute scarce goods and profits from loans to their supporters and also used the system to bind supporters to them via debts. Because of the limited number and accessibility of prime fishing sites, and because labor was the primary constraint on the amount of dried fish that could be produced, accumulators and supporters also appear to have organized themselves into corporate groups. Each group controlled key fishing locations (Romanoff 1985; Teit 1906). These groups undoubtedly vied with each other to attract labor by offering material, security, and entertainment benefits to members, much as the ranked northwest Alaskan Eskimo societies documented by Burch (1975, 1980). Multiple marriages, sponsorship, and slave taking were normal recruitment mechanisms for augmenting or maintaining corporate labor pools (Teit 1906), and it can be expected that high birth rates would have been promoted. I suspect that similar concerns represent the real significance of Venus figurines in the European Upper Paleolithic. In British Columbia, households without access to productive private fishing locations became isolated, "poor," and denigrated (Romanoff 1985; Teit 1906). These families were subject to the greatest stress and "population pressure" during famines.

Other major staples of the area included deer and tubers harvested in the high mountain areas. Deer meat (at least out of season) and domesticated dog meat were labor intensive to procure and therefore scarce local products that were highly sought after for use particularly in feasts (Romanoff 1990). Beyond this, there were many exotic prehistoric and ethnographic imports, including dentalium shells, shell beads, and whalebone artifacts from the coast; copper; obsidian from Anahim Peak; and moose antler from further north. Local materials also were intensively worked into prized items including nephrite adzes, and bone and stone sculptures. All these materials undoubtedly circulated in a potlatch system, and trading was particularly intensive in the Lillooet area (Teit 1906).

The accounts of both resources and native society can be interpreted only in terms of great material abundance for hunter-gatherers. Prehistorically, population levels appear to have reached about one to two people per square kilometer. Ethnographically, there was a quasihereditary class of elites that sometimes monopolized trade in exotic items and held competitive feasts (potlatches). Warfare was endemic and supplied captives who made up the bulk of a slave class (Teit 1906: 326, 243). The large productive fisheries of the area were public domain, and were used primarily for obtaining subsistence varieties of salmon. Smaller but highly productive fishing sites were owned by corporate groups within communities and generally yielded certain varieties of salmon used in trading and debt creation (Romanoff 1985). Even though these fisheries were recognized as belonging to individuals or corporate groups, this recognition appears to have been conditional. In times of famine, poorer individuals in these communities felt that they had the right to demand the use of these fishing locations or a share of the stores of richer households, although the poor still appear to have suffered disproportionately (Romanoff 1985). On the other hand, some of the fishing locations had corporate crests erected on them and were defended against trespass (Teit 1906: 255–56).

In the example of the Lillooet hunter-gatherers, given the establishment of sedentary winter communities with storage facilities and regional trade in prestige items (Richards and Rousseau 1987), it seems that competition and complexity had developed as early as four thousand years ago in the context of abundant resources invulnerable to excessive exploitation (salmon). It seems equally clear that these societies in no sense needed the baubles and bangles that their trading and competitive feasting system brought into the area. That is, complexity does not seem to have developed out of a functionalist need critical for community survival. That these societies did not become even more complex is probably due to the dry environment, the limited range of staples, and the very limited potential for increasing the abundance of that resource base given the restricted number of good fishing sites.

I believe that there are other equally convincing examples of this same basic phenomenon. The Northwest Coast Indians provide some of the most striking examples of complexity among hunter- gatherers anywhere in the world, and their environment is generally characterized as exceptionally rich. Similarly, the Calusa of Florida established some of the most politically and socially complex communities ever known among hunter-gatherers. The resource base and population were extremely rich here as well. Moreover, since the Calusa did not practice significant food storage (Widmer 1988), they demonstrate that counter to suggestions of the central importance of storage for the development of complexity (Soffer 1989; Testart 1982), storage is in fact not an essential factor, but an incidental phenomenon. Eskimo whalers of Point Barrow provide yet another example of rich resources giving rise to socioeconomic complexity among hunter-gatherers (Burch 1975, 1980; Sheehan 1985). In fact, complexity among hunter-gatherers seems to be accompanied by unusually abundant resources invulnerable to excessive exploitation everywhere in the world.

## Conclusion

Archaeologically, I believe that hunter-gatherers were of the simple type throughout most of the Pleistocene era. This is indicated by the low density of sites, the transitory nature of most base camps, the absence of technology for effectively exploiting *r*-selected resources, and the lack of status goods, regional exchange, or other indicators of economically based competition. I feel that technological constraints primarily impeded the full use of Paleolithic food resources. Certainly there appear to have been some exceptions, particularly among the late Upper Paleolithic hunters of southwestern France, Russia, and Ukraine, where finely carved and elaborate prestige items have been recovered from rock shelters and campsites such as Isturitz, La Madeleine, Mas d'Azil, Mezin, and Sungir (Soffer 1985). However, it was only in certain places during the late Upper Paleolithic, and more during the Mesolithic, that abundant resource bases relatively invulnerable to excessive exploitation using stone technologies began to be established. Where this occurred, the same constellation of characteristics appears as in the ethnographic examples: the effective use of one or a few abundant resources relatively invulnerable to excessive exploitation, high densities of population, semisedentism, regional exchange, labor intensive status display objects, rich burials, socioeconomic inequality, and frequently the creation of special structures or areas that can be interpreted as feasting locations. The Jomon of Japan (Aikens and Dumond 1986), the Natufian of the Levant (Henry 1985), the Ertebolle of Denmark (Price and Gebauer 1992), the many rich riverine or coastal archaic cultures of North America (Winters 1969) are all excellent examples. What happened to all of these complex hunter- gatherers? Why were there so few of these cultures left in the world at ethnographic contact? I believe that they embodied the seeds of their own transformations into agricultural societies (Hayden 1990b). Because of the inflationary pressures on resources created by loans and feasting, complex hunter-gatherers rapidly adopted or evolved agriculture wherever the environment was favorable, such as throughout most of temperate America.

Since some ethnologists may be reluctant to accept the proposition that competition and complexity develop under conditions of abundance and invulnerable resource use, it is worth pointing out that Sahlins (1958) has documented clearly the strong relationship between socioeconomic complexity and resource abundance on Pacific Islands. Similarly, the model that I am proposing is consonant with observations and explanations of the dramatic changes that have occurred in Basarwa communities as a result of becoming integrated into permanent camps with more abundant and stable sources of food from farmers or government outlets (Cashdan 1980). In contrast to sharing and egalitarianism, private ownership and competition has emerged in these and similar acculturation situations throughout the world, from the Arctic to the tropics. Both in these situations and in the situations that I have discussed, competition in the form of warfare appears to achieve new levels of intensity precisely where hunter-gatherers exhibit the greatest complexity and resource abundance. Northwest Coast and Calusa warfare (Ferguson 1984; Widmer 1988) are among the best known examples.

Archaeologically, it is in the Mesolithic era that the first cemeteries with evidence of extensive killing occurs (see Wendorf 1968). Logically, and in terms of the ethnographic and archaeological evidence, I believe that there is considerable support for the proposition that competition occurs where abundant resources can be converted into scarcer desirable goods or services. It appears to be primarily via the competitive feasting complex that excess subsistence resources initially are converted into desirable resources among pristine hunter-gatherers, and it is in that same context that ambitious individuals vie with one another for control over excess resources, labor, and the wealth and power that such control confers. Ambitious individuals in competitive feasts are willing to risk death and foment battles in their striving to obtain wealth and control over others, as clearly documented in New Guinea by Strathern (1971). Why should we expect anything less among complex hunter-gatherers? The patterning of resource, prestige, and competitive variables from both ethnology and archaeology, together with theoretical considerations, are now compelling enough to make a strong case for the relationship between competition and complexity on the one hand, and resource abundance and invulnerability on the other.

# Part 5

## Culture Contact

# Editorial

Few human populations have been totally isolated from all others during the roughly four million years of hominid existence. It is true that we do not know this for an absolute fact, since direct evidence on the matter is rarely attainable. But the generalization is known to apply to most other species, including most varieties of nonhuman primates, so it is difficult to believe that it does not apply to species in and near our own lineage as well. Presumably, the relations between and among neighboring hunter-gatherer societies existing in a world of hunter-gatherers spanned the range of intersocietal relations familiar to us today, and included trade, war, alliance, hostility, and neutrality.[1]

Moving forward in time, it also must be true that, ever since the first agrarian societies appeared, perhaps twelve thousand years ago, at least some hunter-gatherer societies have been in contact, both directly and indirectly, with agrarian societies. And again, ever since the first states appeared, some foraging peoples have been in at least indirect contact with states – and so on, up the scale of complexity, to the present.[2]

Whenever the technological sophistication, organizational complexity, and population size of the people on the hunter-gatherer side of the encounter were significantly exceeded in the society on the other side, the foragers were likely to have been influenced by the experience. Just how and to what extent they

1. Theoretical and methodological issues relating to intersocietal relations among hunter-gatherers living in a world of hunter-gatherers have been explored by Schortman (1989), Spielmann (1986), and Wobst (1978). For an ethnographic example in which foragers were surrounded for at least several thousand kilometers by other foragers, see Burch (1970, 1974, 1988c) and Burch and Correll (1972).

2. For discussions of the historic relations between powerful nonforagers, on the one hand, and foragers, on the other, and for criticism of the notion of the "closed society," see Bird-David (1988), Comaroff (1984), Headland and Reid (1989), Leacock and Lee, eds. (1982, Part II), Schrire, ed. (1984), and Woodburn (1988).

were affected, and what the theoretical or methodological significance of the influence might be from the viewpoint of modern science, must be determined on a question-by-question and case-by-
case basis.[3] There must have been many thousands of cases.

It is probably fair to say, however, that never in human history
were unbalanced culture contacts as momentous in their consequences as they were when Europeans began to expand around
the globe, some five hundred years ago. Almost everywhere they
went, but particularly in the New World and Australia, Europeans brought disease (Cartwright and Biddiss 1972; McNeill
1976; R. Wolfe 1982), environmental turmoil (Crosby 1986), and
either a ruthless desire to exploit the people they encountered or
else a holy mission to lead them to eternal life (E. Wolfe 1982).
Whatever their intentions, post-Renaissance Europeans fundamentally altered the nature of culture contact throughout the
world. As we approach the end of the twentieth century, it is
probably fair to say that not a single hunter-gatherer society in
the world has remained unaffected by this process.

It is easy enough to moralize about the negative aspects of
European expansion, with which many people preface their
acknowledgment of the quincentenary of Columbus's "discovery" of the New World. However, other than making people feel
good, or bad, the hand-wringing is of no practical consequence; it
certainly does nothing to help real people with real problems.
What we need instead is careful research into the particular issues
that are involved in actual cases. Only if we understand what
happens during contact will anyone be able to deal effectively
with the disruption attending it. Because contact is now virtually
universal with foragers, and because it almost always leads to
serious problems for them, these matters have now become a central focus of hunter-gatherer studies.

The first paper, by Luís Alberto Borrero, sets the stage with an
example of the limiting case, a classic instance of total disaster. He
reports on the Selk'nam, a foraging people living on an island just
off the southern tip of South America. Although they first
encountered Europeans rather early in the expansion period, they

3. The primary methodological issue is whether one can justifiably extrapolate
from patterns observed in "culturally contaminated" contemporary hunter-gatherers to "pristine" Paleolithic or Mesolithic hunter-gatherers. This issue is at the
substantive heart of the "revisionist" debate outlined in Chapter 1 of this volume.
See that discussion for references; see also Woodburn (1980).

were pretty much left alone until the middle of the nineteenth century. Then, within just a few decades, they were faced with practically the whole array of negative European elements: gold seekers, ranchers, missionaries, settlers, and representatives of uncaring governments. The Selk'nam tried to cope with this onslaught through a series of strategies: avoidance, altered subsistence schemes, alliances with other peoples, and armed resistance. But they were not strong enough to prevail. In the end, centralization, deportation, murder, and, most powerful of all – disease – combined to defeat them. They are now extinct.

Lesley Mearns's paper on Aborigine women's traditional responsibilities in a transformed world is concerned with something much more subtle than the life-and-death struggle of the Selk'nam, and yet in its own way just as powerful. The situation she describes is grounded in the fact that the Australian landscape is endowed with thousands of localities viewed as sacred by the Aborigines. Thirty years ago, developers, miners, and road builders could destroy such sites with impunity. Now there are laws to protect them, and an agency is charged with the responsibility of evaluating development plans in the light of those laws. Thus, in contrast to the Selk'nam case, there is at least a presumption of goodwill on the side of the nonindigenous people involved.

A problem arises from the fact that Aborigines generally make a fundamental distinction between women's knowledge and women's sites, on the one hand, and men's knowledge and men's sites, on the other. For a combination of cultural and historical reasons, most of the decisions regarding sacred sites have been made by men, both Aborigine and otherwise. In order to get the sites protected, women have to share their knowledge of them with men. However, this entails a profound breach of their own moral code. Mearns tells us how they have tried to adhere to their ancient customs in this new and acutely uncomfortable context. That this is by no means a trivial matter is indicated by the fact that some Aborigines have chosen to die without sharing their knowledge of sacred sites and texts with anyone rather than have it fall into the wrong hands.

George Wenzel's paper on the Clyde River Inuit (Eskimos) focuses on a very different problem. In this region of the eastern Canadian Arctic, as in much of the rest of the North American Arctic and subarctic, the indigenous people have become involved in what has been called a "mixed subsistence-market economy" (Wolfe 1984; Wolfe and Walker 1987: 68). In this type of system, both a cash income and a hunting income are necessary for survival. Indeed, and seemingly ironically, a cash income is a prerequisite for a hunting income. The Inuit have been able to make the system work by hunting or trapping species for whose pelts there is a cash market. Wenzel describes how the two aspects of the economy were especially harmonious during the 1960s and 1970s, when there was a good market for the pelt of the ringed seal, the Inuit's primary food source. This market was destroyed abruptly when people in the animal rights movement convinced the countries in the European Common Market to ban the importation of seal skins.[4] This has had profound consequences, not just for the economy, but for many aspects of Inuit life.

Despite their differences, the situations described in all three papers have in common the fact that the relative power of the nonindigenous peoples is much greater than that of the hunter-gatherers. In order to survive culturally (and sometimes even physically, as in the case of the Selk'nam), the foragers are (or were) forced to adjust to agendas set by others, based on priorities appropriate to the cultures of those others; they no longer can really be themselves. This problem is greatly exacerbated when there is direct government involvement in the affairs of indigenous peoples, as described in Part 6 of this volume.

4. The ban had nothing to do with the survival of the seal population, which was never threatened. The animal rights movement generally is a profound threat to contemporary hunter-gatherers, since many of the people involved (for example, Best [1986] and Miller [1984]) advocate what amounts to a program of cultural and economic genocide. In their view, people who hunt for a living are savages, period. They want hunting to be banned – whether or not it means the loss of indigenous cultures or the extinction of the people who depend on hunting for their livelihood. For a comprehensive account of the impact of the animal rights agenda on the life of particular indigenous people, see Wenzel (1991).

# 11

## The Extermination of the Selk'nam

*Luís Alberto Borrero*

The settlement of gold seekers and ranchers on Tierra del Fuego severely disrupted Selk'nam use of space. Historical, ethnographic, and archaeological sources document a change from a highly mobile society, initially using all the north territories, toward a more restricted wandering pattern, practicing an "avoidance strategy" near the center of the island. Finally, a few spatially circumscribed groups sustained tribal life until the complete disintegration of the Selk'nam society occurred.[1]

### Introduction

Space is among the first resources to be affected by the contact between mobile hunter-gatherers and sedentary societies. The long-term use of segments of space characterizing the latter usually conflicts with the customs of systems claiming ownership of mobile resources, such as seasonal ungulates. Such contact has more than one potential result. Solway and Lee (1990: 110) addressed this issue in the following quotation:

> We challenge the notion that contact automatically undermines foragers and that contemporary foragers are to be understood only as degraded cultural residuals created through their marginality to more powerful systems. We consider the possibility that foragers can be autonomous without being isolated and engaged without being incorporated.

This paper will review the case of the Selk'nam (also known as the Ona) and their contact with white colonists at the end of the nineteenth century. It can be seen as an exercise in integrating different lines of research attempting to elucidate the particular evolution of a human population under conditions of contact. It must

1. I wish to express my gratitude to Ernest S. Burch, Jr., for comments on an earlier draft of this paper.

be stressed that an emphasis on contact as a cause for change does not preclude an analysis of the internal dynamics of hunter-gatherer societies, only that in studying the appropriation of land by Western society, specific responses by hunter-gatherers must be isolated (Bicchieri 1990).

The evidence used to discuss this example comes from different kinds of sources, including history, ethnography, and archaeology. The integration of disparate sources within a single research framework is a useful way of attaining cross-disciplinary control (Binford 1989; Jochim 1989).

The case of the Selk'nam is interesting for two reasons. First, because they are often mentioned in classic texts of anthropology as an example of highly territorial hunter-gatherers (i.e., Steward 1955), and second, because they never adopted the horse, continuing instead with their strictly pedestrian way of life into the twentieth century. These conditions suggested to some (such as Lathrap 1968) that the Selk'nam presented an undistorted image of the way of life of ancient hunter-gatherers. We know today that Selk'nam territoriality was not so strict, and that the flexibility of territorial use and delimitation was considerable (Chapman 1986).

It is no longer feasible to defend the view that the Selk'nam, or any other hunter-gatherer people, is in any sense the best analog for prehistoric hunter-gatherers (Bender and Morris 1988; Headland and Reid 1989). However, we do not need to go to the extreme of Wilmsen (1983), and reject any opportunity to learn about the hunter-gatherer way of life from contemporary societies. It is widely recognized that the power of a given analogy does not depend on delimiting a "pristine" source for the analogy, but rather on the logical structure of the analogy itself (Gifford-Gonzalez 1990; Wylie 1982).

The Selk'nam still constitute an exciting choice to study, though they may be neither the best source of analogies, nor an example of Service's (1962) patrilineal band. There are other reasons for a special interest in the study of their history. The Selk'nam lived on an island at the southern tip of South America, encapsulated between two oceans and one strait, making it simple to establish cultural as well as natural boundaries. In addition, historical and ethnographic studies of the Selk'nam are relatively plentiful, presenting an adequate opportunity for the discussion of hypotheses generated by archaeological evidence.

## The Selk'nam

The Selk'nam were terrestrial hunter-gatherers who inhabited the northern portion of Isla Grande of Tierra del Fuego. This is a relatively flat region characterized by huge steppes, which are bounded on the south by dense stands of *Nothofagus* forest. The climate is maritime; cold, humid and windy, and the change of seasons is not very marked.

The Selk'nam used mobile small groups – roughly twenty-five to thirty individuals – to exploit resources that were fairly evenly distributed over the land. Several models of their pattern of movement have been constructed (Borrero 1986; Chapman 1986; Moore 1979-1980; Stuart 1972, 1977), but all conclude that high residential mobility was essential to the functioning of the society. Ethnographic evidence shows that the groups in the nineteenth century usually spent only a few days at each camp, and that they came together in large camps for only limited periods of time, usually for initiation ceremonies or trade (Chapman 1986; Gusinde 1982).

Subsistence was centered on the exploitation of the guanaco (*Lama guanicoe*), a medium-sized ungulate weighing 100 to 120 kilograms. The guanaco was very important for the Selk'nam, and most of the decisions about where to camp and when to move were based on its availability. Guanacos are social animals that live in the open in steppe or prairie environments in continental Patagonia; on Tierra del Fuego they also inhabit forests (Franklin 1983). Guanacos display marked territorial behavior, with a limited home range (Garrido, Amaya, and Kovacs 1981), and live in the same general area all the year round.

The guanaco was supplemented by the consumption of geese (*Chloephaga* species), ducks (*Anas* species) cormorants (*Phalacrocorax* species), small mammals (especially *Ctenomys* species), and plants. Most of the preferred birds were migratory, and spent only the summer months on the island. Thus, bird hunting and trapping, together with plant gathering, were seasonal activities.

Marine resources were also important, including sea lions (*Arctocephalus australis*, *Otaria byronia*), fish, and a variety of mollusks (principally *Patinigera magallanica*) (Massone 1982). Meat and fat from stranded cetaceans (whales, dolphins, porpoises, etc.) also were consumed (Gusinde 1982). Sea mammals in general were important sources of fat, which constituted an essential component of the diet of hunter-gatherers living in high latitudes (Speth and Spielmann 1983). The importance of the fat in the Selk'nam diet was increased by the fact that guanaco meat is very lean.

The Selk'nam commanded a diverse technology, centered on the exploitation of stone, bone, and wood materials. They hunted the guanaco using bows and arrows. Their projectile points were made of stone in prehistoric times, which was replaced by glass introduced by the Europeans near the end of the nineteenth century. The hunting of the guanaco was mainly a solitary task, or was performed by a few individuals at most (Borrero 1986). Ethnographic accounts of sea lion hunting episodes mention the use of nets, sticks, or arrows (Lanata 1990). Sea lions were also pursued on the shore, near their rookeries. Processing sites were located not too far from the kill. Small harpoons made of guanaco bone were used to obtain fish in tidal pools. Fish, mollusks, mushrooms, fruits, and bird eggs were transported in fiber baskets. Whalebone wedges served to extract bark from the trees.

Mechanisms to obtain subsistence goods also included interregional meetings, known as *kuash-ketin*, where different Selk'nam groups came together for several days at a time (Chapman 1986). These meetings also served other social functions, and were the locus for the exchange of essential information concerning the distribution of human groups and the availability of resources.

The neighbors of the Selk'nam were principally "canoe Indians." South of the Andean range were the Yahgan, in the Beagle Channel area, and the Alakaluf, on the Chilean archipelago to the west. Both groups were heavily dependent on maritime resources, and their settlement patterns were confined to the coast. On the north shore of the Magellan Strait were the Tehuelche, pedestrian hunters like the Selk'nam, with whom there was almost no contact.

There is some debate about the ethnic status of a group known under the name of Haush, which inhabited the southeastern part of the island (Lanata 1990). The Haush lived a largely terrestrial life, but sea mammals appear to have played a more important role for them than for the Selk'nam. According to some authors (e.g., Chapman 1986; Vignati 1927), the Haush represented a human population that arrived on the island before the Selk'nam; however, that view is no longer tenable (Lanata 1990). The important point is the general homogeneity of the material culture of the Selk'nam and the Haush; in the absence of any definitive evidence about their status, we will consider them a specialized branch of the Selk'nam (Borrero 1983).

## Archaeology

The archaeology of the north portion of Isla Grande is not very well known, but apparently spans more than ten thousand (radiocarbon) years. At the site of Cerro de los Onas, north of the Sierra Carmen Sylva, an assemblage of extinct and modern animal bones (American horse [*Hippidion* species], giant ground sloth [*Mylodon darwinii*], extinct fox [*Dusicyon avus*], guanaco, and birds) was found in association with stone artifacts, including a fragment of what appears to have been a projectile point. Some of the bones appear to have been butchered. This assemblage has been dated before 10,200 BP (before present) (Massone 1987). At the nearby site of Marazzi, close to Useless Bay, members of a French team uncovered butchered guanaco bones in association with stone artifacts, and dated them at circa 9,000 BP (Laming-Emperaire, Lavallée, and Humbert 1972). Both sites are located on the isthmus between Useless Bay and San Sebastian Bay.

After those occupations, only scanty information on the human use of the area is available. An archaeological gap of almost 8,000 years is interrupted in mid-Holocene times by scattered evidence of humans discovered at Marazzi. It is only within the last thousand years that the information appears to be substantial, since it was obtained at a wide variety of sites. This archaeological gap is probably due to sampling error, and may have nothing to do with the occupational history of the north portion of Isla Grande. The archaeological evidence for the last thousand years may be linked to the populational history of the Selk'nam, and will be discussed later in this paper.

The time depth of contact, as measured by the presence of European goods, is strictly concentrated in the last two hundred years. In most cases the presence of European materials (mostly glass and metal) probably indicates indirect appropriation. Sheep and guanaco bones from the same period also exhibit marks cut by metal tools.

A few general points can be concluded from this quick review of the Fuegian archaeological record. First, the guanaco was a basic resource from the very beginning of human occupation of the island. The other Pleistocene fauna found at Cerro de los Onas represented only a complementary resource. The situation is similar to that of continental Patagonia during the same period. Second, all the available evidence points toward human populations consuming terrestrial resources, whereas marine products constituted only a minor, albeit necessary, part of their diet. Third, archaeological evidence of the replacement of local crafts with European goods is not abundant, although it is widespread, and demonstrates the late impact of European technology.

## Initial Contacts

The strait separating Isla Grande of Tierra del Fuego from continental Patagonia (Strait of Magellan) was discovered by Ferdinand Magellan in 1520, during his famous voyage around the world. Members of the expedition observed several plumes of smoke on the island, which were attributed to the hearths of human groups inhabiting Isla Grande; the toponym "Tierra del Fuego" (Land of Fire) resulted from that observation (see Gusinde 1982: 21–22).

However, it was not until 1580 that the initial contacts between Europeans and Selk'nam occurred. In that year an expedition led by Pedro Sarmiento de Gamboa contacted the Selk'nam at what is now known as Bahia Gente Grande (Tall People Bay), a toponym that resulted from the impression that the tall Selk'nam produced on the shorter Spanish (Sarmiento de Gamboa 1950). This initial contact was an unpleasant one for the Selk'nam, since the Spanish forcefully took one of them to serve as a guide. Unfortunately, this hostile behavior set a pattern for the contacts to follow.

## Contacts in the Nineteenth Century

In the sixteenth and seventeenth centuries only sporadic contacts occurred (see reviews in Chapman 1982; Gusinde 1982), since the interior of Isla Grande, where the Selk'nam spent most of their time, was not explored until the late 1800s. Those sporadic contacts usually resulted in situations similar to the one involving Sarmiento de Gamboa, nearly three hundred years earlier. One encounter, involving the Dutch explorer Oliver van Noort in

1598, is one of the better known episodes, and it ended with the violent death of several Selk'nam.

The main result of these bloody encounters probably was a withdrawal of the Selk'nam toward the interior of Isla Grande. However, there are some cases of shipwrecked Europeans, like those of the *Purísima Concepción* in 1765, and sailors landing to secure water and food, like the Nodal brothers in 1619, that were helped by the Selk'nam or the Haush. But these probably were exceptions, and they did not last long. Members of the Nodal brothers' expedition unsuccessfully tried to capture a Selk'nam to use as a guide, a situation that surely ended any desire to continue helping new landing parties.

## Gold

In 1879, the Chilean explorer Ramon Serrano Montaner conducted the first crossing of the north part of Isla Grande, but he saw only abandoned Selk'nam camps (Braun Menéndez 1975). It is clear that the natives were avoiding contact. An important result of that expedition was that Serrano Montaner discovered alluvial gold (Martinic 1973). This discovery had severe consequences for the natives. The confirmation of the presence of gold in Tierra del Fuego accelerated the immigration of miners of many different origins – Rumanians, Chileans, Argentinians, Italians, and Germans (Martinic 1973). The inevitable contact of the miners with the Selk'nam was violent, and several natives were killed or injured.

In 1886, the Rumanian explorer Julius Popper conducted a second crossing of the north side of the island and explored the Atlantic coast (Popper 1887). This strange character, who later exploited gold in El Paramo, recruited his own army. Conflict with the Selk'nam was inevitable, and Popper even had pictures taken of himself with the dead bodies of Indians after an armed encounter (see Borrero 1957).

Also in 1886, the exploration of the interior by the Argentinian explorer Ramon Lista took its toll of Selk'nam lives. In an armed encounter with the soldiers of Lista's expedition, twenty-six Selk'nam were killed. The Lista expedition also indirectly affected the Selk'nam through the introduction to the island of fifty sheep (Lista 1887).

Starting in 1881, contacts between Selk'nam and white colonists developed around centers of gold exploitation, such as

San Sebastian, El Paramo, Boqueron, and Gente Grande (Bondel 1985; Massone 1982). Around these centers, as well as in occasional contacts with explorers, armed encounters frequently took place. Miners often appropriated Selk'nam women, sometimes killing their husbands. The Selk'nam responded with armed attacks on the miners' settlements. The Chilean regional government finally sent soldiers to Bahia Porvenir in order to control the situation (Martinic 1973: 40).

The mining settlements also operated as centers for the diffusion of diseases such as tuberculosis, pneumonia, measles, diphtheria, and syphilis. Selk'nam women, who sometimes cohabited with miners, spread diseases within the native society.

By the end of the 1880s it was clear that gold was not available in great quantities, and other kinds of exploitation were given priority. After the gold rush of 1883, a strategy of expansion was initiated by the government of Chile, which was soon copied by Argentina (Bondel 1985).

### Sheep, The "White Guanaco"

The Chilean government gave land to Europeans for their personal use. The first concession was to Wehrhmahn & Company, and in 1885 Rodolfo Stubenrauch founded Estancia Gente Grande (*estancia* in this case meant sheep ranch) on those lands. In Argentina, José Menéndez bought lands originally in the possession of Popper, and founded the first *estancia* on the Argentinian side of the border. By 1897 sheep in large numbers had been introduced, mostly from the Islas Malvinas, and the Argentinian government was initiating public land sales.

In 1902, the north side of the island was linked to the Beagle Channel area through a mountain path opened by Lucas Bridges and a group of Selk'nam. Using this path, 2,300 sheep were taken to Estancia Viamonte (founded in 1908), located in the north. Nearly 800,000 sheep were recorded as roaming the island in 1914 (de Goodall 1975). The *estancias* constituted new centers for contact, where intercultural conflict increased. Occasionally, however, some *estancias* – such as Viamonte and Harberton – served as refuges for Selk'nam.

All these developments set the stage for an abrupt change in the perception of territory by the Selk'nam. They were no longer able to follow their traditional movements, since wire fences cut them off (Martinic 1973: 19, 41). In addition, sheep were actively competing with guanacos for pasture (Bondel 1985; Saxon 1979), and the guanacos were at least partially displaced to southern areas. Under these conditions, Selk'nam predation on sheep was more or less forced, since to them animals were not private property (Martinic 1973: 19). At least six hundred sheep were introduced to Estancia Gente Grande, many of which were rapidly dispatched by Selk'nam hunters (Martinic 1973: 18). In 1887, the Indians destroyed the wire fences and continued to hunt sheep. This pattern continued for at least three years (Massone 1982: 89-90). Archaeological evidence of the hunting and processing of sheep by the Selk'nam exists mainly in the form of cut marks on sheep bones, sometimes associated with projectile points made of glass. This evidence, which is slowly increasing, will help in assessing the importance of sheep in the native diet.

The reaction of the *estancieros* (ranch owners) to this pattern of sheep hunting was to hire professional killers. Sometimes the Selk'nam were hunted; otherwise they were captured and sent to the Salesian Mission on Isla Dawson, on the Pacific coast, which was founded in 1889 (Chapman 1982; Martinic 1973; Massone 1982). Sometimes the Selk'nam violently resisted these attacks (Belza 1974), but their resistance was generally unsuccessful.

## The Missions

Between approximately 1875 and 1882 the missionaries unsuccessfully tried to approach the Selk'nam several times (Gusinde 1982: 45). Reverend Thomas Bridges contacted some Selk'nam in Gente Grande and unsuccessfully tried to convince them that sheep belonged to the *estancieros* (Martinic 1973: 19).

In 1893 the Salesian Mission (Misión de la Candelaria) was founded by Monseñor Fagnano on the north bank of the Rio Grande, on the Atlantic coast. The mission was accidentally destroyed by fire in 1896, when at least 230 Selk'nam were living there. In 1897 the mission was reconstructed, this time near Cabo Domingo, and sheep, cattle, and horses were introduced. Many Selk'nam were installed at the mission, sometimes with the help of soldiers.

A more important role in the extinction of the Selk'nam was played by the mission at Isla Dawson (Misión de San Rafael), located to the west of Isla Grande. This was probably the most important concentration camp for the Selk'nam, principally for women and children who survived the armed encounters with gold seekers and professional killers. They were taken to the island in Chilean navy ships or in the missionaries' schooner. The mission was supported by the Socieded Explotadora de Tierra del Fuego, which, since 1893, actively had defended its lands on Isla Grande of Tierra del Fuego (Braun Menéndez 1945: 306; Martinic 1973: 43). By 1896, the only alternatives for the Selk'nam were to escape to the interior, to be killed, or to be deported to Isla Dawson.

The natives lived a difficult life at the mission in Isla Dawson. They were concentrated in barracks, forced to wear European clothing (to which they were not accustomed), and exposed to epidemics. It is no wonder that escape from Isla Dawson was a high priority for the Selk'nam, and that violent attacks on the missionaries occurred (Belza 1974; Braun Menéndez 1945). The Alakaluf, canoe hunter-gatherers of the southern channels, helped several Selk'nam escape from Isla Dawson.

## Selk'nam Strategies

Members of both societies, the Selk'nam and the white colonists, were using available knowledge – knowledge that had been successful in previous situations – in their selection of strategies and tactics to manage interethnic contact. Selk'nam experience had been limited to contact with other hunter-gatherer societies, like the Yahgan or the Alakaluf, while that of the white colonists included dealing with hunter-gatherer populations of the Pampas and Patagonia, as well as other regions.

The initial response of the Selk'nam to the steady intrusion of white colonists was an "avoidance strategy." Avoidance of missionaries by the Indians is explicitly mentioned in the literature (Gusinde 1982: 45). In addition, Martin Gusinde was told that the Selk'nam went to the Fagnano area, to the south, in order to escape contact with the whites (Gusinde 1982: 76). Ethnohistorical information from the end of the nineteenth century describes small camps with very low visibility and with just a few belongings in addition to a windbreak. All the relevant sources from the end of the nineteenth century make it clear that the Indians were avoiding contact (Lista 1887; Popper 1887; Segers 1891). If avoidance had been used in the past to manage contact with the canoe

Indians, it may have been successful. But it was of little use in avoiding contact with a sedentary society.

Elsewhere I have described the "avoidance strategy" as being archaeologically invisible, and have presented a global review of hunter-gatherers who used it in places as different as California, Paraguay, and Southeast Asia (Borrero in press). This strategy has also been evaluated as one of avoiding domination (see Bender and Morris 1988: 12). The main point is that it already had been "tested" in a number of different situations, and that it served only in the short run. It was merely a way to buy time.

Archaeological information concerning sites formed during historic periods is concordant with what is described in ethnohistorical and ethnographic sources. The archaeological sites are small, their maximum size is usually between five and ten meters. Artifacts and ecofacts on these sites are found in small quantities, and all the evidence suggests that they were formed during a period of occupation lasting only a few days (Borrero 1986). The most abundant resource recovered in these sites is shellfish, the consumption of which produces substantial accumulations in a few days. In addition, the distribution of sites suggests that they were preferentially located in the interior. This evidence is taken to mean that high mobility was the norm for late Selk'nam society.

Mobility may be viewed as a short-term strategy (see Moran 1983). For the Selk'nam, it was effective for only a few years, and it failed to stop the process of tribal destruction. The geography of the island was inadequate for long-term success, since only a limited amount of space was available. In the 1890s, many Selk'nam began to visit Estancia Harberton on Beagle Channel regularly, and they became intermixed with the Yahgan (Bridges 1951; Gusinde 1982; Stuart 1980). That was one way to escape, and also to alleviate the competition for space. Harberton was founded in 1886, and the Selk'nam were welcomed to the *estancia*, where they worked for meager wages (Gusinde 1982). The arrangement was convenient for the Selk'nam, who stayed there for the summer, and, after the warm season ended (and human activity in the north declined with the onset of winter), returned to the forest.

To put things in perspective, it must be stressed that during the same period Selk'nam were experiencing other humiliating situations. In 1889, a group was sent for exhibition in the First World Fair in Paris (Borrero 1957), while in 1898 three Selk'nam with their dogs were sent to the Palermo Fair in Buenos Aires. The dogs got rabies, which afterward diffused throughout the island (see Gusinde 1982). Many of the natives, who were exhibited in Europe as "cannibals," fell prey to lung disease and never returned home.

Reduction of the space available to the Indians was progressing almost geometrically downward year after year. Displacement of most of the groups to the southern forests concentrated the human population there, and probably contributed to the intensification of intergroup killing, which was characteristic of the Selk'nam by the end of the nineteenth century (Chapman 1982; Stuart 1980). These conflicts also contributed to Selk'nam disintegration. As Stuart (1980: 280) put it: "When faced with European contact, the Ona first dispersed, then reacted with dramatic self-induced population decline." Somehow this conflict was solved, since in the last male initiation ceremonies (known as *kloketen* or *hain*), people from different groups participated, an unthinkable situation under conditions of war (Chapman 1982, 1986). It is possible that the resolution of intergroup conflict resulted from population decline, which eliminated the earlier overpopulation of the forest area (see Stuart 1980).

By 1900, what was perceived by the whites as the "Selk'nam problem" was ended (Martinic 1973; Stuart 1980), since they no longer threatened the *estancias*. The northern part of Isla Grande had been distributed among a few *estancias* (Bondel 1985). Many Selk'nam escaped to Estancia Viamonte or to the mission in Rio Grande, while others concentrated on Fagnano Lake, in the heart of the forest.

At the turn of the century the whites felt no need to continue removing Selk'nam from their land. The small groups still surviving in the forest or at the missions no longer constituted a threat. Under those conditions, the space still possessed by the Selk'nam was exploited logistically (see Binford 1980).

The new pattern of logistic exploitation of the land appeared as the only one available to the Selk'nam in the twentieth century. They were not allowed the free wandering they had enjoyed in the past, but the use of central base camps appeared to be a realistic way of exploiting the land. This strategy was effected with at least two base camps, one near the Fuego River mouth, and the other near the head of Fagnano Lake. The camp near the Fuego River was dependent on Estancia Viamonte, and, to a minor degree, on Indians attracted to the Salesian Mission at Cabo

Domingo. Located on the Atlantic coast of Tierra del Fuego, this camp was directly exposed to external influences. The base camp at Fagnano Lake was more difficult to approach (see Gusinde 1982), and constituted the last center of tribal life for the Selk'nam.

In 1911 a Salesian mission (Misión de San José) was founded on Fagnano Lake, and in 1925 a reservation for the Selk'nam was established by the government in Argentina (Decree 515,1925). However, by that time there were very few Indians left to use those lands. The mission at Cabo Domingo, where so many natives had sought refuge, was converted in 1942 into the Salesian Agrotechnical School, due to the extinction of the Selk'nam.

## Conclusions

Initial contact with explorers and gold seekers was bloody, but geographically concentrated at coastal points. The core of Selk'nam territory was more affected by the installation and subsequent expansion of the *estancias*, starting in the mid-1880s. Partition of the land with wire fences, and the introduction of sheep, which appeared as new prey for the Selk'nam, precipitated a chaotic situation, which culminated with the Selk'nam being hunted or deported. Both factors were important in the decline of the Selk'nam population. Martinic (1973: 63) calculated that at least two hundred Selk'nam were killed in special raids on the Chilean side of Isla Grande, and at least nine hundred were deported to Isla Dawson, where they succumbed to epidemics. More than one-half of the living Selk'nam population on the Chilean side was lost through epidemics alone. The selective pattern of killing males and deporting women and children was demographically disastrous (Little 1983). Epidemics only exacerbated the trend. In 1924 and 1929, epidemics of measles killed many of the last surviving Selk'nam, since only half-breeds appear to have acquired immunity against that disease (Bridges 1951: 520). The effect of alcohol on the Selk'nam cannot be easily measured, but it certainly contributed to their social disintegration.

According to David Stuart (1980: 280), the most important factor in the Selk'nam decline was "loss of space, purely and simply." Surely it was important, but we cannot easily dismiss the "hunting" of males, the deportation to Isla Dawson, and epidemics. In fact, deportation was a mechanism that allowed more space for the remaining Selk'nam, and it probably made possible the avoidance strategy mentioned above. From what we know from the archaeological record for the period between 1,000 BP and the "Modern" era (*sensu* Stuiver and Polach 1977), it appears safe to assume that strategies of high mobility were within the available cultural repertoire of the inhabitants of northern Isla Grande. In that sense it may be argued that the Selk'nam "reacted to only particular stimuli that triggered age-old and evolutionary *successful* responses to previous conditions of catastrophe" (Stuart 1980: 270; emphasis his) – but the strategy was a complete failure in the new situation.

A cultural system working under the conditions of spatial constraint and exposure to a suite of new diseases lacks resilience – that is, any ability to persist. Even minor additional changes may destroy such a system.

The final move to central base camps can be seen as a forced strategy, imposed from outside. It was maladaptive because the conditions outlined above persisted; the new spatial strategy did nothing to change them. Whatever ecological efficiency the Selk'nam possessed in the nineteenth century and earlier was now absent, for the simple reason that predation was at least partially concentrated on white-owned sheep. Recognition of hunting sheep as a problem was, on the other hand, a mechanism triggering further spatial circumscription. Extinction was the final outcome.

This condensed history of the Selk'nam struggle for survival and final extinction resulted from the analysis of written sources. But the observed changes in the use of space are mainly a result of archaeological research. It is a major point of this paper that archaeology can make a firm contribution to the histories of hunter-gatherer societies, because "its coverage of an enormous time-span and almost total geographical range provide[s] essential evidence on the socioeconomic variability of past gatherer-hunters, and thus [holds] the key to an understanding of the dynamics of long-term change" (Bender and Morris 1988:5).

An "enormous time-span" is the major property of the archaeological record (Binford 1986), which is ideally suited for the study of temporal trends in the use of space. Archaeological research probably constitutes the only way to test models of cultural change such as those proposed by Griffin (1984) or Hoffman (1984).

At the end of the twentieth century the Selk'nam are gone. The written testimonies of ethnographers and travellers about their lives are relatively well integrated within the history of Tierra del Fuego. But our ignorance still exceeds our knowledge of the Selk'nam. Modern ethnohistorical perspectives may shed new light on one or more problems, and some new documents may appear in the future, but it seems that most of our hopes to acquire new knowledge about the Selk'nam are centered in the archaeological record.

# 12

## To Continue the Dreaming: Aboriginal Women's Traditional Responsibilities in a Transformed World

*Lesley Mearns*

As custodians of sacred sites, Aboriginal women in the Northern Territory of Australia must grapple with dilemmas posed by the contemporary social order in fulfilling their responsibility to protect those sites from desecration. In order to maintain tradition they must reinterpret that tradition, thus introducing change to maintain continuity. The complex processes discernible in this situation potentially have implications for all discussions of the continuation of tradition in the modern world.[1]

The terms "tradition" and "traditional" are used in reference to many different forms of social behavior, from those of a society that is perceived as having remained relatively static for generations untold, to dramatic ceremonies of ancient pageantry that stand alone in deliberate stark contrast to the contemporary world in which they are performed. These varied usages are relevant to our understanding of any particular manifestation of tradition – for a word gains its meaning in part from the associations it evokes – but when using so multiplex a term as part of an analysis, it is wise to pay attention to the particular relationship of that term to the context in which it occurs. With this in mind the present chapter examines the notion of tradition as it presents itself in the interaction of an indigenous people, and now ethnic minority, the Aboriginal people of the Northern Territory of Australia, with the wider social order in which they seek to maintain their existence.

1. The original form of this chapter was a paper presented to the Sixth International Conference on Hunting and Gathering Societies held in Fairbanks, Alaska, in 1990. In redrafting the paper I make grateful acknowledgment of comments made by my husband, David Mearns, and by those present at that conference, in particular Mary Edmunds and Harriet Rosenberg.

Throughout the anthropological literature the term "tradition-al" most commonly has been used in reference to those societies that are typified as relatively static and often homogeneous, and as a contrast to societies undergoing a process of rapid change, often referred to as "modernization" or "Westernization." All three of these terms unfortunately have been subject on repeated occasions to the most casual of assumptions by anthropologists, such as the claim of "polarization" between traditional and modern social organization. This is, of course, the popular usage of these terms. In examining the changes that have occurred throughout the world in recent decades, Eisenstadt (1973) concluded that such a dichotomy is analytically misleading and he identified the presence and construction, or reconstruction, of many traditional and neotraditional patterns of social organization within the modern state.

On a smaller scale, John Barnes observed the variable reference to traditional conduct among the Ngoni of southern Africa in the late 1940s, its appearance determined largely by contexts derived from the new social order rather than from any specific intention to conserve past patterns of behavior (Barnes 1951). Similarly, Lindstrom more recently identified the emergence of *kastom* (tradition) as a political symbol in the Pacific, where he maintains that "people today are manipulating this concept in political events in order to reformulate the structures of their existence" (Lindstrom 1982). Indeed, the capacity of a people to evoke tradition in the context of a political struggle frequently has been recorded by anthropologists and historians,[2] but in most instances without reflection on the implications for our understanding of tradition.

In more dramatic form, Hobsbawm and Ranger (1983) have documented the actual invention of traditions in nineteenth- and twentieth-century Britain, and Hanson has focused on the European construction of traditions regarding the Maori Great Fleet and the cult of Io, both of which traditions "have been embraced by Maoris as their authentic heritage" (Hanson 1989: 893). It is therefore not reasonable to assume that, simply because popular thought may attribute both anachronism and unreflective repeti-

---

2. A particularly interesting and relevant example of this can be seen in an article by Irene Silverblatt (1980).

tion to tradition encountered in contemporary society, practice actually mirrors ideology.

When tradition as a term is used specifically in discussions about ethnic minorities, it depicts items of cultural baggage that such minorities are seen to have brought with them from a distant past or distant place, to which they can thus lay legitimate claim as components of a distinctive ethnic identity. It is their common heritage; one that distinguishes that ethnic community from other interspersed communities, and one in which its members have common interests and can claim common rights.

Such traditions theoretically are derived from time-honored practices, but for an ethnic minority it is noticeable that some traditional practices are retained and become venerated traditions, while others disappear from memory or are invoked simply as instances of what one used to do in the old days, long since discarded. Thus traditions can become separated from the total order in which they once took their place and their original meaning, and can be reproduced elsewhere. Such a piecemeal and apparently erratic use of tradition seems a far cry from the images of the harmonious and immutable social order evoked by the term, and yet these mnemonic associations are arguably its greatest strength.

Despite such varied applications of the term, a common theme imbues all reference to tradition and supplies its emotive force: the notion of continuity. Even in focusing on the invention of traditions, Hobsbawm and Ranger (1983: 2) identified invariance and continuous repetition as the defining characteristic of all traditions. Such a concept has value for an ethnic minority seeking to reproduce its identity. It has particular force for an indigenous ethnic minority, both in their self-perception and in perceiving the nonindigenous majority who are by definition more recent arrivals, for indigenous people can lay claim to continuity of place as well as of idea. Indeed, for the Aboriginal people of the Northern Territory, the parallel continuity of space and social organization is of primary cosmological significance.

The social analyst, however, should be cautious of swallowing such an ideology whole, for the reproduction of social organization does not necessarily involve identical repetition. Although components of a minority's older cultural order may offer some semblance of continuity when reproduced in an otherwise radically transformed contemporary setting, some of them may also simultaneously offer reasonable models from which to generate viable social interaction with that new order. We cannot then view the maintenance of traditions by any ethnic minority simplistically, as an internally generated sentimental attachment to the old ways. The reproduction of these old ways is equally stimulated and constrained by the priorities of outside, alien, and sometimes dominant, cultures with which that minority culture must interact, and by the conditions under which that interaction must occur. For such traditions, ideology emphasizes continuity as the basis on which they are incorporated into their new encompassing social environment. Practice inevitably introduces change.

While other discussions mentioned above imply various degrees of intentional manipulation of cultural traditions to achieve new objectives, the present subject matter suggests no such necessary conscious response. Rather, such results flow from a series of processes inherent in and emergent from the new situation. Maintaining a select series of traditions, as opposed to the full body of traditional practices, creates a new set of conditions for the interrelationship of those traditions, both with each other and with their wider context. Where this new set of conditions engenders contradictions in that interrelationship, it sets the stage for reinterpretation. On one level, that reinterpretation may signal change, but at another level it also may facilitate continuity.

This chapter focuses on the paradoxical marriage between continuity and change often found in tradition, and specifically examines the dilemmas of Aboriginal women in the Northern Territory of Australia as they seek to continue and fulfill their traditional responsibilities toward sacred sites.

## Geographical Parameters

Aboriginal people in Australia often are identified by the particular language that they speak, but this chapter focuses not on one set of Aboriginal people speaking one language, but on all those contained within a set of political boundaries established by the wider, and essentially non-Aboriginal, social order.

The Northern Territory covers roughly 1,346,200 square kilometers, and extends from the tropical forests and wetlands of northern Australia to the deserts of the continent's center. Of the Northern Territory's sparse population of approximately 155,000, about 22.4 percent are Aboriginal, of whom almost two-thirds live in rural areas. This distribution stands in stark contrast to the non-Aboriginal population, which is predominantly urban. The Aboriginal population is relatively immobile in terms of permanent change in area of residence, but highly mobile in terms of both circulation within an area and temporary movement between rural and urban settlements. Their average income is low and almost two-thirds of Aboriginal people over fifteen years of age are unemployed.[3] They belong to many different language groups.

It is this unit of population, "Aboriginal," imposed from outside, that is the relevant unit in the present discussion. While the language-sharing group is still a meaningful grouping in Aboriginal culture, it exists within and alongside other classifications, of which the most significant (in contending with the Australian state and its administrative units) are those of "Aboriginal" and "non-Aboriginal." In seeking protection for sacred sites, members of language groups in the Northern Territory ultimately must act as members of the Aboriginal community of the Northern Territory; a grouping that has no traditional precedence.

### The Traditional Responsibilities of Aboriginal Women

Not only the notion of tradition but the very idiom of Aboriginal cosmology is couched in terms of continuity. It is based on a presumption that during an era now called "the Dreamtime," a number of super beings, "Dreamings," traversed the land. These beings were of many forms, from human beings or animals to natural phenomena such as the moon. Through their deeds, including their interactions with each other, these beings created the landscape, the people, and the resources within that landscape, and they established the code of social behavior by which all shall live. This is known in Aboriginal English as "Law" and that Law is represented as unchanging and unchangeable. The Dreamtime thus gave meaning to reality. To maintain the Law established by the Dreamtime is to maintain reality.

It is a mistake, however, to view the Dreamtime simply as a past era. Rather, it is a continuing reality.[4] Indeed the whole concept of the past is problematic in relationship to Aboriginal soci-

---

3. Information taken from Australian Bureau of Statistics, 1990.
4. See the discussions of this issue by Stanner (1965) and Myers (1986).

ety. While I doubt that a written tradition is essential to maintaining historical depth, the absence of a written tradition in Aboriginal society greatly facilitates the rapid merger of the present with the past; a past that fades into uniformity beyond living memory. Aboriginal society places great emphasis on continuity, but that continuity is the consequence of an oral tradition that has recounted Law over the generations, as expressed in the Dreamtime stories and represented in the physical shape of the landscape, over which nomadic Aboriginal people would have traveled repeatedly, and of which they would have gained an intimate knowledge during their lifetime.

The landscape thus stands as a physical representation of the Dreaming, the Law, which underlies all social relationships. Importantly, in the present context, interpretations of traditions revolve around interpretations of the relationship of people to place.

Particular points on the landscape where Dreamings engaged in particular activities, or where they were transformed into that landscape, contain concentrations of the essence, the power, of that Dreaming. These are places of particular religious significance and are referred to in present day terminology as sacred sites. Holding knowledge, or the right to hold knowledge of sacred sites (and thus of the Law that they embody) is the basis and ultimate ratification of social position.

Individuals obtain the right to hold knowledge through a series of processes, of which the most basic is genealogical descent, which ascribes to an individual totem/s, or Dreaming/s. On one level that individual is that Dreaming. The associated knowledge is acquired slowly over a lifetime, as individuals are seen to obtain the social maturity appropriate to such a trust. They hold it and wield it as custodians for the generations that will follow and for those that are past, as well as in demonstration of their own power and authority.

Knowledge of the Law that structures reality is not something that can be obtained or held lightly. To have knowledge for which one is not prepared is extremely dangerous, and to hold that knowledge entails considerable responsibility for its safekeeping, and for ensuring its correct and appropriate transmission and use. Rights and responsibilities in relation to knowledge are inseparable in Aboriginal tradition.

The gender division inherent in Aboriginal society pervades the spiritual realm, although the manner in which this is made manifest varies from one area to another[5] – a factor that has considerable implications for later discussion. While it is very important in relation to Dreaming knowledge to remember that for each group of custodians there is ultimately one common body of knowledge for which they all have some responsibility, in practice certain types of knowledge are more appropriate to one gender or the other. Consequently, certain sacred sites are more the preserve and responsibility of female custodians than of male, and vice versa.

As this knowledge relates to extraordinary powers embedded in the land, only those who appropriately might hold such knowledge, and in practice do so, may have the capacity to deal with such power. Thus, for a man to go where only women should go, or to speak of matters of which only women should speak, or to know things that only women should know, and vice versa, is a dangerous breach of Law that threatens the continuity of the Dreaming and the maintenance of the social order. To break the Law in this way is to invite sanctions of illness or death, visited by either human or supernatural agency on either the perpetrator or the custodians who were responsible for that Dreaming.

The intimate association of individuals with their land has been transformed considerably during the last century, as Aboriginal people increasingly have become incorporated into the spatial organization dictated by the wider Australian society. Many people no longer live on their land, or for much of the time live a relatively stationary existence on only part of it. The process of passing knowledge about "country" (ancestral land) from one generation to another has been disrupted severely. Yet there are those who are old enough to have spent some of their earlier days living on country, or who have since learned much through participation in ritual and through visits to country specifically aimed at the transmission of knowledge.

The continuing importance of traditions associated with the maintenance and protection of sacred knowledge and of sacred sites has carried with it the continuing importance of women's traditional responsibilities. Women have a right to speak on

5. See Kaberry (1939), Berndt (1950), Goodale (1971), Bell (1983), Merlan (1988), and Brock, ed. (1989) for discussions of the varied form this takes throughout this and neighboring regions.

women's knowledge of sacred sites, often known under the wider rubric of "women's business." They also, therefore, have the associated responsibility to do so. No men have the right to speak on women's business, and yet as part of a common Law, both have an interest in the maintenance of such responsibilities. Those responsibilities, however, now operate within a somewhat different environment, and meeting them has new implications, often problematic and sometimes contradictory, for both the women and the men who endeavor to continue the Dreaming.

### The Involvement of Women in Protecting Sacred Sites Under Australian Law

Aboriginal traditions now gain much of their meaning through their articulation in the wider Australian society. In this context, certain traditions become an expression of what is seen as specifically Aboriginal. They are also an accepted basis on which Aboriginal people can express needs and demand to have those needs met.

The operation of successive Northern Territory Aboriginal Sacred Sites Acts (1978, 1989) is one such context through which Aboriginal people in the Northern Territory have had to explore the interaction of existing Aboriginal traditions with the expanding interests of other members of the Australian community. The Acts are intended to provide sacred sites with protection roughly equivalent to that which tradition implies would have been achievable in the past, taking into account the changed circumstances under which that protection must now operate. The Acts have taken two major forms: the first Act, legislated in 1978, and the second Act, created in 1989. The second Act spells out quite specifically in its preamble its intended use:

> To effect a practical balance between the recognized need to preserve and enhance Aboriginal cultural tradition in relation to certain land in the Territory and the aspirations of the Aboriginal and all other peoples of the Territory for their economic, cultural and social advancement. (Australia, *Northern Territory Aboriginal Sacred Sites Act* [1989: 1])

The 1989 Territory Act takes its definition of "sacred site" from the federal *Aboriginal Land Rights (Northern Territory) Act* [1976], through which Aboriginal people may claim land, and to which it is in fact complementary legislation. Thus sacred site means "a site that is sacred to Aboriginals or is otherwise of significance according to Aboriginal tradition" (*Aboriginal Land Rights [Northern Territory] Act* [1976: 3]). This phrasing leaves the definition of sacred site up to Aboriginal people themselves, although they are nevertheless constrained by understandings and misunderstandings previously expounded by non-Aboriginal experts, and by what might or might not be acceptable within a court of law.

Both the federal and the Northern Territory Acts, as is clear from their titles, relate quite specifically to a particular area within Australia, the Northern Territory, and offer opportunities virtually unrivaled throughout much of the rest of Australia for Aboriginal people to regain some level of control over the land once held by their ancestors. The reasons for this are varied, but include a recognition of the number of Aboriginal people in the Territory who have retained a relationship with their land that is in some aspects recognized as traditional. This can be attributed to a number of factors; in particular, the relatively short history of colonization experienced by Aboriginal people in the Northern Territory (for some groups, less than one hundred years), and the low density of the population generally even today.

Particularly important in this context is the fact that many Aboriginal people continue to hold knowledge about sacred sites. Even with regard to the operation of the federal *Aboriginal Land Rights (Northern Territory) Act*, this knowledge has become the primary basis on which Aboriginal people have sought to establish their traditional rights to land and to demonstrate an ongoing relationship to that land. Jeremy Beckett (1988: 207) recently made the pertinent comment that "the Aboriginal claimant for land was cast in the role of homo religiosus rather than homo economicus and the case [was] presented in terms of sacred sites rather than hunting grounds."

Both Acts relate, however, to a much larger area than that encompassed by any one group of Aboriginal people. Thus, while traditions related to sacred sites may vary quite markedly from one group to another, the context to which they have become relevant in recent years, and by which they are potentially affected, extends throughout the administrative area of the Northern Territory. It is to this wider context that I address my discussion of the interaction of such traditions.

The first of the two successive *Northern Territory Aboriginal Sacred Sites Act*s left the Aboriginal composition of the Protection Authority that it established to the decision of existing Aboriginal bodies; that is, to the three original Northern Territory Aboriginal land councils. These land councils were dominated at that time by the presence, and thus also the responsibilities, of Aboriginal men. When they were required to nominate members to the Aboriginal Sacred Sites Protection Authority, as it was known at that time, they nominated only men on the basis that women should not be involved in making decisions or discussing knowledge related to secret men's business.

While this decision removed some of the problems entailed in transferring traditional decision-making processes with regard to men's business into a new context, it made the protection of women's sacred sites highly problematic. In practice, this became a problem not just for women who wished to have their concerns addressed, and who indeed were required by their traditional responsibilities to achieve protection for sites. It also created a dilemma for those men appointed to the Protection Authority who had gained thereby a general responsibility for the preservation of Aboriginal Law in the Northern Territory, but who were threatened by a potential breach of that Law every time protection was requested for a women's site. In light of the rapid development of the Northern Territory they were, moreover, not able simply to ignore the question of women's sites, because increasing numbers of such sites were threatened by the presence of development projects. This paradox remained unresolved for some years.

In the early 1980s, an attempt was made to create a women's committee that would advise the main Protection Authority on matters associated with women's sacred sites. As with the formation of the original Protection Authority, a request was made to the Aboriginal land councils that they nominate women for inclusion on that committee. This process was apparently acceptable to two of the three land councils, both of whom provided nominations as requested. However, the process eventually was vetoed by those members of the third land council who represented regions of the Northern Territory where it was maintained that to have women discussing sacred site matters would not be in accord with Aboriginal cultural policy. This decision was upheld in spite of the fact that several other areas under that same land council's jurisdiction already had made nominations to the committee.

Such a decision highlights a problem inherent in applying one piece of legislation to a large area containing a variety of cultural traditions. The extent of women's involvement in matters related to sacred sites varies throughout the Northern Territory, as does the nature of that involvement, but as the legislation sets up structures that are Territory-wide, the traditions of one group can have considerable impact on the traditions of other quite distinct areas within that region.

In the years following this decision, a range of compromise procedures were adopted by the Protection Authority, by women custodians of sites, and by the professional anthropologists who documented women's sacred sites for registration by the Authority. None of these compromises, however, addressed the fundamental problems of men's deliberation on women's business and of the exclusion of women from the public arena in which decisions were made about matters of religious importance. These processes not only confirmed and reproduced prejudices created by an earlier generation of largely male anthropologists who had denigrated the role of women in sacred matters; they also reduced the effective level of protection available to women's sites while simultaneously compromising in terms of the Law the position of those men who, in accordance with tradition, had been charged with taking care of those sites.

These problems were addressed in a more public forum than the Protection Authority in the late 1980s, when it came under public review. While other issues were canvassed, the area that received the most frequent and consistent criticism was the lack of provision under the Act to ensure the protection of women's sites in a manner equivalent to that accorded men's sites. This was an expression, of course, not just of Aboriginal concern, but of the expansion of feminist ideology in the wider society.

Thus, when the Northern Territory Aboriginal Sacred Sites Act was changed in 1989, sections regulating the required composition of the Protection Authority were altered radically, stipulating from then on that equal numbers of men and women be included within the Aboriginal membership of the new Aboriginal Areas Protection Authority, and that the chairman and deputy chairman be of opposite gender. The practical experience during the 1980s of problems in articulating gender-based traditions was instrumental in ensuring that there was no significant open opposition to this component of the new Act. A quiet revolution had occurred. Now the stage was set for a new experiment in articulating traditional concerns.

## Dilemmas in the Practical Documentation of Women's Business

The dramatic changes enacted on the central legislative stage were closely associated with problems being encountered behind the scenes in the day-to-day discussion and documentation of women's sacred sites. Both concerned issues posed by the ongoing reinterpretation of tradition, discussed here by reference to a few specific examples. It should be noted in this regard that a deliberate effort is made by the author to avoid direct reference to the Dreamings involved and to the location of the sites, because such information is not the property of the author, but rather of the custodians, and the communication of this knowledge might cause offense. Moreover, such information is not crucial to the present discussion. The examples in this discussion come from culturally distinct areas of the Northern Territory, and range from locations where specific women's secret and sacred business is very limited (in comparison with that of men) to regions where women's sites, women's knowledge, and women's ceremonies are considered very powerful Law.

It also should be borne in mind throughout that the author as an employee of the Protection Authority, and others in similar positions, inevitably are actors as well as recorders – an integral part of the context within which, and in response to which, interpretations of tradition are made. I maintain the first person singular throughout the discussion of the specific examples in recognition of this aspect.

### The Male/Female Division of Responsibilities

Debbie Rose previously documented for the Protection Authority a situation in which Aboriginal men, consulted about proposed works to be undertaken in the vicinity of an Aboriginal community, failed either to notify the officials involved that a women's site lay in the path of the proposed work, or to warn the women of the community that such danger threatened. As a result a women's site was damaged (Rose 1985).

This is not an isolated incident and has been repeated in various forms and with various consequences throughout the Northern Territory. As such, it highlights the considerable dilemmas confronted by Aboriginal people when protection for sites entails the translation of practices from their own culture into the procedures of a very alien culture. Yet it is at this interface between Aboriginal culture and the social organization of the wider Australian state that decisions must be made that will have the greatest impact on the continuing existence of Aboriginal traditions.

The area in which Debbie Rose worked places considerable emphasis on the division between men's business and women's business. A similar incident almost occurred, however, in a different region where the division between men's and women's concerns is less distinct in relation to many sacred sites. Nevertheless, there do exist in that region some types of sites that can be discussed publicly only by women, that indeed may contain elements that are known only to women, and perhaps may be seen only by women. This holds true in spite of the fact that the story of the site may be an integral part of a much longer Dreaming track of significance to both sexes. Such sites most commonly deal with the life cycle of women and with the relevant ceremony and Law, but also may relate to other issues that are seen as the particular domain of women.

In this specific instance, a senior male custodian of sites in the area was consulted by both a male and a female representative of interests that sought to mine there, and both understood this custodian to have informed them of the full extent to which sites in the area might be affected by such a proposal.

When, however, the implications of his statements became clear to the body of custodians as a whole, both male and female custodians approached a male staff member of the Protection Authority with whom they had worked for years and explained that they were afraid of potential damage to a women's site that might result from any mining at that specific location. This revelation was a surprise to that staff member, as he had visited the area many times and been told of associated sites, and yet he had not received any indication previously that a women's site was located there. The custodians asked that a female research officer investigate.

I found the site to be an important and fairly extensive one, but the specific section from which men were prohibited entry previously had been well protected by its inaccessibility, and thus priority had been given to the preservation of that knowledge as secret women's knowledge in accordance with tradition. Only an immediate threat to the continued physical existence of the site had forced a reconsideration of the appropriate interpretation of tradition in this regard, and had resulted in a decision to admit the existence of the site to the extent of having it placed on a public register. No man could have made that decision, and thus the custodian who was first approached was unable even to indicate his knowledge of the site's existence, or to express his fears of the consequences to custodians should the site be damaged.

On another occasion in a quite different ethnographic area, women approached by a male consultant failed to indicate to him the presence of a women's site that might potentially be damaged by a proposed development. It was only when the site was actually damaged that a re-evaluation occurred. Even then it required the presence of a female researcher and a female representative of the company involved before the issue could be discussed. The resulting consultation process itself brought out a number of associated issues.

During initial discussions, and before the company representative arrived, all those present at the Aboriginal settlement nearby, with one exception, were female. The one exception was an old man who was both a very important male custodian of the area and the husband of one of the women involved. While considerable effort was made to ensure that he was well supplied with food, he was inevitably left to his own devices for long periods of time while we huddled at the other end of the camp discussing secret women's business. He responded by becoming ill-tempered and eventually sat alone in the dark singing a men's song, which the women present interpreted as a warning that we keep clear of men's concerns both in relation to the knowledge that was being transmitted and in relation to the Dreaming sites that we might visit.

Having completed a documentation of the site that had been damaged, and having been told a coherent story that was commensurate with previous documentation in the area, I was surprised the next morning, just half an hour before the mining company representative arrived, to be told by the wife of this man that the story had been a complete fabrication and that there was no women's site there. This immediately created an argument between the women present; an argument that I needed to resolve quickly, as I had asked the company representative to make a very long journey to attend the meeting.

I noted that the woman who had made this statement seemed to get no support from the other women present and my decision finally was made, at least in the short term, on the basis of the quiet insistence of the most senior woman present (who had distanced herself from the considerable heat generated by the fracas), that everything that they had told me previously about the site had been true.

The next day I discovered from another researcher who recently had worked in that area with the same old man, that in approaching the area identified as the site, the old man had refused to be driven directly across it and instead had insisted on making a long detour around it. His actions had led the researcher to conclude that the area contained a women's sacred site, and indeed the old man's actions had been more circumspect and respectful (or fearful) than those expected by the women who had placed no entry restrictions on the flat land within the site, and had been more concerned by the possibility of damage to hills. A public road already had been built between the hills, thereby crossing the area, and the women had raised no objection to its continued use.

I later documented related sites in that region that fortunately further confirmed the decision I had made at that time. There still remain, however, at least two interesting aspects of this incident that have relevance for the present discussion. Both relate to the old man's annoyance with, and anxiety about, our activities, and both are derived from the ongoing interpretation of tradition that has resulted from the presentation of such information to non-Aboriginal society.

## The Primacy Accorded Male Knowledge

The first of these aspects concerns the lead taken by men in presenting Aboriginal beliefs to non-Aboriginal people. The history of black-white relations in the Northern Territory has given birth to a practice by which men are charged with the responsibility for speaking publicly to non-Aboriginal Australia on matters of religious concern. This is noticeable as early as the beginning of the century, when two researchers, Baldwin Spencer and F. J. Gillen, traveled through virtually uncharted areas of the Territory recording information on the various Aboriginal groups that they encountered. As men, they were informed mostly by men, and, given that Aboriginal tradition now says that it is men's knowledge that should be given by men to men, it is not surprising to find that it was very largely men's business about which they were told, and men's ceremonies that they were allowed to witness.[6]

This process has been experienced repeatedly by the mostly male researchers who followed Spencer and Gillen over the decades and is evidenced in their work, and moreover was reproduced in the interactions of Aboriginal people with the overwhelmingly male administrators who were sent to survive the physical rigors of life in the Northern Territory during the first few decades of this century. Whenever serious matters relating to country, and thus to Dreaming, were discussed, it was inevitably men who came forward to speak. This same point was made by Diane Bell in discussing women's cultural responsibilities in central Australia (Bell 1983: 46).

Tradition would have dictated this course by simple reference to the gender division inherent in the transmission of religious knowledge, regardless of the equality or relative inequality of men and women in the traditional political domain of the time. Although I do not wish to enter the debate about the position of women in Aboriginal society prior to colonization here, I think it reasonable to conclude that these new circumstances fostered an interpretation of tradition that determined that men were thus the most appropriate spokespeople. This tradition now has precedents that extend beyond living memory. "By the time it was proposed that councils should be established on settlements, the die was cast. Men had become the political spokespersons and women the `followers'" (Bell 1983: 46).

The land claim process has reproduced and further elaborated this process. Male dominated land councils have been entrusted with the responsibility of presenting a case that demonstrates traditional ownership of an area of land by a defined group of Aboriginal people. The context in which that traditional ownership

6. See, for example, Spencer and Gillen (1904).

must be demonstrated is, first, an intellectual one in which there is already extensive prior anthropological documentation that supports the seniority of men, and, second, a socially structured one in which the judge and senior legal counsel are all male. Thus Aboriginal men provide the primary evidence on Dreaming association with their land. Meanwhile, women provide supplementary evidence largely confined to traditional foraging practices and similar secondary issues.

Any attempt to demonstrate their religious responsibilities is inevitably limited by the gender composition of the court,[7] and means devised to remedy the situation are fraught with pitfalls. Thus, in some recent land claims[8] the Aboriginal land commissioner has considered it appropriate that his wife (who normally has no jurisdiction in the court) take his place in witnessing women's ceremonial activities submitted as evidence to the court. Men, on the other hand, may expect the presence of the commissioner himself and the status that such a presence endows. Such precedents do little to address the paradox of a body of tradition that now places men as the spokespeople for religious matters but also expects women to maintain their responsibilities to sacred sites and preserve the Law.

As has become clear, it is not just Aboriginal tradition that creates the paradox, but also the social structure of the non-Aboriginal society with which it must interact. Such interaction of tradition with the wider society has further implications, because the role of Aboriginal men as primary political spokespeople has also meant that they have tended to become the initial recipients, and thus the redistributors, of many of the resources that flow from such interactions. While it is not the case that men are the sole recipients of all income from government sources, they do tend to gain resources more readily, such as vehicles or consultation fees. Moreover, because men generally are consulted first, or are the only people consulted, their social standing in the community is further enhanced. Hence the importance that is associated with the primary role that Aboriginal men take in negotiations with the wider society. Hence also the threat posed by any increased role taken by women in this regard.

7. See Rowell (1983) for an extended discussion of this.
8. In particular, I refer to the Jasper Gorge/Kidman Springs and Pigeon Hole Land Claims.

Such concerns may well have played a part in the response of the old man in the incident discussed earlier. It should be noted in this instance that his wife supported his position to the likely detriment of her own. As mentioned earlier, the seniority of men in such public contexts is a tradition established prior to living memory and thus has relevance to women as well as to men, paradoxical though that might prove in certain contexts. As such, it is part of the unbroken Law that must be continued. Other women, placed under slightly different circumstances, reached different conclusions as to how that paradox should be resolved.

*Common Ground*

However, there are also other implications problematic to men, which flow from the incorporation of women into such political consultations, and which may have been relevant to these particular circumstances.

In an attempt to explain the continued relevance of women's responsibilities to Aboriginal culture in spite of the severely limited role women have been able to gain in black-white relations, much has been made by some writers, particularly Bell (1983), of the separation of the domains of men and women. While this approach has considerable value, such an emphasis on separation, and on the relative evaluation of men and women as equal but different, meanwhile has tended to distract attention from an issue that has considerable bearing on the articulation of tradition; that is, the joint incorporation of women and men within a common culture.

Although in theory over the generations women have passed down knowledge to women, and men have passed down knowledge to men, that male and female knowledge is integral to a single body of knowledge, and much of that single body of knowledge is held in common by both. When women recount Dreaming that relates to a women's site they must make reference to that common body. Yet, as noted earlier, it is men who have most successfully laid claim to the right to speak on such issues. Only secret women's knowledge is indisputably within the prerogative of women.

When women evoke their right and responsibility to protect women's sites by providing information on that site to a researcher who is not a custodian, they tread on the responsibilities that generally accrue to men and are the basis of men's social status. Yet both sets of responsibilities are perceived as having their origins in tradition. These contradictions come from the intermeshing of tradition with the present-day context and may at times seem highly problematic to some men, as well as to women.

The perceived dangers are enhanced by the secrecy that is imposed by traditional prohibitions on men being told women's business. The constraints that protect the integrity of men's knowledge also prevent men from finding out what information women have communicated. They potentially fear, therefore, that women have not only told women's knowledge and commonly held knowledge, but that they have also told an outsider secret men's business. This not only threatens the men's power base, it also threatens their well-being if they have thereby failed in their responsibilities as custodians. The complications of intermeshing Aboriginal tradition with an alien culture have moved the processes involved partially beyond their control.

Hence the old man's song as we sat huddled in the dark whispering secrets. The song, as I mentioned above, was interpreted by the women as a threat, telling us to keep away from men's business. Although it related to a site that was spatially separate from the damaged site that we were discussing, indeed several kilometers away, the sites were cognitively connected. While the women in fact conscientiously avoided men's business, I later learned through women's business indications of the probable association in the old man's mind. His fear, then, had real foundations, although at the time it was largely misplaced.

This particular contradiction in the interpretation and maintenance of tradition in relation to sacred sites has even greater potency when the knowledge that must be communicated by women is both common to men and women and of a sensitive nature. This contradiction is especially pertinent when women's sites occur in conjunction with men's sites. Documenting such sites generally requires the acquisition of information from both men and women, and each block of information is likely to contain knowledge that pertains more readily to the domain of the opposite sex.

Moreover, the information is provided with the understanding that some leakage will occur, either indicating the existence of knowledge to which the opposite sex should have no access, or, of more specific relevance to the present discussion, indicating that women have communicated, through necessity, knowledge that men are unwilling to accept as being within their prerogative.

This is perhaps best illustrated by a large and important site that, as part of its associated Dreaming, required discussion of the involvement of women in the initiation of young boys. Previous documentations of the area had unearthed a range of individual Dreamings related to that location, but with no indication of how these might be interrelated. It was only when the site became threatened by extensive mining exploration that a decision was made to resolve this dilemma.

The making of this decision was preceded by a period of impasse, however, when the men documented one small part and then defined the rest of the site (in fact the larger portion) as women's business, while the women were prepared to discuss only small sections of that larger portion on the basis that the men would be angered by what they said.

As it happens, this incident occurred after a period when a few of the more prominent women involved had felt under attack by the men for daring to make reference to anything that might be construed as men's business. In fact, one woman's very serious illness had been attributed to the sorcery of men angered at a remark she had made to another researcher. Not surprisingly, they were reluctant to commit themselves to any discussion of young men's business, and instead laid that responsibility in no uncertain terms at the feet of the men. The men, on the other hand, were similarly reluctant to publicly discuss matters that could be construed as women's business – in this case, the ceremonial responsibilities of women during young men's business.

This impasse was overcome only by the actions of a senior Lawman – of such considerable age, wisdom, and renown that he could carry responsibility for making what was to all intents and purposes a revolutionary decision. He sat down in front of a video camera with an audience of both men and women and told the story of the site. First, he told of the involvement of both men and women in a common ceremony, which thereby integrated both the total area and the range of Dreamings involved; and second, he told the underlying story that explained the extraordinary importance of the site that had previously lain hidden by the exaggerated separation of men's business and women's business that had emerged to meet the modern context, when such knowledge must be communicated to outsiders.

This was an extraordinary and unprecedented act that reversed previous interpretations of the appropriate translation of traditional practice. It not only saved that site by publicly annihilating any possible future denigration of the site's importance, it also established a basis for future cooperative efforts between men and women in defending other sites in that region that might become the focus of mining developments.

A significant part of the present context that creates such dilemmas for the interpretation of tradition stems from the fact that much knowledge is absorbed and transmitted in Aboriginal culture in very different ways from those predominating in the wider Australian society. In this paper, for example, I have tended to treat knowledge as an abstract fact that can be spoken of and then recorded in writing. This is how Australian society records Aboriginal culture and how it deals with the culture in law. As a result, however, I have avoided an integral part of Aboriginal "knowing": that of experience – of seeing a site, of being there and of witnessing or participating in ceremonies that demonstrate Dreaming.

Much knowledge is absorbed during ceremonies, and when the ceremony contains certain public components, these components are absorbed by both men and women. While they may be to some extent differently understood and experienced by each, they also testify to the common heritage that each safeguards for the other. This certainly would have been true of knowledge pertaining to the sacred site mentioned earlier.

Such a context is difficult to reproduce for interaction with an alien culture and attempts to do so in land claim courts have not been entirely successful. Instead, priority has been given to the concept of separation in order to maintain the secrecy necessitated by the detailed and extensive recording of religious knowledge in writing, as opposed to the controlled partial exposure in ceremony.

This very process of creating a permanent, written record is hazardous, for it not only transforms the manner in which knowledge is transmitted from one generation to another, it also potentially places that knowledge within the grasp of other cultures, which do not practice a gender division of knowledge equivalent to that which forms the basis of Aboriginal culture.

## Losing Control of Traditional Knowledge

To transmit knowledge from Aboriginal culture within a context structured by the outside world is to transform the conditions under which it may be evaluated and treated. Although the Aboriginal Areas Protection Authority, which is largely Aboriginal in composition, recognizes this problem and attempts to maintain procedures that reduce the impact as far as possible, it cannot guarantee that circumstances will not change in the future. Thus, to entrust traditional knowledge to an outside body such as the Protection Authority is an act of faith and a decision that cannot be taken lightly.

I have encountered such concerns many times – most vividly in a community where there were very few women's sacred sites, and where, although there had been earlier documentation of men's sites, no previous recording of women's sites had been undertaken. My role there was a new experience for both the men and the women and appeared to cause at least one of the older men a certain amount of consternation, for he discreetly but persistently probed to find out what the women had told me, while also trying to refute the significance of anything they might have said.

The Dreaming that the women had recounted referred to a very important Dreaming that I had encountered elsewhere along its Dreaming track and had found recorded in detail in historical manuscripts dating from early this century. All sources pointed to the considerable importance of this Dreaming in underlying other Dreamings, and confirmed in basic terms the knowledge I had been given by the women.

I found, however, that the earlier documentations by men of one of these sites had made reference only to more superficial stories. This fact led me to consider the possibility that although the women had provided me with only skeleton information in relation to each site, the information I held was not to be relayed to young men or to male outsiders. I am unsure to this day whether the old man's concern was related to a woman such as myself holding such information, or whether his concern related to a more generalized fear that once the knowledge was in the hands of an outsider, its details might become available to men (I suspect it was both).

This particular concern is one that has surfaced repeatedly in the history of legislation associated with sacred sites. Such legislation is nominally intended to facilitate the maintenance of tradition but, in the very process of so doing, it potentially contradicts the basis of that tradition, for it takes knowledge outside the direct control of those people who have been charged by tradition with its safekeeping. The *Northern Territory Aboriginal Sacred Sites Act* (1989) attempts to deal with this in part by ensuring an Aboriginal majority on the board that protects such knowledge from public scrutiny, and by imposing heavy penalties for the disclosure of traditionally secret material. It also provides for the possibility of locally constituted committees to discuss sensitive information.

However, this does not change the fact that the total context in which traditional information is now protected has changed radically. In the past, discrete communities, and indeed individual custodians within those communities, safeguarded that knowledge from inappropriate dissemination and use by outsiders, including Aboriginal outsiders. Now a body selected from across a huge region has that responsibility, only partially reduced symbolically by the prescription that the members of that body should consult with the traditional custodians.

In the past those same custodians controlled the flow and interpretation of that knowledge as it was passed from one generation to another. Indeed, it is generally presumed that since contact with non-Aboriginal society, many senior custodians have decided to die taking their knowledge with them rather than transmit it to a younger generation seen as ill-equipped to receive it. Such decisions have been the prerogative, but also the responsibility, of senior custodians. In Aboriginal society the reservoir of a person's knowledge is the repository of their worth. The knowledge they hold is testimony both to their years of intimate association with their land and to the esteem in which they were held by earlier custodians who saw fit to entrust them with its care. How they equip that trust will be the measure of their future reputation[9]. The option of making a written record and the potential capacity thereby to provide sites with protection that no longer

9. Debates about the control of Ted Strehlow's collection of sacred knowledge and objects revolve around this sensitive issue. Some aspects of this are discussed in McNally (1981).

can be assured by secrecy or by the actions of individual Lawmen and women produces new dilemmas.

While custodians nominally make a conscious choice to cede that control and thus to confirm this new interpretation of tradition, external factors derived from the development aspirations of modern Australia constrain the parameters of that choice. Custodians are left with the alternatives of breaching tradition and Law by standing idly by while their sites are destroyed by forces beyond their control, or accepting an interpretation of tradition that is contrary to previous interpretations, and therefore potentially a breach in the continuity of Law. To continue tradition thus means to change it.

## Conclusions

Although the concept of tradition incorporates an emphasis on continuity, when the traditions under discussion are those of an indigenous ethnic minority, the encompassing social order to which those traditions relate is radically different from the source of those traditions. Such traditions must deal therefore with considerable change. Not only is the meaning they derive from the wider society transformed, but so is the nature of their interrelationship with each other. In their new setting, contradictions may arise in the articulation of those traditions, ultimately requiring a reinterpretation of precisely what should be expressed as traditional practice.

Yet it was pointed out initially that the term "tradition" has wide currency in many different contexts in evoking contrast with the modern world as a perceived medium of incessant change. The processes identified above thus have implications that extend beyond the circumstances of indigenous people, even beyond those all ethnic minorities must confront. They can apply to any discussion of the maintenance of traditional practice in contemporary society, and all such references should be viewed with a critical eye, for common usage clearly disguises many other processes at work.

I have addressed this problem by focusing on the dilemmas that confront Aboriginal women in fulfilling traditional responsibilities to sacred sites. The problems overall for women have proved greater than those for men, largely because the context through which they must resolve those problems already has been structured by men. However, the constraints that they experience are not generated internally simply as a result of their structural position relative to men; rather, they emerge from the interaction of Aboriginal culture with other cultures, in relation to which they are relatively powerless. They are forced to confront the paradoxes that emerge, for these are created by interests that otherwise could threaten the continuing viability of Aboriginal culture. As a result, not just Aboriginal women in one area or even Aboriginal women as a whole must deal with such dilemmas. Rather, the entire Aboriginal community must do so; a process that over time changes the community's interpretation of tradition to meet its traditional responsibilities to continue the Dreaming.

# 13

## Recent Change in Inuit Summer Residence Patterning at Clyde River, East Baffin Island

*George W. Wenzel*

After thirty years of Canadian government relocation policy, Eastern Arctic Inuit maintained into the 1980s a form of summer settlement and community that closely conformed to ethnographic (Boas 1888; Mathiassen 1928) and ethnological (Damas 1963) accounts. Since about 1985, however, this customary pattern of seasonal camping has undergone extensive modification. Notable elements of this change are a constricting of the geographic range of summer camps, and a distinct shift away from the extended family and sociality as the focus of summer camp groups to association centered on nonkin imported resource providers. This paper examines the dynamics of these changes among the Inuit of Clyde River, East Baffin Island, Canada.[1]

### Introduction

Increasingly, descriptions of modernization in the Canadian north (see, for instance, Vallee, Smith, and Cooper 1984) present the view that this process, especially since 1960, has resulted in the near extirpation of what is conventionally referred to as Inuit traditional culture. This is seen as primarily the result of Euro-Canadian sociocultural and technoeconomic initiatives, spearheaded by government agencies, religious organizations, and commercial-industrial interests. In the Eastern Arctic, the govern-

1. This paper is based on research conducted at Clyde River, Northwest Territories, between 1971 and 1990. Primary support for work carried out before 1984 was provided by Carnegie Museum and McMaster University, the Canadian Ethnology Service, and the Department of Indian and Northern Affairs, Canada. Research conducted after 1983 has been supported by the Social Sciences and Humanities Research Council of Canada.

ment-initiated resettlement of Inuit into centralized communities during the 1950s and 1960s has been interpreted as one of the prime components of this wide-scale change.

In fact, many areas of contemporary Inuit life refute the validity of this simplistic "modernization = change" view. This paper is concerned with two key aspects of Inuit traditional culture in the Clyde River region of Eastern Baffin Island and with the conditions that are now operating to weaken them.

The first is the dispersed summer settlement-subsistence pattern still followed by East Baffin Inuit. The other is the structural role of the extended family as a core organizing element of Clyde Inuit ecological and economic activities. Both, as will be shown, are closely interrelated. The third focus is the way these two elements of Clyde traditional culture and society have been progressively weakened by the intervention of a "nontraditional" change agent, the international animal rights movement.

## Background to the Study

The community of Clyde River (see Figure 13.1) is situated on the east coast of Baffin Island and, as of 1988, had an indigenous population of 531 Inuit. There are also roughly fifteen nonnative personnel – principally in the fields of health care, education, and administration – in residence in the settlement for periods of eight to eleven months. Nonnative participation in either the sociocultural or ecological activities of the community is negligible.

The local area used by the Clyde Inuit extends from Buchan Gulf south to Cape Hooper and inland to at least the Barnes Ice Cap, approximately 85,000 square kilometers total (160 sq. km. per person) and roughly conforms to the area known to have been in use from 1920 until intensive government intervention (ca. 1950) in the region. While this large area theoretically is used in its entirety for subsistence purposes, much of the inland area is effectively closed because of unfavorable topography. Rather, the bulk of Clyde Inuit harvesting is concentrated on the waters and landfast ice that touch this complex coastline, and only brief periods (principally in the late winter and early fall) are spent away from the sea (see Table 13.1).

The principal economic orientation of the local Inuit is wildlife harvesting, most notably ringed seals (*Phoca hispida*), caribou (*Rangifer tarandus*), arctic char (*Salvelinus alpinus*), narwhal (*Mon-*

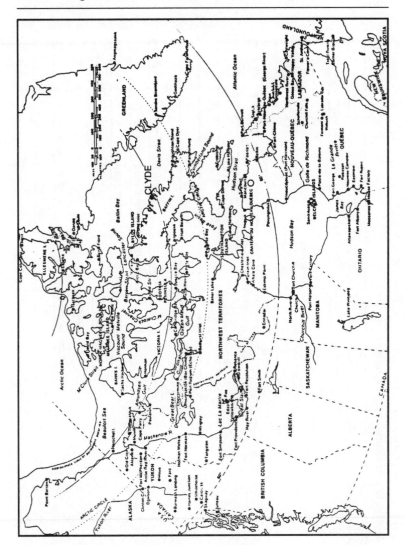

**Figure 13.1:** The Canadian Arctic

*odon monoceros*) and polar bear (*Ursus arcticus*). Of these, the seal, the polar bear, and, to a lesser degree, the narwhal also provide Clyde Inuit with export commodities. The present community was created by the Canadian government in the early 1950s (regional population approximately 190, Clyde River village pop-

**Table 13.1:** Principal Adaptive Relationships in the Clyde System

| SYSTEM COMPONENTS | SEASONAL ASSOCIATIONS | | | | | | | | | | | |
|---|---|---|---|---|---|---|---|---|---|---|---|---|
| | Jun | Jul | Aug | Sep | Oct | Nov | Dec | Jan | Feb | Mar | Apr | May |
| **I. Environmental Set:** | | | | | | | | | | | | |
| **a. physical forms –** | | | | | | | | | | | | |
| 1) usable light | 24 hrs | | | decreasing | | minimal | | | | increasing | | |
| 2) temperature | 0°C | | | -20°C | | below -30°C | | | | -20°C | | |
| 3) sea ice | weak or absent | | | | constant | | | | | | | |
| 4) lake ice | weak | | absent | | | | constant | | | | | |
| 5) snow | little or none | | | | total cover | | | | | | | |
| 6) wind chill | negligible | | | | | major | | | | | | |
| 7) wind speed | | | | | | | major | | | | | |
| **b. biological forms –** | | | | | | | | | | | | |
| 1) ringed seal | basking or swimming | | | | | breathing holes | | | | | basking | |
| 2) polar bear | sea ice / coast (some females inland Nov - Jan/Feb) | | | | | | | | | | | |
| 3) caribou | near coast | | | | inland winter range | | | | | | near coast | |
| 4) narwhal | migrations | | | | | | | | | | | |
| 5) bearded seal | open water | | | | | | | | | | | |
| 6) arctic char | bays and open sea | | | | | inland lakes | | | | | | |
| 7) small game | | | | | | scattered | | | | | | |

**Table 13.1:** *Continued*

| SYSTEM COMPONENTS | SEASONAL ASSOCIATIONS |
| --- | --- |
| | Jun / Jul / Aug / Sep / Oct / Nov / Dec / Jan / Feb / Mar / Apr / May |
| 8) migratory birds | some nesting |
| 9) arctic fox | inland ——————— scattered over land and sea ice |

Material Culture Interface: 1) hunting technology; 2) transportation; 3) shelter; 4) fuel

II. Inuit Action Set:

| | SEASONAL ASSOCIATIONS |
| --- | --- |
| a. marine hunting- | |
| 1) ringed seal | uuttuq and boat hunting ——— mauluqpuq ——— uuttuq |
| 2) narwhal | leads and boats |
| 3) bearded seal | boats |
| 4) polar bear | land and sea ice |
| b. land hunting- | |
| 1) caribou | summer camps ——————— inland journeys |
| 2) small game | occasional |
| c. mixed hunting- | |
| 1) migratory birds | occasional |
| 2) arctic fox | sea ice |
| 3) arctic char | netting ——————— inland ice fishing |

ulation approximately 90) and since 1975 it has been the main residental locus for all but a handful of Inuit (see Wenzel 1981, 1983).

## Clyde Social Organization and Settlement

Before the establishment by the government of a single regional population center, the customary annual winter pattern of settlement consisted of five to eight semipermanent villages (see Figure 13.2). These communities, unlike the sea ice winter village model often presented for Canadian Inuit, were shore sites that afforded maximum access to reliable breathing hole sealing areas in fjords and bays. Polar bear and Arctic fox were also important winter resources, the latter mainly for export rather than for food. Informant information indicates that such winter sites were repeatedly reoccupied; Nitsilsiuk at Scott Inlet, for example, was reoccupied for twenty-six years.

Winter houses were constructed either of snow (*illiuk*) or of canvas, sod, and wood (*qangmaq*), and household organization centered on the nuclear family (*illugariit*). The focal social organizational feature of Clyde winter villages, however, was the consanguineously linked extended family (*ilagiit*), with the oldest resident male providing leadership (*isumataq*) to the local kindred (see Damas 1963: 55; see also Wenzel 1981). In general, the core of such units was male relatedness, with each *illugariit* domiciled separately.

The precentralized summer settlement pattern was characterized by considerable spatial mobility, but the same core kindred unity. Winter villages usually were vacated in May and only reestablished in September and October. Instead, through the spring, summer, and early fall, each group used a number of tent camps and occasionally entered into brief periods of summer coresidence with other *ilagiit*.

In early summer, camp permanence was highly transitory, with some sites used only for a few days. Through June and July, *ilagiit* concentrated subsistence activities on caribou, establishing residence in valleys near the coast and at the heads of fjords. At this time, camp location changed every few days to a week. By late summer, the presence of narwhal and returning arctic char along the now ice-free coast meant a return to a mainly shore-based pattern of camping, with well-located sites being used for up to a month.

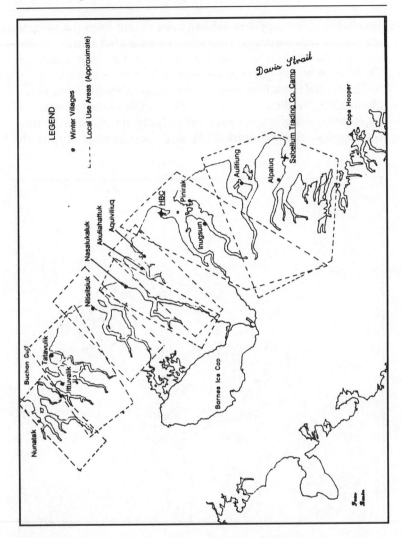

**Figure 13.2:** Clyde Inuit socio-territorial areas, 1920–1945

While the summer season was one of significantly greater territorial and resource dispersal for East Baffin Inuit than winter, Clyde area *ilagiit* maintained a high degree of structural cohesion. Brief periods, especially during caribou season, did occur when one or more households separated from the main unit; however, the "fission-fusion" model said to typify Inuit summer activities (see Balikci 1968) appears to have been absent from the pregovernment Clyde pattern. At Clyde, the extended family, rather than the household, remained the social and economic focus of Clyde subsistence operations in both winter and summer.

The formal Canadian government policy of resettlement began about 1952. By 1965, only two traditional *ilagiit*-based villages, Aqviqtiuq at Eglinton Fjord and Alpatu on Alexander Bay, remained vital (see Figure 13.3), with populations of roughly

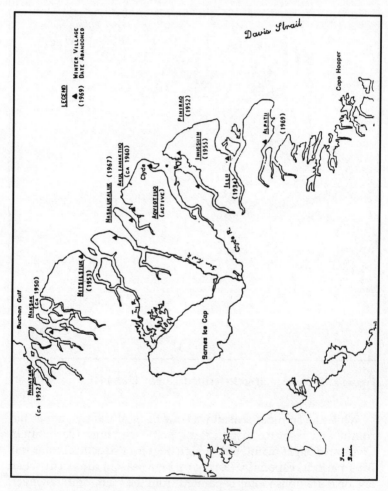

**Figure 13.3:** Clyde winter settlements, 1920-1990

twenty-eight and thirty-five members, respectively. Approximately 150 formerly land-based Inuit by then lived in Clyde settlement. In 1969, due to illness among several elderly members, the Alpatu population also immigrated to Clyde River, Aqviqtiuq community was reduced to one nuclear household by 1975.

## Clyde Ecology and Economy, 1961–1983

The ecology and economy of the Clyde Inuit has retained its traditional subsistence focus into the present, with the ringed seal (*natsiq*) still the primary focus of harvesting. During the pregovernment fur trade era (1923–1945), the region's Inuit were introduced to trapping and incorporated it into their winter activity system, exploiting fox in conjunction with breathing hole sealing. These two activities were compatible (Wenzel 1981) because fox, as a scavenger of seals killed by both Inuit and bears, are a significant presence on the winter sea ice.

Hudson's Bay Company archival sources and Clyde informants indicate that while fox trapping was engaged in for commercial exchange, it had little disruptive effect on local socioeconomic and ecological relations. Goldring's (1986: 171) observation about the Cumberland Sound natives seems to be equally applicable to the Clyde community: "The Cumberland Sound natives' economic strategy was well understood and accepted with resignation by the HBC's managers. The Inuit lived comfortably on seals until they wanted coffee or biscuits, then trapped a few foxes to warrant a trip into Pangnirtung."

Although the fur trade appears to have played a far less significant role in the lives of East Baffin Inuit than is often attributed to it (see Damas 1988), the postwar collapse of the world fox market was strongly felt in the area. This was because, as Goldring (1986) points out, although Inuit had little dependence on the luxuries (coffee, biscuits) such economic contact provided, several decades of intense exchange had made firearms, wood, and iron integral to subsistence operations. The loss of trapping cost Clyde Inuit the exchange commodity that provided access to these ecological necessities.

The Clyde situation, as in other parts of the Canadian Arctic (see Damas 1984), was exacerbated by government postwar policy. As already mentioned, the principal facet of this policy was the relocation of Inuit from traditional villages to government-created settlements in order to provide public health and education services.

Clyde Inuit remember this as a particularly difficult period, economically and ecologically. First, hunters had to adjust to a new area that experienced harvesting pressure far above that of the customary *ilagiit*-based winter situation. It was during winter sealing that this latter facet of the situation became particularly apparent. While the maximum breathing hole hunting group prior to the early 1950s had numbered three to eight men, by 1960 as many as thirty hunters were concentrating their daily efforts in the main sealing area nearest the new settlement.

Directly related to this dilemma was the fact that, unlike the case with customary winter *ilagiit* sealing, post-relocation centralization imposed significantly greater time and distance costs on Clyde hunters (see Table 13.2). While precentralized sealing rarely meant more than a total of two hours of round-trip travel by dogteam for hunters, residence at Clyde River meant sealers at

**Table 13.2:** Time Allocation in Clyde Winter Seal Hunting Sample

| | | TIME (HR:MIN) | | | |
|---|---|---|---|---|---|
| | TRANSPORT | TRAVEL[2] | SEARCH | HUNTING | SEALS |
| **Sample I[1]** | | | | | |
| Aqviqtiuq | dogteam | 1:30 | 1:30 | 2:00 | — |
| | | 1:15 | 2:40 | 1:45 | — |
| | | 1:30 | 1:35 | 4:00 | 1 |
| | | 1:20 | 0:50 | 3:50 | 1 |
| | | 1:30 | 1:05 | 4:45 | 3 |
| | | 1:25 | 1:55 | 3:10 | 1 |
| **Sample II[3]** | | | | | |
| Clyde River | dogteam | 3:45 | 1:55 | 2:05 | 1 |
| | | 3:40 | 2:20 | 2:45 | 2 |
| | | 3:05 | 3:00 | 2:40 | 1 |
| **Sample III[4]** | | | | | |
| Clyde River | snowmobile | 2:00 | 2:35 | 1:20 | 1 |
| | | 2:20 | 1:40 | 2:35 | — |
| | | 2:05 | 3:00 | 2:55 | 2 |
| | | 1:35 | 1:30 | 2:05 | 2 |
| | | 2:20 | 3:10 | 3:05 | 1 |

[1]Activity of one hunter for one week in November 1971.
[2]Travel time calculation based on time to location of first breathing hole and return from same.
[3]Activity of one hunter for one week in February 1974.
[4]Activity of one hunter for one week in March 1985.

least doubled their trip time. Resettlement, therefore, meant a less advantageous ecological situation for harvesters.

Two events combined to alleviate this problem. First, in 1961, sealskins emerged as a commercial replacement for fox furs (see Foote 1967). From 1960 to 1962, skin prices jumped from roughly $0.50 to $4.00 per skin, beginning a general upward trend (see Wenzel 1986a) that lasted until roughly 1983. The second event was the introduction of mechanized forms of winter and summer transport (snowmobiles and outboard equipped wood and canvas canoes, respectively) to Clyde Inuit in the early 1960s.

Although this equipment was costly for the time (approximately $600.00 for a snowmobile, and $1,500.00 for a canoe and engine), this equipment had a marked impact on Clyde Inuit ecological relations. Snow machines provided an effective technological means of offsetting the ecological disadvantages that had attended the early stages of centralization by increasing hunter mobility and reducing time costs. Moreover, since *natsiq* were the central focus of virtually all winter harvesting effort, successful food hunting also provided commercially exchangeable sealskins (and occasional polar bear hides [see Wenzel 1991: 118]).

The outboard powered canoe had an equally important, if slightly different, ecological effect. While the snowmobile allowed hunters to function more effectively with regard to the centralized settlement during winter, motorized water travel permitted Clyde Inuit to reestablish a dispersed *ilagiit*-focused pattern of summer residence that retained a strong marine orientation.

Through the 1950s, the pattern of summer camp distribution underwent a marked change in the East Baffin region. In particular, inhabitants of Clyde Village were forced to adopt a highly restricted pattern that was localized in the Clyde Inlet-Inugsuin Fjord area, contiguous to the government community. This pattern became more pronounced as traditional settlements closed and their members moved to Clyde.

This resettlement occurred for two reasons. First, the cost of the motorized boats used for both the large-scale transport of family groups and hunting was unaffordable after the collapse of the fox trade. Indeed, during this period, all three of the diesel driven whaleboats owned by Clyde Inuit fell into disrepair because of their owners' inability to maintain them. Second, from June to September offered the most reliable time in the settlement to obtain casual or seasonal employment from the government and the Hudson's Bay Company. As a result, *ilagiit* centered camps became fragmented as members of both sexes responded to the wage opportunities present in Clyde village.

Motorized snowmobile and canoe travel provided Clyde Inuit with both winter (over ice) and summer (open-water) access to areas remote to the settlement, while allowing relative ease of return as circumstances dictated. Hunters and their families for the first time were able to resupply even when living in distant camps and, equally important, were able to return to Clyde for brief periods of employment when cash resources were needed for camp maintenance. After more than a decade-long hiatus from dispersed summer settlement, Clyde Inuit were able to return to an extended family pattern of settlement that fully encompassed their former areas of traditional use.

### The Effect of the EC Sealskin Boycott

Ringed seals remained the ecological focus of Clyde Inuit harvesting (see Table 13.3) through the 1970s and early 1980s. They

**Table 13.3:** Importance of Ringed Seal in the Clyde Inuit Diet

| YEAR/SEASON | NUMBER OF SEALS HARVESTED | EDIBLE WEIGHT (KG) | EDIBLE BIOMASS ALL SOURCES (KG) |
|---|---|---|---|
| **1981:** | | | |
| winter | 1,052 | 24,196 | 40,856 |
| spring | 1,317 | 30,291 | 41,517 |
| summer | 697 | 16,031 | 28,662 |
| autumn | 312 | 7,176 | 10,894 |
| **1982:** | | | |
| winter | 812 | 18,676 | 45,092 |
| spring | 947 | 21,781 | 37,485 |
| summer | 544 | 12,512 | 25,769 |
| autumn | 204 | 4,692 | 7,195 |
| **1983:** | | | |
| winter | 932 | 21,436 | 42,337 |
| spring | 689 | 15,847 | 33,197 |
| summer | 763 | 17,549 | 39,813 |
| autumn | 294 | 6,762 | 10,681 |

[1]Source for aggregate harvest data: Baffin Regional Inuit Association Harvest Study n.d.a., n.d.b., n.d.c.
[2]Source of edible weight data: Foote 1967; Wenzel 1983.

also formed the stable cash economic base of the harvesting system, evidenced by their contribution to Clyde hunter income. While the annual sales of harvest products during the 1970s provided only some $1,500 per man (the adult hunting population being male and more than sixteen years of age), the twenty most active Clyde harvesters, in fact, earned an annual average of slightly more than $2,850 from the combined sale of sealskins, polar bear and arctic fox furs, and narwhal ivory. Overall, ringed sealskins amounted to 61.3 percent of the general cash revenue received at Clyde from hunting during the decade.

Although sometimes overlooked by scholars, ringed seals held another important place in the ecologic-economic system of the community between 1961 and 1983. The ringed seal was the only species that provided both food and cash that was not subject to government-imposed harvesting restrictions.

Thus, hunters were able to adjust their sealing efforts in relation to the cash requirements of hunting; for instance, if a downpayment was needed for the purchase of a new snowmobile, a man would increase his short-term pursuit of ringed seals. In addition, ringed sealskin sales provided a means for even young and relatively inexperienced hunters to obtain the money needed to capitalize a modern hunting outfit. By 1975, 71 full-time and part-time Clyde hunters operated an inventory consisting of fifty-two functioning snow machines and thirty-three motorized canoes.

By the latter part of the decade, the pattern of Clyde resource exploitation had become more diversified than at any other time during the centralized settlement period. Late winter hunting now included forays inland of one or more weeks by *ilagiit*-affiliated kinsmen for caribou and arctic char, while summer saw Clyde Inuit disperse into *ilagiit*-based camps from Buchan Gulf to Alexander Bay.

Throughout summer, *ilagiit* remained together, moving to various sites along the coast to seal, fish, and capture narwhal. These same camps provided the base for the periodic dispatch of two to four young and middle-aged men from each family into the hills to hunt caribou.

The European Community's decision in 1983, at the behest of a coalition of animal rights organizations, to ban most Canadian sealskin imports (European Community 1983) – although directed at the northwest Atlantic industrial harp seal hunt (Malouf 1986) – almost immediately affected the economic situation of

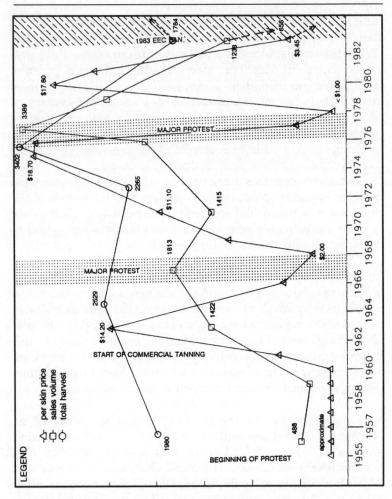

**Figure 13.4:** Clyde seal harvest data, 1955-1982

Inuit communities like Clyde River. As Figure 13.4 shows, the price of ringed sealskins – which, with the exception of two brief fluctuations, had followed a steadily rising course for two decades – suddenly reversed and rapidly fell to pre-1961 levels.

While the loss of sealskin income was felt generally across the community, its most acute impact was on those Clyde Inuit who were full-time, experienced hunters, mainly men between thirty and fifty years old, who were central figures in the extended family organization of the village. This was because *natsiq* represented the base food and cash species pursued by this group. The loss of the cash sales of ringed seal hunting exposed these men to the realities of the cost of imported technology. Almost overnight, the principal hunting cadre in the community was confronted with the loss of its chief revenue source for capitalizing, operating, and maintaining its equipment (see Table 13.4).

In effect, hunters experienced a double bind: not just high equipment costs, but also a suddenly devalued exchange commodity. Moreover, this situation was weakened further by local and international actions that affected two other sectors of the wildlife economy.

The first was a marked reduction in 1985 in the availability of polar bears, the other main cash species in the area, from forty-five animals to fifteen through government regulation (see Freeman 1986; Lloyd 1986). As already shown in Table 13.4, bears represent

**Table 13.4:** Harvester Capital and Operations Costs, Clyde River, NWT[1]

|  | 1975-76 (SSU=$16.40) | 1984-85 (SSU=$4.50) |
|---|---|---|
| 1. Capital Items |  |  |
| snowmobile | $2,300/140 SSU | $2,800/621 SSU |
| canoe | 1,800/110 | 3,000/667 |
| outboard motor | 1,800/110 | 3,300/733 |
| .222 cal rifle | 250/15 | 660/147 |
| .303 cal rifle | 150/9 | 350/78 |
| sleeping bag | 99/6 | 290/65 |
| camp stove | $6,444/393 SSU | $10,470/2327 SSU |
| 2. Snowmobile Parts |  |  |
| track assembly | $200/13 SSU | $390/87 SSU |
| piston | 42/3 | 80/18 |
| spark plug | 2/1 | 4/1 |
| **subtotal** | $244/17 SSU | $474/106 SSU |
| 3. Operational Items |  |  |
| gasoline (227.3 L) | $125/8 SSU | $128/29 SSU |
| avg. annual use = 3409.5 L | 1,875/120 | 1,920/435 |
| ammunition/box: .222 cal x 20 | 8.5/1 | 11.5/3 |
| avg. annual use = 50 boxes (1000) | 425/26 | 575/128 |
| **annual use subtotal** | $2,300/146 SSU | $2,495/563 |
| **Combined Costs** | $7,113/393 SSU | $13,439/2906 SSU |

[1]Costs are depicted in dollars and in sealskin units.

the second largest source of hunter produced cash income. The other involved a boycott of narwhal ivory in the United Kingdom (Harper 1984), ostensibly because narwhal had come to be perceived as an endangered species within that market. Although narwhal harvesting formed only a small element of Clyde Inuit harvesting, mainly from late August to mid-September, the ivory obtained from the tusks of male animals provided hunters with a small, but important, source of cash income at a time of the year when other exchange species were either undesirable or unavailable.

While the economic impact of the European Community's sealskin ban has been widely discussed (Malouf 1986; Wenzel 1986a, 1991), the ecological and sociocultural effects experienced in the Clyde area are only beginning to be recognized. There is a marked reduction in the general level of harvesting activity conducted by men not involved in at least part-time wage labor. Within the group considered to have been full-time hunters during the period between 1970 and 1983, a sample of six men (Wenzel [1986–89]) report that their harvesting efforts are limited to one or two weekly sealing trips during winter, rather than their former average of four such day trips. This group attributed the curtailment in their sealing trips to difficulty in purchasing sufficient quantities of gasoline for more frequent hunting and to an inability to afford replacement parts for old and worn equipment.

The loss of sealskin revenues is even more noticeable for its effect in the region since 1983 on the summer configuring of local land use. Ecologically, the distribution of these seasonal camps has returned to the constricted geographic pattern that it exhibited during the years when Clyde Inuit were adjusting to the loss of the Arctic fox market and wholesale resettlement.

The focal area for camp location once again has become the Clyde Inlet-Inugsuin Fjord area immediately adjacent to Clyde Village. Within this area, Clyde Inuit now establish four to five major summer residence sites, the most distant of which is eighty-five kilometers from Clyde, and the next farthest is less than 60 kilometers. In addition, two "commuter" camps, Supaikajuktuk and Upinavik, both within twenty-five kilometers of Clyde, are now regularly used in summer by households with members whose presence is required in the village on a daily basis.

Even more important than the change in the spatial distribution of summer settlement is the change in the organization of these camps. In all periods prior to 1983–1984 (Wenzel 1981; 1986b), the social focus of multihousehold summer camps was the *ilagiit*, or extended family, affiliation of camp residents (see Figure 13.5). Since 1983, however, there has been an increasing tendency for summer camps to coalesce not around core extended family members (generally genealogically superior older men

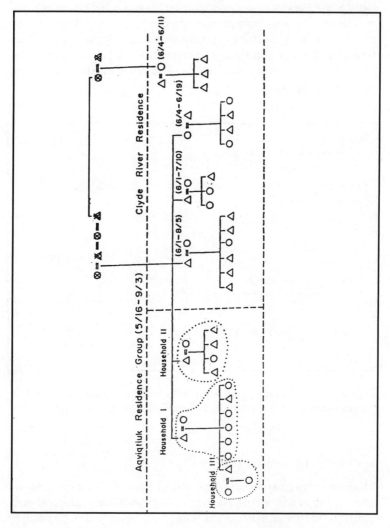

**Figure 13.5:** Eglinton Fiord summer camp group, May-September 1972

[see Damas 1963; Wenzel 1986b]), but around one or two often not linked by kinship men who hold wage positions in Clyde Village and who are, therefore, well-equipped and supplied (see Figure 13.6).

Such individuals have become important because the current money economy (both wage and wildlife exchange) that prevails at Clyde makes it difficult for *ilagiit* to organize, as they did before, the material resources needed for extended summer camp residence. The role of such individuals appears to center on their possession of important capital items of equipment (like large boats) and their ability to ensure that a surplus of otherwise scarce resources, like extra gasoline and oil, is available if needed by other camp residents.

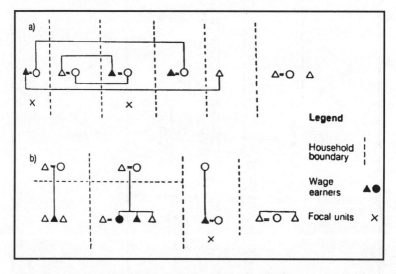

**Figure 13.6:** (a) Suluak camp composition 31 May-5 June 1985 and (b) Nuvuktiapik camp composition, 19 June-26 July 1985

## Summary and Conclusions

Modern ethnographic descriptions of Canadian Eastern Arctic often leave readers with the impression that the ecological-economic relations of modern Inuit have undergone drastic modification since World War II. This brief overview of Clyde River

during the last fifty years suggests, however, that local village situations have been considerably more stable in these areas,
despite significant postwar change to the region's indigenous settlement and demographic structure, than generally has been
assumed. Indeed, as this paper demonstrates, this stability can be
traced to the continuance of traditional ecological activities, albeit
conducted in a mixed economy framework in which the commercial attractiveness of sealskins for Euro-Canadians has been combined with customary local reliance on *natsiq* for food.

As this paper emphasizes, however, the economic, ecological,
and cultural stability of this mixed economy structure lately has
deteriorated, and these negative impacts can be traced to recent
efforts of the animal rights movement regarding commercial seal
hunting. While particular notice has been given to the economic
consequences of the seal protest, there also have been serious ecological and especially social organizational consequences arising
from the protest.

The two main ecological effects have been a serious erosion in
the ability of full-time hunters to participate extensively in all
forms of wildlife harvesting and a constriction of the effective
summer pattern of settlement (see Figure 13.7), and, to a lesser
degree, land use in the region. The latter condition closely resem-
bles the worst conditions experienced by Clyde Inuit during
other poor economic periods in the region.

The effect of the seal controversy on Clyde social organization
is, however, structural in nature and entirely unlike anything previously experienced by Inuit in the region. Because of the effect of
the sealskin market's dilution of local economic power away from
*ilagiit* collective organization to individuals, there has been a partial restructuring of land-based cooperative activities focusing on
economic, rather than social, conditions.

One result of this trend is that summer extra-village residence
and association now might be referred to as a mixed camp form.
These mixed camps roughly resemble what Guemple (1972) has
termed a "DP camp-type" organization. Although *ilagiit* organization remains at the core of Clyde Inuit social and economic
practice, at present it is unclear whether the mixed group pattern
of aggregation that appears to be emerging in place of extended
family-based settlement will continue to affect the summer ecological and socioeconomic relations of Clyde River and other
Eastern Arctic Inuit communities.

**Figure 13.7:** Summer camp type and distribution, 1970–1990

# Part 6

---

# Government Intervention

# Editorial

The territory of every foraging people still in existence falls inside the boundaries of a modern nation state. In most cases the foragers involved are aware of this fact, but the extent to which they have been affected by it varies considerably from one case to another.

As we approach the end of the twentieth century, one of the most crucial issues for foraging peoples (and thus for students of hunter-gatherer societies) is the extent to which they are integrated into the society within whose territory they live. In general, it may be inevitable that they will enter the larger system at the bottom of the economic and political hierarchy. Beyond that, however, as a growing number of studies attest,[1] there is considerable variation, both in the way that the larger societies deal with them and in the ways that the foragers themselves cope with the situation. A good idea of the extent of this variation is conveyed by the papers that follow.

The first paper, by Bwire T. M. Kaare, describes attempts by the government of Tanzania to integrate the Hadzabe (plural of Hadza) with the rest of the nation through the implementation of education and language policies rather than through the more old-fashioned approach of outright coercion. The Hadzabe, however, instead of being seduced or intimidated by the larger system, have remained determinedly independent. Furthermore, they have recognized clearly that they are involved in what the author calls a "struggle for hegemony" with the government. The Hadzabe are committed to this struggle. This is a very important point, for there are many who believe that hunter-gatherers survive today only by default, rather than from a passionate desire to

1. Recent studies of this general subject include Ellanna (1990), Gomes (1990), most of the papers in Altman, ed. (1989), the papers in Part III of Leacock and Lee, eds. (1982), and most of the papers in Wilmsen, ed. (1989).

defend and preserve their traditional way of life. The case also raises an intriguing question: how is it that the Hadzabe, who are the epitome of egalitarian, immediate-return foragers, can resist with such success the efforts of the government of a nation-state to change them, while many larger and more complex societies have crumpled when confronted with such a challenge?[2]

In the situation described by Kenneth Pratt in the second paper, the process of integration is farther along. In this case, which involves the Nunivak Island Eskimos, the natives are already marginal members of U. S. society. For years they were reasonably content with this status because they were still able to hunt, fish, and gather anywhere they wanted in the territory that had been occupied by their ancestors since time immemorial. However, in 1980, under pressure from environmental groups, the U. S. Congress designated the southern half of the island a "wilderness," that is, a land untouched by human hands. Congress thus erased by decree several thousand years of human occupation. Since the land presumably had never been touched by human hands, of course, the Eskimos technically had no right even to be there. Pratt describes additional legislation, bureaucratic incompetence, legal wrangling, and numerous injustices that followed the initial act. Although the Eskimos are legal citizens of a supposedly democratic nation, they never have been consulted about policies that have an enormous impact on their way of life. Pratt's paper also raises another issue: environmentalists often are as threatening to contemporary foragers as animal rights activists are. They perceive the environment to be one order of phenomena and people to be another, even when people have lived unobtrusively in the same area for centuries. All they care about is the environment, as they define it, and they simply are not concerned about the fate of the humans who may be negatively affected by the policies they support.

G. Prakash Reddy's paper, which focuses on several hunter-gatherer peoples in India, outlines a situation that is similar to, but much more complex than, the one in Alaska. As in Alaska, environmentalists have pressured the Indian government into establishing wildlife refuges on land occupied by foragers. The regulations governing activities in refuges seriously limit the for-

---

2. For a pessimistic view of the Hadzabe's future, see Ndagala (1988).

agers' freedom of action to gather and hunt there, despite the fact that their ancestors did so for centuries with little negative impact on the environment. In contrast to the situation on Nunivak Island, many areas in India occupied by foragers are being opened up to development, which is the antithesis of a hunting-gathering way of life. Finally, and also in contrast to the Alaskan situation, many foragers in India are beset by masses of poor farmers desperately seeking land for themselves. Prakash Reddy presents several case studies of the impact of government policies and administrative practices in these situations, and indicates that they are leading rapidly to the extinction of the hunter-gatherer population of the country.

The final paper, by Masami Iwasaki-Goodman and Milton Freeman, concerns small-type coastal whaling in Japan and thus has a very different starting point than the other three. First, the enormous cultural changes associated with industrialization in Japan were not imposed from without, but were initiated by members of its own government during the Meiji Restoration of the 1860s (cf. Kazuko 1975). Second, Japan is not a hunter-gatherer society, but an agrarian nation-state with a history spanning some 2,500 years. Nevertheless, whaling has been practiced in many coastal Japanese villages for at least four hundred years (Takahashi et al. 1989). Over that span of time, whaling and its associated activities acquired considerable importance in many areas of village life. The foragers in this case are integral members of the larger society, but they are also people who have developed a special variant of the general culture.

Small-type coastal whaling was carried on without government intervention until 1947 (Takahashi et al.: 112), but has been under increasingly tight control since then. The moratorium on commercial whaling adopted by the International Whaling Commission in 1982 has been acceded to by the Japanese government, which has meant the loss of a substantial part of the annual catch. This has made it more difficult for people living in whaling villages to celebrate a variety of important ceremonial and social occasions that depend upon the production, exchange, and consumption of edible whale products.

All of the papers included in this section describe politically and economically weak foragers confronting the might of the central governments of nation-states. Rarely are they consulted before, during, or after major policy decisions affecting their lives are made and implemented, and, when disaster occurs, they have little recourse. The government officials involved usually are influenced and supported strongly in these encounters by some combination of relatively powerful modernizers, developers, and environmentalists. But who is there to defend or assist the foragers? Usually no one. It is not surprising that, in such cases, anthropologists familiar with the situation often become involved personally, either as consultants ("applied anthropologists") or as advocates.[3]

3. See Hastrup and Elsass (1990), Maddock (1989), and Paine (1985) for thoughts on anthropological activism.

# 14

## The Impact of Modernization Policies on the Hunter-Gatherer Hadzabe: The Case of Education and Language Policies of Postindependence Tanzania

*Bwire T. M. Kaare*

For the past sixty years, the Hadzabe, a nomadic hunter-gatherer community in Tanzania, have been under pressure to change from their hunting and gathering life to a sedentary agricultural village life. For almost thirty years, in its endeavor to build a Tanzanian nation, the postindependence state has used various strategies to achieve this goal. This chapter looks into how the postindependence state has used language and education policies in attempts to change the Hadzabe. It is argued here that the Hadzabe are aware of the serious dangers posed by the intended changes, that they have resisted them, and that they will go on resisting them until the community becomes completely permeated by the opposing ideology.

### Introduction

After independence, Tanzania embarked on a course of action intended to modernize what generally was considered to be a backward nation. Various policies were formulated with the aim of modernizing political, social, and cultural institutions as the sine qua non for rapid economic development and the construction of a strong and unified nation. In general, the achievements attained in Western Europe and North America were treated as reference points from which the distance from desired development could be measured. Since independence, development usually has been conceived as being analogous to a competitive race in which developed societies have run faster than others (the developing countries). What developing countries such as Tan-

315

zania have to do is to "run while those in front walk" so that some time in the future developing countries can catch up (Nyerere 1971).

But to ensure the change of pace from walking to running, certain conditions are considered necessary. These include the need to rid society of built-in cultural obstacles, such as traditional values, which hinder rapid development. The role of ensuring this rapid development in Tanzania has been assigned for the most part to education and language. Thus, the education and language policies of postindependence Tanzania have been designed to facilitate the process of "nationbuilding." Normally, nationbuilding in the Tanzanian context refers both to rapid economic growth and to social change. To attain this, it was and still is envisaged that the nation should have a system of generalized identification, a civil society wholly integrated economically, institutionally, and culturally, by evolving a single consumption model, a unified education system, and a unifying language.

It can be argued, therefore, that both the language and the education policies of postcolonial Tanzania were promulgated with the intention (on the part of the state) of building a unified nation. In other words, these policies are instruments of the state in the quest for nationhood. They are part and parcel of the process of the "nationbuilding mission." It is due to this requirement that these policies embody particular "ideologies of development." In Tanzania the dominant development ideology always has focused on the contention that the country is economically backward and needs very rapid development. In most cases, this refers to the process of extension and intensification of peasant production and to the expansion of the industrial sector, the government bureaucracy, and the service sector. In economic terms, this amounts to the intensification of the process of producing, selling, and consuming commodities. Furthermore, the Tanzanian state, in quest of rapid development, has assigned the task of extracting the country from its backwardness to peasants and workers. Indeed, it is clearly stipulated in various government policies[1] that Tanzania is a country made up of peasants and

---

1. Government policies are demonstrated by various government pronouncements, which are intended as guidance and statements of action for various (especially educational and cultural) undertakings (e.g., Nyerere 1967).

workers. This peasant/worker categorization is very clear in almost all policy statements in the country.

The peasant/worker categorization represents a clear attempt by the state to define a generalized basis for identification within the nation, but since independence it has undermined the existence of societies within Tanzanian territory that fall outside this simplified construct. Development policies in Tanzania simply ignore the existence of hunter-gatherers. They mention "livestock development" but overlook the existence of pastoralists. Both hunter-gatherer and pastoral societies in Tanzania are inappropriately lumped into the broad category of peasants. It is beyond the scope of this chapter to carry this argument further. Suffice it to say that the project of nationbuilding, coupled with ideologies of development, have had a far-reaching negative impact in Tanzania on those societies that do not fit well into the broad state definition of the categories of Tanzanians who are participating in the "nationbuilding project."

Both education and language policies in Tanzania are designed to imbue the recipients with a world outlook consistent with state intentions for nationbuilding. Indeed, as Nyerere[2] argued, the role of education in Tanzania is to prepare the young generation to fulfill the aspirations of the nation. Thus, the ideological instruments of both education and language have been used as apparatuses for hegemonic control, through which the state asserts its ideological predominance and norms over the ruled, and thereby establishes its legitimacy. Furthermore, it is through language and education that the ideological hegemony of the state and its subsequent praxis of developmentalism is transmitted onto the civil society in the nationbuilding project. The peasant/worker category in Tanzania is, therefore, an attempt by the state to create a generalized identification of society and a means for the state to integrate the country economically. The latter is very important for intensified commodity production. Indeed, as Nyerere (1971) clearly points out, the education system in Tanzania must prepare the young generation to become members of Tanzanian society as peasants or workers. Although Nyerere's conception of education as a socializing agent is rather static, it carries a clear mes-

2. Nyerere argued in *Education for Self-Reliance* (1968) that, among other things, education was supposed to prepare youths in Tanzania to undertake such activities as agriculture and employment in government.

sage about the need for education as an instrument for enhanc-
ing commodity production.

Due to their failure to participate in this economic process,
nomadic groups in Tanzania are singled out for the heaviest dose
of development intervention. The intention is to make these societies "catch up," to adopt peasant life and/or acquire skills that
will enable them to become workers. What prevents these societies from attaining this goal is said to be their "backward attitude," which blocks the infiltration and acceptance of "modern
values." In 1971 President Nyerere (1971: 5) commented on one of
the nomadic groups in the country:

> The Masai know that these things are possible – milk for children,
> clean water, good houses: these things are objective. But the Masai
> don't easily accept the discipline required-work! But it requires
> knowledge, technical know-how. Germany was virtually razed, and
> Japan, but they had the necessary attitude and skills for reconstruc-
> tion. So I have to build these attitudes. But I can't wait to train the
> Masai vets and doctors. I have to bring them trained experts from
> U.S., Germany, U.K., etc.

The notion that certain attitudes are necessary to induce a society's "takeoff" is common in the social sciences. Nyerere was just
replicating ideas dominant in what came to be known as "modernization theory." But what is critical in this short quotation is its
all-encompassing summary of the major tenets of modernization
theory. It is clear from the quotation that development is seen as
unilinear, injected into "backward" societies through diffusion by
unlocking cultural barriers that block "development." The
assignment is given to the already "developed" individuals or
societies to halt "backwardness" and usher in "modernity."
Development is conceived as a series of ruptures or discontinuities in social life that precede the leap into a new stage of
renewed continuity (cf. Rostow 1960). Thus, the question of transforming nomadic societies in Tanzania was interpreted to require
the annihilation of the backward culture.

The postulates of culture and social structure used to be conceived and analyzed by anthropologists and other social scientists in ways that made it difficult to explain change. They often
argued that the introduction of some aspects of Western culture
into "traditional" societies tends to obliterate the latter's culture.
For example, Bohannan (1955, 1959; Bohannan and Bohannan

1968) vehemently claimed that the introduction of Western money into the nonmonetary subsistence economy of the Tiv in Nigeria obliterated spheres of exchange in this society and converted the traditional "multicentric" economy into a "unicentric" economy (see also Bloch and Parry 1989: 13). Others have argued that societies have always changed whenever they encountered foreign cultures. But the problem has been to explain the form of change. For example, according to Sahlins (1985: 31), although a society's culture might appear not to have changed upon the encounter with foreign cultures, in reality the encounter transforms what might appear to be a self-reproducing traditional system. As he aptly argues of the Hawaiian encounter with the Cook expedition:

> [T]he foreigners who were so generously accorded an indigenous status had their own reasons of existence, and no obligations to conform to the preconceptions by which Hawaiians thought them. By encompassing contingent events in received structures, perceiving mythical relationships in historical actions, the system appears merely to reproduce itself in a flexible way. But then . . . "The more it remains the same the more it changes."

What is important in Sahlins's conception of the way in which the "structure is transformed" is his argument that changes may occur even when those involved in the change itself are not conscious of the process.

Contrary to the above argument, Taussig (1980), in his study of the peasants of the Cauca valley, suggests that the "traditional" cultures of such people are practiced in particular historical conjunctures in which they are conscious of the implications of their encounters with foreign culture. Resistance on their part is based on an awareness of the dangers inherent in the foreign culture. "Precapitalist" societies resist capitalism because they "view the bonds between their modern economic activities for what they really are-asymmetrical, non-reciprocal, exploitative, and destructive of relationships between persons-and not as natural relations between forces supposedly inherent in potent things" (Taussig 1980: 38). Taussig shows that people make their history quite consciously on the basis of their shared past life experiences.

This chapter seeks to explain the mode of encounter between the Tanzanian state and the hunter-gatherer Hadzabe people in the state's endeavor to transform the Hadzabe into a sedentary agricultural community. Both language and education have been used as means of integrating this community into the broader Tanzanian "nation-state" society. How have the Hadzabe people responded to government intervention?

## Government Attempts to Change the Hadzabe Way of Life

The Hadzabe (also referred to in the literature as Hadza, Hadzapi, Tindiga, Kindiga, and Kangeju) occupy an area of more than three thousand square kilometers east, south, and west of Lake Eyasi in northern Tanzania (Woodburn 1968a, 1970, 1982). The Hadzabe people are essentially nomadic hunter-gatherers who live at an altitude between 1000 and 1500 meters above sea level in a part of the Rift valley that is arid, yet rich in flora and (formerly) fauna. The land is infested with tsetse flies, although the intensity of the flies has decreased since the 1950s, when the government cleared the flies from the outer areas of Hadzabe land. The whole area to the immediate south and east of Lake Eyasi is an open game reserve that attracts hundreds of illegal as well as legal hunters who have depleted the region's fauna.

The Hadzabe are encapsulated by neighboring communities of peasants, agropastoralists, or pastoralists. Although there is quite a high rate of interaction between the Hadzabe and all their neighbors, it tends to be limited to certain matters of common interest. For example, the Hadzabe trade with their neighbors and exchange meat and honey for cloth, tobacco, and other items. However, the relationship is constrained by stereotypes held by the Hadzabe about their neighbors and vice versa. Except for the pastoral Barbaig, all other Hadzabe neighbors are settled peasants or agropastoralists who have been fully integrated into the "nation-state" framework since colonial times. That is, these communities have been integrated into the system of generalized identification.

The first recorded attempt to sedentarize the Hadzabe people in permanent villages was in 1927 by the British colonial government. In 1925 the colonial administration in Tanzania (then Tanganyika) established "indirect rule" as a method of reorganizing tribes (retribalizing) and reordering the existing social formations to enhance capital accumulation. The policy, however, was a generalized one that had no special reference to particular social formations. In attempting to sedentarize the Hadzabe people, the government's intention was to establish chiefs in the community to enable the collection of a tax and to ease colonial administration. However, these objectives could not be realized because they were incompatible with real practices in the hunting-gathering life of the Hadzabe. Unable to cope with their new life, the Hadzabe resisted government measures to settle them in villages and went back to the bush. Other attempts to settle the Hadzabe in villages were made in 1937 and 1955, but both were futile.

In 1961 Tanzania (still Tanganyika) attained independence from the British. At the top of the new agenda was the quest for rapid development. Various policies were promulgated to facilitate this, fueled by the ambition of building a unified nation. By and large, postindependence policies were directed toward nationbuilding. It is in this context that the policies differed from colonial interventions in Hadzabe life. Postcolonial policies embodied a heavy dose of the ideology of modernization, with a major emphasis on language and education policies.

The use of Swahili as a national language in Tanzania, although traceable to the preindependence period, has been given special attention in the postindependence period. Tanzania is a country with more than 130 ethnic languages. The promotion of Swahili in postindependence Tanzania went along with the nationbuilding project. In this context, the promotion of Swahili was not merely an exercise in developing a lingua franca for the country. Indeed, as Nyerere (1966: 186) argued when justifying why he set up the new Ministry of National Culture and Youth, "I have done this because I believe that culture is the spirit and essence of any nation. A country which lacks its own culture is no more than a collection of people without spirit, which makes them a nation." The newly formed ministry was charged with the responsibility of promoting Swahili not as a mere lingua franca but as part of the culture of the nation. Swahili was promoted as part of the broader project of creating a "Swahili nationality" in the endeavor to build the nation. But as a vehicle through which national culture was to be expressed with particular meanings, Swahili was supposed to transform all the diverse ethnic cultural meanings into a single generalized set of meanings, enshrining the national culture. As is argued below, such endeavors have met with serious obstacles among the Hadzabe.

In the meantime, Swahili was made the official language for government communications and the medium of instruction in all primary education schools (except for less than ten primary schools meant to cater to foreign residents working in Tanzania). To enforce the use of Swahili in schools, it is considered an offense in most of Tanzania's primary schools for people to speak their own ethnic language while on school grounds. So, while undergoing primary education, one is at the same time trained to absorb the culture of the envisaged Swahili nationality. Thus, the introduction of school education among the Hadzabe relates to the state's broad attempt to create a Swahili nationality. To date, almost three decades after independence, the state project of creating a Swahili nationality has had more effect in urban areas than in rural areas. Nomadic groups fare very badly in this project. A number of stigmas and stereotypes have become attached to nomadic groups in Tanzania as a consequence of their resistance to incorporation into the Swahili nationality.

To ensure that "modernity" was imparted to the nomadic Hadzabe community, the government embarked on providing "formal education"[3] for Hadzabe youths and "adult education"[4] for the adults. Whereas the national minimum standard compulsory education was primary education (seven years of schooling), this was not seen as sufficient for the Hadzabe youths and the competitive secondary entrance examinations were waived for them. In 1977, the government admitted twenty-five youths who had completed primary education to various secondary schools in the country. In addition, those youths who previously had undergone primary education were taken to various national institutions as a way of transforming their attitudes to conform to the envisaged national ones. And, although the government never again took other Hadzabe youths to secondary schools after the group of twenty-five, ever since it has been recruiting Hadzabe youths to various learning institutions in order to use them, after they have obtained various educational skills, to change the attitudes of their fellow Hadzabe.

The government has employed various strategies to entice Hadzabe youths and to make their parents willing to let their children attend school. These include providing free school uni-

3. Formal education refers to the schooling system originally introduced by the colonial government, according to which one follows a particular state-regulated curriculum.
4. Adult education is a type of education offered to people who, because of their advanced age, are considered inappropriate for enrollment in formal education.

forms to those attending school, free lunch for pupils, and free food to their parents living in government-sponsored villages. The main prerequisite for youths to attend school has always been the permanent settlement of their parents or guardians in villages. In one of the schools built specifically for the Hadzabe, Munguli primary school, registration and attendance of youths were high only in those years when the community was settled in Munguli village. For example, in 1971, forty Hadzabe youths were registered at this school and all attended. But records show that this number continued to drop as parents or guardians of the registered pupils moved back to the bush. Eleven years later, no Hadzabe youths were attending this school because their parents or guardians had gone back to the bush (Kaare 1985).

Of the twenty-five youths taken to join the four-year secondary education program, only ten managed to complete the program in 1980. The rest dropped out for various reasons. Most of the dropouts joined the community back in the bush. Research conducted in 1984 revealed that, of the twenty-five youths taken to secondary school, only six (about 24 percent) were employed by the government, sixteen (about 64 percent) returned to the community, and three (about 12 percent) died before completing their schooling (Kaare 1988). The government also attempted to train other members of the community in fields such as domestic science. For example, one woman was taken to be trained in community development. On completion of her studies, the government provided her with various working tools, including two sewing machines, cloth, and other supplies. It was intended that this woman should train her female colleagues in various skills related to community development. When interviewed, she complained that her students had little interest in what she taught them. Most women said that their main responsibility was subsistence, such as collecting fruit, and that what they were taught was not relevant for them.

With similar intentions, five Hadzabe youths were registered for a two-year course leading to the award of a teaching certificate. Others were registered at the Community Development Institute for a two-year certificate course in community development. However, in both instances, none of the youths managed to complete the two-year course. All of them dropped out, largely due to failing examinations upon completion of the first year of their studies. But there were other reasons for the failures. These range from failing to cope with school life, bad relationships with fellow students (who often mocked them for their "backward-ness"), and ill health, all of which these youths said was a result of not being able to participate in *epeme* rituals performed by the Hadzabe community. Later, this point was confirmed by the principal of the institute where these youths studied. He said that the students had approached him many times requesting permission to go back home to attend the ritual so as to improve their well-being. Consequently, they were reluctant to return to school after they went back home for holidays. This explains why they performed poorly in their studies.

Furthermore, the government established adult education for those Hadzabe who could not enroll in primary school due to their advanced age. The main purpose of providing adult education in Tanzania is to ensure that adults are able to read and write. It is also anticipated that this education will help them understand their environment better in order to combat problems. Adult education is also viewed by the government as a way to imbue adult members of Tanzanian society at large with political awareness of national political goals so that they will support economic development programs set by the state. In Tanzania, politics is believed to be a mobilizing medium for "mass" involvement in economic development. Adult education classes are designed to provide adult members of society with opportunities to learn reading and writing, and are aimed at inculcating them with political values relevant to nationbuilding. Indeed, the adult education curriculum is heavily loaded with political appeals to adult Tanzanians to participate effectively in nationbuilding.

According to the 1983 Munguli primary school reports, about thirty-four Hadzabe adults registered for and took the adult education program at the school. All thirty-four sat for the national adult education examinations. The government uses the examination as the criterion by which it determines the success of adult education programs. Of the thirty-four Hadzabe who sat for the examinations, six managed to pass at literacy level.[5] Few, if any, of the adults who attended the adult education classes, which emphasized national self-reliance through modern agriculture, have since become effective cultivators. It can be argued that the

---

5. Literacy level is determined by the ability to read, write, and calculate simple arithmetic.

Tanzanian government's attempts between 1971 and 1983 to use education as an agent for change failed to achieve the intended results, and it is unlikely that such attempts will be successful in the foreseeable future. Neither "formal education" nor "adult education" helped transform the Hadzabe from a hunting-gathering community into a community living by sedentary agriculture.

In the meantime, the successive government failures to transform the Hadzabe raised concern in the Ministry of National Culture and Youth. In 1978, the Ministry launched "The Rift Valley Project" with the intention of conducting research on the culture of the Hadzabe, Sonjo, Dorobo, Datog (Barbaig), and Sandawe. According to the Ministry, these communities were considered by the state to be the most "backward." The Ministry of Information and Culture also reported that government officials were discouraged by the communities' "antidevelopment" attitude. Nevertheless, the Ministry (1982: 1) asserted that perhaps these communities actually did desire development:

> Despite the fact that the government claims were basic, it was not true to allege that these communities did not want development. So far no proper strategies have been found to extract these communities from so-called nondevelopment. The aim of the Rift Valley Project is to undertake research on the values and norms of these communities in order to determine how their environment and party and government policies have affected both the communities and government policy implementation. [Translation from Swahili by the author.]

The research was conducted with an emphasis on the need to involve these communities in making decisions on all matters intended to affect them. The Ministry was clearly opposed to the conventional approach of imposing the government's will on the Hadzabe people. Indeed, in its resolutions, the Ministry emphasized the participatory aspect in any future government intervention intentions.

Despite the recognition of the need to avoid government imposition of its will on the Hadzabe, the Ministry's approach still incorporated elements of the state ideology. For example, change was still conceived in terms of transition to sedentary agricultural village life. Furthermore, the Ministry intended to research the possibilities of using Hadzabe culture to transform them. Indeed, some recommendations remained similar to the dominant state ideology of nationbuilding. They still emphasized the authoritarian central role the state was to play as an agent for change, and education was still considered to be an important tool.

Critical here are the implications of using a people's culture to transform them. The assumption is that culture can be manipulated to enforce or to change the hunting-gathering praxis, and that culture can be conceived as an epiphenomenon of the hunting-gathering praxis. Perhaps one reason why it has been difficult for the Ministry to implement these resolutions lies in its attempt to isolate culture from actual foraging. Indeed, seeking to use a people's culture to transform them may pose a difficulty similar to the egg-chicken paradox. The point is that a people's culture is part and parcel of their lives, and thus cannot be singled out as an isolated agent to change them.

Many publications on education programs for nomadic groups have argued that these programs fail because they are incompatible with the nomadic way of life. According to Heron (1983), a lack of objectives and overall understanding of nomadism characterize educational strategies. Turton (1974) argues that efforts to provide schools for the nomadic Somali of Kenya failed to meet the anticipated goals because they were initiated to solve political problems. Generally, arguments posed so far focus on how the traditional value system is threatened by the opposing value system of schools. I argue that this logic is undermined because resistance by nomadic societies to the imposition of schooling systems is rooted in broader issues related to the whole life of nomadic societies, of which values are just an aspect, albeit an important one.

### The Hadzabe Response

The Hadzabe have reacted to the various changes introduced by the government not in relation to how they conflict with their traditional values, but rather in relation to their hunting-gathering praxis and how this praxis should be reproduced. Thus an important focal point must be culture. In this context, culture involves what the Hadzabe consider to be their historical experiences, and the diverse conditions – material and spiritual – that have shaped their struggle for survival. Indeed, many anthropologists agree that an important attribute of culture is learning. In short, learning is the key to human adaptation, and culture labels what is learned (see Fox 1979; Sahlins 1979). Since Hadzabe culture is itself a valued product of their own history, the Hadzabe have been resisting changes that are intended to destroy their culture.

The present way of life of the Hadzabe is a result of their history and their culture. Their historical conditions and experience, their forms of organization, and the local geographical and physical conditions of their environment are what determine the specificity of the community. The community is the bond resulting from the process of common interaction, and the characteristics and identity of its members are a result of this interaction.

In this sense, the individual subject does not predate the community; he or she is constructed by it. Thus, the cultural identity of each member of the community is a result of his or her socialized existence. And, despite the fact that community interaction is done individually, to use individuals (as the Tanzanian state has been trying to do) to transform the community poses a complicated problem of the extent to which individual actors can transform the collective will. Individual actors matter only in situations where conditions are ripe for change.

Hadzabe mythology and folklore clearly support the above argument. Hadzabe myths of origin, from *gelanebe* (the time of the earliest ancestors) to *hamaishonebe* (the current period), emphasize the importance of a shared history and how they have evolved historically. They frequently recite the role of how their god, Haine, has shaped their life. It is Haine who, in this mythology of origin, has invariably contributed to the creation of the egalitarian culture of the community. For example, it is narrated in one of the myths that Haine appeared during the early period and gave instructions on certain taboos related to observing *epeme* rituals, and on the role of women in society who were given the ability to deliver children.

It is narrated further that during the earliest days, the *gelanebe*, Haine called on various tribes to choose implements that would help harness nature for subsistence. It is said that Haine specified conditions before making any choice. Haine put at the disposal of these tribes cattle, hoe, and bow and arrow. Before any tribe chose cattle or hoe, its forefathers had to lick pus first. It is said that Hadzabe forefathers refused the humiliation of licking pus and hence chose the bow and arrow. This is said to be the foundation of the Hadzabe hunting-gathering way of life. The Hadzabe also believe that ancestors influence the well-being of the living people. It is the ancestors who deal with the observance of custom.

Violation of custom may be communicated to the community by ancestors via the elders.

Haine is important in the Hadzabe life. The Hadzabe people communicate with Haine through the sacred *epeme* dance. According to Woodburn (1970: 57):

> Each month on moonless nights the Hadza living in all but the smallest camps perform a sacred dance to which they attach a great deal of importance. They believe that the performing of the dance creates a state of well-being in which men will be successful in their hunting and in which the hazards of illness will be avoided. ... [I]n this dance the emphasis is on harmony and reconciliation, on the interests that link men and women together.

This dance is not merely ceremonial. It includes rituals performed by elders during rites of passage and during extended periods of meat shortage due to poor hunting. On a general level, the dance seeks to reestablish unity with nature as a whole, and by dancing the community stresses harmony and reconciliation and consequently seeks to avoid the danger of not reproducing an egalitarian community.

It is pertinent to ask ourselves why the Hadzabe transmit such myths and folklore to new generations. The reason is that myths and folklore consist of a body of symbols and images capable of evoking sentiments and propelling people to action (Sorel 1961). More significantly, a myth has two components: a statement of goals or objectives, and a commitment to a line of action toward materialization of objectives. A myth, in other words, is an expression of a determination to act. It binds a group of people together, and directs their energy toward specific objectives (Sorel 1961). More important, if we are to understand Hadzabe myths, folklore, and rituals, we must grasp how they control their conditions of social practice and express their relationship with imaginary beings who control the conditions for reproduction of both nature and the world. Ideological social practices both sustain human relationships and are part of the wider symbolic praxis relating to the representation and reproduction of the social order.

Contrary to the conventional belief that failure of the educational programs for nomadic groups is due largely to the incompatibility of schooling values with traditional values, the cultural resistance waged by the Hadzabe (and perhaps by other communities worldwide) emanates from the struggles for the reproduction of their own world order. This means that the opposition represents much more than incompatible value systems. It includes such things as fear of losing the freedom assured in the hunting-gathering life, fear of a breakdown of egalitarianism, and resentment of authoritarian village administration. As argued above, the education policies of postindependence Tanzania were intended to foster "modernization" and simultaneously facilitate nationbuilding. Resistance to these policies by the Hadzabe must be viewed in terms of what these policies really are: asymmetrical, nonreciprocal, and destructive of relationships between persons (see Taussig 1980). Hadzabe resistance is actually based on how they perceive that the intended changes will affect their way of life. Due to this awareness, the Hadzabe people have managed to learn and speak Swahili, the national language. However, they are keen to avoid obliterating cultural meanings attached to certain concepts. For example, they keep a clear distinction between the concept of Mungu, a Swahili word for God, and Hainem, the Hadzabe word for God. They are well aware of the difference in meaning between the two concepts. Thus they use Mungu when referring to the god of others and Haine when speaking of their own god.

We argue, therefore, that the encounter between the Hadzabe and the state involves struggles for hegemony. These are struggles over the ideological predominance of cultural norms, values, and ideas, as well as over the economic ideas of the state intended to capture and transform the Hadzabe in order to establish new "developed" cultural and economic activities different from indigenous Hadzabe activities. The central problem facing the Hadzabe today has arisen out of their commitment to the hunting-gathering way of life, and their consequent opposition to the authoritarian tendencies of the state and its policy for change and "economic development." The Hadzabe, given the environment in which they live, are rational in their awareness of the disadvantages of abandoning their hunting-gathering way of life. The uncertainties of agriculture in this habitat and the dangers of losing their valued egalitarian life compel the Hadzabe to be skeptical of the changes proposed by the government.

The Hadzabe recite their mythology and folklore and perform their rituals as a way of reinforcing the reproduction of their world order. In doing so, they retain their cultural identity as a necessary condition for reproducing their community and avoiding the risks inherent in changes intended by the government. And, as Woodburn (1988) has aptly demonstrated, one reason why the Hadzabe hold certain stereotypes about their neighbors is their own need for cultural identity.

However, it would be simplistic to treat the Hadzabe as an unchanging people holding on obsessively to their past culture. The encounter with the government and their neighbors has led to certain ambiguities. For example, the sense of private property, though still undeveloped, is slowly gaining ground among them. Further, the use of money for exchange, although still confined to transactions between the Hadzabe and outsiders, may inflict profound changes within the community in the future. The Hadzabe, however, will go on maintaining their main cultural and ideological forms even when social circumstances have changed. This is partly due to the fact that other ideologies threaten the principle of reciprocity, which, among the Hadzabe, as in other similar societies, is supported by mystical sanctions and enforced by supernatural penalties (Taussig 1980).

By maintaining myths, rituals, and folklore, the community has effectively avoided the danger of not reproducing an egalitarian society. For example, the importance attached to the *epeme* spiritual dance and Haine have allowed the Hadzabe to abide by their own culture. And it is this need that has enabled the Hadzabe youths who were exposed to formal education to return to their community. Again, it is close contact with the community that ensures a people's well-being. This ultimately perpetuates the reproduction of the hunting-gathering way of life.

## Summary and Conclusion

The postindependence government, with concerted effort, has been trying for the past twenty-five years to settle the Hadzabe through education and language policies. But, contrary to the wishes of the government, the Hadzabe have not changed in the way the government wants. They have not accepted a sedentary agricultural life. At the time of writing this paper, there have been renewed attempts to settle the Hadzabe. But, unlike earlier attempts, the current moves have been initiated by a group of Hadzabe who want to supplement hunting and gathering with agriculture. It is difficult to determine the effect of these moves on Hadzabe life. Their success or failure will depend on the way in which the plan to relocate Hadzabe to sedentary villages is implemented, and on the extent to which this plan conflicts with the immediate and long-term needs of the Hadzabe people.

However, previous experience has shown that the encounter between Hadzabe and the government creates struggles for hegemony. These are struggles about dominating the community and articulating a particular cultural identity for the Hadzabe people. It appears that the Hadzabe people are quite aware of the dangers inherent in government policies. The resistance to these policies is a clear indication of this consciousness. But, at the same time, the looming sense of private property and the use of money pose temptations that may not be easy to resist. This does not mean that any changes will obliterate Hadzabe social organization. The Hadzabe will go on evoking their culture to resist the state until the whole community becomes completely permeated by the opposing ideology.

# 15

# "They Never Ask the People": Native Views About the Nunivak Wilderness

*Kenneth L. Pratt*

This study focuses on the Nunivak Wilderness in southwestern Alaska, and examines the legal definition of wilderness and the wilderness evaluation process relative to indigenous cultural use and occupancy of proposed wilderness lands. The actual effects of the wilderness designation on Nunivak Eskimo land use and land rights are described, and then contrasted to the locally perceived effects. After examining and explaining the obvious discrepancies, I concluded that wilderness legislation ignores indigenous people's concepts of land and land rights, and fails to adequately address their past, present, and future use of designated wilderness lands.[1]

---

We were born here and have lived on this island all our lives. This is our homeland. We dislike for it to be wrongfully taken from us.

*Andrew Noatak (1990)*

## Introduction

As recently as 1920 the Nunivak Eskimos of southwestern Alaska were living an essentially "traditional" lifestyle and had complete control over their homeland and its resources. Since 1920, however, federal and state legislation have steadily eroded local control of Nunivak Island and have restricted Nunivak Eskimo land use and land rights. This study explores the effects of one such legislative action, designation of the Nunivak Wilderness in 1980.

1. Without the cooperation and hospitality I received from the people of Nunivak Island, especially Howard Amos, this essay could not have been written. I also thank my wife Carolyn for her constant support, Victor Kavairlook for the graphics, and Jack Byrne, Robert Drozda, Timothy Hostetler, Matthew O'Leary, and William Sheppard for extremely helpful comments on earlier drafts. Of course, I alone am responsible for the contents of this essay and any errors of fact or interpretation it may contain.

In order to place the Nunivak Wilderness problem in context, the study emphasizes the unique situation of the Nunivak Eskimos regarding the native ownership of land in Alaska. The study critically evaluates federal management of Nunivak lands, and illustrates the cultural insensitivity of wilderness legislation and various conservation land-management policies to indigenous people's historical relationships to and concepts about the land.

## Setting

Nunivak Island is located in the central Bering Sea region of southwestern Alaska (see Figure 15.1). Volcanic in origin, it is roughly ninety-seven kilometers wide (east to west) by sixty-five kilometers long (north to south) and is separated from the Yukon-Kuskokwim mainland by the forty-kilometers-wide Etolin Strait. The island is treeless and its vegetation is dominated by moist tundra communities, in which the tallest shrub is no more than about one meter high. The coastal area of the island is highly diversified. Rocky beaches, peninsulas, and numerous small bays and coves define the northern and eastern coasts. In contrast, the forbidding western coast is dominated by steep cliff formations rising to more than 122 meters high; much of the southern coast consists of smooth sand beaches backed by extensive dune formations, which are usually associated with large, shallow lagoons or estuaries. Nunivak's interior is rocky, dotted with lakes, and characterized by volcanic hills and craters, some of which contain deep lakes and have exposed lava beds. A few scattered peaks rise up from within the southern interior, the highest of which approaches 518 meters in elevation. There are over seventy rivers and streams on the island that originate in the central highlands and flow in a radial pattern to the coasts. Some of these watercourses are substantial and very productive, but all of their upper reaches are shallow and nonnavigable.

Fauna common on Nunivak include: a wide variety of migratory waterfowl and seabirds (large rookeries of which are found on cliffs along the western coast); marine mammals such as walrus and seals; numerous species of fish, including salmon, char, cod, halibut, and tomcod; and a few species of furbearing mammals. Caribou (wild North American reindeer) once roamed Nunivak, but the last of the native herd was killed off sometime before 1900. Thriving populations of introduced reindeer and musk-oxen have since taken the caribou's place as the island's largest land mammals.

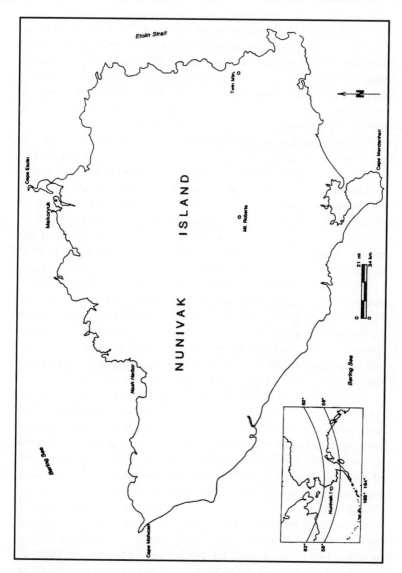

**Figure 15.1:** The study area

## Nunivak Society

It is not possible to estimate accurately the pre-1900 population of Nunivak, but it likely consisted of at least 400 to 500 people (Lantis 1984; Pratt 1990). The aboriginal Nunivak Eskimo economy was based on hunting, fishing, and gathering; marine mammals, fish, and caribou were the most important components of the economy (Lantis 1946, 1984; Nowak 1988; VanStone 1989). A thorough summary of Nunivak Eskimo economy and land-use patterns is provided by VanStone (1989: 1–15).

The most sedentary season of the year for the Nunivak people was winter (October through April), when multiple extended-family groups combined and occupied a limited number of settlements for approximately half of the year. In other seasons, families were dispersed throughout the island in smaller settlements for shorter periods of time. Three specific aspects of aboriginal patterns of land use are of great significance to the topic of the present study. First, since the Nunivak Eskimos did not use tents (Lantis 1946: 162; VanStone 1989: 4), semisubterranean sod houses were present at all settlements. Second, major settlements were located only along the coastal margin of the island, not in the interior; however, the interior was vitally important for subsistence purposes, and also contains the remains of cemeteries, numerous caribou hunting camps and an extensive trail system. And third, although the Nunivak people used virtually every area of the island, the southern half was clearly their "breadbasket."

Today, the roughly 170 Eskimo people living on Nunivak are consolidated in a single village (Mekoryuk), located near the northernmost tip of the island. They live in frame houses equipped with electricity, televisions, and telephones, eat primarily store-bought foods, drive pickup trucks, and enjoy the luxury of daily air service from the mainland community of Bethel. A road system runs through the village and connects it with the local airstrip. Otherwise, transportation throughout the island is accomplished by motorboat as long as open-water conditions prevail, and by snowmobiles during the winter months. Travel by either foot or fixed-wing aircraft is rare. Although the Nunivak people are entrenched in the Western cash economy, the majority continue to engage in traditional, seasonal subsistence activities throughout the year. This is especially evident in summer when – on a punctuated basis – fishing and berry-picking activities take many Mekoryuk residents away from the village for up to a month at a time.

Research in progress by the author has documented an extremely low rate of variability regarding the sites annually occupied by families and individuals for subsistence activities. Most, if not all, Nunivakers now occupy only those sites to which they have a clearly established history of ancestral use.

## Wilderness

The Wilderness Act of 1964 established the National Wilderness Preservation System and authorized the U.S. Congress to designate selected tracts of land as "wilderness," which the act defines in the following way:

> A wilderness, in contrast with those areas where man and his own works dominate the landscape, is hereby recognized as an area where the earth and its community of life are untrammeled by man, where man himself is a visitor who does not remain. An area of wilderness is further defined to mean in this Act an area of undeveloped federal land retaining its primeval character and influence, without permanent improvements or human habitation, which is protected and managed so as to preserve its natural conditions and which (1) generally appears to have been affected primarily by the forces of nature, with the imprint of man's work substantially unnoticeable; (2) has outstanding opportunities for solitude or a primitive and unconfined type of recreation; (3) has at least five thousand acres of land or is of sufficient size as to make practicable its preservation and use in an unimpaired condition; and (4) may also contain ecological, geological, or other features of scientific, educational, scenic, or historical value (U.S. Congress 1964).

In compliance with the Wilderness Act, the Secretary of the U.S. Department of the Interior was required to "review all roadless areas of 5,000 contiguous acres or more and every roadless island within the National Wildlife Refuge System and, within ten years after the effective date of the Act, report to the President of the United States his recommendation as to the suitability or non-suitability of each such area or island as wilderness" (U.S. Fish and Wildlife Service 1972: 8). Because all of Nunivak Island was contained within an existing National Wildlife Refuge when the Wilderness Act was signed, the entire island was evaluated for wilderness suitability by the U.S. Fish and Wildlife Service in 1972–1973.

The definition of wilderness did not include specific guidelines for evaluating lands subject to indigenous customary use and occupancy against the criteria employed to define wilderness (see also Neumann and Reinburg 1989). The most relevant passages emphasize that wilderness should bear little, if any, evidence of human use; but it is unclear what degree of human use of an area is necessary to disqualify it for wilderness status. The Wilderness Society, one of the nation's leading proponents of wilderness preservation, recently contended that "this definition does not require a pristine appearance with no evidence of man's activities whatsoever. Rather, it requires that an area appear to be substantially natural and that the presence of man's imprints not be dominant" (Wilderness Society 1984: 27).

Patterns of land use typical of most hunting-gathering societies are largely nondestructive of the land and leave only minimal physical evidence of human use or occupation. To many, the lands such societies occupy may appear empty and completely "untrammeled" by man. But, "as every ethnographer eventually comes to appreciate, geographical landscapes are never culturally vacant" (Basso 1988: 102). In reference to the territory of the Koyukon Athapaskans of interior northwestern Alaska, Richard Nelson (1983: 246) concludes: "The fact that Westerners identify this remote country as wilderness reflects their inability to conceive of occupying and utilizing an environment without fundamentally altering its natural state."

Nelson's observation could apply to the territories of any number of hunter-gatherer societies worldwide (Brody 1987: 31; White and Cronon 1988: 417; Wilson 1992), but within the United States, both the legal and public conception of wilderness is especially problematic in Alaska. Several points can be made in support of this contention.

First, the majority of Alaska Natives (and many nonnatives) actively pursue a subsistence way of life; this sets Alaska apart from all other states. Thus, even with the comforts of modern conveniences and technology, a significant percentage of Alaska's residents rely on the products of subsistence hunting, fishing, and gathering for their livelihood. It is possible that the Wilderness Act's failure to specifically address customary use and occupancy of the land for subsistence purposes in part may reflect Alaska's anomalous position in regard to contemporary patterns of land use in the United States.

Second, much of the American public perceives Alaska in terms of the famous motto "The Last Frontier." The motto is open to interpretation, but by nearly any interpretation it identifies Alaska as frontier territory and colors the public's image of the state. For instance, to some people Alaska is America's last frontier for resource and economic development; to others it identifies the state as the last bastion of American wilderness and potentially the crown jewel of the National Wilderness Preservation System. The latter point is exemplified in the following passage from a collection of essays published by the Wilderness Society (1989: 64) during its 1989 celebration of the twenty-fifth anniversary of the Wilderness Act:

> [I]n the act of putting . . . millions of acres of Alaska into the National Wilderness Preservation System we are vindicating our history, our willingness to learn, our respect for the land that nurtures and enlightens us even as it stirs the poetry in our souls. This, probably more than any other single thing we can do, would stand as an enduring demonstration of this nation's commitment to the fullest meaning of the Wilderness Act of 1964. Here, finally, we can do it right.

The Nunivak Wilderness (see Figure 15.2), totalling 600,000 acres, was one of thirty-five separate wilderness units created in Alaska and added to the National Wilderness Preservation System under the Alaska National Interest Lands Conservation Act (ANILCA) of 1980. As a result of ANILCA, more than 56 million acres of Alaskan land (or about 15 percent of the state) was designated as wilderness. The U.S. Congress defined wilderness under ANILCA in accordance with the 1964 Wilderness Act, but also specifically recognized the unique relationship of Alaskans to the land:

> Special provisions were made permitting a number of uses which elsewhere have been prohibited by the Wilderness Act and subsequent legislation. ANILCA was carefully worded to make clear that these provisions applied only to Alaskan wilderness. These uses include the construction and/or maintenance of cabins; the use of motorized means of transportation such as snowmobiles, motorboats and aircraft; temporary fishing and hunting encampments; and subsistence uses by natives and non-natives alike. In most cases the agency still maintains the authority to regulate or limit such uses in order to protect wilderness character. (Wilderness Society 1984: 55–56)

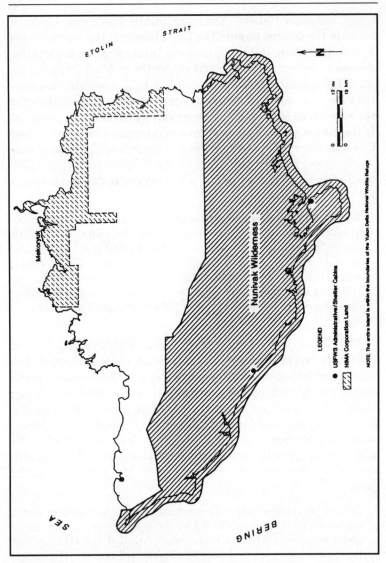

**Figure 15.2:** Nunivak Island land status

## Summary of Nunivak Land Actions, 1920–1986

Local opposition to the Nunivak Wilderness is based upon a sixty-year history of legislation and other actions entirely beyond the scope of local control that have dramatically affected the

Nunivak people's use of and rights to the island. The Nunivak Eskimos believe a common thread runs through all federal legislation and actions that specifically concern Nunivak lands; that is, all occurred without the consent of the Nunivak people. In most cases, the local people were not aware legislation was being drafted or other actions were being planned until after the legislation had become law or the actions had already been taken. Further, local objections to these actions have been ignored consistently or have proven ineffective.

The precursor of all Nunivak land actions was the introduction of (domesticated) reindeer to the island in 1920. According to Stern et al. (1980: 47):

> [I]n 1920, the Bureau of Biological Survey (BBS), in conjunction with the Bureau of Education, began a series of experiments to cross-breed reindeer and caribou on Nunivak Island. Under a cooperative agreement between the Lomens [a private commercial enterprise] and the Bureau of Biological Survey, Nunivak Island was to be used to conduct . . . investigations, experiments and demonstrations for the improvement of the reindeer industry in Alaska. . . . The cooperative agreement providing for the experiment was protested by the island residents. Although the experiments were meant to improve the breeding stock of all herds, island residents objected to the Lomens' presence on Nunivak Island. Lomen and Company claimed the island as their rangeland. Natives claimed that the Lomen-operated store and reindeer herd on Nunivak Island were not being operated in the best interests of the Natives. The later reindeer investigations of the 1930s looked into these charges and counter-charges, but no conclusion was reached. The cross-breeding experiments failed to benefit either the Lomens or the Natives in the long run.

In 1927 a federal statute (44 Statute, 1452) was passed that provided for the protection, development, and utilization of public lands for livestock grazing. The following year, Congress established the Nunivak Island Reservation; the reservation was expanded in 1930 to include offshore islands and submerged lands. These actions withdrew the island from the public domain and led to the creation of the Nunivak National Wildlife Refuge. In addition to providing a preserve and breeding ground for native birds and other wildlife, the Nunivak National Wildlife Refuge supported not only experiments with reindeer and caribou cross-breeding, but also official efforts to reestablish the musk-ox as a native animal of Alaska. (The last of Alaska's native musk-oxen are thought to have been killed near Point Barrow sometime between 1850 and 1860.) Musk-oxen are not native to Nunivak, but four animals were introduced to the island in 1935 and an additional twenty-seven in 1936. The action was intended to provide a nucleus herd from which animals would be available for restocking former musk-ox ranges in the state (U.S. Fish and Wildlife Service 1975: 38).

Nunivak elders say the introduction of musk-oxen to Nunivak occurred in similar fashion to that of the reindeer: A ship simply appeared one day and dropped the animals at the island. The people were given no choice in the matter. Anthropologist Margaret Lantis, who has conducted extensive fieldwork on Nunivak Island since 1939, notes that "[a]n old bull musk-ox was for local people a fearsome animal and in fact all musk-oxen were avoided until 1964" (Lantis 1984: 212). The first musk-oxen terrorized the Nunivak people, entering villages at will and occasionally killing local dogs. Elder Peter Smith remembers the 1936 delivery of musk-oxen to the island and recalls speaking with the ship's men about the animals (Smith 1984): "They told me . . . the musk-oxen . . . [were] for our benefit. They were to be our helpers. But our troubles began with that."

A different set of troubles for the Nunivak people is associated with the 1971 passage of the Alaska Native Claims Settlement Act (ANCSA), which granted Alaska Natives fee simple title to 40 million acres of land in Alaska, and extinguished aboriginal title to any additional lands (Arnold 1978: 146). It is unlikely that the populace of any native village in Alaska fully understood the consequences of ANCSA with respect to their traditional lands (see Berger 1985). A total of 12 Alaska Native regional corporations (with a provision allowing a thirteenth to be added at a later date) and 203 village corporations were created by ANCSA; each of these entities shared in the 40-million-acre land entitlement provided under the Act. The exact acreage entitlements of individual regional and village corporations were determined primarily on the basis of their respective populations.

The Nunivak Island Mekoryuk Alaska (NIMA) village corporation and the Calista (regional) Corporation are those to which the native residents of Nunivak belong. Although the 1971 population of Nunivak entitled the NIMA village corporation to a total land selection of 115,200 acres (five townships), because the island is within a national wildlife refuge, the village corporation was limited to selecting only 60 percent (69,120 acres-only three townships) of its land entitlement on Nunivak Island proper; the remaining "deficiency" lands had to be selected elsewhere (Arnold 1978: 148–150).[2] Further, the ANCSA regulations require a village corporation's land selection to be contiguous. Due to the island's size and Mekoryuk's location at its northern end, the village corporation was essentially prevented from selecting any lands on the southern half of Nunivak (again, see Figure 15.2).

Another very relevant part of ANCSA, Section 14(h)(1), allows the regional corporations to receive a portion of their total acreage entitlements in the form of native historical places and cemetery sites. While Section 14(h)(1) affords Alaska Natives the chance (via their regional corporations) to gain title to sites having local and regional cultural significance, it does not require the regional corporations to make their site selections or associated land-management decisions in accordance with the wishes of local residents. By law, the regional corporations must exist for the purpose of making a profit. They would be hard-pressed to do so with their 14(h)(1) sites because, upon receiving title, the corporations also inherit cultural resource-management responsibilities for protecting the sites. This provision, combined with the fact that many 14(h)(1) sites are located on lands that have considerable trade value with state and federal agencies, makes it clear why corporate executives may in some cases feel it is not in the regional corporation's best financial interest to base its land-management decisions related to Section 14(h)(1) on the concerns of local people. Nunivak Island offers an excellent example of just such a case.

The Calista Corporation applied for 111 14(h)(1) sites on Nunivak Island, representing a total of 1,113 acres. With few exceptions, these sites are all located along the island's coastline; and seventy-six of the applications (or 68 percent) identify lands within the Nunivak Wilderness. The conveyance of Nunivak 14(h)(1) sites to Calista Corporation would constitute private "inholdings" of land within both a national wildlife refuge and a wilder-

2. The NIMA Corporation's deficiency acreage (46,080 acres) is located on the adjacent mainland along the shores of Dall Lake, about 130 kilometers (80 miles) southeast of Mekoryuk. The Nunivak Eskimos never used this area historically and do not use it today.

ness area;[3] both systems discourage, though neither prohibits, private inholdings. This was recognized by the Calista Corporation and the U.S. Fish and Wildlife Service – the federal agency responsible for managing the refuge and the Nunivak Wilderness. In short, the 14(h)(1) sites on Nunivak Island possess trade potential for the Calista Corporation because federal retention of title (and Fish and Wildlife management authority) would help insure the integrity of both the wilderness and the refuge (see U.S. Fish and Wildlife Service 1988: 20–21). This situation led to another land action that occurred without the knowledge of the Nunivak people.

In August 1983 the Calista Corporation entered into what is popularly known as the "Saint Matthew Island Land Exchange Agreement" with the U.S. Fish and Wildlife Service and two other native corporations – Cook Inlet Region, Inc., and the Sea Lion Corporation. As part of this agreement, the Calista Corporation relinquished all rights to the 14(h)(1) sites it had applied for on Nunivak Island in exchange for subsurface rights on Saint Matthew Island (Calista Corporation 1983). This caused the Bureau of Land Management to issue interim conveyance documents of title to the Fish and Wildlife Service for the lands described in the Nunivak 14(h)(1) site applications, which effectively meant that native ownership of the sites was no longer a possibility. At the time this agreement was signed, Saint Matthew Island (located about 175 miles west of Nunivak) was being touted as a potential staging area for offshore oil development in the Bering Sea. On the most basic level then, the exchange resulted in Calista Corporation trading 1,113 acres of land that had little potential to turn a corporate profit for an equivalent amount of land that had exactly the opposite potential. The U.S. Fish and Wildlife Service, however, apparently was prepared to take the risk posed by potential offshore oil development near Saint Matthew Island-which is itself a national wildlife refuge-in exchange for title to the various lands offered by the three participant native corporations (collectively referred to as "The CIRI Group").

The National Audubon Society, an American conservation and environmental group opposed to offshore oil development in the Saint Matthew Island area, brought suit against the United States

3. Inholdings are areas of privately owned land that are located within the boundaries of public land. In this case, they are located within the boundaries of the Nunivak Wilderness/Yukon Delta National Wildlife Refuge.

and the three participating native corporations to prevent the implementation of the exchange agreement.[4] The National Audubon Society won its case and in November 1984 the "Saint Matthew Island Exchange Agreement" was ruled invalid. Accordingly, the Bureau of Land Management reactivated the Nunivak Island 14(h)(1) site applications. Only as a result of field investigations of these sites in the summer of 1986 did the Nunivak people learn of the "Saint Matthew Island Land Exchange Agreement" and become aware that even their own regional corporation could not always be trusted to act in their best interests.[5]

This section of the study rightfully closes with a discussion of the Native Allotment Act of 1906 and its relationship to Nunivak Eskimo land use and land rights. The Act entitled adult natives to obtain title to 160 acres of public land provided they could demonstrate use and occupancy of that land over a five-year period; but subsistence-related use of the land did not count toward satisfying this requirement. The restrictive nature of the use and occupancy requirement and a basic lack of knowledge about the Native Allotment Act among Alaska Natives were significant impediments to their obtaining title to land. Arnold (1978: 98) notes that in 1962, a full fifty-six years after passage of the Act, only 101 allotments had been approved in the state of Alaska. But the process that led to the 1971 settlement of native land claims also generated widespread knowledge of the Native Allotment Act, and several thousand Alaska Natives eventually filed allotment applications. The allotment act remained in effect until

4. The National Audubon Society was the primary plaintiff; all of the following were coplaintiffs: The Bering Sea Fishermen's Association, Trustees for Alaska, The Wilderness Society, Defenders of Wildlife, National Wildlife Refuge Association, Friends of the Earth, and The Natural Resources Defense Council, Inc. Hereafter, "The National Audubon Society" is understood to include all of the plaintiffs.

This case was heard in the United States District Court for the District of Alaska and actually involved three separate lawsuits: *National Audubon Society v. Clark* (No. A 83–425 Civil); *National Audubon Society v. Cook Inlet Region, Inc.* (No. A 84–401 Civil); and *National Audubon Society v. Putz* (No. A 84–402 Civil). All three suits were addressed under a single legal opinion (the "Saint Matthew opinion").

5. Encouragingly, Calista Corporation has recently made a definite commitment to help resolve some of the Nunivak Eskimo's most pressing land problems. In fact, it now seems probable that Calista Corporation will take conveyance of all eligible Alaska Native Claims Settlement Act (ANCSA) 14(h)(1) sites on Nunivak Island then immediately exchange them with the Nunivak Island Mekoryuk Alaska (NIMA) Corporation for an equivalent amount of NIMA's "deficiency" lands around Dall Lake.

December 1971, when it was revoked by the passage of the Alaska Native Claims Settlement Act. Thus, Alaska Natives who did not have allotment applications on file by that date were not eligible for allotments.

In apparent contrast to every other native group in Alaska, not one Nunivak resident owns a native allotment; nor do legal records exist that document the filing of allotment applications by the Nunivak people (see Nunivak Island Mekoryuk Alaska Corp. n.d.).[6] In other words, the entire village of Mekoryuk somehow missed out on the Native Allotment Act. Mekoryuk residents are adamant in their claims that villagers who were eligible to do so actually did complete allotment applications. Local explanations for why applications from Nunivak residents were never officially recorded suggest that the villagers' relative isolation and the absence of outside assistance during the application process were significant factors (Shavings 1975). First, the packet of allotment materials sent to Mekoryuk contained an insufficient number of blank application forms, and also did not include maps showing the entire island, which were necessary for people to clearly identify the lands for which they wished to apply. Requests for more applications and the missing maps apparently went unanswered. Second, numerous Mekoryuk residents claim that a representative of the U.S. Fish and Wildlife Service told the Nunivak people they were not eligible for allotments because they lived in a national wildlife refuge. In both respects, the people's isolation frustrated their efforts to overcome these problems and complete the application process before the deadline had passed. It is not known what happened to the allotment applications that were completed; they appear to have vanished without a trace.

A 1975 letter written by Nunivak resident Hilma Shavings (Shavings 1975) expressed the frustration of the Nunivak people as follows:

> What hurts me the most is that our island was made into a Refuge without even consulting our father[s], maybe because they were so ignorant and did not speak English at that time. That . . . made it impossible for them to even own an acre now. We found out too late, just like an old saying, "closing the barn door, after the horse was stolen." [The] musk-ox is entitled to every acre on the island and my people nothing. My people [have] settled for hunting and fishing on

6. A total of four native allotments *were* filed for lands on Nunivak Island, but each was filed in the mainland community of Bethel by Nunivak Eskimos who no longer lived on the island.

the island, [borrowing the land] under the so- called protection of [the] National Wildlife Refuge, [this] protection includes the native residents, but for how long? [S]ome sympathetic people from the Yukon-Kuskokwim Delta have told me that it is not fair for us, while all the other natives have allotments, none of the islanders own an acre.

Hilma sent copies of this letter to at least twenty different individuals and organizations, including the entire Alaska Congressional delegation and the Secretary of the U.S. Department of the Interior. Apparently, she never received a single response. Though it is now officially a closed case, the allotment issue is still very much alive on Nunivak Island, and the people continue to speak out about it whenever the opportunity arises. The reluctance to accept their lost rights to allotments is poignantly explained by Peter Smith (Smith 1984): "You see, our ancestors owned [the island]. We want Nunivak . . . all of it. . . . [W]e filled out papers in vain, we joined efforts to try to get 120 acres [of] land allotment. However, evidently they lost those papers. There must be someone who is envious of us; the papers were thrown away. We wanted to take our little bit of land. But now we've been brushed aside and it is too late."

## Local Perspectives on the Nunivak Wilderness

The Nunivak Eskimos feel their ancestral lands have been lost not because of their own bad decisions, but because they were never asked to give an opinion or grant their permission before official land actions were undertaken. The only exception was the 1972–73 U.S. Fish and Wildlife Service Nunivak Wilderness Study, the results of which were unanimous: the Nunivak people, Calista Corporation, and the Fish and Wildlife Service opposed any part of Nunivak being designated wilderness. It should be noted that at the time of this study wilderness designation forbade the use of snowmobiles and other motorized vehicles within a wilderness area. Although specific exceptions were written into the Alaska National Interest Lands Conservation Act for Alaska wilderness seven years later, local knowledge of the legislative meaning of wilderness is derived solely from the earlier Nunivak Wilderness Study.

The U.S. Fish and Wildlife Service concluded that the island possessed many wilderness qualities, but opposed wilderness designation for two reasons. First, it would conflict with native subsistence hunting, fishing, and trapping activities because snowmobiles – which were widely used by Nunivak residents for subsistence and reindeer-herding activities – were not permitted within wilderness areas. And second, imbalanced musk-oxen and reindeer populations, inadequate planning to cope with those problems, plus inadequate staffing and budgeting for the refuge suggested that proper management of a wilderness area on Nunivak was impossible (U.S. Fish and Wildlife Service 1972: 77–80; 1973).

Local people publicly expressed numerous objections to the wilderness designation (U.S. Department of the Interior 1973). The use of snowmobiles was often cited, but other reasons are more illuminating of local feelings. The statements of many Nunivak people essentially argued, "If it ain't broke, don't fix it." That is, if Nunivak was considered potentially worthy of wilderness designation, it showed that the people had taken good care of their island and were responsible land stewards. So why was it suddenly necessary for the government to classify the island as wilderness and restrict local people's customary use of the land? Though the wilderness study team assured the people that subsistence use of the island would be relatively unaffected by wilderness designation, it also asked them to identify specific areas that potentially could be designated wilderness without a significant impact on local lifestyles. The Nunivak people contended the entire island was important for subsistence and a person could not draw a line and say "this area is not used." As Walter Amos testified before the wilderness study team: "All the people of Nunivak . . . want to use the island the way they have been using it before without any more restrictions . . . " (U.S. Department of the Interior 1973: 26–27). Clearly, local people believed wilderness designation would constitute a barrier to customary land use. Calista Corporation representatives supported the Nunivakers' opposition to the wilderness, as illustrated in the following quote. "[The Nunivak] people . . . have been preserving the island just as a virgin wilderness, as a virgin island, and it was [a] virgin island when the musk-ox came here. And . . . these people here can . . . preserve the island without the Wilderness Act and take good care of it just as . . . they have been taking care of it before" (U.S. Department of the Interior 1973: 14–15).

Although the 1973 public meeting ended with all in accord that Nunivak should remain free of wilderness designation, some people in attendance were not confident of the final decision. This concern was clearly expressed by Elsie Williams: "[Y]ou people are telling us right now what's going to happen here-everybody's heard what you said. You give us your word that you're going to protect Nunivak from becoming a wilderness area. ... [a] lot of times people ... [have come] here and [told us] what they're going to do and what they're not going to do. But then they go back to work and produce just the opposite of what they tell the people" (U.S. Department of the Interior 1973: 25–26). Obviously, Elsie's concerns were well-founded, for a wilderness area was eventually established on Nunivak Island. That this happened despite the opposition of not only the Nunivak people, but also the federal agency responsible for managing the island's lands reflects the fact that "recommendations to Congress as to which areas qualified as candidates for wilderness ... might or might not be followed by legislation. Moreover, Congress [has] the power to bypass agency recommendations" (Wilderness Society 1989: 6).

It is unclear exactly why Congress bypassed the U.S. Fish and Wildlife Service's recommendation and designated the Nunivak Wilderness, or why the wilderness boundary was drawn to encompass the southern half of the island. One member of the original Nunivak Wilderness study team (Hardy 1986), however, has speculated that the Nunivak Wilderness designation was simply a political compromise aimed at appeasing conservationists, and suggested that the northern half of the island was excluded from such designation out of deference to the local people (so that they would be allowed to use the northern half of the island free of wilderness restrictions). Regardless of the reasoning behind the Nunivak Wilderness designation, local residents view the action as another case in which their concerns were ignored by the government.

Ironically, the refuge staff has taken the brunt of local blame for the wilderness decision, partially because they are the only federal agents with whom the Nunivak people have semi-regular contact, but also because the Nunivakers recognize that the wilderness is an extension of the national wildlife refuge. The U.S. Fish and Wildlife Service has also made several questionable management decisions concerning Nunivak lands, which have damaged its image among island residents. For example, in 1979 (just prior to the creation of the Nunivak Wilderness), the agency forced Nunivak native Fred Don to tear down a cabin he had built two years earlier at a fish camp on the island's southern coast. Fred was told that he had no right to build a cabin on refuge lands and was accused of having built the cabin with the intent of using it for commercial purposes, as a base camp for musk-ox hunters (Don 1990). (Sport hunting of musk-oxen on Nunivak was first permitted by the Fish and Wildlife Service in 1975 in response to the excessive size of the Nunivak herd, and by 1979 Fred had become a certified Assistant Hunting Guide.) Fred denied the agency's accusation, explaining that the cabin was built as a shelter for his family's use while subsistence fishing in the summer. The cabin site had been the summer camp of Fred's mother and stepfather for many years, and had been occupied by his own family for three successive years prior to 1979 (Don 1990). Local people were incensed when the Fish and Wildlife Service ordered the cabin to be torn down.

Although this incident grew out of the Fish and Wildlife Service's refuge cabin policy, many Nunivakers mistakenly attribute it to restrictions imposed by the wilderness designation. The wilderness policies that became applicable after 1980, however, are not inconsistent with the Fish and Wildlife Service's refuge cabin policy: wilderness designations stipulate that only the land-managing agency can construct new cabins in a wilderness area, and then only in limited cases (Wilderness Society 1984: 56). In the summer of 1985, the Fish and Wildlife Service refuge staff began constructing a "cabin" within the Nunivak Wilderness area. This structure really is not a cabin at all, but a semisubterranean sod house. The Nunivak people do not understand why the Fish and Wildlife Service can build such a structure in the wilderness but the local people can not, particularly given their traditional use of semisubterranean sod houses throughout the island.

The Nunivakers' frustration was increased upon learning in the summer of 1986 that the construction of this sod house was in direct violation of federal cultural resource-management laws, as it was dug into the midden of an old village site. Two other cabins built on Nunivak by the Fish and Wildlife Service between 1970 and 1973 are also in violation of such laws. Construction of the sod house in question was undertaken at the direction of the refuge manager and supervised by his staff, but when confronted by the Calista Corporation in the fall of 1986, the agency was extremely reluctant to acknowledge responsibility for its existence, choosing instead to blame the Nunivak people. A refuge official peddled this same story at a village meeting held in Mekoryuk several months later, but eventually admitted the structure's construction was ordered by the agency (Amos 1987). Surprisingly, in a recent visit to the island early in 1990, the refuge staff again stated to local people that the Nunivakers, not the Fish and Wildlife Service, built the sod house (Amos and Kiokun 1990). This attitude only encourages the Nunivak people's distrust of the U.S. Fish and Wildlife Service. Further, the Nunivakers are upset that the agency has not been punished for its known violations of federal law on the island, as explained by Howard Amos (1987): "The natives of Mekoryuk have abided by the rules and regulations of the Fish and Wildlife Service for many years – afraid that if any laws of theirs were violated, they would be incarcerated or fined. Because of the silence of the natives, the Fish and Wildlife Service officials are not prosecuted, nor will they be, unless someone blows the whistle. These [cultural resource management] laws are passed by the U.S. Congress to be enforced by the people who are violating them."

As previously indicated, beginning in 1975 the State of Alaska has allowed sporthunters to harvest a limited number of musk-oxen from the Nunivak herd. These hunts last between thirty and forty-five days in both spring and fall.[7] Weather during the fall hunt is variable but "winter" conditions prevail throughout the spring hunt; and while musk-oxen might be found anywhere on the island in fall, they tend to gather in the southern half of Nunivak during the spring. The hunting of musk-oxen has created economic opportunities for some Nunivak residents, who provide guide and transport services to the hunters. During the past few years, similar services also have been provided to wildlife photographers. Because very few employment opportunities exist for Nunivak residents,

7. Bull musk-oxen can be harvested in either hunt; permits are issued by way of a statewide drawing, so Nunivakers have the same probability of drawing a permit as any other Alaska resident. In contrast, cow musk-oxen are harvested only in the spring, and more than half of all available permits are reserved for Nunivak residents. These "reserved" permits are distributed on a "first- come, first-served" basis by Fish and Wildlife Service officials who travel to Mekoryuk specifically for that purpose. The remaining cow permits are distributed in similar fashion at various regional offices of the Service. The annual number of bulls and cows for which harvest permits are issued is based on herd composition statistics derived from musk-oxen population counts conducted each spring by Fish and Wildlife Service biologists. A maximum of seventy-five animals can be harvested from the Nunivak herd during the 1992–1993 hunts: thirty cows and forty-five bulls (ten in fall, and thirty-five in spring).

Finally, since many of the nonnative hunters of Nunivak musk-oxen are primarily interested in the animals' horns and skins, the local people often receive most of the meat (Fienup-Riordan 1990: 180–181).

the fees charged for guide and transport services represent an important contribution to the annual income of some families. Their importance has become magnified in recent years by serious problems with Nunivaks' commercial herring fishery.

Nunivak guides and transporters claim that restrictions imposed on them by the policies on wilderness and refuge cabins constitute an economic hardship. These policies not only disallow the construction of cabins or other permanent structures on non-private lands throughout the island, but also forbid the use of existing cabins on those lands for commercial activities (see Wilderness Act, Section 4(c); ANILCA, Section 1315(d)). The existing Fish and Wildlife Service cabins on the island can be used by guides and transporters and their clients only in emergency situations (U.S. Fish and Wildlife Service 1989: 11). Further, the refuge staff recently informed Nunivak guides and transporters that they are only allowed to dig into the snow and put a tarp over the resultant chamber as a temporary base on private land (Amos and Kiokun 1990) – there is no private land in the southern half of the island. These restrictions often preclude taking clients on overnight or extended camping trips to the island's southern side.

Additionally, a state law (Alaska Statute 08.54.395) passed in 1989 requires all guides and transporters to carry insurance coverage for their clients, making them solely responsible for their clients' safety.[8] With the unpredictable and frequently severe weather conditions on Nunivak, local operators feel the restrictive cabin policies place their clients in greater danger than is reasonable; and the combination of these policies with the mandatory insurance law makes guiding and transporting an even riskier economic enterprise. Because these commercial operations have been taking place since 1975 (prior to wilderness designation), it is believed they should be exempt from wilderness restrictions. In fact, they may be-but such operations are not exempt from the Fish and Wildlife Service cabin policy. From the Nunivak Eskimo perspective, management of the island's musk-oxen is neatly summed up by this recent remark: "In the present time, my elders state the following; `Animal treated better than humans'" (Amos 1987).

Ultimately, most of the Nunivakers' complaints concerning the wilderness express open confusion about the connection between

8. Guides must be insured by a minimum comprehensive general liability policy of $300,000.00 per occurrence, or $500,000.00 per aggregate. Use of aircraft in guiding operations requires a higher minimum amount of insurance.

wilderness designation and their customary use and occupancy of the land, as well as resentment of the loss of local control of the island. Peter Smith (1984) described the people's loss of ownership to the island in the following way:

> I heard one time that Alaska was going to become a state. When it became a state, [the state powers] . . . came in like nothing, pushing us out and taking our land; the state did just as it pleased in order to take over Alaska, bypassing its own people. And while I was living my life, I heard that we supposedly didn't own the lands which we had been occupying. Oh dear, it looked very bad to me when I thought about having . . . made a sod house in ground that wasn't mine there in the southern part of Nunivak Island. . . . And so now I hear that we the people of Nunivak, down in the wilderness area in the southern part of Nunivak, we can't go there to fish camps of ours without permits. . . . And more and more it's getting to be that way in our land, that you need a permit for everything.

In what may be the most powerful statement against the Nunivak Wilderness, Richard Davis (1989) flatly contends:

> [The south side of Nunivak Island] is not fit for a wilderness, because it has been established on top of the ancestors' old living places. Even on the tops of mountains. Mountaintop houses were used not just for caribou hunting, but also for reindeer herding, one to three months at a time. Just about any mountain you look on has the remains of these shelters. There are also graves on many of these places. If you walk across this island you will see evidence of graves and houses everywhere. Even people that are gone today, their blood stains the land all over the south side.

## Discussion and Conclusions

The Nunivak Eskimos' perceptions of the impacts of wilderness designation on their land-use rights are exaggerated beyond their actual scope for two main reasons. The first is their deep-seated distrust of the state and federal governments, an attitude based on legislation and land-management policies enacted since the late 1920s that have substantially eroded local control of Nunivak lands. A second reason is the abysmally poor implementation of the wilderness by the U.S. Fish and Wildlife Service, and its consequent role in fostering local misunderstandings. The fact that many of the wilderness impacts perceived by the Nunivak people are incorrect-such as a ban on the use of snowmobiles and chainsaws-indicates that the Fish and Wildlife Service has failed in its duty to adequately inform the people of the exceptions that the Alaska National Interest Lands Conservation Act (ANILCA) allows in Alaska wilderness. In the Nunivak case, perceptions have now become real; this has contributed to the development of a powerful anti-wilderness attitude among the local people.

In one form or another, the entirety of Nunivak Island bears evidence of indigenous cultural use (see VanStone 1989: 42), which may partly explain the fact that the concept of "wilderness" in the Western sense is foreign to the Nunivak people. In the Western concept of wilderness, geographic boundaries are implicit. Wilderness is a conceptual compartment that segregates the landscape in a unique way by specifically separating man from the land. But in the Nunivak world view, man is conceptually embodied in the land, even in uninhabited areas. This reflects a fundamental difference in cultural views of and toward the land; a difference that is completely obscured by the wilderness label.

The author has not located a single passage in the wilderness legislation that specifically discusses the relationship of wilderness to indigenous people's traditional and customary land use and land rights.[9] The American public's distorted image of Native Americans as the "original conservationists . . . people so intimately bound to the land that they left no mark upon it" (White and Cronon 1988: 417; see also Wilson 1992), and the historical tendency of anthropologists to insist that land was not owned [in Western conceptual terms] in hunting-gathering societies (Myers 1988: 264; Voget 1975: 288–310, 631) no doubt have contributed to the neglect of native concepts of land and land use (see Momaday 1976) in the relevant legislation.

This lack of representation, by extension, suggests legislators consider hunting-gathering peoples to be truly a part of nature (just like other animals) and implies that their presence does not leave lasting "imprints" on the land. This thought is especially intriguing in relation to the Nunivak Wilderness, which contains the remains of more than forty habitation sites (all having physical evidence of permanent semisubterranean structures), scores of caribou hunting camps, and hundreds of burials. Perhaps in wilderness evaluations the imprints native peoples have left on the landscape are deemed

9. The Alaska director of the Wilderness Society (A. E. Smith 1990) told the author that in his more than twenty years of experience working with wilderness issues, he does not recall ever seeing any written discussion of this sort.

insignificant once permanent settlements have been abandoned? If so, continued seasonal use of the land may be equated with that of other anadromous or migratory species.

But if native peoples are as much a part of the wilderness as other species, then wilderness proponents should put forth an equivalent effort to conserve their lifestyles. Physical imprints aside, what does the existence of extensive native place – names in a wilderness area say about the degree of human presence in the landscape? Research on Nunivak ethnogeography to date has documented more than nine hundred native place-names on the island, more than half of which are located within the Nunivak Wilderness (Drozda and Pratt n.d.). The names are evidence of the Nunivak Eskimos' land-use history, and forge a link between the island's present inhabitants and their ancestors through the medium of land. Whereas the American public in general has divorced itself from the land, the Nunivak Eskimos maintain a symbolic relationship with their island that is reciprocal and nurturing; neither can be complete or healthy without the other. In this sense, the people retain "traditional" values toward the land in spite of technological and economic changes that have greatly altered the surface character of Nunivak Eskimo life on the land.

The Nunivak people consider the wilderness designation a rejection of their own personal relationship with the land, as well as a denial of their ancestors' existence on and past use of the island. Nunivakers clearly perceive "wilderness" as a threat to their culture, and resent that it casts them as trespassers on much of their ancestral land. Together with their loss of ownership and control of the island over the past sixty years, this sentiment has prevented the Nunivak Eskimos from recognizing the primary benefit of wilderness designation: it protects the land and its natural resources from exploitation and potentially harmful development, thereby constituting a buffer against numerous activities that could seriously endanger their contemporary subsistence way of life. It should be remembered, however, that this attribute of wilderness designation is applicable only to Alaska; and it is naive to think this exception was created for any reason other than the need for wilderness advocates and other conservationists to make concessions to assure passage of the ANILCA legislation. If the opinion of a Sierra Club Executive Committee member that berry picking is a "trivial activity" (McCargo 1985) is any indication, the protection of Alaska Native land and subsistence rights will continue to be a rallying point for conservationists only when it can be used to fight particularly controversial development plans.

It is not necessary to repeal the wilderness designation to resolve the Nunivak Wilderness problem; in the final analysis, wilderness designation is a relatively small part of the problem. Resolution can be achieved through increased communication, cooperation, and understanding between government agents and the Nunivak people (see Oswalt 1961: 13), as well as the adoption of more flexible management policies for federal conservation lands. The responsibility for initiating such changes rests squarely with the U.S. Fish and Wildlife Service; the probability that it will take action of this sort in the immediate future, however, seems remote.

The agency has long been aware of the Nunivakers' negative opinions about the wilderness designation and various refuge-management issues, but has given no indication that it considers this an important management problem. It apparently interprets the Nunivak people's hostility regarding the wilderness as simply a misunderstanding about how it affects their access to the land and its resources; the cultural values, heritage, and land-use history of the people have not been linked to this and other Nunivak management problems. Agencies such as the Fish and Wildlife Service should heed Fall's (1990: 88) point that "[a] management system that is responsive to traditional uses and needs is more likely to build cooperation and trust than one that ignores local knowledge or imposes inappropriate regulatory regimes on traditional systems of hunting and fishing." Yet, comparatively speaking, the Fish and Wildlife Service probably is not much different from other land-managing agencies (in Alaska and elsewhere) having authority over the homelands of contemporary hunters and gatherers; most agencies find it difficult to hear or respond to an indigenous voice. But it is increasingly urgent that these voices be heard, for the preservation of hunting-gathering peoples is at stake.

The case examined in this essay reveals that the basic identity of such a society is inextricably tied to the land – and the Nunivak Eskimos are very likely the most land-poor of all Alaska Native groups. Understandably, this predicament has created a pervasive feeling of insecurity among these people and is a primary factor in their bitter opposition to the Nunivak Wilderness.

# 16

# Hunter-Gatherers and the Politics of Environment and Development in India

*G. Prakash Reddy*

There are a number of hunting-gathering communities in India. Widely known among them are the Chenchu of the eastern Ghats Mountains and the Onge of the Andaman and Nicobar Islands. While the mainland hunter-gatherers are going through a phase of transition, one not necessarily beneficial to them, the Andaman and Nicobar groups are declining, and a few are on the verge of extinction. The present deplorable state of affairs in these communities, on both the mainland and the islands, is due mainly to the unimaginative policies of the government in relation to the environment, industrialization, development, and even the welfare measures in these districts.

## Introduction

Once upon a time, not all that long ago, most of the tribal communities on the Indian subcontinent were hunters and gatherers. Today, their number has declined, and many of the survivors have become shifting and settled cultivators who practice hunting and gathering as subsidiary occupations. Unfortunately, a few groups unable to make this transition have become extinct.

A decade ago the Government of India (1982) declared that seventy-two tribal communities were so primitive that they required special development efforts. The most important feature of these communities was that hunting and gathering still dominated their lives. For a few, like the Onge, Jarawa, Sentinalese, and Shompen of the Andaman and Nicobar Islands, hunting and gathering is the exclusive subsistence activity. For the Chenchu of the eastern Ghats, the Birhor of Bihar, the Kadar of Kerala, and many others, foraging is important, along with forest labor and primitive cultivation. There are also hunter-gatherers that depend exclusively on one species, who may be called "specialized foragers." For instance, the Phasepardhi hunt only deer, while the Vaidu depend only on small carnivores, and the Nandiwalla hunt porcupines (Malhotra, Khomne, and Gadgil 1983). An interesting aspect of contemporary hunter-gatherers in India is that at least one community, namely, the Sentinalese, who number an estimated two hundred people and who inhabit Sentinal Island in the Andaman chain, that has not yet been contacted by modern people. On the same islands, two other hunter-gatherer communities, the Jarawa of South Andaman and the Shompen of Great Nicobar, have been only partially contacted.

The hunter-gatherer communities in India are passing through a critical phase in their history. They are gradually being marginalized and displaced, and a few are even moving toward extinction. The situation among the Andaman and Nicobar Negrito and Mongoloid hunter-gatherers gives particular cause for concern. A few groups have already become extinct, while others are declining at an alarming rate. The Andamanese of Strait Island are on the way to extinction, with only twenty-eight survivors as of 1990.

The condition of the hunter-gatherer communities on mainland India is not much better. They are not necessarily declining in population, but they are being displaced and marginalized, and losing access to their traditional resource base.

The sad state of affairs in these communities is due to four factors: the deforestation of India's tropical and subtropical forests and the consequent environmental degradation and resource depletion; programs to control environmental degradation and ecological imbalance; unimaginative development programs; and programs, developmental and otherwise, in the name of the national interest.

## Deforestation

India is losing its forest cover at an alarming rate. The British began the commercial exploitation of India's forests, but the belief has persisted in both the national and state governments that forests exist only for exploitation. The result has been both the legal and illegal devastation of much of the country. Data released in 1984 by India's National Remote Sensing Agency show that the country lost 1.3 million hectares of forest each year between 1972 and 1982. Satellite data show that in 1972, 16.89 percent of the land was forested. Today the forested area of the country is estimated to be less than 14 percent of the total land area.

The reasons for this massive destruction of forests are obvious. In addition to the increasing commercial exploitation of forests, the establishment of forest-based and heavy industries and the construction of irrigation dams and hydroelectric projects have all had a negative impact. The population explosion has created land hunger leading to illegal encroachment into the forests, and this has further undermined the quality and quantity of the forests.[1] This massive and rapid deforestation, which has caused ecological disasters (flash floods, soil erosion), climatic changes, drought and famine, has endangered the very survival of the tribal communities dwelling in the forests.

*Awareness Among the Tribes*

The tribal communities located in central India, as well as those in other states – such as Orissa, Bihar, Gujarat and Andhra Pradesh, are very conscious of the destruction of their habitat. They have organized countless protests, and in a few areas have even taken up arms. These protests have fallen on deaf ears, and sometimes have been greeted with bullets. In 1981, police firing on the tribals of the Adilabad District in Andhra Pradesh killed nearly one hundred Gond and Kolam people (Prakash Reddy 1987). In the same year, in the Singhbhum District of Bihar, police bullets felled more than twenty-five protesting tribals. These are but two of many examples of the brutal suppression of the protests of forest dwellers. The attitude of the police and the administration is clearly presented by Bose (1984: 71): "[After the fighting in Bihar] curfew was immediately imposed and [a] news blackout was attempted. It was learned that during the week armed police visited several villages and local hospitals and killed injured tribals in cold blood."

1. Many small towns have emerged in the tribal areas (forests) of the country, causing further deforestation. A look at the settlement pattern of these towns reveals both stratification and the real culprits who are destroying the forests. Tops of hills are invariably dotted with government offices and with residential and guest houses of important officials. Beneath these houses, at successively lower levels, are the neighborhoods of lower officials, nontribal immigrants, and, at the bottom, the settlements of the original inhabitants, the tribal communities.

There are a number of hunter-gatherers, like the Birhor, Kolam, and Raji, whose fate is tied to the shifting and settled cultivators who occupy the same habitat. Other groups – isolated hunter-gatherers like the Negritos and Mongoloids of the Andaman and Nicobar Islands, and the Chenchu of Nallamalais in the eastern Ghats – are so few in number and so geographically remote that, except for some grumbling, they have never really protested. Ramachandra Guha and Madhav Gadgil (1988), two Indian environmental experts, have described the effects of deforestation on Indian hunter-gatherers as going "from decline to extinction." They point out that many hunting-gathering communities were not large enough to actively resist the social and economic changes that followed the introduction of state forest management.

Everyone in India is aware of who the real culprits are behind the destruction and devastation of the forests. But the government, the Forest Department, the forest contractors and even the National Commission on Agriculture make the tribal communities the scapegoats at every available opportunity, ignoring the fact that the tribals are protesting and have taken up arms to protect the forests and their way of life.

I shall illustrate the process of pauperization and marginalization that has begun to occur among the hunting- gathering communities of India as a result of deforestation with some specific case studies.

### The Hill Kharia

The Hill Kharia inhabit the forests of the Singhbhum District of west Bengal. Once gatherer-hunters, they had made the transition to shifting cultivation supplemented by hunting and gathering. Over the course of time, however, they withdrew more and more into the interior of the forest, and once again became full time food gatherers and hunters. As in almost all the forested areas of the country, the Forest Department adopted a double standard here. While it placed restrictions on shifting cultivation considered harmful to the forest, it closed its eyes to the encroachment of nontribal populations into the forest for settlement and illegal cultivation. The nontribals, in addition to illegally clearing the forest and planting crops, also become competitors of the Kharia in their hunting-gathering activities.

Even in the interior, the Kharia could not continue their hunting and gathering because of further encroachment by the nontribals. They were forced for sheer survival to take up agricultural labor to supplement the little hunting and gathering they did. But the combination of these activities failed to provide them with even minimum food requirements. This was evident during the periods from February to June, and from September to October, when the food supply is critically low, causing starvation for days on end (Dikshit 1984).

## Andaman Islanders

If the fate of Hill Kharia was the result of deforestation and the encroachment of nontribals, the Negrito hunters and gatherers of the Andaman Islands are the best examples of a deliberate policy of encroachment and annihilation. This policy was initiated by the colonial government; it is still followed by the present government, but in a different way. The situation is a textbook case of the consequences of deforestation for hunter-gatherers, and of the impact of sudden contact with outsiders and land imperialism that governments in many parts of the world are imposing on indigenous populations (Prakash Reddy and Sudarsen 1989).

Before the British colonized the islands, all the hunter-gatherer tribes roamed freely over the entire area. The limit of their habitat started decreasing with the establishment of a penal settlement and the town of Port Blair. In 1956 remnants (kitchen middens) of their occupation were found on the outskirts of Port Blair by Lidio Cipriani, an Italian anthropologist. Today, Port Blair has grown so much that these remnants have been destroyed. An anthropologist who worked among the Onge of Little Andaman in 1956 estimated their population to be around five hundred; as of 1990 their number was only ninety-nine. The fate of the Great Andamanese, who now number at most twenty-eight, was entirely at the mercy of forest contractors until they were settled on Strait Island.

The Jarawa, another Negrito hunter-gatherer population, are estimated to have once numbered between 150 and 200 people on South Andaman Island. They initially were friendly toward the colonizers, but gradually became hostile. This may have been due to the British policy of befriending the Jarawa's enemies. The

British even sent punitive expeditions against the Jarawa. As more and more forest area was cleared, they were pushed from the island's east coast, where water was abundant. They now live in a reserve on thin slices of land about 128 kilometers long and 35 kilometers wide, on the two main islands. After the country's independence, the position of the Jarawa became more precarious. A portion of the original Jarawa reserve (demarcated in 1929 by the British) was cleared of forest, and refugees from east Bengal were settled there. This action of the administration further infuriated the Jarawa and, in retaliation, they occasionally raided the refugee settlements. To give protection to the settlers, the administration created a special police force and called it the "bush police." Their posts now surround the Jarawa reserve.

Another act of the administration, which further reduced the habitat of the Jarawa, was the laying of the Great Andaman trunk road through the virgin forest in the midst of their territory. Besides this planned destruction, the tropical forest on both sides of the road became completely denuded. This affects the productive capacity of Jarawa territory, and provides easy access to poachers.

There are some indications that the Jarawa, confined to their small stretch of forest, face scarcity of food and drinking water during the summer months. Earlier, when the Jarawa raided the refugee settlements, they never touched any food in either the fields or the houses. During the past decade, however, they have visited the water sources near the refugee settlements and have stolen food. During these visits, the Jarawa also cut the banana crops of the settlers for their own use, although little damage was done because of their habit of collecting just enough for one day. The deforestation and encroachment of immigrants into the forest for cultivation seem to have harmed the perennial water sources in Jarawa territory. Poaching by forest laborers and immigrants has increased in recent times. Poachers have even killed Jarawa children and set fire to Jarawa huts.[2]

2. The modus operandi of the poachers is inhuman. To scare away the Jarawa, poachers nearing their settlement let loose firecrackers. The Jarawa flee, and the poachers ransack the huts and then set fire to them. Another disturbing fact that recently came to my notice is that nontribal immigrants are putting pressure on the Andaman administration for licenses to buy firearms to defend themselves against the Jarawa. If the administration yields to this pressure, the Jarawa will cease to exist.

One of the recent administrators of the Andaman and Nicobar Islands, writing about the present situation of the Jarawa, says that the scarcity of food and water in the summer impels them to go in search of water sources. Their raids have taken place along rivers and streams. The jungle in the present Jarawa area contains neither edible roots nor fruits (Bhatt 1987).

The Andaman administration has succeeded in establishing contact with one group of Jarawa by leaving gifts, such as coconuts, bananas, and cooked rice, on the edge of their territory. It hopes to "befriend" them and to settle them in a small area in tin-roofed sheds. This process is correctly termed by the ecologist Romulus Whitaker (1985) as "spreading the seed to trap the birds." It has been rumored that the Forest Department on the islands has already divided Jarawa territory into blocks in their working plans, and is ready to move in for commercial exploitation the moment the people have been resettled.

One cannot help but think that the Jarawa will suffer the same fate as the Onge of Little Andaman if they are fully "befriended." The Onge have lost their freedom entirely, and are housed in tin-roofed sheds at Dugong Creek, on Little Andaman Island. Deforestation started when 700 square kilometers of Onge land was cleared and allotted to immigrant settlers in 1971, and to the Forest Development Corporation in 1977. Further deforestation occurred when a jetty was constructed and a road twenty-one kilometers long was laid on the island. Nearly 25,000 hectares of forest were cleared for the purpose of agriculture and oil palm plantation. Forest was cleared again in 1975 for settling Nicobarese brought in from the Nicobar Islands. A matchstick factory was established on the island in the 1970s (Venkatesan 1988).

## Environmental Programs

Awareness of environmental devastation has increased in recent years, both among the people and in the government. No one disputes the fact that, unless the environment is protected and ecological balance maintained, people's survival is at stake. But the environmental experts and the government often forget that people are also part of the ecosystem, and it is they who protect or destroy the environment. This attitude on the part of environmentalists and the government is clearly shown in the programs designed and implemented for environmental protection. For example, as part of environmental protection programs, "animal sanctuaries" and "biosphere reserves" are being established indiscriminately throughout the country, undermining the rights of tribal communities in general, and of hunters and gatherers in particular. It is ironic that the hunter-gatherers in India are caught between deforestation, on the one hand, and environmental restoration programs, on the other. A brief examination of the impact of animal sanctuaries on these communities will illustrate their plight.

Hundreds of wildlife sanctuaries and a few national parks have been established in various parts of the country over the past decade. Unfortunately, many of them are located in the heart of tribal areas and, in many cases, they were established over the protests of the tribal communities. In the state of Orissa in central India, tribals were so enraged at the establishment of a sanctuary at Simlihal that they invaded the sanctuary and started killing the animals in it.

Of all the wildlife sanctuaries so far established, the most damaging to the interests of these tribal peoples are tiger sanctuaries. These are created under the name of Project Tiger, and there are fifteen of them in the country. The general situation is illustrated by an example from the state of Andhra Pradesh.

In the state of Andhra Pradesh alone there are fifteen wildlife sanctuaries, five of which are located in the heart of tribal territories. The Chenchu inhabit two of the five. In the remaining three are found the Koya, Kolam, Gond, and Konda Reddy, who supplement their subsistence activity with hunting and gathering. Two of these five sanctuaries are tiger sanctuaries established under Project Tiger. A brief examination of the impact of the tiger reserve of Srisailam on the hunter-gatherer community of the Chenchu illustrates the general pattern.

The Chenchu number a few thousand people. They are a well-known hunting-gathering community studied by anthropologist Christopher von Fürer-Haimendorf. He described Chenchu territory as "leafless in the summer, offering no shade to man or beast; while underfoot the ground, robbed of its grassy cloak, lay charred, barren and black, the stony surface radiating the sun's heat" (von Fürer-Haimendorf 1943). By the end of May, almost the whole forest is clad in new foliage, and grass carpets the ground in level, shady places. In the winter it is a luxurious jungle in the rainy season, and an arid sun-baked desert in hot weather. Professor von Fürer-Haimendorf, then Tribal Welfare Adviser to the Nizam's government,[3] wanted the District to be declared an exclusive sanctuary for the Chenchu. It has become a reserve for tigers instead.

The tiger sanctuary came into existence in 1980. Chenchu settlements are located in the core and on fringe areas of the sanctuary, and in both areas people have problems with the reserve. After it was established, the tiger population increased, and movement of Chenchu in the core area was restricted because of tiger attacks. The one or two goats kept by each Chenchu family, and many of the cattle given to them by the government, have become prey to tigers. Even the officials of the Tribal Welfare Department are not allowed to enter the core area because of the danger. The result has been that no assistance, not even medical care, can be given to the Chenchu in time of need.

The Chenchu on the sanctuary's fringe, in addition to hunting and gathering, have begun farming in a limited way. Since the establishment of the sanctuary they have not been allowed to enter the core area. This restriction has deprived them of the benefits of hunting and gathering. Before the establishment of the sanctuary, their cattle grazed freely in the forest. The cattle can no longer graze freely, which has resulted in fodder shortage. Furthermore, the Chenchu families that are really interested in agriculture cannot be assigned any land on the fringe areas of the reserve. The land offered at a distance from the forest is not to the Chenchu's liking. Prior to the establishment of the reserve, Chenchu used to be employed in bamboo cutting for daily wages by the Forest Department and by private contractors. This additional source of income has also vanished.

Rehabilitation of the Chenchu families from both the core and fringe areas started recently under the supervision of the Forest Department. The families that have already been rehabilitated are miserable. Given a choice, they would prefer to return to their old settlements, but the government would never agree to this. Many Chenchu question the establishment of a tiger sanctuary in their midst, saying that the "government prefers tigers to human beings."

3. The Nizam was the ruler of the Hyderabad region, where some of the Chenchu lived.

## Development Programs

The development programs launched among hunter-gatherers by the various tribal development agencies at both the national and state levels have brought misery instead of improvement. In the name of development, the freedom of the hunter-gatherers has been curtailed further.

A review of the development programs for hunter-gatherers initiated up to now clearly indicates the basic thinking and approach of the government. Colonization is considered the answer to bring development and "progress" to these communities. "Colonize them and turn them into cultivators" seems to be the slogan. What happened and what is happening in the settlements created for the hunter-gatherers can be understood if we examine the examples of the Chenchu of the eastern Ghats and the Onge of the Andaman Islands.

### The Chenchu

In 1957, Chenchu resettlement was started as a centrally sponsored scheme at the Byrluti and Nagaluti Chenchu village of Atmakur Taluk in the Kurnool district (this area also includes the tiger reserve of Srisailam). There were three main features of the scheme: resettlement of one hundred Chenchu families in houses built by the government; reclamation of five hundred acres of forest to be distributed to the Chenchu for their cultivation by providing each family with a pair of bullocks; and repairing the existing irrigation tank for providing water to the lands given to the Chenchu.

The project management could persuade only forty Chenchu families to move to the new settlement, but even those families would not take up cultivation. Moreover, the families who moved there could not hold onto the lands given to them under the project. Within no time, their lands had passed into the hands of surrounding nontribals. The nontribals exploited these families in various ways. A few Chenchu men and women got addicted to country liquor because of the influence of nontribals, so much so that there was even a case of a Chenchu man selling his grown daughter for a bottle of liquor.[4] Ultimately, the project, which was

---

4. Such cases are not unheard of in these communities. In a tribal area of Tamil Nadu, I once came across a tribal giving away an acre of land in exchange for a

managed by the Department of Cooperation, was closed down, leaving the forty Chenchu families to their own fate and to the influence of unscrupulous forest contractors, traders, money-lenders, and land grabbers (Prakash Reddy 1979).

The rampant deforestation of the Chenchu habitat and the movement of Chenchu to places far away from the forest have affected their nutritional standards. Consequently, the population has fallen prey to various diseases. Chenchu children with bloated stomachs, thin hands and legs, and dilated eyes are a constant sight in Chenchu villages. According to a recent visiting medical team, many of the elders suffer from tuberculosis.

Immediately after independence, when the land colonization programs were initiated as one of the development measures, officials used only persuasion to resettle tribal families. The administration promised various incentives to these families, and resettlement was portrayed as a way to acquire comfort and security. Even those families who were persuaded to move quickly realized that it was a mistake. The promised incentives never materialized, and the families were abandoned to fend for themselves. The resettlement of hunter-gatherers by the administration continues even today, but persuasion has given way to force. During the 1960s, faced with an extremist movement that emerged as a response to the injustices perpetrated by the government and the nontribal immigrants, hundreds of tribal settlements in the eastern Ghats were moved nearer to the police and administrative headquarters. This was done under the guise of providing them with better welfare and development opportunities. Today, these villages are called "regrouped villages."

## The Onge of Little Andaman

In the name of resettlement, the Andaman administration herded the Onge into a corner of the island locally called Dugong Creek and settled them in tin-roofed houses. The resettled Onge are supposed to look after the fifty-year-old, seventy-five acre coconut plantation under the supervision of a social worker. Every morning the social worker tries to herd them into the plantation for

---

square meal. It is hunger and starvation that push the tribals into the hands of nontribal moneylenders and traders.

work, but so far these efforts have been only partially successful.

The administration doles out rations every day to the Onge families, including wheat flour, rice, and sugar, which the Onge neither produce nor have the capacity to buy. If this ration is discontinued, the Onge probably would not suffer, but the officials in charge of the program would experience a major financial loss.

The administration tried to introduce pig rearing, but the Onge refused to take it up on the ground that pigs eat human feces. Next came the scheme of teaching the Onge how to keep cows for milk. For this purpose a cow was provided, but only the social worker benefited, since the Onge were not interested in either the cow or its milk.

In the name of Onge development and welfare, many officials are stationed in the Dugong Creek colony. They try to teach all sorts of new habits to the Onge. It is a kind of cultural assault in which the Onge are treated with utter disrespect and contempt.

In the political arena, the administration introduced the franchise to the community; the people were to elect their own leader. In the first election, they chose their traditional headman as leader. If the process of imposed elections continues in this small community of ninety-nine people, no one knows what the outcome will be if factions emerge.

One of the important duties of the officials stationed at Dugong Creek is to herd the Onge, dressed in pants and shirts, before visiting "VIPs". The VIPs present the Onge with gifts (such as colored pieces of cloth, a few bunches of coconuts, or bananas), and pose for photographs with them to show their friends and relatives back home.

On the whole, by restricting the Onge to a corner of the island, and by doling out daily rations, the administration is teaching them a parasitic life. If this continues for long, I fear that they are going to lose their will to survive. And if that happens, no one can prevent their extinction. One well-meaning official who acted as director of tribal welfare privately agreed with me that the policies and measures of the Andaman administration towards these communities were proving genocidal.

### The National Interest

Programs created in the name of the national interest are perhaps the worst offenders – not only to the hunting-gathering communities, but also to other tribal communities in the country. There are innumerable programs in the name of the national interest that have uprooted and displaced thousands of tribal communities. Here I limit myself to a single example of a hunter-gatherer community affected by one of these programs, the Yanadi of Andhra Pradesh.[5]

The Yanadi, who inhabit the coastal district of Andhra Pradesh, are a very numerous tribe. They are divided into two endogamous groups, the Challa Yanadi and the Manchi Yanadi. The Challa group depends entirely on hunting and gathering and scavenging dead animals, while the Manchi subsist on agricultural labor and domestic work in the households of landowners.

This case study will focus on the Challa Yanadi of Sriharikota Island. Sriharikota Island is a small island, 56 kilometers long (north to south) and 9.6 kilometers wide (east to west) at the widest point. The island is the biggest of five that are separated from the mainland by a backwater of the Bay of Bengal known as Pulicat Lake or Chilakasamudram; it is between the Tamil Nadu and Andhra Pradesh coasts. It is located eighteen kilometers from Sulurpet, under which administrative jurisdiction it falls. The island is covered with a thick equatorial forest, within which are several freshwater ponds that provide sustenance to both man and beast. The ponds also contain a variety of fishes, crabs, tortoises, and other food sources.

The Yanadi have inhabited Sriharikota Island for centuries. All Yanadi, even those living outside the island, believe that the Yanadi people originated there. Until the end of the nineteenth century, they were the sole inhabitants of this island, foraging in the forest and fishing in the ponds and backwaters. During the last quarter of the nineteenth century, non-Yanadi immigrants (caste groups) from coastal villages started finding their way onto the island. By 1971, the immigrants had established eleven villages, with a total population of about 2,500. At that time, the Yanadi numbered around 250.

5. Displacement of the tribal communities (due to the construction of irrigation and hydroelectric projects and to the nearby location of industries) and the resultant protest movements organized against them are numerous and well publicized. Many tribal communities, both food-gathering and otherwise, have received wide public attention. On the other hand, the Yanadi, a large gathering-hunting group, are little known even within India. The displacement of Yanadi families due to a program of "national interest" is also little known, which is the main reason I include this case study here.

The immigrants cleared a part of the forest for cultivation. The Forest Department also arrived on the island around the same time as the immigrants. Despite the immigrant population and the many restrictions placed on them by the Forest Department, the Yanadi managed to carve out a niche in the island's ecosystem. This way of life sustained them in a relatively comfortable position.

The serene and contented life of this food-gathering community was disturbed in 1968 when the island was selected for the construction of a rocket launching station. All the inhabitants, including the Yanadi, were asked to evacuate the island. According to the agreement reached with the central government, the government of Andhra Pradesh based the compensation paid the evacuees on people's fixed assets and the deeds they had to their lands. With the connivance of the officials, the caste population organized a pressure group that was able to extract more compensation than its fair share. But the Yanadi, who had neither fixed assets nor deeds, were left with nothing. However, the government, as a matter of charity, was prepared to resettle the Yanadi families to places outside the island. Even before the resettlement program was announced, half of the Yanadi families left, receiving neither compensation nor relocation. No one knows where they went.[6] Ultimately, only seventy-nine Yanadi families were relocated to two places in Sulurpet. After two months, all of them abandoned these settlements. Reddy (1981: 176), who has made a thorough study of the resettlement program of these people, says that "the Yanadi could not adopt to the conditions of the colonies, owing to environmental, sociocultural, administrative and psychological factors."

## Policies and Attitudes

To understand more clearly the plight of tribal communities in general, and of hunting-gathering communities in particular, it would be useful to consider some of India's policies as a reflection of the attitudes of officials and nontribals toward tribals.

6. The government officials handling the compensation payment and the rehabilitation program were aware that many Yanadi families were leaving the island without receiving any compensation and without waiting to be relocated. But they never made any attempt to stop them or to inform them of the government program and plans for relocation (Reddy 1981: 193–94).

From ancient times, Indian forests have played an important role in the economy. Their use was regulated through local customs and traditions. Many rural and tribal communities maintained what are known as "sacred groves," which were not to be touched by anyone except in dire need. The commercial exploitation of India's forests started with the British. For them, communal ownership of land and forest was anathema, because the land held resources that the state could usurp and claim as state property.

After 1857 the British seriously considered the nationalizing of India's forests. The primary reason was that the British were laying a great network of railway lines, and for that they required an enormous quantity of wood. The government realized that, without regulating the use of the forests, it would not be able to acquire the necessary quantity of timber (Gadgil and Malhotra 1985: 10). Thus, the categories of reserved and nonreserved forests came into existence through the passage of the first Forest Act in 1885. With the promulgation of this act, the collective rights of communities were transformed into privileges for individuals. With one stroke, the tribals lost the right of collective ownership of their habitat, while as individuals they were given certain privileges to utilize forest products. The tribals protested and expressed their resentment, but to no avail.[7]

In independent India, the national forest policy was formulated in 1952. This policy hit the forest dwellers much harder than the British policy, because the "privileges" were further diluted and called "concessions." The attitudes of the people governing the country toward the forests and its inhabitants in independent India were similar to those of the British. These people did not learn any lessons from the consequences of misguided forest policy implemented by the British.

In 1988 the government of India promulgated a new forest policy, prompting the following comment from Walter Fernandes (1989: 37): "[A] policy that affects the very life support system of the tribals and other rural poor has been formulated without their

7. The larger tribes, like the Santhal, Bagata, and Kondadora, who are shifting cultivators, organized armed rebellions that were put down brutally by the British as well as by successive governments after the British left. Hunting-gathering tribes, like the Chenchu, occasionally showed their resentment against the oppressive methods used by the officials of the Forest Department by felling trees indiscriminately.

participation. This perhaps is indicative of the attitude of the decision makers towards these marginalized groups."

The Forest Department, as well as governments at both the state and national levels, have always discriminated against tribal communities in favor of nontribal communities. It is a sad irony that people who were born and brought up in forests and whose cultures are intertwined with forests are not allowed to utilize forest resources; indeed, many of them have been physically relocated away from their forest homes. At the same time, nontribals are allowed to move into forest reserves and clear them for cultivation. The politicians and the governments have not only turned a blind eye to these illegal encroachments, but have conferred legitimacy on the perpetrators through government orders, not just once, but many times in all parts of the country (Prakash Reddy 1990).

When the tribals and the poor collect wood for fuel, the governments put the blame on them for deforestation. The National Commission on Agriculture blames the tribals and the poor for deforestation, which evoked the following comment from Walter Fernandes (1989: 38):

> [T]he way the causes of depletion, such as fuel, fodder, etc., have been mentioned, creates the impression that the policy makers continue to consider the forest dwellers and other rural poor as the main destroyers of forests. In fact, industry and raw materials have not been mentioned directly among the causes of deforestation. Hence one is left with the impression that even while being aware of it, the policy makers do not analyze adequately the role of the industrial commercial complex that started this vicious circle of clear felling vast tracts of forests, impoverishment of the people, and their destructive dependence on forests.

Government policy declares that the prime consideration in forest management is environmental stability. All other aspects, including the establishment of industries, are said to be subordinate. Unfortunately, however, industries, both private and state owned, are the major culprits destroying India's forests. Industries have played havoc with the lives of tribal peoples. The largest concentration of industries is found in the heart of the tribal area of central India. The benefits from these industries go to nontribals, while the tribals lose their land, habitat, and social cohesion. Even on the small island of Little Andaman, where the Onge live, a matchstick factory has been built that uses the soft wood from the local forest. The wild mango trees, whose fruit gave sustenance to the Chenchu, Savara, Konda Reddy, and their food-gathering communities in summer, have been felled because of their suitability for manufacturing plywood.

Every irrigation dam and hydroelectric project in India has caused the submergence of millions of hectares of forest area and the displacement of millions of people, mostly tribals. Environmental policy says that prior clearance from the government is a necessary condition for planning new irrigation and hydroelectric projects, but it is never put into practice. In fact, most of the projects that were vetoed by environmental experts and the committees set up by the ministry itself have been carried out anyway. For instance, the first committee constituted by the Department of the Environment on the proposed Narmada Valley irrigation and hydroelectric project vetoed it on both human and environmental grounds. But the government struck committee after committee until it received a favorable report.

It is pertinent to note that if the proposed Narmada Valley project comes into existence, one million tribals, including a few gathering-hunting communities, will be displaced and uprooted, while the benefits of the project will be enjoyed by the nontribal communities. When questions of building irrigation dams and hydroelectric projects and establishing industries arise, the forest and its inhabitants are expendable; where these projects are not planned, the tribal peoples are expendable for the creation of biosphere reserves and animal sanctuaries.

The meaning of "national interest" changes according to the caste, creed, religion, and status of individuals and groups. The government, the officials, and the politicians always make a distinction between the needs of the tribal communities and those of everyone else. What the tribals require are called "people's needs," while the requirements of the industrialists and other vested interests are called "national needs" – despite the declaration in the 1952 forest policy act that *all* needs require equal attention.

Consider, for instance, the demand for self-rule by the tribal communities of central India (Jharkand movement). The government has conferred self-rule on almost every tribe in northeast India, but it is not willing to concede the same right to the central Indian tribes whose populations and territories are greater than those of all the northeastern states put together. This discrepancy exists because central India is the area of the richest mineral wealth. So, in the name of national interest, the tribals' demand for self-rule cannot be granted.[8]

The Andaman and Nicobar Islands are still rich in forest resources, and, according to geologists, the possibility of finding oil there is encouraging. These islands are also important for purposes of defense, so the rights of the hunting- gathering communities over their territory cannot be recognized. However, they can be resettled and granted daily rations in the name of the national interest.

## Entitlements of Hunter-Gatherers in India

From historical, anthropological, and sociological points of view, and according to the definition of the United Nations, the Andaman/Nicobar hunter-gatherers cannot be classified into any category other than "indigenous populations." Each community maintains its distinct identity through its language, its culture, and its occupation of a distinct territory. The British colonial government, the successive Indian governments, and the nontribal immigrants, cannot but be termed usurpers of the territories and the resources of these communities, not only on the islands but also on the mainland.

Some tribal communities in mainland India successfully articulated the argument that they are indigenous people and are entitled to the resources in their territories. These communities were even able to internationalize the issue by raising it at the United Nations Indigenous Population Conference of August 3–7, 1987.

The state is the most important institution in modern times. It usurps the rights and entitlements of indigenous populations throughout the world, and the Indian state is no exception. The vast differences in perception between the indigenous groups and the state about the nature of rights over land and resources has always existed, and the legal experts are aware of this (Prakash Reddy 1988a). For indigenous people, territory and land

8. Jharkand literally means "land of the forests." The Jharkand region of central India is the richest in mineral and forest wealth. According to Bose, "in 1971–72 India's mineral output was [rupees] 5,426 million and timber Rs. 989 million, a total of Rs. 6,415 million. As much as 85 percent of India's mineral and forest wealth comes from the southeast resources triangle of (central India) Orissa, east Madhya Pradesh, parts of west Bengal and the Chotanagapur area of southern Bihar" (Bose 1984: 73).

are associated not only with an economy but also with a political unit. Justice M. Hidayatullah (1975: 22) of India recognized this when he said that "it is well to remember that property in lands always links political functions of a group with its social economy." But the state invariably separates the individual from the community. Consequently, where no individual rights exist, particularly with regard to land, it becomes the property of the state (Prakash Reddy 1988b).

According to Roy Burman (1989: 59), property in land has a dual meaning to aboriginal groups. Devolution of property is from the community to the individual, and this devolution is subject to the control of the community. It can be argued, then, that it belongs simultaneously to the community and to individuals, either alone or in family units. But the state is blind to this argument.

Here it would be appropriate to mention two legal concepts: *lex loci* and *res nullius*. *Lex loci* concerns the law of the place where something is located; by this law, indigenous groups hold rights over the resources and territories in which they live and whose resources they exploit. Unfortunately, the state always applies the law of *res nullius* in the case of indigenous groups. *Res nullius* refers to the right of property accrued to individuals from the property of nobody. By the extension of this concept, the state claims superior rights over the land. Not only the colonial government, but also the present government, thinks that indigenous groups are too barbaric to have *lex loci* rights recognizable by the courts, and so they are deprived of their land and their territories.

Indeed there is no doubt that, within the third world, there is a fourth world.

# 17

## Social and Cultural Significance of Whaling in Contemporary Japan: A Case Study of Small-Type Coastal Whaling

*Masami Iwasaki-Goodman and Milton M. R. Freeman*

In contemporary Japan, small-type coastal whaling (STCW), a regulated small-scale coastal fishery that harvests mainly minke whale, continues to demonstrate the historical importance of whaling in the local communities where STCW is based. Abiding by the decision of the International Whaling Commission, the catching of minke whale has been suspended by the Government of Japan since the end of the 1987 whaling season. This paper discusses the production, distribution, and consumption of whale resources in STCW communities, through which the social, cultural, and economic significance of STCW operations and the various impacts of the international suspension of commercial whaling will be analyzed.

A moratorium on all commercial whaling was adopted by the International Whaling Commission in 1982. This action reflected growth in the political sophistication of those concerned with the protection of whales and, at the same time, marked the beginning of an era of great uncertainty for the small whaling towns in Japan.

Pelagic (open-sea) whaling in Antarctic waters, the best known form of Japanese whaling, and large-type coastal whaling (LTCW), the large-scale shore-based commercial operation harvesting large whales in Japanese coastal waters, have both ceased, and the operating companies were dissolved in 1987. The third, and least known form of whaling, namely small-type coastal whaling (STCW), was severely affected by the moratorium. Small-type coastal whaling (STCW), which in previous years harvested about four hundred whales of three or four different species, lost a substantial part of the annual catch quota (see Table 17.1) and, under domestic regulation, has been continuing with a limited harvest of small cetaceans (marine mammals) that are not affected by the international whaling ban.

**Table 17.1:** Minke whale catch by STCW since 1982

| | |
|---|---|
| 1982 – 324 | 1987 – 304 |
| 1983 – 290 | 1988 – 0 |
| 1984 – 367 | 1990 – 0 |
| 1985 – 327 | 1991 – 0 |
| 1986 – 311 | 1992 – 0 |

SOURCE: Japan Small-type Whaling Association

Despite the end of industrial-scale whaling, which in the past satisfied a national market for whale meat and other products, there persists an intensive effort by the community people in various parts of Japan to conserve their endangered whaling culture for future generations. This tendency is stronger in the communities where STCW is based, due to the localized focus and the sociocultural significance of this particular whaling operation.[1] Besides the efforts of the local people to promote an understanding of the significance of continued whaling, there have been about thirty academic research projects undertaken in order to examine the social, cultural, and economic aspects of STCW. These studies have provided the basis of discussions on Japanese STCW and the socioeconomic implications of the moratorium at the International Whaling Commission since 1988 (see Akimichi et al. 1988; Bestor 1989; Braund et al. 1989; Japan 1989, 1990, 1991, 1992; Kalland 1989; Takahashi et al. 1989).

Current discussions about STCW at the International Whaling Commission are focused on the role of coastal whaling in meeting

---

1. Kalland and Moeran (1992: 18) define a whaling community as "a group of people directly or indirectly involved in whaling related activities (such as the catching, flensing, processing, and/or marketing of whales and whale products), and for whom whaling related activities are important elements in the establishment of their self-identity." In the case of the STCW fishery, the whaling communities are the subcultural groups within an administrative unit (Abashiri, Oshika, Wada, and Taiji) that are identifiable within the concept of the Japanese whaling cultural complex.

local residents' "human needs" in these small, and often remote, whaling communities. "Human needs" are defined in relation to various social, cultural, nutritional, and economic aspects of contemporary life in these coastal communities. One of the more important aspects in understanding "human needs" relates to the use of the whale carcass for human consumption. This use of the whale primarily as food makes Japanese whaling unique among the industrialized whaling countries that have engaged in intensive large-scale commercial whaling in the past primarily for the production of oil for industrial use.

## Theoretical Discussion

A series of anthropological studies on Japanese STCW have been conducted since 1988, when the issue of the sociocultural dimensions of localized STCW was first discussed extensively at the forty-first annual meeting of the International Whaling Commission. The nature of Japanese STCW had been mostly unknown outside of Japan until a comprehensive research project was undertaken by an international group of anthropologists in 1988 (Akimichi et al. 1988). One major contribution of this collaborative research appears to be the establishment of an important anthropological concept, namely, the Japanese whaling culture complex.

The concept of the whaling culture complex placed localized STCW in an appropriate national and historical context. Focusing on earlier work (Kalland 1986) on the history of Japanese whaling during the late-feudal Tokugawa period (1603–1868), Akimichi et al. (1988) reviewed the historic accounts of Japanese whaling, which revealed the continuation of several forms of coastal whaling through transmission of knowledge and the migration of whalers over the centuries. Such a long history of coastal whaling resulted in the development of three diversified forms of whaling (STCW, LTCW, and pelagic whaling) in the modern period (Akimichi et al.: 10–16).

The geographical spread of the whaling culture over the years was examined more extensively by Kalland (1989), who focused on the migration of whalers out of the established whaling communities in southwestern Japan to the newly opened whaling areas in the north. Thus STCW is the most recently established form of the developing Japanese whaling complex. Dating from the 1930s, STCW focused upon the catching of several small

species of whale, thereby ensuring continuity with various traditional whaling- related social and cultural institutions in the local
whaling communities. The historical importance of STCW as the
most recent operating phase of the long-established Japanese
whaling cultural complex is recognized by many Japanese, especially in the various whaling districts.

The concept of a whaling culture also made later research on
STCW coherent with respect to verifying the social and cultural
interactions occurring in the whaling communities. Akimichi et
al. (1988) described all phases of STCW: production, processing,
distribution, consumption, and celebration, through which
important social and cultural institutions such as gifting and religious observances have been sustained. Akimichi et al. (1988: 75)
define the whaling culture:

> [T]he shared knowledge of whaling transmitted across generations.
> This shared knowledge consists of a number of different socio-cultural
> inputs: a common heritage and world view, an understanding of eco-
> logical (including spiritual) and technological relations between human
> beings and whales, special distribution processes, and a food culture.

This definition was confirmed by Takahashi et al. (1989), who
compared the production and processing involved in premodern
whaling with three types of modern whaling. Discussion of continuities, similarities, and the linkages among the different forms of
whaling demonstrates the existence of an integrated whaling culture in Japan (see also Braund et al. 1989; Kalland and Moeran
1992: 134–73).

The localized nature of STCW, unlike other forms of modern
whaling, has also been given attention. Four STCW communities
(Abashiri, Ayukawa, Wada, and Taiji) have been examined by
anthropologists, some of whom have produced papers on particular communities (e.g. Akimichi et al. 1988: Appendix 2; Iwasaki
1988; Manderson and Hardacre 1989a, 1989b; Takahashi 1987,
1991;). These varied studies confirm the important material and
symbolic functions of whales and whaling in these communities,
and in some cases conclude that "the end to whaling means the
end of these towns as viable communities" (Manderson and
Hardacre, 1989b: 28).

Social scientists have also investigated the local and nationwide
impact associated with the current pause in commercial whaling
that affected coastal whaling operations in Japan after the end of

the 1987 season. A thorough assessment of the socioeconomic impact of the moratorium on all modern forms of whaling operations in Japan was completed (Japan 1989). This study reported a series of negative impacts at the individual, family, community, and national levels. At the conclusion of a discussion of this report at the 1989 International Whaling Commission meeting, it was noted in the *International Whaling Commission Chairman's Report of the 41st Meeting* that "the impacts pose a serious threat to the continued survival of these traditional small communities" (International Whaling Commission 1989: 4). This report further concludes that the impacts are more seriously damaging to STCW communities because of the localized nature of the whaling operation and the limited economic alternatives for the laid-off whalers in this particular fishery (see also Takahashi 1991).

An intensive discussion on the issue of whale-based local food culture took place at the forty-second and forty-third annual meetings of the International Whaling Commission. Various academic papers provided the bases for critical discussion of the issue, the principal paper being a detailed quantitative assessment of the social and cultural significance of the consumption of whale meat in several STCW-dependent communities in Miyagi Prefecture (Braund et al. 1990).

In response to questions raised at the forty-second annual meeting, further examination of the cultural significance of the consumption of whale meat in everyday meals occurred at the forty-third International Whaling Commission meeting. Theoretical and empirical analyses of the social and cultural importance of everyday meals indicated the critical role played by whale meat and blubber. The report concluded: "[T]hese cultural values are rooted in a variety of historical, symbolic, aesthetic, social and locational considerations" (Japan 1991: 13). Ashkenazi and Jacob (1991) have independently examined the general Japanese dietary patterns; their study confirms the role of whale meat as an integral part of the Japanese customary diet, and the fact that whale-based cuisine provides the basis for the distinctive regional identity of members of Japanese STCW communities.

More recently, an international study group for small-type whaling examined small-scale whaling activities in Greenland, Iceland, Japan, and Norway, and reported their findings at the forty-fourth meeting of the International Whaling Commission (Japan 1992). This report proposed a resource management strategy directed at minke whale and founded upon two principles, namely "the widely-recognized goal of sustainable development [which] requires broadening our understanding of human/environment relations" and "greater sensitivity toward the importance of marine living resources in the livelihoods of diverse coastal communities" (Japan 1992: 1). The study group, having demonstrated significant similarities in small-scale whaling in these four countries, points out that, while the International Whaling Commission recognizes the Greenlandic whaling operation as subsistence whaling, it has failed to recognize the similar nature of small-scale whaling operations in Japan, Norway, and Iceland.

This intensive anthropological research conducted recently on Japanese whaling and summarized above provides a theoretical framework for future studies on different aspects of the three distinct forms of Japanese whaling. More important, an accumulation of the social science data on Japanese whaling has confirmed two major roles that modern whaling, and especially STCW, have played in the contemporary Japanese context. First, whaling plays a strong integrative role in the economic, social, and cultural institutions in these small whaling communities, making continued whaling indispensable for the social vitality and economic viability of these communities. And second, modern whaling continues to fulfill its traditional role as a human food supplier, which is one of the key elements in satisfying "human needs" in these particular communities.

### Small-Type Coastal Whaling

Small-scale coastal whaling operations, harvesting about 350 minke whales each year within fifty miles of shore (until the zero-catch quota was imposed in 1988) has its major whaling bases in three communities along the Japanese Pacific coast and one on the Okhotsk Sea coast (see Figure 17.1). Small-type coastal whaling has been a stable supplier of fresh (unfrozen) minke whale meat, Baird's beaked whale meat, and pilot whale meat – the necessary ingredients for the distinctive local cuisine and various important ceremonial dishes (see Akimichi et al. 1988: 66–74, 92–95; Braund et al. 1990; Kalland and Moeran 1992: 145–49). Considering the harvest level and the number of participating boats, STCW has been a notably stable fishery, regulated by both the national government and the International Whaling Commission.

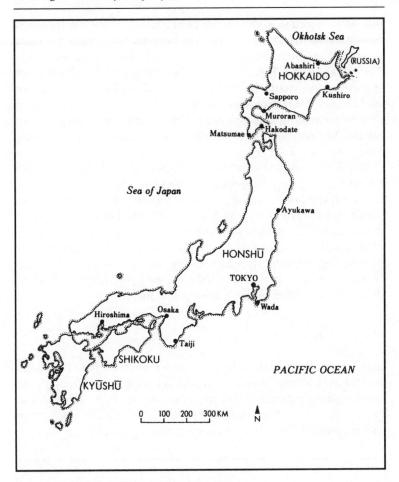

**Figure 17.1:** Place names mentioned in the text

It is the localized nature of this whaling operation, and particularly the sociocultural significance of the consumption, distribution, and production phases of this type of whaling operation that critically distinguishes it from industrial-scale whaling.

## Consumption of Whale Meat

The whale, a locally available and relatively abundant natural resource, has been long valued, hunted, and utilized in numerous ways in order to satisfy the varied needs of society throughout Japanese history. However, the primary and most consistent use of the whale has been as human food (Baba 1942; Fukumoto 1960; Maeda and Teraoka 1952; Tôyô Hogei 1989). The following comment made by a sixty-year-old male local historian (field notes 1986) provides a common description of whale consumption among the Japanese: "We don't waste any part of whale. We eat meat and blubber and use bone for fertilizer. Every part is used."

Small-type coastal whaling was started around 1930 to supply the local needs for whale meat and blubber, and since that time it has been the sole supplier of fresh minke whale meat. Minke whale meat produced in the STCW fishery is distinguished from that produced by pelagic whaling by the fact that it is cut from the freshly killed carcass and kept chilled with ice from the time of butchering (shortly after harvesting) until it reaches the local retail stores, where it is labelled as *nama kujira* (fresh whale) to differentiate it from frozen minke whale meat.

*Five Parts of the Minke Whale*

In the recent past, minke whale was consumed mostly in Hokkaido and the area around Ayukawa in Miyagi prefecture. Although the consumption patterns differ from one region to the other, some generalities can be identified. Minke whale is divided roughly into five parts according to its preparation (see Figure 17.2).

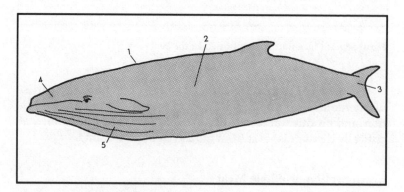

**Figure 17.2:** The five main parts of the minke whale according to the type of preparation

1) *Kawa* (blubber) is eaten both raw and cooked. Some blubber is salted for preservation, and then becomes an ingredient for a New Year's ceremonial dish called *Kujirajiru* (a vegetable stew cooked with salted blubber). Although in the past whale oil was extracted from blubber for industrial use, in recent years blubber has been sold exclusively as human food (Kalland and Moeran 1992: 110).

2) *Kujiraniku* (whale meat) is cut up and graded into four ranks, depending on the shape of the cuts and the quality of the meat. In addition to these four ranks of meat, occasionally minke whales provide a small quantity of localized marbled meat called *onomi*. However, *onomi* is usually associated with the large species of whale than the minke whale. Whale meat is enjoyed mostly as *sashimi* (raw slices).

3) *Oba, obaike, obaki,* or *obake* (tail fluke) is sliced thinly and made into a dish called *sarashikujira*. Fluke is also used as an offering on the whaleboat's Shinto altar where, in accordance with tradition, the distal three centimeters of the fluke is placed on the altar each time a whale is caught.

4) *Saezuri* (tongue) is a local delicacy, especially in the Osaka region.

5) *Unesu* (ventral groove) is processed into whale bacon. In some cases, *unesu* is eaten raw as *sashimi*.

Whalers and their families also enjoy other parts of the whale, such as the internal organs and meat scraped from the chin bone. In Ayukawa, such parts are cooked for sale at the local fish stores, as well as for private consumption by the crew and boat owners (see also Akimichi et al. 1988: 66–74 for further variation in STCW town diets).

## Whale Dishes

The above-mentioned five parts of the minke whale have significantly different texture and flavor, and are prepared in order to satisfy the nutritional, social, and cultural needs of consumers. In whaling communities, *sashimi* has been the major preparation choice for minke whale meat and blubber since late Meiji times (1868–1912), when whaling became established in the region. *Kujiraniku* is sliced thinly (roughly 0.5 centimeters thick) into bite-size pieces, which are placed on a bed of shredded cabbage or a few pieces of roughly cut crispy lettuce. In Ayukawa, red meat is often served with white blubber, presenting an aesthetically pleasing and appetizing color contrast.

The data gathered through interviews as well as research results published by other social scientists (Akimichi et al. 1988; Iwasaki 1988; Manderson and Hardacre 1989a,1989b; Braund et al. 1990; Japan 1991) demonstrate that minke whale has been eaten for three principle purposes: for ceremonial occasions, such as New Year's eve and day, weddings, and local festivals; for marking visits and community gatherings; and for everyday meals at home and in such public institutions as schools and hospitals. Within these broad categories, Braund et al. (1990) identified thirty culturally significant food occasions requiring the use of minke whale meat in STCW-associated communities in Miyagi Prefecture.

At wedding receptions, for example, a large plate of assorted *sashimi*, in which *kujiraniku* and *kawa* are placed as a centerpiece, is served to highlight the occasion. Whale dishes are a significant part of the menu served at local shrine festivities and religious gatherings. The local priest in Ayukawa states: "From the old days we have had whale meat and regard this as necessary: we offer to the gods whale meat despite the usual injunction [against] red meat. . . . So it's necessary to have whale meat for this [ritual] meal" (Manderson and Hardacre 1989a: 39).

*Kujirajiru* has been a regional New Year's meal in Hokkaido. This regional dish has been passed down through several generations in the southwestern part of Hokkaido. The subsequent migration of people to other areas on Hokkaido has resulted in the widespread appeal of *kujirajiru* throughout the island. Presently, those with ancestral ties to the Matsumae and Esashi areas, but not presently living in geographical proximity to those areas, continue to value *kujirajiru* as a necessary dish at New Year's celebrations. *Kujirajiru* is also symbolically appropriate for the occasion because whales are normally associated with wealth, growth, and happiness. For the same reason, *sarashikujira* is enjoyed as a necessary part of the New Year's meal.

Whale dishes are served when local people gather together for private or public purposes, or when relatives and guests from distant communities visit the whaling communities. Fresh *kujiraniku* or *unesu*, or frozen reserves of these foods in the whaling off-season, are prepared in order to welcome guests to whaling towns where whale dishes are considered *meibutsu* (the local speciality), and therefore appropriate food for these occasions (see Kalland and Moeran 1992: 147–48).

Substantial use is made of minke whale products as a part of everyday meals during the whaling season. *Kujiraniku* is often served at dinner as *sashimi* while fresh meat is abundant and reasonably priced. People are motivated to prepare whale dishes because of their familiarity with the taste of whale, a result of having lived in the whaling towns and of having been exposed to the local whale-based cuisine. Whale meat provided the major source of animal protein during the period of food shortage immediately after World War II. At that time, people relied heavily upon whale meat for maintenance of their nutritional balance, and some people in Abashiri still recall the hardship of daily life during that period (field notes 1986): "At that time, whale was almost a staple food. There was not enough of other food to eat. If it had not been for whale, we would have been starved." However, some who associate whale dishes with the food shortages of those times tend to have a negative image of whale meat as a cheap and tasteless meat substitute.

In Ayukawa, apart from its extensive use in everyday meals, minke whale meat is served at public institutions as a part of the regular menu. Whale dishes are considered nutritionally and culturally appropriate food to be served to those with special needs in places such as hospitals and schools.

## Distribution

Consumers, including whalers and their families, generally acquire whale meat through two distribution channels: customary sharing and gifting, and commercial distribution.

### Customary Sharing and Gifting

Formal gift-giving is an established social and cultural institution observed throughout Japan (Befu 1968). In the case of STCW communities, whale meat and blubber perform a key function in the exercise of this important institution. The first of a series of whaling-associated gifting ceremonies is carried out at the beginning of the whaling season. Gifts given to boat owners to celebrate *funaoroshi* (bringing a boat to the harbor) and *hatsuryoiwai* (the first-catch celebration) are reciprocated by the gift of a share of the first whale caught for that year (Akimichi et al. 1988: 43–51).

Gifting of whale products continues throughout the whaling season. Whaling crews, factory workers, and boat owners each receive their share of whale meat and blubber when a whale is caught. Further distribution also takes place from these original recipients to their relatives, neighbors, friends, and business partners. One elderly woman expressed the importance of such exchanges (field notes 1986): "We are farmers. So we give next door neighbors our vegetables. They give us some whale meat and blubber."

Seasonal gifting, such as *seibo* (the end of year gift) and *chugen* (the mid summer gift), are also important occasions when whale products are exchanged, as are other gift items. Customary sharing of whale products is more common locally in the whaling communities, but also extends outside of the local community, functioning as a mechanism to promote social solidarity, alliance, and identity (Akimichi et al. 1988: 41–51; Iwasaki 1988: 47–55; Manderson and Hardacre 1989b: 19–22; Kalland and Moeran 1992: 141–45, 156):

> I have relatives in Yoichi where people have to have *kujirajiru* for New Year's. Every year they wait for me to send them some salted blubber. My son, a whaler, buys me some from *oyakata* (boss) so that I can send it to my relatives. (seventy-year old wife of a whaler, quoted in Iwasaki 1988: 49)

Customary gifting may involve both commercial and noncommercial distribution. Producers of whale meat and those in their gifting network engage in exchanges involving whale meat; such transactions do not involve cash, and thus are essentially noncommercial in nature. However, the commercial distribution of whale products may itself fulfill socially and culturally important roles when, for example, a person is required to buy whale meat and blubber in order to give an appropriate gift to his or her gifting partner. Therefore, edible whale products, whether obtained through noncommercial or commercial channels may be functionally similar in social and cultural terms in ensuring that customary gifting is appropriately celebrated.

### Commercial Distribution

Whale products are mostly distributed through established commercial networks, with a very small portion sold directly by the whalers to the consumers, when, for example, the local people visit the flensing station or the meat-boxing factory. (However, changes are occurring as a result of the whaling moratorium; see Takahashi 1991). In Ayukawa, the local Fishery Cooperative Association, which is responsible for distributing whale products, auctions variable-sized lots to local wholesalers. The Abashiri whaling companies on the other hand, sell their products directly to local distributors who deal with the local markets as well as other markets throughout Hokkaido (Bestor 1989).

An important feature in the commercial distribution of the STCW-produced whale product is that it represents a highly localized distribution, which differs significantly from the centralized marketing systems that distributed whale products formerly produced by the large-scale whaling corporations. (For differences between the distribution system operating in Japanese STCW and LTCW, see Japan 1990.) In the case of STCW, the small geographical distance from the flensing station or landing port to the local market enables the local distributors to maintain a regular supply of high quality fresh (unfrozen) minke whale meat throughout the whaling season. As mentioned above, it is the nature of this "fresh minke" that clearly separates the STCW-derived minke whale meat from the other minke whale meat (from the Antarctic), which is held, shipped, and sold frozen.

The commercial distribution of whale products is closely connected with regionally-specific events having social and cultural significance. In Hokkaido, most of the whale products are consumed within the Hokkaido region, with high demand in Abashiri and the neighboring communities. A small quantity of *oba*, *unesu*, and *saezuri* are sent out to those areas where the demands are especially great (see Figure 17.3). In the Matsumae and Esashi area, *kujirajiru* is the traditional dinner for New Year's Eve and Day. Throughout Hokkaido, *kujirajiru* is often served on these occasions and salted blubber is one of the gift items at *seibo*. Salted blubber is sold at fish stores or supermarkets in most cities and towns in Hokkaido just before New Year's Eve. While some salted blubber is sold directly to the fishermen from Matsumae and Esashi who fish from Abashiri port, the remainder is sold through the distributors in Abashiri and Kushiro, which are both government-designated landing ports for minke whale.

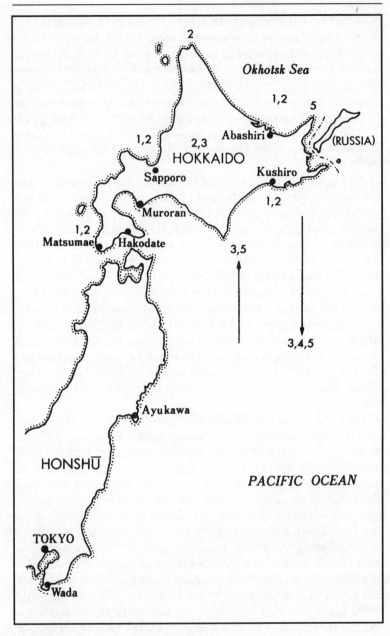

**Figure 17.3:** Consumption and distribution patterns of minke whale in Hokkaido according to whale product categories (see p. 385 for number descriptions).

*Oba* is another item that is sold just before New Year's Eve at local fish stores or supermarkets in the cities and towns in Hokkaido for use in *osechi* (the New Year's dish).

*Kujiraniku* constitutes a major part of total minke whale production. To be distributed to consumers, *kujiraniku* is further divided into four grades according to the shape and quality of the meat: highest grade A, second highest B, third highest C, and the lowest D. Meat judged to be of A or C quality is likely sold to the central cities in Hokkaido, and meat of B or D quality tends to be sold locally or in the neighboring communities around Abashiri.

In the case of Hokkaido, the localities where whale consumption is most pronounced are widely scattered around the coastal area throughout the prefecture. The reason for this is that there have been a large number of whaling bases for both large-type coastal whaling and small-type coastal whaling all around the coastal area in Hokkaido during the last fifty years (see Figure 17.4; see also Tatô 1985). Whale dishes therefore, were adopted into the local diet and continue to be favored dishes for people living in these former whaling districts up to the present day.

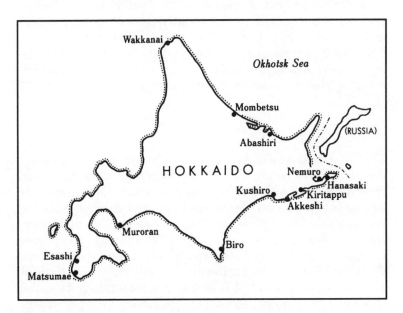

**Figure 17.4:** Whaling station locations in Hokkaido from 1900 to the present (after Terry 1950)

One minke whale product is exported from Hokkaido. This is *saezuri*, especially favored in the Osaka region in central Japan. However, in terms of both product weight and value, the quantity of export is quite small. It is also important to note that some proportion of the whale product exported from Hokkaido returns, as in the case of *sarashikujira* and *unesu*.

## Production

The STCW operational strategy has been dictated by weather, variable whale distribution and behavior patterns and, to a large degree, by the national government's "Ministerial Ordinance for Licenses and Regulation of Designated Fisheries." This ordinance defines permissible operational details, including, for example, the length of the whaling season, the caliber of the cannons, specifications of landing and flensing stations, and prohibitions about catching lactating female whales.

In STCW the scale of production is extremely limited compared to the other forms of whaling in Japan. Consistent with the consumption and distribution patterns of STCW, the production phase is also localized, in that a high degree of social, cultural, and economic integration occurs within the local community. A description of crew composition, company structure, and hunting activities will be presented in order to provide a better understanding of operational aspects of this fishery.

### Crew Composition

The STCW boat crew usually includes a harpooner, captain, engineer, a few deck hands, and a cook. In addition to the boat crew, there are a small number of specialized flensers and temporary assistants who process the carcass at the land station. Before the ban on minke whaling, seventy-five full-time workers and thirty-eight seasonal helpers were employed by the eight companies engaged in STCW in Japan (Japan 1989: 6). The social characteristics of the STCW employees characteristically differ from those of whalers engaged in both LTCW and pelagic whaling. First, the crews generally consist of local people having their permanent residence in a STCW community. Second, kinship appears to play an important role in crew composition, for often crew members are related to others on the boat or to the boat owner's family. Kin ties are frequent in the wider network that includes the crew, the boat owners, and their immediate and extended families (see Kalland and Moeran 1992: 123–33 for discussion of recruitment patterns in STCW).

Traditionally, promotion over the years from cook to deck hand, and, in some cases, finally to harpooner took place on a STCW boat, though the succession could involve various employment moves between STCW, LTCW, and pelagic whaling boats. However, as the number of whaling boats in all three forms of whaling in Japan was successively reduced due to domestic as well as international regulation, the total number of whaling-crew openings also became reduced. Thus, chances for promotion became scarce. A decided status hierarchy exists in the crew, with the position of harpooner being the most prestigious.

## STCW Companies

The nine STCW boats are mostly owned by small, family-business enterprises established in the whaling communities. For the past several years, seven of the eight companies each owned one boat, and one company owned two boats. One of the nine boats is operated by the local Fishery Cooperative Association.

The STCW boat owners are mostly heirs of the family business: their continued dedication to the whaling enterprise consequently stems from the pride and obligation boat owners have toward maintaining the family business that their ancestors have established. Such feelings are expressed in statements like the following: "If the time comes that whaling must stop completely, then I feel that my ancestor's work and history and culture will be gone" (former Taiji harpooner with thirty years of whaling experience, as reported in *San Francisco Examiner* 1988: 36).

The family tradition involves harpooners and other whaling boat crewmen as well as meat processors, flensers, and retailers. Manderson and Hardacre (1989a: 49–52) report on an Ayukawa-area family of specialized processors of *kabura* (a dish prepared from whale cartilage) who learned the techniques from Taiji whalers. This family passed on their business for four generations through adoptions, in the absence of biological sons, to maintain the family line. Small-scale family businesses such as this, involved with processing whale products, constitute an integral and important part of the local economy in STCW communities, by providing stable employment opportunities to local people.

Through socialization, the younger members of the whaling communities develop understanding and knowledge involved in whaling and other whaling-related work, as a seventy-year-old widow of a whaler explained (field notes 1986):

> Two of my sons, now both whalers, loved visiting their father on the boat. They spent hours and hours playing around the boat and dreamt to be whalers just like their father . . . [and] when their father was hospitalized for three months before he died, these sons went to ask him more about whaling. I remember my husband giving directions to them in his bed.

It is through this process of occupational socialization that the continued recruitment and maintenance of STCW in the whaling towns has been assured.

Small-type coastal whaling also helped the financial well-being of the whaling towns by providing predictability and stability for the local economy; a steady harvest of the strictly controlled annual quota and a guaranteed local market for the product ensured economic stability. The local community clearly benefited from such economic security, especially when the other coastal fishing industries have shown recent evidence of serious decline. Another apparent economic gain from STCW was the revenue to the local Fishery Cooperative Association that STCW provided in some whaling towns. The most noticeable case is found in Ayukawa, where STCW companies provided the Oshika Fishery Cooperative Association 79 percent of its total annual revenues in 1987 (Bestor 1989; see also Japan 1989: 24–32 for data on similar situations in other STCW communities).

*Harvest Activities*

In STCW, the catching operation is usually completed in one day. On rare occasions, when weather and ocean conditions permit, boats may stay overnight on the whaling ground if the hunt has been unsuccessful during the day. Small-type coastal whaling boats hunt whales within about fifty miles of the coast, due to the boats' limited range and in order to avoid possible accidents caused by sudden sea or weather changes. Another reason for limiting the area of operation is that STCW boats generally return immediately to the flensing station (or to the government-approved landing port when sailing in Hokkaido waters), so the whale meat reaches consumers in as fresh a condition as possible.

Whaling operations start with the search for a whale. Because STCW boats are not equipped with the electronic whale-locating devices used on LTCW and pelagic whaling boats, human eyesight and binoculars are the means used to locate whales from the masthead. Thus, good weather and relatively calm sea conditions are essential for a successful whale search. Sighting the whale is of great importance in STCW operations, as it grants a boat the exclusive right to harvest that particular whale. Therefore, a differential bonus system has been developed to reward a crew for sighting different species of whale (Japan 1989: Appendix II).

Once a whale is sighted, a boat moves into the area near the whale to enable the harpooner to aim at it. In approaching a whale, a small motorboat may be used to help turn the whale toward the whaling boat, thus reducing pursuit time and the chance of missing the whale, and overall, significantly increasing the efficiency of the whaling operation (Kalland and Moeran 1992: 105–106).

Shooting a harpoon successfully requires long-term training and experience. The prestige associated with success as a harpooner is consistent throughout the history of Japanese whaling (Fukumoto 1960). Similarly, harpooners on STCW boats are granted exclusive authority to coordinate the details of all sailing and hunting activities once a whale is being pursued. At the moment of shooting a harpoon, other crew members on board assist the harpooner, who aims at the whale and pulls the trigger with a silent prayer.

Flensing is carried out in two different ways, depending on the whaling ground. In coastal areas near Ayukawa, the whales are towed to the designated flensing station where land workers who specialize in flensing expertly cut up the whale. In Hokkaido waters, initial butchering is done on board,[2] with the whale meat subsequently shaped and boxed in a factory near the government-designated landing port. Workers who are engaged in flensing or boxing are often retired whalers, or women or neighbors who come to help on a part-time or seasonal basis in order to

---

2. Special permission is granted by the Japanese whaling authorities for on-board flensing during minke whaling operations only in Hokkaido waters.

receive a share of whale meat as payment, in addition to cash, for the work performed.

## Small-Type Coastal Whaling Since the Moratorium

In 1985 the International Whaling Commission instituted a ban on the commercial harvest of those species internationally accepted as falling under the Commission's management competence. The Japanese government agreed to implement this decision at the close of the 1987 season for the STCW minke whale fishery. As a consequence of this decision, the minke whale quota for the Japanese small-scale coastal whale fishery was reduced to zero, resulting in an overall harvest reduction of about 46 percent by weight in 1988 compared to the previous year (Japan 1989: 1). As a further consequence, the annual harvest activity of STCW became concentrated on the catch of Baird's beaked whale and pilot whale, both of which continue to be regulated by the Japanese government. The number of registered boats and STCW licenses have not changed: eight STCW companies continue to operate and nine STCW boats are licensed to operate, as in the past twenty years.

However, in order to rationalize operating costs under the currently reduced harvest quota, the STCW operators have been operating a reduced number of boats: six boats in the 1988 whaling season, and four in the 1989, 1990, and 1991 seasons. This reduced number of boats is sufficient to harvest the authorized annual quota of sixty Baird's beaked whale (reduced to fifty-four in 1990 and 1991) and fifty pilot whales. In 1989, a newly opened southern whaling ground, also with a quota of fifty pilot whales, was authorized by the Japanese authorities. However, so far the hunt in this new area has proved unsuccessful.

The supply of minke whale meat is extremely limited at present. Currently, the only source comes from the national distribution of the by-products from the annual Antarctic scientific research program (see Japan [1989: Appendix I] for organization details of this distribution system, and Ward [1992: 30–33] for an economic analysis of this activity).

However, frozen minke whale meat from the Antarctic is not an appropriate substitute for fresh minke whale meat because of the difference in quality. Furthermore, the limited amount of meat resulting from the research is insufficient to satisfy both the local demand in STCW communities and the total national demand for whale meat. Whale dishes are now often referred to as *natsukashii tabemono* (nostalgic food). Strong sentiments concerning whale dishes were repeatedly expressed by consumers like this sixty-five-year-old male (nonwhaler) who reported (field notes 1986): "We never get tired of whale dishes. It makes me feel sad to think it is no longer available. We really miss the taste of minke whale."

The interruption in supplies of whale products has compromised the integrity of various local community institutions. The exchange of gifts necessarily occurs less frequently since the ban on minke whaling, with a consequent weakening of social solidarity. Some of the other ceremonies ordinarily strengthening the symbolic function of whale and whaling in some STCW communities have been dramatically reduced in the absence of whaling activities in their coastal waters. In the case of Ayukawa, where the whale-based cuisine and whaling provided the basis for local tourism, the loss of whaling has negatively effected a wide range of local businesses, such as shops, inns, and restaurants. With the ensuing economic distress caused by the loss of jobs and reduced revenues of the Fishery Cooperative Association and local businesses, consequent social dislocations have variously and seriously undermined the continued vitality and viability of these whaling communities (Japan 1989: 40).

Despite the drastic changes occasioned by the restricted supply of minke whale meat, the local people in STCW communities continue to seek ways to normalize the small-scale whaling operations. The request for an exemption from the moratorium on commercial whaling was first presented at the International Whaling Commission meeting in 1986, at which time the many social and cultural similarities between small-scale Japanese coastal whaling and North American and Greenlandic subsistence whaling (carried out by aboriginal people) were presented (Japan 1986). In 1988, a thorough documentation of Japanese STCW accompanied by a petition from the local townspeople was presented at the International Whaling Commission meeting. A special effort was made at the forty-first International Whaling Commission meeting in 1989 by the mayor of Oshika township, within which the Ayukawa whaling community is situated. The mayor presented a plea for the resumption of minke whaling and was accompanied at that meeting by all eight whaling boat owners. Statements by the mayor and boat owners included detailed explanations of the impacts of zero quotas, and these explanations were again offered at the forty-second, forty-third, and forty-fourth meetings in the three following years. The persistence with which efforts are made to continue STCW signals the importance of whaling and whaling- related activities in these coastal communities.

## Discussion and Conclusion

An examination of three phases of STCW operations – consumption, distribution, and production – as well as the description of the current situation during the hiatus in minke whaling caused by the moratorium, has indicated some important characteristics found in this form of whaling. An examination of consumption patterns of minke whale meat and blubber demonstrates the total utilization of the whale carcass for human consumption. Five main parts of the minke whale carcass are prepared and subsequently consumed in various localities where whale products are favored. The most common preparation of STCW products at present is *sashimi*, which is eaten both as a ceremonial dish and as an everyday meal during the whaling season. Small-type coastal whaling is the sole supplier of fresh minke meat, the most preferred ingredient for *kujira sashimi*, which consumers distinguish from frozen minke whale meat produced in other whaling operations. It was also noted that minke whale consumption patterns are deeply rooted in the historical, social, and cultural accounts of the local peoples' lives. Not only does the preferred taste for whale dishes motivate consumers to prepare them, but symbolic values attached to the whale make such dishes appropriate for particular social or ceremonial occasions. This is often reinforced by means of a past and present association with a whale-meat diet and with whaling. The whale-based cuisine involves important social dimensions, as socially and ceremonially important gatherings and visiting in whaling towns are often celebrated by sharing whale dishes.

Whale products are distributed through commercial and noncommercial means, allowing consumers to satisfy a variety of socially and culturally significant consumption needs. People who have both direct and indirect ties with the whalers participate in gift exchanging, during which whale is the main gift item.

Through such social interaction with the whalers, local people have access to whale meat and blubber. Another means of access is provided by middlemen who distribute the meat commercially. Regardless of the degree of commercialism involved in the means of distribution, the consumers are socially and culturally motivated to make use of the STCW products, which, in turn, sustain traditional institutions and values.

The most important characteristic of the commercial distribution of STCW products is that it is highly localized. The initial distribution takes place at the landing port and involves local distributors who market the products primarily in the whaling community, and also in those neighboring communities that have historic, social, and cultural links with the whaling community. Such an efficient distribution system enables fresh minke whale meat to reach consumers in the best condition. The localized nature of the distribution, furthermore, makes STCW an integral and essential part of the local economy.

The production phase of the STCW operation can be characterized by its high efficiency. STCW production operations are small-scale in order to achieve optimal production, during which a whale carcass is kept chilled to maintain the high quality required to meet exacting culinary standards. Harvest activities are conducted within a limited coastal area involving a minimum number of local crews so that efficiency in production is maximized. The social dimension of the production phase of whaling is also noteworthy; an intimate work situation creates a close unity among the crew members. Such unity is further reinforced by the fact that kinship has traditionally, and currently to a certain degree, played an important role in recruitment of whalers. Such intimate social unity is a vehicle for the transmission of whaling knowledge and technology from generation to generation.

What, then, is the social and cultural significance of the STCW operation in present-day Japan? The answer becomes more apparent when the three phases of STCW are viewed in the context of the Japanese whaling cultural complex. The activities in the three phases of STCW operations are concentrated in the present STCW communities and extend to other areas identifiable within the whaling cultural complex. The analysis of consumption patterns demonstrates the existence of a diversified regional minke whale-based cuisine maintained in the northern part of Japan. Historical development of Japanese whaling has fostered widespread whale-eating customs in different regions. The minke whale cuisine forms a part of this historical diversity, and remains vital for the maintenance of the continually changing Japanese whaling culture.

STCW provides a regular and reliable supply of fresh minke whale meat in these regions through localized commercial and noncommercial distribution networks. Distribution of minke whale products originated in the local whaling community and extended to the area where socially and culturally identifiable needs for minke whale meat and blubber were maintained. The STCW distribution system ensured a continuous supply of fresh minke whale meat in the area where whaling and the associated whale-based food culture has fostered consumption needs for whale meat.

Practical considerations involved in producing fresh minke whale meat place limitations upon the scale and area of operation. STCW boats operate from the government-designated ports within a limited distance, which allows them to return to port while the meat stays fresh.

A locally developed distinctive whale-based cuisine, efficient coastal whaling operations, and localized distribution network together form a cohesive system that sustains important social, cultural, economic, and nutritional needs of the local community. Such an adaptive system, though relatively recent in origin and technologically modern in some important respects, nevertheless serves to maintain the long-established, culturally varied, and yet clearly identifiable Japanese whaling culture in contemporary Japan.

The present distress observed in the STCW communities demonstrates the obvious negative impacts of the International Whaling Commission's decision to prolong the pause imposed on all commercial whaling. The persistence with which the local people have been appealing for the normalization of their small-scale coastal minke whale fishery has its roots in all of the critical social, cultural, and economic relationships linking this fishery to the survival of these small distinctive coastal communities.

# Part 7

## Native Perspectives

# Editorial

Throughout the growth of sociocultural anthropology as a discipline, methods and theories have been developed for gathering data on and comprehending the perspectives of the people that are the focus of anthropological research. It has been much less common for anthropologists to inquire how subjects feel about being the objects of such research. However, in recent years – goaded by native authors such as Vine Deloria (1969) – indigenous peoples' thoughts about Western influences on their culture in general, and the effects of anthropological inquiry in particular, have gained a more central position among the concerns of the discipline.

In the not-too-distant past, theories of cultural change depicted hunter-gatherers (and other indigenous peoples) as being indiscriminating recipients of the objects, social institutions, and world views of assimilating societies. However, as we have seen in the papers in Parts 5 and 6, that is by no means always the case. Indigenous peoples frequently are active players in the processes and outcomes of assimilation and, more recently, modernization. It is now recognized that, whenever they have enough freedom of action to make choices, indigenous peoples make conscious decisions concerning the taking, adapting, modifying, incorporating, or rejecting the elements of Western culture to which they have been exposed. These decisions are conditioned by indigenous values, knowledge, and logic systems that have functioned to sustain the peoples involved for countless generations.

Alaska Natives, like most other hunter-gatherers, experienced an onslaught of assimilative agents with multiple interests, commencing in the eighteenth century with Russian fur hunters and traders and proselytizing clergy. After the United States acquired control of Alaska in 1867, official government policy toward the natives was overtly assimilationist. The Alaska Native Claims Settlement Act of 1971 (ANCSA) was regarded by representatives of the dominant Western population of the United States to be the culmination of this assimilation process. Almost immediately, however, many natives rejected that view. It had been their understanding that ANCSA would give them not only land, but the resources to control their own destinies – the means to keep from being fully assimilated. Events have shown that it was not quite that simple. Alaska Natives continue to experience many of the tribulations suffered by indigenous peoples in other parts of the world.

Certainly a great deal of assimilation has occurred in Alaska, as elsewhere. This has enabled some indigenous people to move between their native languages and cultures and those of the Western world with an ease and sophistication rarely achieved by anthropologists. These individuals have acquired an unusual ability to see the situation from both sides, and they have become effective intermediaries. Larry Merculieff is one such person.

Merculieff is a university educated Alaska Native leader with strong ties to his Aleut cultural traditions. An astute observer of the processes of interaction between the indigenous peoples of Alaska and Westerners, he is often critical of the latter. In the chapter that follows, he expresses frustration and bitterness, but he presents his views in a reasoned critique that should be understood and appreciated by everyone who has studied traditional foragers.

In contrast to many native authors, Merculieff does not focus his attention on the government in general or on anthropologists in particular. Instead, his anger is directed at two other groups: animal rights activists, who threaten the economic base on which his people have depended for generations; and wildlife managers, who treat with contempt the knowledge traditional hunters have of game populations. His sentiments on these issues probably reflect those of contemporary hunter-gatherers throughout the world. The questions he raises and the challenges he makes should be considered among the core issues of hunter-gatherer research today.

Merculieff's views were originally conveyed in an address to the Sixth International Conference on Hunting and Gathering Societies. In its written version, it retains the flavor of the original presentation.

# 18

# Western Society's Linear Systems and Aboriginal Cultures: The Need for Two-Way Exchanges for the Sake of Survival

*Ilarion (Larry) Merculieff*

Western scientific regimes, which are built upon deeply ingrained linear structures and ways of understanding, currently dominate efforts to address global environmental and economic distress. Difficulties in cross-cultural communication cause the exclusion of knowledge possessed by indigenous peoples because such knowledge draws upon a cyclical understanding of the world. To avoid progressing completely into a global mono-culture and to avoid single-minded, increasingly destructive, and unsustainable approaches to the problems faced by humans today, serious and concerted efforts must be made to include the depth of experience and knowledge indigenous peoples have gained from centuries of intensive interaction with their environments. We must recognize that cultural and bioeconomic diversity are as vital to human survival as genetic diversity is to the survival of the biosphere.

---

For those of you who don't know me, I am an Aleut, one of three distinct aboriginal races in Alaska. I was born and raised on the Pribilof Islands, a group of tiny islands in the middle of the Bering Sea. My people have lived in the same region of Alaska for almost ten thousand years. Although I have been certified by the state of Alaska as an expert on Aleut history and culture, I am not a scientist by Western standards, so please bear with me and look not to the scientific construct of what I am about to say but to the concepts I wish to convey. These concepts deal with the linear systems of Western society, cyclical systems of many aboriginal societies, and the challenges both pose to communication and to the transfer of knowledge that is essential to maximizing the probabilities of human survival.

About five years ago I attended the World Conservation Strategy Conference in Ottawa. Among the delegates from throughout the world were representatives of aboriginal groups from Africa, Australia, North and South America, the South Pacific, and Europe. The World Conservation Strategy, adopted by 134 nation-states, is a blueprint for the protection of the environment and sustainable economic development. The strategy was of interest to the indigenous peoples' representatives not so much for what it included as for what it did not include – the knowledge and experience that indigenous peoples can contribute to the goals of the World Conservation Strategy. This omission gave the representatives a focus for action, so they held a caucus. During the caucus, each representative, in turn, gave a description of the basic thrust of their own cultural system and the issues they faced. Much to our amazement, we found a substantial degree of commonality. Differences existed only in degree, not in substance. This commonality formed the basis for a global coalition of aboriginal or indigenous peoples for the purpose of amending a folio of the World Conservation Strategy. The amendment would formally recognize that linkages with aboriginal peoples who have had sustained contact with their immediate environment for generations are important to the ultimate success of the strategy.

I was astonished that the original document, created by some of the best minds in the world concerned about environment and development, did not already incorporate the policy of linkage with aboriginal people. Since I was privileged to have had a very traditional Aleut upbringing, I am keenly aware of the depth of knowledge and experience about the environment inherent in my own cultural system. It did not occur to me that we would need to convince the intellectual powers behind this influential document of the utility of such knowledge and experience. But that is exactly what we had to do. After five years of effort, the United Nations will consider our amendment to the World Conservation Strategy folio.

This encounter caused me to reevaluate my life experience regarding how, when, and if institutions deal with aboriginal peoples. I already know that prejudices, misperceptions, misconceptions, ethnocentrism, and racism are obstacles to recognition of a people's value. Some of that may have been at work here, but there was also something else involved. I was not able to put my finger on it until I realized that there was a definite pattern in the breakdown of communication between aboriginal peoples and well-intentioned, well-meaning mainstream individuals in positions of power, authority, or professional standing in Westernized institutions throughout the world. I will attempt to explain what is behind this breakdown in communication. I realize I have just made a statement of sweeping generality, but I put it in these terms in order to highlight something to which we all should be alerted.

I can best communicate what I mean by recounting something that happened in a remote village in Alaska where scientists, land and resource managers, and seven tribal chiefs met last year to discuss subsistence. The seven tribal chiefs represented people in villages highly dependent upon hunting and trapping for survival.

The chiefs invited state wildlife management officials and their field biologist to make presentations and to engage in discussions. One of the state representatives gave a forty- five-minute presentation on how they were going to conduct a field reconnaissance on moose to determine the health of the local population. The individual gave a good description of the state's methodology, and indicated that the reason this particular study was important was that the current bull-to-female ratio and the overall size of the moose population indicated that it was at a critical threshold of sustainability. Further negative changes might jeopardize the health of the moose population. The state game official completed his presentation and asked for questions.

The lead spokesperson for the traditional governing group did not ask any questions except in a rhetorical sense; he also gave a forty-five-minute dissertation. He said that people in all the surrounding villages had noticed a distinct drop in marshland water levels. He noted that the food sources for moose in the marshlands were adversely affected. He asked if anyone from the state had counted the number of beaver in these areas or the number of dams these beavers had built. He noted that at least twenty small tributaries to the Yukon River were dammed. He commented that the Alaska Department of Fish and Game might propose to cut villagers' subsistence take of moose as their answer to the problem, but that no studies were planned on beaver. The leader said, "It seems to me you should listen to us and find ways to work together." The state game official responded that they should go to their regional game advisory board, which would consider this information and, if it chose, give recommendations to the state Board of Game, which had the ultimate decision-making powers.

Both sides of this dialogue left the meeting feeling that they never connected – because they didn't connect. The scientist had a script to follow of proper scientific procedure. His job was to collect limited field data on moose only. The native groups provided information that went beyond the training of the field scientist and the scope of his field assignment. The native groups fully understood that the final decision-making body – the state Board of Game – had a mandate to scientifically manage the state's wildlife populations and habitat, and that this mandate requires that heavy weight be given to scientific field data and minimizes the importance of what appears to be anecdotal information. As a result, the native voice was never heard.

I choose to recount this exchange because it is a microcosm of how cross-cultural communication breaks down when people do not understand that each comes from a different world view, a different frame of reference, which leads people to different conclusions because they use different facts to interpret the same issue. I have witnessed this breakdown many times around the world. The cost of such breakdowns is dramatic in human terms: massive institutional failures in attempting to help indigenous peoples in education, economic development, law enforcement, governmental structures, social services, environmental concerns, and resource and wildlife management.

In this microcosmic example, the two world views could be described as linear, on the one hand, and cyclical, on the other. The scientist is indoctrinated in the linear construct, as are most Westernized people. In the educational system, one begins with kindergarten, first grade, second grade, and progresses to college and graduate school, until one ends up with a doctorate. It is inherent in this linear progression that anything in the beginning of the line is inferior to anything at the end of that line: a Ph.D. is superior to a Master's degree, which is superior to a four-year college degree, and so forth. In technology development, we developed the sun dial, then the pendulum clock, then pocket watches, then wristwatches, and finally computerized watches. Again, anything earlier in the technological line is inferior to whatever follows it. In science, the linear progression evolved into scientific specialization and the continued refinement of scientific methodology from its origins of simple logic, common sense, and visual observation. All such constructs may have had their beginnings in Christian religions: Alpha to Omega, Genesis to Revelations. Whatever the case, this way of thinking is inherent in much of what one can observe in Westernized societies.

Contrast this way of life with those people who live their lives by the seasons and in response to their immediate environment. Theirs is a world in which the interdependence of humans, animals, plants, water, and earth – the total picture – is always immediate, always present. And the total picture – every day, every season, every year – is seen as a circle. Everything is connected: the marshlands to the beaver, the beaver dams to altered conditions, the new conditions to the moose herd, the moose herd to the marshlands. Each affects the other, and it is this intimate knowledge of the environment (all of the curves in the circle) that has allowed these people to survive for hundreds of generations.

In the chief's presentation, he described a specific sequence of events that his people had observed that demonstrated their world view of connectedness; details that the specialized scientist could not admit into his education. The scientist's job was to make methodical aerial transects of an area, count the number of male and female moose in each, and record the data. Scientific data carry more weight in management forums than the empirical evidence presented by natives, which evidence is often considered anecdotal in the scientific community. What is overlooked by dismissing such information is that the native comes from a community of people who have had sustained contact with their immediate environment for thousands of years, and who, through a cultural information system, have passed on their visual observations, knowledge, and experience to each successive generation. In this context, the native information is anything but anecdotal. It comes from an individual with an invaluable storehouse of knowledge about the environment that is irreplaceable and cannot be replicated. This knowledge tells the person, for example, that environments are in a constant state of flux. By the time the scientist formulates data with an adequate time series to make the information useful, the model probably will be outdated. In addition, the knowledge tells the person that periodic chaos accompanies the symmetry in nature, and that scientific models have yet to become sophisticated enough to incorporate the predictability of such chaos and its effect on the symmetry. As such, native people respect intelligent visual observations more than scientific models. They have to – their lives and their children's lives literally depend on it.

If individuals in decision-making positions would acknowledge information passed on by native peoples, it could save them time, money, and effort. I am reminded of when I read a story about a scientific study that was conducted by the University of California. Hundreds of thousands of dollars were spent to send researchers down in a submarine to make visual observations of halibut to determine if they ever fed above the ocean floor. Ever since I was a child, I knew halibut fed off the ocean floor because of what I was taught and what I observed. Frequently, we would catch halibut after pulling our subsistence fishing line up halfway from the sea bottom, so we knew that the fish were mobile and would follow prey a great distance off the sea bottom. We even found shallow diving birds in halibut stomachs and we caught halibut that were feeding above substantially elevated underwater terrain. Halibut coloring alone should have told the researchers something; the fish are black on top and white on the bottom to better camouflage them from predators. If halibut only stayed on the bottom of the sea, they would be entirely black, since predators looking down toward the bottom would see a dark environment. Looking upward from the bottom of the ocean, the view is lighter; thus halibut are lighter on their bottom to protect them as they swim up from the sea floor. We could have saved the scientists money or, better yet, they could have paid us for the information.

In the true stories I have recounted about the tribal chiefs and the situation with the World Conservation Strategy, it occurs to me that decision makers indoctrinated in the linear systems of Westernized societies regard many aboriginal groups as primitive and consider their knowledge base inferior because they have not progressed according to linear principles. That is the definite pattern I referred to earlier that at the time I could not identify precisely. It is no wonder that aboriginal groups feel they are simply engaging in powerless politics, that their voices and their knowledge of the environment are falling on deaf ears.

The end result of these kinds of dynamics is what we are witnessing today, the creation of a monoculture: one dominant culture that subsumes the other and tells the other, in no uncertain terms, that it must conform to the linear world view if it wants to be heard. For the cyclically based aboriginal cultures, this message heralds inevitable destruction if they acquiesce. Some would call this acquiscence progress – a view that requires examination.

We have all heard about the animal rights movement. This movement is born of a linear model. People who subscribe to animal rights believe that humans have now evolved to the point that we are the only animal capable of making moral choices. In accordance with this belief, then, it is incumbent upon us to recognize that it is immoral and inhumane to kill animals or to allow them to suffer at our hands. Societies that kill animals are brutal and primitive. This line of thinking has made tremendous inroads around the world and it threatens every culture that uses biological resources as part of its economic activity.

The animal rights movement was the primary factor in destroying the traditional way of life in my home in the Pribilof Islands. My people harvested fur seals on a sustainable basis for two hundred years on two tiny islands that are currently home to one million fur seals, three million birds, and seven hundred Aleuts. During those two centuries and for a millennium before, Aleuts worked within their own environmental ethics: all life on the Pribilof Islands thrived, including the fur seals. But, beginning in 1976, the fur seal population began to decline. The animal rights coalition blamed our taking of sixteen thousand nonbreeding male seals (from the population of one million) as the cause of the decline. Our people said they noticed some bird species and sea lions also declining and said that these declines were probably connected. But the animal rights groups, in true linear thinking, ignored these observations and simply focused on the seals. With a well-funded campaign aimed at stirring up the emotions of the public, the animal rights groups succeeded in stopping the seal harvest five years ago and, in the process, destroyed our only economic base. To replace it, we are developing a regional bottomfish port that will bring in thousands of transients and massive development. This new economy may do more to destroy our habitat and disrupt the wildlife than anything in the island's history, and it has the capacity to accomplish this destruction within a single generation.

I find it supremely ironic that, in Alaska today, scientists and others are beginning to notice with alarm the decline of all the species observed by my people, and are scurrying to find answers. If any of these species becomes endangered, it could shut down all major fisheries in the state. U.S. law requires the elimination of any human activity that results in disruptive contact with endangered species.

Historically, my people were the stewards of the Pribilof Islands; we lived close to land and sea, using those resources wisely and adjusting our take of animals according to our knowledge and experience. This way of life is fast disappearing as the need to earn hard cash to survive outweighs the need to be concerned about the environment. The termination of the seal harvest in the Pribilofs has severed the economic and cultural link between the people and the seals. It was this economic and cultural link that ensured a truly symbiotic and functional relationship between man and animal. It was this linkage that provided the human incentive to be stewards. People who have not had sustained interaction with their immediate environment over generations have difficulty understanding a vital principle underlying successful aboriginal cultures: these cultures are banks of extensive, invaluable knowledge and experience about how to sustain ecosystems, and they exist according to the economics of survival.

The U.S. Congress took action against this seal harvest in response to a large public outcry about what was viewed as a brutal, archaic practice. Now, Aleuts can kill seals for subsistence, but we cannot use any part for commercial purposes. The law even allows us to kill seals at sea if we use a traditional craft manned by no more than five people, with no firearms – but harpoons are allowed. Engines are forbidden; we must use oars. This was the Congressional version of Aleutian traditional seal hunting practice. No one thought about how ridiculously cumbersome this at-sea method would be, especially when one considers that there are hundreds of thousands of seals on land. Meanwhile, the seal herd continues to decline along with the sea lions and certain bird populations. All of these are being studied as separate, disconnected problems – despite the fact that all of these animals have a common food base. And the renewable, biodegradable products (sealskin garments) are no longer available; instead, they are replaced with nonbiodegradable, nonrenewable, petroleum-based synthetics.

It may be nice to glamorize aboriginal cultures, to insist that such cultures help preserve wildlife by stagnating their hunting technologies, to promulgate laws that totally eliminate economic incentives. Sadly, this philosophy, intended to somehow protect wildlife, leads to the greater destruction of wildlife. It most certainly ensures that people living in some of the most pristine and delicate wilderness areas of the world lose what is at the root of all successful cultures: the ability to grow and adapt as required for survival, and the knowledge to seek out and enhance strategies for economic survival according to their location. Show me a culture without these two elements and I will show you a people that are dead or dying.

To digress again, this new law, dictating how Aleuts are to deal with seals, replaces traditional laws. In this instance, and indeed in all such instances, wildlife and habitat are or were protected because the aboriginal people had the power to decide for themselves what to incorporate into their culture, language, and laws. As a result, protection of wildlife and habitat became synonymous with ensuring the survival of cultures. Again, the story comes full circle. The primary difference between such aboriginal laws and laws in the current legal context is that aboriginal laws are intricately woven into everyday life. Enforcement occurs through the social pressure to conform to societal norms, not by threat of punitive action. The approach of interjecting outside authority based upon noncyclical constructs very quietly, but very forcefully, erodes the utility of incorporating management of wildlife and habitat into culture and everyday life. In effect, this destroys ways of living that are successful models of as much harmony with nature as humans are capable of achieving. Can we accept this as a price of progress?

Everyone is struggling to find effective scientific models for managing ecosystems because we are disrupting them on a massive scale. We are disrupting them because humans, unlike most life on Earth, have no niche. Without a niche, we stumble into and disrupt natural systems all around us. The fact is that cultural systems that have, as a paradigm, an intimate interaction with the environment are the closest humankind will come to having a niche. I suggest that the humane, morally proper, and most efficient laws must complement, supplement, and enhance those rational local systems already in place.

Alaska's experiences are similar to those of the rest of the world in terms of its successes (or more appropriately, its failures) in dealing with issues that directly affect aboriginal peoples. In Alaska, the vast majority of villages are not economically self-sufficient and, indeed, have become increasingly dependent upon government transfer payments, government grants, and government jobs, despite the untold millions and millions of dollars that have been poured into rural economic development. The scores of most young native people are between the twentieth and the thirtieth percentile level in national standardized academic achievement tests. Over thirty percent of these students fail to complete high school when they leave their villages to attend urban schools. Alaska Natives represent between 12 to 15 percent of the statewide population, but approximately 25 percent of all persons arrested, 25 percent of all persons convicted of felonies, and 34 percent of all persons incarcerated are native. Suicide rates, alcohol abuse, and fetal alcohol syndrome are all far above national norms. They are at crisis levels. Given all of this, there is, in the native community, a growing sense of disenfranchisement and distrust of Western institutions, with a consequent growth of legal and civil confrontations. I maintain that Alaska is not atypical of what is happening to indigenous groups around the world (in addition to malnutrition, starvation, and overt violation of human rights). I further maintain that part of these failures can be attributed to the lack of understanding of the difference in world views and the role of this disjuncture in the success or failure of all of our attempted solutions to human survival. These are not just failures that hurt one particular group of people. They are forcing a singular world view, a monoculture if you will, which could mean the destruction of humankind on Earth.

The United Nations is beginning to recognize the value of indigenous knowledge, as are some scientists. They are beginning to understand that cultural diversity and bioeconomic diversity may be just as essential as genetic diversity in achieving accommodation with the environment in a way that enhances the chances for human survival. Cultural and bioeconomic diversity are rapidly disappearing. Aboriginal peoples in the South Pacific, South America, North America, Africa, India, and the circumpolar north are all experiencing the same challenges to their cultural viability. They are only different by degrees, but the principles undermining their cultures are virtually identical. These principles include the subtle or overt destruction of intimate links with their immediate environments, and the replacement of these links with inappropriate economic activities that are based on a singular world view. The result of this destruction is environmental degradation, the destruction of habitat and wildlife, the development of huge economic development projects, and the irreplaceable loss of invaluable knowledge and experience.

As professionals involved with hunting-gathering societies, it is incumbent upon us to try to understand what is happening. We all must become vocal advocates of cultural and bioeconomic diversity if we hope to prevent the extinction of humanity. For my part, I am collaborating with two Canadians who are research associates with the Arctic Institute of North America, Susan Swibold and Helen Corbett. We have been involved in a decade-long research project that examines human interactions with the environment in high latitude ecosystems. We have produced four documentary films as part of a lecture series that we are taking around the world to stimulate critical public thinking about these issues. We utilize the visual medium, with bicultural narration, as a means of taking people out of their cultural milieu. We find this a necessary step to remove the cultural blinders that hinder mutual understanding when discussing humans, environment, and development.

# Part 8

New Problems in
Hunter-Gatherer Research

# Editorial

A quarter of a century has passed since *Man the Hunter* (Lee and DeVore 1968) appeared. More field research on foragers was carried out during this period than in the entire previous history of anthropology. This work resulted in the accumulation of an enormous quantity of new information.

The need for more direct communication among the many scholars engaged in hunter-gatherer research spawned a series of International Conferences on Hunting and Gathering Societies (since 1988 abbreviated "CHAGS," followed by the number of the conference): in Paris, France, in 1978 (Leacock and Lee, eds. 1982); in Quebec, Canada, in 1980; in Bad Homburg, Germany, in 1983 (Schrire, ed. 1984; Wilmsen, ed. 1989); in London, England, in 1986 (Ingold, Riches, and Woodburn, eds. 1988a, 1988b); in Darwin, Australia, in 1988 (Altman, ed. 1989; Meehan and White, eds. 1990), and in Fairbanks, Alaska, in 1990 (E. A. Smith 1991a). These conferences have been supplemented by others focusing on hunting-gathering societies (such as Koyama and Thomas, eds. 1981; Williams and Hunn, eds. 1982), volumes intended for undergraduate use (Bicchieri, ed. 1972; Coon 1971; Service 1979), a general review in *Current Anthropology* (Testart 1988b), four separate treatments in the *Annual Review of Anthropology* (Barnard 1983; Bettinger 1987; Flanagan 1989; Myers 1988) within a mere six-year span, and innumerable symposia at the annual meetings of national and regional anthropological associations.

By 1990, hunter-gatherer research could legitimately be considered a distinct specialty within anthropology, a subfield encompassing the work of literally hundreds of scholars in all parts of the world. However, there are reasons to believe that the next twenty-five years will see profound changes in hunter-gatherer studies, and possibly even their demise. The conditions under which fieldwork is conducted are changing very rapidly, and many researchers are calling into question some of the fundamental assumptions upon which hunter-gatherer research is based. Some of the more philosophical of the latter were discussed in a recent article by Richard Lee (1992). Several of the basic conceptual, methodological, and practical problems of hunter-gatherer research are discussed in the two papers that conclude this volume.

In the first paper, Harvey Feit examines a number of generally accepted models of social relations, relations to land and resources, and particularly the orientation to time of hunter-gatherers. He evaluates the models in the light of empirical evidence – particularly from the Waswanipi Cree – and finds the models wanting. In each area, Feit asks if hunter-gatherer societies really are as distinct from other types of society as most writers claim, and in each case he concludes that they are not. If societies of foragers are not particularly distinct from any others, then there is no justification for a separate field of hunter-gatherer studies.

In the final paper, which is an essay rather than an empirical study, Burch reviews a number of practical, methodological, and conceptual issues facing hunter-gatherer research. In the practical realm, he notes that extremely rapid social change already has made it nearly impossible to do the kinds of field studies that were conducted only a few years ago, and he discusses the implications of this fact. With regard to methodology, he discusses the extent to which one can generalize from data on recent hunter-gatherers to patterns that might have prevailed thousands of years ago. Finally, in the conceptual realm, Burch, like Feit, asks whether the concept of hunter-gatherer is really useful as an analytical category. And like Feit, he concludes that it is not. If they are right – and others have argued the same point – one may expect major changes in hunter-gatherer research in the years ahead.

# 19

# The Enduring Pursuit: Land, Time, and Social Relationships in Anthropological Models of Hunter-Gatherers and in Subarctic Hunters' Images

*Harvey A. Feit*

This paper examines recent models that have sought to characterize the distinctive features of hunter-gatherer societies that distinguish them from small-scale agricultural or pastoral societies. The survey shows that distinctive features have clustered around questions of land and resource use, and around concomitant social institutions. The survey also shows that hunter-gatherers are repeatedly portrayed as living in a distinctive temporal frame, one in which the juxtaposition of a lengthy past and an instantaneous present obviate an enduring present oriented to a future shaped by human agency. I consider these models in relation to some long-established and recent ethnographic and ethnohistoric counter evidence, which I suggest has broad implications; and in relation to the cultural images crafted by subarctic Waswanipi Cree Indian hunters in Quebec. This survey concludes that there is no distinctive social feature of substance or consequence with which to distinguish hunter-gatherer societies.[1]

1. Earlier versions of this paper were read at the 1989 meeting of the American Ethnology Society, Santa Fe, New Mexico, 5–9 April; and in 1990 at the Sixth International Conference on Hunting and Gathering Societies, Fairbanks, Alaska, 28 May–1 June. I have been assisted by comments from the floor at both meetings, as well as from colleagues who have responded to the written versions. Although they do not necessarily agree with the final form, I want to thank the following people for improving this paper: Bernard Arcand, Nurit Bird-David, Ann Fienup-Reardon, Tim Ingold, Steve Langdon, Harriet Rosenberg, Colin Scott, and Estellie Smith. The paper draws on research funded by the Social Sciences and Humanities Research Council of Canada (Grants 410–87–0715, 410–88–0535, and 410–90–0802), and from the McMaster University Arts Research Board. I also want to thank the U.S. National Science Foundation for a conference travel grant to attend one of the sessions.

**Introduction**

In this paper I review recurrent major themes in some of the recent efforts of hunter-gatherer specialists to define what distinguishes hunter-gatherer societies from other "simple" agricultural and pastoral societies. What I show first is that the initial plausibility of the anthropological distinctions is often based on models that employ ambiguous and conflicting characterizations of hunter-gatherer relations to land and resources, of the temporal dimensions of hunter-gatherers' lives, and of hunter-gatherer social relationships. I then claim that these recent efforts to radically separate the hunter-gatherers, based on models of their distinctive productive and social relations, stand in rather tenuous relationship to the available ethnographic evidence. In a final part of the paper I examine some hunters' images as a contrast to anthropological models, and emphasize that hunters' views need to be given more consideration, a viewpoint previously asserted but infrequently pursued.

My aim in this paper is to share reflections for consideration rather than to demonstrate conclusions, and my approach is explicitly selective; I use widely cited models and case examples I know well. In my conclusions, I suggest, as others have suggested before, that a universal concept of socially distinctive hunter-gatherer societies may not be a credible anthropological category.[2]

As has been noted frequently in recent years, anthropology as a Western intellectual enterprise constructs images of "the other" that help to define ourselves (Boon 1982; Marcus and Fischer 1986). Today images of others provide one kind of powerful comparative framework within which much analysis is undertaken. In the world of the human past, probably the most important others that scholars construct, at the most distant places of time and space, are the hunter-gatherers.

**Ambiguities in Anthropological Models of Hunter-Others**

One key dimension of the core image of the hunter-gatherers is reflected in what has probably become the most widely quoted assertion of the relevance of hunter-gatherers to us, the opening

2. For earlier reviews of the issues and the literature see Arcand (1988) and Myers (1988). The present arguments are directed more specifically to recent theorizing, and to temporal dimensions of social reproduction, than the earlier discussions.

words of the *Man the Hunter* volume, "Cultural Man has been on earth for some 2,000,000 years; for over 99 percent of this period he has lived as a hunter-gatherer" (Lee and DeVore 1968: 3). This dramatic image of hunter-gatherer peoples occupying all but the last fifteen minutes of the cultural human's day contrasts paradoxically with a second well-established temporal image of hunter-gatherers: that they are bound to the momentary present.

An early version of this latter view is the assertion that hunter-gatherers are preoccupied with the daily food supply, they face unresolvable difficulties of storage, and they use relatively simple productive equipment. In accordance with this view the economist Alfred Marshall (1936) wrote that "We find savages living under the dominion of custom and impulse, scarcely ever striking out new lines for themselves, never forecasting the distant future, and seldom making provision for the near future; fitful in spite of their servitude to custom, governed by the fancy of the moment" (cited in Herskovits 1952: 88). Daryll Forde and Mary Douglas (1956: 322) wrote in a similar vein in their review of primitive economics: "In short, the productive effort of a primitive economy is capable of anticipating its future needs only for a very brief span. Accumulation is difficult, long-term planning impossible."

Each of these images both separates us from hunter-gatherers, and links them to us. The ecologically oriented *Man the Hunter* statement calls attention to the idea that we have radically transformed ourselves within a very short duration of time, and that we live in fundamentally different types of human societies as a result of having crossed the neolithic and industrial rubicons; yet this transformation must have been profoundly shaped by the immense span of time in which our ancestors lived as hunter-gatherers. Thus, hunter-gatherers are both other and kin.

At the same time, the Man the Hunter Conference, held in Chicago, 1966, announced a challenge to the popular conviction, and anthropological opinion, that hunter-gatherers never had the leisure time to "build culture" (see references in Sahlins 1972: 3). Marshall Sahlins's discussion of original affluence signaled the turnabout in these aspects of the anthropological conceptions of hunter-gatherers. Nevertheless, these transformations did not reject the images of hunter-gatherers' radical, if ambiguous, distinctiveness from us. Sahlins offers an image of affluence by the Zen route of few and easily satisfied wants within the context of mobile social groupings. In Sahlins's revision of our models of hunter-gatherer economy, comparisons between us and them play the central role in both the evidence mustered and in the consciously polemical rhetoric of the argument. For example, how much they work and how much they own are made significant by reference to our own patterns of labor and consumption.

The ambiguity of the relationship is highlighted in Sahlins' discussion of the conceptual problems raised by hunters' attitudes toward their condition. Sahlins (1972: 30) consciously exaggerates the ambiguities in his phrasing of their views: "Oriented forever to the present, without the slightest thought of, or care for, what the morrow may bring (Spencer and Gillen 1899: 53) the hunter seems unwilling to husband supplies, incapable of a planned response to the doom surely awaiting him." As primary support for the prodigal nature of hunter-gatherers, Sahlins (1972: 30) cites the seventeenth-century Jesuit missionary Père LeJeune, who commented on his winter among Montagnais hunters in 1633–1634: "I told them that they did not manage well, and that it would be better to reserve these feasts for future days, and that in doing this they would not be so pressed with hunger. They laughed at me. 'Tomorrow' (they said) 'we shall make another feast with what we shall capture.' Yes, but more often they capture only cold and wind."

While noting that some have tried to rationalize hunter-gatherer prodigality, Sahlins (1972: 31) implores us to attend to the Montagnais' explanation of their feasting, that tomorrow will bring more of the same. And he argues that hunter-gatherer survival attests that the hunters' view must have some objective basis. Despite the reassurance, here the hunter-gatherer is made into the other, par excellence.

Sahlins, however, is not solely bound to the radical separations that might be drawn from this view. While hunters may not plan in his models, they do engage in rationalities of diminishing returns and domestic modes of production. He tells us that they weigh the advantages of owning more than a minimal tool kit, or storing surplus subsistence, or using resources more intensively, or having numerous young offspring, or increasing local group size, against the diminishing returns of staying put when there are fresh lands to forage if one can move relatively efficiently. And he does open the door for hunter-gatherers to be analyzed as examples of domestic economies, along with agriculturalists and pastoralists.

Nevertheless, among these alternative perspectives, he leaves us, as do others, with a vision that hunters and gatherers inhabit a special world, connected yet other; people with a short vision and a long history.

## Recent Models of Hunter-Gatherer Distinctiveness

While discussions of the separation of hunter-gatherers as a form of human society have continued in the anthropological literature, the primary focus has shifted in recent years from the separations between them and us to the separations between hunter-gatherers and small-scale agricultural and pastoral societies. These discussions owe as much to Meillassoux as to Sahlins and the "Man the Hunter" tradition. But there are continuities that cut across different theoretical and national traditions, as will be discussed later.

Claude Meillassoux (1973) made land use and temporality central to the constitution of the self-sustaining mode of production of the hunting band, thereby spinning one of the central threads in the ongoing series of debates. His essay, published originally in French in 1967, contrasted the generalized African hunting economy with his model of agricultural economy, drawing heavily from the Pygmy ethnography of Colin Turnbull (1965b), and his own ethnography of the agricultural Guro.

The main difference between hunters and agriculturalists, Meillassoux (1973: 192) argued, is that for the former land is the "subject of labor" rather than the "object." That is, hunters accept nature's bounty, "without any attempts toward maintenance or reclamation." He goes on to claim that such a mode of exploitation of the land does not lead to "any lasting organization and arrangement of the landscape," and it "results in a kind of roving within a loose area." A major implication of this way of living, claims Meillassoux (1973: 192–93), is the following: "For want of investment in the land, labor applied to it yields an *instantaneous* return, not a deferred one. This mode of exploitation involves discontinuous undertakings of a limited duration, independent of each other and whose product is obtained immediately at the end of each venture. Supplies are provided through these repeated operations, carried out at brief intervals, usually daily" (emphasis in original).

Citing Turnbull's claim that Mbuti have an "*almost* complete lack of concern for the past as for the future," Meillassoux (1973: 194) generalizes that: "The shortness and the sporadic repetition of activities lead to a way of life which is tied *to the present*, without any duration or continuity. The way of life is 'instantaneous'" (emphasis in Meillassoux).

By contrast, Meillassoux later says (1973: 198) that in agricultural societies, "where duration, expectation and cyclical repetition – that is time – are paramount, the future becomes a concern and, along with it, the problem of reproduction."

Here, hunters stand by definition in a distinct relation to land and the products of labor, to time, and to the reproduction of social life. Indeed, Meillassoux (1973: 201) goes on in his closing comments to effectively remove hunters from evolutionary time. He constructs so radical an opposition between hunting societies and farming societies that he cannot resolve how a changeover from one system to the other could have occurred, and he concludes that "hunting may well be unable to develop into any other mode of production." As for the stages of human evolution preceding agriculture, he suggests that "the origins of agriculture should be looked for among other activities, such as fishing" (1973: 201).

Hunters thus not only live without a sense of future, they do not produce a real future, that is, a future with the potential to be anything but a continuation of the present instant. This is a temporal mode of determination with a dialectical vengeance, since it undermines the evolutionary temporality that is part of its motivational sources.

These formulations have generated significant debates among hunter-gatherer scholars (including some limited revisions by Meillassoux 1981). James Woodburn (1980) has independently proposed a classification of all hunting-gathering societies into immediate-return systems and delayed-return or delayed-yield systems. The former are characterized by being strongly oriented toward the present with a lack of concern for past or future. The few examples include the Mbuti, !Kung, and the Hadza, among whom Woodburn worked and from which he draws much of his evidence. Woodburn (1980: 113) goes on to suggest that historically, delayed-return systems must have been based on immediate-return systems.

But Woodburn also notes that delayed-return hunter-gatherer systems are by far the most common, and that agricultural and pastoral systems are, of course, all delayed-return systems. Alain Testart (1982, 1988b) has independently developed a classification based on whether significant storage of seasonal staples occurs in the context of annual economic planning. He also has suggested that the transition to storage based societies helps to dissolve the single rubicon created by the idea of a neolithic revolution based on a single stage transition to agropastoralism.

More recently, Tim Ingold (1987: 198) has reviewed the debates arguing that the socially important diagnostic of hunter-gatherer societies lies in "whether or not people are bound to one another by enduring relations in respect of the control and distribution of the means of subsistence." He goes on to point out that the two criteria by which hunting-gathering societies have been commonly distinguished are that labor is not invested in the expectation of a delayed return, and that there is little or no food storage, because the time lags involved in either would create the basis for lasting mutual dependencies. As he puts it, "Time ties people down" (Ingold 1987: 199).

He points out that ethnographic instances now abound of considerable prior investment of labor in technology and artifice for harvesting wild foods, and of cases with extensive storage of hunter-gatherers' harvests. He argues, however, that hunter-gatherer societies are distinctive. What differentiates them is that social dependencies on specific other people do not develop, because hunters maintain collective access as opposed to restricted appropriation of resources.[3]

Noting the prevalence of delayed-return hunter-gatherers, Ingold (1987: 200) distinguishes between types of delayed-return systems based on the different "time-lag associated on the one hand with the practical staggering of production and consumption schedules, and on the other with the deferment of access to socially appropriated resources." He argues that only when there is an appropriative movement as opposed to collective access to resources does delay invest social relations with a quality of durability, and such investment with appropriation is definitive of agricultural and pastoral production. "In a purely extractive hunting and gathering economy . . . whether or not it entails practical delays, social relations have the character of immediacy – in the sense that 'People are not dependent on *specific* other people for access to basic requirements'" (Ingold 1987: 200; citing Woodburn 1982: 434. Emphasis in Woodburn).

3. In his most recent and as yet unpublished work, Ingold has gone on to revise these views.

That is, even delayed-return hunter-gatherer systems share the social character of immediate-return systems, for their dependence on each other is of a generalized kind. Ingold (1986: 216) thus tries to recover some theoretical significance for what he calls "the much maligned category of `hunting and gathering.'" Ingold (1987: 217–18) ends his discussion by noting that researchers have yet to include the "much more complicated" issue of "the categories of the people themselves." In emic terms, a common view is that present returns on hunting are viewed as the outcome of previous hunts in the past, so that what may be constructed by an observer as an immediate-return system may be a delayed-return system to the hunters themselves.

These polemics have made explicit just how profoundly the very existence or significance of the category of hunter-gatherers has come to hinge on conceptual constructs of resource utilization, labor, temporality, and their social concomitants, far removed from the apparent obviousness of the category "hunter-gatherer." While the variations and nuances now involved in the debates are not done justice by this summary review, I will stop here to consider the basic case which is being made.

## Land and Resource Use, Time, and Anthropological Evidence

In the next sections of this paper I want to assess these accounts of hunter-gatherer distinctiveness by considering the kinds of evidence on which they rest, and by considering an ethnographic case of the hunters' own models. The first section considers the supposed distinctive importance of immediate-return, a task partly accomplished by Woodburn and Ingold, and therefore only briefly reviewed here. I will then consider the distinctiveness of processes of change in hunter-gatherer societies, before returning to the issue of social relations and dependencies, as articulated in some hunters' views.

At the core of Meillassoux's assumption that hunters and gatherers in general have little thought for the morrow, and that they live almost solely in the present instant, is the widely shared assumption that there is a radical disconnection between hunter-gatherers' present actions and labor, and their ability to provide subsistence for the morrow. By contrast with pastoralists and agriculturalists, it is still often claimed that nothing that the hunter-gatherers can do on one day will assure when, where, or whether food will be harvested on the next. And this appears to be considered especially true of game hunters.

But to acknowledge that the harvest is not as predictable or certain as that of peoples with domesticated food sources does not support the assumption that there are no real or observable consequences of today's labor for tomorrow's harvest. The harvest of plants or animals in particular places and numbers today often shapes the pattern of abundance and the spatial distribution the gatherer or hunter can expect to find tomorrow. This point would be trivial were not the relations between present activities and future harvests so complex and subtle.

James Woodburn (1980: 101) has summarized the case:

> Hunters and gatherers may control their food supplies by culling game animals selectively, by operating restrictions on hunting which have the effect of providing a close season, by using vegetable resources with discretion and replanting portions of the root so that the plants regenerate, by extracting only part of the honey from wild bees' nests so that the sites are not deserted and by many similar techniques of conservation which suggest that the distinction between hunting and gathering as a system of unplanned extraction, and cultivation as a system of planned production is not valid.

I have previously pointed out that studies in wildlife management show that hunting and fishing by humans is one of the most significant factors affecting wildlife populations (Feit 1973). For many species, the present harvests taken by hunters – whether sport hunters, commercial hunters, or hunter-gatherers – will change the wildlife population's age structure, sex balance, production rates, yields, and often the average size and health of the animals in the harvested population. Studies of the impacts of fishing show similar relationships. One does not have to demonstrate that hunters are conservationists to make the point that their present activities are profoundly connected to the outcomes of their future harvesting activities, and that those connections in many cases can be easily observed in the changing rates of encounters with animals over time.

Therefore, it would be surprising if hunter-gatherers were completely unaware of all such connections, and if they really gave no thought for the resources or for the morrow. Indeed, much of what they do shows just such considerations, changing hunting areas periodically or on rotation, and burning areas to initiate vegetation and animal population changes. In many of these cases the consequences of their present changes in harvest patterns will not be observed the next day or week; rather, the morrow will be the next year, at the next annual fish run or waterfowl migration. We also find that many hunter-gatherers are aware that the cycles of vegetation regeneration following fires take many years to complete, and realize the associated changes in animal populations. In many areas there are reports of intentional burning by hunter-gatherers to improve or select habitats (Lewis 1982). These intentional burnings may involve annual repetitions, or they may occur once every several decades as cycles of forest or grassland regeneration are set in motion with each burn.

The conditions of productive labor therefore provide important opportunities for hunter-gatherers to experience and respond to the connections between current activity and future consequence, which may extend from days to decades ahead. Thus, even in cases where technology and artifice may not involve delayed return on labor inputs, the hunt itself, when conceived as an enduring set of practices that extend over seasons or years, involves both immediate and delayed returns on present labor inputs. If hunter-gatherers, in particular circumstances, give no thought to the morrow, then this fact needs as much explanation as does their frequent planning.

### Neighbors, World Markets, and Time in Anthropological Models

Recent research examining the histories of hunter-gatherer societies and their linkages with neighboring agricultural or pastoral peoples, or with world markets, also is relevant for the assessment of both the immediacy of hunter-gatherers' lives, and the potential for appropriation in hunter-gatherer social relations.

Let me quickly review the ambiguities that have emerged in the accounts of the supposed atemporality of earlier hunters and gatherers. Meillassoux depended heavily on Turnbull's early ethnographic accounts of the Mbuti. This, it has turned out, is problematic because in later ethnographies it has been found that Mbuti institutions have not only been shaped by their relationships to neighboring agricultural people, but by the rapid changes brought by European colonization (Bahuchet and Guillaume 1982).

This has important implications for Meillassoux's models. The immediacy of the political tactics of the Mbuti to a rapidly changing colonial context implies a longer-term strategy: resistance. That is, not only is the relevance of Mbuti short-term decision making to general hunter-gatherer society in doubt because it is a strategy adopted in relation to neighbors and colonization, but we must also question their supposed indifference to longer-term considerations. Thus, the simple fact of immediate response needs to be interpreted carefully, as it may conceal longer-term strategizing.

The reading of both time and appropriation are also problems in other contexts where the expansion of the world market is implicated. Sahlins depends most heavily for evidence of hunters' lack of thought for the morrow on LeJeune's extended account of his sojourn among the Montagnais from Tadoussac during the winter of 1633–1634. He is aware of the difficulties in constructing hunter-gatherer economies and societies from the ethnohistorical and ethnographic records, and he comments on these at the beginning and end of his essay. Sahlins (1972: 8–9) notes, for example, that even explorer and missionary accounts may be speaking of "afflicted economies" (referring to Service 1962), and he notes that the eastern Canadian hunters were committed to the fur trade in the early seventeenth century according to the *Jesuit Relations*.

Nevertheless, one can question his use of LeJeune as a source on Algonquian culture as it might have been before significant contact with Europeans. As I have reviewed in a recent paper (Feit [under revision]), Eleanor Leacock (1954: 10, 1969: 1) who also cited LeJeune's account extensively, noted that fur trading with eastern Algonquians actually began by the early 1500s, and specialized trading ships were frequenting the east coast of North America by the middle of the sixteenth century. Trading had begun at Tadoussac by 1550, and it became the main summer trading center for the St. Lawrence Valley from about 1580 to 1608 (Biggar 1965 [1901]: 23, 27, 29, 32; Trigger 1976, vol. 1: 210).

Given the still prevailing anthropological images of hunter-gatherer temporality and change, the seventy-five years of seasonal contact with the fur traders prior to LeJeune's account may seem unlikely to have fundamentally transformed Montagnais conceptions or behavior patterns. But I believe that here we are judging plausibility based on models that have convinced us that there are distinct temporal dimensions of change in hunter-gath-

erer societies. For who would argue that seventy-five years after
direct intermittent trade with Europeans, there were not important changes among New Guinea highland peoples, or among the
seventeenth century Iroquois?

As it turns out, there is clear evidence that, by the 1630s, the
Tadoussac Montagnais had experienced a major displacement of
native goods with trade goods, and that they had become middlemen in the fur trade, and were no longer just subsistence
hunters or fur producers.[4] It is reported by Trigger (1976) and Bailey (1937) that the Montagnais middlemen were defending access
to the harbor of Tadoussac against other bands, that they were the
center of a trade network extending some hundreds of miles into
the interior, that they had formed alliances with other Montagnais and Algonquian groups (with whom they were trying to
drive the Iroquois out of the St. Lawrence Valley), and that they
could muster over a thousand people to Tadoussac for Champlain's visit in the spring of 1603. Trigger (1976, vol. 1: 235) argues
that the hardships and starving condition of the Indians witnessed by Champlain upriver at Quebec in 1608 was likely the
result of the disruption of traditional subsistence patterns.

This evidence of shifts from subsistence production to trade middlemen, of extended market trade alliance formation, of trade motivated warfare, and of appropriating and limiting accessibility to
trading sites, does not suggest that LeJeune was residing with a society comprised solely of the highly fluid hunting bands with unre-
stricted access to resources that have been assumed to be the subjects
of his observations. Nor does it suggest that these were people who
lacked foresight, planning, long-term strategies, or even cunning.

I suggest that the initial failure of some anthropologists to see
the changes brought about by early contact is due in part to the
extra-long time horizon, and the presumed slow changes we associate with hunter-gatherers. Thus anthropological perceptions of
hunter-gatherers have been shaped by a presumed long period of
slow change in hunting societies, just as they have been shaped by
the presumed synchronicity of hunter-gatherer objectives.

While these may seem like contradictory views, they are actually complementary in important ways. Both the assumption of
very slow change and the assumption of the immediacy of action

4. A fuller account of these data is developed in Feit [under revision]. See also
Feit (1991).

construct hunter-gatherers who are outside of time, for they are simultaneously caught in the momentary present without foresight, and they are relatively unchanging.

## Hunters' Views of Social Relations and Differentiation

What, then, are hunters' views? I cannot generalize about what hunter-gatherers think with respect to their temporality and social distinctiveness, but I can offer one example with some general implications for questions of social relations and forms of lasting mutual dependencies.

Waswanipi Cree Indian hunters in subarctic Quebec have a profound awareness that they do not control the morrow's harvest, but this is closely linked to the view that what they do today will nevertheless significantly affect that harvest. These two views may be common among circumpolar hunters, although Waswanipi constructions of the issues are certainly distinctive.

The Waswanipi express this dual relationship through the linking of the concepts of reciprocity[5] and knowledge to future time. This structural connection is embedded for the Waswanipi in the continuity, change, and differentiation of social relationships. I will set out the structural and processual frameworks sequentially in this summary account.[6]

It is widely said by Waswanipi that what they catch is a "gift"; animals are *chimiikonow* or *chashimikonow* ("it is being given to us" or "it is being given to us to eat"). What these statements emphasize is that the killing of animals by humans is not solely the result of the knowledge, will, or action of human persons. Calling animals "gifts" places the emphasis on the opposite pole. Hunting is not in this view solely an application of human labor to passive resources. Animals are spoken of as being "like persons." When questioned about who gives the gift, Waswanipi hunters, who now are all Christians, respond with either "God," or the category names of various spirit beings, or they say the animals give themselves.

But the gift implies obligation and reciprocity. "When we have food, and we are living with others, we give them half our food, and it seems we find more to replace it." A series of proverbs

5. On the pervasive concept of reciprocity among Cree see Scott (1989).
6. Much of the material in this section is drawn from previously published ethnographic papers, especially Feit (1986). It dates to an ethnographic present covering the period from 1968 to about 1985.

emphasizes how one must give food to others in order to receive more gifts from spirits and animals. The same reciprocity is found in injunctions not to kill too much, and to kill only what is given. A piece of the meat is burned in the stove each day, and this offering is thereby given back up the stove pipe to the wind and animal spirits as a sign of respect, and to "tell" them to give more animals in the future.

Mary Black (1977) has suggested that the Ojibwa term usually glossed as "living beings" would be better glossed as "powerful beings," and a cognate terminology is used at Waswanipi. God is said to be all powerful, and the boss, or leader, of all things. Human beings receive power from spirits, and differ from each other as power increases with age and with the care and attention individuals give to interpreting and cultivating knowledge. Power is linked to status, hunting leadership, and to the stewardship of hunting territories.

When asked to explain the power of God, the most common statement is that what God thinks, happens. When asked to explain their own power, hunters' most common statement is that they sometimes know what will happen, that what they think sometimes comes true. In hunting, when the things a hunter thinks about actually come to be in the future, he is said to have *miiyopayiw*, or "good luck." And when they do not come to be, he has *matsiipaio*, or "bad luck." Luck or power is thus not a matter of chance, but of an ebb and flow of connections between human lives and a personalized universe, and many proverbial statements attest to this perception, and to the danger of too much luck or power. This is said to be "God's way."

Power is most often manifested in *niikanchischeyihtan*, literally "future knowledge." Forms of knowledge of the future are actively sought in dreams, conjuring, scapulamancy, divination, and various other "traditional" practices that have their roots, if not their present forms, in pre-Christian Cree practices.

We typically think of power as the ability to control others or the world. For the Cree, power involves less control and more a quest, an openness to truth or knowledge that comes to be in the world. Future knowledge is not the passive acquisition of knowledge, it is described as "looking to find what one knows," much as hunting involves looking for signs that game are willing to give themselves. Power is a coincidence between the knowledge a person has and a future configuration in the world. The coming to be of that configuration is anticipated in knowledge, and created by the diverse powerful beings in the world; and humans can participate in it. The model, then, is that humans do not ultimately control life, but intimately and respectfully link their thought and action to those other powerful beings who create the conjunctures of life.

Humans who try to actualize understandings in social praxis sometimes integrate their thoughts and actions with other beings in such a way that they participate in the power of the becoming of the world. Hunting is a participation in power. In this sense, human life is itself a process of participating in ongoing power, by which the world comes into being through time, and the essence of hunting (as that of life) is the experience of linking present anticipation and future events.

One of the processual dimensions of this system of meaning and practice is thus in the organizing and interpreting of hunting itself. Another processual dimension, however, lies in the quest for social reputation and in intergenerational socialization and social relations.

Elder hunters often tell stories of their important hunting experiences, stories with themes such as killing animals everyone knew were there but could not find; or sending others out with instructions on where to look, and the success of those they advised; or the time they made a big catch and broke a period of hardship or hunger for many people.

These stories have a self-aggrandizing dimension quite out of keeping with aspects of the most common Waswanipi model of the hunter, outlined above. Yet, they are stories consistent with the outline in other respects, for they are stories about the actualization of power – personal, social, and spiritual. And they are explicit demonstrations of the contributions of elders to the hunt, and of their claim to respect.

Most young Waswanipi men learn these stories not just as moving personal tales, but as part of their educational process as hunters. Both the stories and the models of reciprocity and power outlined above are communicated by elders in the context of showing the teenagers how to be effective hunters. Young men sometimes comment that they have better hunts when they live with an elder hunter. And they are frequently concerned with learning hunting well and developing good reputations, which are bestowed by their elders.

In the contemporary historical context, the stories are explicitly mobilized by the elders in opposition to the assumptions and learning the young men bring with them to the bush, after having spent varying durations in the public school system. Comments by those young men who take up hunting as their primary activity tend to confirm that the views of the elders contrast sharply with what they have learned in school. The presentation of animals and natural occurrences as social beings, the emphasis on harvests as gifts to be reciprocated with spirits and kin, and the assertion that power is knowing the future all contradict school learning.

The difference is encapsulated in what I take to be an intended contrast between Waswanipi usage of the terms "good luck" and "bad luck" as expressions of the cycles of power, and the school taught notion of "luck" as unexplainable chance occurrence. Knowledge derived from the elders is central to the young hunters' efforts to make sense of their experiences in the bush, where "good luck" and "bad luck" are demonstrated and explained by elders in convincing ways. The elders try to construct for the young hunters a world that the latter's schooling neither taught them to expect, nor is capable of explaining.

The process of passing on the hunting culture and practice to succeeding generations thus not only regenerates the hunt, it reproduces the social system of relations, including the social differentiations that both hierarchically separate and link generations. The temporally binding image of power, linking present to future, is central to this process, for it is through learning the ways of power that young men become respected hunters. For Waswanipi hunters, it is a common conception that the hunt is a lifelong quest for knowledge and power, an enduring pursuit.

### Conclusion: Social Differentiation and the Distinctiveness of Hunter-Gatherers

The Waswanipi therefore remind us of an essential social temporality, that hunting as experienced events and as practical activity is embedded in recreation across generations of social relations. Is the Waswanipi case relevant to other hunter-gatherers, and to the period before Christianity or exchange with the world market? There can be no definitive answer, but the problems of social "reproduction" exist throughout social history, although not in identical forms, and there are grounds for considering specific features of the Waswanipi data in a more general perspective.

It is clear that the Waswanipi are not reflecting just post-fur trade, post-missionization or post-schooling values, although each of these has had its impacts. Daily practices of social reciprocity and egalitarianism do not have roots in market exchanges or formal schools. Daily pursuit of power does not have roots in Christianity. Nevertheless, extrapolation is treacherous, for these values have been shaped and reshaped as responses to such exchanges. Some suggestions are appropriate here.

Emphasis on reciprocity is widely reported among living hunter-gatherers. And it is clear that the profound concern with the coming to be of the future, as reflected in practices such as dream seeking and interpretation, shamanistic practices, conjuring, and divination have deep historical roots and are widely reported among contemporary and earlier hunting-gathering peoples. However, the social distribution of such practices is not typically uniform across generations. There are therefore prima facie grounds for considering the implications of the Waswanipi findings in broader historical and geographical contexts, subject to further analyses.

In general, the hunt is in some respects short, but the quests of which it is a part may be enduring. And it is in that endurance, as an experience, and as a construction of the world by socially located elders who actively construct authoritative meanings, that power is displayed, socialization occurs, and unequal social relationships of consequence may be actualized. Such relationships create and make public claims and rights to resources and/or to knowledge, and they create real social dependencies between individuals and generations.

Ingold, it seems to me, is wrong, at least for the kind of cases I have cited here, to assert that the distinctive feature of hunter-gatherers is that social relations have the character solely of immediacy, in the sense that people are not dependent on specific others for access to basic requirements. Social relations themselves are reproduced through time via the same processes by which the knowledge and practice of hunting are reproduced. These processes depend on specific linkages and dependencies that endure in the form of intergenerational transmission of knowledge, and therefore differentiation. Ingold has viewed hunters through a temporally shallow horizon that isolates production from knowledge, and social relations from full social reproduction, including primary and secondary socialization.

In conclusion, I would suggest that the link between production on the land, the transmission of knowledge, and the reproduction of social formations among hunters-gatherers may not universally distinguish hunter-gatherers from small-scale agricultural or pastoral societies. We have yet to define a rubicon with social consequence and substance that can systematically differentiate these societies.

## Epilogue – The Mirror of Distinctiveness

Returning to the all too frequent attempts to fit hunter-gatherers into the long human past or the short-term present, there is an irony. Anthropological constructions of hunter-gatherers are implicitly and in substantial terms disempowering, for the anthropological models deny the planning and the everyday processes of change that are essential to both effective intentional action and to the human role in historical process. In short, we construct hunters who have a past and a momentary present, but who lack a real future, one with possibilities they might set about constructing as social actors. The political implications of such anthropological models are important, whether intended or not.

But there is a further irony, because these views are mirrored by the reflections of some hunters, who express similar bewilderment at the temporal frameworks that limit the vision of some of the people of European descent with whom they deal.

The Waswanipi Cree hunters are constantly amazed at the short-term view taken by Canadian resource exploitation projects-forestry, mining, and hydroelectric developments – which then cause long-term or permanent environmental degradation for what appear to the Cree to be short-term benefits. In many cases the Cree are convinced that the destruction can never be reversed. Yet they see companies come and go, mines open and close. Hydroelectric dams may last longer, but plans and operations are constantly changing. The impact of each operation consistently exposes the lie in the companies' claims that the impact is short term and well contained. The Cree live with the consequences.

The Cree hunters are often confounded at the kind of society and beliefs that can generate what they consider to be irresponsible behavior, for they know that they have lived on these lands since times before the present era. The stewards of the hunting territories emphasize that the land was inherited from their fathers and grandfathers, and will be passed on to their children and their grandchildren. Their time horizon thus stretches over at least a century as they consider their present. Cree hunters occasionally say they have trouble understanding how Euro-Canadians can ignore the past and the future generations when they destroy the land.

The issues are reflected in a quote from an elder Waswanipi hunter, the late Jacob Happyjack (1983), who was universally respected in the community.[7] Speaking through an interpreter who quotes Jacob in the third person, he answered a question about what he expected in the future:

He's been hunting for fifty years, and he has been keeping track of his land, and he finally realizes how much damage the white man has been doing to his land. He thinks all the damage that has been done is irreversible, the land will never be the same as it's been before.

It's gonna be really different, won't be able to survive as good as before. Like when he was hunting he used to live alone in the bush, and they would have their children alone in the bush, and when the bush was good that's how they managed to survive. Since he was born he has never had a job and he has never worked, and he has still raised his sons and daughters to be full grown from the bush. Now that the land has been ruined, he doesn't think any of his sons could raise their families like he did when the land was still good.

What he did before on the land, he wasn't thinking about himself but about the younger generation – so they could survive as he did. What he learned from the bush, he didn't learn from his father; he taught himself in the bush. When he was growing up for [in] his family, many times he used to think about that, and [he] thought about times he didn't see his dad. Sometimes when he was out hunting he just stood there and thought about his dad, and he used to cry. Then he finally got better and better at hunting. Then he finally [learned(?)].

When he looked at tracks of other people and he knew they didn't have no food, he went to their camp and it was true they didn't have no food. And he went to his camp to get a toboggan load of food and he took it to them. He can't do that [now], he's too old and he's getting sick. Sometimes when he looks at his son he wishes his son could do the same thing he did in his younger days.

7. He was nevertheless somewhat distinctive in the community because, having lost his father when he was young, he could claim to have painfully taught himself more about how to hunt than most men of his generation.

# 20

# The Future of Hunter-Gatherer Research

*Ernest S. Burch, Jr.*

Hunter-gatherer research has enjoyed a tremendous expansion in interest and involvement among anthropologists over the past thirty years. However, as we approach the end of the century, the field faces a major crisis. This paper reviews the practical, methodological and conceptual dimensions of this crisis and discusses the implications of the trends in each. Research on foraging societies is likely to be very different in the next quarter century than it was in the last, and hunter-gatherer studies may cease to exist as a distinct specialty within sociocultural anthropology.[1]

---

The history of every scientific field is characterized by cycles, each of which has periods of growth, crisis, and renewal (Kuhn 1970). The field of hunter-gatherer studies has experienced extraordinary growth since the conferences that spawned it a quarter of a century ago. Now, however, there is reason to believe that it is approaching a time of crisis. As is true in science generally, this crisis is in many respects a consequence of the enormous increase in knowledge that occurred during its period of growth. In contrast to the usual situation in the more advanced sciences, however, where critical periods typically involve a growing disjunction between theory and evidence, the crisis in hunter-gatherer studies is multidimensional. Richard Lee's (1992) recent discussion of this crisis dealt primarily with its philosophical aspects. In the present paper, I discuss its practical, methodological, and conceptual aspects. Each of these problem areas is distinct and needs to be discussed separately.

1. I thank Bernard Arcand, Harvey A. Feit, Richard B. Lee, Marion J. Levy, Jr., Carmel Schrire, Eric A. Smith, and Edwin S. Wilmsen for comments on an earlier version of this paper. All of the views expressed here are, of course, my own.

## Practical Problems

The practical problems in hunter-gatherer research are due to the fact that there are few if any societies of foragers left in the world that have not been profoundly affected by, and to some extent integrated into, much larger-scale systems (see Peterson 1991a, 1991b). In short, the very subject matter of our investigations is disappearing. This problem has been with us since the beginning, but each year it becomes more acute than it was previously.

One of the most important consequences of the disappearance of viable, autonomous foraging societies is that, in most cases, it is difficult, if not impossible, to replicate earlier research. Lee (1992: 38) commented on this problem:

> [F]ieldworkers who arrive in the 1980s and 1990s and observe [the current] appalling conditions [in Botswana] find it unbelievable that 30, 20, or even 10 years earlier, observers could have found societies with [traditional] band structure, kinship, and subsistence patterns still functioning. Instead of reflecting on the magnitude of the changes in the 10- or 20- year period, these revisionists immediately assume that the earlier studies were wrong and they go on to blithely project the contemporary patterns . . . back into the past.

In my judgment this is an enormous problem in contemporary hunter-gatherer research, and it is likely to get worse in the future. I also think it is worth more emphasis than Lee gave it.[2]

The problem of replicability is clearly illustrated by my own experience. During the winter of 1969-1970 I made a major effort to reconstruct the nineteenth-century social history of northern and northwestern Alaska, an area of approximately 170,000 square miles occupied primarily by Iñupiat Eskimos. I was thrilled to find that, of the roughly eleven thousand Iñupiat living in the region at the time, perhaps two hundred could still speak knowledgeably about various aspects of life during their grand-parents' and great-grandparents' times. Of those, perhaps thirty commanded reasonably authoritative (and mutually consistent) information on early and mid-nineteenth century social bound-aries, intersocietal relations, population movements, historical changes, and other phenomena in which I was interested. I had the privilege of working with about half of the larger group, and

2. For similarly brief but telling comments on the rate of change in foraging soci-eties and on the implications of this change for research, see C. Berndt (1981: 170-71) and Silberbauer (1991: 97, 98). For a debate on the subject, see Birdsell (1970).

two-thirds of the experts. Indeed, it was the latter who really taught me how to do historical research (Burch 1991).

By 1990, one generation later, almost everyone in the earlier pool of informants was either dead or else too old to be of help, and all of the experts were gone. Their descendants knew little or nothing about the subjects on which their own parents and grand-parents had been so informative, and most of them found my questions to be incomprehensible. In short, by 1990 I could not replicate even my own research of twenty years before. How, then, is a graduate student just beginning work in northern Alaska to know whether or not what I have written has any basis in empiri-cal fact? Where my findings disagree with those of other authors, how is anyone to determine who is correct? These problems, of course, pervade social scientific research, but they are much more acute for students of small-scale societies than for anyone else.

Fortunately for me, there is enough information in the records of early nineteenth-century European explorers of northern Alas-ka to corroborate at least the basic outlines of the picture present-ed to me by Iñupiat elders in 1970. Most other parts of the world inhabited in recent decades by foraging societies are not so well endowed with useful early historic sources. It seems to me that the only recourse for future investigators in those areas, and to a large extent even in northern Alaska, is anthropologically orient-ed but otherwise standard historiographic research, in which the original field notes of earlier field investigators serve as primary sources.[3] In order for this to be possible, these notes have to be accessible to future generations of researchers, and also to the descendants of the people with whom they are concerned. In order for them to be accessible they must be donated to an archive where they can be properly curated, on the one hand, and made available to interested parties, on the other.[4]

3. It will, of course, be possible for investigators to doctor their field notes. Fab-ricated "original" documents are a common concern in historiography, and they sometimes appear in the natural sciences as well. They are unlikely to be any worse in anthropology than in any other field. One way to make the authenticity of one's own notes more convincing to future scholars is to keep the originals on file after they have been transcribed in more elegant fashion.

4. I was pleased to note that the participants in a recent Wenner-Gren sympo-sium on preserving anthropological records also came to this conclusion (*Anthro-pology Newsletter* 1992: 8; Silverman [1993]). As this volume goes to press (in early 1994), a number of anthropological associations around the world are considering whether or not to pass resolutions embodying the conclusions of this symposium.

The disposition of field notes should not be left to the discretion of heirs. There is an unfortunate tendency among heirs to think that anthropological field notes can be sold for vast sums of money. That is virtually never the case. While waiting for this illusory windfall to come about, the notes (including photographs, maps, tapes, etc.) may not be properly stored, and they certainly will not be made accessible to others. Eventually the heirs may give up in disgust and throw them out, or they might donate them to an archive many years later or they might not do anything but have them included in their own estate. The only satisfactory solution is for the author to bequeath them to an appropriate archive, and to do so immediately.[5]

These considerations suggest that hunter-gatherer research may soon become historically oriented rather than field oriented. But before I continue with this topic, there is another one that should be mentioned, namely, "readback."

Readback is a term used by some in Alaska to refer to the phenomenon of native informants giving anthropologists information on their ancestors' way of life that they themselves acquired from reading anthropological reports and publications.[6] In other words, they are "reading back" the results of previous anthropological research, rather than sharing knowledge acquired directly from elders among their own people. Reading may actually be helpful if it stimulates young people to question their elders about customs no longer practiced, and thus become independently informed. More often, however, it results in anthropologists essentially talking to each other (or even to themselves) through the intermediary and filter of a native informant. Newcomers to an area where people are literate must pay particular attention to this possibility. One may suspect that the problem exists when (literate) teenagers and young adults seem to know more about the old ways than their (nonliterate) elders do.

Returning to the question of the temporal orientation of hunter-gatherer research, I believe it is fair to say that the extremely rapid change that has characterized the few remaining

5. Copyright to the notes should also be part of the bequest, since the transfer of the physical material does not convey ownership of the copyright. Otherwise, researchers will have to track down all of the heirs of the deceased anthropologist and get written releases from them prior to any extensive use of unpublished material. The directors of any established archive may be expected to use good judgment regarding the use of the material under their care.

6. I am grateful to Edwin S. Hall, Jr., for introducing me to the concept of readback.

foraging societies over the past twenty-five years does indeed mean that it will become primarily retrospective in nature. I agree with Eric Smith (1991b: 3) that foraging as an activity is still amenable to fruitful study now, and it probably will be for many years to come. But the hunting involved will be carried out by marginal members of large-scale social systems, rather than by core members of small-scale systems. Other elements of forager life may persist as well, but hunter-gatherer ways of life as coherent systems are no longer amenable to direct observation, except in very few cases.

There are at least two ways for scholars to deal with this problem. One way is to shift the primary research procedure from participant-observation in an ongoing system to the reconstruction of a previously existing one. To some extent, this is possible through ethnographic research (Burch 1988b; Henige 1982), but even the best reconstruction cannot yield the kind of observational details and nonmaterial nuances that gave the studies of the Basarwa carried out in the 1960s, for example, their enduring value.[7] As time passes and even more changes occur, archival and archaeological research will steadily replace ethnographic fieldwork as the major means of testing theories about the structure of hunter-gatherer societies.

A sign that the trend is already underway is the growing involvement of prehistorians (e.g., Bettinger 1987, 1991; Davis and Reeves, eds. 1990; Jochim 1976; Price and Brown, eds. 1985; Williams 1974) in systematic research on theoretical questions relating to foraging societies. In addition, many archaeological journals are at least as likely to publish papers dealing with theoretical questions about foraging societies as more ethnographically oriented journals.

Another way for scholars to deal with the dramatic changes occurring among contemporary hunting-gathering peoples is to shift the focus of their attention from the structure of such societies to social change. In studies with this orientation, theoretical interest inevitably shifts away from the ultimate objective of

---

7. Whatever the outcome of the revisionist debate regarding evolutionary questions, the basic ethnographic data published by Richard Lee (e.g., 1979, 1984) and his colleagues (e.g., Lee and DeVore, eds. 1976), George Silberbauer (1981) and Jiro Tanaka (1980), will have a permanent place in the anthropological literature. The same can be said about all of the good field studies that were carried out during the early modern period of hunter-gatherer research.

developing generalizations about foraging societies to formulating theories about social change. Often the shift is even greater: from theoretical concerns of any kind to real world problems of applied research. It is in this area, it seems to me, that the future of ethnographic fieldwork among hunter-gatherers lies.

The extent to which research on the structure of foraging societies has been replaced by a concern with the survival problems of contemporary hunter-gatherers has been dramatically demonstrated at the International Conferences on Hunting and Gathering Societies (CHAGS). Many of the papers included in the published collections of papers from CHAGS-4 (Ingold, Riches, and Woodburn, eds. 1988a, 1988b) are oriented to this problem area, and those from CHAGS-1 (Leacock and Lee, eds. 1982), CHAGS-3 (Schrire, ed. 1984; Wilmsen, ed. 1989) and one of the volumes from CHAGS-5 (Altman, ed. 1989) focus on this issue. At CHAGS-6, by my count, some 55 percent of the papers dealt with social change; if the papers based primarily on archaeological data are excluded, the proportion rises to nearly 70 percent. One must conclude from these figures that social change and practical problems already have become the dominant foci in studies of contemporary hunter-gatherers.

## The Methodological Problem

The second major problem confronting hunter-gatherer studies is methodological: to what extent can a general model of foraging societies be developed on the basis of research on recent or contemporary foragers? The basic answer to that question is very simple: a model can be developed on the basis of any data, or even through pure intuition. The critical issue is not the basis on which a model is developed, but the extent to which it increases our understanding of the relevant phenomena in an empirically supportable way.

The fundamental principles here are as follows: if a measurably distinct class of societies – e.g., foraging societies – can be delineated, and if an empirically testable model of that class can be developed, then the model should apply to all members of that class, regardless of when they existed in time (cf. Schrire 1980; Woodburn 1980). The same would be true of any other class of societies – industrialized, agrarian, and state. To this effect, Lewis Binford was recently quoted by Bower (1989: 264): "It is obvious that there are no pristine hunter-gatherers [living today], but to say you cannot generalize in any way to the past because modern behavior is unique is, in essence, an attack on science." I agree.

A model that purports to be a truly general representation of the structure of gatherer-hunter societies should be tested against evidence from simple, intermediate, and complex foraging societies, both historic and prehistoric. To my knowledge, no model encompassing this range has ever been produced. Most of the theoretical work has been at the simple end of the continuum, particularly in the immediate-return category. At this level examples abound.[8] Whether or not any of these models holds up against data from the Upper Paleolithic era or some other early time period remains an open question.

The extent to which one may extrapolate from historic foraging societies to ancient ones is one of the main issues in the current revisionist debate (see Chapter 1, this volume). On one side, the generalists (Richard Lee in particular [e.g., 1979: 432]), hold that a general model of the structure of foraging societies can be developed, at least in principle.[9] To the extent that it is developed, it should apply equally to both ancient and contemporary systems of foragers. On the other side, the historical particularists (Headland and Reid 1989; Schrire 1980; Wilmsen 1983, 1989a, 1989b; Wilmsen and Denbow 1990) argue that contemporary foraging peoples in general, and the Basarwa in particular, have long histories during which all or most of them have been in direct or indirect contact with pastoralists or agriculturalists of various kinds.[10] These contacts have significantly affected the way they operate, they say, and thus cannot be equated in any way with societies that were in existence several millennia ago.

Unfortunately, most of the people engaged in this debate lack the comparative macrosociological perspective (Fallers 1968: 564)

8. The focus here is on models of the structure of entire societies. Examples include Birdsell (1958, 1968, 1970, 1973), Ingold (1980, 1987, 1988), Jochim (1976), Lee (1968, 1976, 1979, 1981a, 1981b, 1984, 1988, 1990), Sahlins (1968b, 1972), Service (1962, 1975, 1979), Testart (1982), Williams (1974), and Woodburn (1968a, 1972, 1979, 1982; Barnard and Woodburn 1988). Models of aspects of societies, such as foraging strategy, camp distribution, and local group size, are too numerous to mention here.

9. This is the general issue in the debate. Two more specific ones, which are too detailed to discuss here, are the extent to which the specific model based on the Basarwa actually applies to the Paleolithic era, and the extent to which it has been claimed by its developers to apply to the Paleolithic era.

10. The label "historical particularism" is taken from Lewin (1988: 1148).

that is most relevant here. Insofar as the argument concerns entire societies, the basic issues are the following: (1) Is the specific unit under study a separate society or a subsystem of some other society? (2) If it is a separate society, does it meet the defining criteria of the class of foraging societies? If the system in question is a society, and if it meets the defining criteria of the foraging type, then one may legitimately use data on that system in critiquing or building general models of hunter-gatherer societies – regardless of how long the society in question has been in contact with agriculturalists, and regardless of whether it had an agrarian subsistence base itself at some earlier point in time.[11] If either criterion is not met, however, then the data cannot be used in that way. But in order to use this approach, one must employ the concept of society in a serious way.

"Society" is one of the most fundamental and widely used concepts in the social sciences, yet it is probably employed with less consistency than any other. Ingold (in Solway and Lee 1990: 131) recently maintained that the concept should not be applied to foragers at all because "the very notion of 'society' locks the people into an externally imposed frame that is structured by relations of domination and subordination." After having spent three decades studying more than thirty early historic Eskimo societies (Burch 1980, 1986) that were not dominated by or subordinate to anyone, I find this an untenable assertion.

Of course much depends on how one defines society. Ingold did not indicate the definition that guided his remarks. The definition that has proven useful to me was formulated by Marion J. Levy, Jr. (1952: 113), quoted here from a later work (1966: 20–21):

> A society is a system of social action: (1) that involves a plurality of interacting individuals whose actions are [carried out] in terms of the system concerned and who are recruited at least in part by their own sexual reproduction, (2) that constitutes a set of social structures such that action in terms of them is at least in theory capable of self-sufficiency for the maintenance of the plurality of individuals involved, and (3) that is capable of existing long enough for the production of stable adult members of the system of action from the infants of the members.

11. If enough foraging societies could be identified so that there would be samples of those not in contact with agrarian societies and with no history of agrarian production, those in contact with agrarian societies, and those that had an agrarian economy at some previous time – it would be interesting to see if there were systematic differences among them. If there are, then the historical particularist position would gain in credence.

A society is essentially what most of us think of as a country, in the modern world; with hunter-gatherers and other small-scale societies, the referent is often less apparent, especially to outsiders such as anthropologists.

It is not appropriate here to discuss all of the implications of this definition, but a few are so frequently distorted or misunderstood (e.g., by Mayhew 1968) that some comments are in order. First, since a society is defined as a type of system, like every kind of system, it has a boundary, a singular discontinuity between it and its social and material environments (Sim and Smallen 1972: 2). Just how a society's boundary is manifested is not specified or implied by the definition, and hence may vary from one case to another. The definition does not state or even imply that a society is a closed system, which would be nonsense; if there is such a thing as a closed system, it is the universe as a whole. However, it does imply that if a given social system is a society, then its members will have the means of dealing sufficiently effectively with external phenomena (e.g., members of other societies, the nonhuman environment) to persist long enough for infants to become stable adults. The length of the maturation period will vary from one case to another, but presumably it will be at least eighteen years in the case of immediate-return hunter-gatherers, and twice that (or more) in the case of highly modernized societies.

Second, the definition does not state or imply that a society is self-sufficient for any commodity. However, it clearly implies that if a given social system is a society, its members will have available a means of acquiring from elsewhere the commodities they need that they cannot produce in sufficient quantities themselves for the system to persist for the specified time period.

Third, the stipulation about "stable adults" does not indicate a set of psychological superpersons or optimally adapted individuals of some kind. It merely requires a set of individuals who are capable of filling the various roles differentiated in the system successfully enough for the system to persist for the length of time stipulated by the definition.

Finally, it is appropriate to note that, unlike most definitions of society, this one does not contain a provision for a discrete territory. Thus, conceivably, it would be possible to have a society without any territory at all, societies with interlocking territories, or a society whose territory is enclosed within that of a larger system.

If Gypsies are or were members of one or more distinct societies, they would be examples of the first possibility. Australian Aborigine societies, with widely scattered sacred sites, might be an example of the second possibility. And most historically documented hunter-gatherer societies definitely were examples of the third possibility. In any event, given this definition, whether or not a society is associated with a discrete territory is a matter of empirical observation, not of definition.

The major weaknesses of Levy's definition derive from measurement problems. How does one definitively determine, for example, whether a given system of action is "at least in theory capable of self-sufficiency for the maintenance" of a set of individuals, or whether a system is "capable of existing long enough" to produce stable adults? These problems are particularly acute at opposite ends of the complexity continuum: with highly modernized societies, which are highly interdependent, and with very small-scale societies (such as most hunter-gatherer societies), where even extended families are highly self-sufficient.

Many of my students and colleagues have told me that the measurement problems are fatal to this definition. My response is to challenge them to demonstrate either that we do not need a concept of "society" (by whatever name) in the social sciences, or to come up with a more fruitful definition themselves. So far they have done neither. If measurement difficulties are considered fatal to a concept in the social sciences, then we must get rid of many others as well: power, responsibility, fear, affection, role, love, belief, centralization, solidarity, cognition, complexity – the list goes on and on. But no one is suggesting that we discard these concepts for the very good reason that they are important for an understanding of human affairs.

As a final comment on this particular issue, I wish to point out that if physicists had discarded theoretically significant concepts simply because their referents were difficult to measure, the most highly advanced of all sciences would still be back in the stone age. When physicists are confronted with a measurement problem relating to a theoretically significant issue, they get to work and try to devise ways to solve the problem. Sometimes it takes decades of strenuous effort by some of the best minds in the business. Social scientists should have the same attitude.

One of the major virtues of Levy's definition is its usefulness in determining the level of generalization on which comparisons and theoretical statements can be made. Given his definition, all social systems are either (1) societies (e.g., the United States, Japan), (2) subsystems of societies (e.g., the U.S. Congress, the John Doe family), or (3) systems interrelating the members of two or more societies (e.g., the United Nations, CHAGS-6) (cf. Etzioni 1970: 71). This is an issue that few writers have confronted, yet it is clear that if we are ever to speak about such things as band societies and industrialized societies, then we must have either a definition of society that encompasses both, or some other concept that serves exactly the same purpose. Theoretical work will not make much progress if such a fundamental term is held to mean one thing in one context and something quite different in another.

The society issue fits into the context of the revisionist debate in the following way. If it can be shown that a given population of historic foragers – the Dobe !Kung of the early 1960s, for example – constituted the membership of a distinct society (as opposed to a subsystem of a larger society), then information about it is appropriate for use in formulating or testing theories about the structure of any and all hunter-gatherer societies, past, present, or future.[12] If, however, they already had been incorporated into a larger system, then their appropriateness becomes problematic. I suspect that when Lee, Marshall, Silberbauer, and Tanaka did their work among the Basarwa in the 1950s and 1960s, at least some indigenous societies were still in operation. By the time the revisionists got there, just a few years later, that was no longer the case. It does not take very long for the transition to be made.[13]

I predict that, unless and until this issue is sorted out, both in general and in many specific empirical cases, hunter-gatherer studies will not contribute much in the way of general theory to social science as a whole.

---

12. Recently Binford (1990: 137) maintained that "most of the historically documented [foragers] are irrelevant as analogs for Pleistocene terrestrial hunters." If he is correct about the importance of aquatic resources in the historic period and the lack thereof in the Pleistocene era, he may be right-insofar as direct analogs are concerned. It does not follow that the general structure of forager societies differed between the two periods.

13. See, e.g., Sugawara (1991) and Tanaka (1991). In the case of my own research among the Eskimos of northwestern Alaska and the central Canadian subarctic, most of the societies ceased to exist some 110 and 65 years ago, respectively.

## The Conceptual Problem

The third and final major element in the crisis facing hunter-gatherer studies concerns the very concept of "hunter-gatherer society." The issues here occur at two levels. At the more general level, the question is, does a class of empirical referents for the concept hunter-gatherer society exist? Arcand (1981: 39; 1988) has answered this question in the negative. At the more specific level, the question is, even if a class of empirical referents for the hunter-gatherer society concept can be shown to exist, is there anything distinctive enough about the societies in it for the class to have any analytic utility or theoretical significance? Arcand (1981, 1988) and Hamilton (1982), among others, have also answered this question in the negative. In their general reviews of the state of hunter-gatherer studies, both Barnard (1983) and Myers (1988) have, not surprisingly, regarded these questions as being of fundamental importance: if hunting-gathering societies do not exist, or if there is nothing distinctive about them even if they do exist, then the whole subfield of hunter-gatherer research is based on a mirage.

It seems to me that the question concerning the existence of hunter-gatherer societies, in contradiction to Arcand, must be answered positively. If they do not exist now as distinct societies, surely they did at one time; I have studied nearly three dozen of them myself. But regarding whether foraging societies constitute a class that is distinctive in significant ways from all other types of society, I have to agree with Arcand and Hamilton: they do not.

A few authors have formulated alternative classifications of small-scale societies (see the discussions in Barnard 1983 and Myers 1988), but no one has dealt with the entire range from the simplest to the most complex within the framework of a single scheme. As Arcand (1981: 41) noted, the differences across this range are so great that in *The Hunters*, Elman Service (1979: 3) had to exclude most foraging societies from his purview; the book would have been more accurately titled "band societies." The problem is compounded by the apparent fact that many simple agrarian societies have more in common with foraging societies than they do with other agrarian systems, while just the reverse is true of complex foraging societies.[14]

14. Just why some agrarian societies should be less complex than any foraging societies is an interesting question that needs to be investigated.

It is easy to understand why most anthropologists have had difficulty confronting this issue. We know that foraging societies occurred first in human history. There is also no doubt that the agrarian revolution came much later and that it led to enormous changes in human affairs. Given these facts, it does not take much of a creative leap to conclude that foraging and agrarian societies must somehow be fundamentally different from one another. This view is supported by the Marxist obsession with modes of production, with an obvious division between foraging and agrarian modes (Ingold 1988; Keenan 1977; Lee 1981a, 1990; Meillassoux 1973).

In my judgment, the most definitive division of small-scale societies identified so far is not between foraging and agrarian, but between immediate-return and delayed-return societies, in Woodburn's (1972, 1979, 1982; Barnard and Woodburn 1988) terms, or nonstoring and storing societies in Testart's terms (1982). As Testart (1982: 530) put it,

> Agriculturalists and storing hunter-gatherers together are neatly in opposition to nonstoring hunter-gatherers. The conclusion to be drawn is certainly not the presence of agriculture or its absence which is the relevant factor when dealing with such societies, but rather the presence or absence of an economy with intensive storage as its cornerstone.

Immediate-return or "generalized" hunter-gatherer societies are so unlike all others that, as Birdsell (1973: 338) once noted, it is difficult even for anthropologists who have not personally experienced one to conceive how they can exist; it is almost impossible for nonanthropologists to do so.

Having set off immediate-return societies at the simple end of the range of complexity from all other foraging societies, the next question is what to do with the rest – which includes all other societies in world history. I think that Service (1975: 70) correctly identified the next dividing line when he distinguished between segmental and (by implication) nonsegmental societies. He defined the former as those "composed of equal and similar component groups (normally kin groups like clans or lineages)." Segmental societies thus lack both an office (chief) and a subsystem (council) having a society-wide span of control (or authority); they consist entirely of networks of segments. Nothing is stated or implied about their economic base, so presumably foraging, pastoral, and agricultural economies are all possible within the

· storing segmental sphere. However, it is one thing to assert that this division makes sense, and quite another to demonstrate it – which I do not have the space to do here, and which I have not done elsewhere. This distinction thus must be regarded as being of hypothetical significance until its ramifications are worked out and tested.

Just what label should be used to identify the class of small-scale societies that are not segmental was not specified by Service. The next category included in his scheme (1975: 71 ff.) was chiefdoms, which are societies in which an office associated with a society-wide span of authority is differentiated. This strikes me as a reasonable possibility, although there may be cases in which a council, rather than an office, is the unifying element in the system. Whatever the label, the important point is that even at this level of complexity, both hunter-gatherer and agrarian societies belong to the same class.

One could proceed in this manner right on up the scale of complexity. At some point – certainly once industrialized societies have been reached, but probably well before that –hunter-gatherer societies would eventually drop out of consideration. There is no need for present purposes to pursue the matter further. The basic point has been made already: there is too much variation within the class of hunter-gatherer societies to make it a useful category for theoretical purposes.

### Conclusions

This essay began with an assertion that, despite the enormous recent growth of the field, hunter-gatherer research is approaching a time of crisis. This crisis involves three main elements: (1) the likelihood that much of the subject matter of the field is about to disappear; (2) a profound disagreement about the logic used in extrapolating from field studies to general theory; and (3) the likelihood that the field is based on an unfruitful concept in the first place. Any one of these factors could be enough to destroy a field; the three together may prove to be overwhelming.

Colleagues who reviewed a draft of this paper were appalled at these seemingly negative conclusions. One even expressed the view that they are a repudiation of all of the research that has been done over the past thirty years. In bringing the paper to a close, it is appropriate to address these concerns.

In the first place, I did not use the term "crisis" by accident. Because of the problems outlined above, I feel quite safe in saying that hunter-gatherer research in the next quarter century will be a fundamentally different enterprise than it was in the last. If crisis is too alarming a word, perhaps "threshold" will do, but it does not convey the tension I see growing in the field.

Second, far from repudiating all the work that has been done in the last thirty years, the crisis I have outlined is a tribute to it. Although hunter-gatherer studies have hardly reached the level of theoretical sophistication of the fields discussed in Kuhn's *Structure of Scientific Revolutions* (1970), our crisis, like those that have occurred over the centuries in physics, is the result of our success. We have learned so much in the last three decades that the framework of inquiry and debate has changed fundamentally. We now must rethink the whole enterprise.

# References

Aikens, C. Melvin, and Don Dumond 1986 Convergence and common heritage: Some parallels in the archaeology of Japan and western North America. In *Windows on the Japanese past.* R. Pearson, ed., pp. 163–78. Ann Arbor: University of Michigan, Center for Japanese Studies.

Akimichi, T., et al. 1988 *Small-type coastal whaling in Japan: Report of an international workshop.* Edmonton: Boreal Institute for Northern Studies. (Occasional publication no. 27.)

Allison, M., D. Mendoza, and A. Pezzia 1978 A radiographic approach to childhood illness in pre-Columbian inhabitants of southern Peru. *American Journal of Physical Anthropology* 40:409–415.

Altman, John C. 1984 Hunter-gatherer subsistence production in Arnhem Land: The original affluence hypothesis re-examined. *Mankind* 14(3):179–190.

Altman, John C., ed. 1989 *Emergent inequalities in Aboriginal Australia.* Sydney: University of Sydney. (Oceania monograph no. 38.)

Ames, Kenneth M. 1985 Hierarchies, stress and logistical strategies among hunter-gatherers in northwestern North America. In *Prehistoric hunter-gatherers: The emergence of cultural complexity.* T. Douglas Price and James A. Brown, eds., pp. 155–80. Orlando: Academic Press.

———, 1991 Sedentism: A temporal shift or a transitional change in hunter-gatherer mobility patterns. In *Between bands and states.* Susan A. Greed, ed., pp. 108–34. Carbondale: Southern Illinois University at Carbondale, Center for Archaeological Investigations. (Occasional paper no. 9.)

Amos, Howard 1987 Letter dated 9 January to Ted Stevens, United States Senator. Copy in author's [Kenneth Pratt's] possession.

Amos, Howard, and Hultman Kiokuh 1990 Personal communications to Kenneth Pratt dated April 1, 3, and 5, 1990. Mekoryuk, Alaska.

Anderson, H. Dewey, and Walter C. Eels 1935 *Alaska natives: A survey of their sociological and educational status.* Stanford: Stanford University Press.

Andrews, Elizabeth F. 1989 The *Akulmiut*: Territorial dimensions of a Yup'ik Eskimo society. Ph.D. dis. University of Alaska Fairbanks.

*Anthropology Newsletter* 1992 Preserving anthropological records. *Anthropology Newsletter* [of the American Anthropological Association], special edition, June 1992, p.8.

Antropova, V. V. 1949a Rasselenije Itel'menov v pervoj polovine XVIII veki [Itel'mens' settlement pattern during early eighteenth century]. *Izvestija Vsesojuznogo Geograficheskogo Obshchestva* [Transactions of the All-Union Geographical Society] 81(4):414–419.

———, 1949b Starinnyje Kamchadalskije sani [Old Kamchadalan sledge]. *Sbornik Muzeja Antropoligii i Etnografii* [Essays of the Museum of Anthropology and Ethnography] 10:47–92.

———, 1971 *Kul'tura i byt Korjakov* [Culture and everyday life of the Koriaks]. Leningrad: Nauka.

Arcand, Bernard 1981 The Negritos and the Penan will never be Cuiva. *Folk* 23:37–43.

———, 1988 Il n'y a jamais eu de société de chasseurs-cueilleurs. *Anthropologie et Sociétés* 12(1):39–58.

Arnold, Jeanne E. 1992 Complex hunter-gatherer-fishers of prehistoric California: Chiefs, specialists, and maritime adaptations of the Channel Islands. *American Antiquity* 57(1):60–84.

Arnold, Robert D. 1978 *Alaska native land claims*. Anchorage: The Alaska Native Foundation.

Aro, K. V., and M. P. Shepard 1967 Pacific salmon in Canada. Part IV, Salmon of the north Pacific Ocean: Spawning populations of north Pacific salmon. *International North Pacific Fisheries Commission Bulletin* 23.

Arsen'yev, V. 1925 Gizhiginskij promyslovyj rajon [Gizhiga economic region]. *Ekonomicheskaja Zhizn' Dal'nego Vostoka* [Economic Life of the Far East] 5:17–37.

Ashkenazi, Michael, and Jeanne Jacob 1991 Whale meat as a component of the changing Japanese diet in Hokkaido. Report on file, The Institute of Cetacean Research, Tokyo.

Atwood, M. 1972 *Survival: A thematic guide to Canadian literature*. Toronto: Anansi.

Australia, Bureau of Statistics 1990 *Aboriginal People in the Northern Territory*. Canberra: Australian Government.

Australia, Government of 1976 *Aboriginal Land Rights (Northern Territory) Act.*, Canberra, Australia.

Australia, Northern Territory Government
1978 *Northern Territory Aboriginal Sacred Sites Act*. Northern Territory, Australia.

———, 1989 *Northern Territory Aboriginal Sacred Sites Act*. Northern Territory, Australia.

Baba, Komoa 1942 *Hogei* [Whaling]. Tokyo: Tennensha.

Bahuchet, Serge 1985 *Les pygmees Aka et la forêt Centrafricaine*. Selaf, CNRS, Paris .

———, 1988 Food supply uncertainty among the Aka Pygmies. In *Coping with uncertainty in food supply*. I. deGarine and G. Harrison, eds., pp. 118–149. Oxford: Clarendon Press.

Bahuchet, Serge, and Henri Guillaume 1982 Aka-farmer relations in the northwest Congo Basin. In Eleanor Leacock and Richard B. Lee, eds., *Politics and History in Band Societies*. New York: Cambridge University Press.

Bailey, Alfred G. 1937 *The conflict of European and eastern Algonkian cultures, 1504–1700. A study in Canadian civilization*. New Brunswick: New Brunswick Museum Publications, Monograph Series 2.

Bailey, R. C. 1988 The significance of hypergyny for understanding subsistence behaviour among contemporary hunters and gatherers. In *Diet and Subsistence: Current Archaeological Perspectives. Proceedings of the Nineteenth Annual Chacmool Conference*. Brenda V. Kennedy and Genevieve M. LeMoine, eds. Calgary, Alberta: University of Calgary Archaeological Association.

Bain, Margaret S. [In press] *Crossed wires: The Aboriginal/white encounter*. Dallas: Summer Institute of Linguistics.

Bain, Margaret S., and Barbara J. Sayers 1990 Degrees of abstraction and cross-cultural communication in Australia. Paper presented to the Sixth International Conference on Hunting and Gathering Societies. Fairbanks, Alaska.

Balikci, Asen 1968 The Netsilik Eskimos: Adaptive processes. In *Man the hunter*. Richard B. Lee and Irven DeVore, eds., pp. 78–82. Chicago: Aldine Publishing Company.

Barnard, Alan 1983 Contemporary hunter-gatherers: Current theoretical issues in ecology and social organization. *Annual Review of Anthropology* 12:193–214.

————, 1992 *The Kalahari debate: a bibliographical essay*. Edinburgh: Centre for African Studies, Edinburgh University.

Barnard, Alan, and James Woodburn 1988 Property, power and ideology in hunter-gathering societies: An introduction. In *Hunters and gatherers 2: property, power and ideology*. Tim Ingold, David Riches, and James Woodburn, eds., pp. 4–31. Oxford: Berg Publishers Limited.

Barnes, J. A. 1951 History in a changing society. *Journal of the Rhodes Livingstone Institute* 11:1–9.

Barnicot, N.A., et al. 1972 Blood pressure and serum cholesterol in the Hadza of Tanzania. *Human Biology* 44:87–116.

Basgall, Mark E. 1987 Resource intensification among hunter-gatherers: Acorn economies in prehistoric California. *Research in Economic Anthropology* 9:21–52.

Basso, Keith H. 1988 "Speaking with names": Language and landscape among the western Apache. *Cultural Anthropology* 3(2):99–130.

Beardsley, Richard K., et al. 1956 Functional and evolutionary implications of community patterning: Seminars in archaeology, 1955. *Memoirs of the Society for American Archaeology* 11:130–157.

Beaver, George 1982 How children received their names. In *Yup'ik lore: Oral tradition of an Eskimo people [Yuut Qanemciit]*. Edward A. Tennant and Joseph N. Bitar, eds., pp. 61–63. Bethel, Alaska: Lower Kuskokwim School District.

Beckett, Jeremy R. 1988 The past in the present; the present in the past! In *Past and Present*. Jeremy R. Beckett, ed. Canberra: Aboriginal Studies Press.

Befu, H. 1968 Gift-giving in modernizing Japan. *Monumenta Nipponica* 23:444–456.

Begler, Elsie B. 1978 Sex, status and authority in egalitarian society. *American Anthropologist* 80(3):571–588.

Bell, Diane 1983 *Daughters of the Dreaming*. Sydney: George Allen and Unwin.

Belovsky, Gary E. 1988 An optimal foraging-based model of hunter-gatherer population dynamics. *Journal of Anthropological Archaeology* 7(4):329–372.

Belza, Juan E. 1974 *En la Isla del Fuego*. Buenos Aires: Instituto de Investigaciones Historicas de Tierra del Fuego.

Bender, Barbara 1981 Gatherer-hunter intensification. In *Economic archaeology*. Alison Sheridan and Geoff Bailey, eds., pp. 149–157. Oxford: British Archaeological Reports. (International series no. 96.)

———, 1990 The dynamics of nonhierarchical societies. In *The evolution of political systems: Sociopolitics in small-scale sedentary societies*. Steadman Upham, ed., pp. 247–63. New York: Cambridge University Press.

Bender, Barbara, and Brian Morris 1988 Twenty years of history, evolution and social change in gatherer-hunter studies. In *Hunters and gatherers 1: History, evolution and social change*. Tim Ingold, David Riches, and James Woodburn, eds., pp. 4–14. Oxford: Berg Publishers Limited.

Bennett, F. J., N. A. Barnicott, J. C. Woodburn, M. S. Pereira, and B. E. Henderson 1975 Studies on viral, bacterial, rickettsial, and treponemal diseases of the Hadza of Tanzania, and a note on injuries. *Human Biology* 2:61–68.

Bennett, F., I. Kagan, N. Barnicott, and J. Woodburn 1970 Helminth and protozoal parasites of the Hadza of Tanzania. *Transactions of the Royal Society of Tropical Medicine and Hygiene* 64:857–80.

Berg, L. S. 1948 *Ryby presnykh vod SSR i sopredel'nykh stran, 1* [Fresh-water fish species of the USSR and adjacent countries, part 1]. Moscow-Leningrad: U.S.S.R. Academy of Sciences.

Berger, Thomas R. 1985 *Village journey: The report of the Alaska Native Review Commission*. New York: Hill and Wang.

Bern, J. 1979 Ideology and domination: Toward a reconstruction of Australian Aboriginal social formations. *Oceania* 50(2): 118–32.

Berndt, Catherine H. 1950 Women's changing ceremonies in northern Australia. *L'Homme* 1:1–87.

———, 1981 Interpretations and "facts" in aboriginal Australia. In *Woman the gatherer*. Frances Dahlberg, ed., pp. 153–203. New Haven: Yale University Press.

Berndt, Ronald M. 1959 The concept of "the tribe" in the Western Desert of Australia. *Oceania* 30(2):81–107.

Berndt, Ronald M., ed. 1982 *Aboriginal sites, rights, and resource development*. Perth: University of Western Australia.

Best, Stephen 1986 The animal rights viewpoint. In *Native people and renewable resource management*. J. Green and J. Smith, eds., pp. 197–213. Edmonton: Alberta Society of Professional Biologists.

Bestor, T. C. 1989 *Socio-economic implications of a zero-catch limit on distribution channels and related activities in Hokkaido and Miyagi prefectures*. International Whaling Commission, Cambridge. (Document IWC41/SE1.)

Bettinger, Robert L. 1987 Archaeological approaches to hunter-gatherers. *Annual Review of Anthropology* 16:121–42.

———, 1991 *Hunter-gatherers: Archaeological and evolutionary theory*. New York: Plenum Press.

Bhatt, V. V. 1987 Hostile Jarawa and Sentinalese. In *Studies in island cultures of India*. G. Prakash Reddy and V. Sudarsen, eds., pp. 75–84. Hyudeabad: Goutami Educational Society.

Bicchieri, Marco G. 1990 Comment on "Foragers, genuine or spurious?" *Current Anthropology* 31(2):123.

Bicchieri, Marco G., ed. 1972 *Hunters and gatherers today*. New York: Holt, Rinehart and Winston.

Biggar, H. P. 1965 [1901] *The early fur trading companies of New France: A contribution to the history of commerce and discovery in North America*. (reprint) New York: Argonaut Press, Ltd.

Binford, Lewis R., 1978 Dimensional analysis of behavior and site structure: Learning from an Eskimo hunting stand. *American Antiquity* 43:330–61.

———, 1980 Willow smoke and dog's tails: Hunter-gatherer settlement systems and archaeological site formation. *American Antiquity* 45:4–20.

———, 1986 In pursuit of the future. In *American Archaeology: Past and Future*, David J. Meltzer, Don D. Fowler and Jeremy A. Sabloff, eds., pp. 459–479. Washington, D.C.: Smithsonian Institution Press.

———, 1989 Multidimensional analysis of sheep and goats: Baa-ck and forth. In *Debating archaeology*. Lewis R. Binford, ed., pp. 267–81. San Diego: Academic Press.

———, 1990 Mobility, housing, and environment: A comparative study. *Journal of Anthropological Research* 46(2):119–52.

Binford, Lewis R., et al. 1968 Does hunting bring happiness? Discussions, Part 2. In *Man the hunter*. Richard B. Lee and Irven DeVore, eds., pp. 89–92. New York: Aldine Publishing Company.

Bird-David, Nurit H. 1988 Hunters and gatherers and other people – a re-examination. In *Hunters and gatherers 1: History, evolution and social change*. Tim Ingold, David Riches, and James Woodburn, eds., pp. 17–30. Oxford: Berg Publishers Limited.

————, 1992 Beyond "the original affluent society." *Current Anthropology* 33(1):25–47.

Birdsell, Joseph B. 1953 Some environmental and cultural factors influencing the structuring of Australian Aboriginal populations. *American Naturalist* 87:171–207.

————, 1958 On population structure in generalized hunting and collecting populations. *Evolution* 12(2):189–205.

————, 1968 Some predictions for the Pleistocene based on equilibrium systems among recent hunter-gatherers. In *Man the hunter*. Richard B. Lee and Irven DeVore, eds., pp. 229–40. Chicago: Aldine Publishing Company.

————, 1970 Local group composition among the Australian Aborigines: A critique of the evidence from fieldwork conducted since 1930. *Current Anthropology* 11(2):115–142.

————, 1971 Ecology, spacing mechanisms, and adaptive behaviour among Australian Aborigines. In *Land tenure in the South Pacific*. Ron Crocombe, ed., pp. 334–61. Melbourne: Oxford University Press.

————, 1973 A basic demographic unit. *Current Anthropology* 14(4):337–56.

Black, Mary B. 1977 Ojibwa power belief system. In *The Anthropology of Power*, R. D. Fogelson and R. N. Adams, eds. New York: Academic Press.

Bleek, D. F. 1931 The Hadzapi or Watindega of Tanganyika Territory. *Africa* 4(3):273–86.

Bloch, M., and J. Parry. 1989 Introduction: Money and the Morality of Exchange. In *Money and the Morality of Exchange*. J. Parry and M. Bloch, eds., pp. 1–32. Cambridge: Cambridge University Press.

Blurton Jones, Nicholas G. 1986 Bushman birth spacing: A test for optimal inter-birth intervals. *Ethology and Sociobiology* 7(2):91–105.

————, 1993 The lives of hunter-gatherer children: effects of parental behavior and reproductive strategy. In M. Perreira and L. Fairbanks, eds., *Primate Juveniles*. New York: Oxford University Press.

Blurton Jones, Nicholas G., Kristen Hawkes, and James F. O'Connell 1989 Modelling and measuring costs of children in two foraging societies. In *Comparative socioecology*. V. Standen and R. Foley, eds. Oxford: Blackwell.

Blurton Jones, Nicholas G., and M. J. Konner 1976 !Kung knowledge of animal behavior. In *Kalahari hunter-gatherers: Studies of the !Kung San and their neighbors*. Richard B. Lee and Irven DeVore, eds., pp. 325–48. Cambridge: Harvard University Press.

Blurton Jones, Nicholas G., and R. M. Sibly 1978 Testing adaptiveness of culturally determined behaviour: Do bushman women maximise their reproductive success by spacing births widely and foraging seldom? In *Human behaviour and adaptation*. (Society for study of human biology symposium no. 18.) N. Blurton Jones and V. Reynolds, eds., pp. 135–58. London: Taylor and Francis.

Blurton Jones, Nicholas G., et al. 1992 Demography of the Hadza, an increasing and high density population of savanna foragers. *American Journal of Physical Anthropology* 89:159–81.

Boas, Franz 1888 The central Eskimo. In *Sixth annual report of the Bureau of American Ethnology . . . 1884–1885*, pp. 399–668. Washington, D.C.: Government Printing Office.

Bodenhorn, Barbara 1990 "I am not the great hunter, my wife is": Iñupiat and anthropological models of gender. Etudes/Inuit/Studies 14 (1–2):55–74.

Bohannan, Paul 1955 Some principles of exchange and investment among the Tiv. *American Anthropologist* 57(1):60–70.

———, 1959 The impact of money on an African subsistence economy. *The Journal of Economic History* 19(4):491–503.

Bohannan, Paul, and L. Bohannan 1968 *Tiv economy*. London: Longmans.

Bondel, Conrado S. 1985 *Tierra del Fuego (Argentina): La organización de su espacio*. Ushuaia: CADIC.

Boon, James 1982 *Other tribes, other scribes*. Ithaca: Cornell University Press.

Borrero, José M. 1957 *La Patagonia trágica*. Buenos Aires: Editorial Americana.

Borrero, Luís Alberto 1983 On cultural adaptation in the subantarctic zone. *Current Anthropology* 24(2):241–42.

———, 1986 La economía prehistorica de los habitantes del Norte de la Isla Grande de Tierra del Fuego. Tesis de Doctorado [Ph.D. Diss.], Universidad de Buenos Aires.

———, In Press. Los 'Modelos de Situaciones excepcionales' y el estudio de las sociedades de cazadores-recolectores. *Comechingonia* 10.

Bose, Tapan K. 1984 India: Ecopolitics and Adivasis. *IWGIA Newsletter* 39:69–81.

Bouey, Paul D. 1987 The intensification of hunter-gatherer economies in the southern north coast ranges of California. *Research in Economic Anthropology* 8:53–101.

Bourque, Bruce J., Steven L. Cox, and Arthur E. Spiess 1983 Cultural complexity in maritime cultures: Evidence from Penobscot Bay, Maine. In *The evolution of maritime cultures on the northeast and northwest coasts of America*. Ronald J. Nash, ed. Burnaby, B.C.: Simon Fraser University, Department of Archaeology Publication No. 11.

Boursier, D. 1984 Enquête sur l'anthropologie Baka. Texte roneographie á diffusion limitée.

Bower, Bruce 1989 A world that never existed. *Science News* 135(17):264–66.

Braun Menéndez, A. 1945 *Pequeña historia Fueguina*. Buenos Aires: Emece.

———, 1975 Primera expedición cientifica al interior de Tierra a del Fuego. *Karukinka* 13:17–26.

Braund, Stephen R., Milton M. R. Freeman, and Masami Iwasaki 1989 *Contemporary sociocultural characteristics of Japanese small-type coastal whaling*. Cambridge: International Whaling Commission, Document TC/41/STW1.

Braund, Stephen R., et al. 1990 *Quantification of local need for minke whale meat for the Ayukawa-based minke whale fishery*. International Whaling Commission, Cambridge. (Document TC/42/SEST8.)

Brett, J. R. 1952 Skeena River sockeye escapement and distribution. *Journal of the Fisheries Research Board of Canada* 8:453–68.

Brice-Bennett, Carol, ed. 1977 *Our footprints are everywhere: Inuit land use and occupancy in Labrador*. Nain: Labrador Inuit Association.

Bridges, E. L. 1951 *Uttermost part of the earth*. London: Hodder and Stoughton.

Briggs, Jean L. 1982 Living dangerously: The contradictory foundations of value in Canadian Inuit society. In *Politics and history in band societies*. Eleanor Leacock and Richard Lee, eds., pp. 109–31. Cambridge: Cambridge University Press.

Brock, Peggy, ed. 1989 *Women, rites and sites: Aboriginal women's cultural knowledge*. Sydney: Allen and Unwin.

Brody, Hugh 1987 *Living Arctic: Hunters of the Canadian north*. Boston: Faber and Faber.

Brown, James A. 1985 Long-term trends to sedentism and the emergence of complexity in the American midwest. In *Prehistoric hunter- gatherers: The emergence of cultural complexity*. T. Douglas Price and James A. Brown, eds., pp. 201–31. New York: Academic Press.

Budagjan, F. E., ed. 1961 *Tablitsy khimicheskogo sostava i pitatel'noj tsennosti pishchevykh produktov* [Tables of the foodstuffs' chemical content and nutritional value]. Moscow: Medgiz.

Buikstra, Jane E. 1976 The Caribou Eskimo: General and specific disease. *American Journal of Physical Anthropology* 45(3):351–68.

Burch, Ernest S., Jr. 1970 The Eskimo trading partnership in north Alaska: A study in "balanced reciprocity." *Anthropological Papers of the University of Alaska* 15(1):49–80.

———, 1972 The caribou/wild reindeer as a human resource. *American Antiquity* 37(3):339–68.

———, 1974 Eskimo warfare in Northwest Alaska. *Anthropological Papers of the University of Alaska* 16(2):1–14.

———, 1975 *Eskimo kinsmen: Changing family relationships in northwest Alaska*. Saint Paul: West Publishing Co. (American Ethnological Society monograph 59.)

———, 1980 Traditional Eskimo societies in northwest Alaska. *Senri Ethnological Studies* 4:253–304.

———, 1981 *The traditional Eskimo hunters of Point Hope, Alaska: 1800–1875*. Barrow, Alaska: The North Slope Borough.

———, 1986 The Caribou Inuit. In *Native peoples: The Canadian experience.* R. Bruce Morrison and C. Roderick Wilson, eds., pp. 106–33. Toronto: McClelland and Stewart.

———, 1988a Modes of exchange in North-West Alaska. In *Hunters and gatherers 2: Property, power and ideology.* Tim Ingold, David Riches, and James Woodburn, eds., pp. 95–109. Oxford: Berg Publishers Limited.

———, 1988b The method of ethnographic reconstruction. Paper presented at the Sixth Inuit Studies Conference. Copenhagen, Denmark. 17–20 October.

———, 1988c War and trade. In *Crossroads of continents: Cultures of Siberia and Alaska.* William W. Fitzhugh and Aron Crowell, eds., pp. 227–40. Washington, D.C.: Smithsonian Institution Press.

———, 1991 From skeptic to believer: The making of an oral historian. *Alaska History* 6(1):1–16.

Burch, Ernest S., Jr., and Thomas C. Correll 1972 Alliance and conflict: Inter-regional relations in north Alaska. In *Alliance in Eskimo society: Proceedings of the American Ethnological Society, 1971, supplement.* D. L. Guemple, ed., pp. 17–39. Seattle: University of Washington Press.

Burman, Roy B. K. 1989 *Tribal profiles and issues for further studies.* New Delhi: ICSSR.

Burns, John James 1964 The ecology, economics and management of mink in the Yukon-Kuskokwim Delta, Alaska. M.S. thes. University of Alaska, Fairbanks.

Butzer, Karl 1986 Paleolithic adaptations and settlement in Cantabrian Spain. *Advances in World Archaeology* 5:201–52.

Calista Corporation 1983 Letter dated 10 August to the state director, Bureau of Land Management, Alaska state office. Anchorage.

Carneiro, Robert 1970 A theory of the origin of the state. *Science* 169:733–38.

Carter, R. M. 1974 *Chipewyan semantics: Form and meaning in the language and culture of an Athapaskan-speaking people of Canada.* Ann Arbor: University Microfilms.

Cartwright, Frederick F., in collaboration with Michael D. Biddiss 1972 *Disease and history: The influence of disease in shaping the great events of history.* New York: Thomas Y. Crowell Company.

Cashdan, Elizabeth A. 1980 Egalitarianism among hunters and gatherers. *American Anthropologist* 82(1):116–20.

———, 1983 Territoriality among human foragers: Ecological models and an application to four Bushman groups. *Current Anthropology* 24(1):47–66.

———, 1984 G//ana territorial organization. *Human Ecology* 12(4):443–63.

Cashdan, Elizabeth, ed. 1990 *Risk and uncertainty in tribal and peasant economies.* Boulder, Colorado: Westview Press.

Chang, K.-C. 1962 A typology of settlement and community patterns in some circumpolar societies. *Arctic Anthropology* 1(1):28–41.

Chapman, Anne 1982 *Drama and power in a hunting society.* Cambridge: Cambridge University Press.

———, 1986 *Los Selk'nam: La Vida de los Años.* Buenos Aires: Emece.

Cheater, Angela P. 1989 Personal communication to George Silberbauer, May 5, 1989.

Childe, V. Gordon 1925 *Dawn of European civilization.* London: Kegan, Paul, Trench, Trubner and Company.

———, 1951 *Social evolution.* London: Watts and Company.

Cohen, Mark Nathan 1981 Pacific coast foragers: Affluent or overcrowded? *Senri Ethnological Studies* 9:275–95.

———, 1985 Prehistoric hunter-gatherers: The meaning of social complexity. In *Prehistoric hunter-gatherers: The emergence of cultural complexity.* T. Douglas Price and James A. Brown, eds., pp. 99–119. Orlando: Academic Press.

Cohen, Mark N., and George J. Armelagos 1984 Paleopathology at the origins of agriculture: Editors' summation. In *Paleopathology at the origins of agriculture.* Mark N. Cohen and George J. Armelagos, eds., pp. 586–601. New York: Academic Press.

Comaroff, John L. 1984 The closed society and its critics: Historical transformations in African ethnography. *American Ethnologist* 11(3):571–83.

Cook, Della Collins 1984 Subsistence and health in the lower Illinois valley: Osteological evidence. In *Paleopathology at the origins of agriculture.* Mark N. Cohen and George J. Armelagos, eds., pp. 235–69. New York: Academic Press.

Coon, Carleton S. 1971 *The hunting peoples.* Boston: Little, Brown and Company.

Cooper, B. 1949 The Kindiga. *Tanganyika Notes and Records* 27:8–15.

Coveney, P., and R. Highfield 1990 *The arrow of time.* New York: Ballantine.

Cowgill, George L. 1975 On causes and consequences of ancient and modern population changes. *American Anthropologist* 77(3):505–25.

Crosby, Alfred W. 1986 *Ecological imperialism: the biological expansion of Europe, 900–1900.* Cambridge: Cambridge University Press.

Cybulski, J. S. 1977 Cribra orbitalia: A possible sign of anemia in early historic native populations of the British Columbia coast. *American Journal of Physical Anthropology* 47(1):31–39.

Dahlberg, Frances, ed. 1981 *Woman the gatherer.* New Haven: Yale University Press.

Damas, David 1963 *Igluligmiut kinship and local groupings: A structural approach.* Ottawa: National Museums of Canada. (Bulletin 196.)

———, 1968 The diversity of Eskimo societies. In *Man the Hunter.* Richard B. Lee and Irven DeVore, eds., pp. 111–17. Chicago: Aldine Publishing Company.

———, 1969 Characteristics of central Eskimo band structure. In *Contributions to anthropology: Band societies, proceedings of the conference on band organization.* David Damas, ed., pp. 116–38. Ottawa: National Museums of Canada. (Bulletin 228.)

———, 1984 Central Eskimo: Introduction. In *Handbook of North American Indians*, vol. 5., *The Arctic*. David Damas, ed., pp. 391–96. Washington, D.C.: Smithsonian Institution.

———, 1988 The contact-traditional horizon of the central Arctic: Reassessment of a concept and reexamination of an era. *Arctic Anthropology* 25(2):101–38.

Damas, David, ed. 1969a *Contributions to anthropology: Band societies.* Ottawa: National Museums of Canada. (Bulletin 228.)

———, 1969b *Contributions to anthropology: Ecological essays*. Ottawa: National Museums of Canada. (Bulletin 230.)

Davies, Nicholas, and Alasdair Houston 1984 Territory economics. In *Behavioural ecology: An evolutionary approach*, 2d ed. J. R. Krebs and N. B. Davies, eds., pp. 148–69. Oxford: Blackwell Scientific Publications.

Davis, Leslie B., and Brian O. K. Reeves, eds. 1990 *Hunters of the recent past*. Boston: Unwin Hyman. (One world archaeology 15.)

Davis, Richard 1989 Personal communication to Kenneth Pratt, 4 April. Mekoryuk, Alaska.

Dawson, G. M. 1887 Notes and observations on the Kwakiool people of the northern part of Vancouver Island, and adjacent coasts, made during the summer of 1885, with a vocabulary of about 700 words. *Proceedings and Transactions of the Royal Society of Canada* 5:63–98.

de Goodall, R. N. P. 1975 *Tierra del Fuego*. Ushuaia: Ediciones Shanamaiin.

Deloria, Vine 1969 *Custer died for your sins; an Indian manifesto*. New York: Macmillan.

DeVore, Irven, ed. 1965 *Primate behavior: Field studies of monkeys and apes*. New York: Holt, Rinehart and Winston.

Dickel, David N., Peter D. Schulz, and Henry N. McHenry 1984 Central California: Prehistoric subsistence changes and health. In *Paleopathology at the origins of agriculture*. Mark N. Cohen and George J. Armelagos, eds., pp. 439–61. New York: Academic Press.

Dikshit, Sinha 1984 *The Hill Kharia of Purulia*. Calcutta: ASI.

Dirks, Robert 1980 Social responses during severe food shortages and famine. *Current Anthropology* 21(1):21–44.

Dodd, Robert 1984 Rituals and the maintenance of internal cooperation among the Baka hunters and gatherers. Paper presented at the Third International Conference on Hunting and Gathering Societies. Bad Homburg, Germany.

Dolgikh, B. O. 1960 *Rodovoj i plemennᴄj sostav narodov Sibiri v XVIII veke*. [Clan and tribal structure of the Siberian peoples in eighteenth century]. Moscow: Nauka.

Don, Fred 1990 Personal communication, 4 April. Mekoryuk, Alaska.

Donald, Leland 1987 Slave raiding on the north Pacific coast. In *Native peoples, native lands*. B. Cox, ed., pp. 161–72. Ottawa: Carleton University Press.

Donald, Leland, and Donald H. Mitchell 1975 Some correlates of local group rank among the southern Kwakiutl. *Ethnology* 14(4):325–46.

Draper, Patricia 1976 Social and economic constraints on child life among the !Kung. In *Kalahari hunter-gatherers: Studies of the !Kung San and their neighbors*. Richard B. Lee and Irven DeVore, eds., pp. 199–217. Cambridge: Harvard University Press.

Draper, Patricia, and Elizabeth A. Cashdan 1988 Technological change and child behavior among the !Kung. *Ethnology* 27(4):339–65.

Drozda, Robert M., and Kenneth L. Pratt [n.d.] Nunivak place names. Unpublished collection in author's possession.

Drucker, P. and R.F. Heizer 1967 *To make my name good: A re-examination of the southern Kwakiutl potlatch*. Berkeley: University of California Press.

Dunn, Frederick L. 1968 Epidemiological factors: Health and disease in hunter-gatherers. In *Man the hunter*. Richard B. Lee and Irven DeVore, eds., pp. 221–28. New York: Aldine Publishing Company.

Durham, William H.1981 Overview: Optimal foraging analysis in human ecology. In *Hunter-gatherer foraging strategies: Ethnographic and archeological analyses*. Bruce Winterhalder and Eric A. Smith, eds., pp. 218–31. Chicago: University of Chicago Press.

Durkheim, E. 1964 *The division of labor in society*. New York: Macmillan.

———, 1965 *The elementary forms of religious life*. New York:Macmillan.

Dyck, Noel 1980 Booze, barrooms and scrapping: Masculinity and violence in a western Canadian town. *Canadian Journal of Anthropology* 1(2):191–98.

———, 1983 The negotiation of Indian treaties and land rights in Saskatchewan. In *Aborigines, land and land rights*. Nicolas Peterson and Marcia Langaton, eds., pp. 405–15. Canberra: Australian Institute of Aboriginal Studies.

Dyson, T. 1977 The demography of the Hadza in historical perspective. In *African historical demography*. University of Edinburgh, Centre for African Studies.

Dyson-Hudson, Rada, and Eric Alden Smith 1978 Human territoriality: An ecological reassessment. *American Anthropologist* 80(1):21–41.

Edwards, W. H. 1987 Leadership in Aboriginal society. In *Traditional aboriginal society: A reader*. W. H. Edwards, ed., pp. 153–73. Melbourne: Macmillan.

Eisenstadt, S. N. 1973 *Tradition, change, and modernity*. New York: John Wiley and Sons.

Elkin, A. P. 1950 The complexity of social organization in southwestern Arnhem Land. *Southwestern Journal of Anthropology* 6(1):1–20.

———, 1953 Murngin kinship re-examined, and remarks on some generalizations. *American Anthropologist* 55(3):412–19.

Ellanna, Linda J. 1983 *Bering Strait insular Eskimo: a diachronic study of ecol-*

*ogy and population structure.* Juneau: Alaska Department of Fish and Game, Division of Subsistence, Technical Paper No. 77.

————, 1990 Demographic change, sedentism, and western contact: An inland Dena'ina Athabaskan case study. In *Hunter-gatherer demography, past and present.* Betty Meehan and Neville White, eds., pp. 101–16. Sydney: University of Sydney. (Oceania monograph no. 39.)

Ellanna, Linda J., George K. Sherrod, and Steven J. Langdon 1985 Subsistence mapping: An evaluation and methodological guidelines. Juneau: Alaska Department of Fish and Game, Division of Subsistence. (Technical paper no. 125.)

Epstein, A. L., ed. 1967 *The craft of social anthropology.* London: Tavistock.

Estioko-Griffin, Agnes, and P. Bion Griffin 1981 Woman the hunter: The Agta. In *Woman the gatherer.* Frances Dahlberg, ed., pp. 121–51. New Haven: Yale University Press.

Etzioni, Amitai 1970 Toward a macrosociology. In *Theoretical sociology: Perspectives and developments.* John C. McKinney and Edward A. Tiryakian, eds., pp. 69–97. New York: Meredith Corporation.

European Community 1983 Council directive of 28 March 1983 concerning the importation into member states of skins of certain seal pups and products derived therefrom. Brussels. (83/129/EEC.)

Fall, James A. 1990 The division of subsistence of the Alaska Department of Fish and Game: An overview of its research program and findings, 1980–1990. *Arctic Anthropology* 27(2):68–92.

Fallers, Lloyd A. 1968 Societal analysis. In *International encyclopedia of the social sciences*, vol. 14. David L. Sills, ed., pp. 562–72. New York: Macmillan Free Press.

Feit, Harvey A. 1973 The ethno-ecology of the Waswanipi Cree, or how hunters can manage their resources. In *Cultural ecology: Readings on the Canadian Indians and Eskimos.* Bruce Cox, ed. Toronto: McClelland and Stewart.

————, 1976 *James Bay debates: A bibliography.* Montreal: The Grand Council of Crees (of Quebec).

————, 1983 Negotiating recognition of aboriginal rights: History, strategies and reactions to the James Bay and Northern Quebec agreement. In *Aborigines, land and land rights.* Nicolas Peterson and Marcia Langton, eds., pp. 416–38. Canberra: Australian Institute of Aboriginal Studies.

————, 1986 Hunting and the quest for power: The James Bay Cree and whitemen in the twentieth century. In *Native peoples: The Canadian experience.* R. Bruce Morrison and C. Roderick Wilson, eds., pp. 171–207. Toronto: McClelland and Stewart.

————, 1989 James Bay Cree self-governance and land management. In *We are here: politics of aboriginal land tenure.* Edwin N. Wilmsen, ed. Pp. 68–98. Berkeley and Los Angeles: University of California Press.

————, 1991 The construction of Algonquian hunting territories: Private property as moral lesson, policy advocacy, and ethnographic error. In *Colonial situations: Essays on the contextualization of ethnographic knowledge*. George W. Stocking, Jr., ed. Madison: University of Wisconsin Press. (History of anthropology series, vol. 7.)

[Under revision] Algonkian hunting territories before contact? Critical review of the history of the arguments and of the evidence. *Ethnohistory*.

Ferguson, R. Brian 1984 A reexamination of the causes of Northwest Coast warfare. In *Warfare, culture and environment*. R. Brian Ferguson, ed., pp. 267–328. New York: Academic Press.

Fernandes, Walter 1989 The Forest Policy and the Forest Conservation (Amendment) Act, 1988. *Lokayan* (January-February):37–46.

Fienup-Riordan, Ann 1984 Regional groups on the Yukon-Kuskokwim Delta. *Etudes/Inuit/Studies* 8 (supplementary issue):63–93.

———, 1989 Eskimo war and peace: The history of bow and arrow warfare and interpersonal violence among the Yup'ik Eskimos of western Alaska. In *Keynote speeches from the Sixth Inuit Studies Conference, Copenhagen, October, 1988*. Jens Dahl, ed., pp. 90–107. Copenhagen: Kobenhavns Universitet. (Institut for Eskimologi no. 14.)

———, 1990 *Eskimo essays: Yup'ik lives and how we see them*. London: Rutgers University Press.

Flanagan, James 1989 Hierarchy in simple "egalitarian" societies. *Annual Review of Anthropology* 18:245–66.

Foerster, R. E. 1968 The sockeye salmon, *Oncorhynchus nerka*. Ottawa: *Fisheries Research Board of Canada*. (Bulletin 162.)

Foote, Don Charles 1967 Remarks on Eskimo sealing and the harp seal controversy. *Arctic* 20(4):267–68.

Ford, Richard I. 1972 Barter, gift, or violence. *University of Michigan Museum of Anthropology Papers* 46:21–45.

———, 1977 Evolutionary ecology and the evolution of human ecosystems: A case study from the midwestern U.S.A. In *Explanation of prehistoric change*. James N. Hill, ed., pp. 153–84. Albuquerque: University of New Mexico Press.

Forde, Daryll, and Mary Douglas 1956 Primitive economics. In *Man, culture and society*. Harry L. Shapiro, ed., pp. 330–44. New York: Oxford University Press.

Fox, R. 1979 The cultural animal. In *Issues in cultural anthropology*. B. W. McCurdy and J. P. Spradley, eds. Toronto: Little, Brown and Company.

Franklin, W. L. 1983 Contrasting socioecologies of South America's wild camelids: The vicuña and the guanaco. *Advances in the Study of Mammalian Behavior* 7:573–629.

Freeman, Milton M. R. 1976 *Report: Inuit land use and occupancy project*. 3 vols. Ottawa: Department of Indian and Northern Affairs.

———, 1986 Renewable resources, economics and native communities. In *Native people and renewable resource management*. J. Green and J.

Smith, eds., pp. 29–37. Edmonton: Alberta Society of Professional Biologists.

Fukumoto, Kazuo 1960 *Nihon hogei shiwa* [History of Japanese whaling]. Tokyo: Hôsei University Press.

Gadgil, Madhav, and K. C. Malhotra 1985 Ecology for the people. *South Asian Anthropologist* 6(1):1–13.

Galbraith, John Kenneth 1958 *The affluent society*. Boston: Houghton Mifflin.

Gale, Fay, ed. 1978 *Woman's role in aboriginal society*. Canberra: Australian Institute of Aboriginal Studies.

Garrido, J. L., J. N. Amaya, and Z. Kovacs 1981 *Territorialidad, comportamiento individual y actividad diaria de una población de guanacos en la Reserve Faunistica de Cabo Dos Bahías*. Puerto Madryn: SECIT-CON-ICET-CNP.

Geineman, B. A. 1912 Ocherk rybolovstva na Kamchatke [On the fishery in Kamchatka]. Lenin Library Archives, St. Petersburg.

Gifford-Gonzalez, Diane P. 1990 Modern analogues: Developing an interpretive framework. In *Bone modification*. Robson Bonnichsen and Marcella Sorg, eds., pp. 43–52. Orono: University of Maine, Center for the Study of the First Peopling of the Americas.

Gill, E. 1968 Examination of Harris lines in recent and fossil Australian aboriginal bones. *Current Anthropology* 9(2/3):215.

Gilman, Antonio 1981 The development of social stratification in Bronze Age Europe. *Current Anthropology* 22:1–24.

Godelier, Maurice 1977 *Perspectives in Marxist anthropology*. Cambridge: Cambridge University Press.

Goland, Carol 1991 The ecological context of hunter-gatherer storage: Environmental predictability and environmental risk. In *Foragers in context: Long-term, regional, and historical perspectives in hunter-gatherer studies*. Preston T. Miracle, Lynn E. Fisher, and Jody Brown, eds. Ann Arbor: University of Michigan. (Discussions in anthropology no. 10.)

Goldring, Phillip 1986 Inuit economic responses to Euro-american contacts: southeast Baffin Island, 1924–1940. In *Historical Papers/Communications Historiques*, pp. 146–72.

Gomes, Alberto G. 1990 Demographic implications of villagisation among the Semang of Malaysia. In *Hunter-gatherer demography, past and present*. Betty Meehan and Neville White, eds., pp. 126–38. Sydney: University of Sydney. (Oceania mcnograph no. 39.)

Goodale, Jane C. 1971 *Tiwi wives*. Seattle: University of Washington Press.

Goodman, Alan H., et al. 1984 Indications of stress from bone and teeth. In *Paleopathology at the origins of agriculture*. Mark N. Cohen and George J. Armelagos, eds., pp. 13–49. New York: Academic Press.

Gosden, Chris 1989 Debt, production, and prehistory. *Journal of Anthropological Archaeology* 8:355–87.

Gould, Richard A. 1982 To have and have not: The ecology of sharing among hunter-gatherers. In *Resource managers: North American and Australian hunter-gatherers*. Nancy M. Williams and Eugene S. Hunn, eds, pp. 69–91. Boulder: Westview Press, Inc. (AAAS selected symposium 67.)

Graburn, Nelson H. H., and B. Stephen Strong 1973 *Circumpolar peoples: An anthropological perspective*. Pacific Palisades, California: Goodyear Publishing Company, Inc.

Griffin, P. B. 1984 Forager resource and land use in the humid tropics: The Agta of N. E. Luzon, the Philippines. In *Past and present in hunter-gatherer studies*. C. Schrire, ed., pp. 95–121. New York: Academic Press.

Gubser, Nicholas J. 1965 *The Nunamiut Eskimos: Hunters of caribou*. New Haven: Yale University Press.

Guemple, Lee 1972 Eskimo band organization and the "DP camp hypothesis." *Arctic Anthropology* 9(2):80–112.

Guha, Ramachandra, and Madhav Gadgil 1988 *State forestry and social conflict in British India: A study in the ecological bases of agrarian protest*. Bangalore: Indian Institute of Science.

Gurvich, I. S. 1963 Russkije starozhily doliny reki Kamchatka [Russian old-settlers of the Kamchatka River valley]. *Sovetskaja Etnografija* [Soviet Ethnography] 3:31–41.

Gurvich, I. S., ed. 1987 *Etnicheskoje razvitije narodnostej Severa v sovietskij period* [Ethnic development of the Northern peoples in Soviet time]. Moscow: Nauka.

Gusinde, Martin 1982 *Los Indios de Tierra del Fuego, 1: Los Selk'nam*. Buenos Aires: CAEA/CONICET.

Hamilton, Annette 1982 The unity of hunting-gathering societies: Reflections on economic forms and resource management. In *Resource managers: Northern American and Australian hunter-gatherers*. Nancy M. Williams and Eugene S. Hunn, eds., pp. 229–47. Boulder: Westview Press, Inc. (AAAS selected symposium 67.)

Hamilton, Nathan D. 1988 Ceremonialism associated with the Moshier Island burial site, Casco Bay, Maine. Paper presented to the Society for American Archaeology. Phoenix, Arizona.

Hanson, F. Allan 1989 The making of the Maori: Culture invention and its logic. *American Anthropologist* 91:890–902.

Happyjack, Jacob 1983 Personal communication to H.A. Feit, 30 August.

Harako, Reizo 1976 The Mbuti as hunters – a study of ecological anthropology of the Mbuti pygmies. *Kyoto University African Studies* 10:37–99.

Hardy, Clay 1986 Personal communication to Kenneth Pratt, 12 September. Anchorage.

Harper, Kenn [1984] Narwhal ivory in England. Mimeographed manuscript.

Harris, Marvin 1968 *The rise of anthropological theory*. New York: Crowell.
———, 1971 *Culture, man and nature*. New York: Crowell.
Hart, J. L. 1973 Pacific fishes of Canada. Ottawa: *Fisheries Research Board of Canada*. (Bulletin 180.)
Hastrup, Kirsen, and Peter Elsass 1990 Anthropological advocacy: A contradiction in terms? *Current Anthropology* 31(3):301–11.
Hawkes, Kristen 1990 Why do men hunt? Some benefits for risky strategies. In *Risk and uncertainty in tribal and peasant economies*. E. Cashdan, ed., pp. 145–66. Boulder: Westview Press.
———, 1991 Showing off: Tests of a hypothesis about men's foraging goals. *Ethology and Sociobiology* 12:29–54.
Hawkes, Kristen, Kim Hill, and James F. O'Connell 1982 Why hunters gather: Optimal foraging and the Aché of eastern Paraguay. *American Ethnologist* 9(2):379–98.
Hawkes, Kristen, and James F. O'Connell 1981 Affluent hunters? Some comments in light of the Alyawara case. *American Anthropologist* 83(3):622–26.
Hawkes, Kristen, James F. O'Connell, and Nicholas G. Blurton Jones 1989 Hardworking Hadza grandmothers. In *Comparative socioecology: The behavioral ecology of humans and other mammals*. V. Standen and R. Foley, eds., pp. 341–66. Oxford: Blackwell.
———, 1991 Hunting income patterns among the Hadza: Big game, common goods, foraging goals and the evolution of the human diet. *Philosophical Transactions of the Royal Society of London* B334:243–51.
Hawkes, Kristen, et al. 1985 How much is enough? Hunters and limited needs. *Ethology and Sociobiology* 6(1):3–15.
Hayden, Brian D. 1981 Research and development in the Stone Age: Technological transitions among hunter/gatherers. *Current Anthropology* 22:519–48.
———, 1982 Interaction parameters and the demise of Paleo-Indian craftmanship. *Plains Anthropology* 27:109–23.
———, 1987 Alliances and ritual ecstasy: Human responses to resource stress. *Journal for the Scientific Study of Religion* 26(1):81–91.
———, 1990a The right rub: Hide working in high ranking households. In *The interpretative possibilities of microwear studies*. Bo Graslund, ed., pp. 89–102. Uppsala: Societas Archaeologica Upsaliensis. (Aun 14.)
———, 1990b Nimrods, piscators, pluckers and planters: The emergence of food production. *Journal of Anthropological Archaeology* 9(1):31–69.
Hayden, Brian, and Rob Gargett 1990c Big man, big heart? A Mesoamerican view of the emergence of complex society. *Ancient Mesoamerica* 1(1)3–20.
Headland, Thomas N., and Lawrence A. Reid 1989 Hunter-gatherers and their neighbors from prehistory to the present. *Current Anthropology* 30(1):43–66.

Hearne, S. 1971 [1795] *A journey from Prince of Wales's fort in Hudson's Bay to the northern ocean*. Edmonton, Alberta: M. G. Hurtig, Ltd.

Helm, June 1975 Bilaterality in the socio-territorial organization of the Arctic drainage Dene. *Ethnology* 4(4):361–85.

Henige, David 1982 *Oral historiography*. Essex: Longman Group U.K. Ltd.

Hennigh, Lawrence 1983 North Alaskan Eskimo alliance structure. *Arctic Anthropology* 20(1)23–32.

Henry, Donald 1985 Preagricultural sedentism: The Natufian example. In *Prehistoric hunter-gatherers: The emergence of cultural complexity*. T. Douglas Price and James A. Brown, eds., pp. 365–84. Orlando: Academic Press.

Heron, P. 1983 Education for nomads. *Nomadic Peoples* 13:61–68.

Herskovits, Melville J. 1952 *Economic anthropology: The economic life of primitive peoples*. New York: W. W. Norton.

Hewlett, Barry S. 1987 Intimate fathers: Patterns of paternal holding among Aka Pygmies. In *The father's role: Cross-cultural perspectives*. Michael E. Lamb, ed., pp. 295–330. Hillsdale, N.J.: Lawrence Erlbaum Associates.

———, 1988 Sexual selection and paternal investment among Aka Pygmies. In *Human reproductive behavior*. L. Betzig, P. Turke, and M. Borgerhoff-Mulder, eds. Cambridge: Cambridge University Press.

Hiatt, L. R. 1962 Local organization among the Australian Aborigines. *Oceania* 32(4):267–86.

———, 1965 *Kinship and conflict: A study of an Aboriginal community in northern Arnhem Land*. Canberra: Australian National University.

———, 1966 The lost horde. *Oceania* 37(2):81–92. 1984 Traditional land tenure and contemporary land claims. In *Aboriginal landowners: Contemporary issues in the determination of traditional Aboriginal land ownership*. L. R. Hiatt, ed., pp. 11–23. Sydney: University of Sydney Press. (Oceania monograph no. 27.)

———, 1989 Aboriginal land tenure and contemporary claims in Australia. In *We are here: Politics of aboriginal land tenure*. Edwin N. Wilmsen, ed., pp. 99–117. Berkeley and Los Angeles: University of California Press.

Hiatt, L. R., ed. 1984 *Aboriginal landowners: Contemporary issues in the determination of traditional Aboriginal landownership*. Sydney: University of Sydney Press. (Oceania monograph no. 27.)

Hidayatullah, M. 1975 *Right to property and the Indian Constitution*. New Delhi: Arnold Herman.

Hiernaux, J., and C. Boehdi Hartono 1980 Physical measurements of the adult Hadza of Tanzania. *Annals of Human Biology* 7(4):339–46.

Hill, Kim, Barbara J. King, and Elizabeth Cashdan 1983 On territoriality in hunter-gatherers. *Current Anthropology* 24(4):534–37.

Hobsbawm, Eric, and Terry Ranger 1983 *The invention of tradition*. Cambridge: Cambridge University Press.

Hoffman, C. 1984 Punan foragers in the trading networks of southeast Asia. In *Past and present in hunter-gatherer studies*. C. Schrire, ed., pp. 123–49. New York: Academic Press.

Holmberg, Heinrich Johan 1985 *Holmberg's ethnographic sketches*. Fritz Jaensch, trans. Marvin W. Falk, ed. Fairbanks: University of Alaska Press.

Howell, N. 1976 The population of the Dobe area !Kung. In *Kalahari hunter-gatherers: Studies of the !Kung San and their neighbors*. Richard B. Lee and Irven DeVore, eds., pp. 137–51. Cambridge: Harvard University Press.

———, 1979 *Demography of the Dobe area !Kung*. New York: Academic Press.

Hunn, Eugene S. 1981 On the relative contribution of men and women to subsistence among hunter-gatherers of the Columbia plateau: A comparison with ethnographic atlas summaries. *Journal of Ethnobiology* 1(1):124–34.

Hunter, J. G. 1959 Survival and production of pink and chum salmon in a coastal stream. *Journal of the Fisheries Research Board of Canada* 16:835–86.

Huntington, W. R. 1973 *Religion and social organization of the Bara people of Madagascar*. Ann Arbor: University Microfilms.

Ichikawa, Mitsuo 1978 The residential groups of the Mbuti Pygmies. *Senri Ethnological Studies* 1:131–88.

———, 1983 An examination of the hunting-dependent life of the Mbuti Pygmies, eastern Zaire. *African Study Monographs* 4:55–76.

India, Government of 1982 Report of committee on forest and tribals in India. Ministry of Home Affairs, New Delhi.

Ingold, Tim 1980 *Hunters, pastoralists and ranchers: Reindeer economies and their transformations*. Cambridge: Cambridge University Press.

———, 1987 *The appropriation of nature: Essays on human ecology and social relations*. Iowa City: University of Iowa Press.

———, 1988 Notes on the foraging mode of production. In *Hunters and gatherers 1: History, evolution and social change*. Tim Ingold, David Riches, and James Woodburn, eds., pp. 269–85. Oxford: Berg Publishers Ltd.

Ingold, Tim, David Riches, and James Woodburn, eds. 1988a *Hunters and gatherers 1: History, evolution and social change*. Oxford: Berg Publishers Ltd.

———, 1988b *Hunters and gatherers 2: Property, power and ideology*. Oxford: Berg Publishers Limited.

International Whaling Commission 1989 *Chairman's report of the 41st meeting*. International Whaling Commission, Cambridge.

Irimoto, T. 1981 Chipewyan ecology: Group structure and caribou hunting. *Senri Ethnological Studies* 8.

Iwasaki, Masami 1988 Cultural significance of whaling in a whaling community in Abashiri. M.A. thes., University of Alberta, Edmonton.

Jacobsen, Johan Adrian 1977 *Alaska voyage, 1881–1883*. Erna Gunther, trans. and ed. Chicago: University of Chicago Press.

Jacobson, Steven A., comp. 1984 *Yup'ik Eskimo dictionary*. Fairbanks: University of Alaska, Alaska Native Language Center.

Japan 1986 *Small-type whaling in Japan's coastal seas*. International Whaling Commission, Cambridge. (Document TC/38/AS2.)

———, 1989 *Report to the working group on the socio-economic implications of a zero-catch limit*. International Whaling Commission, Cambridge. (Document IWC/41/21.)

———, 1990 *Distinguishing between Japanese STCW and LTCW in relation to coastal whaling fishery management*. International Whaling Commission, Cambridge. (Document TC/43/SEST3.)

———, 1991 *The cultural significance of everyday foods*. International Whaling Commission, Cambridge. (Document TC/43/SEST1.)

———, 1992 *Similarities and diversity in coastal whaling operations*. International Whaling Commission, Cambridge. (Document IWC/44/SEST6.)

Jarvenpa, R. 1976 Spatial and ecological factors in the annual economic cycle of the English River band of Chipewyan. *Arctic Anthropology* 18(1):45–60.

———, 1980 *The trappers of Patuanak: Toward a spatial ecology of modern hunters*. Ottawa: National Museum of Man. (Canadian Ethnology Service, Mercury series paper no. 67.)

———, 1982 Intergroup behavior and imagery: The case of Chipewyan and Cree. *Ethnology* 31(4):283–99.

Jelliffe, D. B., et al. 1962 The children of the Hadza hunters. *Tropical Paediatrics* 60:907–13.

Jochim, Michael A. 1976 *Hunter-gatherer subsistence and settlement: A predictive model*. New York: Academic Press.

———, 1988 Optimal foraging and the division of labor. *American Anthropologist* 90(1):130–36.

———, 1989 Optimization and stone tool studies: Problems and potentials. In *Time, energy and stone tools*. R. Torrence, ed., pp. 106–11. Cambridge: Cambridge University Press.

Joiris, Veronique 1986 Elements of techno-economic changes among the sedentarized BaGyeli Pygmies (south-west Cameroun). Paper presented at the Fourth International Conference on Hunting and Gathering Societies. London, England.

———, 1990 Ritual participation by Baka women of southern Cameroon in activities considered exclusively masculine. Paper presented at the Sixth International Conference on Hunting and Gathering Societies. Fairbanks, Alaska.

Jordan, Richard 1987 Koniag Eskimos: Complex hunter-gatherers of southcentral Alaska. Paper presented to the Society for American Archaeology, Toronto, Canada.

Kaare, Bwire T. M. 1985 Problems of using education as means of transforming hunter-gatherers. Unpublished manuscript on file. University of Dar-es-Salaam.

————, [1988] The Hadzabe and the Tanzanian state: problem of transformation in a hunting-gathering community. Unpublished paper delivered at the Fifth International Conference on Hunting and Gathering Societies, Darwin, Australia.

Kaberry, Phyllis M. 1939 *Aboriginal woman*. London: George Routledge and Sons.

Kabo, V. R. 1986 *Pervobytnaja dozemledel'cheskaja obshchina* [Primeval prefarming community]. Moscow: Nauka.

Kaganovskij, A. G. 1949 Nekotoryje voprosy biologii i dinamiki chislennosti gorbushy [Some problems of the pink salmon biology and population dynamics]. *Izvestija Tikhookeanskogo Nauchno-Issledovatel'skogo Instituta Rybnogo Khoziajstva i Okeanografii* [Transactions of the Pacific Ocean Scientific-Researching Institute of Fishery and Oceanography] 31:3–57.

Kalland, A. 1986 Pre-modern whaling in northern Kyûshû. *Bonner Zeitschrift für Japanologie* 8:29–50.

————, 1989 *The spread of whaling culture in Japan*. International Whaling Commission, Cambridge. (Document TC/41/STW3.)

Kalland, A., and B. Moeran 1992 *Japanese whaling: End of an era?* London: Curzon Press.

Kaplan, Hillard, and Kim Hill 1985 Food sharing among Ache foragers: Tests of explanatory hypotheses. *Current Anthropology* 26(2):223–46.

Kazuko, Tsurumi 1975 Yanagita Kunio's work as a model of endogenous development. *Japan Quarterly* 22 (3):223–238.

Keeley, Lawrence H. 1988 Hunter-gatherer economic complexity and "population pressure": A cross-cultural analysis. *Journal of Anthropological Archaeology* 7(4):373–411.

Keen, Ian 1989 Aboriginal governance. In *Emergent inequalities in aboriginal Australia*. John C. Altman, ed., pp. 17–42. Sydney: University of Sydney. (Oceania monograph no. 28.)

Keenan, Jeremy 1977 The concept of the mode of production of hunter-gatherer societies. *African Studies* 36(1):57–69.

Keene, Arthur 1983 Biology, behavior, and borrowing: A critical examination of optimal foraging models in archaeology. In *Archaeological hammers and theories*. A. Keene and J. Moore, eds., pp. 137–55. New York: Academic Press.

————, 1985 Nutrition and economy: Models for the study of prehistoric diet. Robert I. Gilbert and James H. Mielke, eds., *The Analysis of Prehistoric Diets*. New York: Academic Press.

Kelly, Robert L. 1991 Sedentism, sociopolitical inequality, and resource fluctuations. In *Between bands and states*. Susan A. Gregg, ed., pp.

135–58. Carbondale: Southern Illinois University at Carbondale, Center for Archaeological Investigations. (Occasional paper no. 9.)

Kent, Susan 1992 The current forager controversy: Real versus ideal views of hunter-gatherers. *Man* 27(1):25–70.

Kilbuck, John H. ca. 1890–1910 Something about the Innuit of the Kuskokwim. Typescript. Bethel, Alaska: Moravian Seminary and Archives.

Kisliuk, Michelle 1991 Confronting the quintessential: Singing, dancing, and everyday life among the Biaka Pygmies (Central African Republic). Ph.D. diss. New York University.

Klein, David R. 1966 Waterfowl in the economy of the Eskimos of the Yukon-Kuskokwim delta, Alaska. *Arctic* 19(4):319–36.

Kleindienst, Maxine R., and Patty Jo Watson 1956 Action archaeology: The archaeological inventory of a living community. *Anthropology Tomorrow* 5(1):75–78.

Kocen, R. S. 1984 Virus infections of the nervous system. In *Oxford Textbook of Medicine*. D. J. Weatherall, J. G. G. Ledingham, and D. A. Warrell, eds. Oxford: Oxford University Press.

Kohl-Larsen, Ludwig 1958 *Wildbeuter in ost-Afrika: Die Tindiga, ein Jäger- und Sammlervolk*. Berlin: Dietrich Reimer.

Kolig, Erich 1989 The powers that be and those who aspire to them: Knowledge and reputation in Australian Aboriginal society. In *Emergent inequalities in Aboriginal Australia*. John C. Altman, ed., pp. 43–65. Sydney: University of Sydney. (Oceania monograph no. 28.)

Komarov, V. L. 1912 O Russkom naselenii Kamchatki [On the Russian inhabitants of Kamchatka]. *Russkij Antropologicheskij Zhurnal* [Russian Anthropological Journal] 2–3:100–36.

Koyama, Shuzo, and David Hurst Thomas, eds. 1981 Affluent foragers: Pacific coasts east and west. Osaka: *Senri Ethnological Studies 9*.

Krasheninnikov, S. P. 1949 *Opisanije zemli Kamchatki* [Description of Kamchatka land]. Moscow-Leningrad: AN SSSR Press.

Krejnovich, E. A. 1973 *Nivkhgu*. Moscow: Nauka.

Krjukov, N. A. 1894 Nekotoryje dannyje o polozhenii rybolovstva v Priamurskom kraje [Some data on the state of fishery in Amur region]. *Zapiski Priamurskogo Otdela Ruskogo Geograficheskogo Obshchestva* [Notes of the Amur Department of the Russian Geographical Society] 1(1):1–87.

Kroeber, Alfred L. 1935 History and science in anthropology. *American Anthropologist* 37(4):539–69.

Krogius, F. V., and E. M. Krokhin 1956 Rezul'taty issledovanij biologii nerki-krasnoj, sostojanije jejo zpasov i kolebanij chislennosti v vodakh Kamchatki [The result of the studies concerning nerka-red biology, state of its population and quantity fluctuations in Kamchatka waters]. *Voprosy Ikhtiologii* [Problems of Ichthyology] 7:3–20.

Krupnik, Igor I. 1989 *Arkticheskaja etnoekologija* [Arctic ethnoecology]. Moscow: Nauka.

Krynin, P. P. 1913 *Otchot po rekognostsirovochnym issledovanijam v 1909 g. rek Kamchatskogo poluostrova Kamchatki, Bol'shoj i Avachi* [Report on the preliminary investigations of Kamchatka Peninsular rivers Kamchatka, Bol'shaya and Avacha in 1909]. St. Petersburg: Upravlenije vnutrennikh vodnykh putej i shossejnykh dorog po otdeleniju vodnykh i shossejnykh soobshchenij.

Kuhn, Thomas S. 1970 *The structure of scientific revolutions.* 2d ed. Chicago: University of Chicago Press. (International encyclopedia of unified science, vol. 2, no. 2.)

Laming-Emperaire, Annette, Danièle Lavalée, and Roger Humbert 1972 Le site de Marazzi en Terre de Feu. *Objets et Mondes* 12(2):225–44.

Lamphere, Louise 1974 Strategies, cooperation, and conflict among women in domestic groups. In *Woman, culture and society.* Michelle Zimbalist Rosaldo and Louise Lamphere, eds., pp. 97–112. Stanford: Stanford University Press.

Lanata, José L. 1990 Humans and terrestrial and sea mammals at Peninsula Mitre, Tierra del Fuego. In *Hunters of the recent past.* L. B. Davis and B. O. K. Reeves, eds., pp. 400–406. London: Unwin Hyman.

Langdon, Stephen J. 1979 Comparative Tlingit and Haida adaptation to the west coast of the Prince of Wales Archipelago. *Ethnology* 18(2): 101–20.

Lantis, Margaret 1946 The social culture of the Nunivak Eskimo. *Transactions of the American Philosophical Society* 35(3):151–323.

———, 1984 Nunivak Eskimo. In *Handbook of North American Indians,* vol. 5, *The Arctic.* David Damas, ed., pp. 209–23. Washington, D. C.: Smithsonian Institution.

Lathrap, D. W. 1968 Discussion. In *Man the hunter.* Richard B. Lee and Irven Devore, eds., pp. 93–94. Chicago: Aldine Publishing Company.

Leacock, Eleanor 1954 *The Montagnais hunting territory and the fur trade.* Washington, D.C.: American Anthropological Association. (Memoir 78.)

———, 1969 The Montagnais-Naskapi band. In *Contributions to Anthropology: Band societies.* David Damas, ed., pp. 1–17. Ottawa: National Museums of Canada. (Bulletin 228.)

———, 1978 Women's status in egalitarian society: Implications for social evolution. *Current Anthropology* 19(2):247–75.

Leacock, Eleanor, and Richard B. Lee 1982 Introduction. In *Politics and history in band societies.* Eleanor Leacock and Richard B. Lee, eds., pp. 1–20. Cambridge: Cambridge University Press.

Leacock, Eleanor, and Richard B. Lee, eds. 1982 *Politics and history in band societies.* New York: Cambridge University Press.

Lee, Richard B. 1968 What hunters do for a living, or, how to make out on scarce resources. In *Man the hunter.* Richard B. Lee and Irven DeVore, eds., pp. 30–48. Chicago: Aldine Publishing Company.

————, 1972a Population growth and the beginnings of sedentary life among the !Kung bushmen. In *Population growth: Anthropological implications*. B. Spooner, ed., pp. 329–42. Cambridge: M.I.T. Press.

————, 1972b Work effort, group structure and land-use in contemporary hunter-gatherers. In *Man, settlement and urbanism*. Peter J. Ucko, Ruth Tringham, and G. W. Dimbleby, eds., pp. 177–85. London: Duckworth.

————, 1976 !Kung spatial organization. In *Kalahari hunter-gatherers: Studies of the !Kung San and their neighbors*. Richard B. Lee and Irven DeVore, eds., pp. 73–97. Cambridge: Harvard University Press.

————, 1979 The *!Kung San: men, women and work in a foraging society*. Cambridge: Cambridge University Press.

————, 1981a Is there a foraging mode of production? *Canadian Journal of Anthropology* 2(1):13–19.

————, 1981b Politics, sexual and nonsexual, in an egalitarian society: The !Kung San. In *Social inequality: Comparative and developmental approaches*. Gerald D. Berreman, ed., pp. 83–102. New York: Academic Press.

————, 1982 Politics, sexual and non-sexual, in an egalitarian society. In *Politics and history in band societies*. Eleanor Leacock and Richard B. Lee, eds., pp. 37–59. Cambridge: Cambridge University Press.

————, 1984 *The Dobe !Kung*. New York: Holt, Rinehart and Winston.

————, 1988 Reflections on primitive communism. In *Hunters and gatherers 1: History, evolution and social change*. Tim Ingold, David Riches, and James Woodburn, eds., pp. 252–68. Oxford: Berg Publishers Limited.

————, 1990 Primitive communism and the origin of social inequality. In *The evolution of political systems: Sociopolitics in small-scale sedentary societies*. Steadman Upham, ed., pp. 225–46. Cambridge: Cambridge University Press.

————, 1992 Art, science or politics? The crisis in hunter-gatherer studies. *American Anthropologist* 94(1):31–54.

Lee, Richard B., and Mathias Guenther 1991 Oxen or onions? The search for trade (and truth) in the Kalahari. *Current Anthropology* 32(5):592–601.

Lee, Richard B., A. Pilling, and L. R. Hiatt 1968 Territorial boundaries. In *Man the hunter*. Richard B. Lee and Irven DeVore, eds., pp. 156–57. Chicago: Aldine Publishing Company.

Lee, Richard B., and Irven DeVore, eds. 1968 *Man the hunter*. Chicago: Aldine Publishing Company.

————, 1976 *Kalahari hunter-gatherers: Studies of the !Kung San and their neighbors*. Cambridge: Harvard University Press.

Lesseps, J. B. 1801 *Lessepsovo puteshestvije po Kamchatke i juzhnoj storone Sibiri, 1* [Lesseps's travels in Kamchatka and southern part of Siberia, part 1]. Moscow: Gubernskaja tipografija u A. Reshetnikova.

Levy, Marion J., Jr. 1952 *The structure of society.* Princeton: Princeton University Press.

———, 1966 *Modernization and the structure of societies: A setting for international affairs.* Princeton: Princeton University Press.

Lewin, Roger 1988 New views emerge on hunters and gatherers. *Science* 240(4856):1146–48.

Lewis, Henry 1982 Fire technology and resource management in aboriginal North America and Australia. In *Resource managers: North American and Australian hunter-gatherers.* Nancy M. Williams and Eugene S. Hunn, eds., pp. 45–67. Boulder: Westview Press, Inc. (AAAS selected symposium 67.)

Lindstrom, Lamont 1982 Leftamap Kastom: The political history of tradition on Tanna (Vanuatu). *Mankind* 13:316–29.

Linton, Sally 1971 Woman the gatherer. In *Women in perspective: A guide for cross-cultural studies.* Sue-Ellen Jacobs, ed. Urbana: University of Illinois Press.

Lista, R. 1887 *Viaje al país de los Onas.* Buenos Aires: Establecimiento Tipográfic o de Alberto Nuñez.

Little, M. A. 1983 An overview of adaptation. In *Rethinking human adaptation.* R. Dyson-Hudson and M. A. Little, eds., pp. 137–47. Boulder: Westview Press.

Lloyd, Kevin 1986 Cooperative management of polar bears on northeast Baffin Island. In *Native people and renewable resource management.* J. Green and J. Smith, eds., pp. 108–16. Edmonton: Alberta Society of Professional Biologists.

Lobdell, John E. 1980 *Prehistoric human populations and resource utilization in Kachemak Bay, Gulf of Alaska.* Ann Arbor: University Microfilms.

———, 1984 Harris lines: Markers of nutrition and disease at prehistoric Utqiagvik village. *Arctic Anthropology* 21(1): 109–16.

Lourandos, Harry 1985 Intensification and Australian prehistory. In *Prehistoric hunter-gatherers: The emergence of cultural complexity.* T. Douglas Price and James A. Brown, eds., pp. 385–423. Orlando: Academic Press.

———, 1988 Palaeopolitics: Resource intensification in Aboriginal Australia and Papua New Guinea. In *Hunters and gatherers 1: History, evolution and social change.* Tim Ingold, David Riches, and James Woodburn, eds., pp. 148–60. Oxford: Berg Publishers Ltd.

Lovell, Nancy, et al. 1986 Prehistoric salmon consumption in interior British Columbia. *Canadian Journal of Archaeology* 10:99–106.

MacNeish, June Helm 1956 Leadership among the northeastern Athabascans. *Anthropologica* o.s. 2:131–163.

Macpherson, R.K. 1966 Physiological adaptation, fitness, and nutrition in the peoples of the Australian and New Guinea regions. In *The biology of human adaptability.* Paul T. Baker and J. S. Weiner, eds. Oxford: Clarendon Press.

Maddock, Kenneth 1982 *The Australian aborigines: A portrait of their society*. 2d ed. Ringwood, Victoria, Australia: Penguin Books.

———, 1989 Involved anthropologists. In *We are here: Politics of aboriginal land tenure*. Edwin N. Wilmsen, ed., pp. 138–76. Berkeley: University of California Press.

Maeda, Kêjirô, and Y. Teraoka 1952 *Hogei* [Whaling]. Tokyo: Suisan Shûhôsha.

Maine, H. 1972 [1861] *Ancient law*. New York: Dutton.

Malhotra, K. C., S. B. Kohmne, and Madhav Gadgil 1983 Hunting strategies among three non-pastoral nomadic groups of Maharashtra. *Man in India* 63:21–39.

Malouf, Albert 1986 *Seals and sealing in Canada: Report of the Royal Commission*, vol. 2., pp. 217–85. Ottawa: Supply and Services Canada for the Royal Commission on Seals and the Sealing Industry in Canada.

Manderson, L., and H. Hardacre 1989a Small-type coastal whaling in Ayukawa: Draft report of research, December 1988–January 1990. Report on file. The Institute of Cetacean Research, Tokyo.

———, 1989b Gender, space and seasons: Occupation and identity in Japanese whaling villages. Unpublished manuscript.

Marciniak, Arkadiusz, Hitoshi Watanabe, and Alain Testart 1988 On the social anthropology of hunter-gatherers. *Current Anthropology* 29(3):488–91.

Marcus, George, and Michael Fischer 1986 *Anthropology as cultural critique*. Chicago: University of Chicago Press.

Marquardt, William H. 1988 Politics and production among the Calusa of south Florida. In *Hunters and gatherers 1: History, evolution and social change*. Tim Ingold, David Riches, and James Woodburn, eds., pp. 161–88. Oxford: Berg Publishers Limited.

Marshall, Alfred 1936 *Principles of economics*. 8th ed. London: Macmillan.

Marshall, Lorna 1976a Sharing, talking and giving. In *Kalahari hunter-gatherers: Studies of the !Kung San and their neighbors*. Richard B. Lee and Irven DeVore, eds., pp. 349–71. Cambridge: Harvard University Press.

———, 1976b *The !Kung of Nyae Nyae*. Cambridge: Harvard University Press.

Martin, John F. 1983 Optimal foraging theory: A review of some models and their applications. *American Anthropologist* 85(3):612–29.

Martinic, M. 1973 Panorama de la colonización en Tierra del Fuego entre 1881 y 1900. *Anales del Instituto de la Patagonia* 4:5–70.

Massone, Mauricio 1982 *Cultura Selknam (Ona)*. Santiago: Departamento de Extension Cultural del Ministerio de Educación.

———, 1987 Los cazadores paleoindios de Tres Arroyos (Tierra del Fuego). *Anales del Instituto de la Patagonia* 17:47–60.

Mathiassen, Therkel 1928 Material culture of the Iglulik Eskimo. In

*Report of the Fifth Thule Expedition, 1921–24*, vol. 6, no. 1. Copenhagen: Gyldendalske Boghandel.

Matson, R. G. 1985 The relationship between sedentism and status inequalities among hunters and gatherers. In *Status, structure and stratification*. Marc Thompson, Maria Teresa Garcia, and François Kense, eds., pp. 245–52. Calgary: Archaeological Association of the University of Calgary.

Mauss, M. 1967 *The gift*. New York: W. W. Norton and Co.

Mayhew, Leon W. 1968 Society. In *International Encyclopedia of the Social Sciences*. David L. Sills, ed., pp. 577–86. New York: Macmillan Free Press.

McCargo, Dave 1985 Allotments threaten public lands. *Sierra Borealis* (Spring): 6.

McCarthy, Frederick D., and Margaret McArthur 1960 The food quest and the time factor in aboriginal economic life. In *Records of the American-Australian scientific expedition to Arnhem Land*, vol. 2, *Anthropology and nutrition*. Charles P. Mountford, ed. Melbourne: Melbourne University Press.

McCreedy, Marion 1987 Biaka dance and society. Paper presented at the eighty-sixth annual meeting of the American Anthropological Association. Chicago.

———, 1989 Unpublished field notes from Djoko, August, 1989. Originals in possession of the author.

McDowell, W. A. 1981 A brief history of the Mangola Hadza. Report for the Rift Valley project. Dar-es-Salaam: Tanzania Ministry of Information and Culture.

McHenry, Henry M. 1968 Transverse lines in long bones of prehistoric California Indians. *American Journal of Physical Anthropology* 29(1):1–18.

McHenry, Henry M., and Peter D. Schulz 1976 The association between Harris lines and enamel hypoplasia in prehistoric California Indians. *American Journal of Physical Anthropology* 44:507–12.

———, 1978 Harris lines, enamel hypoplasia, and subsistence change in prehistoric central California. *Ballena Press Publications in Archaeology, Ethnography, and History* 11:35–49.

McNally, Ward 1981 *Aborigines, artifacts and anguish*. Adelaide: Lutheran Publishing House.

McNeill, William H. 1976 *Plagues and peoples*. Garden City, N.Y.: Anchor Press/Doubleday.

Meehan, Betty 1982 *Shell bed to shell midden*. Canberra: Australian Institute of Aboriginal Studies.

Meehan, Betty, and Neville White, eds. 1990 *Hunter-gatherer demography: Past and present*. Sydney: University of Sydney. (Oceania monograph no. 39.)

Meggitt, Mervyn J. 1962 *Desert people: A study of the Walbiri Aborigines of central Australia*. Sydney: Angus and Robertson.

———, 1966 Indigenous forms of government among Australian Aborigines. In *Readings in Australian and Pacific anthropology*. Ian Hogbin and L. Hiatt, eds., pp. 57–74. Melbourne: Melbourne University Press.

Mehlman, M. 1988 Later quaternary archaeological sequences in northern Tanzania. Ph.D. diss. University of Illinois, Champaign-Urbana.

Meiklejohn, Christopher, et al. 1984 Socioeconomic change and patterns of pathology and variation in the Mesolithic and Neolithic of western Europe: Some suggestions. In *Paleopathology at the origins of agriculture*. Mark N. Cohen and George J. Armelagos, eds., pp. 75–100. New York: Academic Press.

Meillassoux, Claude 1973 On the mode of production of the hunting band. In *French perspectives in African studies*. Pierre Alexandre, ed., pp. 187–203. Oxford: Oxford University Press for the International African Institute.

———, 1981 *Maidens, meal and money: Capitalism and the domestic community*. Cambridge: Cambridge University Press.

Mensforth, R. P., et al. 1981 The role of constitutional factors, diet, and infectious disease in the etiology of porotic hyperostosis and periosteal reactions in prehistoric infants and children. *Medical Anthropology* 2(1):1–59.

Merlan, Francesca 1988 Gender in Aboriginal social life: A review. In *Social anthropology and Australian Aboriginal studies: A contemporary overview*. Ronald M. Berndt and R. Tonkinson, eds., pp. 17–76. Canberra: Aboriginal Studies Press.

Michael, Henry N., ed. 1967 *Lieutenant Zagoskin's travels in Russian America, 1842–44*. Toronto: University of Toronto Press. (Anthropology of the North, translations from Russian sources no. 7.)

Miller, Vicki [1984] Untitled essay in *The Ark·II Activist: Canadian Animal Rights Network*. [4 pp.]

Minc, Leah 1986 Scarcity and survival: The role of oral tradition in mediating subsistence crises. *Journal of Anthropological Archaeology* 5(1):39–113.

Mitchell, Donald H. 1984 Predatory warfare, social status, and the north Pacific slave trade. *Ethnology* 23(1):39–48.

Mitchell, Donald H., and Leland Donald 1988 Archaeology and the study of Northwest Coast economies. Prehistoric economies of the Pacific Northwest Coast. *Research in Economic Anthropology* supplement 3:293–351.

Moise, Robert 1992 "A mo kila!" [I refuse!]: Living autonomously in a Biaka community. M.A. thes. New York University.

Momaday, N. Scott 1976 Native American attitudes to the environment. In *Seeing with a native eye: Essays on native American religions*. Walter H. Capps, ed., pp. 79–85. New York: Harper and Row.

Moore, K. M. 1979–80 Archaeological correlates of the Ona: Hunter-gatherers of the sub-antarctic. In *The archaeological correlates of hunter-gatherer societies: Studies from the ethnographic record.* F. E. Smiley, et al., eds. Michigan Discussions in Anthropology 5:62–77.

Moran, Emilio F. 1983 Mobility as a negative factor in human adaptability: the case of South American tropical forest populations. In *Rethinking Human Adaptation*, R. Dyson-Hudson and M. A. Little, eds., pp. 117–135. Boulder: Westview Press.

Morgan, R. C. 1981 The economic basis of Nootka polities. *Canberra Anthropology* 4(2):29–44.

Morrow, Phyllis 1984 It is time for drumming: A summary of recent research on Yup'ik ceremonialism. *Etudes/Inuit-Studies* 8 (supplementary issue): 113–40.

Murashko, O. A. 1985 Starozhily Kamchatki v istoriko-demograficheskoj i sotsial'no-ekonomicheskoj perspektive [Kamchatka old-settlers in historical-demographic and social-economic perspective]. In *Mezhetnicheskije kontakty i razvitije natsional'nykh kul'tur* [Interethnic contacts and ethnic cultures' development]. Igor Krupnik, ed., pp. 77–88. Moscow: Soviet Academy of Sciences, Institute of Ethnography.

Myers, Fred R. 1982 Always ask: Resource use and land ownership among Pintupi Aborigines of the Australian Western Desert. In *Resource managers: North American and Australian hunter-gatherers.* Nancy M. Williams and Eugene S. Hunn, eds., pp. 173–96. Boulder, Colorado: Westview Press, Inc. (AAAS selected symposium 67.)

———, 1986 *Pintupi country, Pintupi self: Sentiment, place, and politics among Western Desert Aborigines.* Washington, D.C.: Smithsonian Institution Press/Canberra: Australian Institute of Aboriginal Studies.

———, 1988 Critical trends in the study of hunter-gatherers *Annual Review of Anthropology* 17:261–82.

Ndagala, Daniel K. 1988 Free or doomed? Images of the Hadzabe hunters and gatherers of Tanzania. In *Hunters and gatherers 1: history, evolution and social change.* Tim Ingold, David Riches and James Woodburn, eds., pp. 65–72. Oxford: Berg Publishers Limited.

Neave, F. 1953 Principles affecting the size of pink and chum salmon populations in British Columbia. *Journal of the Fisheries Research Board of Canada* 9:450–91.

Needham, R. N. 1972 *Belief, language, and experience.* Oxford: Basil Blackwell.

———, 1975 Polythetic classification: Convergence and consequence. *Man* 10:349–69.

Nelson, E. W. 1882 A sledge journey in the delta of the Yukon, northern Alaska. *Proceedings of the Royal Geographic Society* n.s. 4:660–70.

———, 1899 The Eskimo about Bering Strait. In *Bureau of AmericanEthnology. 18th Annual Report, Part 1, 1896–97*, pp. 3–518. Washington, D.C.: Government Printing Office.

Nelson, Richard K. 1983 *Make prayers to the raven: A Koyukon view of the northern forest*. Chicago: University of Chicago Press.

Neumann, Loretta, and Kathleen M. Reinburg 1989 Cultural resources and wilderness: The white hats versus the white hats. *Journal of Forestry* 87(10):10–16.

Noatak, Andrew 1990 Personal communication to Kenneth Pratt, 3 April. Mekoryuk, Alaska.

Nowak, Michael 1988 Sea mammals in a mixed economy: A southwestern Alaskan case. *Arctic Anthropology* 25(1):44–51.

Nunivak Island Mekoryuk Alaska (NIMA) Corporation [n.d.] Draft petition to the Secretary, U.S. Department of the Interior, concerning Nunivak Island land withdrawals and native allotments. Copy in author's [Kenneth Pratt's] possession.

Nyerere, Julius K. 1966 *Freedom and Unity*. Dar-es-Salaam: Oxford University Press.

———, 1967 *After the Arusha Declaration*. Dar-es-Salaam. Ministry of Information and Tourism.

———, 1968 Education for self-reliance. In *Ujamaa: Essays on socialism*. Julius K. Nyerere, ed., pp. 44–75. London: Oxford University Press.

———, 1971 We must run while they walk. In *Nyerere of Tanzania*. William E. Smith, ed. New York: Random Press.

Obst, E. 1912 Von Mkalama ins land der Wakindiga. *Mitteilungen der Geographischen Geselleschaft in Hamburg* 26:3–45.

O'Connell, James F., Kristen Hawkes, and Nicholas Blurton Jones 1988a Hadza scavenging: Implications for plio-pleistocene hominid subsistence. *Current Anthropology* 29(2):356–63.

———, 1988b Hadza hunting, butchering, and bone transport and their archaeological implications. *Journal of Anthropological Research* 44(2):113–62.

———, 1990 Reanalysis of large mammal body part transport among the Hadza. *Journal of Archaeological Science* 17(3):301–16.

———, 1991 Distribution of refuse-producing activities at Hadza residential base camps: Implications for analyses of archaeological site structure. In *The interpretation of archaeological spatial patterning*. Ellen M. Kroll and T. Douglas Price, eds., pp. 61–76. New York: Plenum Publishing Corporation.

Ogryzko, I. I. 1961 Rasselenije i chislennost' Itel'menov i Kamchatskikh Koriakov v kontse XVII v. [Itel'mens' and Kamchatka Koriaks' settlement pattern and population numbers at the end of seventeenth century]. *Uchonyje Zapiski Leningradskogo Gosudarstvennogo Pedagogicheskogo Instituta* [Scientific Papers of Leningrad National Pedagogical Institute] 222:171–208.

Orekhov, A. A. 1987 *Drevniaja kul'tura severo-zapadnogo Beringomorja* [Ancient culture of northwestern side of Bering Sea region]. Moscow: Nauka.

Oswalt, Wendell H. 1961 The new Alaskan Eskimo. *Americas* 13(9):10–13.

———, 1963 *Napaskiak: An Alaskan Eskimo community*. Tucson: University of Arizona Press.

———, 1967 *Alaskan Eskimos*. San Francisco: Chandler Publishing Company.

———, 1980 *Kolmakovskiy redoubt: The ethnoarchaeology of a Russian fort in Alaska*. Los Angeles: University of California, Institute of Archaeology. (Monumenta Archaeologica 8.)

Paine, Robert, ed. 1985 *Advocacy and anthropology, first encounters*. St. John's: Memorial University of Newfoundland, Institute of Social and Economic Research.

Paynter, Robert 1989 The archaeology of equality and inequality. *Annual Review of Anthropology* 18:369–99.

Pedersen, Jon, and Espen Wæhle 1986 The complexities of residential organization among the Efe (Mbuti) and the Bamgombi (Baka): A critical view of the notion of "flux" in hunter and gatherer societies. In *Hunters and gatherers 1: History, evolution and social change*. Tim Ingold, David Riches, and James Woodburn, eds., pp. 75–90. Oxford: Berg Publishers Limited.

Pennington, Renee, and Henry Harpending 1988 Fitness and fertility among Kalahari !Kung. *American Journal of Physical Anthropology* 77(3):303–19.

Pete, Mary C., Daniel E. Albrecht, and Ronald E. Kreher 1987 Subsistence herring fishing in the Nelson Island district and northern Kuskokwim Bay, 1987. Juneau: Alaska Department of Fish and Game, Division of Subsistence. (Technical paper no. 160.)

Peterson, Nicolas 1991a Introduction: cash, commoditisation and changing foragers. *Senri Ethnological Studies* 30:1–16.

———, 1991b Cash, commoditisation and authenticity: When do Aboriginal people stop being hunter-gatherers? *Senri Ethnological Studies* 30:67–90.

Peterson, Nicolas, and Jeremy Long 1986 *Australian territorial organization: A band perspective*. Sydney: University of Sydney. (Oceania monograph no. 30.)

Peterson, Nicolas, ed. 1976 *Tribes and boundaries in Australia*. Canberra: Australian Institute of Aboriginal Studies. (Social anthropology series no. 10.)

Peterson, Nicolas, and Marcia Langton, eds. 1983 *Aborigines, land and land rights*. Canberra: Australian Institute of Aboriginal Studies.

Petroff, Ivan 1884 Report on the population and resources of Alaska. In *Tenth United States census, 1880*. Washington, D.C.: Government Printing Office.

Ponomarenko, A. K. 1985 *Drevniaja kul'tura Itel'menov Vostochnoj Kamchatki* [Ancient culture of Eastern Kamchatka Itel'mens]. Moscow: Nauka.

Popper, J. A. 1887 Exploración de la Tierra del Fuego. *Boletín del Instituto Geográfico Argentino* 8:74–115.

Prakash Reddy, G. 1979 Introducing agriculture in a tribal community: The case of Chenchus. *Man and Life* 5(1–2):81–92.

———, 1987 *Politics of tribal exploitation.* New Delhi: Mittal Publications.

———, 1988a Hunters and gatherers and the tropical habitat of Andaman and Nicobars: A study into their declining relationship. *South Asian Anthropologist* 9(2):171–79.

———, 1988b *The rights and entitlements of indigenous populations of Andaman and Nicobar Islands: Symposium on ecology and environment.* Port Blair: INTECH.

———, 1990 Pre and post independent government of India and the native communities of Andaman and Nicobar Islands. Paper presented to the National Seminar on Andaman and Nicobar Islands. November 9–10. University of Madras, Madras.

Prakash Reddy, G., and V. Sudarsen 1989 In the death trap: The hunting and gathering communities of Andaman and Nicobar Islands. *IWGIA Newsletter* 58:67–81.

Pratt, Kenneth 1984 Classification of Eskimo groupings in the Yukon-Kuskokwim region: A critical analysis. *Etudes/Inuit/Studies* 8 (supplementary issue):46–62.

———, 1990 Economic and social aspects of Nunivak Eskimo "Cliff-Hanging." *Arctic Anthropology* 27(1):75–86.

Pravdin, I. F. 1928 Ocherk zapadno-kamchatskogo rybolovstva v sviazi s obshchimi voprosami Dal'nevostochnoj rybopromyshlennosti [Notes on the Western Kamchatka fishery in regards to general problems of Far-Eastern fish industry]. Vladivostok: *Izvestija Tikhookeanskoj Nauchno-Promyslovoj stantsii* [Papers of the Scientific-Industrial station] 1 (1):169–266.

Price, Barbara 1984 Competition, productive intensification, and ranked society: Speculations from evolutionary theory. In *Warfare, culture and environment.* R. Brian Ferguson, ed., pp. 209–40. New York: Academic Press.

Price, T. Douglas, and James A. Brown 1985 Aspects of hunter-gatherer complexity. In *Prehistoric hunter-gatherers: The emergence of social complexity.* T. Douglas Price and James A. Brown, eds., pp.3–20. Orlando: Academic Press.

Price, T. Douglas, and Anne Gebauer 1992 The final frontier: First farmers in northern Europe. In *Transitions to agriculture in prehistory.* Anne Gebauer and T. Douglas Price, eds., pp. 97–116. Madison, Wisconsin: Prehistory Press.

Price, T. Douglas, and James A. Brown, eds. 1985 *Prehistoric hunter-gatherers: The emergence of cultural complexity.* Orlando: Academic Press, Inc.

Prozorov, A. A. 1902 *Ekonomicheskij obzor Okhotsko-Kamchatskogo kraja* [Economic review on the Okhotsk-Kamchatka region]. St. Petersburg: Trud.

Putnam, Patrick 1948 The Pygmies of the Ituri forest. In *A reader in general anthropology.* C. Coon, ed., pp. 322–42. New York: Holt, Rinehart and Williams.

Radcliffe-Brown, A. R. 1918 Notes on the social organization of Australian tribes. *Journal of the Royal Anthropological Institute of Great Britain and Ireland* 48:222–53.

———, 1930 The social organization of Australian tribes, parts I and II. *Oceania* 1(1):34–63; (2):206–46.

———, 1931 *The social organization of Australian tribes.* Melbourne: Oceania Monographs 1.

———, 1954 Australian local organization. *American Anthropologist* 56(1):105–106.

———, 1956 On Australian local organization. *American Anthropologist* 58(2):363–67.

Rainey, Froelich G. 1947 The whale hunters of Tigara. *Anthropological Papers of the American Museum of Natural History* 41(2): 231–83.

Rathje, William 1972 Praise the gods and pass the metates. In *Contemporary archaeology.* Mark Leone, ed., pp. 365–92. Carbondale: Southern Illinois University Press.

Ray, Dorothy Jean 1967 Land tenure and polity of the Bering Strait Eskimos. *Journal of the West* 6(3):371–94.

———, 1975 *The Eskimo of Bering Strait, 1650–1898.* Seattle: University of Washington Press.

Reddy, Sudhakar P. 1981 The displaced Yanadi of Sriharikota Island: A study in socio-cultural continuity and change. Ph.D. diss. S. V. University, Tirupati.

Renouf, M. A. P. 1991 Sedentary hunter-gatherers: A case for northern coasts. In *Between bands and states.* Susan A. Gregg, ed., pp. 89–107. Carbondale: Southern Illinois University at Carbondale. (Center for Archaeological Investigations occasional paper no. 9.)

Reynolds, R. G., W. D. Watson, and D. J. Collins 1983 *Water resources aspects of drought in Australia. Water 2000: Consultants report no. 13.* Canberra: Government Publishing Service.

Richards, Thomas, and Michael Rousseau 1987 *Late prehistoric cultural horizons on the Canadian plateau.* Burnaby, British Columbia: Simon Fraser University. (Department of Archaeology publication no. 16.)

Ridington, R. 1988 *Trail to heaven.* Iowa City: University of Iowa.

———, 1990 *Little bit know something.* Iowa City: University of Iowa.

Rogers, Edward 1969 Band organization among the Indians of eastern subarctic Canada. In *Contributions to anthropology: Band societies, proceedings of the conference on band organization.* David Damas, ed., pp. 21–50. Ottawa: National Museums of Canada, 1969. (Bulletin 228.)

Romanoff, Steven 1985 Fraser Lillooet salmon fishing. *Northwest Anthropological Research Notes* 19:119–60.

———, 1990 The cultural ecology of hunting and potlatches among the Lillooet Indians. *Northwest Anthropological Research Notes* 22:1–35.

Rosaldo, Michelle Zimbalist, and Louise Lamphere 1974 Introduction. In *Woman, culture and society*. Michelle Zimbalist Rosaldo and Louise Lamphere, eds., pp. 1–15. Stanford: Stanford University Press.

Rose, Deborah Bird 1985 Social and cultural management of a sacred site in the VRD area. Unpublished manuscript on file. Aboriginal Areas Protection Authority, Darwin.

Rostow, W. W. 1960 *The stages of economic growth*. Cambridge: Cambridge University Press.

Rouland, Norbert 1979 Les modes juridiques de solution des conflits chez les Inuit. *Etudes/Inuit/Studies*, vol. 3 (special issue).

Rowell, Meredith 1983 Women and land claims in the Northern Territory. In *Aborigines, land and land rights*. Nicholas Peterson and Marcia Langton, eds. Canberra: Australian Institute of Aboriginal Studies.

Sahlins, Marshall 1958 *Social stratification in Polynesia*. Seattle: University of Washington Press.

———, 1968a Notes on the original affluent society. In *Man the hunter*. Richard B. Lee and Irven DeVore, eds., pp. 85–89. Chicago: Aldine Publishing Company.

———, 1968b *Tribesmen*. Englewood Cliffs: Prentice-Hall.

———, 1972 *Stone age economics*. Chicago: Aldine-Atherton, Inc.

———, 1979 The uses and abuses of biology. In *Issues in cultural anthropology*. D. W. McCurdy and J. P. Spradley, eds. Toronto: Little, Brown and Company.

———, 1985 *Islands of History*. Chicago: University of Chicago Press.

*San Francisco Examiner* 1988 Japanese remember tale of whale. (World news section,) December 4.

Sanday, Peggy R. 1974 Female status in the public domain. In *Woman, culture and society*. Michelle Zimbalist Rosaldo and Louise Lamphere, eds., pp. 189–206. Stanford: Stanford University Press.

Sanger, David 1975 Cultural change as an adaptive process in the Maine-Maritimes region. *Arctic Anthropology* 12(2):60–75.

Sarmiento de Gamboa, Pedro 1950 *Viajes al Estrecho de Magallanes (1579-1584)*. Buenos Aires: Emece.

Saxon, Earl C. 1979 Natural prehistory: The archaeology of Fuego-Patagonian ecology. *Quaternaria* 21:329–56.

Schalk, Randall F. 1977 The structure of an anadromous fish resource. In *For theory building in archaeology*. Lewis R. Binford, ed., pp. 207–49. New York: Academic Press.

———, 1981 Land use and organizational complexity among foragers of northwestern North America. *Senri Ethnological Studies* 9:53–75.

Schebesta, Paul 1933 *Among Congo pygmies*. London: Hutchinson.

Schortman, Edward M. 1989 Interregional interaction in prehistory: The need for a new perspective. *American Antiquity* 54(1):52–65.

Schrire, Carmel 1980 An inquiry into the evolutionary status and apparent identity of San hunter-gatherers. *Human Ecology* 8(1):9–32.

———, 1984 Wild surmises on savage thoughts. In *Past and present in hunter gatherer studies: Selections from the proceedings of the Third International Conferences on Hunter-Gatherers.* Carmel Schrire, ed., pp. 1–25. New York: Academic Press.

Schrire, Carmel, ed. 1984 *Past and present in hunter gatherer studies.* New York: Academic Press.

Schultz, J. 1971 *Agrarlandschaftliche veranderungen in Tanzania (Mbulu/ Hanang districts).* Hamburg: Weltform Verlag.

Scollon, R., and S. Scollon 1989 Fang Kuei Li (1902–1987). *American Anthropologist* 91(4):1008–9.

Scott, Colin 1989 Ideology of reciprocity between the James Bay Cree and the whiteman state. In *Outwitting the state.* Peter Skalník, ed., pp. 81–108. New Brunswick, N.J.: Transaction Publishers.

Segers, Polidoro A. 1891 Hábitos y costumbres de los indios Aonas. *Boletín del Instituto Geográfico Argentino* 12(69):56–82.

Sergeev, M. A. 1936 *Narodnoje khoziajstvo Kamchatskogo kraja* [National economy of Kamchatka region]. Moscow-Leningrad: AN SSSR Press.

Service, Elman R. 1962 *Primitive social organization: An evolutionary perspective.* New York: Random House.

———, 1975 *Origins of the state and civilization: The process of cultural evolution.* New York: W. W. Norton, Inc.

———, 1979 *The hunters.* 2d ed. Englewood Cliffs, N.J.: Prentice-Hall.

Sharp, Henry S. 1975 Introducing the sororate to a northern Saskatchewan Chipewyan village. *Ethnology* 14(1):71–82.

———, 1976 Man:wolf::woman:dog. *Arctic Anthropology* 13(1):25–34.

———, 1977 The Chipewyan hunting unit. *American Ethnologist* 4(2):377–93.

———, 1979 *Chipewyan marriage.* Ottawa: National Museum of Man. (Canadian Ethnology Service, Mercury series paper no. 58.)

———, 1981 The null case: the Chipewyan. In *Woman the gatherer.* F. Dahlberg, ed., pp. 221–44. New Haven: Yale University Press.

———, 1982 Some problems in wolf sociology. In *Wolves of the world.* F. H. Harrington and P. C. Paquet, eds., pp. 423–33. Park Ridge, N.J.: Noyes.

———, 1986 Shared experience and magical death: Chipewyan explanations of a prophet's decline. *Ethnology* 25(4):257–70.

———, 1987 Giant otters, giant fish, and dinosaurs: "Apparently irrational beliefs" in a Chipewyan community. *American Ethnologist* 14(2):226–35.

———, 1988a *The transformation of Bigfoot: Maleness, power, and belief among the Chipewyan.* Washington, D.C.: Smithsonian Institution Press.

———, 1988b Dry meat and gender: The absence of ritual for the regulation of animal numbers and hunting in Chipewyan society. In *Hunters and Gatherers 2: Property, power and ideology*. Tim Ingold, David Riches, and James Woodburn, eds., pp. 183–91. London: Berg Publishers Limited.

———, 1991 Memory, meaning and imaginary time. *Ethnohistory* 35(2): 149–75.

———, [In press (a)] Inverted sacrifice. In *Religion and ecology in northern Eurasia and North America*. T. Irimoto, ed. Tokyo: University of Tokyo Press.

———, [In press (b)] Asymmetric equals? Gender equality among the Chipewyan. In *Gender and power in native North America*. L. Klein and L. Ackerman, eds. Norman: University of Oklahoma Press.

Sharp, R. Lauriston 1958 People without politics. In *Systems of political control and bureaucracy in human societies: Proceedings of the 1958 annual spring meeting of the American Ethnological Society*. Verne F. Ray, ed., pp. 1–8. Seattle: American Ethnological Society.

Shavings, Hilma 1975 Letter dated 28 June. On file. NIMA Corporation, Mekoryuk, Alaska.

Sheehan, Glenn 1985 Whaling as an organizing focus in northwestern Alaskan Eskimo societies. In *Prehistoric hunter-gatherers: The emergence of cultural complexity*. T. Douglas Price and James A. Brown, eds., pp. 123–54. Orlando: Academic Press.

Shinkwin, Anne, and Mary Pete 1984 Yup'ik Eskimo societies: A case study. *Etudes/Inuit/Studies* 8 (supplementary issue):95–112.

Shnirelman, Victor A. 1986 "Neoliticheskaja revolutsija" i neravnomernost' istoricheskogo razvitija [Neolithic revolution and unevenness of the historical development]. In *Problemy perekhodnogo perioda i perekhodnykh obshchestvennykh otnoshenij* [Problems of the transitional period and transitional social relations]. Yu. K. Pletnikov, ed., pp. 119–34. Moscow: AN SSSR, Institute of Philosophy.

———, 1989 *Vozniknovenije proizvodiaschego khoziajstva*. Moscow: Nauka.

Sih, Andrew, and Katherine A. Milton 1982 Optimal diet theory: Should the !Kung eat mongongos? *American Anthropologist* 87(2):395–401.

Silberbauer, George B. 1981 *Hunter and habitat in the central Kalahari Desert*. Cambridge: Cambridge University Press.

———, 1982 Political process in G/wi Bands. In *Politics and history in band societies*. Eleanor Leacock and Richard Lee, eds., pp. 23–35. Cambridge: Cambridge University Press.

———, 1991 Morbid reflexivity and overgeneralization in Mosarwa studies. *Current Anthropology* 32(1):96–99.

Silverblatt, Irene 1980 "The universe has turned inside out ... there is no justice for us here": Andean women under Spanish rule. In *Women and colonization: Anthropological perspectives*. Mona Etienne and Eleanor Leacock, eds. New York: Praeger.

Silverman, Sydel 1993 Preserving the anthropological record. *Current Anthropology* 34 (1):100–102.

Sim, Francis M., and David Smallen 1972 Defining system boundaries. Paper presented at the annual meeting of the Canadian Sociology and Anthropology Association. May 31. Montreal.

Slobodin, R. 1962 *Band organization of the Peel River Kutchin*. Ottawa: National Museums of Canada. (Bulletin 179.)

———, 1969 Leadership and participation in a Kutchin trapping party. In *Contributions to anthropology: Band societies*, pp. 93–115. Ottawa: National Museums of Canada. (Bulletin 228)

———, 1970 Kutchin concepts of reincarnation. *Western Canadian Journal of Anthropology* 2(1):67–79.

———, 1975 Without fire: A Kutchin tale of warfare, survival, and vengeance. In *Proceedings: Northern Athapaskan Conference, 1971*, vol. 1. A. M. Clark, ed., pp. 259–301. Ottawa: National Museum of Man. (Canadian Ethnology Service, Mercury series paper no. 27.)

Slunin, N. V. 1895 *Promyslovyje bogatstva Kamchatki, Sakhalina i Kommandorskikh ostrovov* [The richness of the wildlife of Kamchatka, Sakhalin and Commander Islands]. St. Petersburg: V. F. Kirshbaum.

———, 1900 *Okhotski-Kamchatskij kraj* [Okhotsk-Kamchatka region]. 2 vols. S. Petersburg: Ministry of France.

Smith, Allen E. 1990 Personal communication to Kenneth Pratt. 8 January. Anchorage.

Smith, David M. 1973 *I$^n$ko$^n$ze: Magico-religious beliefs of contact-traditional Chipewyan trading at Fort Resolution, NWT, Canada*. Ottawa: National Museum of Man. (Canadian Ethnology Service, Mercury series paper no. 6.)

———, 1982 *Moose-Deer Island house people: A history of the Native people of Fort Resolution*. Ottawa: National Museum of Man. (Canadian Ethnology Service, Mercury series paper no. 81.)

———, 1985 Big stone foundations: Manifest meaning in Chipewyan myths. *Journal of American Culture* 18(1):73–77.

———, 1990a The Chipewyan medicine-fight in cultural and ecological context. In *Culture and the anthropological tradition*. Robert H. Winthrop, ed., pp. 153–75. New York: University Press of America.

———, 1990b Personal oral communication to H. S. Sharp, November 25, 1990.

Smith, Eric Alden 1987a On fitness maximisation, limited needs, and hunter-gatherer time allocation. *Ethology and Sociobiology* 8(1): 73–85.

———, 1987b Optimization theory in anthropology: Applications and critiques. In *The latest on the best: Essays on evolution and optimality*. John Dupré, ed., pp. 201–49. Cambridge, Massachusetts: Bradford Books/MIT Press.

———, 1988 Risk and uncertainty in the "original affluent society": Evolutionary ecology of resource-sharing and land tenure. In *Hunters and gatherers 1: History, evolution and social change*. Tim Ingold, David Riches, and James Woodburn, eds., pp. 222–51. Oxford: Berg Publishers Ltd.

———, 1991a The current state of hunter-gatherer studies. *Current Anthropology* 32(1):72–75.

———, 1991b *Inujjuamiut foraging strategies: Evolutionary ecology of an Arctic hunting community*. New York: Aldine De Gruyter.

Smith, Eric Alden, and Bruce Winterhalder 1985 On the logic and application of optimal foraging theory: A brief reply to Martin. *American Anthropologist* 87(3): 645–48.

———, 1992 *Evolutionary ecology and human behavior*. Chicago: Aldine de Gruyter.

Smith, J. G. E. 1970 The Chipewyan hunting group in a village context. *Western Canadian Journal of Anthropology* 2(1):60–66.

———, 1978 The emergence of the micro-urban village among the caribou-eater Chipewyan. *Human Organization* 37(1):38–49.

Smith, Peter 1984 Testimony before the Alaska Native Review Commission. 24 February. Tununak, Alaska.

Smoliak, A. V. 1989 Personal communication to V. A. Shnirelman, February 5, 1989.

Soffer, Olga 1985 *The upper Paleolithic of the central Russian plain*. Orlando: Academic Press.

———, 1989 Storage, sedentism and the Eurasian Palaeolithic record. *Antiquity* 63(241):719–32.

Solway, Jacqueline S., and Richard B. Lee 1990 Foragers, genuine or spurious? Situating the Kalahari San in history. *Current Anthropology* 31(2):109–46.

Sorel, G. 1961 *Social evolution and states*. Cambridge: Cambridge University Press.

Spencer, Baldwin, and F. Gillen 1899 *The native tribes of central Australia*. London: Macmillan and Company.

———, 1904 *The northern tribes of northern Australia*. London: Macmillan and Company.

Spencer, Robert F. 1959 *The North Alaskan Eskimo: A study in ecology and society*. Washington, D.C.: Smithsonian Institution Press. (Bureau of American Ethnology bulletin 171.)

Speth, John D., and Katherine A. Spielmann 1983 Energy source, protein metabolism and hunter-gatherer subsistence strategies. *Journal of Anthropological Archaeology* 2(1):1–31.

Spielmann, Katherine Ann 1986 Interdependence among egalitarian societies. *Journal of Anthropological Archaeology* 5(4):279–312.

Stanner, W. E. H. 1956 The dreaming. In *Australian signpost*. T. A. G. Hungerford, ed. Melbourne: F. W. Cheshire.

———, 1962 Aboriginal territorial organization: Estate, range, domain and regime. *Oceania* 36(1):1–26.

———, 1965 Religion, totemism and symbolism. In *Aboriginal man in Australia*. R. M. Berndt and C. H. Berndt, eds. Sydney: Angus and Robertson.

————, 1966 *On aboriginal religion*. Sydney: Sydney University Press. (Oceania monograph no. 11.)

Starkova, N. K. 1976 *Itel'meny: Material'naja kul'tura XVIII–60–e gg. XX v* [Itel'mens: Their material culture from the eighteenth century to the 1960s]. Moscow: Nauka.

————, 1978 Rybolovstvo i orudija promysla u itel'menov (konets XIX–nachalo XX vv.) [Fishing and fishing gear among the Itel'men (from the end of the nineteenth century to the beginning of the twentieth century)]. In *Kul'tura nardov Dal'nego Vostoka SSSR (XIX–XX vv.)* [Culture of the Far-Eastern USSR peoples (nineteenth-twentieth centuries)]. L. I. Sem, ed., pp. 75–80. Vladivostok: DVNTs AN SSSR.

Steller, G. V. 1927 *Iz Kamchatki v Ameriku: Byt i nravy Kamchadalov v XVIII v.* [From Kamchatka to America: Every-day life and customs of Kamchadals in eighteenth century]. Leningrad: P. P. Sojkin Press.

Stern, Richard O., et al. 1980 *Eskimos, reindeer and land*. Fairbanks: University of Alaska, School of Agriculture and Land Resources Management, Agricultural Experiment Station. (Bulletin 59.)

Steward, Julian H. 1936 The economic and social basis of primitive bands. In *Essays in anthropology in honor of A. L. Kroeber*. R. H. Lowie, ed., pp. 331–50. Berkeley: University of California Press.

————, 1938 *Basin-plateau aboriginal sociopolitical groups*. Washington, D.C.: Smithsonian Institution. (Bureau of American Ethnology bulletin no. 120.)

————, 1955 *Theory of culture change: The methodology of multilinear evolution*. Urbana: University of Illinois Press.

Stickney, Alice 1984 *Coastal ecology and wild resource use in the central Bering Sea area: Hooper Bay and Kwigillingok*. Juneau: Alaska Department of Fish and Game, Division of Subsistence. (Technical paper no. 85.)

Stiles, Daniel 1992 The hunter-gatherer "revisionist" debate. *Anthropology Today* 8(2):13–17.

Strathern, Andrew 1971 *The rope of Moka*. Cambridge: Cambridge University Press.

Strathern, Marilyn 1981 Some implications of Hagen gender imagery. In *Sexual meanings*. Sherry B. Ortner and Harriet Whitehead, eds., pp. 166–91. Cambridge: Cambridge University Press.

Strehlow, T. G. H. 1947 *Aranda traditions*. Melbourne: Melbourne University Press.

————, 1965 Culture, social structure, and environment in aboriginal central Australia. In *Aboriginal man in Australia*. R. M. Berndt and C. H. Berndt, eds., pp. 121–45. Sydney: Angus and Robertson.

Stuart, David E. 1972 Band structure and ecological variability: The Ona and Yahgan of Tierra del Fuego. Ph.D. diss. University of New Mexico.

————, 1977 Seasonal phases in Ona subsistence, territorial distribution and organization: Implications for the archeological record. In *For the-*

*ory building in Archaeology.* Lewis R. Binford, ed., pp. 251–83. New York: Academic Press.

————, 1980 Kinship and social organization in Tierra del Fuego: Evolutionary consequences. In *The versatility of kinship.* Linda S. Cordell and Stephen J. Beckerman, eds., pp. 269–84. New York: Academic Press.

Stuiver, M., and H. Polach 1977 Discussion: Reporting of 14 C dates. *Radiocarbon* 19:355–63.

Sugawara, Kazuyoshi 1991 The economics of social life among the central Kalahari San (G//anakhwe and G/wikhwe) in the sedentary community at !Koi!kom. *Senri Ethnological Studies* 30:91–116.

Suttles, Wayne 1960 Affinal ties, subsistence, and prestige among the Coast Salish. *American Anthropologist* 62(2):296–305.

————, 1962 Variation in habitat and culture on the northwest coast. In *Proceedings of the 34th International Congress of Americanists*, pp. 533–37. Vienna.

————, 1968 Coping with abundance: Subsistence on the northwest coast. In *Man the hunter*. Richard B. Lee and Irven DeVore, eds., p. 56–68. Chicago: Aldine Publishing Company.

Swadesh, Morris 1948 Motivations in Nootka warfare. *Southwestern Journal of Anthropology* 4:76–91.

Takahashi, Junichi 1987 Hogei no machi no chômin aidentîtî to shimboru no shiyô ni tsuite [People's identity and the use of symbol in a whaling town]. *Minzokugaku Kenkyû* 52(2):158–67.

————, 1991 Socio-economic implications of the international whaling ban on a nationally regulated small-scale local fishery: A case study of Baird's beaked whale fishery in Japan. *Resource Management and Optimization* 8(3–4):227–34.

Takahashi, Junichi, et al. 1989 Japanese whaling culture: Continuities and diversities. *Maritime Anthropological Studies* 2(2):105–33.

Tanaka, Jiro 1980 *The San, hunter-gatherers of the Kalahari: A study in ecological anthropology.* David W. Hughes, trans. Tokyo: University of Tokyo Press.

————, 1991 Egalitarianism and the cash economy among the central Kalahari San. *Senri Ethnological Studies* 30:117–34.

Tanner, Nancy Makepeace 1981 *On becoming human.* Cambridge: Cambridge University Press.

————, 1983 Hunters, gathering and sex roles in space and time. *American Anthropologist* 85(2):335–41.

Tanno, Tadashi 1976 The Mbuti net-hunters in the Ituri forest, eastern Zaire: Their hunting activities and band composition. *Kyoto University African Studies* 10:101–35.

Tanzania, Ministry of Information and Culture 1982 *Mradi wa Bonde la Ufa: Kumbukumbu za Warsha juu ya Wahadzabe* [The Rift Valley Project: Report on the Workshops about the Hadzabe]. Dar-es-Salaam: Government Printer.

Tatô, Seitoku 1985 *Hogei no kekishi to shiroyô* [History and statistics of whaling]. Tokyo: Suisansha.

Taussig, Michael T. 1980 *The devil and commodity fetishism in Latin America*. Chapel Hill: University of Carolina Press.

Teit, James Alexander 1906 The Lillooet Indians. *Memoirs of the American Museum of Natural History*, vol. II, part 5.

Terashima, Hideaki 1983 Mota and other hunting activities of the Mbuti archers: A socio-ecological study of subsistence technology. *African Studies Monographs* 3:71–85.

Terry, William M. 1950 *Japanese whaling industry prior to 1940*. Tokyo: SCAP. (Natural resource section report no. 126.)

Testart, Alain 1982 The significance of food storage among hunter-gatherers: Residence patterns, population densities, and social inequalities. *Current Anthropology* 23(5):523–37.

———, 1987 Game sharing systems and kinship systems among hunter–gatherers. *Man* 22(2):287–304.

———, 1988a Food storage among hunter-gatherers: More or less security in the way of life? In *Coping with uncertainty in the food supply*, I. de Garine and G. A. Harrison, eds., pp. 170–74. Oxford: Clarendon Press.

———, 1988b Some major problems in the social anthropology of hunter-gatherers. *Current Anthropology* 29(1):1–31.

Thomas, David Hurst 1981 Complexity among Great Basin Shoshoneans: The world's least affluent hunter-gatherers? *Senri Ethnological Studies* 9:19–52.

Tjushov, V. N. 1906 Po zapadnomu beregu Kamchataki [Along the western side of Kamchatka]. *Zapiski Imperatorskogo Russkogo Geograficheskogo Obshchestva po Obshchej Geografii* [Notes of the Emperor's Russian Geographical Society, Department of Geography] 37(2).

Tomita, K. 1966 The sources of food for the Hadzapi tribe: The life of a hunting tribe in east Africa. *Kyoto University African Studies* 1:157–73.

Tonkinson, Robert 1988 "Ideology and domination" in Aboriginal Australia: A Western Desert test case. In *Hunters and gatherers 2: Property, power and ideology*. Tim Ingold, David Riches and James Woodburn, eds., pp. 150–64. Oxford: Berg Publishers Limited.

Townsend, Joan B. 1980 Ranked societies of the Alaskan Pacific rim. *Senri Ethnological Studies* 4:123–56.

———, 1985 The autonomous village and the development of chiefdoms. In *Development and decline: The evolution of sociopolitical organization*. Henri J. M. Claessen, Pieter van de Velde, and M. Estellie Smith, eds., pp. 141–55. South Hadley, Massachusetts: Bergin and Garvey.

Tôyô, Hogei 1989 *Nihon hogeishi* [History of Japanese whaling]. Tokuyama.

Trigger, Bruce 1976 *The children of Aataenstsic: A history of the Huron people to 1660*. 2 vols. Montreal: McGill-Queen's University Press.

Trusswell, A. Stewart, and John D. L. Hansen 1976 Medical research among the !Kung. In *Kalahari hunter-gatherers: Studies of the !Kung San and their neighbors*. Richard B. Lee and Irven DeVore, eds., pp. 166–94. Cambridge: Harvard University Press.

Tsikoyak, Andrew 1987a Interview with Andrew Tsikoyak by Elizabeth Andrews. Mary C. Pete, translator. Nunaputchuk, Alaska, August 27, 1987. Transcript in possession of E. Andrews.

———, 1987b Interview with Andrew Tsikoyak by Elizabeth Andrews. Mary C. Pete, translator. Nunapitchuk, Alaska, October 7, 1987. Transcript in possession of E. Andrews.

Tsurumi, Kazuko 1975 Yanagita Kunio's work as a model of endogenous development. *Japan Quarterly* 22(3):223–38.

Turnbull, Colin M. 1961 *The Forest People*. New York: Natural History Press.

———, 1965a The Mbuti pygmies: An ethnographic survey. *Anthropological Papers of the American Museum of Natural History*, New York.

———, 1965b *Wayward servants: Two worlds of the African pygmies*. New York: Natural History Press.

———, 1972 *The mountain people*. New York: Simon and Schuster.

———, 1978 The politics of non-aggression. In *Learning non-aggression*. Ashley Montague, ed., pp. 161–221. New York: Oxford University Press.

———, 1981 Mbuti womanhood. In *Woman the gatherer*. Frances Dahlberg, ed., pp. 205–19. New Haven: Yale University Press.

Turton, E. R. 1974 The introduction and development of educational facilities for the Somali of Kenya. *History of Education Quarterly* (Fall): 69–90.

United States, Congress 1964 The Wilderness Act. Public Law 88–577 (78 Statutes 890). 88th. Congress, 2nd. Session.

United States Department of the Interior 1973 Nunivak wilderness study-public hearing at Mekoryuk, Alaska, 18 October. On file. NIMA Corporation. Mekoryuk, Alaska.

United States Fish and Wildlife Service 1972 Nunivak National Wildlife Refuge wilderness study report (preliminary draft). On file. NIMA Corporation. Mekoryuk, Alaska.

———, 1973 *Nunivak wilderness study summary*. Anchorage: U.S. Fish and Wildlife Service, Bureau of Sport Fisheries and Wildlife.

———, 1975 Environmental assessment-proposed management of muskox on the Nunivak National Wildlife Refuge, Alaska. Anchorage: United States Fish and Wildlife Service.

———, 1988 Yukon Delta National Wildlife Refuge: Comprehensive conservation plan, environmental impact statement, wilderness review and wild river plan (final). Anchorage: U.S. Fish and Wildlife Service, region 7.

———, 1989 Cabin management policy on national wildlife refuges in Alaska. Anchorage: U.S. Fish and Wildlife Service, region 7.

Unterberger, P. F. 1912 Priamurskij kraj, 1906–1910 [Amur region, 1906–1910]. In *Zapiski Imperatorskogo Russkogo Geograficheskogo Obshchestva po Otdeleniju Statistiki* 13 [Notes of the Emperor's Russian

Geographical Society, Department of Statistics], pp. 1–428. S. Petersburg: V. F. Kirshbaum.

Vallee, Frank, Derek G. Smith, and Joseph D. Cooper 1984 Contemporary
Canadian Inuit. In *Handbook of North American Indians*, vol. 5, *The Arctic*.
David Damas, ed., pp. 662–75. Washington, D.C.: Smithsonian Insti-
tution.

VanStone, James W. 1965 *The changing culture of the Snowdrift Chipewyan*.
Ottawa: National Museums of Canada. (Bulletin 209.)

———, 1989 Nunivak Island Eskimo (Yuit) technology and material culture. *Fieldiana Anthropology* n.s., vol. 12.

VanStone, James W., ed. 1973 V. S. Khromchenko's coastal explorations
in southwestern Alaska, 1822. David H. Kraus, trans. *Fieldiana Anthropology* vol. 64.

Vasil'evskii, R. S. 1977 *Proiskhozhdenije i drevnjaja kul'tura Koriakov* [Origin
and ancient culture of the Koriak]. Novosibirsk: Nauka.

Vayda, Andrew 1974 Warfare in ecological perspective. *Annual Review of
Ecology and Systematics* 5:183–93.

Vayda, Andrew, ed. 1976 *War in ecological perspective*. New York: Plenum
Press.

Venkatesan, D. 1988 The island foragers: Ecology, subsistence and social
organisation of Onge. Ph.D. diss. University of Madras, Madras.

Vignati, M. A. 1927 Arqueología y antropología de los conchales
fueguinos. *Revista del Museo de La Plata* 30:79–143.

Vincent, Anne S. 1985 Plant foods in savanna environments: A preliminary report of tubers eaten by the Hadza of northern Tanzania. *World
Archaeology* 17(2):131–48.

Voget, Fred W. 1975 *A history of ethnology*. New York: Holt, Rinehart and
Winston.

von Fürer-Haimendorf, Christopher 1943 *The Chenchus: Aboriginal tribes
of Hyderabad*, vol. 1. London: Macmillan.

Wagner, R. 1981 *The invention of culture*. Chicago: University of Chicago
Press.

Ward, S. 1992 *Biological samples and balance sheets*. Tokyo. The Institute of
Cetacean Research.

Washburn, Sherwood L., and C. S. Lancaster 1968 The evolution of hunting. In *Man the hunter*. Richard B. Lee and Irven DeVore, eds., pp.
293–303. Chicago: Aldine Publishing Company.

Waskey, Frank 1950 Tribal division of the Eskimo of western Alaska. Ivar
Skarland collection. University of Alaska Archives, Rasmuson
Library, Fairbanks.

Webb, Stephen 1989 *Prehistoric stress in Australian aborigines: A
palaeopathological study*. Oxford: British Archaeological Reports. (International series no. 490.)

Weltfish, G. 1965 *The lost universe: The way of life of the Pawnee*. New York:
Ballantine.

Wendorf, Fred 1968 Site 177: A Nubian final Paleolithic graveyard near Jebel Sahaba, Sudan. In *The prehistory of Nubia*, vol. 2. Fred Wendorf, ed., pp. 954–95. Taos, New Mexico: Fort Burgwin Research Center.

Wenzel, George W. 1981 *Clyde Inuit adaptation and ecology: The organization of subsistence*. Ottawa: National Museum of Man. (Canadian Ethnology Service, Mercury series paper no. 77.)

———, 1983 Kinship as an economic and ecological integrator among Inuit on the east Baffin coast circa 1920–1960. Report on file, the Canadian Ethnology Service, Ottawa.

———, 1986a Canadian Inuit in a mixed economy: Thoughts on seals, snowmobiles and animal rights. *Native Studies Review* 2(1):69–82.

———, 1986b Resource harvesting and the social structure of native communities. In *Native people and renewable resource management*. J. Green and J. Smith, eds., pp. 10–22. Edmonton: Alberta Society of Professional Biologists.

———, [1986–89] Unpublished field notes from Clyde River, in possession of the author.

———, 1991 *Animal rights, human rights: Ecology, economy and ideology in the Canadian Arctic*. Toronto: University of Toronto Press.

Whitaker, Romulus 1985 *Endangered Andamans*. Environmental service group, World Wildlife Fund and MAB, India.

White, Richard, and William Cronon 1988 Ecological change and Indian-White relations. In *Handbook of North American Indians*, vol. 4, *History of Indian-White relations*. Wilcomb E. Washburn, ed., pp. 417–29. Washington, D.C.: Smithsonian Institution.

Widmer, Randolph J. 1988 *The evolution of the Calusa: A nonagricultural chiefdom of the southwest Florida coast*. Tuscaloosa: University of Alabama Press.

Wiessner, Pauline 1977 Hxaro: A regional system of reciprocity for reducing risk among the !Kung San. Ph.D. diss., University of Michigan, Ann Arbor.

Wilderness Society, The 1984 *The Wilderness Act Handbook*. Washington, D.C.: The Wilderness Society.

———, 1989 A special report-wilderness America: A vision for the future of the nation's wildlands. *Wilderness* 52(184).

Williams, B. J. 1974 A model of band society. *American Antiquity* 39(4) part 2. (Memoir 29.)

Williams, Nancy M. 1986 *The Yolngu and their land: A system of land tenure and the fight for its recognition*. Canberra: Australian Institute of Aboriginal Studies.

Williams, Nancy M., and Eugene S. Hunn, eds. 1982 *Resource managers: North American and Australian hunter-gatherers*. Boulder: Westview Press, Inc. (AAAS selected symposium 67.)

Wilmsen, Edwin N. 1983 The ecology of illusion: Anthropological foraging in the Kalahari. *Reviews in Anthropology* 10(1):9–20.

————, 1989a *Land filled with flies: A political economy of the Kalahari.* Chicago: University of Chicago Press.

————, 1989b Those who have each other: San relations to land. In *We are here: Politics of aboriginal land tenure.* Edwin N. Wilmsen, ed., pp. 43–67. Berkeley: University of California Press.

Wilmsen, Edwin N., and James R. Denbow 1990 Paradigmatic history of San-speaking peoples and current attempts at revision. *Current Anthropology* 31(5):489–524.

Wilmsen, Edwin N., ed. 1989 *We are here: Politics of aboriginal land tenure.* Berkeley: University of California Press.

Wilson, Edward O. 1975 *Sociobiology: The new synthesis.* Cambridge: Harvard University Press.

Wilson, Samuel M. 1992 That unmanned wild countrey [sic]. *Natural History* 5/92:16–17.

Winterhalder, Bruce 1983 Opportunity-cost foraging models for stationary and mobile predators. *American Naturalist* 122(1):73–84.

————, 1986 Diet choice, risk, and food sharing in a stochastic environment. *Journal of Anthropological Archaeology* 5(4):369–92.

Winterhalder, Bruce, William Baillargeon, Francesca Cappelletto, I. Randolph Daniel, Jr., and Chris Prescott 1988 The population ecology of hunter-gatherers and their prey. *Journal of Anthropological Archaeology* 7(4):289–328.

Winterhalder, Bruce, and Eric Alden Smith, eds. 1981 *Hunter-gatherer foraging strategies: Ethnographic and archaeological analyses.* Chicago: University of Chicago Press.

Winters, Howard 1969 *The Riverton culture.* Springfield: Illinois State Museum. (Reports of Investigations no. 13.)

Wittfogel, Karl 1957 *Oriental despotism: A comparative study of total power.* New Haven: Yale University Press.

Wizara ya Habari na Utamaduni [Ministry of Information and Culture] 1982 *Mradi wa Bonde la Ufa: Kumbukumbu za warsha juu ya Wahadzabe* [The Rift Valley project: Report on the workshops about the Hadzabe]. Dar-es-Salaam: Government Printer.

Wobst, H. Martin 1978 The archaeo-ethnology of hunter-gatherers or the tyranny of the ethnographic record in archaeology. *American Antiquity* 43(2):303–309.

Wolfe, Eric R. 1982 *Europe and the people without history.* Berkeley: University of Los Angeles Press.

Wolfe, Robert J. 1979 Food production in a Western Eskimo society. Ph.D. diss. University of California, Los Angeles.

————, 1982 Alaska's great sickness, 1900: An epidemic of measles and influenza in a virgin soil population. *Proceedings of the American Philosophical Society* 126(2):90–121.

————, 1984 Commercial fishing in the hunting-gathering economy of a

Yukon River Yup'ik society. *Etudes/Inuit/Studies* 8 (supplemental issue): 159–83.

Wolfe, Robert J., and Robert J. Walker 1987 Subsistence economies in Alaska: Productivity, geography, and development impacts. *Arctic Anthropology* 24(2):56–81.

Wood, Alan 1970 Personal communication. February 25. Interview by L. Donald and D. Mitchell at Department of Fisheries, Vancouver.

Woodburn, James C. 1964 The social organisation of the Hadza of north Tanganyika. Ph.D. diss. University of Cambridge.

———, 1968a An introduction to Hadza ecology. In *Man the hunter*. Richard B. Lee and Irven DeVore, eds., pp. 49–55. Chicago: Aldine Publishing Company.

———, 1968b Stability and flexibility in Hadza residential groupings. In *Man the hunter*. Richard B. Lee and Irven DeVore, eds., pp. 103–10. Chicago: Aldine Publishing Company.

———, 1970 *Hunters and gatherers: The material culture of the nomadic Hadza*. London: British Museum.

———, 1972 Ecology, nomadic movement and the composition of the local group among hunters and gatherers: An east African example and its implications. In *Man, settlement and urbanism*. Peter J. Ucko, Ruth Tringham, and G. W. Dimbleby, eds., pp. 194–206. London: Duckworth.

———, 1979 Minimal politics: The political organization of the Hadza of North Tanzania. In *Politics in leadership: A comparative perspective*. William A. Shack and Percy S. Cohen, eds., pp. 244–46. Oxford: Clarendon Press.

———, 1980 Hunters and gatherers today and reconstruction of the past. In *Soviet and Western Anthropology*. Ernest Gellner, ed., pp. 95–117. London: Duckworth.

———, 1982 Egalitarian societies. *Man* 17(3):431–51.

———, 1988 African hunter-gatherer social organization: Is it best understood as a product of encapsulation? In *Hunters and gatherers 1: History, evolution and social change*. Tim Ingold, David Riches, and James Woodburn, eds., pp. 31–64. Oxford: Berg Publishers Limited.

———, 1990 Personal communication to N. Blurton Jones, May.

Woodburn, James C., and S. Hudson 1966 The Hadza: The food quest of a hunting and gathering tribe of Tanzania. [16 mm film.] London School of Economics, London.

Woodbury, Anthony 1984 Eskimo and Aleut languages. In *Handbook of North American Indians*, vol. 5, *The Arctic*. David Damas, ed., pp. 49–63. Washington, D.C.: Smithsonian Institution.

Workman, William B. 1980 Continuity and change in the prehistoric record from southern Alaska. *Senri Ethnological Studies* 4:49–101.

Workman, William B., John E. Lobdell, and Karen W. Workman 1980

Recent archaeological work in Kachemak Bay, Gulf of Alaska. *Arctic* 33(3):385–99.

Workman, William B., and Karen W. Workman 1988 The last 1300 years of prehistory in Kachemak Bay: Where later is less. In *The late prehistoric development of Alaska's native people*. Robert D. Shaw, Roger K. Harritt, and Don E. Dumond, eds. Anchorage: Alaska Anthropological Association. (Aurora no. 4.)

Wrangell, Ferdinand Petrovich 1980 *Russian America, statistical and ethnographic information.* Mary Sadouski, trans. Richard A. Pierce, ed. Kingston, Ontario: The Limestone Press. (Materials for the study of Alaska history, no. 15.)

Wylie, A. 1982 An analogy by any other name is just as analogical: A commentary on the Gould-Watson dialogue. *Journal of Anthropological Archaeology* 1:382–401.

Wyndham, C. H. 1966 Southern African ethnic adaptation to temperature and exercise. In *The biology of human adaptability*. Paul T. Baker and J. S. Weiner, eds. Oxford: Clarendon Press.

Yellen, John E. 1977 *Archaeological approaches to the present*. New York: Academic Press.

———, 1990 The present and future of hunter-gatherer studies. In *Archaeological thought in America*. C. C. Lamberg-Karlovsky, ed., pp. 103–16. New York: Cambridge University Press.

Yellen, John E., and Richard B. Lee 1976 The Dobe-Du/da environment: Background to a hunting and gathering way of life. In *Kalahari hunter-gatherers: studies of the !Kung San and their neighbors*. Richard B. Lee and Irven DeVore, eds., pp. 27–46. Cambridge: Harvard University Press.

Yengoyan, Aram 1976 Structure, event and ecology in aboriginal Australia. In *Tribes and boundaries in Australia*. Nicolas Peterson, ed., pp. 121–32. Canberra: Australian Institute of Aboriginal Studies. (Social anthropology series no. 10.)

Yesner, David R. 1977 Resource diversity and population stability among hunter-gatherers. *Western Canadian Journal of Anthropology* 7:18–59.

———, 1980 Maritime hunter-gatherers: Ecology and prehistory. *Current Anthropology* 21(6):727–50.

———, 1983 On explaining changes in prehistoric coastal economies: The view from Casco Bay. In *The evolution of maritime cultures on the Northeast and Northwest Coasts of America*. Ronald J. Nash, ed. Burnaby, British Columbia: Simon Fraser University. (Department of Archaeology publication no. 11.)

———, 1984 Population pressure in coastal environments: An archaeological test. *World Archaeology* 16:108–27.

———, 1987 Life in the "Garden of Eden": Constraints on the adoption of marine diets by human societies. In *Food and evolution*. Marvin Harris and Eric B. Ross, eds. Philadelphia: Temple University Press.

————, 1988 Island biogeography and prehistoric human adaptation on the southern coast of Maine (USA). In *The archaeology of prehistoric coastlines*. Geoff N. Bailey and John E. Parkington, eds. Cambridge: Cambridge University Press.

————, 1989 Subsistence and diet in north-temperate coastal hunter-gatherers: Evidence from the Moshier Island burial site, southwestern Maine. In *Diet and subsistence: Current archaeological perspectives*. Brenda V. Kennedy and Genevieve M. LeMoine, eds. Calgary: University of Calgary Archaeological Association.

————, 1990 Osteological remains from Larsen Bay, Kodiak Island, Alaska. *Arctic Anthropology* 26(2):96–106.

————, 1992 Evolution of subsistence in the Kachemak Tradition: evaluating the North Pacific maritime stability model. *Arctic Anthropology* 29 (2):167–181.

Zihlman, Adrienne L. 1981 Women as shapers of the human adaptation. In *Woman the gatherer*. Frances Dahlberg, ed., pp. 75–120. New Haven: Yale University Press.

# Notes on Contributors

ELIZABETH F. ANDREWS is Subsistence Regional Program Manager for the interior, western, and Arctic regions of the Alaska Department of Fish and Game. She received her Ph.D. in anthropology from the University of Alaska Fairbanks in 1989. She has conducted research on historic and contemporary land and resource use among Alaskan Athapaskan groups in interior Alaska since 1975, and among Yup'ik Eskimo groups in western Alaska since 1982. Currently, she is responsible for coordinating and conducting applied research on contemporary subsistence in the numerous and predominantly native communities within the coastal, riverine, and Arctic regions of northern Alaska.

NICHOLAS G. BLURTON JONES is Professor in the Departments of Education, Psychiatry, and Anthropology at the University of California, Los Angeles. He received his Ph.D. in zoology at the University of Oxford in 1964 and has conducted field and laboratory studies in a variety of locations on several species. Relevant to this paper is his fieldwork on the !Kung with Melvin Konner and Marjorie Shostak in 1970, with his coauthors and Henry Harpending in 1988, and a series of visits to the Hadza between 1982 and 1990.

LUÍS ALBERTO BORRERO is Professor of Archaeology at the Universidad de Buenos Aires and Researcher at the Consejo Nacional de Investigaciones Cientificas y Técnicas (CONICET), Argentina. He received his Ph.D. in anthropology from the Universidad de Buenos Aires in 1986. His dissertation field research was carried out in Tierra del Fuego. In 1987–1988, he was Postdoctoral Visiting Scholar at the University of Nevada, Reno, and at the University of California, Santa Cruz. He is now undertaking extensive archaeological research on the evolution of Patagonian and Fuegian hunter-gatherers.

ERNEST S. ("Tiger") BURCH, JR., is Research Associate in Anthropology with the Smithsonian Institution, Washington, D.C. He received his B.A. in sociology from Princeton University, and his Ph.D. in anthropology from the University of Chicago. For most of his professional career he has pursued his interest in the macrosociology of hunting-gathering societies through ethnographic and historical studies of early historic Eskimo populations. His research has focused primarily on northern Alaska and the central Canadian subarctic.

504

LELAND DONALD is Professor in the Department of Anthropology at the University of Victoria, British Columbia, where he has taught since 1969. He received his Ph.D. in anthropology from the University of Oregon in 1968. He has conducted ethnographic field research among the Navajo of northern Arizona and the Yalunka of Sierra Leone. He has been engaged in ethnohistoric research on the aboriginal peoples of the north Pacific coast of North America since the early 1970s. He and Donald Mitchell have reported jointly and separately on various aspects of their enquiries into the aboriginal Northwest Coast resource base and its use, social inequality (especially slavery), and intergroup relations (especially warfare and trade) in this region.

Professor PATRICIA DRAPER has a joint appointment in the Departments of Anthropology and Human Development at Pennsylvania State University. She obtained her Ph.D. in anthropology at Harvard University after fieldwork on !Kung children during 1968–1970. She has returned several times to the !Kung for intensive studies of aging and of contemporary changes in demographic and reproductive patterns.

LINDA J. ELLANNA received her M.A. in anthropology from the University of Wyoming, and her Ph.D. in biobehavioral sciences and biological anthropology from the University of Connecticut. She has conducted extensive ethnographic fieldwork among several different native groups in Alaska, but particularly among the Iñupiat (Eskimos) of the western and northwestern part of the state. She has also studied the relationships between the subsistence and market sectors of the economics of Alaska natives and the Aborigines of northern Australia. She organized the Sixth International Conference on Hunting-Gathering Societies (CHAGS-6) in 1990, and is coorganizer of CHAGS-7, to be held in Moscow in 1993. Currently she is Associate Professor of Anthropology at the University of Alaska, Fairbanks.

HARVEY A. FEIT is Professor of Anthropology at McMaster University, in Hamilton, Ontario, Canada. He has done fieldwork among James Bay Cree from 1968 to 1970 and seasonally from 1981 to 1984. From 1974 to 1978 he was Senior Social Science Advisor to the Grand Council of the Crees (of Quebec) during the negotiation and initial implementation of the James Bay and Northern Quebec Agreement, the first modern "treaty" in Canada. His most intensive Cree research is on political and symbolic ecology. He has also done research on environmentalism and social movements in North America and Europe, and has written on the history of Algonquianist anthropology. He has been a consultant to indigenous organizations across Canada and to several government agencies. He is presently working on a monograph on the Waswanipi Cree entitled *Hunting with the North Wind*.

MILTON M. R. FREEMAN is Henry Marshall Tory Professor of Anthropology at the University of Alberta. He obtained his Ph.D. at McGill University in 1965. He has a long-standing interest in maritime hunting societies, and was chairman of an international committee, which, in 1979 advised the International Whaling Commission on the sociocultural significance of subsistence whaling in Alaska and Greenland. In 1988 he chaired an international panel of anthropologists undertaking a similar task in connection with small-type coastal whaling in Japan.

KRISTEN HAWKES is Professor in the Department of Anthropology at the University of Utah. She received her Ph.D. in anthropology at the University of Washington after fieldwork in highland New Guinea. Her recent fieldwork has included studies of the ecology of Ache hunter-gatherers in Paraguay, and research on ecology, time allocation, and food sharing among the Hadza in Tanzania. Most recently she conducted an experimental study of hunting and prey selection among the Hazda.

BRIAN HAYDEN is Professor in the Department of Archaeology, Simon Fraser University, Burnaby, British Columbia. He has focused much of his research on ethnoarchaeological work among Australian Aborigines, Highland Maya Indians, and most recently among the Indians of interior British Columbia. He has a long-standing interest in hunter-gatherer adaptations, and during the last six years he has been investigating the development of both prehistoric and ethnographic complex hunter-gatherers near Lillooet, British Columbia.

MASAMI IWASAKI-GOODMAN is presently a doctoral student in the Department of Anthropology, University of Alberta. She has Master's degrees from the University of Minnesota and the University of Alberta, where she was Premier Lougheed Scholar, 1984–1987. She has held teaching posts at Sapporo University, Fuji Women's College, and Hokusei Gakuen College. Her publications include work on Japanese prehistory, Ainu folklore, and social and cultural analyses of small-type coastal whaling in Japan, and comparisons between Japanese and Alaskan small-scale coastal whaling.

BWIRE T. M. KAARE has been Assistant Lecturer in Behavioral Sciences at the Institute of Finance Management in Dar-es-Salaam, Tanzania, since 1988. He conducted field research among the Hadzabe of Tanzania in 1987. Currently, he is working on his Ph.D. in social anthropology at the London School of Economics, and is planning field research among the Akie Dorobo of Tanzania.

MARION McCREEDY is an artist and anthropologist. She received her B.F.A. from the Art Institute of Chicago in 1978, and her M.A. in anthropology from the University of Illinois at Chicago in 1989, and is contemplating continued Ph.D. work in anthropology. She originally went to the Central African Republic to shoot a film on the Biaka pygmies and her lengthy field trip generated a deepening interest in anthropology. She is presently enjoying motherhood while trying to complete her documentary film.

LESLEY MEARNS is Senior Anthropologist at the Aboriginal Areas Protection Authority in Darwin, Australia. She received an M.A. in social anthropology from the University of Manchester, England, in 1975. She undertook research for a Ph.D. at the University of Adelaide, South Australia, before moving to Darwin, where she took up a post as Lecturer in Anthropology at the Darwin Institute of Technology in 1984. In 1986 she joined the Authority, then known as the Aboriginal Sacred Sites Protection Authority.

ILARION (Larry) MERCULIEFF is a native Aleut from S. Paul Island, in the Bering Sea. His ancestors were among many who were forcibly relocated by Russian fur traders from their ancestral homeland in the Aleutian Islands to the previously uninhabited Pribilof Islands, roughly two hundred years ago. He was raised in the traditional Aleut manner, but became actively involved in regional and state politics during the native rights movement of the 1960s. Since then he has worked in the fields of rural economic development, business and resource management, cultural preservation, and subsistence resource and environmental management. He has held a number of important posts in the S. Paul Village Corporation, the Aleut Regional Corporation, and the Alaska state government. Currently he is collaborating with the Arctic Institute of North America in a long-term study of high- latitude island ecosystems and a culture in rapid and involuntary transition.

DONALD H. MITCHELL is Professor of Anthropology at the University of Victoria, and has taught there since 1965. He received his Ph.D. in anthropology from the University of Oregon in 1968. His doctoral research was based on excavations at sites in southwestern British Columbia's Gulf Islands. Since then he has been involved with further archaeological work in the south and central portions of coastal British Columbia, and has maintained a program of ethnohistorical and ethnological research largely on Northwest Coast economies.

KENNETH L. PRATT received his B.A. and M.A. degrees in anthropology from Western Washington University, and is currently a Ph.D. candidate in cultural anthropology at the University of Oregon. Since 1980 he has worked as an anthropologist and archaeologist for the University of Alaska and the United States Bureau of Indian Affairs, in connection with the Alaska Native Claims Settlement Act (ANCSA) of 1971. He has conducted ethnographic, ethnohistorical, and archaeological research throughout southwest Alaska, mainly devoted to documenting the cultural heritage and land use histories of local native groups. His ongoing work with the Nunivak Eskimos began in 1986.

G. PRAKASH REDDY is Professor in the Department of Social Anthropology at Sri Venkateswara University, Tirupati, India. He received his Ph.D. in social anthropology from Andhra University in 1978. He has undertaken extensive studies of hunting-gathering communities on the Andaman and Nicobar Islands and in mainland India. He has also studied social unrest among the tribal communities of India, and has made two ethnographic films on a tribe in Andhra Pradesh. His most recent work involved a field study of a small village in Denmark, which resulted in both a book and a film.

HENRY S. SHARP is currently Scholar-in-Residence in the Department of Anthropology at the University of Virginia. He has worked with the Chipewyan of the central Canadian subarctic since initiating work for his doctorate at Duke University in 1969. His most active period of field research was during the 1970s, but he has returned to the field several times since then. He taught in Canada at Simon Fraser University and the University of Victoria before coming to the University of Virginia.

VICTOR A. SHNIRELMAN is Senior Researcher at the Institute of Ethnology and Anthropology of the Russian Academy of Sciences, Moscow. He received his candidate of history degree in 1977 and doctor of history degree in 1990, both from the Institute of Ethnography of the Academy of Sciences of the former USSR. His early research dealt with the origins of pastoralism and the emergence of food-producing economies, combining the approaches of archaeology, social and cultural anthropology, palaeoclimatology, palaeoethnobotany, and archaeozoology. More recently he has investigated problems of ethnicity, both in the past and under present conditions. He also has studied the modernization process among the Tlingit Indians of southeastern Alaska, and the changes that occurred among the small indigenous peoples of eastern Siberia under the Soviet regime.

GEORGE B. SILBERBAUER, after studying at Stellenbosch and London Universities, joined the British Colonial Service, serving as District Commissioner of Ngamiland and Ghanzi. After further work at the University of the Witwatersrand, he conducted a decade of fieldwork as Bushman Survey Officer in Botswana. After retiring, he went to Monash University's Department of Anthropology and Sociology as Senior Lecturer, where he obtained a Ph.D. He has done research in central Australia, further work among Basarwa on Ghanzi ranches, research on his own village's response to the destructive bush fires of 1983, more general disaster studies, and work on socioecological aspects of the Western Port Rivers Management Study in Victoria.

GEORGE W. WENZEL is affiliated with the Department of Geography, McGill University, Montreal, Canada. Trained in anthropology and geography, his field research has concentrated on the role of social relations in Inuit ecological adaptation, focusing particularly on the Canadian eastern Arctic and west-central Greenland. His current research focuses on the role of money in modern Inuit subsistence.

DAVID R. YESNER is Associate Professor of Anthropology at the University of Alaska, Anchorage. His major interest is in the ecology and subsistence of hunter-gatherers of both past and present, particularly maritime hunter-gatherers of the subarctic and subantarctic regions. He received his B.A. from Cornell University in 1971, and his Ph.D. from the University of Connecticut in 1977. His dissertation work in the eastern Aleutian Islands involved the reconstruction of prehistoric subsistence and settlement patterns based on archaeological faunal remains. Since that time, he has undertaken fieldwork in Maine (1978–1987) and Argentine Tierra del Fuego (1985 to the present), and has continued working in southcentral Alaska, where he is currently codirector of the Broken Mammoth archaeological project

# Index